INDIVIDUATION IN SCHOLASTICISM

SUNY SERIES IN PHILOSOPHY
GEORGE R. LUCAS, JR., EDITOR

Individuation in Scholasticism

The Later Middle Ages and the Counter-Reformation 1150–1650

Edited by
Jorge J. E. Gracia

State University of New York Press

Published by
State University of New York Press, Albany

© 1994 State University of New York

For information, address State University of New York Press,
State University Plaza, Albany, NY 12246

Production by M. R. Mulholland
Marketing by Nancy Farrell

Library of Congress Cataloging-in-Publication Data
Individuation in scholasticism : the later Middle Ages and the counter
-reformation (1150–1650) / edited by Jorge J. E. Gracia.
p. cm.—(SUNY series in philosophy)
Includes bibliographical references and indexes.
ISBN 0-7914-1859-6 (cloth : alk. paper).—ISBN 0-7914-1860-X
(pbk. : alk. paper)
1. Individuation (Philosophy)—History. 2. Scholasticism.
I. Gracia, Jorge J. E. II. Series
BD394 .I53 1994
126—dc20   93-15483
                                                    CIP

10 9 8 7 6 5 4 3 2 1

"[L'individuazione] investe la questione essenziale della Filosofia, e non 'e un semplice tema di esercitazioni intellettuali, come di solito vengono considerati i problemi per cui si appassionarono i filosofi medioevali."

—Giovanni Gentile, *Teoria generale dello Spirito come atto puro*, Laterza, 1924, p. 57.

CONTENTS

PROLOGUE

The need for an introductory study of the problem of individuation in the scholasticism of the later Middle Ages and the Counter-Reformation should require no justification. Although there are some studies of individuation as it appears in a few individual authors from these periods, so far no one has attempted a general study of the development of this problem in scholasticism from 1150 to 1650. Yet, individuation is not only one of the major philosophical problems of all times, a fact amply demonstrated by the continued attraction it has exercised on philosophers, but it is one that has especial fascination for late medieval and Counter-Reformation scholastics. Indeed, most scholastic authors of those periods dealt with individuation in one way or another, and the number of questions, disputations and treatises devoted to it is impressive.

The fascination that the problem of individuation had for scholastics can be explained not only on the basis of its perennial philosophical interest and the implications that it has for other philosophical issues such as the problem of universals, but also because of its substantial theological ramifications. In an age where theology was regarded as the queen of the sciences and philosophy as the handmaiden of theology, any philosophical issue that had theological bearing necessarily acquired importance. The theological doctrines to which the problem of individuation is related are many, but five in particular stand out: the Trinity, original sin, the immortality of the soul, the resurrection of the body, and the nature of angels. Individuation had to do with trinitarian doctrine because, according to orthodox Christian belief, God was both one and three. Christian authors from the very beginning of the Christian era realized the need to express this belief in intelligible philosophical terms and to do so it became necessary to discuss the nature of individuality and the principle of individuation. The doctrine of original sin was also related to individuation, because it required an explanation of how sin can be committed by one individual and its effects passed down to others. In the thirteenth century medieval authors became particularly sensitive to the importance of the problem of individuation for the problem of personal immortality. To account for the preservation of the individual person after death and for just punishments and rewards, it was necessary to understand what individuality is, how it is brought about, and how it is preserved. Related to immortality was the doctrine of the resurrection of the body. This doctrine raised important questions concerning the identity and individuality of the body and the composite of soul and body. Finally, the question concerned with the explanation of the uniqueness of purely spiritual entities and the differences among various angelic natures prompted scholastics, particularly in the thirteenth century and later, to raise questions related to their individuation.

Nevertheless, in spite of the importance that the problem of individuation had for scholastics and the need to understand its development in the later Middle Ages and the Counter-Reformation, no study attempts to present an overview of its historical development at the time. The reasons are obvious. Not only is this a very long stretch of time, covering half a millenium, but it is crowded with major philosophical thinkers. It is difficult enough to try to understand and present a clear exposition of the thought on this issue of any major scholastic figure such as Thomas Aquinas or Duns Scotus, let alone attempt to do so with several of them. Moreover, the 500 years in question witnessed great changes in philosophical and theological outlook as well as major institutional developments whose impact was felt, directly or indirectly, in the perception of and solution given to various philosophical problems, including the problem of individuation. The changes were so many and of such magnitude that even their mere enumeration would be out of place in an introductory preface such as this. But at least those that had the greatest impact on the age must be mentioned in passing: the translations of Arabic and Greek philosophical and scientific works into Latin, the foundation of the universities and major religious orders, the official ecclesiastical condemnations of ideas perceived as dangerous and heretical, the rise of humanism, and finally the Reformation and Counter-Reformation. It would be foolish, then, for anyone to attempt single-handedly a study that takes into account the historical development of scholastic views on individuation throughout a period as long and complex as that constituted by the later Middle Ages and the Counter-Reformation. Nor could any single work aspire to cover the thought of the many figures who discussed this topic. What to do, then? Should one simply give up and regard the history of the problem of individuation during this key period in the West as unchartable and the attempt to understand its major developments as impossible?

To answer the last question affirmatively would be, I believe, a serious mistake. True, no individual scholar could undertake the task, and no single work could hope to discuss fully all the figures involved in the scholastic controversies surrounding individuation. But there is another procedure that, although not so ambitious, may be of use to future scholars and that has been adopted in this volume. What we have attempted to do here is to present an introductory, selective account of the major developments in the period. Two principles have guided the procedure. First of all, the number of scholastic figures to be discussed was reduced to a manageable number. All towering figures are included, but only some lesser thinkers are discussed; they are included to help explain the transitions among the major figures and make clear the climate of opinion at particular times during the period. The application of this principle in the composition of this work has resulted in a collection of articles on various authors that serves as an introduction to the history of the problem of individuation by establishing the main parameters of that history. Second, the work was divided among scholars well acquainted with particular authors, for only those familiar with their thought can hope to understand, on the one hand, the role that the problem of individuation played in the development of their ideas and, on the other, the way their overall perspective affected their views on individuation.

The disadvantages of the procedure we have followed should be clear. This book is not a comprehensive and complete study of the history of the problem of individuation in the scholasticism of the later Middle Ages and the Counter-Reformation; many and important gaps remain and need to be filled, but we hope the book will encourage others to study this matter further. Moreover, as with any collective work, it contains differences of terminology, style, emphasis, and method. I have tried to promote cohesiveness and coordination not only by making appropriate editorial suggestions to the contributing authors, but also by circulating semifinal versions of the articles among the contributors. I have not, however, asked that the authors adhere to a definite format and structure or that they adopt a determined terminology or methodology. Rather, I have allowed the contributing scholars to follow their own counsel on these matters with the hope that such procedure would produce both a more accurate rendition of the views of the scholastic authors discussed and a better picture of diverse approaches used in current medieval and Counter-Reformation scholarship. There are, therefore, some disadvantages to the procedure adopted, but I trust the indicated advantages, together with the benefit of having an initial chart of the development of an important problem whose course has lain largely uncharted until now, will overide the minor problems which the reader will find in the volume.

The temporal boundaries of the book have not been established arbitrarily. Obvious historical reasons justify them. The middle of the twelfth century marks an important beginning in the history not only of the problem of individuation but of scholastic thought in general. In the second half of the twelfth century the impact of the translations from Arabic and Greek sources began to be felt in the West, and it is well known that this impact changed the course of Western philosophical and theological thought in various ways. The introduction of previously unknown texts from Aristotle and the commentaries on those texts by Islamic and Jewish writers initiated Latin medieval authors into philosophical problems and ideas of which they were ignorant.

These texts and commentaries also provided them with conceptual tools to address not only new problems, but also many issues with which they had already dealt. The middle of the twelfth century, therefore, is an appropriate starting point. On the other hand, the middle of the seventeenth century marks a good point at which to end the book for two reasons. First, this was the time at which the last and most complete scholastic synthesis became a standard reference work on metaphysics in European universities. I am referring to Francis Suárez's *Disputationes metaphysicae* (1597). And, second, the year 1644 saw the death of the last major scholastic to have a substantial impact on the future course of mainstream European philosophy, John of St. Thomas. Scholasticism and scholastic influence did not end with Suárez and John of St. Thomas, of course. Indeed, Suárez's thought in general and his *Metaphysical Disputations* in particular, as well as the work of John of St. Thomas and many of their scholastic contemporaries and predecessors, had considerable impact in the philosophical speculations of later centuries. Scholastic thought continued to be influential in many ways, as the writings of most modern thinkers such as Descartes, Spinoza, and Leibniz indicate. But it can hardly be denied that after 1650 scholasticism ceased to be the primary philosophical current of the times; philosophy was moving in new directions. It is appropriate, then, that a study of scholastic views on individuation end at the middle of the seventeenth century.

The unavoidable temporal and spatial limitations imposed on the study mean that some important materials having a bearing on scholastic views on individuation have been left out. The thought on individuation produced by nonscholastic Renaissance and Counter-Reformation figures, for example, has not been taken into account. Moreover, except for one illustrative article at the end, no attempt has been made at studying the important influence of scholastic thought concerning individuation on early modern philosophers; that will be the subject of a different volume to appear in this series. Nor has it been possible to make explicit the relation between the problem of individuation with the other philosophical and theological issues of concern to scholastics. All such areas require research and thinking, but they have been left untouched here for the aforementioned reasons.

In accordance with the stated general policy, my original plan was to invite a dozen scholars to write articles on two dozen late medieval figures, but the volume grew to include contributions from sixteen scholars, who deal with more than twenty-five different scholastic authors. The body of the volume is composed of eighteen articles covering the thought of various scholastic figures. These articles are preceded by four propaedeutic pieces and followed by an article illustrating the impact of scholasticism on modern philosophy and an epilogue. The first of the propaedeutic pieces is a short Introduction in which the problem of individuation is systematically presented.

Its purpose is to make it easier to understand both the issues involved in individuation and the relations among the various positions that philosophers have adopted with respect to it. I have taken the opportunity to identify in the footnotes some of the contemporary writers who hold versions of those positions in order to facilitate the research of those readers whose philosophical interests are not parochial to the Middle Ages and the Counter-Reformation. Although the Introduction presents a systematic framework that naturally entails certain philosophical views, I have tried to keep it as neutral as possible with respect to philosophical commitments and I have neither asked nor expected in any way that contributors to the volume adhere to it or interpret the authors they study in its terms. Indeed, the Introduction was written as an aid to readers rather than as a guide for contributors. The other three propaedeutic articles are historical rather than systematic. The aim of the first two is to provide some background to the currents of thought that were at work in the middle of the twelfth century and which were to influence the future course of scholastic discussions of individuation. The aim of the third is to acquaint the reader with a current of thought that flourished alongside that of the Latin West. The first summarizes the state of medieval discussions of individuation prior to 1150. The second article deals with the Islamic background, and particularly with Avicenna and Averroes, the two Islamic thinkers who had the greatest influence on later Latin philosophy. The third article discusses the thought of Maimonides and two later members of the Jewish tradition whose thought should help to illustrate the cross-fertilization between Jewish and Christian ideas in the area of individuation at the time. At the end of the volume a short piece on Leibniz has been added; its aim is to illustrate with one example the impact that scholastic discussions on individuation had on modern philosophy. Finally, the Epilogue aims to draw together a very general picture of the development of the problem of individuation from 1150 to 1650 and to indicate areas where particular research is needed. The Bibliography contains the titles of the sources used in the book; it is not meant as an exhaustive list of sources on individuation in the later Middle Ages, but rather as a tool for the location of references. Indices of authors and subjects have been added at the end for the convenience of readers. The volume closes with short biographical notes on the contributors.

The particular choice of major scholastic authors to be discussed in this book posed no serious difficulty, they are easily identifiable, but the decision as to which minor figures to include and which to leave out was difficult. The final list of inclusions and assigments was the product of discussions between the editor and the contributors. As far as the choice of contributing authors is concerned, I decided at the beginning to include both senior scholars as well as representatives from younger generations. This approach should help to present a more accurate panorama of the different styles used by those interested in the problem of individuation and gives an indication of the past, present, and future course of scholarship on the history of scholastic philosophy.

In closing, I would like to express my gratitude to all those who have cooperated in this project. In particular I would like to thank the authors of the articles for meeting the deadlines I established, for their willingness to accept as well as to offer suggestions for the improvement of the book and for correcting the page proofs of their articles. In addition, I would like to thank Paul V. Spade, Alfred J. Freddoso, John F. Quinn, and Marilyn McCord Adams for their suggestions of possible contributing authors. I should also mention that five of the articles included here are based partly on previously published material, although in all cases, with the exception of Wippel's article, substantial modifications have been introduced. The article by John F. Wippel on Godfrey of Fontaines, Peter of Auvergne, and John Baconthorpe was originally published in *Essays Honoring Allan B. Wolter,* Ed. William A. Frank and Girard J. Etzkorn (St. Bonaventure, NY: The Franciscan Institute, 1985, pp. 309–349). Part of the discussion of Gerson by Tamar Rudavsky is based on an article published in *The New Scholasticism* 56 (1982), pp. 30–50. My discussion of Suárez is indebted to the Introduction to my *Suárez on Individuation* (Milwaukee: Marquette University Press, 1982), pp. 1–27. And both the systematic introduction and the piece on the legacy of the early Middle Ages use materials contained in my *Introduction to the Problem of Individuation in the Early Middle Ages* (Munich and Washington, DC: Philosophia Verlag and The Catholic University of America Press, 1984; 2nd rev. ed., Philosophia Verlag, 1988). I would like to thank, therefore, the editors and publishers of the pertinent texts for their gracious permission to use them. I would like to express my appreciation to Ky Herreid for proofreading the parts of the volume written by me as well as for his many helpful stylistic suggestions, and to Marie Fleischauer and Eileen McNamara for the patience and expertise with which they typed various drafts of parts of this volume. Finally, I also wish to thank Peter H. Hare, chair of the Department of Philosophy at Buffalo, for his unwaivering support of this project.

Jorge J. E. Gracia
1988

1

INTRODUCTION: THE PROBLEM
OF INDIVIDUATION

JORGE J. E. GRACIA

The study of the history of a philosophical problem profits considerably from a systematic understanding of that problem, and the study of the historical development of the problem of individuation in the scholasticism of the later Middle Ages and the Counter-Reformation is no exception to that rule. Consequently, this Introduction will present a brief systematic analysis of the issues involved in the problem of individuation together with a schematic classification of the most general positions that have been taken with respect to it in the history of philosophy. It will be brief because a similar, more detailed discussion has already been presented in another volume published a few years ago.[1] Therefore, I have dispensed with much of the detail contained in that work and particularly with the arguments usually given in favor of the various positions adopted with respect to individuation and related issues. The present discussion is intended primarily for those who have no immediate access to that volume. It is not meant to supercede or take the place of the earlier discussion, although in several instances some changes of outlook and approach have been introduced.

For most of those philosophers who adopt an Aristotelian perspective, the aim of science in general and philosophy in particular is the identification of causes and principles.[2] To know something scientifically is to be able to identify the causes that brought it about and the principles that play a role in its makeup. Thus, to know human nature, for example, is to be able to identify the causes that produce it and the elements of which it is composed. Likewise, to know individuality is to be able to determine the causes and principles that are responsible for it. The determination of the causes and principles of individuality is in fact what is usually called "the problem of individuation". What is it, for example, that accounts for the individuality of

Socrates, or this chair, or the color of Socrates' hair (for those who accept the individuality of qualities such as hair color)? This is what most scholastic authors understood as the central issue concerning individuation, since most of them had been exposed to and influenced by the Aristotelian conception of science.

There are important differences, acknowledged in many cases by scholastics, between causes and principles. Within the Aristotelian oriented metaphysical framework that dominated mainstream scholastic thought from the thirteenth to the seventeenth centuries, causes were identified with the four physical causes that according to Aristotle were responsible for change: efficient, formal, material, and final. However, the term 'principle' was used more broadly to refer not only to the four causes, but also to metaphysical notions such as essence, existence, substance, and accident and to logical notions such as the principles of identity and noncontradiction. The term 'principle' is much more pliable because of these various uses and, perhaps because of it, was the preferred term that scholastics employed when discussing individuation. Indeed, it allowed the kind of range of interpretation that would accommodate the widely different views concerning individuation developed at that time. It should also be noted that, although the problem of individuation surfaced as early as Boethius, as we shall see in the next chapter, the use of the term 'principle' did not become established in the literature until the thirteenth century. For the sake of convenience, then, I shall use the term 'principle' throughout this Introduction, although it should be kept in mind that not all authors used the term, different authors interpreted it differently, and there was no uniform understanding of the term among scholastics.

The solution to the problem of individuation depends to a great extent on (1) the interpretation of individuality, (2) the things considered to be individual, and (3) the ontological status accorded to individuality in the individual. That it depends on the interpretation of individuality should not be difficult to see, for, if individuality is interpreted, for example, as the relation of difference or distinction among things, as many authors argue,[3] then the principle of individuation must consist in whatever makes individual things different or distinct from one another. But, on the other hand, if individuality is conceived as indivisibility into units similar in nature to the original, as others contend,[4] then the principle of individuation must be what accounts for such lack of division and not necessarily for difference or distinction.

Furthermore, the extension of 'individual' also plays a role in the problem of individuation. If everything is individual, including the features of Aristotelian primary substances, such as the black hair color of a human being or the weight of a cat, the principles that go to make something individual would probably be different than if the term 'individual' extended only to primary substances. And there will be important differences as well if both physical and nonphysical entities are involved or if individuality is restricted to physical entities. For example, in the case of physical entities, matter could be a candidate for the principle of individuation, but it would never do in the case of nonphysical entities.

Finally, the ontological status accorded to individuality in the individual, whether it be that of a real feature to be found in things or merely that of a concept present in the mind of the observer, also affects the solution to the problem of individuation. For it is one thing to account for a real feature in a thing and another to account for a concept in a mind.

We shall have occasion to return to these matters in a moment. At this point what is important for us to note is that, instead of a single issue, the problem of individuation involves at least four different but closely connected philosophical issues whose solutions are interdependent. And there are two other issues as well that have not been mentioned but to which some reference will be made later: discernibility of and reference to individuals. I shall not discuss these last two to any great extent in this Introduction both because the concern of this volume is primarily with the metaphysical problem of individuation, whereas these other issues are not metaphysical, and because the authors discussed here did not generally deal with them in that context.

Let me turn, then, to the examination of each of these issues and of the main solutions that have been given to them in the history of Western philosophy.

I. The Conception of Individuality

Of all the issues mentioned, perhaps the one that most influences the solution to the problem of individuation has to do with the conception of individuality. The question it raises is the following: What is it for something to be individual? If Socrates and this sheet of paper on which I am writing are individual, what does it mean to say that they are so? What features or characteristics are involved in being individual? In short, what is at stake is the analysis of the intension of 'individual'. In more traditional terms we could say that the issue concerns the definition of individuality. Just as, for example, a definition of "human being" consists in its analysis into rational animal, to use the most popular scholastic definition of it, so the analysis of "individuality" would involve the identification of those features that are involved in being individual, the necessary and sufficient conditions of individuality.

Throughout the history of Western philosophy, including the medieval period, individuality has been understood in a variety of ways. But at least six stand out: indivisibility, distinction, division of the species, identity, impredicability, and noninstantiability. Practically all of these views of individuality, taken alone or in some combination, are found in scholastic discussions of individuation.

Indivisibility is one of the most popular ways of understanding individuality, not only among scholastics, but throughout the history of Western thought.[5] The individual is conceived as that which cannot be divided. However, there are at least two important versions of this view. Some hold what may be characterized as an absolute notion of indivisibility: a thing is individual if and only if it cannot be divided. This view, of course, has serious problems, since we ordinarily regard many things that are divisible as individual, such as for example, this piece of paper on which I am writing or the body of the writer of these words. Obviously, something seems to be lost in the process of division of these things, but that does not make the things in question less individual. These considerations have led to modifications of the view of individuality as absolute indivisibility, in favor of a more moderate position that interprets indivisibility in relative terms. Those who favor a modified conception of individuality as indivisibility hold that individual things are indivisible in the sense that if they are divided they lose their being or their nature. For example, the body of the writer of these words is individual because, if divided, it ceases to be a body, becoming a pile of bodily parts. Still, others maintain what became an important view in the later Middle Ages, namely, that individuality consists in indivisibility into entities of the same specific nature as the original. Thus, for example, a cat is individual because it cannot be divided into cats even if it can be divided into organs, limbs, and other parts.

Another feature that has traditionally been used in the analysis of individuality has been what might be called "distinction" or "difference".[6] For those who favor this position either by itself or in conjunction with any of the others discussed here, to be individual is to be distinct or different from other things. The existence of a distinction or difference among things, then, is what constitutes the individuality of things. That Socrates and Aristotle are individual means that they are distinct from one another and from other things; Socrates is something other than Aristotle and vice versa, and likewise with the other individual things that exist in our world, such as cats, trees, and their features, if those features are considered to be individual. The distinction involved is not a distinction of genus or species, but what is usually called a "numerical distinction". The generic distinction exists among things that belong to different genera, such as a plant and a monkey. And the specific distinction holds among things that belong to different species, such as a man and a cat. However, the numerical distinction holds not only among things that differ in genus and species, but also among things that belong to the same genera and species, such as Plato and Aristotle. It is called "numerical'' precisely to differentiate it from the other two and to indicate that each of the things distinguished is one unit separate from others.

Distinction and difference as understood in this context should not be confused with diversity. Although the notion of diversity was controversial and different medieval authors proposed different understandings of it, for many scholastics things were diverse only if they had no nature in common.[7] Thus, for example, accidental features belonging to different categories, such as red and tall, were said to be diverse, not different. Difference or distinction implied some common ground or nature among the things said to be different or distinct. Nor is difference to be confused with the specific difference that, together with the genus, makes up the *definiens* of the definition of the species. The difference or distinction in question does not play the role that rationality, for example, plays in the definition of human being.

A third feature frequently associated with individuality is that individual things divide or, as scholastics preferred to say, ''multiply'' the species, creating what they called ''a plurality''.[8] Individual human beings, for example, multiply the species ''human being'', and the same, so it was argued, is the case with all other individuals and their respective species. Obviously, if individuality is taken to involve the division (or multiplication) of the species, and this is taken as a necessary condition of individuality, then the possibility of species with only one member is ruled out. This consequence was going to undermine this view of individuality in the eyes of those who, like Thomas Aquinas, maintained that each angel constitutes a complete species.

The notion of identity has also been frequently associated with individuality.[9] By identity here is meant the capacity of things to remain the same through time and some changes. For example, the sheet of paper on which I am writing was white and clean a few minutes ago, but now it has black marks all over it, and with time even the parts that are now white will probably turn yellow. Yet the sheet of paper will remain fundamentally the same: It will have endured through time, the changes I made on it, and the conditions that affected its color. Individuals, according to many authors, seem to have this capacity of endurance. But if this position is adopted and identity becomes a necessary condition of individuality, beings that do not experience time or change, such as God according to most scholastics, cannot be individual.

Another feature frequently associated with individuals is impredicability.[10] It is said that individuals cannot be predicated of other things although universals can. But impredicability can be understood in two ways, metaphysically and logically, depending on what one means by 'predication'. Nowadays most philosophers hold that predication is a relation between words. When one says that something is ''predicable'' or ''impredicable'' of something else one is speaking about a relation between words. This is a logical interpretation of predication that extends to impredicability. If one adopts this understanding of impredicability and at the same time holds that individuality involves impredicability, one is forced to concede that the individuals in question are words. And indeed, much of the contemporary discussion of individuality has been concerned with so-called individual or singular words such as proper names and indexicals.

On the other hand, prior to this century it was common to understand predication in such a way that it applied to things in addition to words.[11] In this sense, that something is predicable of something else means that it inheres in or adheres to it, as happens when something has a particular color or dimension.

Although some scholastics interpreted predicability and impredicability in purely logical terms, many of them used the notion of predication metaphysically and associated it with individuality. One popular formula during the period referred to individuals as "not being predicable of many" and another referred to them as "being predicable of only one".[12]

Finally, there are those who conceive individuality as noninstantiability, that is, as the impossibility for individuals to become instantiated in the way universals can.[13] Thus Socrates, for example, cannot be instantiated into other human beings or any other things for that matter, unlike "human being", which can be instantiated into Socrates, Aristotle, and the readers of this book. Scholastics developed a notion similar to this, but they called it "incommunicability".[14] This is in every way the most successful understanding of individuality in my opinion.

As mentioned earlier, these various understandings of individuality are used either singly or in combination throughout the late medieval period and the Counter-Reformation. But many authors did not separate their discussions from other issues related to individuation, and a substantial number of them did not make explicit their views on individuality. Their ideas in this regard are nevertheless implicit in their discussions and affect in important ways their perspectives concerning the principle of individuation.

II. The Extension of 'Individual'

A second philosophical issue closely related to the problem of individuation has to do with the extension of 'individual'. What is involved here is (1) the determination of whether there are any things that are individual, and (2) if there are any, which are those things. This issue is closely related to the problem of universals; namely, the problem of whether there are any things that are universal and, if there are any, which are universal and which are not. Indeed, for those philosophers who maintain, as many do, that the notions of universality and individuality are exhaustive and mutually exclusive, the problem of the extension of 'individual' and the problem of universals are one and the same.[15] For, if everything is either universal or individual, but cannot be both, to determine the extension of 'individual' is indirectly to determine the extension of 'universal' and vice versa. It is perhaps for this reason, together with the overwhelming concern that philosophers have had with universals ever since Plato, that this issue has generally been discussed in the context of universals and that few philosophers have dealt with it in the context of individuation. Yet, as stated earlier, the matter of extension has important implications for individuation, a fact that did not escape many late scholastics.

The variety of opinions in the history of Western philosophy concerning this problem is staggering. But three fundamental views have divided the philosophical community, even if within those three general views are found many variations. One (I) holds that nothing that exists is individual and, therefore, that everything that exists is universal. A second view (II) maintains that everything that exists is individual and, therefore, that there are no such things as universals. And a third position (III) finds a place in existence for both individuals and universals. Traditionally, the first view has been regarded as a very strong form of realism; the second view has been given the name of nominalism (although some versions of it as we shall see border on realism); and the third view has been regarded as a moderate form of realism.

Very few authors in the history of Western thought have held a clear and uncompromising version of the first position (I). Individuality seems too obvious in our experience to dismiss it as mere appearance, as the defenders of this position must do. It is difficult to maintain that the real world of existing beings is composed only of universals such as justice, humanity, redness, and the like and that individuals such as Socrates, Aristotle, and the chair on which I am sitting at this moment are devoid of real existence. Yet, there were and are proponents of this position, although they do not agree with each other.

There is a group of authors who, following a traditional interpretation of Plato, maintain (I-A) that there are as it were two separate realms. One is the realm composed of ideas or universal notions accessible only through reason. The other is the realm of experience, composed of individuals. The realm of universals is what constitutes reality, while the realm of individuals is a mere illusion. For example, the individual Socrates is an illusion, but the universals humanity, knowledge, and justice are real existents in a world separate from what is perceived by the senses. I do not know of anyone who today strictly adheres to this position, but it does seem that Plato was committed to some version of this view.

A different and more acceptable version of this position maintains (I-B) the same basic tenets of the first, except that it does not posit two separate realms but rather one that appears individual through sensation even though in reality is composed of universals.[16] Thus, Socrates is still an illusion if considered something other than the universal features of which he is composed.

Because of the emphasis on the transcendent character of universals, I like to call the first view (I-A) Transcendental Realism. The second (I-B) I call Immanent Realism because it brings the universals back into our world. In both cases the key to the understanding of the positions lies in the notions of reality and existence and how they are interpreted.

The second view (II), although as radical as the first in the uncompromising nature of its claim, has been paid lip service by many more philosophers.[17] Authors abound who say, for example, that everything that exists is individual or that nothing that exists is universal. But, when one pays closer attention to their position, it becomes clear that many of them substantially diminish the radicality of their claim. Indeed, as with the previous view, two basic versions of this position can be identified. According to one (II-A), the most radical and uncompromising version of the two, everything is individual and it is individual essentially. To be is by nature to be individual, and this applies to Aristotelian primary substances, to their features and components, and to anything else that might have some entitative status in the universe. There are no entities such as justice, humanity, or baldness apart from or even in Socrates that are not individual, because to be what they are requires by nature that they be individual. And it is these individual features and the things of which they are features that are real. The rest is an illusion. This version of the position clearly adheres to the letter of the formula given previously, and in the Middle Ages it was frequently attributed to William of Ockham and his followers.

But there is a second (II-B), more moderate interpretation of that formula, which holds that everything is indeed individual, but that the individuality in question is derived. In other words, things are not individual essentially; they are so as a result of something other than their natures. Socrates is not individual because to be a human being entails being individual, and the color of his beard is not individual because to be a color similarly entails being individual; rather Socrates and the color of his beard are individual because they have been individuated by something else. Socrates may have been individuated, for example, by the matter out of which he is composed, and the color of his beard may have been individuated because it belongs to him—the identification of the exact principle of individuation constitutes a separate issue. What is important to note is that this version of the second view (II) is moderate and opens itself up to all sorts of moves that can imply granting ontological status to universals even if, strictly speaking, they are denied existence. This openness has led many to call this position a type of moderate realism, depending on the status that its supporters give to universals, although it could as well be called a form of moderate nominalism. Indeed, the views of both Thomas Aquinas and Duns Scotus could be subsumed under this position, even though they are substantially different.

The third position (III) holds a middle ground between the other two outlined: both universals and individuals exist, although how their existence is interpreted varies considerably from author to author. The most frequent interpretation of the view, quite current in contemporary philosophy, holds that Aristotelian substances are individual but that their features and characteristics are not.[18] Thus, Socrates is individual, but the color of his beard and the texture of his skin, for example, are not. Interestingly enough, in the early Middle Ages this position was most widespread, but in the later Middle Ages, the moderate form of the second position discussed earlier (II-B) was most favored. Most authors accepted the individuality of both substances and their features, although they differed as to whether it was derived or essential and gave different emphases to the reality of natures.

III. Ontological Status of Individuality

A third issue closely related to individuation concerns the ontological status of individuality. It involves two questions. The first has to do with the ontological characterization of individuality. An ontological characterization consists in a description of the ontological type to which something belongs. For example, an ontological characterization of "the color red" within an Aristotelian metaphysics consists in its classification as a quality, and the ontological characterization of "human being" will state that human beings are substances. "Fatherhood", on the other hand, is a relation, and "one meter long" is a quantity. An ontological characterization of individuality, then, involves a determination of the fundamental ontological type to which individuality belongs.

The second question depends to a great extent on the answer to the first, for it has to do with the kind of distinction that there is between the individuality of an individual and its other components, principles, and characteristics. Take the individual Socrates. The issue this question raises in the case of Socrates concerns the type of distinction that there is between Socrates's individuality and Socrates's color of hair, benevolence, materiality, and so on.

These two questions did not become explicit in the early Middle Ages, but in the latter part of the age they were frequently addressed under the general question of "Whether in a thing the individual adds something to the common nature."[19] By "individual" sometimes it was meant the individual considered as a whole, that is, the composite of the common nature and individuality; and at other times it was meant only the individuality of the individual. The latter usage of the term 'individual' was quite frequent and created some confusion in the discussions of this issue.[20]

Many answers have been given to the first question in the history of Western philosophy, but seven of these are most important. Individuality has been characterized at various times as a substratum, a feature, a relation, a set or collection of features, a mode, nothing but the individual itself, and a concept external to the individual. These will be discussed in more detail later.

The answers to the second question show some variety but not nearly as much as the answers to the first question. Fundamentally the answers to it can be grouped into three basic positions. One holds that individuality is really distinct from the nature of the individual and therefore that one can distinguish in an individual thing two realities, its nature and its individuality. These come together to constitute the individual: Socrates's individuality and his humanity (his nature in this case) are really distinct but come together to constitute Socrates.

The second position holds that there is only a conceptual distinction between the individuality of the individual and its nature. In reality the individuality of the individual and its nature are one and the same thing, but mentally one can separate them and consider them as two. Socrates's humanity and Socrates's individuality are one and the same thing; there are no two things that come together to constitute Socrates. The distinction between Socrates's individuality and his nature is only the result of someone's mental consideration.

Finally, there is a position that tries to bridge the gap between these two. It is known by various names. Duns Scotus introduced the term 'formal distinction' and Suárez and others used terms such as 'modal distinction' and 'distinction *ex natura rei*' to refer to it. Although one must be careful not to equate these and other versions of the view, since there are important differences among them, in general the position can be described as holding that the distinction between the nature and the individuality of an individual is something less than real but more than conceptual. How 'more' and 'less' are unpacked depends very much on the author and has been the subject of much controversy, but it need not concern us at this point. Socrates's nature and individuality, then, are not separate or separable things in reality; they are inseparable, yet, as Scotus seems to have suggested, their intensional analyses are different. A thing's individuality is not the same as its nature. Now, since the view that authors take of the distinction between an individual's nature and its individuality depends to a great extent on the view they take of the ontological status of individuality, we need first to discuss the seven mentioned theories of the status of individuality, if only briefly, dealing with the distinction between the nature and the individuality of the individual in that context.

First, the view of individuality as a substratum goes back to the well-known *haecceitas* of Duns Scotus and has received considerable attention in this century under the name of the Bare Particular View.[21] It proposes to understand individuality as a decharacterized entity, sometimes regarded as a formality, in the individual, whose only function is to individuate the nature. Thus Socrates is composed not only of his properties and accidental characteristics but also of a decharacterized principle that is responsible for the individuality of both Socrates and his features. Most traditional authors who adhered to this position held that there is no empirical verification of this substratum; it is postulated purely on dialectical considerations based on the need to account for the individuality of individuals. But others claim some empirical acquaintance with it.[22] Again, most philosophers who favor this view accept the middle sort of position described earlier concerning the distinction between individuality and the nature: the nature and individuality are distinguished formally, modally, *ex natura rei,* or in a similar fashion. The distinction between Socrates's humanity and his individuality is formal, that is, Socrates's humanity cannot be separated from his individuality, but it is not his individuality: their intensional analyses are different.

A second view of individuality, also popular, interprets it as a feature.[23] Thus, individuality, like redness or tallness, characterizes individual things. Sometimes this feature is conceived as a first-order feature along with the other features that characterize an individual, and at other times it is conceived as a second-order feature of individuals. In either case the distinction between the feature in question and the nature of the individual is taken to be real or at least something intermediate between real and conceptual, since it is a distinction between two real things. What makes Socrates individual is a feature similar to what makes him heavy, for example, and as such Socrates's individuality must be really distinct from his humanity and the other features belonging to him.

Third, others interpret individuality as a relation, making it dependent on things other than the individual itself or its components.[24] In the example of Socrates, his individuality would in this view be a relation between him and some other things. By himself Socrates would not be individual; he is so only in relation to something else. In this case the type of distinction holding between the individuality and the nature of the individual will depend on the view of relations adopted. For those who accept the reality of relations, the distinction will be at least intermediate and most likely real. But for those who interpret relations as mental beings, then the distinction could be conceptual.

Fourth, a more popular ontological view of individuality, which goes back to some texts of Boethius and is found in authors of the early Middle Ages, conceives it as a set or collection of features.[25] Thus, we are told that the individuality of Socrates, for example, is his Socrateity and that such Socrateity is composed of the features and characteristics that compose the individual Socrates. Individuality in this sense becomes a bundle of features. This is what has given rise to the name Bundle View, although this view is not only about the ontological status of individuality, but also about the principle of individuation, as we shall see later. Those who adopt this position usually make only a conceptual distinction between the individual and its nature. If the individuality of the individual is identified with the set or collection of its features, there is nothing left in the individual from which its individuality could be distinguished. The distinction between something's individuality and its nature, then, becomes a purely conceptual matter resulting from the way an observer looks at things.

A fifth view interprets individuality as nothing other than the individual itself.[26] This position differs from the one just mentioned in that it does not accept that the individual is composed of features or natures that taken together form its individuality. Having a nominalistic origin, the position rejects the existence of natures and features in the individual and so, in identifying the individuality of the individual with the individual itself, does not reduce individuality to a set or collection of features. Naturally, the most likely distinction that this view will accept between the individuality of the individual and its nature is conceptual, since there is only one thing in reality, which is conceived in two different ways. However, I say "most likely" because there have been some authors, such as Suárez, for example, who have challenged this view of the distinction between the individuality of the individual and its nature and who have made the attempt to find an intermediate sort of distinction between them.

For those who hold that individuals have no real existence, there is a sixth point of view concerning the ontological status of individuality, in which individuality is understood as a concept external to a thing resulting from some mental consideration.[27] Individuality, then, is nothing in an individual thing, but rather it is a kind of fiction based on a subject's perception of the thing. Socrates, as an individual, is an illusion. As with the previous position, those who adhere to this point of view generally find only a conceptual distinction between the individuality of a thing and its nature, in the sense that the concept of individuality has no real counterpart in the thing. It should be noted, however, that the concept as such, considered as present in a subject, can be conceived as something real and distinct from the thing that it purports to represent. But that, of course, is an entirely different matter with no particular bearing on the issue at stake here.

Finally, there is the mode theory, which I believe is the best way to understand individuality.[28] As a mode, individuality can be inseparable but still conceptually distinct from the individual and its features. For modes are not realities independent of the things they modify, but nevertheless are intensionally distinct from them. Thus a mode of walking, say quickly, is nothing other in fact than walking, but it is something intensionally distinct from just walking, since walking can also be done slowly. Thus, to say that individuality is a mode is to say that it is inseparable, but still conceptually distinct, from the individual and its features.

IV. The Principle of Individuation

The core of the problem of individuation involves the identification of the principle of individuation. However, as we already saw, different conceptions of individuality will yield a search for different principles. For it is one thing to ask for a principle of indivisibility and another to ask for a principle of difference and distinction. And likewise with multiplication (or division), identity, impredicability, and noninstantiability. Not every author in the Middle Ages and the Counter-Reformation observed these distinctions, but some were aware of at least some of them, thus keeping separate, for example, the search for a principle of individuation considered as indivisibility or distinction on the one hand, and the search for the principle of multiplication, on the other.

Likewise, as already mentioned, different extensional and ontological views of individuality will affect the kinds of answers that will be found adequate by different authors. So it is important to try to understand exactly what an author's views are on these matters before one examines and evaluates the author's position concerning the principle of individuation.

Another matter that needs to be kept in mind while discussing individuation is that in the later Middle Ages and the Counter-Reformation the distinction between substance and accident was generally accepted, and most authors also accepted the individuality of accidents and other features of substances. As a result, the individuation of both substances and accidents were subjects of discussion during the period. In this analysis I shall adopt that distinction and keep the discussion of the individuation of substances separate from the discussion of the individuation of accidents. I shall not discuss the individuation of other entities, such as events and propositions, because most scholastics would analyze them in substance-accident terms.

1. Individuation of Substances

There are five different types of theories concerning the individuation of substances. They may be classified as follows: (1) bundle theories, (2) accidental theories, (3) essential theories, (4) existential theories, and (5) external theories.

Although there are different varieties of (1) bundle theories of individuation, most agree that the principle of individuation is the bundle of features that a thing has.[29] Thus, in Socrates, for example, his individuality is a result of the color of his beard, his having a snubnose, his dimensions and weight, and so forth; that is, the bundle of all the features he has. Note that the features in question include what Aristotelians call properties as well as accidents. Properties are the features that always accompany the members of the species, while accidents are features that an individual belonging to a particular species may or may not have.[30]

In contrast with bundle theories of individuation, (2) the accidental theory holds that only certain accidental features are responsible for individuality. There are various versions of this theory, depending on the accidental characteristics identified as individuators, but the most commonly found are spatio-temporal and quantitative theories.

Spatio-temporal theories have in common that they identify spatial, temporal, or spatio-temporal coordinates as individuators.[31] Socrates is said to be individual because he occupies a particular space or because he lives at a particular time, or because he is both here and now. Clearly, the strongest version of these theories is the one that combines space and time, and indeed many of the views that seem to be concerned exclusively with space frequently assume time as well. It is important to note that the theories vary also with respect to what they understand by space. Some of them interpret space as location or position, that is, the spatial relation of something to other things. According to this view space is understood as a relation. But others understand by space a nonrelational feature of things, more like the inner boundary of a thing. Understood in the latter way, what individuates Socrates is not, as in the previous view, the location or position he has with respect to the things that surround him but the portion of space he occupies. Taken in this way, the spatio-temporal view is very similar to a quantitative view of individuation, since it boils down to the dimensions of a thing.[32] Socrates's individuator would be the dimensions he has.

In contrast with the theories of accidental individuation, others choose (3) features essential to a thing as individuators. And again there are different varieties of this point of view. Three in particular stand out. The first, frequently found in the history of philosophy, argues that it is the matter in things that individuates them.[33] Thus the flesh and bones of Socrates account for his individuality, and the marble in this statue of Aphrodite makes it individual. Obviously, this view restricts individuality to material entities. In most cases the view is understood to refer to matter considered by itself, but sometimes matter has been combined with an accident, such as dimensions, to account for individuality. Thomas Aquinas, for example, maintained a view of the latter sort.

Another view of individuation that relies on essential features adopts form as individuator.[34] Socrates is individual owing to his form. The form is the inner structure of a being, involves its essential features, and according to some, is what gives it being. Therefore, it must be responsible for individuality. In a human being, for example, the form is the humanity of the being and should account not only for the thing being the type of thing it is, but also for its being individual. This position was usually attributed to Averroes in the Middle Ages, but several scholastics also favored it, as will become evident in some of the chapters included in this volume.

The third most popular view of essential individuation holds that individuation is due to a sui generis principle in things whose function is only to individuate and that has no characteristics of its own. Because it is decharacterized the principle has been called a "bare particular" by some contemporary authors.[35] In the Middle Ages, Scotists referred to it as *haecceitas*, that is, "thisness". In Socrates, for example, it is the thisness that turns humanity into this humanity, that is, into Socrates's humanity.

Much less popular than these theories is (4) the theory of existential individuation, which in the Middle Ages was usually attributed to Avicenna. According to this view, a version of which I have recently defended, the principle of individuation is the existence of a thing.[36] Naturally, fundamental to the understanding of this view is the analysis of existence. For those who interpret existence essentially, this view becomes either a formal view or a substantial view, depending on the relation of essence to form and substance. And for those who interpret existence as an act, it is the act that individuates. In either case, existence becomes a necessary and sufficient condition of something being individual.

Finally, some authors have tried to find the source of individuation in (5) principles external to a thing, such as the natural or supernatural agents that produced it. They argue that Socrates, for example, is individual owing to his parents (natural causes) or to God's activity (supernatural cause). But these views have not been frequently defended in the history of philosophy and are very deficient from a theoretical point of view.[37]

2. Individuation of Accidents

The aforementioned views, I believe, are the most important with respect to the individuation of substances, and most other views can be reduced to one of them. Now, those who hold, as most later scholastics did, that not only Aristotelian primary substances but also accidents are subject to indi-

viduation have devised three basic types of theories to account for their individuation. The first maintains that accidents are individuated through the
substance in which they are found.[38] Thus, for example, the gray color of
Socrates's beard is individuated through the fact that it belongs to Socrates.
This may be described, then, as a substantial view of the individuation of
accidents, and it was popular with a host of scholastics including Thomas
Aquinas. Another theory holds that accidents are individuated through other
features of the substance. And here there can be a variety of opinions, depending on whether the features are taken altogether as a bundle or whether
specific features, such as spatio-temporal location, are taken to individuate.
And, finally, there is a theory, a favorite of nominalists such as Ockham and
maintained by Suárez among others, that argues that accidents are individuated by themselves.[39] This brings us to the end of the discussion of the four
fundamental issues that I claimed were involved in individuation. However,
two other issues were mentioned earlier that need to be introduced, although
they are not metaphysical issues strictly speaking and therefore their discussion need not be detailed: the discernibility of and reference to individuals.

V. Discernibility of Individuals

The issue of the discernibility of individuals is epistemic, although it is
frequently confused or purposefully identified with the issue of individuation.[40] The issue of individuation involves the question of the principle that
accounts for individuality. The issue of the discernibility of individuals, on
the other hand, is concerned with the principles that make possible the identification of an individual by a knower: How and by what means are we able
to discern individuals qua individuals?

Obviously, the two issues are closely related, but there is a clear logical
distinction between the two. The close relation between the issues has made
possible their frequent confusion in the history of philosophy. But there are
authors who do not confuse them. Some of them, however, particularly in
contemporary circles, believe that the only legitimate issue for philosophers
is the epistemic one. Be that as it may, it will become clear in the course of
this volume that some scholastics distinguished the two issues and identified
principles of discernibility different from principles of individuation, whereas
others did not. With respect to the principles that philosophers have identified as principles of discernibility, we find as many theories as there are of
individuation, and they follow along pretty much the same lines. There are
bundle theories, accidental and essential theories, and even sui generis theories. Since similar views have been presented earlier in the context of individuation, and since our concern in this book is not epistemic, there is no
need to deal with them at this point.

VI. Reference to Individuals

Another problem that needs to be mentioned, if only briefly and in passing, is the issue of the reference to individuals. As users of language, we refer to individuals with various terms. Therefore, a complete treatment of individuation would have to include some discussion of the terms used to refer to individuals, the function of these terms, and how they work. These issues have been the source of much discussion in contemporary circles, owing to the linguistic turn introduced into philosophy by the analytic movement at the beginning of this century. But in the Middle Ages and the Counter-Reformation they did not occupy as important a position. While all the other issues that have been mentioned here were explicitly discussed to some extent in the context of individuation, the issue of reference was frequently ignored altogether or taken up in contexts other than individuation. For these reasons there is no need to discuss it in detail in this Introduction, although at least one author discussed in this volume pays some attention to it.

Having discussed the various issues that are related to the problem of individuation, we are ready to turn to the positions of the authors who are discussed in this volume. Before we do that, however, it would be useful to say something about the development of the problem of individuation in the early Middle Ages. In that way we will be able to understand better the point of departure of twelfth century scholastics with respect to this issue. The chapter that follows presents a sketch of such development.

Notes

1. *Introduction to the Problem of Individuation in the Early Middle Ages,* Analytica Series (Munich, Vienna, and Washington, DC: Philosophia Verlag and Catholic University of America Press, 1984). Elsewhere I have a systematic study of individuality and individuation in which I present my own ideas on the subject while referring to both contemporary and scholastic positions: *Individuality: An Essay on the Foundations of Metaphysics* (Albany: SUNY Press, 1988).

2. Aristotle, *Posterior Analytics* 2, no. 11 (94a20). I have also provided a justification of the historiographical approach I use here in Chapter 5 of *Philosophy and Its History: Issues in Philosophical Historiography* (Albany: SUNY Press, 1991).

3. This view was widespread in the early Middle Ages as I have shown in *Introduction to the Problem of Individuation.* For some contemporary discussions of this position, see Max Black, "The Identity of Indiscernibles", *Mind* 61 (1952); rep. in *Problems of Analysis* (Ithaca, NY: Cornell University Press, 1954). Also A. J. Ayer, "The Identity of Indiscernibles", in *Philosophical Essays* (London: Macmillan and Co., 1954), pp. 26 ff.; and P. F. Strawson, "On Particular and General", *Proceedings*

of the Aristotelian Society 54 (1953–54); rep. in M. J. Loux, ed., *Universals and Particulars* (Notre Dame, IN: Notre Dame University Press, 1976), p. 67; and *Individuals* 3, 4 (London: Methuen and Co., 1959).

4. This view is scholastic in origin and it is primarily in scholastic texts that one finds it explicitly stated as will become clear in this volume. However, there are some contemporary non-scholastic authors who have views that have some parallels with this position. For example, cf. Nelson Goodman, "A World of Individuals", in *The Problem of Universals*, ed. Charles Landesman (Notre Dame, IN: Notre Dame University Press, 1956), p. 296.

5. *Ibid.*

6. See n. 3.

7. For various understandings of diversity in the early medieval period, see my *Introduction to the Problem of Individuation*, p. 3.

8. Gustav Bergmann appears to include plurality in his understanding of individuality in *Logic and Reality* (Madison: University of Wisconsin Press, 1964), pp. 159 ff.

9. Henry Veatch, "Essentialism and the Problem of Individuation", *Proceedings of the American Catholic Philosophical Association* 47 (1974): 64–73.

10. P. F. Strawson, *Individuals* 5 (London: Methuen and Co., 1959).

11. John of Salisbury, *Metalogicon* 2, 17, ed. Clemens C. Webb (Oxford, 1929), p. 92. More recently, Michael Loux has argued against a purely linguistic view of predication in *Substance and Attribute: A Study in Ontology* (Dordrecht, Holland, and Boston: Reidel, 1978), p. 90.

12. Boethius, *In librum Aristotelis De interpretatione, editio secunda*, in *PL* 64, pp. 318–319. For Aristotle's text, see *On Interpretation* 7 (17a38).

13. I have argued for this position in "Individuals as Instances", *Review of Metaphysics* 37 (1983): 39–59, and in *Introduction to the Problem of Individuation*.

14. This term was introduced in this context by Boethius in *De interpretatione, PL* 64: 462–464.

15. For arguments against the view that universality and individuality are exhaustive and mutually exclusive, see A. J. Ayer, "Individuals", in *Philosophical Essays* (London: Macmillan and Co., 1954), pp. 1–25.

16. For contemporary discussions of versions of this position, see Bertrand Russell, *The Problems of Philosophy* (Oxford: Clarendon Press, 1912), *An Inquiry into Meaning and Truth* 6 (London: Allen and Unwin, 1940), p. 93, and *Human Knowledge: Its Scope and Limits* (New York: Simon and Schuster, 1948), pp. 77 ff. and 292 ff. Also Ayer, "The Identity of Indiscernibles", in *Philosophical Essays,*

pp. 26 ff. Very few scholastics adhered to versions (A) or (B) of (I), but there are some early medieval figures who did as we shall see in the next chapter.

17. D. C. Williams, "The Elements of Being", *Review of Metaphysics* 7 (1953), pp. 3–18 and 171–192; Nicholas Wolterstorff, *On Universals* (Chicago: University of Chicago Press, 1970), pp. 133 ff; Wilfrid Sellars, *Science and Metaphysics* (London: Routledge and Kegan Paul, 1967), p. 107; and W. V. O. Quine, *From a Logical Point of View* (Cambridge, MA: Harvard University Press, 1953), p. 10.

18. P. F. Strawson, *Individuals*, p. 2; Gustav Bergmann, *Realism, A Critique of Brentano and Meinong* (Madison: University of Wisconsin Press, 1967), p. 24; D. C. Long, "Particulars and Their Qualities", *Philosophical Quarterly* 18 (1968); rep. in M. Loux, ed., *Universals and Particulars* (New York: Anchor Books, 1970), pp. 280–281.

19. Francisco Suárez, *Disputatio metaphysica* V, sect. 2.

20. Gracia, *Introduction to the Problem of Individuation*, p. 34.

21. Edwin B. Allaire, "Bare Particulars", *Philosophical Studies* 14 (1963): 1–7. The similarities between the two positions should not be overstressed, however. See Woosuk Park, "Haecceitas and the Bare Particular", *Review of Metaphysics* 46 (1990): 375–398.

22. See Allaire's article cited in n. 21.

23. Ayer, "The Identity of Indiscernibles".

24. B. J. Martine, *Individuation and Individuality* (Albany: SUNY Press, 1984), pp. 4, 10, 72–73, and 75. Also Héctor-Neri Castañeda, "Individuation and Non-Identity", *American Philosophical Quarterly* 12 (1975): 131–140.

25. Boethius, *De interpretatione, PL* 64: 318 ff.; Thierry of Chartres and Gilbert of Poitiers, in Gracia, *Introduction to the Problem of Individuation* 3; and Ayer, "The Identity of Indiscernibles".

26. See n. 17.

27. This would be the ontological counterpart of the extensional view described earlier as Realism.

28. *Individuality* 3.

29. See n. 16.

30. These formulae are found in Boethius' translation of Porphyry's *Isagoge*, second edition, 4, 17, ed. Samuel Brandt, in *CSEL* (Vienna: Tempsky, 1906; rep. New York: Johnson, 1966), vol. 48, pp. 275 and 280.

31. K. R. Popper, "The Principle of Individuation", *Proceedings of the Aristotelian Society* 27 (1953): 107–112; J. W. Meiland, "Do Relations Individuate?"

Philosophical Studies 17 (1966): 65–69; V. C. Chappell, "Particulars Re-clothed", *Philosophical Studies* 15 (1964): 60–64. The origin of this view in the Middle Ages can be traced to texts of Boethius and Porphyry, as we shall see in the next chapter.

32. I have found no contemporary authors who subscribe to a quantitative view of individuation, but in the later Middle Ages some attributed this position to Thomas. See Suárez, Disp. V, sect. 3, in Gracia, *Suárez on Individuation* (Milwaukee: Marquette University Press, 1982), pp. 81 and 95.

33. G. E. M. Anscombe, "The Principle of Individuation", *Berkeley and Modern Problems, Proceedings of the Aristotelian Society,* suppl. vol. 27 (1953): 83–96; A. C. Lloyd, "Aristotle's Principle of Individuation", *Mind* 79 (1970): 519–529.

34. David Wiggins, *Sameness and Substance* (Oxford: Basil Blackwell, 1980), p. 92; J. Lukasiewicz, "The Principle of Individuation", *Proceedings of the Aristotelian Society,* suppl. vol. 27 (1953): 81.

35. G. Bergmann, *Logic and Reality* (Madison: University of Wisconsin Press, 1964), pp. 133, 288, 318 ff., and *The Metaphysics of Logical Positivism* (London: Longmans, Green and Co., 1954), pp. 197 ff. Also Allaire, "Bare Particulars", pp. 1–7.

36. Gracia, *Individuality* 4.

37. I have found no contemporary authors who adhere to this position, but some scholastics speak this way.

38. D. C. Long, "Particulars and Their Qualities", pp. 264–284; A. Quinton, *The Nature of Things* (London: Routledge and Kegan Paul, 1973), pp. 28 ff.

39. G. F. Stout, "The Nature of Universals and Propositions", *Proceedings of the British Academy* 10 (1921); rep. in Charles Landesman, ed., *The Problem of Universals,* pp. 153–166.

40. Bertrand Russell, *Human Knowledge,* pp. 292 ff.; and P. F. Strawson, *Individuals,* pp. 2 ff.

2

THE LEGACY OF THE EARLY
MIDDLE AGES

JORGE J. E. GRACIA

I. Boethius (b. ca. 480; d. ca. 524)

Medieval discussion of the problem of individuation began with Boethius. However, one should not expect to find in his writings a systematic analysis of the problem that distinguishes the various issues discussed in the Introduction to this book. Nor should one expect to find precise formulations of the various questions involved in those issues or of the solutions to those questions that later scholastics gave. Indeed, even the terminology that Boethius used differs in many ways from the terminology that was used in later centuries to deal with individuation. Still, it is in Boethius's texts that we find the first explicit references in the medieval period to the problem of individuation as well as views that, although not worked out in detail, became the subject of important controversies later on. In particular, Boethian formulae became well-entrenched in the early Middle Ages and were often repeated and used by subsequent authors. In many cases, Boethius's authority in these matters was regarded as so important that even those writers in the early medieval period who clearly disagreed with him felt the need to interpret his views in order not to have them clash with their own positions. In short, Boethius's influence in the area of individuation was extraordinary, a fact that can be explained in part because most of the discussions of individuation until the twelfth century occur precisely in commentaries on Boethian works or on works by Aristotle and Porphyry that Boethius had translated and on which he had commented.

The texts where Boethius refers to individuation fall into two different categories, which give rise to two textual and philosophical currents in subsequent discussions of individuation. The first comprises his logical works;

namely, the commentaries on works by Porphyry and Aristotle to which reference has already been made. This group includes the two important editions of his translation of and commentary on Porphyry's *Isagoge,* the translation of and commentary on Aristotle's *Categories,* and the two editions of the translation of and commentary on Aristotle's *De interpretatione.*[1] The second group comprises his theological tractates, including *De trinitate, Utrum pater et filius, Quomodo substantiae, De fide catholica,* and *Contra Eutychen.*[2]

Not all of Boethius's logical and theological works, however, had the same impact upon subsequent writers. Of the logical works, the *Commentary on Porphyry's "Isagoge",* particularly the second, more detailed edition, was most influential. Although the other logical works also contained important views on individuation, the commentaries on Aristotle's *Categories* and *De interpretatione* were not used as much as the commentary on Porphyry.[3] Likewise, in the context of individuation there was one theological work that exercised particular influence, *De trinitate,* although *Contra Eutychen* also had some influence. The reason for the greater impact of *De trinitate* was not that the other theological tractates were used less, but rather that only in *De trinitate* did Boethius discuss matters relevant to individuation to any serious extent. Relevant comments are also found in *Contra Eutychen,* but they are few and have to do primarily with persons rather than with individuals as such.[4]

There are three important ways in which Boethius's thought affected subsequent discussions of individuation. The first (A) concerns the introduction and passing down of terminology; the second (B) has to do with Boethius's own philosophical views related to individuation; and the third (C) involves the way in which the two groups of works already mentioned influenced discussions of individuation in different ways, creating two currents of development that used different approaches.

The number of terms that Boethius used in the discussion of individuation is substantial. Many of these terms had been used by other thinkers in their own texts or in their translations of Greek terms into Latin, although Boethius was responsible for the introduction of others. But, regardless of whether Boethius introduced them for the first time in technical philosophical discourse or not, it was largely due to his use of them and it was with the connotations that he attached to them, that they entered the philosophical vocabulary of later generations of medieval authors. Many of these terms are not particularly or especially related to individuation. Terms and expressions such as *unum* (one), *substantia* (substance), *subsistentia* (subsistence), *subiectum* (subject), *accidens* (accident), *forma* (form), *materia* (matter), *proprietas* and *proprium* (property), *id quod est* (that which something is), *id quo est* (that whereby something is), *praedicare* (to predicate), *dividire* (to divide), and the like are not parochial to discussions of individuation. None-theless, they are basic terms whose understanding often affects in important ways the views that might be held concerning individuation. There are other terms and expressions, however, whose use is primarily related to discussions of individuation. Among the most important ones in Boethius's works are the following: *individuum* (individual), *particulare* (particular), *singulare* (singu-lar), *numero* (number), *differentia numerica* (numerical difference), *alteritas* (otherness), *diversitas* (diversity), *differentia* (difference), *indifferentia* (in-difference), *incommunicabile* (incommunicable), *communicabile* (communi-cable), *non praedicabile* (impredicable), *universale* (universal), *idem* (same), *pluralitas* and *multitudo* (plurality), *varietas accidentium* (variety of acci-dents), and *collectio proprietatum* (bundle or collection of properties). These and other terms and expressions, as well as their derivatives, were not always used in the same way by Boethius and later thinkers, and often disputes arose precisely concerning their proper understanding or because of their under-standing. Yet, the introduction or use of so much technical terminology was to have a substantial impact on future discussions of individuation.

The second way (B) in which Boethius's impact upon discussions of individuation was felt was through the ideas he proposed concerning this topic. For although, as mentioned earlier, many of his views did not enjoy wide acceptance and others were insufficiently developed, most of them had some influence on the thought of those who discussed individuation. Perhaps the most important of these ideas was his view concerning the principle of individuation, although it should be kept in mind that he did not use the ex-pression 'principle of individuation' (*principium individuationis*).[5] That ter-minology was developed much later. Boethius spoke rather of what causes (*facit*) numerical difference.[6] Also important to note is that there are certain variations in how he expressed his position that could have given rise to dif-ferent interpretations. On the one hand, in the *Commentary on the Isagoge* the analysis suggests two different views of the individuation of substances: an accidental view in which the individuality of individual accidents individ-uates the substance, and a bundle view, in which the uniqueness of a set of features considered together is responsible for the individuation of substance.[7] Accidents themselves, as well as other properties and features, are individuated by the substance in which they are found.[8] And this view concerning the individuation of accidents is repeated in the *Commentary on the Categories*.[9] On the other hand, although in *De trinitate* there is no men-tion of individuation as such, Boethius provides us with a very clear state-ment to the effect that the variety of accidents (*accidentium varietas*), and place (*locus*) if all else fails, makes a substance numerically different.[10] The similarity between this view and the one suggested by statements in the *Com-*

mentaries is striking and may have been the reason why most of Boethius's commentators concluded that in his opinion the principle of individuation and the principle of numerical difference were one and the same. Indeed, most of them did not make a distinction between individuality and numerical difference.

This brings us to the conception of individuality, another area of Boethian thought where his ideas had considerable impact upon the development of the problem of individuation. The difficulty here, however, is that Boethius does not always favor or use the same conception of individuality, and when he does, he speaks about it in different terms. In particular three ways in which Boethius speaks of individuality are important for understanding subsequent developments. In the logical commentaries he speaks of individuality as indivisibility, although often the indivisibility involved is of different sorts. But he also uses the notions of nontransferability, incommunicability, and impredicability. Moreover, although he never analyzes individuality in terms of numerical difference in those works, he discusses numerical difference in the context of individuality. And what looks like the principle of individuation in the logical commentaries and what is regarded as the cause of numerical difference in *De trinitate* are very similar if not the same. All of this led subsequent thinkers to equate individuality and numerical difference, as suggested earlier. The conception of individuality as impredicability is prevalent in the *Commentary on the Isagoge*.[11] There are also comments there about indivisibility and nontransferability, but the overriding emphasis seems to be on impredicability.[12] The notion of incommunicability is used elsewhere, in the *Commentary on De interpretatione*, but as already stated, that work did not have much influence in the early Middle Ages.[13] As will become evident in some of the chapters contained in this volume, however, the notion of incommunicability was reintroduced in the thirteenth century in connection with individuality. Finally, although there is some discussion of numerical difference in the logical works,[14] the discussion found in *De trinitate* 1 is very clear and makes no mention of impredicability.[15]

A third important area where Boethius's thought on individuality had a marked impact upon subsequent discussions has to do with the extension of 'individual'. For, although Boethius does not seem to adopt a clear position on this in all instances, there are many places where he makes comments relevant to this issue. In some works he clearly accepts not only Aristotelian primary substances but also their features as individual.[16] In other places, however, he seems to speak as if some features of substances, and indeed substances themselves, were not individual.[17] In the area of the ontology of individuality, Boethius does not say anything very clear, but he speaks of the "property" and "quality" of individuals.[18] And he distinguishes between real number, which is a kind of unity in things, and the number by which we count, which presumably is something mental.[19] These ideas were discussed by others later.

Another important legacy of the Boethian discussions of individuality was that they contain no attempt to distinguish between the metaphysical issue of individuation and the epistemic problem of the discernibility of individuals. There are texts that seem to be speaking about one and not the other, but there are others that seem to be speaking about both of them at once.[20]

Finally, in spite of Boethius's interest in logic and logical subjects, one can find relatively little about the topic of reference in his works. Moreover, the little that one can find is confined to the logical works.[21]

Apart from terminology and specific doctrines, there is a third way (C) in which Boethius's legacy substantially influenced subsequent discussions of individuation. Largely as a result of his influence, the discussion of individuation in the early Middle Ages developed along two different lines. The first followed a generally metaphysical approach that viewed individuality as characterizing things in the world. Those who adopted this approach usually devised theories about the nature and principle of individuation. The other approach had a primarily logical bent and was interested in individuality mainly as characterizing words or concepts. Consequently, those who fall into this group devised views about individuality that were largely logical in character. Those thinkers who followed the former approach posed questions, for example, about the principle of individuation: What is it that makes Socrates individual? But those who adopted the second approach were concerned with questions about the terms employed to refer to individuals and how they are used and function: How does 'Socrates' function and how is it capable of picking out the individual Socrates?

These two lines of development do not seem to be the result of a conscious effort on the part of Boethius to separate the metaphysical and logical issues involved in individuation. In fact, it does not seem that he was very conscious of two different sets of questions and often he seems to have mixed logical and metaphysical issues without any qualms.[22] These lines of development are only an indirect consequence of the way Boethius approached individuality and related issues in different works. In the logical works the notion of individuality as impredicability seems to have the upper hand, and therefore, authors who read and commented on those works tended to discuss the aspects of individuality that had to do with logic, even if they did not always restrict themselves to those issues. On the other hand, it is clear that in *De trinitate* the central question raised in the context of individuality is the metaphysical issue of what causes numerical difference. Those authors, then, who commented on *De trinitate* tended to deal with individuality or numerical difference metaphysically, frequently ignoring the logical issues that concerned the commentators on the logical works.

II. The Standard Theory of Individuality

The dichotomy between the metaphysical and logical approaches is especially evident in the rise of a largely self-contained metaphysical tradition in discussions of individuality and in particular of what I have called elsewhere "the Standard Theory of Individuality".[23] This theory was metaphysical and dominated most of the thinking about individuality in the early Middle Ages. It was held in one form or another by John Eriugena, Odo of Tournai, Anselm of Aosta, Adelard of Bath, Clarembald of Arras, William of Champeaux, Thierry of Chartres, and in modified forms, by Gilbert of Poitiers and John of Salisbury, among others. It had four main aspects: the conception of individuality as difference or distinction, the restriction of the extension of 'individual' to Aristotelian primary substances, the lack of distinction between the problem of individuation and the problem concerned with the discernibility of individuals, and finally, most important of all, the identification of the principle of individuation either (1) with one or more accidents (usually place) of a substance or (2) with the collection of all features (including nonaccidental ones) belonging to the substance.

The view that individuality is some kind of difference or distinction was not often stated explicitly or clearly. And most likely many authors were not conscious of the intensional issue it involved. But the fact that there were some authors, like Odo of Tournai and Gilbert of Poitiers, who explicitly discussed what they considered to be the proper understanding of individuality and tried to distinguish it from other notions, such as singularity, indicates that this was a problem with which at least some authors were concerned.[24]

The understanding of individuality as a kind of difference had its origin in Boethian texts. It is true that Boethius did not say that individuality consists in a kind of difference, or that it is the same thing as numerical difference, as most supporters of the Standard Theory of Individuality understood it to be. But there are statements in Boethius's logical works in which there is a suggestion of at least a close relation between individuality and difference in general and between individuality and numerical difference in particular. Moreover, the fact that Boethius maintained in *De trinitate* that what makes something numerically different is the variety of accidents, and also presented in the logical works what looked like accidental and bundle theories of individuation, must have contributed to the identification of the two notions by many subsequent authors.

Whereas the first aspect of the Standard Theory was most often only implicit, the view that individuality is restricted to Aristotelian primary substances and, therefore, that the accidents and features of things are not individual, was not only explicitly stated but also openly defended by many authors. Interestingly enough, although some statements of Boethius may be interpreted as supporting this view, in general it is clear from the works we have mentioned that, according to him, not only substances but also accidents and other features of substances can be individual. The sources of this position concerning accidents and features of substances must be found, then, in the strong neo-Platonic currents at work during the early medieval period rather than in the Boethian texts.

As with the first aspect of the Standard Theory, the lack of distinction between individuation and the discernibility of individuals was not explicitly held during this period. The closest that one gets to an explicit statement of this point of view is in John Eriugena.[25] But at least one author, Gilbert of Poitiers, presented a different view, a fact that indicates an awareness of the problem and suggests the existence of different ideas on the subject at the time. The background of this aspect of the Standard Theory can be found in Boethius, for in many of his texts epistemic language about discernibility is mixed with metaphysical language about individuation. For example, he wrote frequently and even in the same passage as if "that whereby things *are called* individual or *are known* to be individual" were the same as "that whereby things *are caused* to be individual".[26] Whether he did this consciously or not must remain a matter of scholarly interpretation, since the texts are inconclusive. However, what is important to note is that the ambiguity of his texts surely must have helped to preserve the lack of distinction between the two issues in the minds of later writers.

The fourth and most basic aspect of the Standard Theory was, like the second, regularly and explicitly defended by many authors, who adopted a bundle or accidental view of individuation. According to them, the principle of individuation of Aristotelian primary substances is either (1) one or more accidents (usually place) of the substance or (2) the collection of all features (including nonaccidental ones) belonging to the substance. This aspect of the theory can be traced back directly to Boethius's statement in *De trinitate* that "the variety of accidents causes numerical difference" and to some statements in the *Commentary on Porphyry's Isagoge* that it is accidents and the collection of features (*proprietates*) that cause individuation.[27] Since the authors who supported this view did not generally make a distinction between numerical distinction and individuality, they found strong support for their view in both the logical and theological works of Boethius.

All this illustrates the strong metaphysical character of the Standard Theory. It also indicates the influence of Boethius's *De trinitate* in shaping it. Indeed, it is in commentaries on that work and to a lesser extent in commentaries on other Boethian theological tractates that the strongest and clearest statements of the Standard Theory appear. True, there are also pertinent statements in other theological contexts and even in discussions of Boethius's logical works, but the most explicit statements and argumentation in favor of the Standard Theory are present in commentaries on *De trinitate* or in works that deal with the subject matter of that work and were influenced by Boethius's treatise.

These claims can be illustrated by a discussion of Thierry of Chartres (d. ante 1155). Although Thierry introduced some modifications in the Standard Theory and his view was more developed than the bare-bones position outlined here, he did adhere to the main aspects of the Standard Theory. His views are presented in his *Commentaries* on Boethius's theological works: *Commentum super Boethii librum De trinitate, Fragmentum admuntense: De hebdomadibus, Lectiones in Boethii librum De trinitate, Fragmentum londinense: Contra Eutychen,* and *Glosa super Boethii librum De trinitate.*[28] There is also some indirect confirmation of his views in several other works belonging to his school but of doubtful authorship.[29]

Thierry treated individuality and numerical difference as equivalent notions, but he distinguished various kinds of differences and separated them from the notion of diversity. He stated very clearly that accidents are not numerically different, although they cause numerical difference in the things in which they are present. He refered to the principle that "number comes from accidents but is not found in accidents" as an "indisputable principle of philosophy", thus clearly adhering to the most basic aspect of the Standard Theory.[30] And, finally, he made no distinction between individuation and the discernibility of individuals. Thierry, therefore, exemplifies well the Standard Theory of Individuality.[31]

The Standard Theory did not go unchallenged in the early Middle Ages, although it was not until the eleventh century that we find explicit and serious attacks on its various aspects. These attacks came both from within and from without the metaphysical tradition springing from Boethius's *De trinitate.* The two most important critics of it were Gilbert of Poitiers and Peter Abailard. Gilbert criticized and modified the Standard Theory in radical ways but continued to work within a primarily metaphysical framework and tried to find answers to the metaphysical questions that had prompted the development of the theory. Peter Abailard, on the other hand, presented a stinging criticism of the two most basic foundations of the theory and turned his constructive philosophical attention primarily to the logical issues involved in individuality.

III. Gilbert of Poitiers (b. ca. 1076; d. 1154)

Gilbert's views on individuation were principally presented in his *Commentaries* on Boethius's *De trinitate* and *Contra Eutychen* and to a lesser extent in his *Commentary on De hebdomadibus.*[32] They rely on a complex metaphysical position, the details of which are too involved to be discussed here.[33] We can, however, point out those elements of his view that indicate clearly his position concerning individuation. There are three areas in which Gilbert modified the Standard Theory of Individuality. First, he distinguished singularity, diversity (including numerical diversity, also called "numerical difference"), and individuality. Second, he abandoned the Boethian view that accidents and ultimately place are the source of numerical difference. And, third, he introduced a distinction between the principle of numerical diversity and the principle of the discernibility of numerical diversity, which indicates that he was aware of and accepted a distinction between individuation (or numerical diversity) and the discernibility of individuals (or discernibility of numerically diverse things).

All three of these views represent major departures from the Standard Theory. The only view he shared completely with the Standard Theory is the notion that individuality is a kind of difference: for him, to be individual is to be dissimilar to other things.[34] Individuality is opposed to what he called, borrowing a Ciceronian term that had not been used in a long time, "dividuality", which in turn consists in similarity or conformity.[35] But he went on to distinguish individuality from diversity and singularity from both. Diversity, which is opposed to sameness (*idem*), has to do with plurality and it can be subdivided into generic, specific, or numerical.[36] Singularity, moreover, is distinguished from individuality and diversity, but Gilbert did not provide an analysis of it, giving the impression that he might have regarded it as what we now call a primitive notion.

With respect to the principle of individuation, Gilbert's views were as follows.[37] First of all, the principle of individuation of an Aristotelian primary substance (he called a primary substance *id quod* using a term derived from the Boethian expression *id quod est*) is either its total property or some of its partial properties. Gilbert used the term 'property' to mean feature, extending it both to accidents and to what Aristotelians consider properties strictly speaking. A total property is the collection of all of the features of a thing. But, although he accepted the individuality of total properties, he did not specify what makes the total property of an *id quod* individual. On the other hand, it is quite clear what he thought concerning the principle of the numerical diversity of numerically diverse things: for Aristotelian primary substances, that is, *id quods,* it is the numerical diversity of their features (he also called each of those features an *id quo*). In features that are total properties, numerical diversity is due either to the numerical diversity of their components or to the singularity of the total property. In features that are partial properties, it is due to their respective singularities. Singularity, therefore, is ultimately the principle of numerical diversity. It should be clear that accidents or place play no role in individuation or numerical difference for Gilbert.

With respect to the discernibility of individuals specifically, Gilbert did not say anything, but he did claim that accidents and location "prove" rather than "cause" numerical difference.[38] This indicates that he was aware of the distinction between the epistemic issue of discernibility and the metaphysical issue of the source of numerical diversity.

The situation with respect to the remaining fundamental aspect of the Standard Theory of Individuality is not so clear. Gilbert modified that aspect, but clearly he did not reject it altogether. His view was that only primary substances and their total properties are individual. Partial properties, whether simple or complex, are not individual, but dividual.[39] And since individuality consists in dissimilarity for Gilbert, neither primary substances nor their total properties are similar to anything. On the other hand, primary substances and their total and partial properties are numerically diverse, although it is not clear whether numerical diversity extends also to God.[40] But singularity extends to everything, including God.[41]

The changes that Gilbert introduced in the Standard Theory of Individuality were so drastic and profound that his position cannot really be considered as a version of that theory. Rather, it should be taken as a departure from it that laid the foundations for a different conception of individuality and related notions as well as for a new theory of individuation. Without a doubt, not all of Gilbert's views were acceptable to subsequent authors, but they provided a point of departure for more profound metaphysical analyses. On the one hand, for example, the distinction between singularity and individuality and the use of the notion of dividual was not adopted by later thinkers. But, on the other hand, the distinction he introduced between the problem of discernibility and the problem of individuation, as well as Gilbert's view that not only primary substances (*id quods*) but also their features (which he called total and partial *id quos* or properties) are numerically diverse, seem to have survived into the next century.

IV. Peter Abailard (b. 1079; d. 1142)

The second challenge to the Standard Theory of Individuality did not come from within the metaphysical tradition; it was posed by the views of those who adopted a primarily logical approach to individuality. The best representative of this group was Peter Abailard, as already stated. He provided a virulent attack on the most basic aspects of the Standard Theory of Individuality and opened up the discussion of individuality to more logical concerns, although he was by no means indifferent to metaphysical considerations. His views were presented primarily in two logical works that are known as *Logica ingredientibus* and *Logica nostrorum*.[42] Both are introductory logical treatises in which Abailard used extensively Porphyry's *Isagoge* and Boethius's *Commentaries* on that work.

Abailard explicitly rejected two important aspects of the Standard Theory of Individuality. According to one of these aspects some things in the universe are not individual, and these things are the features of substances. But Abailard opposed the notion of universal entities and favored the view that any accidents and forms found in an individual are also individual and that their individuality is not derived.[43] According to the other aspect of the Standard Theory that Abailard rejected, the principle of individuation of substances is to be found in the accidents of the substances in question. By contrast, for Abailard substances are individual essentially and of themselves and therefore need nothing other than themselves for their individuation.[44]

Although Abailard attacked these aspects of the Standard Theory of Individuality in various ways, two criticisms in particular were fundamental and may have had a decisive impact on subsequent authors. The first was directed against the view that an individual is composed of a material essence and a cluster of forms attached to it. The essence, which in this context means "thing" or "substance", is the same for all individuals who belong to the same species or genus. Socrates and Plato are not just men, but are essentially (i.e., substantially or at bottom) the same man. And the same is the case with the donkey Brunellus and Socrates, since both are animals. Now, since Socrates, Plato, and Brunellus are the same essentially, their differences must be accidental. Accordingly, they differ in the type and number of accidents (although not in the accidents themselves as long as the accidents are of the same type).[45] For example, Socrates and Plato are the same in that they are human, have a body, and so forth, and they differ in that Socrates is bald and has a snub nose, whereas Plato has hair on his head and an aquiline nose.

Abailard's criticism of this position consists in pointing out that if the components of things are at bottom the same, then things must be at bottom the same, for all things can be grouped into the same general categories: substance, quantity, quality, and so on; and therefore, the things in question would have to end up being, like their components and features, at bottom the same.[46] Clearly, under these conditions individuality, when conceived as Abailard conceives it as a kind of difference and discreteness,[47] cannot be accounted for.

This criticism is not conclusive upon closer examination, however. For the whole point of the Standard Theory was precisely to maintain that things are essentially, or, as Abailard put it, at bottom, the same and that they differ only accidentally. Although Socrates and Plato may be the same insofar as they are human or have noses, they are different insofar as their noses have different shapes. But, regardless of its validity, this criticism may have impressed future generations of medieval authors in that it clearly brought to the fore the accidental and derivative character of individuality as portrayed by the Standard Theory.

The second criticism is more important than the one just mentioned. It argues that, in a substance-accident ontology of the Aristotelian sort, an accidental view of individuation is contradictory.[48] In this kind of ontology, accidents depend on and are posterior to substance and not vice versa; therefore, accidents cannot be responsible for the individuation of the substance. In substance-accident ontologies Socrates's black color of hair, for example, does not exist except through Socrates, while Socrates does not depend on the color of his hair. Indeed, he could have different colors of hair at different times or even at the same time on different parts of his head (substances can have contrary features). But the Standard Theory requires a reversal of this relation, making Socrates dependent on his accidental features.

Again, this argument begs the question insofar as those who wish to maintain the Standard Theory can point out that their view of substance and the accidents of substance is not Aristotelian and, therefore, that they are not bound to accept the consequences of such a view. Still, in the thirteenth century most authors accepted the Aristotelian view of substance and accidents and, therefore, could not ignore its consequences for a theory of individuation as pointed out by Abailard. The result is that they tried to find the source of individuation in something substantial rather than in accidents, contrary to what the Standard Theory had proposed. Indeed, as we shall see in this volume, the most important theories of individuation in the later Middle Ages identified substantial principles such as substantial form, matter, existence, or entity as principles of individuation. And even those views that preserved an accidental element, as was the case with Thomas Aquinas's view of individuation as brought about by designated matter, clearly added a substantial element to avoid the kind of objection voiced by Abailard.

Abailard's own concerns, apart from his criticism of some of the two aforementioned aspects of the Standard Theory, were primarily logical. He did not dispute the understanding of individuality as difference and distinction that permeated the Standard Theory, although he changed the terminology slightly, preferring the term 'discreteness' to describe what is fundamental in individuality. Nor did he make an effort to establish a distinction, as Gilbert had done, between the problems of discernibility and individuation. His efforts were directed rather to the development of a theory about the words used to refer to individuals, which he called individual, singular, and particular words. But, since this aspect of his thought does not seem to have had a great impact on later theories of individuation, which were primarily metaphysical in approach, there is no need to dwell on these matters here.[49]

The Legacy of the Early Middle Ages[50]

From what we have seen in the preceding pages we can reach two general conclusions. First, the early Middle Ages saw a growing awareness of the complexity of the issues and problems related to individuation. Although a few authors, such as Clarembald and John of Salisbury, kept repeating well-known formulae concerning these issues at the end of the period, many dealt with the problem of individuation in a deliberate and philosophically sophisticated fashion. The almost casual remarks characteristic of some early authors, such as Eriugena, became quite insufficient for many. Second, there seemed to be not only a greater understanding of individuality but also a growing awareness that individuality is much more important than had been thought before and that its place and role in a complete ontology would have to be accounted for at greater length. Indeed, there was a tendency toward a more nominalistic approach in which individuality was considered at least as important as universality in the makeup of the universe and its description. This was, however, still far from the time when, as with Suárez, individuality was regarded as more fundamental than universality and, consequently, as requiring prior treatment. But, nonetheless, the first signs of a change in that direction were present in Abailard's and Gilbert's challenges to some of the basic aspects of the Standard Theory of Individuality.

The growing concern with individuality as well as the progressive movement toward nominalism and away from the realism of the earlier period prepared the ground for discussions in the later Middle Ages. The impact of the early Middle Ages was not restricted to general attitudes. The particular ideas of Gilbert, Abailard, Thierry, and others no doubt had some influence on the work of thirteenth and fourteenth century authors. Although some of the early terminology was never adopted, particularly the very idiosyncratic nomenclature adopted by Gilbert, still many of the ideas of the period survived even though every one of the four fundamental aspects of the popular Standard Theory was rejected. Indeed, to consider the first aspect in the thirteenth century and later we find a slow but concerted effort to distinguish individuality from numerical difference and to separate the logical notion of a subject (impredicable) and predicate (predicable) from the metaphysical notions of individual (incommunicable) and universal (communicable). True, these distinctions were not always observed, but nonetheless they were introduced and gradually gained widespread recognition. In this sense, then, the work of authors like Gilbert in particular was not lost.

Something similar happened with the second fundamental aspect of the Standard Theory, which maintained the individuality of primary substances and the universality of properties and accidents. In the later Middle Ages the views on the extension of 'individual' became much more complex than they had been in the earlier period. The newly popularized terminology of natures, for example, made possible new distinctions. Still, the criticism that we find among twelfth century writers of the naive realism of earlier authors seems to have had a role to play in the abandonment of the view that the features of substances are universal. Even such authors as Duns Scotus would have insisted that everything found in the individual substance is individual, although not everyone accepted that such individuality was, as I have surmised to be Abailard's view, essential. Some, like Ockham, adopted views similar to that of Abailard, but Thomas and Scotus, among others, shied away from this stricter form of nominalism. For them substances and their features are individual, but their individuality is derived, not *per se*.

Also rejected was the third fundamental aspect of the Standard Theory of Individuality, the lack of distinction between individuation and individual discernibility. Although this distinction was ignored by most early medieval figures with the exception of Gilbert, many later writers explicitly acknowledged it, or at least made use of it implicitly. In some instances later writers discussed the issues of individual discernibility in some detail, although not all scholastics paid attention to them. We do not know whether Gilbert's statements were instrumental in this respect, but one suspects that they probably were, given his popularity and stature.

The fourth fundamental aspect of the Standard Theory, concerned with the principle of individuation, suffered a similar fate. For there were no major scholastics who adhered to it in the form favored in the early Middle Ages. Abailard's criticism, we may surmise, had done its job. Indeed, even those authors like Thomas, who tended to preserve some role for accidents in individuation, added other principles to avoid the difficulties raised in the twelfth century and repeated later. With time, even the modest role Thomas gave them in individuation was dropped completely; all later major figures, such as Scotus, Ockham, and Suárez, followed this path. Even Thomists, as we shall see in John of St. Thomas, tried to move away from an accidental theory of individuation.

From this it is clear that, for all practical purposes, by the close of the twelfth century the Standard Theory of Individuality had ceased to be the powerful force it had been in the early period—mainstream thought had moved in a different direction.

Apart from the Standard Theory and its criticism, the work of early medieval authors was to prove influential in two of the other problems involved in individuation identified in the Introduction. The first has to do with the ontological status of individuality. As already mentioned, this was an area of important developments in the later Middle Ages but of little consequence in the early period. Nevertheless, in spite of the scant discussion of this problem, early medieval authors used terminology and made passing remarks that resemble some of the terminology and positions taken by later authors. Some seem to have treated individuality as a form, simple or complex, a position that has some similarities with Scotism. And others either spoke of individuality as if it were nothing, or argued against it being anything in the individual or apart from it (the Ockhamist position). In both cases elaboration was lacking but the seeds of future developments perhaps had been planted.

In the area of singular terms such as proper names and indexicals, some important ideas also circulated in the early period among grammarians and those who worked primarily with Boethius's logical works. These ideas no doubt played a role in the surge of logical theory in the later Middle Ages, but generally they were discussed in contexts other than individuation.

Let me finish by summarizing three important aspects that characterize the legacy of the early Middle Ages to the later Middle Ages concerning individuation: first, a fairly clear formulation of the problem of individuation as well as the development of some awareness concerning various issues related to it; second, a body of terminology and formulae that continued to be used whenever individuation was discussed in later centuries; third, a powerful case built in the later part of the early Middle Ages against the Standard Theory of Individuality, a theory prevalent throughout most of the period. With this in mind we can now turn to two other important sources of ideas concerning the problem of individuation for the later Middle Ages: Islamic and Jewish thought.

Notes

1. *In Isagogen Porphyrii commenta,* ed. Samuel Brandt, in *CSEL,* vol. 48 (Vienna: Tempsky, 1906; rep. New York: Johnson, 1966); *In Categorias Aristotelis libri quatuor,* ed. J. P. Migne, in *PL,* vol. 64 (Paris, 1891); *In librum Aristotelis De interpretatione,* ed. J. P. Migne, in *PL,* vol. 64 (Paris, 1891).

2. Ed. and trans. H. F. Stewart and E. K. Rand, in *Boethius: The Theological Tractates, The Consolation of Philosophy* (Cambridge, MA: Harvard University Press, 1968).

3. John Marenbon, *From the Circle of Alcuin to the School of Auxerre* 1 (Cambridge: Cambridge University Press, 1981), pp. 17–18. See also Osmund Lewry, "Boethian Logic in the Medieval West", in *Boethius: His Life, Thought and Influence,* ed. Margaret Gibson (Oxford: Basil Blackwell, 1981), pp. 90–134.

4. Primarily in relation to his definition of a person as "persona uero ratio-nabilis naturae indiuidua substantia". *Contra Eutychen* 4, p. 92.

5. In the important passage of *De trinitate* where he speaks about numerical difference and what causes it, he mentions "the principle of plurality" (*principium pluralitatis*). This surely was a factor in the development of the later terminology. *De trinitate*, p. 6.

6. *Ibid.*

7. *In Isagogen*, pp. 235–236 (*PL* 64.114). In Gracia, *Introduction to the Problem of Individuation* 2, p. 77.

8. *Ibid.*, pp. 183–196 (*PL* 64.92-93). In Gracia, *Introduction to the Problem of Individuation* 2, p. 78.

9. *In Categorias, PL* 64.171–172.

10. *De trinitate* 1, p. 6.

11. *In Isagogen*, pp. 49, 195, 233–234 (*PL* 64.30, 97 and 113–14).

12. *Ibid.* and pp. 81–82 (*PL* 64.47–48).

13. *In librum De interpretatione, PL* 64.462–464.

14. *In Isagogen*, pp. 190–191 (*PL* 64.95–96).

15. *De trinitate* 1, p. 6.

16. See n. 8 for pertinent texts.

17. *Contra Eutychen*, p. 84, and *In Categorias, PL* 64.182.

18. *In Isagogen*, pp. 81–82 (*PL* 64.47–48) and *In librum De interpretatione, PL* 64.462–464.

19. *De trinitate* 2, pp. 12–14.

20. *In Isagogen*, pp. 233–234 (*PL* 64.113–114), and Gracia, *Introduction to the Problem of Individuation* 2, pp. 75–76.

21. *Ibid.* and *In librum De interpretatione, PL* 64.462–464.

22. For Marenbon, his "logical terms are loaded with metaphysical and theological implications". *From the Circle of Alcuin*, p. 1.

23. Gracia, *Introduction to the Problem of Individuation* 2.

24. Gilbert's views will be summarized briefly later. For Odo, see Gracia, *Introduction to the Problem of Individuation* 3, pp. 135–141.

25. Gracia, *Introduction to the Problem of Individuation* 3, pp. 131–132.

26. *In Isagogen*, pp. 233–234 (*PL* 64.113–114) and pp. 183–196 (*PL* 64.92–93). My emphasis.

27. In Boethius's translation in *In Isagogen*, pp. 231 and 234–235 (*PL* 64.112 and 114).

28. Thierry of Chartres, *Commentaries on Boethius*, ed. N. M. Häring (Toronto: PIMS, 1971).

29. *Ibid*.

30. *Lectiones, ibid.*, pp. 150.6–151.49.

31. For a general discussion of Thierry's view, see Gracia, *Introduction to the Problem of Individuation* 3, pp. 142–155.

32. Gilbert of Poitiers, *The Commentaries on Boethius*, ed. N. Häring (Toronto: PIMS, 1966).

33. See Gracia, *Introduction to the Problem of Individuation* 3, pp. 155–178.

34. *De trinitate*, pp. 143–144 (*PL* 64.1293–1294).

35. *Ibid*. For Cicero, see *De deorum natura* 3, 12, 29.

36. *De trinitate*, pp. 74.20–75.40 (*PL* 64.1262).

37. For texts in support of the interpretation given here see Gracia, *Introduction to the Problem of Individuation* 3, pp. 157–170.

38. *De trinitate*, pp. 77.80–78.19 (*PL* 64.1264).

39. *Contra Eutychen*, p. 274.75–94 (*PL* 64.1372).

40. *De trinitate*, p. 58.43 (*PL* 64.1255). See also Gracia, *Introduction to the Problem of Individuation* 3, p. 192, n. 137.

41. *Contra Eutychen*, p. 270.70–80 (*PL* 64.1371).

42. They have been edited by B. Geyer with the titles *Incipiunt Glossae secundum magistrum Petrum Abaelardum super Porphyrium* and *Logica nostrorum petitioni sociorum* in BGPM 21, Nos. 1–3 and 4 (1919–1927 and 1933).

43. *Logica ingredientibus*, pp. 119 and 13.

44. *Ibid.*, p. 13.

45. *Logica ingredientibus*, pp. 10–11 and 63; and *Logica nostrorum*, p. 515.

46. *Logica ingredientibus*, p. 12.

47. *Ibid.*, p. 64.

48. *Ibid.*, pp. 13 and 64.

49. For their discussion see Gracia, *Introduction to the Problem of Individuation* 4, pp. 215–27.

50. The remarks that follow are taken almost verbatim from the conclusions to Chapter 5 of my *Introduction to the Problem of Individuation*.

3

THE ISLAMIC BACKGROUND: AVICENNA (B. 980; D. 1037) AND AVERROES (B. 1126; D. 1198)

ALLAN BÄCK

My topic in this chapter is the problem of individuation in Islamic philosophy, to the extent that Islamic philosophers influenced Latin medieval philosophy on this issue. Therefore, I shall be concentrating on those works by Islamic philosophers that were available, in Latin translation, to the West, although I shall work from both the Arabic texts and their Latin translations. I shall also limit my discussion to Ibn Sina (Avicenna) and Ibn Rushd (Averroes), due to limits of space and time, although there were other Islamic philosophers who were read in the West and who wrote on this topic (al-Farabi and al-Ghazali in particular, in their *Metaphysics*). The focus of my discussion will be the positions that Avicenna and Averroes take on the various facets of the problem of individuation, as distinguished by Jorge J. E. Gracia in the Introduction to this book. I shall not be able here to do justice to the historical background of their doctrines, in Greek and in earlier Islamic philosophy, nor to the arguments that are brought forth in support of those doctrines. Still, I intend to present the theory, and make some progress in presenting its justification.

Avicenna and Averroes are, by common consensus, the most important Islamic philosophers for the Latin medieval philosophy of the High Middle Ages and later. Averroes was known as "the Commentator", as his commentaries on Aristotle accompanied early Latin translations of Aristotle's complete corpus around the beginning of the thirteenth century. In this way, medieval philosophers received Aristotle along with Averroes's commentaries. Averroes stuck quite closely to the text of Aristotle, and so his commentaries were viewed as a great help in understanding Aristotle. Whatever views Averroes had that differed from Aristotle (these often derived from

Alexander of Aphrodisias, John Philoponus, and earlier Islamic philosophers like al-Farabi and Avicenna) were then given serious consideration by
association.

    Avicenna, in contrast, did not follow Aristotle closely, in content or in
organization; in fact he makes a point that he is interested in the truth, not in
presenting Aristotle's views.[1] Some of the writings of Avicenna (namely,
some parts of his encyclopedia, the *Shif'ā,* known as the *Sufficientia*[2]) were
received by the Latin West in translation about the same time as Aristotle's
works with Averroes's commentaries.[3] The attraction of Avicenna's thought,
despite its great difficulty, was, and is, that Avicenna offers a grand synthesis
of Aristotelian and Platonic philosophy, where the insights of both are retained, but the conflicts supposedly eliminated. Thus for the Latin West,
which had to reconcile its older, mostly neo-Platonic tradition with the new
Aristotelian tradition, Avicenna's work offered sophisticated solutions to serious, pressing problems. The importance of Avicenna's philosophy for medieval philosophy is great, though probably not thoroughly appreciated today,
since his work is not read much these days. To give some examples, Aquinas's *De ente et essentia* is mostly a paraphrase of Avicenna's *Metaphysica.*
Again, in the problem of universals, which has been called the main problem
of medieval philosophy, Aquinas, Scotus, and Ockham all cite Avicenna (the
same passage!) in support of their respective positions.[4] What has often happened with Avicenna's views, as with many others, is that those who repeat
them are given credit for being brilliant and having originated them.

I. Avicenna: The Great Synthesizer

    I now turn to the views of Avicenna on individuation. I shall, as I have
said, be concerned mainly with presenting his results or doctrines, and not
with his arguments for them, nor with their historical antecedents.

    As a preliminary, it is important to note that the views Avicenna gives
in his *Shif'ā* and the only ones available to the Latin West are not necessarily
his own views. At any rate, Avicenna claims that in that work he just is presenting the views of the Western Aristotelians, while his own philosophy, the
"philosophy of the Orientals", differs from these views.[5] I have suggested
elsewhere, though, that, at least in terms of his extant writings, his "Western" and his "Eastern" do not differ much: even in the *Shif'ā,* after presenting a common view on a topic, Avicenna then gives his own view.[6] In any
case, as we are concerned here with the *Avicenna Latinus,* I shall just present
the views of the *Shif'ā.*

1. Types of Individuals

    Avicenna insists that there are two types of existence, existence in in-
dividuals (*in re*) and existence in the mind (*in intellectu*).[7] It is absurd, he

says, for us to be concerned with what does not exist at all, in neither way, for we would never have a way to know it.[8] Rather we have to be able to know something. So everything exists, at least potentially *in intellectu*. To say that a chimera does not exist just means that it does not exist *in re;* a chimera does exist *in intellectu,* since we have, or can acquire, an idea of a chimera.

This doctrine is important for the problem of individuation because in accordance with it Avicenna recognizes two sorts of individuals, the sensible and the intelligible. The existence of both types of individuals has a central place in Avicenna's philosophy. For example, in discussing the problem of universals, Avicenna defines a universal in the standard way, as "that which is said of many". However, there is then the problem that some universal terms are not, in fact, said of many individuals and, in some cases, cannot be said of many individual things existing *in re.* For example, 'heptagonal house' is a universal term, but there are not, have not, nor probably will there be any heptagonal houses. Again 'sun' (in ancient astronomy) or 'universe' can be said truly of only one thing in the natural, physical world. How can such terms be universal? Avicenna says that they are said of many individuals that exist *in intellectu* but not *in re;* the imagination creates them, mostly from components given in sense perception.[9] So there are individuals that exist both *in re* and *in intellectu,* and individuals that exist only *in intellectu.* Avicenna then is faced with the problem of giving a theory of individuation that handles both sorts of individuals satisfactorily.

It is common in dealing with the problem of individuation just to concentrate on sensible individuals. Yet any theory of individuation seems to have to face the issue of the individuation of nonsensible individuals as well. Indeed, I have just pointed out the need for doing so to give a satisfactory definition of 'universal'. Furthermore, in particular, for Avicenna as for most other philosophers, pure mathematical objects like numbers are not sensible. Avicenna, not being a Platonist, holds that mathematical objects have existence only *in intellectu.*[10] The problem is that to do mathematics there must be able to be different instances or individuals of the same number. For example, in '2 + 2 = 4', the number or type, '2', has two instances or tokens. For the equation to make any sense, these two tokens must be individuated, since, without multiplicity, a number cannot be added to "itself". Thus there has also to be an account of the individuation of intelligible individuals, including mathematical objects. Still, I shall begin with what is better known to us, sensible individuals. More precisely, I shall be concerned with sensible individual substances subject to generation and corruption, that is, substances in the sublunary sphere according to Aristotle's cosmology. Avicenna himself develops his views on individuation most fully and clearly for this case. Later I shall consider briefly how Avicenna's account applies to other individuals existing *in re,* like celestial substances and individual accidents, and to intelligible individuals.

2. Individual Substances and the Bundle Theory

What is it to be an individual sensible corruptible substance for Avicenna? He says, repeatedly, that such an individual is a substantial form in a compound with matter and accidents.[11] As the substantial form and the matter, be it prime or proximate, is common to all individuals of the same species, it might be concluded that the accidents then must constitute the individual: an individual would in this view be a unique collection of accidents belonging to a substantial form that has come to exist really in matter. Avicenna ends up not endorsing this view, which makes the principle of individuation the presence of a unique set of accidents. However, as his own view differs only subtly from it and develops from it, let me continue to develop it.

In the Aristotelian view, Socrates is composed of matter, not only the brute stuff, but the proximate, organic matter suitable for human beings, and the substantial form, humanity.[12] Socrates, being a compound of matter and form, is then able to receive accidental attributes, like being white, snub-nosed, large, Greek, the husband of Xanthippe, being in the agora at a certain time, standing, and so forth. Now any other human being is also a compound of the human organic matter and the substantial form of humanity. To be sure, Socrates and Plato are not composed of the same hunk of matter. But to attribute individuality to being different hunks of matter would require us to provide criteria for the individuation of different hunks of matter, which we would have to do in terms of matter, the form, or the accidents. But then we would start a vicious regress (if we keep on looking for a more basic matter) or a vicious circle (if we return to the analysis of matter and form to individuate the hunks of matter). So what makes an individual an individual in this analysis of matter and form does not appear to be the form, which is common to all members of the species, nor the matter. Thus, in this Aristotelian analysis of the individual substance being a compound of matter of form, it looks quite reasonable for Avicenna to say that the accidents provide the ground of individuation. Indeed, he seems to say this explicitly, repeatedly.[13]

3. The Threefold Distinction of Quiddity

Yet, despite this apparent endorsement of a bundle theory of individuation, Avicenna does not hold that an individual is an individual in virtue of its accidents. To understand his position, we must look at his views on individual substance. Indeed, Avicenna is well known for his detailed account of the structure of an individual thing and its attributes. Avicenna says that a universal or, more strictly, a quiddity (the *to ti ēn einai*) has three respects: in itself, in individuals, and in the mind. This doctrine is known, somewhat inaccurately, as the "threefold distinction of quiddity" (*triplex status naturae*). I shall now present, in summary form, those features of the doctrine of the *triplex status* useful for understanding Avicenna's views on individuality. The following is Avicenna's most explicit statement of this doctrine:

> And the quiddities of things may be in individual things, and they may be in the mind; so they have three respects: the respect of quiddity inasmuch as it is that quiddity is not added to one of the two modes of existence, nor to what is attached to the quiddity, insofar as it is in this respect. And quiddity has a respect insofar as it is in individuals. And there accidents which make particular its existence in that are attached to it. And it has a respect insofar as it is in the mind. So there accidents that make particular its existence in that are attached to it; e.g., being a subject and being a predicate, and universality and particularity in predication . . . [14]

In general, a quiddity is an essence. The term 'quiddity' (*mahīyyāt*) is a direct translation of '*to ti ēn einai*', which is usually translated as '*substantia*' in some medieval translations of Aristotle, and as 'essence' in some modern ones.[15] But Avicenna says that whiteness is a quiddity in itself just as much as humanity.[16] As whiteness is not a substance, it is best to understand quiddities more generally: a quiddity is what is signified by a universal term, a term said of many. What is signified by a universal term, substantial or not, I am calling an 'essence'. The doctrine of the threefold distinction of quiddity thus claims that there are three modes of signification of a universal term, not that there are three referents of a universal term. If there were three referents, the universal term would be merely ambiguous and name three things. In contrast, according to this doctrine, the same thing is being talked about somehow, yet in three different ways.[17]

So for Avicenna quiddities have three respects: in themselves, in things, and in the mind. Quiddities in themselves have no accidents, whereas quiddities in individuals and in the mind each have accidents proper to them in their respect. Quiddities in individuals and quiddities in the mind exist, in different ways, whereas quiddities in themselves do not exist, yet are real.

To speak of the quiddity in itself is to stipulate that the universal term is to be considered solely with respect to its definition.[18] 'Man', taken to represent a quiddity in itself, signifies only what being a man is. To be a man is to be, let us suppose, a rational animal, and hence also to be what it is to be an animal. The quiddity in itself will thus include the definition of the universal term and the definitions of the parts of that definition.[19] Avicenna is quite explicit that even those attributes that are necessarily inseparable from the definition—the *propria* or proper accidents—do not constitute the quiddity in itself.[20] Because the quiddity in itself consists only of the quiddity's definition (the *ti esti*), Avicenna often refers to the quiddity in itself by an abstract term; instead of 'being human', 'being animal', he says 'humanity', 'animality'. Thus humanity is a quiddity in itself, and it is rational animality, that is, rational animal corporeal substantiality.[21]

Quiddities in individuals, that is, individual things or substances, are individual material objects. These individuals have quiddities in themselves. Thus, for example, this man, Socrates, is a man, is white, is just. Matter, a substratum, is able to receive many compatible quiddities in themselves— humanity, whiteness, justice. Quiddities come to be associated here with quiddities that are not contained in their definitions.[22] In this way, "accidents happen" to quiddities in themselves. Quiddities in individuals are normally signified by concrete terms used concretely. Thus, 'man' in general is not a quiddity in individuals; rather, 'this man' or 'a man' is. Quiddities are said to exist in individuals because they are instantiated in matter. Matter here functions as a ground or substratum for the reception of a type of accidents. The sort of accidents received by individuals are those of first intention, that is, those in the Aristotelian categories. I shall call such accidents "material accidents", and the sort of existence enjoyed by quiddities having such accidents "material existence".

Two warnings are in order at this point. First, Avicenna insists that, although Socrates and Plato, being men, may both be said to have the quiddity humanity, there is not a single humanity that is in both Socrates and Plato, strictly speaking. That is, there is not a Form of humanity in which Socrates and Plato participate. Indeed, strictly speaking, there are no common properties in the respect of quiddities in individuals.[23] We may note common properties and consider different individuals to belong to the same species, defined with respect to a quiddity in itself. But we note this similarity with respect to our perception of those individuals, that is, with respect to the quiddities existing in the mind.[24] Whatever exists *in re,* be it essential or accidental, is individual. Second, individuals are what they are, all their quiddities. That is, the individual is not separate from the quiddities that it has, be they essential or accidental. Although some quiddities appear essential to the individual substance and others accidental, still, with respect to quiddities in individuals, there is no such distinction. A thing has all of its attributes and cannot be divorced from any of them as long as it has them. But some attributes, which are called "essential," must remain permanently with the individual substance, as long as it exists, while those called "accidental" need not remain. Like the notion of having common attributes, this distinction of essence and accident is made only in another respect, namely, that of quiddities in the mind.

Quiddities in the mind are, in a broad sense, concepts.[25] These quiddities are abstracted, via sense perception and imagination, from quiddities in individuals. Being abstractions, quiddities in the mind have a dual nature. On the one hand, they represent individual as well as common features of quiddities in individuals. Thus two real individual substances, Socrates and Plato, are both human, and each may be called 'man'. On the other hand, abstractions have certain formal features not found in the things from which the abstractions arose. Thus man is a common notion, is essential to things that are men, and indeed is a species. Being a common notion, being essential, being a species are formal attributes or accidents that apply to the abstractions but not to the things.[26] Quiddities in the mind are strictly signified by concrete terms used abstractly. Thus, 'man is a species', 'man is animal', and 'Socrates is man' (as distinct from 'Socrates is a man') are true claims about quiddities in the mind. Given that quiddities in the mind have a distinct type of accidents, formal accidents, and that for each such type there corresponds a distinctive sort of matter and existence, it is clear why Avicenna says that quiddities in the mind exist in a distinctive way. We may call that sort of existence "formal", to distinguish it from the material existence of quiddities in individuals.[27]

According to the threefold distinction of quiddity, types of true statements accumulate as we move from the respect of quiddities in themselves to the one in individuals to the one in the mind. Definitions alone are true of quiddities in themselves; definitional and materially accidental statements are true of quiddities in individuals; definitional and materially and formally accidental statements are true of quiddities in the mind. Of course, these statements, when made strictly, will have distinctive forms relative to each respect: consider the different subject terms, 'humanity', 'men', 'man'.

4. The Individuation of Sensible Substances

Fortified with this account of Avicenna's doctrine of quiddities, let us return to his views on individuation. A sensible individual is, in terms of the threefold distinction of quiddity, a quiddity in individuals, that is, *in re*. Individual substances of the same species differ from one another not in virtue of having the quiddity in itself proper to that species, for example, humanity for Socrates and Plato, but in virtue of that quiddity's having a material existence. I now shall consider further Avicenna's account of material existence.

Strictly, all that matter seems to be for Avicenna is the potentiality that a quiddity in itself has to be joined to others. Quiddities in themselves that are in the category of substance are prior to those in other categories, not in respect of being quiddities in themselves, but in respect of the order of instantiation, of coming to exist *in re* (*wujūd,* generally translated as *esse*). The subject or substratum for the reception of diverse quiddities in themselves into the sensible individual must be composed of a quiddity from the category of substance put into a state receptive of other quiddities, that is, put into matter. This is Avicenna's way of putting the standard Aristotelian view that only substances can have properties: 'the white' (in Avicenna's terms, the quiddity in itself, whiteness coming to be *in re*) cannot exist apart from substance (a quiddity in itself in the category of substance made able to receive accidents), for to say 'the white' implicitly supposes a thing that is white, and a thing is a substance.[28] So matter is just a certain state of a substantial quiddity in itself, where that quiddity is able to be conjoined with other quiddities.

Avicenna sees a certain necessary progression in the coming to be of a sensible individual substance, that is, in the association of quiddities in themselves into a complex existing materially.[29] First, as said previously, a quiddity in the category of substance, on the most specific level, is put into a state able to have other quiddities attached to it. This receptive state is the matter.[30] Then, Avicenna says, for sensible individuals, it is necessary that the quiddity in itself of corporeity, or being a body, be attached to the complex in formation.[31] By corporeity, all Avicenna means is three-dimensionality, the ability to come to have a definite three-dimensional shape.[32] In short, a substantial quiddity in itself when it comes to exist *in re* is put into a state of being in space—a space suspiciously like Newtonian space and less like Aristotelian place.[33] Only later on does the sensible individual assume the full range of features of a physical body, including such quantitative accidents as having a certain size and weight at each point in time when it exists. Unlike the specific size that a sensible individual has, which may change during the career of that individual's existence, being three-dimensional in general is a condition essential for material existence and so for the reception of accidents.

But the exact status of corporeity in Avicenna's scheme is obscure. To be sure, corporeity is the material form, the structure of the matter that is the substratum for the reception of accidental quiddities in themselves by the substantial quiddities. And, like Aristotle, Avicenna holds that the matter is substance. So corporeity appears to belong to the category of substance, and so to consist in those features that define the substantial genus, body. But I find two possible accounts. The first, simpler one is that corporeity is in the category of substance. Then corporeity would be an essential constituent of, for example, animality and humanity. and the process of a sensible individual substance coming to be *in re* would consist in corporeity's being put into matter, a state receptive of accidental quiddities.[34] In the second account, corporeity, that is, three-dimensionality, is not essential to the substantial quiddity in itself but only to its material existence.[35] In this account, Avicenna would be holding that corporeity is a *proprium,* a necessary accident of material existence, but not a genus, of the individual sensible substance. Body, the genus in the category of substance, would be just the propensity to receive dimensional properties, that is, it would be being spatial, with no further specification of what dimensional properties are to be received. So occupying space would be part of the definition of 'humanity', whereas being three-dimensional would be a *proprium* of the substance 'man', and having a specific three-dimensional shape would be an accident in the category of quantity. (To make this point more plausible, consider Kant, who claims that 'a body is extended' is analytic, true by definition, whereas 'a body is three-dimensional' is synthetic, not true by definition.[36])

The texts are sufficiently obscure for either account to be what Avicenna intended. Still, judging by the complexity of his discussions, I am inclined toward the second. In either account, corporeity will belong to the category of substance. If corporeity belonged to the definitions of substances, it would be a constituent of quiddities in themselves like humanity. But then a quiddity in itself would itself have a substratum able to receive other quiddities accidental to it, and there would consequently be no difference between a quiddity in itself and a quiddity in individuals: the quiddity in itself, having a substratum provided by corporeity, would already be receptive of accidents. So, rather, corporeity in the sense of three-dimensionality, like risibility, is a *proprium* of substantial quiddities in themselves.[37]

Once the emerging complex of quiddities that is coming to be the sensible individual substance has the association of the substantial specific form with corporeity, quiddities in other categories can come to be attached to that complex.[38] So, whiteness, snubness, being in the agora, can come to be attached to that complex, at which point the sensible individual substance has come to be. That complex then forms the substratum, and the other quiddities can come and go in it at different times; in short, the complex of the substantial quiddity in itself plus corporeity is what persists through change as the material individual; the change consists in the reception of different accidents. But what individuates one member of a species from another is precisely the possession of a unique collection of accidental quiddities at each point in time. Every individual man has the substantial form, humanity, in matter, which is the state receptive of other quiddities, in connection with corporeity. The accidents are what make different men, the same in species, but distinct, or different in number.

This process of the coming to be of sensible individual substances from quiddities in themselves is not a necessary process of emanation. Rather, Avicenna insists, sensible individuals are contingent; they need not exist at all nor have the history that they come to have. The putting of quiddities in themselves into a state able to form complexes requires an external cause.

This process is called 'creation', and its cause God. God is necessary being and the ultimate cause of the coming to be of individuals.[39]

This picture of what a sensible individual substance is makes Avicenna look Platonist. For, according to it, an individual seems here to be a bundle of Forms (quiddities in themselves) put into complex combination, just as it happens with Forms in the receptacle described in Plato's *Timaeus,* which looks very much like Avicenna's conception of matter. Indeed, Avicenna, like other Islamic philosophers, has been routinely accused of just having a mixture of Plato and Aristotle in a hodgepodge, and of having been led to this mistake through neo-Platonic works like the *Liber de causis* being attributed to Aristotle.[40]

Yet there are several reasons not to regard Avicenna as a Platonist.[41] First, as we have seen, he insists that quiddities in themselves do not exist, though they have a sort of reality. The things that exist are individuals *in re,* and the individuals abstracted from them *in intellectu.* Quiddities in themselves are some sort of active principle or aspect of reality, but do not exist apart from existing individuals.[42] Like Aristotle, Avicenna staunchly affirms that Socrates's parents caused him to come to be.[43] His parents are sensible individual substances, not quiddities in themselves. The parents themselves are only the efficient cause and contain in them the formal cause of Socrates's coming to be, namely, the substantial form that is already in matter potentially in the seed.[44] In short, though I shall not be able to develop this point here, Avicenna's account of individuality in terms of the threefold distinction of quiddity needs to be viewed in light of his extensive work in Aristotelian natural philosophy, where the emphasis on substance is on the concrete individual, namely, on substance in the sense of a compound of matter and form, generated from other concrete individuals.

A second point, however, I shall discuss more fully. Avicenna, despite all his views that I have presented thus far, does not hold that individual substances are individual because they have a unique bundle of attributes. He does hold that every individual must have a unique complex of accidents at every time; after all, otherwise two sensible individual substances would occupy the same space. Yet, he insists, it is wrong to conclude that the individual, qua individual, is just a unique bundle of accidents.

His reason for this position is quite contemporary. Working out the implications of a bundle theory of individuality, he then notes that it would then appear possible to define sensible individuals, by listing some or all of the accidents in the bundle:

> So if you say: Zayd is the handsome, tall, literate so- and-so [man]—as many attributes as you like, still the individuality of Zayd has not been determined for you in the intellect. Rather it is possible for the concept

consisting of the totality of all that to belong to more than one. Rather, however, existence and the demonstration of an individual concept determines Zayd, as when you say that he is the son of so-and-so, is what is existent at a certain time, is tall, is the philosopher. And then it would have occurred that at that time there is not something sharing with him in those attributes, and you would have already had this knowledge also by this occurrence, and that is through a consciousness analogous to what is demonstrated by sensation, in some mode demonstrating the very same so-and-so at the very same time. Here you would be verifying the individuality of Zayd, and this statement would be significative of his individuality.[45]

So Socrates, say, is the man who is tall, a philosopher, literate, the son of Sophroniscus, sitting on that chair now, and so forth at this time, and so on. Since every individual has a different set of accidents, such a list would then distinguish Socrates from all other individuals, including all other human beings. Nevertheless Avicenna rejects the possibility of defining individuals. He admits that every (sensible) individual substance can be uniquely characterized by its unique accidents, in what today would be called a definite description.[46] However, he denies that such descriptions are definitions, because it is possible for them not to apply to the individual described. Socrates would still be Socrates if he were not a philosopher, but instead only a mason. Accidental features are just that: accidental. So, since it is not necessary for an individual to have the accidents that it has, it is not possible to define an individual as the being that has exactly those accidents. To be sure, every individual must have accidents, a complete and unique set of them at each point in time. That is why definite descriptions are possible. But the identity of the individual is not determined by the accidents that it in fact happens to have.

A similar result holds for our knowledge of individuals. Avicenna would deny that we know a sensible individual substance to be individual through the perception of a unique complex of accidental features.[47] We may use such complexes to help ourselves pick out one individual among many: "Which one is Socrates?" "The one with the snub nose without shoes." But this use of the unique accidental features of an individual would not enable us to recognize the individual, the thing that persists through the changes of accidental features over time. Rather, Avicenna says, we have a direct, intuitive experience of the existence and individuality of a sensible individual. Our conception of being a real, singular existence is immediate and given by direct acquaintance.[48]

So the individuality of a sensible individual substance is an intrinsic feature of its existence *in re*. This individuality has the consequence of every individual's having a unique set of accidents at each time. But it is the material existence of the individual substance, the presence of the substantial form in matter that provides the active principle of persisting through time with a unique, though constantly changing, set of accidents.[49] The same account will apply to individual celestial sensible substances, with the difference that their sort of material existence has a more limited scope for change: only the accidents related to circular motion can change.[50]

5. The Individuation of Intelligible Individuals

The same account applies to intelligible individuals, mutatis mutandis. As I have noted in discussing the threefold distinction of quiddity, things that exist in the mind are concepts, generally derived from sense perceptions of quiddities that exist in individuals, that is, from our experience of individual material substances, like Socrates and that statue. So we have a conception of Socrates, that is, of a thing composed of a substantial form with material accidents like being snubnosed and being a philosopher. But in the mind, due largely to the abstraction processes of cognition, there arise other, formal accidents, like being a species or being an individual, and being an essence or an accident. So intelligible individuals are individuated in a way similar to the way in which sensible individual substances are individuated: the quiddity in the mind essential to that individual is the substantial form and so provides the basis for the identity of the individual over time with different accidents. Still, the intelligible individual comes from the sensible individual, and so that substantial quiddity is perceived in connection with its material accidents. Further, once existing in the mind, the intelligible individual also has another ground for the reception of a different type of accidents, formal accidents, of the sort studied in logic; that is, the intelligible individual has "intelligible matter". Because of this intelligible matter, an individual existing in the mind can come to constitute multiple abstract conceptions that do not directly correspond to sensible individuals existing *in re*. So, for example, 'animal' in general, what Avicenna calls the 'logical genus', has the property of being predicated of many, although no individual man existing *in re* has that property. Likewise, Socrates and Plato, considered in the mind in a certain way, have the property of being two men, although, in reality, there is no dyad of human beings, but rather only this man and that man.[51] Again, in an equation like '$2 + 2 = 4$', the different occurrences of '2' are distinguished by conceptual, formal features. Avicenna thus makes many distinctions of quiddities existing in the mind according to their formal features.[52] As might well be imagined, the discussion gets quite complex and quite obscure. But it is clear throughout his procedure that a difference in the formal accidents of a quiddity in the mind suffices for him to establish the presence of different concepts, that is, different intelligible individuals. So the multiplicity of individuals existing *in intellectu* is explained along the same lines as the multiplicity of individuals existing *in re:* in each case, the substantial form's presence in matter gives the individuality, which may then be recognized by its consequence, having a unique collection of accidents at each point of its history.[53] (In the case of quiddities in the mind, Avicenna does not see much in the way of temporal change, since for him, as for Aristotle, scientific knowledge is of the unchangeable and eternal. So just being a unique collection of accidents, be they formal or material, suffices here.)

But, unlike the case of sensible individuals, these accidental properties that individuate, say, different instances of the number '2', as they do not change and are universal, can be used to define intelligible individuals. Here there is no possibility of the individual, that is, the concept, changing. Each intelligible individual has its own definition and so is a distinctive bundle of properties.[54] So each intelligible individual is a distinct species; the "accidental" properties are not accidental to the individual qua individual, but only to the individual qua member of a more general species. There are many instances of the number '2', many angels if you like, and each has a distinct definition, while at the same time satisfying the definition of '2' or 'angel'.

6. The Individuation of Accidents

Avicenna gives roughly the same account for the individuality of accidents. On the level of quiddities in themselves, there is no difference between the substantial and the accidental: whiteness and humanity are equally quiddities in themselves. As for the substantial, so for the accidental: as more than one white thing exists, how are quiddities like whiteness individuated? A quiddity in itself that comes to exist as an accident, like whiteness, is individuated by existence, be it material or formal. But here its individuality depends on the individuality of the substance, since the substance has to provide a substratum for the existence of the accidental quiddity; the only way for an accident to exist is for there to be an individual substance in which to exist.[55]

7. The Concept of Individuality

Avicenna also has a sophisticated discussion of the concept of individuality.[56] As he notes, the term 'individual' is peculiar.[57] On the one hand, it is supposed to denote just what is distinctive of a particular thing: to view something as an individual and not as a member of a species is to view it concretely, as it itself is. On the other hand, 'individual' is a term that applies equally to all particular things: it is as universal as any other transcendental term, like 'existent' or 'good'. In this sense, to say that Socrates is an individual, is not to claim that Socrates is Socrates, but to say that Socrates is a quiddity in itself (in his case, humanity), coming to exist in a material state able to receive accidents. This description holds of any other quiddity that exists *in re* or *in intellectu*.[58]

As for the existing things that are individuals in the former sense, Avicenna has already explained why they are individuals: it is not because they have associated with them a quiddity or form of individuality; rather it is because of their material existence. He still needs to explain how it is that 'individuality' comes to be a universal term. For him, 'individuality' is a universal term, just like 'one' or 'species': it is a formal accident, associated with the conception of the material thing in the mind.[59] In fact, Avicenna takes 'individuality' to be just a certain notion of unity, and unity for him, like all other numerical entities, exists only in the mind, as formal accidents—abstract patterns of things existing *in re*.

So in the mind, we have a conception of the species man, that is, 'rational animal', pure and simple; we also have a conception of the individual man, that is 'individual rational animal', which would be the concept of the species man with its attendant particularizing matter and consequent accidents. Yet, 'individual man', like 'beautiful man', does not name a distinctive species of man, because there is nothing existing *in re* corresponding to it: beautiful man is not a compound that persists over time and generates its own kind. Likewise, Avicenna says that individual man is a distinctive concept, namely, an intelligible individual, separate from the concept of the species man: the two concepts are two separate quiddities existing *in intellectu*, but denote the same things existing *in re*.[60] 'Individual' is a formal accident that may be attached to a general concept, like 'man', abstracted from perceptions of individual men.

8. Ending Remarks

So Avicenna has a vast, sweeping, comprehensive theory of individuation. I have done here little more than to outline it; I have not discussed much how he argues for it. Yet its very inclusiveness makes it attractive. Of course, one problem with such a theory is whether it be systematic or even consistent; a common view of Islamic philosophers like Avicenna is that they present a mere hodgepodge of earlier views with no unity. Even if this were true, at the least, the depth of Avicenna's views enabled nearly all the later Latin medieval philosophers to use and borrow something from them. Perhaps they took only what is consistent or valuable from his views; on the other hand, it may well be that Avicenna is a profound thinker of the caliber of Aristotle or Plato, whose profundity his followers only partially grasped.

Or, perhaps Avicenna missed what was profound in Aristotle's thought and so offered additions and emendations to what was but an inadequate and impoverished view of Aristotle's thought. To a large extent, Averroes can be viewed as having taken this position; Averroes is known mostly as a detailed commentator and supporter of the original Aristotelian position and to his views we now turn.

II. Averroes: The Great Commentator

As with Avicenna, there are some major difficulties in ascertaining just what Averroes's views are. One such difficulty concerns the character of what he wrote. Averroes apparently was engaged in writing his own version of Aristotelian philosophy (*The Incoherence of the Incoherence* is the best known such work) when he accepted a commission to write extensive commentaries on all of Aristotle's works. Earlier commentaries were thought to be incomplete or inadequate (as with al-Farabi's work) or to diverge too far from the text (as with Avicenna's). Averroes thus devoted much of his career to explicating each of the texts of Aristotle in a series of commentaries, known as the long, the middle, and the short (or epitome).[61] The problem is that most of the material written by Averroes that we have consists in these commentaries, and so the question might well be raised whether what Averroes says in them represents his own views. Yet, most scholars conclude that they generally do.[62] In particular, in the epitomes, Averroes diverges from the text enough to answer later objections to Aristotle's views and add material, such as his discussions of the agent intellect in his epitome of *Metaphysics* XII.[63] Still, there and also in his other work, Averroes generally presents views in agreement with a fairly literal interpretation of Aristotle. At any rate, as Averroes's main influence on the Latin West was through his commentaries, I shall confine myself to presenting the doctrines on individuation contained in them.

A second problem with Averroes's writings concerns the state of the text.[64] Many of Averroes's works are lost in the original Arabic and preserved only in Latin, or even Hebrew or Spanish, translations. So there is some problem in working from uncritical translations to determine Averroes's position. But, as the topic here concerns Averroes's influence on Latin medieval theories of individuation, the *Averroes latinus* is most pertinent to this discussion, and so the problem of dealing with translations will not create much difficulty.

1. The Principle of Individuation

On the whole, Averroes's position on the problem of individuation follows what can be gleaned from a fairly literal reading of Aristotle's works, *Metaphysics* VII in particular. Averroes endorses the various Aristotelian descriptions of an individual as what is not predicated of many, as what cannot be divided further, as what is the same in species but different in number.[65] Individual substances are also not in a subject and remain the same through change, as they provide a substratum for change. Averroes, however, also admits the existence of individual accidents, which, of course, exist only in a substance as subject, and so the criteria for individual substances should not be regarded as criteria for individuality *simpliciter.*[66]

Like Avicenna and, presumably, Aristotle, Averroes recognizes existence both *in re* and *in intellectu.* So he will recognize both sensible and intelligible individuals.[67] Again, following the Aristotelian tradition, Averroes distinguishes sensible substantial individuals into the eternal celestial and the corruptible terrestial. As I have done with Avicenna, I shall concentrate on Averroes's account of the sensible terrestial substantial individual, as this is the central case discussed, and then remark later on how the account is to be applied to the other types of individuals recognized by Averroes.

Following Aristotle, Averroes holds that only individuals exist, and in the primary sense, only individual substances exist. Universals, though, have a sort of reality, insofar as they are the active principles or causes of the generation of individuals. Yet these universals, the Aristotelian substantial forms, do not exist apart, independent of the individual exemplifying them, but always exist as instantiated, *in rebus.*[68] What actually exists, *in re,* is the substantial individual, the compound of matter and substantial form. The substantial individual can take on various accidents at different times, while retaining its identity. Individual accidents exist only insofar as they are in individual substances.

So for Averroes to be an individual is to be a compound of form and matter.[69] Like Aristotle, he holds that a substantial individual is identical to its quiddity; Socrates is just what it is to be Socrates, namely the substantial form of man.[70] The presence of this substantial form in matter causes the individual to persist and change in regular ways, just as a child grows up to be an adult human being. However, the substantial form does not come to be present in matter by coming from a transcendent, noumenal realm. Rather, "man generates man": one substantial form, present in matter, causes another substantial form of the same species to come to be present in matter.[71] More precisely, the substantial individual that is the cause causes the new substantial individual to come to be by joining a preexisting substantial form that is already present in matter to some other material that promotes the development of a new member of that species. Thus, for a human being, some man contains the substantial form of another human being in potency, that is, has a sperm which is a substantial form of another human being in seminal matter. When that man implants the sperm in the womb, then the sperm is put in contact with other matter that promotes the growth and development of another human being. So, in natural generation, the new substantial individual comes to exist in act, whereas it had already existed in potency in a seminal form.[72]

Likewise, in artistic production, the substantial form of the artifact has already existed before the artifact is produced, as a form in the mind of the artist.[73] Here again the substantial form exists in matter, but here in the "intellective" or "fictive" matter in the mind of the artist.[74] Artistic production is a process whereby the substantial form existing in the intellect, say, the shape of a sphere, is transferred to other matter existing *in re,* say, the bronze, which then comes to lose its previous shape or form, and then comes to have the shape of a sphere.[75]

So for Averroes, as indeed for Aristotle, the substantial form is the active principle of individuation: it is that by which the individual comes to be and that by which the individual retains its identity.[76] The substantial form, when it exists, namely, when it is in matter, provides a substratum for the reception of various accidents at different times. In this way, then, the substantial form can be thought to be that by which one individual differs from another individual, even of the same species, as its presence provides identity for the thing and a substratum for receiving accidents.

Yet the reason why there are many individuals of the same species, that is, that have the substantial form, is the presence of matter. Matter is not the active principle, or formal cause, of an individual's coming to be and being what it is. Still, its presence enables a substantial form to exist at all and to constitute a substratum for the reception of accidents. Like Aristotle, Averroes distinguishes prime from proximate matter. A substantial form, like humanity, needs the appropriate proximate matter, like flesh and bones, to exist. The proximate matter, as it has properties, already has a substantial form of a sort. If we were to abstract away all properties and forms from proximate matter, we would be left with prime matter, which is just a bare receptacle for the instantiation of substantial forms. But, like the substantial form, prime matter does not exist apart, separate from form. Rather these principles, substantial form and prime matter, are separated and distinct only in abstract thought. So, abstractly, it can be said that matter provides a ground for the individuation of beings of the same species, that is, makes difference in number possible, just as the substantial form can be said to be the active principle for an individual's having an identity and persisting through change.

2. The Individuation of Other Types of Individuals

Such is Averroes's account of the individuation of sensible corruptible substances. For the sensible celestial individuals, Averroes gives generally the same account, except that he insists that the matter there is "simple" and allows only change in place.[77] As I have mentioned, he gives the same account for intelligible individuals, for which he postulates an intelligible, or fictive, matter. So, again, an intelligible individual is composed of a substantial form in matter, although this time the matter and the resulting existence is found *in intellectu* and not *in re*.[78] In some cases, the intelligible individuals will be conceptions of sensible individuals, such as my idea of Socrates; other times, they will be abstracted patterns derived from sensible individuals, as with mathematical objects and the forms in the imagination that enable the artist to produce artifacts.[79] The individuality of accidents depends on the existence of individual substances: an individual accident exists only in a subject, in a compound of matter and form.[80]

3. The Concept of Individuality

Like Aristotle, Averroes discusses the concept of individuality in discussing senses of the term 'one'. He distinguishes senses of 'one', just as Aristotle does in *Metaphysics VI*. In particular, Avicenna says, "the concept of numerical unity has existence *in intellectu* only."[81] On the other hand, there is a transcendental notion of oneness, or unity or perhaps individuality, that is coextensive with the notion of being: every item, in any category whatsoever, has being and is one, single individual. The difference between 'one' and 'being'—'individual' and 'existent' if you like—consists simply in a matter of emphasis.[82]

4. Objections Against Avicenna

In short, then, Averroes closely follows the text of Aristotle and offers views on individuation derived from a close reading of that text. As Aristotle is difficult to understand on many topics, Averroes's presentation thus was invaluable to Latin medieval philosophers. Further, Averroes apparently sought to distinguish the original position of Aristotle from its later modifications and extensions, including those like that of Avicenna. After all, Avicenna might well claim that he accepts Aristotle's doctrine and view his own work as extending or supplementing it. For Avicenna could accept most of what Averroes attributes to Aristotle. However, there are some differences on which Averroes defends Aristotle against Avicenna, and thereby seeks to distinguish Aristotle's position from Avicenna's.[83]

So, for example, Averroes attacks Avicenna for claiming that corporeity attaches first and primarily (in a logical or conceptual order at least) to the complex of the substantial quiddity in itself and prime matter.[84] Averroes's main point seems to be that there is nothing in particular that this corporeity could be. Avicenna himself admits that this corporeity is not the body that is a genus in the category of substance, nor the particular quantitative accidents that come to be in the material substance. So, Averroes asks, what then is corporeity? Averroes argues that there is nothing that it can be in Aristotelian terms: the quantitative features are but accidents and do not compose the material substratum, as Avicenna would have it; the features like body are in the category of substance and so already are present in the complex of the substantial quiddity in itself and prime matter.[85] Moreover, there would be a move from potency to act, without the presence of the form, in the complex (the substantial quiddity in itself plus corporeity) then coming to have a definite, actual shape. Therefore, Averroes rejects Avicenna's account of the priority of corporeity.

In reply, it might be said that Avicenna is simply trying to get more detail in the relation between the substantial form, as given in the definition and formula, and the substratum. What Avicenna has said is certainly not present in the texts of Aristotle explicitly. As I have noted, Avicenna does not care much about following Aristotle at the expense of truth. Still, some texts of Aristotle do support Avicenna's account: Aristotle's remark in the *Categories* that quantity is that accidental category which most resembles substance; Aristotle's very notion of prime matter, which suggests some sort of presence in space. Moreover, I have already suggested that Avicenna is groping toward a conception of space beyond the Aristotelian notion of place, and that the second interpretation of Avicenna's position I have given earlier avoids this objection. So, though Averroes is right that Aristotle's scheme taken literally as already complete has no place for Avicenna's conception of corporeity, it still might be that Aristotle's account needs to be completed in such a way.

Again, Averroes criticizes Avicenna's account of the conception of 'one' (or 'individual') for giving it merely a mental status.[86] As we have seen, Avicenna sees unity or individuality as a formal accident of a quiddity, that is, as a quiddity existing only in the mind (a second intention). So unity, or individuality, is not a real characteristic but only a mental one. Averroes, taking Aristotle's side, objects. For 'one' and 'being' are coextensive, transcendental terms that describe the reality common to all individual items in all categories. We know this reality of individuals via sense perception.[87] So individuality denotes something real, not something existing merely *in intellectu*.

In reply, Avicenna might observe that he too recognizes a reality to which 'individuality' refers. For, as we have seen, he too claims that we have a direct intuition of a real individual as real individual. So there is, to be sure, an immediate conception of the individuality and being of things existing *in re*. Yet, this account by itself does not explain the peculiar features of the concept 'individual' or 'one', how it can be both the most general and the most particular description of a thing, yet does not occur explicitly in its definition.[88]

So, again, Avicenna's account can be seen to be a supplement for Aristotle's theory, to answer new questions, or, at least to augment bare hints and answers given by Aristotle. On the other hand, Averroes will succeed in his objections if it can be determined either that Aristotle's account is adequate by itself, or that the supplements offered by Avicenna are inconsistent with Aristotle's philosophy.

III. Conclusions

I shall now summarize Avicenna's views on individuality in terms of the structure provided by the Introduction to this volume.

1. Avicenna

Displaying his syncretism, Avicenna'a conception of individuality has a place for all the notions that Gracia lists in the Introduction. An individual for Avicenna is indivisible in the sense that there can be no further compounding of quiddities on the level of quiddities in themselves beyond it. The individual man, for example, has the nature of rational animality, and no other quiddities can be added on the level of things in themselves to make a "lower", or more determinate, species. Individuality is that by which one thing differs from other things, where the difference may be both one in species or genus, or in number. Individuals multiply the species: the substantial form can come to exist in more than one instance. An individual is that which remains the same through change. Further, on the logical level, of quiddities in the mind, an individual cannot be predicated of another; it must be remembered that Avicenna holds predication and similar relations not to concern quiddities *in re* directly.

Regarding the extension of individuals, Avicenna is what Gracia would call a "moderate realist". Everything that exists is an individual, where the existence may be *in re* or *in intellectu*. Still, universals have some sort of reality or being, though they do not exist: there is the respect of quiddities in themselves and also, perhaps, formal universals, like individuality, existing in the mind.

As for the ontological status of individuality, Avicenna appears to hold something like Gracia's modal view. Existence is a necessary condition for something to be individual. The act of existence itself individuates, but itself depends on the presence of a quiddity in itself coming to be a substantial form, that is, a quiddity in the category of substance materially receptive of other quiddities. In this position, Avicenna is then able to accomodate in his syncretist fashion the other accounts of individuation: the bundle of properties that a thing has do individuate it for us. The individuators, strictly speaking, are the accidents of the thing, whose combination is unique, but, since accidents must be in some subject, a substance, they presuppose the essential properties (the *propria* and the attributes in the category of substance). Thus, in a way, all the thing's attributes are in the bundle that individuates it. Again, Avicenna would have a prominent place for spatial accidents, since corporeity is a first requirement for the coming to be of an individual sensible substance. Again, in a way, it is the matter that individuates, for the matter is just the ability or potency for quiddities in themselves in different categories to come into connection. Thus matter makes it possible for there to be a unique collection of accidents, for there to be numerical difference and a direct intuition of individuality. Since Avicenna holds that we can have this direct intuition of individuals qua individual, in a sense he might be taken to endorse haecceities: he does in fact use terms like 'Socrateity' and 'Platonicity'. Still, it is the material presence of the substantial form that makes possible for the thing to be unique and to retain its identity through change. So Avicenna has a quite comprehensive view that accomodates features of many different theories of individuation.

Finally, Avicenna does discuss at great length the conception of individuality, both in regard to its formal features and its features as a quiddity existing in the mind. He wants to make some distinctions to explain how the term 'individual' can function both as the most particular description that can be given of something and as the most general. He also offers an explanation why every individual thing is necessarily individual, even though 'individual' does not appear in the formula defining its substantial form.

2. Averroes

I now shall summarize Averroes's position. Like Avicenna, Averroes has a conception of individuality that includes all the features that Gracia mentions, though it does stress impredicability more than the other features. Like Aristotle, Averroes holds that only individuals, the compounds of matter and form, exist, though universals do have a sort of being, as active principles and features of individuals. So Averroes is a moderate realist. Averroes recognizes both individual substances and accidents, and individuals both eternal and corruptible, both *in re* and *in intellectu*. Individuality for Averroes is a transcendental notion, like 'being'. There is only at best a conceptual or perhaps a formal distinction between the individuality of a thing and its quiddity: for a thing to be an individual is for it to be the thing that it is. As for the principle of individuation, Averroes holds that the substantial form, as present in matter, makes something an individual. In a way, this principle can be said to be "existential", since for something to exist is just for there to be this substantial form in this matter. Still, it is the presence of matter that enables there to be things having the same substantial form but differing in number. Accidents are individuated probably derivatively, via their being in individual substances. Averroes does not discuss the issue of discernibility much, but subscribes to Aristotle's theory of sense perception, where we perceive the form of the individual thing in the mind. That form in the mind has fictive matter, and so matter again provides the distinction of individuals differing only in number. Averroes discusses the conception of unity and individuality, and distinguishes various senses. In the primary sense, 'individual' denotes a transcendental concept, like 'being'.

I have now presented, in outline, the views of Avicenna and Averroes on the problem of individuation. On the one hand, Averroes offered to the Latin medieval West of the High Middle Ages a cogent, fairly systematic presentation of Aristotle's philosophy closely in accord with the text. The main virtue of his account lies in his showing just how far one can go in solving philosophical problems largely within the confines of Aristotle's text.[89] On the other hand, Avicenna offered an audacious synthesis of Aristotelian philosophy with other traditions, including the Platonist, Stoic, and the Asharite. This synthesis too was attractive to the Latin West, which also had to digest the Aristotelian corpus within its own, similar traditions. I would have to conclude, though, that Avicenna's position on the problem of individuation is more interesting than Averroes's, as it is more original, while the latter mainly just expounds and defends Aristotle's position.

Let me end with a note on the influence of these two Islamic philosophers on Aquinas's theory of individuation.[90] Aquinas, as well as Albert the Great, needs to be read with reference to Avicenna in particular.[91] In his contribution to this volume, Joseph Owens claims that Aquinas tends not to discuss individuation as a topic in its own right, especially during his later years. I submit that a reason for this is that Aquinas was relying heavily on the Islamic material and did not feel a need to rehash it. Many of the problems that can be found in Aquinas's theory can be solved by referring to it.[92]

The picture that Owens presents of Aquinas's position on individuation has him following Avicenna mainly. The cause of individuation of sensible substances is existence, given by an external agent, namely God, who causes the form to come to have a material existence. Sensible substances, Owens says, are individuated by undefined quantitative dimensions. Again, this is approximately Avicenna's view of the function of corporeity. Again, Aquinas's view of the signification of 'individual' paraphrases Avicenna's doctrine.

Still, Aquinas is also influenced by Averroes. The most prominent similarity is his insistence that matter is the principle of individuation. As I have discussed, Averroes insists, in an orthodox Aristotelian fashion, that matter provides the ability for specific forms to exist in many individuals different only in number. Aquinas has the same view, except that he does not stress the role of substantial form as much as Averroes does.[93] Avicenna, in contrast, would hold that matter by itself does not individuate, since all members of the same species have the same complex of form and matter. So for Avicenna the *materia signata quantitate interminata,* Aquinas's principle of individuation, does not individuate, but only provides a necessary condition for the reception of individual accidents, notably the quantitative, which do individuate.[94] Perhaps Aquinas intended to say what Avicenna had said, but his scattered remarks, without a supplement from his Islamic predecessors, do not suffice.

Notes

1. Avicenna, *Al-Maqūlāt*, 7, 7–8; 18, 4–6.

2. The *Avicenna Latinus* is misleading: that part of Avicenna's *Opera omnia* known as the *Sufficientia* is actually just the part of the *Shif'ā* on the *Physics.*

3. See F. Van Steenberghen, *Aristote en Occident;* A. -M. Goichon, *La Philosophie D'Avicenne et son influence en Europe Médiévale.* On the reception of Aristotle together with Islamic commentaries by the Latin medieval West, see B. Dod, "Aristotles Latinus", pp. 47–48; 71; 74–79; F. Copleston, *A History of Medieval Philosophy* (1972), pp. 106; 153–154.

4. Just compare *De ente et essentia* 3–4 with Avicenna's *Metaphysica*, V.1–2! On the problem of universals in medieval philosophy, cf. M. De Wulf, *A History of Medieval Philosophy,* vol. 1, p. 100. The passage of Avicenna in question is *Il.*, 196, 6–11; *Met.* 86v, col. 1. For a discussion of the use of this passage in Latin medieval philosophy, see my *On Reduplication*, ch. 12.

5. Majid Fakhry, *A History of Islamic Philosophy,* pp. 147–152.

6. Allan Bäck, "Avicenna on Existence", p. 355, n. 18.

7. Avicenna, *Ilāhīyyāt*, 22, 8–10; 23, 10–11; *Metaphysica* 71v, col. 1.

8. *Il.*, 32, 8–12; *Met.*, 72v, col. 1.

9. *Il.*, 195, 6–15; *Met.*, 86v, col. 1.

10. *Il.*, 119, 4–9; *Met.*, 80r, col. 2A. Cf. Aristotle, *Physics,* 193b31–5.

11. By 'substantial form', I mean the form in composition with matter, i.e., the quiddity in itself existing *in re*. It is in this sense that Avicenna says that the humanity in Socrates is not the humanity in Plato, *Il.*, 198, 7–199,3; 208, 10–209,2; *Met.*, 86v, col. 2; 87v, col. 2; *The Metaphysica of Avicenna*, p. 33 [12]. Cf. A. -M. Goichon, *La distinction de l'essence et de l'existence d'après Ibn Sina,* pp. 409–410. At *Il.*, 31, 5; 34, 2, *Met.*, 72v, col. 2, the substantial form seems to be the essence plus the *propria.*

12. Aristotle,*Metaphysics*, 1029a5; 1033a1–10; 1041b11–13;*Physics*, 193a10–b6.

13. *Il.*, 201,10; 220, 9–12; 228,9; *Met.*, 87r, col. 2; 88v, col. 1; 89r, col. 1; *Al-Madkhal*, 29, 8; 42, 3–5; 31, 4; *Logica*, 4r, col. 1; 5v, col. 1; 4r, col. 1. In particular, *Al-Madkhal*, 70,8–10; *Log.*, 12v, col. 1: "Individuum autem non fit individuum nisi cum adiungitur naturae speciei proprietates extraeneae concomitantes aut non concomitantes, et designaretur ei aliqua materia haec vel illa."

14. *Al-Madkhal*, 15, 1–6; *Logica*, 2r, col. 2. I translate from the Arabic; the Latin translation differs significantly: "Essentiae vero rerum aut sunt in ipsis rebus, aut sunt in intellectu, unde habent tres respectus: unus respectus essentiae est secundum quod ipsa est non relata ad aliquid tertium esse, nec ad id quod sequitur eam

secundum quod ipsa est sic. Alius respectus est secundum quod est in his singularibus. Et alius secundum quod est in intellectu. Et tunc sequuntur eam accidentia quae sunt propria istius sui esse, sicut est suppositio et predicatio et universalitas et particularitas in praedicando et essentialitas et accidentalitas in praedicando et cetera eorum quae postea scies.''

15. E.g., *Metaphysics* 1032b14, ''legō d'ousian aneu to ti ēn einai'' is translated as ''I call the essence substance without matter'' in *The Complete Works of Aristotle*, ed. J. Barnes, and as 'et dico substantiam', Averroes, *In Met.*, 173D: cf. 174E: ''Deinde dicit 'et dico substantiam' et forte intendit: et dico substantiam, id est, formam sine materia formam quae est in anima. . .''

16. *Il.*, 202, 3–8; 218, 10–13; 220, 9–12; 235, 1–5; 353, 2–5; *Met.*, 87r, col. 2; 88r, col. 2; 88v, col. 1; 90v, col. 1; 99v, col. 2.

17. *The Metaphysics of Avicenna*, p. 33 [12].

18. *Il.*, 201, 7–13; *Met.*, 87r, col. 2. At *Il.*, 201, 10 (*Met.*, 87r, col. 1), Avicenna says that the quiddity in itself ''precedes in existence (*wujūd*)'', but this use is careless, I think. At *Il.*, 205, 2 (*Met.*, 87r, col. 2) he says that this ''existence'' of the essence is the divine existence; i.e., the essence is from God and exists in God's mind. In the usual sense of 'existence', Avicenna insists that existence belongs solely to individuals that have quiddities (*Il.*, 207, 5–12; 209, 3–9; *Met.*, 87v, col. 1). The discussion is complicated because 'universal' and 'individual' concern quiddities in the mind, strictly speaking, although the basis for the presence of universals in the mind lies with the quiddities in themselves.

19. *Al-Madkhal*, 36, 8; 48; 15; *Logica*, 4v, col. 2; 6r, col. 1.

20. The differentiae alone belong to the quiddity in itself and bring it into existence (*Il.*, 354, 1–8; *Net.*, 99v, col. 2). On the status of *propria*, cf. *Al-Najāt*, 6, 17; *Al-Madkhal*, 29, 15–30, 1; *Logica*, 4r, col. 1.

21. *Il.*, 236, 6–8; 241, 5–16; *Met.*, 90r, col. 2; 90v, col. 2; *Al-Madkhal*, 28, 13–29, 6; *Log.*, 3v, col. 2.

22. *Il.*, 202, 3–8; 204, 16–205, 2; *Met.*, 89r, col. 2.

23. *Il.*, 198, 7–199, 3; *Met.*, 86v, col. 2; *The Metaphysica of Avicenna*, p. 33 [12].

24. *Il.*, 207, 10–12; *Met.*, 87r, col. 1.

25. The standard term is ‹*māʿnān*›, often though not always translated as *intentio*. The literal sense is ''what is meant'', i.e., the Stoic *lekton*.

26. So Avicenna says that horseness (a quiddity in itself) is neither one nor many, *Il.*, 197, 1ff.; *Met.*, 86v, cols. 1–2; *Al-Madkhal*, 65, 8; *Logica*, 9r, col. 1. Likewise horses like Bucephalus are neither one nor many, *Il.*, 197, 13–198, 2; *Met.*, 87v, col. 2 (this is the passage referred to at *Al-Madkhal*, 66, 1–5; *Logica*, 9r, col. 2). Such

formal attributes belong only to quiddities in the mind (*Il.*, 109, 10–110, 3; *Met.*, 79v, cols. 1–2); being one and being many are "extrinsic inseparable accidents" (i.e., *propria*) (*Il.*, 201, 14–207, 2; *Met.*, 87r, col. 2). Cf. Alexander, *In Met.*, 483, 26–38. The horse example comes from Aristotle, *Metaphysics*, 1031b15.

27. On this distinction, see *Il.*, 156, 1–5; *Met.*, 83v, col. 1D; *Al-Madkhal*, 23, 14–15; *Logica*, 3r, col. 2; Alfarabi, *Kitāb Al-Ḥurūf*, 65, 22.

28. *Il.*, 85, 12; *Met.*, 9v, col. 1. Cf. Aristotle, *Metaphysics*, 1030a1–2; 1031b21–8.

29. *Il.* 208, 5–9; *Met.*, 87v, col. 1; *Al-Madkhal*, 74, 11–75, 21; *Logica*, 8v, col. 2.

30. *Al-Najāt*, 451; *Al-Ishārāt*, 101–102. Cf. A. -M. Goichon, *La Distinction*, pp. 468 and 470–473.

31. *Il.*, 64, 6–12; *Met.*, 75v, col. 1: "Corporeitas igitur vera est forma continuationis recipiens id quod diximus de positione trium dimensionum, et haec intentio est extra mensuram et extra coporeitatem disciplinalem. Hoc enim corpus secundum hanc formam non differt ab alio corpore sive sit maius, sive sit minus, nec comparatur ei sive sit aequale, sive sit numeratum per illud, sive communicans ei, sive incommunicans. Hoc enim non est ei nisi inquantum est mensuratum et inquantum aliqua pars eius numerat illud. Et haec omnia considerantur in eo absque consideratione corporeitatis quam assignavimus." Cf. *Il.*, 61, 16–62, 6; 72, 1–2; 196, 6ff.; *Met.*, 75r, col. 2; 76r, col. 2; 86v, col. 1; *Al-Ishārāt*, 98; *The Metaphysica*, p. 24 [8]. On earlier views of corporeity, cf. Plotinus, *Enneads*, II.4.12.

32. By 'three-dimensionality' I mean, strictly speaking, the ability to be three-dimensional, i.e., the ability to exist as an object with a definite magnitude in three-dimensional space. So Avicenna sees corporeity as an *inclinatio* for being a three-dimensional object. Only when an individual substance has a definite actual shape is it in fact three-dimensional in the full sense (*Il.*, 214, 3; *Met.*, 88r, col. 1; *Sufficientia*, 14r, col. 1). Cf. Léon Gauthier, *Ibn Rochd*, p. 73; H. A. Wolfson, *Crescas' Critique of Aristotle*, pp. 101 and 584.

33. To make this point less anachronistically, Avicenna had three major traditions on the nature of space available to him: the Aristotelian, the atomistic (in Democritus and more readily in the philosophy of the Kalām), and the dimensional (in Philoponus). I am claiming that Avicenna embraced the dimensional in his conception of corporeity, although he may have kept the Aristotelian in his discussion of the category of place. Cf. Max Jammer, *Concepts of Space*, pp. 54–57; Gauthier, *Ibn Rochd*, p. 76. Avicenna definitely rejects the atomist view (*Il.*, 65, 16ff.; *Met.*, 75v, col. 1; Goichon, *La Distinction*, p. 426).

34. *The Metaphysica*, p. 17 [4]: "its bodily form will always persist, whereas these three dimensions do not persist. Thus these three dimensions are accidents to the wax, while its form is another attribute. Bodies differ not with respect to form because, by belonging to one kind of category, all bodies are identical with respect to the

possibility of being described by these three dimensions in the aforesaid manner." Cf. Morewedge, in his translation of *The "Metaphysica,"* p. 115: "Intensionally ibn Sina does not equate 'having a form and substratum-matter' with 'having a dimension' . . . he affirms that 'dimensionality' is a necessary feature of 'any given body though it is not the essence of that body'; hence 'the meaning of a body' cannot be equated with 'dimensionality'." So corporeity is not the shape of a body (its "measure", cf. *Il.*, 80, 4–10; *Met.*, 79v, col. 1). Rather it is the receptivity of the substantial quiddity in itself to acquire a shape. Morewedge is urging that corporeity (dimensionality) is not part of the definition, i.e., an essential consitutent, of the substantial quiddity in itself.

35. *Il.*, 214, 1–216, 9; 219, 11; 239, 13; *Met.*, 88r, col.1; 88v, col. 1; 89v, col. 1. The distinction is between body as genus and body as matter: the former is a predicate, in the definition of an individual sensible substance; the latter is not. E. Gilson, *History of Christian Philosophy in the Middle Ages*, p. 193, seems to agree with my second account: "Each being then is made up of two forms, that of corporeity and, for instance, that of animality." Again, p. 208: "Corporeal substance . . . is continuous and extended in space, according to the three dimensions. The form which enables it to receive the dimensions is the corporeal form." Cf. *Sufficientia*, I.2, 14r, cols. 1ff.

36. Kant, *Prolegomena* § 15.

37. Here I differ with Goichon, *La Distinction*, pp. 430–431, where she claims that the form of corporeity belongs to the category of substance, i.e., to the substantial quiddity in itself. Yet what is in a quiddity in itself in the category of substance cannot perform the function of relating such a quiddity to quiddities in other categories. This is what corporeity (being three-dimensional and being able to be divided) does. After the connection of corporeity to a specific substantial quiddity, then individual accidents of quantity, etc., like shape, can be received. (This refinement of the second account also largely defuses Averroes's criticism—discussed later—as a potency (*inclinatio*) that comes to actuality with no external cause.)

38. *Il.*, 221, 10–11; *Met.*, 88v, col. 1.

39. *Il.*, 47, 1–15; *Met.*, 74r, col. 1; *Al-Madkhal*, 69, 3–18; *Logica*, 12v, col. 1.

40. F. Copleston, *A History of Medieval Philosophy*, pp. 106–107; F. van Steenberghen, *Aristotle in the West*, pp. 17–19; E. Gilson, *History of Christian Philosophy in the Middle Ages*, pp. 181–182.

41. At *Il.*, 311, 6; 314, 16ff.; *Met.*, 96r, col. 2, Avicenna discusses fallacies committed by Platonists. Also see *Al-Najāt*, 451; *Al-Ishārāt*, 101–102.

42. At *Il.*, 89, 6–7; *Met.*, 77v, col. 2, Avicenna claims that the material form does not exist apart from matter: "Forma igitur non habet esse nisi in ulē. Hoc autem quod ulē causa est sui esse et quod ipsa est in ulē. . ." See *Il./Met.* II.3 for the relation of matter and form in composite substance.

43. *Il.*, 135, 10–15; 201, 4–7; *Met.*, 81v, col. 2; 87r, col. 1.

44. *Il.*, 174, 16ff.; *Met.*, 85r, cols. 1–2.

45. *Al-Madkhal*, 70, 12–20; *Logica*, 12v, col. 1: "Si enim diceres quod Plato est longus, scriptor, pulcher, talis et talis, quotquot proprietates apposuerit, non tamen describeretur per illas in intellectu individualitas Platonis. Possibile est enim ut intentio quae componitur ex his omnibus habeatur a pluribus quam ab uno. Non autem demonstrat tibi eum nisi esse, et ostensio intentionis individualis. Velut si diceretur quod est filius illius et est in tali hora longus philosophus, contingeret illa hora nullum aliorum cum eo in illis proprietatibus, et contingeret te sure hunc visum, tunc scieres eius individualitas, quemadmodum scieres id quod est sensibile si digito ostenderetur tibi. Veluti si ostenderetur Platonem hora tertia, tunc enim certificaretur tibi individualitas illius, et hoc esset tibi ostendens individualitatem eius."

46. *Il.*, 246, 8–247, 6; *Met.*, 90r, col. 1.

47. This is the individual as we perceive it, the "natural man", the composite of form and matter and accidents (*Il.*, 200, 13–201, 3; *Met.*, 87r, col. 1).

48. *Il.*, 29, 5–6; *Met.*, 72r, col. 2; *The Metaphysica*, p. 15 [3].

49. *Il.*, 205, 3–5; *Met.*, 87r, col. 2. Goichon, *La Distinction*, p. 468, claims that for Avicenna having a unique set of accidents is a necessary consequence but not a cause of individuation.

50. Terrestial and celestial substances do not differ in corporeity (*Il.*, 68, 17–69, 6; *Met.*, 76r, col. 1). However, there is no potentiality for the celestial (*Il.*, 186, 6ff.; *Met.*, 85v, col. 2). Avicenna holds that the causes of celestial sensible substances are intelligences or souls, commonly known as 'angels'. These causes are individuated like the intelligible individuals in the mind, by properties. So every angel will constitute a separate species, as in Aquinas.

51. So Avicenna claims that numbers exist both *in re* and *in intellectu:* the numbers of mathematics are structural features abstracted from real objects (*Il.*, 119, 6–9; *Met.*, 80r, col. 2).

52. *Il.*, 205, 5–206, 5; *Met.*, 87r, col. 2; *Al-Madkhal*, 15, 7; *Logica*, 9r, col. 1; *Al-Maqūlāt*, 15, 7.

53. *A-Madkhal*, 34, 5–35, 9; *Logica*, 4v, col. 1.

54. *Il.*, 143, 9–144, 6; *Met.*, 82v, col. 1. So Avicenna ends up embracing a bundle theory for intelligible individuals. Yet he is thereby no Platonist. The main reason why Avicenna seems to be a Platonist is that his discussions of sensible individuals are generally put in terms of our ideas of them, and thus the features of intelligible individuals are constantly being related to those of the sensible.

55. *Il.*, 57, 12ff.; 93, 11–94, 4; 135, 7–10; *Met.*, 74v, col. 2; 78r, col. 1; 81v, col. 2–82r, col. 1; *Al-Madkhal*, 85, 12–15; *Logica*, 9v, col. 1.

56. *Il.*, 97, 1ff.; 211, 9–16; *Met.*, 78v, col. 1; 87v, col. 2.

57. *Al-Madkhal,* 71, 1–72, 2; *Logica,* 12v, col. 2.

58. Avicenna also discusses individual terms at *Al-Madkhal,* 27, 1–16; *Logica,* 3v col.1, where he notes that 'Zayd' is an individual and not a universal term, although many people are called by the name, 'Zayd', for the intended concept is individual.

59. *Al-Madkhal,* 65, 8ff.; *Logica,* 12r, col. 1.

60. *Al-Madkhal,* 72, 2–7; *Logica,* 12v, col. 2. Avicenna sharply distinguishes the *individuum vaguum* and the *individuum determinatum:* the former ('man' in general) is a quiddity in the mind, while the latter ('a certain man') is a quiddity in individuals. This distinction is clearly marked for 'man' in Arabic; cf. Goichon, *La Distinction,* pp. 463–464.

61. For an overview, see Edward Booth, *Aristotelian Aporetic Ontology in Islamic and Christian Thinkers,* pp. 127–128 and 281.

62. *Ibid.,* pp. 127–128; E. Gilson, *History of Christian Philosophy,* pp. 217–220. Also, some of Averroes's commentaries are printed with annotations by Gersonides inserted frequently into the text. Still, to investigate the *Averroes latinus,* it is not necessary for me to distinguish sharply these annotations from Averroes's own words, as we are interested in Averroes's medieval influence.

63. At *In Met.,* 181B–D, and *Epitome,* 394Hff., Averroes says that Aristotle does not hold the view given by Alexander, Themistius, and Avicenna, that the forms are given by the active intellect in a process of creation. Averroes seems to side with this view against Aristotle. Cf. Ernest Renan, *Averroès et L'averroïsme,* pp. 108–111.

64. For a summary of the problems, see E. Booth, *Aristotle's Aporetic,* p. 126, n. 122.

65. *Epitome,* 159K–160D; 160I; *In Met.,* 111B–113H.

66. *In Met.,* 153K.

67. *Epitome,* 371I–K.

68. *Epitome,* 372A.

69. *Epitome,* 370E; 370L; *In Met.,* 174F; 178A–B; 197D; 197K.

70. *In Met.,* 169F; 169K–L; 170G.

71. *Epitome,* 367B–I; 368B; *In Met.,* 177C.

72. *In Met.,* 180C–G.

73. *In Met.,* 173I–174A; 180B.

74. *Epitome,* 371F–G.

75. *Epitome*, 366L; *In Met.*, 160L. Cf. Alexander, *In Met.*, 465, 7–8; 472, 16–17; 489, 13–14.

76. *In Met.*, 168L–159D.

77. *Epitome*, 372E.

78. *In Met.*, 185C; 185K; 191H–I.

79. *In Met.*, 189G; 190G; 191H–K.

80. *Praedicamenta*, 24h; 24L (which is a comment by Gersonides).

81. *Epitome*, 380D.

82. *Epitome*, 379E.

83. Still, note that Averroes often follows Avicenna. E.g., Averroes's *Epitome* II strongly resembles Avicenna's *Metaphysica* III.

84. *Epitome*, 364K–365L; 373H–374E.

85. L. Gauthier, *Ibn Rochd*, pp. 70–74.

86. *Epitome*, 160F–H; 379L–380E; *De substantia orbis*, p. 321.

87. *In Met.*, 185H–I; 202E.

88. Avicenna makes a similar point about 'existent' at *Il.* 232, 7; *Met.*, 90r, col. 2; *Al-Madkhal* 64, 4; *Logica*, 8r, col. 1.

89. L. Gauthier, *Ibn Rochd*, pp. 257ff.

90. In addition to the materials cited by Owens, see M. Anawati, ''St. Thomas et la Métaphysique d'Avicenne''; Y. Chisaka, ''St. Thomas Aquinas et Avicenne''.

91. Generally, Albert and Aquinas are supposed to be different: ''Albert doit tout à Avicenne; saint Thomas, comme philosophe, doit presque tout à Averroes,'' E. Renan, *Averroés*, p. 236.

92. Goichon, *La Distinction*, p. 468, n. 2, criticizes Roland-Gosselin, *Le ''De ente et essentia'' de S. Thomas D'Aquin*, pp. 59–66, for conflating points of Avicenna's doctrine that he was careful to keep apart. I suggest that Roland-Gosselin was following the pattern set by Aquinas.

93. E. Renan, *Averroés*, pp. 241–242.

94. Goichon, *La Distinction*, pp. 475–476: ''Pour saint Thomas, la matière en tant que principe d'individuation doit etre marqueé par une quantité indéterminée, *signata quantitate interminata*. C'est la condition nécessaire et suffisante. Pour Ibn Sina, c'est une condition nécessaire, mais insuffisante.''

4

The Jewish Tradition: Maimonides (b. 1135; d. 1204), Gersonides (b. 1288; d. 1344), and Bedersi (b. 1270; d. 1340)

Tamar M. Rudavsky

I. Introduction

In this chapter I shall examine the views of three representative Jewish thinkers: Maimonides (1135–1204), Gersonides (1288–1344) and Yedayah Bedersi (ca. 1270–1340). Of the three, Maimonides is the best known and most influential writer in that his works influenced the majority of subsequent Jewish philosophers. However, both Gersonides and Bedersi are important figures as well. Unlike Maimonides, who was rooted in the Islamic philosophical tradition, Gersonides and Bedersi illustrate the important influences of scholastic thought upon Jewish philosophy.[1]

Before turning to the detailed discussions of these three thinkers, however, we should point out some of the differences in scope between Jewish and scholastic discussions of issues of individuation. Part of the difference is due to the fact that until the fourteenth century Jewish writers had little access to the logical writings of Aristotle, and so the specific logical issues related to individuation that arose out of the *Categories* and *On Interpretation* were of little direct concern to them. Not until the commentaries of Alfarabi and Averroes were translated into Hebrew in the mid-twelfth–early thirteenth centuries were Jewish philosophers exposed to specifically logical concerns. In fact, with the exception of Maimonides's early treatise on logic, which relied heavily upon Alfarabi's books,[2] there are few Jewish writings prior to the fourteenth century devoted to matters of logic.[3] Second, inasmuch as Jewish philosophers were obviously not concerned with those ontological issues that arose out of a trinitarian conception of God, they did not feel as obliged as did their scholastic counterparts to construct elaborate theories of identity and individuation to account for the unity within diversity of the Godhead.[4]

In general, problems associated with individuation occured more readily for Jewish thinkers within the context of cosmological and psychological concerns. More specifically, starting with Ibn Gabirol's characterization of a universal hylomorphism[5] and continuing throughout the Jewish neo-Platonic tradition, Jewish philosophers were concerned with the following sorts of issues: What is the ultimate composition of particular entities? Is matter sufficient to particularize these entities? And, can particular entities be known by God and by humans? The neo-Platonic emanation scheme forced philosophers to offer an explanation for the very existence of material entities: How, within an ontology that emphasizes the unity of the whole of substance, does one account for the proliferation of entities within a predominantly nonphysical hierarchy?[6]

These ontological concerns carried with them theological ramifications that were manifested in the examination of God's knowledge of these particulars. For if, as the majority of Jewish philosophers were wont to argue, God is an immaterial Being and not subject to change, then how can He know the world of changing, material particulars? Concomitantly, if these particulars are in some way individuated on the basis of their matter alone, then in what sense can God individuate them? And if God cannot individuate particulars, how can He bestow providence upon them? For, within the medieval Jewish tradition, divine providence is bestowed only upon individuals who satisfy certain criteria, that is, moral and intellectual qualities.

Finally, Jewish philosophers raised issues of individuation within the context of theories of personal immortality. Here they were clearly influenced by the Islamic controversy over the unity/plurality of forms.[7] Jewish discussions took several dimensions. First, in light of the fact that the soul is the form of the body, does it retain its individuality upon separation from the body? And second, philosophers were concerned with the implications of their views with respect to the process of knowledge; that is, the connection, if any, between human intellect and the Active Intellect, as characterized by Avicenna and Averroes.[8]

We cannot, in our brief discussion here, examine all of these issues in detail. Therefore I have tried to concentrate upon the more salient and influential of these issues in our three philosophers. I shall first present the views of Maimonides and Gersonides, who represent the two major Jewish figures of the twelfth and fourteenth centuries, respectively. I shall then briefly discuss the work of Bedersi, who, although not as major a figure, nevertheless contributed to subsequent developments in the topic of individuation in the fourteenth century.

II. Maimonides

1. Introduction

I have chosen to concentrate upon Maimonides's major philosophical work, *Guide of the Perplexed,* for this discussion. Although not a systematic work, nevertheless it represents Maimonides's paramount attempt to integrate the philosophical and theological domains, particularly with respect to such thorny issues as the creation of the universe, divine predication, prophecy, and natural science. Unfortunately, however, reading this work is no easy task, for as is well known, Maimonides himself gave impetus to the contention that the ostensibly orthodox views espoused in the *Guide of the Perplexed* are not necessarily his own. In the Introduction to the *Guide* Maimonides distinguishes two levels of interpretation, exoteric and esoteric, and suggests that it is sometimes incumbent upon a philosopher to conceal his own esoteric position behind the veil of exoteric doctrine.[9] Maimonides further describes seven sorts of contradictions commonly found in philosophical works and suggests that two of these (#5 and #7) may be used specifically to conceal potentially controversial or even heretical doctrines from the masses.[10] He then states that any contradictions found in the *Guide* itself are intentional and are of type #5 or #7.[11] Finally, Maimonides characterizes certain doctrines, such as that of creation, as potentially volatile, and certainly extremely challenging. So that when readers of the *Guide* turn to those chapters, they have already been forewarned by the author to expect at least a modicum of ambiguity at best, or outright deception at worst.

Maimonides does not devote separate chapters to problems of individuation and particulars; rather, his comments are scattered throughout his work and must be reconstructed in light of several main concerns: his critique of Kalam thought;[12] his discussion of creation; and his assessment of Aristotelian metaphysics. My own presentation, then, will concentrate upon two sets of issues: Maimonides's characterization of matter and form and his concern with the particularization of entities within his cosmological system.

2. Matter and Form, Potency and Privation

Unlike his scholastic contemporaries, Maimonides does not develop the notions of matter and form into a cohesive theory. His characterization of matter and form, albeit sketchy, is a mixture of Aristotelian and neo-Platonic elements. This characterization has important implications not only for his theory of creation of the world but for the doctrine of individuation as well, for it affects the way Maimonides regards both material and immaterial things. Maimonides's views are borne out in several representative contexts which I should like to examine.

In Part II of the *Guide,* after summarizing the salient aspects of Aristotelianism, Maimonides suggests that he accepts the bulk of Aristotle's
metaphysical scheme. The hylomorphic composition of things is described in
Guide II, prop. 22, as follows: "Every body is necessarily composed of two
things and is necessarily accompanied by accidents. The two things constituting it are its matter (*homer*) and its form (*tsurah*); and the accidents accompanying it are quantity, shape and position."[13] And again, in II, prop. 25,
Maimonides reiterates that "the principles of an individual compound substance are matter and form."[14]

That matter is the principle of possibility is expressed in II, prop. 24:
"Whatsoever is something in potentia is necessarily endowed with matter, for
possibility is always in matter."[15] The passivity of matter as contrasted to the
activity of form is emphasized in the following passage: "Matter, as you
know, is always receptive and passive, if one considers its essence, and is not
active except by accident. Form, on the other hand, is in its essence always
active, . . . and is passive only by accident."[16]

But Maimonides superimposes this Aristotelian characterization with
neo-Platonic elements. In *Guide* III, 10, Maimonides argues that matter and
evil are ultimately nonexistent. Having claimed that matter is a veil separat-
ing the ultimate apprehension of formal reality,[17] Maimonides goes on to argue that evil, and in particular its material instantiation, is a privation: "all
the evils are privations with which an act is only connected in the way we
have explained: namely, through the fact that God has brought matter into
existence provided with the nature it has—namely a nature that consists in
matter always being a concomitant of privation, as is known."[18] What does
it mean to say that the material instantiation of evil is a privation? This statement has ontological as well as ethical significance. Ontologically, Maimonides is suggesting that ultimately matter has no positive status of its own.
That is, echoing Plotinus, Maimonides characterizes matter as the "nonexistent", a "nothing which is not nothingness".[19]

The ethical connotations are amply borne out in Maimonides's commentary upon the extended analogy developed in *Proverbs* 7:6-21. In this
passage, according to Maimonides, King Solomon likens matter to a married
harlot in that, "all the hindrances keeping man from his ultimate perfection,
every deficiency affecting him and every disobedience, come to him from his
matter".[20] Echoing the neo-Platonic dictum that matter is the root of corporeal evil, Maimonides urges man not to follow his bestial or material nature,
for "the proximate matter of man is identical with the proximate matter of
the other living beings".[21] In this passage Maimonides is alluding to a distinction made in his logical work, *Millot Hahigayon,* between "proximate
substance" and "remote substance".[22] In both passages Maimonides claims
that inasmuch as the former substance more closely approaches the individual

nature of man than the latter, humans ought not to associate themselves with this "remote substance".

In III, 8, Solomon's parable is expanded further in light of the inherent corruptibility of matter:

> The nature and the true reality of matter are such that it never ceases to be joined to privation; hence no form remains constantly in it, for it perpetually puts off one form and puts on another. . . . It has then become clear that all passing-away and corruption or deficiency are due solely to matter. . . . Similarly every living being dies and becomes ill solely because of its matter and not because of its form. All man's acts of disobedience and sins are consequent upon his matter and not upon his form, whereas all his virtues are consequent upon his form.[23]

Just as a harlot is never satisfied with just one man, so too Maimonides construes matter as constantly flitting from one form to another; and just as a harlot is responsible for indulgence and vice in a man, so too is matter seen as the principle of evil and decay in humans.

In short, Maimonides has presented a hylomorphic picture according to which things are composed of both a material and a formal principle. Following Aristotle, matter is associated with potentiality and form with actuality. Matter represents absolute privation or lack of being. One ramification of this neo-Platonic chord is that on an ontological level material things, inasmuch as they are composed of matter, are not accorded as much reality as purely formal things.

3. The Particularization of Material and Formal Things

Having examined the hylomorphic composition of objects, let us turn to their particularization. Maimonides addresses this issue in two contexts, that of the creation of material entities, and the immortality of the soul. In *Guide* II, 19, the problem of particularization is raised in terms of the difference among things: given that all things in the sublunar universe have one common substance, why, then, are the species, as well as the individuals within each species, different from one another?[24] Maimonides first summarizes the Aristotelian response according to which prime matter is transformed into the four elements each with different qualities; these in turn form the basis for the myriad compounds found in the sublunar spheres. Since matter has great latitude with respect to its specific forms, "the individuals of the species differ in a way corresponding to this latitude, as has been elucidated in the natural science".[25]

Maimonides agrees with Aristotle that differences in the spherical motions imply that they have different forms. However, unlike Aristotle, he is concerned as well with where these differentiating forms originate. "Since every substratum in [the heavenly spheres] has been particularized so as to receive a certain form other than the forms received by the others, who is it that has particularized these substrata and has predisposed them to receive various forms?"[26]

Kalam philosophers had developed their own response to this issue, which Maimonides summarizes in I, 74. For the Mutakalimun maintained that the very fact that a thing has been determined in terms of one particular size, place, location, and so forth is proof that there exists a being that freely chooses these determinations. Inasmuch as objects, in the atomist ontology, do not have specific natures, the fact that they exhibit one set of characteristics rather than another must be explained.[27] Hence the Mutakalimun concluded that a Being must be responsible for the characterization of each entity in the universe: "Thus the world as a whole requires someone to particularize it as a whole and each of its parts by means of one of the various admissible possibilities."[28] Although Maimonides rejects atomist occasionalism as a metaphysical doctrine, he agrees with its conclusion, namely that the fact that there is particularization is evidence of a particularizer.

This doctrine of particularization is developed further in I, 72, where Maimonides draws a comparison between the universe as a whole and the human entity. According to this analogy, the universe is "one individual being" whose parts constitute a single entity. Just as the members of the human body cannot exist by themselves, so too the parts of the universe cannot exist independent of one another.[29] However, with respect to the heavenly spheres, Maimonides has several important stipulations. Although the heavens are material, "its matter is not like that which is in us".[30] And further the terms 'matter' and 'body', when used of us and of the heavenly bodies, are equivocal; that is, they have totally different referents.[31] This is not to say that the spheres are individuated on the basis of their matter; rather, Maimonides follows the Aristotelian doctrine that each heavenly sphere is a separate intelligence.[32] Inasmuch as the motions of the spheres differ from one another, it stands to reason that the explanation of these differences must rest in their form. In effect, following Aristotle, Maimonides claims that "there exist separate intellects whose number is equal to that of the spheres, that every sphere desires the intellect that is its principle and is the mover causing it to move according to the movement proper to it, and that that intellect is the mover of that sphere."[33]

Inasmuch as these intellects are separate from matter, "no multiplicity due to a difference between their essences is at all possible with regard to them because they are not bodies".[34] Maimonides concludes that every intellect, and hence every sphere, is distinguished from the others with respect to its motive powers.[35]

Can this characterization of the spheres be used to understand the issue of immortality of the soul? Interestingly enough, Maimonides devotes very little space in the *Guide* to the issue of immortality. His main discussion of this issue is contained in a short work entitled *Treatise on Resurrection,* in which he is concerned primarily to refute the doctrine of bodily resurrection.[36] In *Guide* I, 41, Maimonides distinguishes three meanings to the term *'nefesh,'* or soul, and suggests that only in the third sense, that is, as a rational intellect, can the soul be considered immortal. However, the soul that survives after death is not like that a person has when alive, for the former enjoys a separate existence after death and is a distinct ontological reality:

> For that which comes into being at the time a man is generated is merely the faculty consisting in preparedness, whereas the thing that after death is separate from matter is the thing that has become actual and not the soul that also comes into being; the latter is identical with the spirit that comes into being.[37]

In this passage Maimonides seems to be suggesting that when separated from the body, the immortal soul enjoys a special sort of existence akin to the Active Intellect. For, like the Active Intellect, this soul has no personal features.

But if there are no such personal features, how are immortal, incorporeal souls individuated? Maimonides does not expressly address this issue, as will Gersonides. We can only infer his view from what he has to say about his predecessors. Maimonides does mention the view of Avicenna according to whom there must be a distinction of cause and effect among souls:

> Now you know that regarding the things separate from matter—I mean those that are neither bodies nor forces in bodies, but intellects—there can be no thought of multiplicity of any mode whatever, except that some of them are the causes of the existence of others and that thus there is a difference among them since one is the cause and the other the effect.[38]

It is not clear from this passage, however, whether Maimonides accepts Avicenna's view. On the contrary, some contextual evidence suggests that he rejects it in favor of the doctrine of the unity of intellect as propounded by Ibn Bajja. For inasmuch as what remains of one soul is neither the cause nor the effect of another, Maimonides suggests that "all are one in number" as Ibn Bajja was wont to suggest.[39] This interpretation is supported by II, prop. 16, in which Maimonides states that multiplicity is ultimately founded upon materiality.

In whatsoever is not a body, multiplicity cannot be cognized by the intellect, unless the thing in question is a force in a body, for then the
multiplicity of the individual forces would subsist in virtue of the multiplicity of the matters or substances in which these forces are to be
found. Hence no multiplicity at all can be cognized by the intellect in
the separate things, which are neither a body nor a force in a body, except when they are causes and effects.[40]

Regardless of whether this proposition is read as a metaphysical or an
epistemological claim, it upholds the contention that, inasmuch as immortal
souls have no causal or motive features, they (unlike the heavenly spheres)
are not individuated after death.[41]

The main features of Maimonides's views on individuation can now be
summarized. Having distinguished between material and purely formal
things, Maimonides posits different criteria for each. Generally he seems to
regard individuation in terms of multiplicity within the species. Material
things are individuated on the basis of their matter, as evidenced by the proliferation of entities in the sublunar world. The heavenly spheres are individuated on the basis of formal considerations, that is, the motive powers of
the intellect. However, inasmuch as souls have neither a material element nor
a motive power, they are not individuated after the death of the body; rather
all immaterial souls form a united whole. We see, therefore, that several distinct strands have been interwoven into his discussion. Although Maimonides
himself has not explored the implications of these strands fully, his successor
Gersonides develops them further.

III. Gersonides

1. Introduction

For Gersonides, writing in fourteenth century southern France, considerations of an epistemological nature prompted his interest in individuation:
more specifically, the question of whether God knows future contingents
raised a number of questions concerning the nature of particulars, the distinction between individuals and particulars, and problems associated with
the individuation of forms. Gersonides spent several years in the papal court
in Avignon and may at that time have come into contact with the views of
Ockham and other fourteenth century scholastics. His major work, *Milhamot
Adonai*, is a sustained examination of the major philosophical issues of the
day.[42] In this work Gersonides tries to reconcile traditional Jewish beliefs
with what he feels are the strongest points in Aristotle; although a synthesis
of these systems is his ultimate goal, the strictures of philosophy often win
out at the expense of theology.

Having posited in *Milhamot* III that divine knowledge and human knowledge are univocal (in the sense that both God and created persons can be said to "know" in the same way), Gersonides must explain how God can be said to have knowledge of particulars. In a certain sense, he argues, God does know particulars. In an attempt to mediate between the view of Aristotle, who claimed that God does not know particulars, and that of Maimonides, who claimed that he does, Gersonides adopts a compromise position claiming that "there remains no alternative but that in one way He knows them [particulars] and in another respect He does not. The respect in which God knows contingents is the respect in which they are ordered—that is, God knows their essences."[43]

Gersonides's point is that God does not know particulars in their particularity, but rather that He knows them insofar as they are ordered. By 'ordered,' he is suggesting that God knows the essences or universal natures of particulars without knowing them qua particulars. That is, God's knowledge extends only to the domain of species and genera. God knows individual persons, for example, only through knowing the species man. Ultimately what God knows are the constitutive properties of concepts; these properties are then applied to the domain of particulars.[44] The upshot of this discussion is that particulars must be understood from two aspects: from one aspect they are material and not known by God; from the second, they are internally ordered and capable of being known even by God.

Gersonides's discussion of divine knowledge raises the general question concerning the role individuals and particulars assume in his ontology. To assess this role, three issues must be examined: the material constitution of particulars; formal considerations concerning immortality and individuality; and epistemological considerations centering around the relation between knowledge of universals.

2. Gersonides' Conception of Matter

In contrast to Maimonides, for whom matter was largely a privative principle, Gersonides upholds a theory of the positive status of prime matter. This theory is developed primarily within the context of his discussion of the creation of the universe, in *Milhamot* 6. Having posited that the world was created outside of time by a freely willing agent, Gersonides must decide whether the world was engendered ex nihilo or out of a preexistent matter. Arguing that ex nihilo creation is incompatible with the facts of physical reality, he adopts a Platonic model of matter drawn ultimately from the *Timaeus*. The opening verses of *Genesis* I are used to distinguish two types of material reality: *geshem* and *homer rishon*.[45] Totally devoid of form, *geshem* is the primordial matter out of which the universe was created. Since it is not informed, it is not capable of motion or rest; and since it is characterized by

negation, *geshem* is inert and chaotic.[46] This primordial matter is identified
with the "primeval waters" described in *Genesis* I, 2 (*tohu, tehom and
mayim*). However, Gersonides points out that *geshem* does not itself exemplify absolute nonbeing, but rather is an intermediary between being and
nonbeing.[47]

In contrast to *geshem, ḥomer rishon* is the second type of reality.
Homer rishon is understood in the Aristotelian sense as a substratum that is
allied to form. *Ḥomer rishon,* or matter, is inferior to form and hence cannot
be known in itself. It contains within itself the potentiality to receive forms,
yet has no actuality of its own.[48] Inasmuch as it does not contain its own actuality, *ḥomer rishon* is not an ontologically independent entity. Rather, Gersonides is wont to refer to it as "the matter that does not keep its shape".[49]
In *Milhamot* VI, pt. 2, ch. 7, Gersonides compares this matter to darkness,
for just as darkness is the absence of light, so too this matter represents the
absence of form or shape.

On the basis of this conception of matter, Gersonides adheres to the following distinction between individual (*y'ḥidi*) and particular (*p'rati*): the individual is the unitary instance of a species, that is, one of the units into
which a species can be divided, whereas the particular is a material
individual.[50] Existent individuals are subject to unique reference. However,
whereas all particulars are individual, not all individuals are particular. The
intelligibles, for example, are individual without being particular.

3. Immortality, Individuality and Unity of Form

The implications of this view of the status of matter and form for issues
of individuation become apparent when we turn to the complicated issue of
personal immortality. It is within this discussion that Gersonides's views on
the logical, ontological and epistemological status of individuals are most developed. In our examination, I shall concentrate upon three areas: the arguments used by Gersonides against his Greek and Arabic predecessors, which
arguments depend to a large extent upon considerations of individuation; the
logic of universals and particulars; and finally the principle of individuation
and its relation to individuals and particulars.

Gersonides's discussion of the immortality of the soul, contained primarily in *Milhamot* I, must be understood against the backdrop of Greek and
Arabic commentators on Aristotle's notoriously difficult passage in *De anima* 3:5:

And in fact mind as we have described it is what it is by virtue of becoming all things, while there is another which is what it is by virtue of
making all things: this is a sort of positive state like light; for in a sense
light makes potential colors into actual colors. Mind in this sense of it

is separable, impassible, unmixed, since it is in its essential nature activity. . . . When mind is set free from its present conditions it appears as just what it is and nothing more: this alone is immortal and eternal . . . and without it nothing thinks.[51]

In this passage Aristotle seems to postulate the existence of an active intellect that is separable from the passive intellect and that is primarily responsible for the intellectual activities of the human mind. But what is the relation between the active and passive intellects, and which, if either, of the two is immortal?[52] In answer to these questions, Gersonides first summarizes four representative positions as follows:

1. *The view of Alexander of Aphrodisias;* according to whom the material intellect is in the individual soul in its entirety; this intellect is ''nothing but a disposition'', that is, a passive receptor. In contrast, the ''other intellect'' is identified with the divine Agent Intellect, which is eternal and totally separate from humans. This latter intellect represents the total intellectual cognitions acquired by an individual and is to some extent immortal.[53]

2. *The view of Themistius;* according to whom the material intellect itself is a ''separable intellect that is neither generated nor corruptible'';[54] in other words, the material intellect is incorporeal and eternal, and ultimately identifiable with the Agent Intellect.[55]

3. *The view of Averroes* is a conflation of 1 and 2 in that the material intellect is a separate substance and identified with the Agent Intellect, but ''insofar as it attaches itself to the human soul, it is a disposition and has a potentiality for knowledge''.[56] That is, both the Agent Intellect and the material intellect are ultimately one and the same in all men.[57]

4. *The view of the ''moderns'':* according to whom the material intellect is ''a separable intellect that is generated essentially but not from something else''.[58]

Inasmuch as Gersonides's own position reflects that of Alexander, he raises a number of objections to the other accounts. A full examination of these arguments is beyond the scope of this chapter; I should, however, like to examine briefly those arguments that pertain most directly to issues of individuation.

Against Themistius's position that the Agent and material intellects are equivalent, Gersonides raises the following sorts of objections. First, he argues that Themistius's position is unable to account for the individuation of persons on the grounds that separate forms cannot be numerically individuated:

[Material] form is individuated in so far as it is manifested by different
subjects, so that, for example, this form of Reuben is numerically different from the form of Simon. If this were not so, one and the same
form would be both knowledgeable and ignorant at the same time on
the same point. . . . But this is utterly absurd. And so individuation of
this form can be accounted for on Alexander's hypothesis, but this is
not the case on Themistius's hypothesis, for separate substances cannot
be numerically individuated, except if they differ as species, as has
been demonstrated by arguments proper to this subject.[59]

Gersonides's point can be restated as follows. If both Reuben and Simon share the same material form, and this form is reflected in cognitive
abilities, then when Reuben knows p and Simon is ignorant of p, it follows
that one and the same form both knows and fails to know p. Hence, Gersonides concludes that there must be another criterion for individuating these
cognitive processes.

Themistius attempted to minimize these difficulties by claiming that
Alexander is unable to account for the identity of the act of knowing and that
which is known. Gersonides, however, claims that Themistius's gambit is insufficient on the grounds that epistemological identity does not necessarily
presuppose that the intellect be a separate form, as Themistius insists. Rather,
Gersonides supports Alexander's attempt to account for this identity on the
grounds that cognition need not be of particulars, but can be of general natures that are identified with the material intellect.

Gersonides then turns to various considerations that undermine the
Averroist position, according to which the same material intellect is found in
all persons. He first points out that, in Averroes's position, two things that
have different definitions would be numerically one. But this according to
Gersonides is absurd on the grounds that "it is evident that the definition and
essence of the Agent Intellect differ from that of the material intellect. But if
we were to claim that the two are identical, then two things of different natures would be numerically identical, which is absolutely absurd. For it is
impossible for them to be one in species; all the more so is it impossible for
them to be numerically identical."[60]

And if, as Averroes claims, the material intellect is identical with the
Agent Intellect, then one of two situations must arise: either "insofar as it is
conjoined with us it is numerically one . . . or, insofar as it is conjoined with
us it is numerically many".[61]

Gersonides argues, however, that both options are untenable. The first
is rejected on grounds similar to those used previously against Themistius;
namely, that the very same intellect would be both knowledgeable and ignorant with respect to the same question.[62]

The second option raises a number of problems having to do with individuating particulars. Most important, Gersonides raises the important issue of the separability of these separate forms:

> The separate forms differ from other forms because they differ only qualitatively, whereas material forms differ among themselves both qualitatively and quantitatively. Qualitative diversity, for example, is illustrated in the sentence, 'The form of a horse is different from the form of an ass'. Quantitative diversity, for example, is illustrated in the sentence, 'The form of this horse is different from the form of a second horse'. Accordingly, since the material intellect can be diversified quantitatively . . . it is thereby not separate; for a separate form is not multiplied according to the diversity of subjects of which it is the form. But it has been alleged that the material intellect is identical with the Agent Intellect, which is separate. This is absolutely false.[63]

What Gersonides has in mind in this passage is that, according to the view that the Agent Intellect is numerically diverse when conjoined to humans, there would be no individuating principle to account for this diversity except on quantitative grounds; but inasmuch as quantitative considerations do not apply to the Agent Intellect and individuation must at least take into account material features, it follows that the Agent Intellect cannot be numerically diverse. Gersonides therefore rejects Averroes's position.

Finally, the "modernist" view, according to which the material intellect is generated but not from anything else, is rejected for a variety of reasons. For example, this view propounds two separate generations for an individual, one for the individual intellect and another for its body. But this entails that one man be actually two insofar as his parts exist independently. Gersonides rejects this position as well on the grounds that, when there is no unity between the parts of the definition, the defined entity is actually two things.[64]

The import of Gersonides's critique of his predecessors can be reduced to three main issues. From a theological perspective it is clear that the doctrine of unity of intellect threatens the notion of personal immortality. For if all humans share the same intellect, then upon physical death, all that remains of the person is an unindividualized intellect. Epistemologically, the doctrine is unable to account for how it is that two (or more) knowers can entertain contrary items of knowledge; or more stringently, how one person can be in error of an item that another person knows. And from a metaphysical perspective, the main problem is how to individuate this separate intellect when it is manifested in many individuals: for if it is individuated materially on the basis that individual bodies differ, then the substance is no longer incorporeal or separate. As Feldman has pointed out, in this theory an incorporeal substance either is a unique member of a species or is not a member of a species at all.[65]

Let us turn, then, to Gersonides's own position with respect to immortality. As we have seen, Gersonides agrees with Alexander that immortality consists in the intellectual perfection of the material intellect. However, he disagrees with Alexander over the precise nature of this intellectual attainment. For Alexander (according to Gersonides) had claimed that immortality is achieved when the intellect acquires knowledge of the Agent Intellect (hence the term 'acquired intellect' is introduced). Immortality is thus understood by Alexander as a form of conjunction between the Agent and acquired intellects. "They [the followers of Alexander] maintain that the material intellect is capable of immortality and subsistence when it reaches that level of perfection where the objects of knowledge that it appprehends are themselves intellects, in particular the Agent Intellect . . . [material intellect] is immortal when it is united with the Agent Intellect."[66]

Gersonides rejects this notion of conjunction, however, and replaces it with a model of immortality according to which it is the content of knowledge of the acquired intellect that matters. When the content of the acquired intellect mirrors the rational ordering of the Agent Intellect, immortality is achieved.

What is the content of this knowledge? The Agent Intellect must possess complete knowledge of the sublunary world; that is, it "contains a conception of the rational order obtaining in all individuals".[67] The anti-Platonic tenor of this position is emphasized when Gersonides describes in more detail what it is that the Agent Intellect knows. For according to Gersonides the knowledge of the Agent Intellect must be grounded in the domain of particulars.

> Universality accrues to [this order] by virtue of its grounding in perceived particulars existing outside the mind. . . . The definition is the very order that is in the mind of Agent Intellect according to which the genus is generated. This order is exhibited in some sense in each and every individual instance of that genus, as we have seen. It does not follow from this, however, that all these individuals are numerically one, as would be the case for those who believe in [Platonic] universals. In this manner knowledge of accidental properties also is established, not just of essential properties . . . [68]

In this important passage Gersonides suggests that his position avoids the epistemological difficulties apparent in a realist ontology. Inasmuch as the material intellect reflects the knowledge inherent in the Agent Intellect and inasmuch as this knowledge is grounded in particulars, it follows that humans can have knowledge of particulars.

To appreciate more fully the scope of this theory, we must say more about Gersonides's theory of concepts and universals, which ultimately forms the backbone of this intellectualist doctrine of individual immortality.

4. Universals, Particulars, and Concepts: A Logical Analysis

Gersonides's rejection of Platonic realism suggests that particulars are ontologically prior to universals. In *Milhamot* I, 10, Gersonides addresses the specific question of how intelligibles signify extramental entities. His attack is directed at the view, attributed to Alexander, that intelligibles are universal in nature. His own view, which depends upon the distinction drawn by earlier Arabic logicians between concepts and universals, is that concepts are characterized in the context of a linguistic framework that reflects a metaphysical adherence to essences.[69]

Gersonides first divides the intelligible (*muskal*) into two logical sub-headings, the simple concept (*tsiyur*) and its verification or true judgment (*immut*).[70] The concept "answers the question 'what is it' and represents the true understanding of the essence of a thing".[71] In other words, it expresses the essence of every individual to which the definition in question applies. The verification, on the other hand, is the affirmation or denial of the concept and is usually expressed in a syllogism.[72]

Both the concept and its verification are contrasted with the universal. Gersonides specifies two senses of universal: it is understood either as something that both comprehends and encompasses individuals, or else as the total or conjunction of individuals.[73] That is, as a unity the universal comprises both genus and species, embracing the multiplicity of particulars; whereas as a plurality it refers to the particulars themselves taken as a group of individuals. Gersonides then goes to identify conception and verification with definition and statement, respectively. To determine whether the intelligibles are universal, he need only examine whether definitions and statements are universal.[74]

That the concept, or the definition of a thing, is not a universal taken as a unity is demonstrated in the following sort of argument:

> If the definition were the definition of a universal, it would be so in so far as the universal is a unit; for there is no plurality in a definition. For example, in the definition of man it is not stated, 'men are rational animals', but 'man is a rational animal'. Hence, it would appear that the definition defines a single thing. Now when it shall be proved that it is

impossible for a definition to be a definition of a universal as a unit, it
will be thereby shown that the definition cannot be a definition of a universal at all.[75]

Not only can the concept not denote the universal without losing its referential
relation to individuals, but Gersonides maintains further that the verification
or judgment must be distinguished from the universal as well. For if the judgment is nothing but a proposition about something that has been
conceptualized,[76] then the proposition cannot refer to a universal. A number
of considerations based on the nature of universal propositions (of the form
"All *S* is *P*") are adduced to demonstrate the absurdity of postulating that
universal judgments refer directly to universals taken in the first sense.[77]

Having refuted the position that universal judgments, or their corresponding concepts, refer either to species/genus or to the plurality of individuals, Gersonides presents his own position; namely that "the universal
proposition refers distributively to each individual that falls within the range
of this proposition".[78] For example, in the proposition 'all men are rational',
the universal term 'man' applies to each individual man. The main implication of this position, as Gersonides describes it, is that universal objects of
knowledge exist extramentally in the same way that they are conceived; that
is, the intelligible does not differ essentially from its extramental existent, for
both are ultimately *individual* in nature. "Accordingly it is evident that the
object of knowledge as such does not refer to each and every one of an infinite
number of individuals; rather it denotes an individual only as any individual
whatever, and this is a thing that could exist outside the mind."[79]

5. Individuation in Gersonides

What, then, can we conclude about individuation on the basis of this
discussion? We have seen that Gersonides's ontology comprises universals,
particulars, and individuals. Particulars are material individuals, such as the
particular man, while the universal refers distributively to each individual
within its range. Gersonides agrees with his Jewish predecessors, for example, Maimonides, that in principle there is no need for more than one instance
within each species. If this is so, why the existence of a multiplicity? Numerical differentiation, he argues, results from matter: "when essences are
construed as abstracted from matter they cannot be conceived as being enumerated at all."[80] For example, when a corporeal form is abstracted from
matter, plurality does not accrue to it. Corporeal forms are multiplied by virtue of the multiplication of their subjects: "[Material forms] are not multiplied in terms of the multiplication of the subjects in which they inhere. But
they are multiplied insofar as they are particular and embodied in matter.
This latter follows from their being material forms."[81]

Ultimately multiplicity in the sublunar domain arises as an effect of the Agent Intellect: "God knows particulars since the Agent Intellect and the Celestial bodies are the instruments through which He produces these actions (i.e. particulars) . . . a Separated Intellect acts upon everything which is capable of receiving its activity without itself having a perception of particulars (*qua* particulars). . . . In this way the Agent Intellect produces these things."[82]

Echoing Maimonides, Gersonides's point is that the concrete particular is multiplied through the instrumental causality of the Agent Intellect, deriving its particularity through matter. Thus matter is responsible for the multiplication of the form into many instances. In other words, matter pluralizes what was previously one.

On this level, individuation is viewed as the process of differentiating one particular from another; to this end matter is a necessary condition. However, inasmuch as matter itself is unknowable, Gersonides suggests that it is not the individual qua particular that is known, but rather the internal ordering of the particular: when the matter of the thing in question is removed, what remains is no longer particular although it is still individual.[83] Hence with respect to the self-identity of things, Gersonides claims that matter is not a sufficient condition for individuation, for reasons suggested in the following passage:

> The definition which best individuates an object from others besides it is that which gives the most complete knowledge of the thing, even though it does not individuate it completely. I.e., one would say concerning a boat that it is a substance, made of wood, made through a craft, hollowed out and uncovered. Each one of these specifications increases the knowledge, since it removes confusion from everything included in the individual which preceded it, which is not included in it, even though not one completely specifies the boat from other things.[84]

In this passage Gersonides is concerned with two processes: differentiation and self-identity of a thing. In listing its descriptive properties, he attempts to circumscribe the thing in question in order not only to distinguish it from other similar things, but to individuate it as well. It should be noted that Gersonides's example is ambiguous, however. For although the aforementioned specifications (i.e., being a substance, made of wood) do help us to distinguish a boat from something that is not a boat, they obviously fail to help us identify one of two boats sitting side by side. What emerges from this example is that for Gersonides the process of self-identity must comprise nonessential elements.

Ultimately Gersonides's point is that it is not possible to individuate things in terms of their unique self-identity. This does not mean that they cannot be differentiated one from the other, for surely their matter accomplishes that. This can be seen as the process of particularization. However, the uniqueness of things cannot be accounted for along traditional lines. Gersonides has enumerated a list of descriptive items that enter into a specification of a thing's essence, while at the same time suggesting that these items need not, indeed cannot, be used to individuate that thing. Although it does particularize objects, matter alone cannot individuate them. Yet unless an individuating principle contains at least one nonessential characteristic, it fails to account for a thing's self-identity.[85] It remains for Yedayah Bedersi to supply this characteristic.

IV. Yedayah Bedersi

1. Introduction

The last individual in our survey is Yedayah ben Abraham Bedersi ha-Penini, who lived primarily in Southern France (Perpignon and Montpellier). His reputation during the Middle Ages was based on his extremely popular book of moral sentences, *Sefer Behinat Ha-Olam (Examination of the Universe),* of which more than seventy editions have been published.[86] In addition, he wrote numerous philosophical treatises, including *Ketav Hitnazlut (The Letter of Apology)*, a defense of philosophy against its theological critics.[87] Of his purely philosophical works, I should like to concentrate upon a short treatise, *A Treatise upon Personal or Individual Forms,* which appears only in manuscript form.[88]

In this treatise Bedersi examines the issue of individual forms, a topic that had not been hitherto posed in Jewish philosophy. In upholding the existence of personal and individual forms, Bedersi places himself directly in the Scotistic camp. Hence he stands in contradistinction to Judaeo-Arabic thinkers who followed the Aristotelian tradition according to which forms by definition are general and not individual. For, according to Scotus and in contrast to Aristotle, individual differences are explained in terms of a thing's *haecceitas;* although Scotus himself did not identify this *haecceitas* with "personal forms", his later disciples tended to obscure the distinction.[89]

It should be noted that nowhere in this treatise does Bedersi quote Scotus or other scholastics directly; nevertheless, both Pines and Sirat have emphasized the obvious Scotistic element in his discussion.[90] What is not clear is whether Bedersi took his sources from an unknown scholastic work or whether he was influenced by general scholastic discussions and then developed the details of his theory on his own.[91] In any event, even a brief examination of Bedersi's treatise reveals a new dimension in Jewish discussions of individuation.

2. Individuation and Personal Forms

Bedersi opens his treatise by stating the object of his investigation; namely, "to investigate of the individuals which fall under one species, whether when they change their accidents they change their personal forms as well, or whether they retain their personal forms and change form only in number, such that the individuals change only in their accidents".[92] The question posed by Bedersi is one that was popularly discussed in thirteenth century scholastic circles; namely, whether individuals have their own personal forms in addition to those that accrue to the species. Bedersi is allowing for two possibilities: in the first option, each individual has its own personal form that is superadded to the form of the species in question; whereas in the second, individuals belonging to the same species have no difference of individual form with the exception of numerical diversity. This second view, which explains the difference among individuals on the basis of accidents, is the position that was interpreted as belonging to Aristotle and was largely adopted in the Judaeo-Arabic tradition.[93] Bedersi subjects this view to criticism and ultimately rejects it in favor of the former.

In its support, Bedersi raises a number of considerations pertinent to our discussion. For example, in 66a–66b he draws a parallel between those qualities that exist between the forms of a species that fall under a particular genus, and those forms of individuals that belong to a particular species. That is, individual forms are ontologically analogous to "species forms": for just as the members of one genus differ from those members of another genus by virtue of a specific form, so too does each member of a particular species differ by virtue of a specific individual form.[94] However, Bedersi points out that in contradistinction to species forms, which are intellectual in nature, the individual forms cannot be known, for they are ultimately rooted in matter. The difference among individual members of a species is based upon a material element, and so is not entirely general in the way that is required for intellection. Hence Bedersi suggests that ultimately these individual members can be defined only in terms of the species. "Individuals are not intellected under the rubric of the species, that is, their individual forms; for what is intellected is always general and separate from the material element. Hence individuals are not definable except in terms of the species."[95]

Furthermore, Bedersi refers to the Aristotelian principle that nature does nothing in vain to support his espousal of individual forms. For the fact that a plurality of individual forms identify with one another in all respects save that of number is evidence that individual forms must exist.[96]

Other arguments based upon Aristotelian considerations of heavenly motion, the celestial spheres and the nature of material objects are offered as well.[97] For example, Bedersi accepts the Aristotelian characterization of material objects as a hylomorphic compound of matter and form. However, for matter itself to support corporeality, it must have predicated of it the accident of corporeity.[98] Forms too have their own accidents that account for their being principles of activity.[99] And finally there exists a class of accidents, such as motion, that pertain both to form and to matter.

How does Bedersi account for the problem of change of personal forms? Changes in general occur only with respect to individuals of three categories: humans, other animals, and plants.[100] Only with respect to individuals that belong to a single species, however, is change explainable in these terms.[101] It does not apply to change of parts of individuals or to parts that have been separated from a particular individual. Bedersi distinguishes further between simple substances that are composed of one of the four elements and those more complex substances that constitute a mixture of elements. In each case different criteria for change apply.[102]

We have seen that Bedersi's major contention is that the difference between members of a species derives in large part from the forms that inhere in the individual species; on this basis he has postulated the existence of personal forms.[103] This theory does not accord with the Aristotelian tenor of his Jewish and Islamic predecessors. Rather it is here that Bedersi most clearly approaches Scotistic thought. For both Bedersi and Scotus understand the process of individuation not as something derived primarily from matter, but rather as rooted in form. This does not mean that individuation eschews matter entirely.

According to Scotus the individual differs from the universal formally as well as virtually: "Similiter forma individualis determinat naturam specificam ut sit haec vere; non tamen illa forma est proprie haec, sive hoc aliquid, quia si sic, tunc sequitur quod differentia esset species."[104] However, the principle of individuation contains both a a formal and a material element.[105] Although matter plays a role for both Scotus and Bedersi, in both cases, the ultimate difference with regard to individuals is formal: it is individual forms that individuate an entity.

V. Conclusion

In this study we have examined those concerns within the Jewish philosophical tradition that are related to problems of individuation and individuality. In particular, those problems associated with a hylomorphic ontology, divine providence, and immortality of the soul have raised issues having to do with individuality. Maimonides paved the way for future understanding of how immaterial substances could be individuated. Not until Gersonides, however, were such issues discussed in their logical context. In his examination of the relation between universals and particulars, and in his insistence upon the primacy of individuals, Gersonides allowed for nominalist tendencies to take root in fourteenth century Jewish thought. Bedersi reflected most strongly the influence of scholastic discussions of individuation, with his reflection of Scotistic conceptions of *haecceitas* and personal forms. By the mid-fourteenth century Averroes's Middle Commentaries on Aristotle's *Organon* were translated into Hebrew, and the influence of scholastic logic was felt in Jewish philosophy. The works of Jewish philosophers such as Narboni, ibn Kaspi, and others working within this new intellectual climate contributed further to discussions of individuality; their developments culminated in the systematic enterprise of Hasdai Crescas. That, however, is a separate story.

Notes

1. The influence of scholastic thought upon Jewish philosophers has been examined by S. Pines in his important article "Scholasticism After Thomas Aquinas and the Teachings of Hasdai Crescas and His Predecessors", *Proceedings of the Israel Academy of Sciences and Humanities* 1, no. 10 (Jerusalem, 1967): 1–101.

2. Moses Maimonides, "Maimonides' Arabic Treatise on Logic", ed. I. Efros, *Proceedings of the American Academy for Jewish Research* (*PAAJR*) 34 (1966), supplementing a previous publication in 8 (1938).

3. For a discussion of the development of logic within Jewish philosophy and its outgrowth from Islamic and scholastic sources, see S. Rosenberg, "Logic and Ontology in Jewish Philosophy in the Fourteenth Century," Ph.D. dissertation (Hebrew University, 1974).

4. A succinct discussion of the theological importance of the problem of individuation can be found in Jorge J.E. Gracia, *Introduction to the Problem of Individuation in the Early Middle Ages* 2nd rev. ed. (Munich, 1988), pp. 255ff.

5. Ibn Gabirol's metaphysical system is developed in his major philosophical work *Mekor Hayyim* (*Fountain of Life*), which can be found in A. Munk, "La Source de Vie", in *Mélanges de philosophie juive et arabe*, (Paris, 1857, repr. 1955); see also J. Schlanger, *La philosophie de Salomon Ibn-Gabirol* (Leyden, 1968), for a study of this system.

6. A helpful discussion of this problem can be found in H. A. Wolfson, *The Philosophy of Spinoza*, 2 vols. (New York, 1969), pp. 390ff.

7. A preliminary summary of this problem in Islamic thought, and its implications for Jewish and scholastic discussions, can be found in D. Callus, "The Ori-

gins of the Problem of the Unity of Form'', *Thomist* 24 (1961): 257–285; O. Hamelin, *La théorie de l'intellect d'apres Aristote et ses commentateurs* (Paris, 1953).

8. The 'active' (or 'agent') intellect is a term that refers back to Aristotle's actual intellect as described in *De anima* III.5. The term was transmitted to Jewish and scholastic writers through Islamic philosophers, and it came to represent not only a part of the human soul but the domain of Divine intellectual cognition as well.

9. The Arabic text, *Le Dalalat Al-Hayarin* was edited by S. Munk in *Le Guide des Egarées*, (Paris, 1856–66); a widely used modern Hebrew translation *Moreh Nevukhim* was edited by E. Shemuel (Jerusalem, 1959). In this chapter, page references to the *Guide* will be to S. Pines's English translation, *The Guide of the Perplexed* (Chicago; 1963). Note the following passages in the Introduction to the *Guide:* "For my purpose is that the truths be glimpsed and then again be concealed, so as not to oppose that divine purpose which one cannot possibly oppose and which has concealed from the vulgar among the people those truths especially requisite for His apprehension" (pp. 6–7) Also, "God, may He be exalted, knows that I have never ceased to be exceedingly apprehensive about setting down those things that I wish to set down in this treatise. For they are concealed things; none of them has been set down in any book. . ." (p. 16).

10. The fifth cause of contradictory or contrary statements arises from the necessity of teaching difficult and obscure material. Occasionally the teacher must resort to oversimplifying the material "in accord with the listener's imagination that the latter will understand only what he now wants him to understand. Afterwards, in the appropriate place, that obscure matter is stated in exact terms and explained as it truly is." *Guide*, Intro., p. 18. The seventh cause is the most important for our purposes, and is used, when "speaking about very obscure matters . . . to conceal some parts and to disclose others. . . . In such cases the vulgar must in no way be aware of the contradiction; the author accordingly uses some device to conceal it by all means." *Guide*, Intro, p. 18.

11. "Divergences that are to be found in this Treatise are due to the fifth cause and the seventh. Know this, grasp its true meaning, and remember it very well so as not to become perplexed by some of its remarks." *Guide*, Intro., p. 20.

12. The term 'Kalam' refers to a particular system of thought that arose in Islam prior to the philosopher al-Kindi (d. 873). Its exponents, the Mutakalimun, were contrasted with straightforward philosophers. For a detailed discussion of standard Kalam doctrines, see M. Fakhry, *A History of Islamic Philosophy* (New York, 1983); H. A. Wolfson, *The Philosophy of the Kalam* (Cambridge, MA, 1976).

13. *Guide* II, Intro., p. 238.

14. *Guide* II, Intro., p. 239.

15. *Guide* II, Intro., p. 239. Maimonides clearly rejects a Platonic conception of the relation between matter and form in favor of the Aristotelian view according to

which privation plays an important role: "Thus Plato and his predecessors designated Matter as the female and Form as the male. Now you know that the principles of the existents subject to generation and corruption are three: Matter, Form and Particularized Privation, which is always conjoined with Matter. For, were it not for this conjunction with Privation, Matter would not receive Form." *Guide*, p. 43. Maimonides bases his understanding on Aristotle's *Metaphysics* 12, 2 (1069b 32–34).

16. *Guide* I, 28, p. 61.

17. *Guide* III, 9, p 436.

18. *Guide* III, 9, p.440.

19. For further discussion of the Plotinian elements in Maimonides's conception of matter, see A. Ivry, "Maimonides on Creation", in *Creation and the End of Days*, ed. N. Samuelson and D. Novak (New York, 1986), pp. 185–214.

20. *Guide*, Introd., p. 13.

21. *Guide* Introd., p. 14.

22. This distinction is shown in the following example: "in regard to the material cause, a person's proximate matter is his limbs; more remote are his four humours of which the limbs are composed." See "Maimonides' Arabic Treatise on Logic," p. 50.

23. *Guide* III, 8, pp. 430–431.

24. For further elucidation of this notion of individuation in terms of difference, see Jorge J. E. Gracia's discussion in the Introduction to this volume.

25. *Guide* II, 19, p.304.

26. *Guide* II, 19, p.306.

27. This discussion is dependent upon the Kalam doctrine of "admissibility", which is described by Maimonides in *Guide* I, 73, and III, 15. According to this technical notion, certain states of affairs are admissible on ontological grounds and others on logical grounds. For a description of this notion of "admissibility", see A. Ivry, "Maimonides on Possibility" in J. Reinhartz et al., eds., *Mystics, Philosophers and Politicians* (Durham, NC, 1982), pp. 77ff; and H. A. Wolfson, *The Philosophy of the Kalam*, pp. 43ff.

28. *Guide* I, 74 pp. 218–219.

29. *Guide* I, 72 p. 184. Compare this analogy to similar ones drawn in Aristotle's *De caelo* I, chs. 7, 8.

30. *Guide* I, 58, p 136.

31. *Guide* III, 19, p. 305.

32. *Guide* II, 4, p. 256.

33. *Guide* II, 4, p. 257.

34. *Guide* II, 4, p. 258.

35. *Guide* II, 4, p. 259; compare with Aristotle's *De caelo* II, 2. For a discussion of this topic, see H. A. Wolfson, *Crescas' Critique of Aristotle*, p. 598.

36. See the version by L. N. Goldfeld, *Moses Maimonides' Treatise on Resurrection: An Inquiry into Its Authenticity* (New York, 1986); see also Maimonides's *Ma'amar tehiyyat ha-meytim (Treatise on Resurrection,)* ed. J. Finkel (New York, 1939), a new translation of which has appeared by A. Halkin (New York, 1984).

37. *Guide* I, 70, p. 174.

38. *Guide* I, 74, p. 221.

39. *Guide* I, 74, p. 221. For a discussion of the influences of Ibn Bajja upon Maimonides, see A. Altmann, ''Ibn-Bajja on Man's Ultimate Felicity'', S. Pines's Introduction to the *Guide*, pp. ciii ff.

40. *Guide* II, prop. 16, p. 237.

41. See the discussion in H. A. Wolfson, *Crescas' Critique of Aristotle*, p. 108.

42. In this chapter, references to *Sefer Milhamot Adonai* (*Wars of the Lord*) will be made either to the complete Hebrew edition [*Milhamot ha-shem*] which was reprinted in Leipzig in 1866, or to the partial English translations [*Wars*] prepared by S. Feldman, *The Wars of the Lord Book I* (Philadelphia, 1984) and N. Samuelson, *Gersonides: The Wars of the Lord; Treatise Three: On God's Knowledge* (Toronto, 1977). In both cases, references will be to treatise, chapter, and page number. For an extensive bibliography of recent scholarly works on Gersonides, see M. Kellner, ''R. Levi ben Gerson: A Bibliographical Essay'', *Studies in Bibliography and Booklore* 12 (1979): 13–23.

43. Wars III, 4 (N. Samuelson, trans.), p. 232.

44. For an extended discussion of the problem of divine omniscience in Gersonides, see N. Samuelson, ''Gersonides' Account of God's Knowledge of Particulars'', *The Journal of the History of Philosophy* 10 (1972): 399–416; T. M. Rudavsky, ''Divine Omniscience and Future Contingents in Gersonides'', *The Journal of the History of Philosophy* 21 (1983): 513–536.

45. *Milhamot* VI, 1, ch. 17, pp. 267–271. In *Milhamot* V, 2, ch. 2 pp. 193–194, Gersonides argues that this formless matter accounts for various astronomical phenomena. For general discussions of Gersonides's theory of creation and matter, see S. Feldman, ''Gersonides' Proofs for the Creation of the Universe'', *Proceedings American Academy for Jewish Research* (1967): 113–137; S. Feldman, ''Platonic Themes in Gersonides' Cosmology'', in *Salo Whitmayer Baron Jubilee Volume* (Jerusalem, 1975), pp. 383–405.

46. *Milhamot* VI, 1, ch. 17, pp. 367–368; 374. For further elaboration of these arguments, see S. Feldman, "Platonic Themes", pp. 394–395.

47. *Milhamot* VI, 1, ch. 18, p. 372.

48. *Milhamot* VI, 1, ch. 17, p. 367.

49. *Milhamot* V, 2, ch. 1; VI, 6, pt. 2, ch. 4.

50. For further discussion of this distinction, see *Wars* (N. Samuelson, trans.) pp. 52–53; 64; 154n; 174n.

51. Aristotle, *De anima* III, 5, 430a 10–25, trans. J. A. Smith in *Basic Works of Aristotle*, ed. R. McKeon (New York, 1941).

52. A discussion of these questions, and the positions of representative commentators, can be found in the introduction by B. Zedler to Thomas Aquinas's *On the Unity of the Intellect Against the Averroists* (Milwaukee, 1968).

53. *Wars* I, 1 (S. Feldman trans.), p. 110; see Feldman's discussion on page 72.

54. *Wars,* I, 1 (S. Feldman trans.), p. 110.

55. For further discussion of this position, see *Wars* (S. Feldman trans.), p. 72; also O. Hamelin *La théorie de l'intellect d'apres Aristote et ses commentateurs,* pp. 38–43.

56. *Wars* I, 1 (S. Feldman trans.), p. 110.

57. For further discussion, see *Wars* (S. Feldman trans.), p. 74; also A. Ivry "Averroes on Intellection and Conjunction", *Journal of the American Oriental Society* 86 (1966): 76–85.

58. *Wars* I, 10 (S. Feldman trans.), p. 110. This view has been identified by some with Christian thinkers of Gersonides's day. See *Wars* (S. Feldman trans.), p. 75, n. 10.

59. *Wars* I, 2 (S. Feldman trans.), pp. 114–115.

60. *Wars* I, 4 (S. Feldman trans.), p. 134.

61. *Wars* I, 4 (S. Feldman trans.), p. 137.

62. *Wars* I, 4 (S. Feldman trans.), p. 138.

63. *Wars* I, 4 (S. Feldman trans.), p. 138.

64. *Wars* I, 4 (S. Feldman trans.), p. 139.

65. *Wars* (S. Feldman trans.), p. 79.

66. *Wars* I, 8 (S. Feldman trans.), p. 170.

67. *Wars* I, 4 (S. Feldman trans.), p. 136; see also *ibid.*, p. 170.

68. *Wars* I, 6 (S. Feldman trans.), pp. 162–163.

69. Arabic logicians distinguished between the extension and comprehension of a concept as follows: a concept's extension consisted in the individuals to which it referred, while its comprehension referred to its connotation within a particular linguistic system. For further discussion of the notion of concepts in Arabic logic, see I, Madkour *L'Organon d'Aristote dans le monde arabe* (Paris, 1934), pp. 57–65.

70. *Wars* I, 10 (S. Feldman trans.), p. 186.

71. *Wars* I, 10 (S. Feldman trans.), p. 186.

72. *Wars* I, 10 (S. Feldman trans.), pp. 186–187.

73. *Wars* I, 10 (S. Feldman trans.), p. 187.

74. Manekin notes that this move from intelligible to definition and statement represents a move from psychological to logical considerations. See C. Manekin, *The Logic of Gersonides* (Dordrect: Kluwer Academic Publ., 1992), p. 30.

75. *Wars* I, 10 (S. Feldman trans.), p. 187.

76. *Wars* I, 10 (S. Feldman trans.), p. 188.

77. *Wars* I, 10 (S. Feldman trans.), pp. 188–189.

78. *Wars* I, 10 (S. Feldman trans.), p. 193.

79. *Wars* I, 10 (S. Feldman trans.), p. 194. In his doctoral dissertation Manekin notes that Gersonides's reading is reminiscent of the distributive reading of the universal quantifier in traditional logic. For further discussion of the implications of such an interpretation, see C. Manekin, "The Logic of Gersonides," pp. 76ff. In other words, Gersonides is presenting a quasi-nominalist position according to which both the intelligible and its extramental referent are individuals in the sense that only they represent ultimate realities. Gersonides follows Aristotle in positing individuals as causally prior to universals.

80. *Wars* I, 6 (S. Feldman trans.), p. 156.

81. *Wars* I, 10 (S. Feldman trans.), p. 179.

82. *Milhamot* III, 4, p. 139.

83. See the discussion in N. Samuelson, "Gersonides' Account of God's Knowledge", p. 409.

84. *Milhamot* III, 2, p. 130. For Samuelson's discussion of this passage, see *Wars* (N. Samuelson trans.), pp. 172–173.

85. See N. Samuelson, "Gersonides' Account of God's Knowledge", p. 410. It is here that Gersonides most closely approaches the view of Duns Scotus. For a

discussion of the similarities between the two theories, see T. M. Rudavsky, "Individuals and the Doctrine of Individuation in Gersonides", *The New Scholasticism* 51 (1982): 30–50.

86. J. Bedersi, *Sefer Behinat Olam,* first printed in Mantua, before 1480.

87. *The Letter of Apology* was printed in *She'elot u-Tchuvot . . . Rabbenu Shelomo ben Adret* (Hanover, 1610), 65d–67a (416–418). For a recent study of this work, see A. S. Halkin, "Yedaiah Bedersi's Apology", in A. Altmann, ed., *Jewish Medieval and Renaissance Studies* (Cambridge, MA, 1967), pp. 165–184.

88. Y. Bedersi, *A Treatise upon Personal or Individual Forms* is found in Paris, Bibliothèque Nationale Man. 984 Heb. fol. 66a–93b. A synopsis of the contents of this treatise can be found in S. Pines, "Individual Forms in the Thought of Yedaya Bedarsi", in *Harry A. Wolfson Jubilee Volume* (Jerusalem, 1965), pp. 187–201 [Hebrew]. For a discussion of Bedersi's life and other works, see E. Renan, *Les écrivains juifs francais du XIVe siècle* (Paris, 1877), pp. 13–56; C. Sirat, *A History of Jewish Philosophy in the Middle Ages* (Paris, 1985), pp. 274–277.

89. For a discussion of the early history of the doctrine of personal forms, see D. Callus, "The Origins of the Problem of the Unity of Form", *Thomist* 24 (1961): 257–285.

90. Sirat, *History,* p. 277; Pines, "Individual Forms", p. 5. Pines, for example, states that "the personal forms serving as the subject of [Bedersi's] deliberations are but a variant of the concept accepted by the disciples of Duns Scotus . . . his stand in this matter is comprehensible only if one assumes that he was decisively influenced on this point by Scotist teachings, for he could not have a hold in any other theory and most decidedly not in the Islamic-Jewish philosophical teachings".

91. See Pines, "Individual Forms", pp. 11–12; 21. Pines suggests that there may have been a literary tradition, possibly due to perceived persecution, according to which late medieval Jewish philosophers did not directly mention their Christian sources.

92. *Treatise,* 66a.

93. Pines, "Individual Forms", p. 3.

94. *Treatise* 66a.

95. *Treatise,* 66b; see the comment in Pines, "Individual Forms", p. 3.

96. Treatise 67a.

97. See *Treatise* 67a–72a.

98. *Treatise,* 69b.

99. *Treatise,* 71a.

100. *Treatise,* 73a.

101. *Treatise,* 75a.

102. See *Treatise,* 76a–77a, for further discussion.

103. See the discussion of this point in Pines, "Individual Forms", pp. 9–10.

104. Duns Scotus *In Met.* I, vii, 213, n. 16.

105. The material component of *haecceitas* is seen clearly in the passage quoted by Wolter in this volume, p. 290.

5

ALBERT THE GREAT (B. 1200; D. 1280)

JEREMIAH M. G. HACKETT

I. Introduction

Albert the Great was a very prolific writer.[1] There are references to the problem of individuation in many of his works, which date from the late 1230s or early 1240s up to the 1270s. The range of texts, topics, and places in the works of Albert that have some reference to the problem of individuation is vast. Nevertheless, there is a remarkable consistency about Albert's treatment of individuation. For Albert the Great, matter is the principle of individuation. More specifically, matter is the principle of individuation of material bodies. The individuation of simple substances is explained in terms of the distinction of *quod est* and *quo est*. I will speak only in passing concerning the individuation of simple substances.

The early views of Albert on individuation are found in the context of the discussion of person in theology.[2] The works in which these discussions are found are normally dated to the 1240s. There are some references to individuation in the commentaries on Aristotle, which are dated to the 1250s.[3] Finally, there are treatments of individuation in the *Metaphysics* (1260s) and the *Summa theologiae* (1260s).

The reader will find that a variety of aspects of the problem of individuality is discussed by Albert. For example, in the early works, much emphasis is placed on incommunicability; in the logical and physical works issues relating to indivisibility, impredicability, individuality and multiplicity of species, and specific and numerical distinction arise. I will order my presentation in such a manner that the reader can see that context often dictates Albert's emphases. Still, although I will make reference to a variety of topics in works of very diverse content, a large part of my presentation will be taken from the *De predicabilibus*.[4] Much of the treatment of individuation in the *Metaphysica* presupposes this latter work, and further, the treatment in the *Metaphyisca* is often related to topics other than individuation.

The following is the order of presentation: Individuation and person in the early theological works, the *Commentary on the Sentences,* and the *Summa de creaturis;* nature, universal and individual: *De predicabilibus;* individual and species: *De predicabilibus;* critical evaluation: Albertus and Bacon.

II. Individuation in the Early Theological Works, the *Commentary on the Sentences,* and the *Summa de creaturis* (1240s).

The concept of individuality in these theological works is closely tied to Albert's treatment of the concept of person. Indeed, one might see the concept of person as one of the main influences on his understanding of individuality. This emphasis clearly follows from the fact that in these early works, Albert is speaking as a theologian who had inherited centuries of Christian speculation on the notion of person. In *Summa de creaturis* and *Commentary on the Sentences,* Albert raises the following two questions. First, "what, according to definition, is a person ?" and "The question is asked concerning the definition of this name 'person'?"[5] It is important to note that in asking for a definition of 'person', Albert is not looking for a nominal definition. Rather, he is asking for a definition of the thing itself, the reality that is named "person". The definitions of person that are given by Albert are important for the subsequent definition of the individual. Some central traits of the definition of individual occur in the five definitions of person that are listed by Albert. It is, therefore, appropriate to list these definitions here.

The first definition is the classical definition of person found in Boethius: Person is an individual substance of a rational nature. The next three definitions are taken from Richard of St. Victor, *De trinitate:* (1) We say that the person is something that alone is discrete (distinct from) all other things due to its singular characteristic; (2) the Divine Person is the existence of the divine incommunicability; (3) person is that which alone exists through itself according to the singular mode of the existence of rational nature. The fifth definition is taken from the "Magistri": Person is the hypostasis with distinct characteristics pertaining to dignity.[6] Already, one will note that distinctiveness, incommunicability, and singularity are involved in the notion of person.

Albert gives some very long and extended expansions of these definitions. He raises a host of important issues such as these: (1) Is 'person' said univocally of creatures and God? (2) Is person the same as individual? (His answer is negative.) (3) Is person by definition something that is not communicable? That is, is "incommunicability" a typical characteristic of person, which is only found in persons, or is "incommunicability" something that all individuals, personal or nonpersonal, have as a specific feature? In all of this, there are many serious theological issues that have had a long history. For example, if incommunicability is the essential definition of being a person, how can the second person of the Trinity unite, that is, be communicated to, human nature?

In all of his discussion of person in divinity, Albert is more than careful to distinguish between person as used in divinity and person as used in nature and human matters. Even within the theological discussion, Albert presents an explicit philosophical account of the relationship of person and hypostasis in relationship to individual being in natural matters (*in inferioribus*). Yet, one must note carefully that a theological doctrine of creation and Trinity as well as a metaphysics of light and participation are always on the background of Albert's philosophical reflections on the nature of essence, person and individual. In these early theological works, one representative passage on individuation stands out.

> Truly it ought to be noted that one thing is signified by the word 'hypostasis' and another thing by the word 'person'. And in order to understand this, it should be pointed out that in the things of nature (*in inferioribus*) there are four things, namely, *res naturae, subiectum, suppositum, individuum,* to which also in things of a rational nature there is added a fifth, namely person. By the thing of nature, we understand that which is a composite from matter and form or from *quod est* and *quo est,* in nature and under a common nature, and this is *a this something* (a *hoc aliquid*) in nature. The *suppositum,* however, is added to the thing of nature in relation to the common nature to which it supposits as the incommunicable. The subject, however, as the Philosopher says, is a being which is complete in itself, [and] the occasion of another existing in it: this has a relation to accident, although it is not understood in its name by the habit of accident: And this is called ''substance'' by Aristotle, and, by the Greeks, it is called ''hypostasis''. *An individual, however, is that which has individuating accidents.* Person, however, expresses in a rational nature that which is incommunicable according to that mode, inconsistent solely with the understanding of composite things, which is not found in divine realities. Among the holy writers, one finds four things, that is, a thing of nature (*res naturae*) which St. Hilary posited, and supposit, hypostasis, and person: for an *individuum* and a singular (*singulare*) are not properly present in divine matters (in God). And a thing of nature will be *in divinis* in the way ''someone'' or ''what'' are in the divine nature: supposit, however will be there through the *habitudinem ad proprietatem:* But person will be there as a hypostasis according to a distinct characteristic.[7]

One can speak therefore of a hierarchy or ordering of reality from *res naturae, suppositum, subjectum, individuum, persona*. The *res naturae* is the concrete nature, the *hoc aliquid,* whether the result of natural generation or the creation of God. The *res naturae* is the supposit in reference to the universal nature that is its cause. As a being, complete in itself and the subject of accidents, we can name it subject, substance or hypostasis, "three terms which are synonymous. The individual is the substance or hypostasis considered in its relation to the accidents which individualize, that is to say, in its relation to the 'collection of accidents'. . . ."[8] To be an individual is "to have individuating accidents". Finally, the person brings to the individual substance the dignity of a rational nature, which confers on it a perfect incommunicability.

Unity arises from the matter; singularity from the individuating accidents; incommunicability, however, from the highest, most complete, and perfecting distinction. Thus, although the individual arises due to being a *res naturae* determined by the reciprocal relationship of matter and form, potency and act, the individual as such arises due to the "collection of accidents" (the so-called Avicennian *appenditiae materiae*) by means of which a substance is recognized as an individual.[9]

In all of this treatment in Albert, a whole theory of matter and form, universal, and nature as well as of substance is presupposed. It would be a mistake to think that Albert did not know and use Aristotle's philosophy prior to his composition of his commentaries in the 1250s. Already, in these theological works from the 1240s, one finds an explicit and conscious use of Aristotelian philosophy.

Nature, Universal, and Individual: *De predicabilibus*

1. Nature and Universal

A number of important issues arise out of Albert's strong emphasis on form in his account of composite material beings. For example, if nothing exists but individual beings and they exist on account of form, how can one account for the element of universality in predication? One finds an answer to this problem in the early theological works. Moreover, the main elements of this answer are repeated in *De predicabilibus*. In the latter, particular attention is given to the relationship of nature, the universal, and the individual.

In brief outline, the position in the early theological works is as follows: The universal is reached through abstraction. That universality is found in the *forma totius* (the form of the whole that gives reality and essence) when it is disengaged from all individuating restrictions. Therefore, for an individual to be intelligible for us, we must have an abstraction of the universal apart from all individuating factors. Hence, Albert commonly speaks of the *species in hoc individuo particulari*. The *forma totius* is the "*species in hoc individuo particulari*".[10] Within the individual, the species is not universal. According to Albert, one cannot talk about it as a Platonic thing in itself. The process of abstraction will disentangle the form or species and disclose the simplicity of the universal. One consequence of all of this is that, although the individual being alone is a *res naturae*, a *hoc aliquid*, and a substance, it is in itself unintelligible. That is, without the abstraction of the *forma totius* one would not know the individual as such. What one knows is the *forma totius*, the species in the individual. And as Albert never tires of saying, the species is the whole *esse* of individual things. He even adds that "Whatever is after the species is part of the individuating [elements]." It is this thesis of Boethius, as interpreted by Albert, that Roger Bacon will attack in his *Communia naturalium*.[11] Bacon was concerned with the implications of this thesis. To him, the designation of the individual being as a great unknown was a scandal; his response was to place greater emphasis on the ontological priority of the individual as such over *genera* and *species*.

The problem of universals in Albert has already received critical study. Some aspects of this doctrine in *De predicabilibus* have been carefully analyzed.[12] For the purposes of this account of individuation, I wish simply to present a brief account of universals in this tract, and then proceed to analyze the relation of universal, nature, species, and individual. Albert elsewhere tells us that the universal is not a Platonic form existing in itself. Rather, he wishes to rule out the idea that the universal is a pure product of abstraction, and therefore, he wishes to uphold the ontological status of the universal as the basis of *scientia*.[13]

In terms of logic, concerning which *De predicabilibus* was written, the universal is examined in the context of argument.[14] For something to be truly predicated of many, it must be in many. The universal, then, in this sense is the basis of predication. And in the view of Albert individual being is a composite with an element that makes universal predication possible. Part of the problem concerning whether or not Albert's solution is Platonic or Aristotelian arises from the peculiar relation between "nature" and "universal" that Albert received from Avicenna.[15] Most treatments of the universal in Albert give a broad account of this relationship, but I will confine my remarks to the bare essentials. The universal can be seen in relation to form. According to Albert's treatment, the universal considered in itself can be considered as an image of light in the thing of nature. When it is understood as being in this or that thing or incorporated in them, "it is a particular substance and being in the substantial being (*esse*) and essence of the singular thing." To interpret the universal in this manner is to go beyond a consideration of the universal as a second intention, as part of logic. It is to view the universal metaphysically as "a specific nature". Something can be said to be in something in a number of ways. First, the universal is said to be present in the many in the manner in which humanity is present in many men such that the whole nature is multiplied in many individuals. Second, something can be said to be present in only one thing. Third, something can be present in many and not just in one thing as the case of an aptitude that can be in many.

This allows Albert, following Avicenna, to argue that the universal can be considered in three ways: (1) as a simple essence in itself (a *natura simplex*), (2) as existing in things, (3) as the abstracted universal in the mind. As Albert would put it, there is the universal *ante rem, in re,* and *post rem.*[16] The universal *ante rem* can mean either the universal in the mind of God or the universal that arises in time with the thing. Albert calls the latter the form or the nature. One notices here the close connection between "form" and "nature". But again note the ambiguity. Nature may mean (1) matter insofar as it is an *incohatio formae,* or (2) more properly speaking, it is "the nature of existing things and the substance, which is the form of things and the quiddity". This close connection between matter, form, and nature shows that the form is not a self-standing independent Platonic essence. It is the nature as the basis of both matter and form in the composite and of the composite itself.

The universal *in re* is the universal as particularized and individuated, multiplied and incorporated. Thus, it is the subject of an infinite number of characteristics on account of matter. The universal *post rem* is the universal as it exists in the intellect. It is the product of abstraction. However, Albert is concerned to argue that the universal in the mind does not cause the universal nature. It knows it abstractly. The universal *ante rem et in re* is the basis of the objectivity of abstract cognition.

Perhaps, the most important thing to say here is that the universal and the singular need to be distinguished from the simple nature. The simple nature considered as the basis of being, essence, and name is not the singular or the universal. It is on the basis of the simple nature considered as such in its threefold mode, *ante rem, in re, et post rem,* that universal predication is metaphysically possible. When this simple nature is referred to many things, it is called "universal" or "common". Moreover, singularity or individuality arises from the fact that the simple nature is individualized, particularized, multiplied and incorporated in the things of nature.

2. *De predicabilibus:* Species and Number

In *De predicabilibus,* Albert informs us that, in opposition to nominalist and Platonist views of universality, he intends to follow the opinion that appears to be most probable: that of the Peripatetics. He then asks the question: "Whether universals and especially genera and species, that are signified subsist in nature according to a being that is separate from the intellect. Or do they not subsist as such but are placed as sole, bare, pure intellectual forms?'' The question is important, and as we shall see, it has major implications for the theory of individuation.

The whole point of this section of *De predicabilibus* is to attack the Platonic theory of self-subsistent forms. Some of this account has direct reference to the problem of individuation. Objection three notes that, if everything that exists separately in nature is a particular and an individual such that every form which is in an individual is itself an individual, any universal that subsists outside the intellect in its particular will be particular. Hence, it will not be a true universal since it would not be predicable of many. Albert solves the problem by reference to his distinction of the universal *ante rem, in re, post rem,* which we have noted already. The answer to objection three, however, provides a good example of Albert's views on individuation.

To the objection of Avicenna that everything which is in an individual (insofar as it is an individual) is singular, one can say that nothing in an individual properly speaking prevents the presence of a universal. The latter is a this kind (*quale quid*) and not a *hoc aliquid*. Again, if someone were to say that what is in the individual is present in the individual *per modum individui,* the person might wish to argue that the universal is a singular and a this something. Albert is not satisfied with this argument. He says: ''That which is in an individual is not always in it according to the mode of being of the individual, but sometimes through the mode of being of the principles of the individual.''[17]

One should note that Albert rejects the ideas of the Platonists (the so-called *amici Platonis*) that universals are pure intelligibles that are not found in singular, material things. Rather, they flow from the universal agent intellect after the manner of light. This rejection has implications that Albert draws immediately. In the next chapter, he rejects utterly the Platonist teaching that ''mathematical lines and surfaces are certain separate beings from which mathematical bodies are composed, just as every divisible is said to be composed from indivisibles, taking these from the Epicureans who began to philosophize before him. Melissus, however, and Parmenides said these same things, and so did certain others. They said that all *material quantity* arose from small and great mathematical objects.''[18] One should note here that throughout the references to individuation in the *Metaphysica* there is an intense preoccupation with the implications of the Platonist views on matter for the problem of individuation.

The issue is crucial for understanding the difference between individuation in Albert and in the *amici Platonis;* namely, those Oxford Platonists such as Grosseteste, Kilwardby, and their Parisian follower, Roger Bacon.[19] Following the views of Plato, they held ''that certain universals were constituted in mathematical reasonings and forms''. Or as Albert presents it in the *Metaphysica,* they ''said that natural things are founded on mathematical, and mathematical being founded on divine, just as the third cause is dependent on the second, and the second on the first; and so [Plato] said that the principles of natural being are mathematical, which is completely false.''[20]

The Platonic error was twofold. First, as we have just seen, the object of knowledge was the eternally subsistent ideas. Second, antecedent to subsistent ideas are the formal generative principles, formal number, the number that is the principle of being. The subsisting figures and numbers are the proper subjects of mathematics. Above this, is subsisting unity, God. What Albert rejects, then, is a particular philosophy. We saw previously that he rejected the view that universals were pure intelligibles in a separate world. Here, he will deny mathematical being is self-subsistent and independent from matter. Further, he will argue that numerical unity is entirely distinct from metaphysical unity. The strictness of this distinction marks Albert's account of individuation out from the *amici Platonis.*

In *De predicabilibus,* Albert presents three Platonic arguments for the view that the numerical unity of material things is due to quantity and basic mathematical entities that precede real, physical being. He counters these arguments with his own Aristotelian arguments that propose that the principles of being precede mathematical being.

In Albert's view, all the Platonic arguments miss the mark: They fail to see that the universal is said of many and is a function of the possible intellect. The universal, therefore, is ''a simple notion and nature separated from all quantitative dimension''. The result is that genera and species are not determined quantitatively to this or that thing. If they were so determined, they would not be universals, but would be singular things. Thus, according to Albert, ''A universal principle is not a mathematical quantity in those things which are corporeal. But it is a simple nature constituted in genus and species, providing name and definition.''[21]

In the *Metaphysica,* Albert returns to this theme. There, he describes the error as the ''error of the Pythagoreans''. There also, he strongly argues against a confusion between ''principles'' and ''things''. Whatever principles of things are, they are not atomic particles, nor are they self-subsistent forms. In this, he consciously attacks most forms of ancient Greek philosophy that hold a non-Aristotelian views of change.[22]

The universal, above all, for Albert, expresses the aspect of things that is communicable. Its being is a being apart from singulars. ''Universal being is a common being suited to be in many and communicable to many. This however cannot be had from singulars; because singulars are discrete and incommunicable. The universal does not receive its communicable being from the singular.''[23]

One might then ask: What is the origin of the singular? Albert answers: The universal exists in the singular. The universal has its own rationale. Similarly, the singular has its own nature. In a distinction, which is also found in Roger Bacon, Albert argues that the universal is in the singular in a twofold manner: in a determinate mode and an indeterminate mode. One should also note in passing that this treatment of individual and universal is given in a context of light and multiplication of light. In all of this, Albert goes to great length to argue that individuals are only multiplied within a species. The individual does not immediately participate in the genus. Again, "species is the whole being of individuals or the essential similitude of individuals".[24] This comment leads into a series of extended comments on individuation in *De predicabilibus*.

III. *De predicabilibus:* Individual and Species

'Species' is sometimes defined in a vulgar manner as *forma vel formositas*. Yet, in strict terms, "genus is that to which species is supposited, and thus genus is defined through species and species through genus". Many, however, and especially the Peripatetics whom Albert says he follows here define species in such a manner that "species is that which is placed under genus, and concerning which genus is essentially predicated".[25] This is especially important for the understanding of an individual. Someone might argue that an individual is placed under the genus animal, for example, in respect of its essential predication: thus the individual would seem to be the defined species. One can say in reply: The individual is not placed in an immediate position under the genus. Rather, the species is placed in such a position.

Albert finds the solution to the problem of the relation of species and individual in the doctrine of participation. Species is placed under genus in the line of participation. The individual is not caused by the genus; it is the result of matter.

Species, therefore, is what is predicated essentially of many things that are different in number. That which is predicated is predicated as that which is participated. Thus, the individual does not participate except through the species, and it is not predicated immediately of things that differ numerically except through the species. And the difference in number arises from matter. The name 'species', according to Albert, applies to the most special species and not to the subalternate species. Albert talks about "species" and "individual" as follows:

> Because as Boethius says, the species is the whole *esse* of individuals or is the essential similitude of individuals. And so an individual can be

defined in a twofold manner. First, as a materially determined particular or as a *res naturae,* in which something common stands: or in
which a *fluxus naturae* stands, which is a diffusion of nature and so the
individual is taken to mean "some man", and this individual properly
speaking and in itself is a subject, and is the subject to the species. And
in this manner, the species is first predicated of it. And insofar as it is
destined to be in many according to its total being, the species is the
universal. Species, therefore, is that which is placed under the genus
and concerning which the genus is essentially predicated. For it is predicated as substance and subject in a species, which is individuated by
the constitutive difference, and is formed in the species, which is the
nature of a species and not a this something.[26]

   Thus, the species is a *formale quid* of individuals, and their "total being". But, "that being which is after the species in individuals, is concerned
with the individuating traits, and is not the same as simple being, because
matter gives no being, nor is it properly called being, but is the act of essence
in that which is matter".[27] Thus, matter is not predicable. What is predicable
is the *forma totius.* How then are the inferior individuals related to a species?
Albert remarks: "The species of inferior individuals contain the individuals;
that is, they contain them in that they unite them in the form of the species,
which in turn is the total being of the individuals according to all perfection
of their power."[28] Albert again states the relation of species to individuals as
follows:

   Differences are not divided according to the relationship that species
   have to individuals, as if part of their power were in individuals, but it
   is in each individual according to its total essence, and according to all
   its power: this belongs to species and not to genus, and not just as species but as the most special species, which has nothing beneath it except the individual, which is only numerable through matter and not
   through form. Form is diffused totally in that which can be and in that
   which is matter. . . . And so the division only takes place through matter. And as Aristotle says, division is the cause of number, and the division of matter is the cause of the numbering of material things; it
   follows that species is predicated of many differences only by the number of matter in respect of what they are: because it is in itself the *quid*
   and *quiddity* of individuals and the total being of these.[29]

   In the remainder of this section of *De predicabilibus,* there are two significant treatments of individuation. In the first, Albert examines the role of
species and individual in the descending and ascending lines of influence on

the Porphyrian tree. And in the second, he draws heavily on the *Isagoge* of Porphyry for this account of individuals.

The particular and the singular insofar as they are particular and singular are always manifold (*in multitudine*). The cause of this multiplicity is the division of matter. Thus, in a manner contrary to the way in which a collection is united in a common nature of a species, that which is one in nature is divided into many, "not, however, by a division of form but by a division of matter". What follows is important in that it shows the universal scope of Albert's outlook: he is presenting an account of the total division of nature. He remarks:

> The totality of the division of nature, which is divided through being, nature and form, is divided according as its essence and potentiality is in singular things. And on the contrary, the species unites and gathers many divided things into a unity: for by participation through species, many men are one man. It is not the case, however, that *this man* who is one man through matter is the same as many men divided through their matter and their supposits. Rather, the many participate in one, that is, in one nature and essence. And this is the same as if one were to say that Socrates and Plato and other singular men are one in being man according as "man" expresses the nature of the species which is predicated of them. Yet, from the fact that many men are one man due to the participation of species, it does not follow that simply speaking many men are one man. Many men or one man, simply speaking, are named from the plurality or unity of material subjects. On the other hand, in regard to particular things or men who are particular through matter, the one "man", nature, or form brings about many men according to a singular being. Thus, the universal or common nature or form, while remaining undivided in itself, is divided in all particular things through the subject. Yet, that which is singular and determined according to being and subject is always divided according to that which is common to its proximate and determinate being. And what is common and universal is always the unifying and gathering principle.[30]

One notices again the dominance of species, form, and nature in the determination of the individual. And above all, one notices that participation is the metaphysical determinant of the conditions of finite individual being. At the end of his account of species, Albert explicitly takes up the issue of the status of an individual.

Concerning the individual, Albert repeats what he had said earlier about genus, species, and individual. He then notes that an individual is not predicated except of one discrete and designated thing by means of an improper predication. Yet, one must distinguish a complete individual from an incomplete individual (*individuum vagum*). The latter will be predicated of many by a predication of species, and not by a predication of the individual. Albert continues:

> For the individuals which are distinguished (*discernitur*) from other particulars placed under the same common nature, are formed in a two-fold manner: for substance is formed through the accidents, which are the signs of such distinction, as used for example in the proper name, Socrates. Yet, because *accident is not individuated except through substance,* so an individual accident (*individuum accidentium*) is designated (*designatur*) by pointing (*demonstratio*) at the thing standing under the accident, such as this white substance or this one arriving, so that the accident, with or without time and motion, is designated. In another way it is distinguished through a circumlocution, as for example the way in which the distinguishing characteristic of Socrates is designated through his parents, as when we say "the son of Sophroniscus". If Socrates is the only son of Sophronicus, this leads to a more definite description than the name Socrates. There may be two individuals who bear the name Socrates.[31]

Clearly, the "collection of accidents" helps identify an individual as an individual. Yet, these accidents are not self-standing; rather, they are individuated through the principles of substance. Again, a circumlocution pointing to "origin" as in "son of Sophroniscus" *point* to that aspect of individuality which is basic: There cannot be two similar individuals. That is, there can be only one "son of Sophronicus" with the name 'Socrates'. But there is nothing distinct about the name 'Socrates': There could be two persons bearing this name.

Albert continues, individuals are called first substances because individuals are taken separately; not based on characteristics that have a kind of vague reference to one substance. Rather, their division arises from those characteristics whose collection or union in one substance is not found in any other substance. These characteristics according to Albert, who follows Boethius, are sevenfold: proper form, proper figure, proper origin, proper nomenclature arising from the appropriately imposed accident, one's proper country of origin, proper time of origin, and proper place of origin. These characteristics cannot be abstracted from the concrete thing. They are in the concrete thing as this, that, and now.[32]

Albert firmly distinguishes "accidents" and "substance". Matter is the principle of individuation and a part of the individual substance. The "accidents'' make us aware of the distinguishing marks of the individual substance. If an individual is regarded not as a ''substance'' but as a ''definite'' something (*discretum*), and the word '*discretum*' designates this thing, the accidents are names in the concepts of reason and part of the essence of the designated individual. Yet, the accidents *are not* parts of the substance. The latter is composed only of matter and form.[33]

Other ''common characteristics'' are shared by all men such as the ability to laugh, to be of good cheer, and so forth. These are found in particular men. ''They are in those particular men through that which is common in them, and they belong to them in sofar as they are men.''[34] Now, according to the order of the predicables, the individual is contained under man or more generally under the species, man; and the species man is contained under the genus, animal. The genus, then, is the total universal.

> The individual, however, is not the total, but only a subjective part of the total universal. The species which is the medium is between the genus and the individual and is the total being compared with the diverse parts. . . . Rather, the species is the totality of all other individuals, because according to Boethius, it is the total being in individuals. Nor are individuals related to the species as part of the species, but as singulars according to being and power, having and participating the species in themselves.[35]

It follows, therefore, ''that the individual as an individual, is a certain part. The species, however, is the totality and the part''.[36]

It is important, then, to notice this interdependence of species and individual in the context of species, nature, and participation. It provides the necessary metaphysical background for an understanding of individuation in Albert. Apart from the preceding account of the discernibility of individuals, one should note the dominant role which predication plays in his theory.

IV. Critical Evaluation: Bacon and Albert on Individuation

De predicabilibus of Albert may postdate the Parisian Commentaries of Roger Bacon. And from an examination of topics such as matter and form, universals and individuation, it seems clear that common sources, topics, and concerns abound. It would not be rash to argue that Albert knew and responded to the Parisian Commentaries of Roger Bacon.

Both writers are firmly set against any thesis of the homogeneity of matter. They provide much polemic against the view that holds that matter is one in number in all things. Bacon's ideas on matter developed: He moved from an initial attachment to a kind of unity of matter to the argument that matter differs from matter as form differs from form. It is clear, however, that Bacon in his Parisian Commentaries and his later works is opposed to the view that "form alone divides". For Bacon, individuals are divided through matter. There is no formal division through universals, whether differences or species. Individuals have their own proper form and matter. It seems clear then that, in this central position, Albert and Bacon are opposed from the very beginning. Yet, there is some agreement among them on the fact that "accidents" are not the cause of individuation. Rather, the principles of substance are the causes of individuation. And both authors, although they stress that matter is the cause of individuation, have a role for form. In Bacon, form with matter is the cocause of individuation. And in Albert, we saw that he also has a role for form in individuation, for accidents are the signs of the individual. Both writers distinguish between the incomplete and complete individuals.

There is a major difference between them concerning number and numerical unity. Bacon criticizes the notion that accidents can serve as the basis of numerical unity. Bacon based numerical unity on mathematical quantity. We saw earlier that Albert criticizes this position. For Albert, numerical unity follows specific unity.

One should note above all the crucial role that the Avicennian *common nature* plays in the theory of universality and individuality in both Albert and Bacon. The relation of universal being to individual being is one of participation; that is, participative similitude and not one of mere imitation. The notion of communicability and incommunicability plays a major part in Albert's theory. Again, one should notice the crucial heuristic role that predicability plays in both authors.

The crucial difference between Albert and Bacon is acknowledged by Bacon himself in the *Communia naturalium*. According to Bacon, the view of Albert and others is foolish because it supposes that nothing else except species and something added to species causes the individual. In Bacon's view, the individual has its own singular principles that define it, just as a universal has its own principles. In the end, Bacon finds the issue of individuality to be less problematic than that of universality. God simply makes the nature that is peculiar to each individual to be individual. Thus, an individual, in Bacon's view, as an individual, "naturally has its own true being and essence first, before its universal arises. And thus, neither a universal nor anything added to it makes an individual".

Albert, however, argues that "species is the whole essence of individuals". This is the first thesis on individuation that is rejected by Roger Bacon in *Communia naturalium*. Now, it is clear that Albert does not deny the reality of an individual; after all, it is the supposit to a common nature. But he does give such an important role to form and species that he can say that the species is the whole essence of individuals. Bacon's answer, that the individual has its own true being prior to the universal or species, was written in direct opposition to Albert's views on individuation, and it laid the basis for a very different future development of the topic; namely, the views of Scotus and Ockham.

Notes

1. Albert the Great was born in 1200. He studied in Cologne, lectured in various German cities, studied theology at Paris (1245–48). He taught at Cologne 1248–54, was at the Papal Court in 1256. He was Bishop of Regensburg 1261–62. He died in Cologne on November 15, 1280.

2. These views are found in the two works, the *Commentary on the Sentences* and the *Summa de creaturis.* The latter work is not yet edited in a modern edition. Hence, I will refer to the seventeenth century edition: Petrus Jammay, Opera B. Alberti Magni (Lugduni Sumptibus Claudii Prist 1651, vol. 19: *Summa de Creaturis divisa in duas partes.* Prior to the contemporary Cologne edition of the works of Albert, the standard edition has been that of August Borgnet, *B. Alberti Magni Opera omnia,* (Paris, 1890). The contemporary critical edition of the works of Albert began in 1951. Albertus Magnus, *Opera omnia,* ed. Institutum Alberti Magni Coloniense. Münster im Westphalia, 1951). Where possible, I will refer to the latter. Yet, due to lack of access to all of the latter and parts of the Borgnet edition, I will need to refer to the Jammay edition for references to the early works of Albert.

3. For present purposes in this chapter, I have omitted major treatment of individuation in the Aristotelian commentaries. The references to individuation in these works need a major analysis. Many of the discussions are linked to topics other than individuation. In general, one notices a preoccupation on the part of Albert with the problem of matter. Especially in the *Metaphysica, De generation,* and *De caelo,* Albert presents a strong polemic against Platonic, Stoic, and Epicurean views of matter. And he discusses individuation in this context. I will treat this topic in another study.

4. Albert, *De predicabilibus,* ed. Borgnet, vol. 1, pp. 1–148. My reasons for this procedure are as follows. The *De predicabilibus* is more than a work on logic; it has also metaphysical import. Moreover, there are extended treatments of individuation in this work, whereas in the *Metaphysica, De anima,* or the *Summa theologiae* individuation is discussed in brief and in the context of other topics. Further, one notices that the metaphysics of light, a concern with the status of universals, especially with the status of genera and species, provides the specific philosophical context for Albert's later application of his ideas on universality and individuality in his Aristotelian commentaries. One important aspect of this work will become clear toward the end of the chapter. The *De predicabilibus* of Albert appears to presuppose a knowledge of Roger Bacon's Parisian *questiones* insofar as these deal with individuation.

And Roger Bacon's *Communia naturalium* from the 1260s definitely presupposes a knowledge of the ideas of Albert on individuation and universality as expressed in the *De predicabilibus*.

5. Albert, *I Sent.* d.25, a.1 (Jammay 14, 382); *Summa de creaturis*, I, q. 44, m.2, (Jammay 17, 295). For a thorough and comprehensive treatment see Alfons Hufnagel, *Das Person-Problem bei Albertus Magnus*, in *Studia Albertinia: Festschrift für Bernhard Geyer Zum 70. Geburtstage*, ed. Heinrich Ostlender, (Münster im Westphalia, 1952) Beiträge zur Geschichte der Philosophie und Theologie des Mittelalters, supplemental vol. 4.

6. Albert, *I Sent.* a.1. ad.1, (Jammay 14, 382): Latin, nb.i. "Persona est rationalis naturae individua substantia"; ii. "Personam dicimus aliquem solum a caeteris omnibus singulari proprietate discretum"; iii. "Persona divina est divinae naturae incommunicabilis existentia"; iv. "Persona est existens per se solum iuxta singularem rationalis naturae existentiae modum."

7. Albert, *I Sent.* d.26 a.4 (Jammay 14, 396a–b): "Verum est tamen quod aliter significatur per nomen hypostasis et aliter per nomen personae. Et ad hoc intelligendum, notandum quod in inferioribus sunt quatuor, scilicet, res naturae, subiectum, suppositum, individuum, quibus etiam in natura rationali adiicitur quintum quod est persona: et rem naturae intelligimus compositum ex materia et forma, vel quod est et quo est, in natura et sub natura communi, et hoc est hoc aliquid in natura. Suppositum autem addit rei naturae respectum ad naturam communem, cui supponitur ut incommunicabile. Subjectum, autem, ut dicit Philosophus, est ens in se completum, occasio alteri existendi in eo: et hoc habet respectum ad accidens, licet non fit in intellectu sui nominis habitu accidentis: et hoc vocatur ab Aristotele substantia, et a Graecis hypostasis."

8. M.-D. Roland-Gosselin, *Le "De ente et essentia" de S. Thomas D'Aquin*, Paris, 1948) (Bibliothèque Thomiste, VIII), p. 91: "Considérée comme un être complet en soi, sufet des accidents, elle est dite: sufet, substance ou hypostase, ces trois termes étant synonymes. L'individu, c'est la substance ou hypostase considérée dans son rapport aux accidents qui L'individualisent, c'est-à-dire dans son rapport à ces accidents dont la (collection) ne se retrouve nulle part allieurs."

9. *Ibid.*, p. 92 n. 2.

10. Albert, *3 sent.* d.10, a.1, questiuncula 2, sed contra 2 and response; *De predicabilibus* (see later). The same expression is found throughout the Aristotelian commentaries, especially in the *Metaphysica*. It is repeated many times.

11. See Jeremiah Hackett, "Roger Bacon," chapter 6 in this volume.

12. Ralph McInerny, "Albert on Universals", in *Albert the Great Commemoration Essays*, ed. Francis J. Kovach and Robert W. Shahan (Norman, OK, 1980), pp. 3–18.

13. Albert, *De predicabilibus*, Tr. II, ch. 2, p. 20a.

14. *Ibid.*, Tr. I, ch. 4, p. 7b: "Logicae subjectum est argumentatio." See Richard F. Washell, "Logic, Language and Albert the Great," *Journal of the History of Ideas* 34, no. 3 (1973).

15. *Ibid.*, Tr. II, ch. 1, p. 17.

16. *Ibid.*, Tr. II, ch. 3, p. 24.

17. *Ibid.*, 25a–b: "Ad id quod tertio inducunt per dictum Avicennae, *dicendum quod omne quod est in individuo (secundum quod est in individuo) singulare est.* Sed id quod in individuo est, nil prohibet esse universale, non secundum quod est in individuo acceptum: hoc enim secundum se acceptum, nihil prohibet esse quale quid, et non hoc aliquid. Si quis autem sic objiciat, *Quod est in individuo est in eo per modum individui. Individuum autem est hoc aliquid. Ergo illud quod est in individuo, est singulare et hoc aliquid. Non valet argumentum. Quod enim est in individuo, non semper est in eo per modum esse individui, sed aliquando per modum principii individui. Et non oportet quod hoc secundum id quod est, sit individuum et hoc aliquid:* quia potest esse quale quid. Et ideo in argumento paralogismus est figurae dictionis: quia interpretatur quale quid ut hoc aliquid."

18. *Ibid.*, Tr. II, C. 4, 26a–b: "Secunda autem quaestio est, an universalia sint incorporalia vel corporalia? quae ex Platonicis inducta est sicut prima. Dicebat enim Plato mathematicas lineas et superficiem esse separate quaedam, ex quibus corpora mathematica componuntur: sicut omne divisibile ex indivisibilibus dicebat componi, accipiens haec ab Epicureis qui ante philosophare coeperunt. Melissus autem et Parmenides talia dicebant, et quidam alii. Ex mathematicis autem magnis et parvis omnem materialem dicebant constare quantitatem."

19. See James A. Weisheipl, "Albertus Magnus and the Oxford Platonists," *Proceedings of the American Catholic Philosophical Association* 32 (1958): 124–139.

20. Albert, *Metaphysica,* Tr. I, C.1, 2a (Cologne ed., vol. XV1, 1; Bernahardus Geyer ed., 1960), p. 2a: "Cavendus autem hic error Platonis, qui dixit naturalia fundari in mathematicis et mathematica in divinis, sicut tertia causa fundatur in secunda et secunda fundatur in primaria, et ideo dixit mathematica principia esse naturalium, quod omnino falsum est. . . ."

21. *Ibid.*, 28b: "Et hoc principium constituens speciem et genus quantitatis non est quantitas vel quantum, sed potius quantitatis natura simplex et ratio. Et haec natura sic simplicitate sua accepta est universale. . . . Sed hoc principium non est mathematica quantitas in his quae corporea sunt: sed est natura simplex constituens in genere et specie, et dans nomen et rationem."

22. *Ibid.*, I, Tr. 10, chs. 5, 7, pp. 436–438; 439–441.

23. Albert, *De predicabilibus,* Tr. III, c. 4, 30b–31a: "Hoc etiam sic probatur: Esse universalis est esse commune aptum natum esse in pluribus et multis communicabile. Hoc autem esse non potest habere a singulari: quia singularia sunt discreta et

incommunicabilia. Communicabilia ergo esse quod est esse universalis, universale non habet a singulari.''

24. See Albert, *Metaphysica*, I. 3, Tr. 3, ch. 8–10, pp. 146a–149b (Cologne ed.).

25. *Ibid.*, 57a: ''Plurimi autem, et maxime Peripatetici quos hic imitamur, adhuc etiam sic assignant diffinientes speciem, dicentes quod species est quae ponitur sub genere, et de qua genus in eo quod quid sit praedicatur.''

26. *Ibid.*, 60a–60b: ''Et quod dicitur, quod species specialissima non praedicatur nisi de his quae differunt numero solo, in quibus speciei accidit esse, dicendum quod non sic accidit species esse in individuis, quod sit accidens eis, vel accidens in ipsis: quia, sicut dicit Boethius, species est totum esse individuorum, vel individuorum essentialis similitudo.'' etc.

27. *Ibid.*, 61a: ''Esse enim quod est post speciem in individuis, est et de individuantibus, et non est idem esse simpliciter, quia materia nulli dat esse, nec est proprie de esse: sed est actus essentiae in eo quod est materia.''

28. *Ibid.*, 63b: ''Species autem inferiorum individuorum sicut continet individua: continet autem in hoc, quod adunat ea in forma speciei, quod est totum esse individuorum secundum omnem suae potestatis perfectionem.''

29. Albert, *De praedicabilibus*, Tr. 4, ch. 5, pp. 67b–68a: ''Secundum autem habitudinem quem habet ad individua, non dividitur differentiis, ut secundum partem suae potestatis sit in inferioribus. . .'' etc.

30. *Ibid.*, 73a: ''Dividitur autem totius universalis divisione, quod divisum per esse dividitur, et per naturam et formam, secundum totum suam essentiam et potentiam est in singulis.'' etc.

31. *Ibid.*, Tr. 4, Ch. 7, p. 77a–b: ''Individuum autem quod est certum, non praedicatur, nisi de uno solo discreto et signato, illa praedicatione quae in antehabitis determinata est: quamvis individuum vagum de pluribus praedicatur, hoc est, praedicatione speciei, et non individui, ut dictum est. Individuum enim quod discernitur ab aliis sub eodem communi positis particularibus, dupliciter formatur: substantia enim formatur per accidentia quae signa sunt talia discretionis, quae in proprio nomine importantur, ut cum dicitur Socrates.'' etc.

32. *Ibid.*, p. 77b.

33. *Ibid.*, pp. 77b–78a.

34. *Ibid.*, Tr. 4, Ch. 7, p. 78a: ''. . . sunt enim in eis per commune quod est in eis, et ideo conveniunt eis in eo quod homines sunt. . .''

35. *Ibid.*, p. 78a: ''Individuum autem non est totum, sed tantum pars subjectiva totius universalis. Species vero quae est in medio, est inter genus et individuum, et totum est et pars diversis comparata: sed pars quidem alterius generis quod est totum

ad ipsum. . . . Totum autem est species, non totius alicuius: quia nihil participat eam secundum partem suae potestatis, sicut ipsa species participat genus, sed est totum omnibus aliis individuis: qui ipsa species, ut dicit Boethius, totum esse est in individuis. Nec referuntur individua ad speciem ut partes ipsius, sed potius ut singularia secundum totum esse et potestatem, in se habentia speciem et participantia.''

36. *Ibid.*, p. 78B ''Individuum autem secundum quod individuum est, pars quaedam. Species vero est et totum et pars.''

6

ROGER BACON (B. CA. 1214/20; D. 1292)

JEREMIAH M. G. HACKETT

Roger Bacon[1] treats the problem of individuation in two places. First, one finds a presentation of the problem in his early Parisian lectures (ca. 1240–1247).[2] Second, there is an examination of the problem in his works from the mid-1260s.[3] The most polemical account is found in the *Communia naturalium*.[4]

Naturally, the problem of individuation is connected with other topics in Bacon's philosophy such as universals, matter and form, nature and agency. Clemens Baeumker in his study, *Roger Bacons Naturphilosophie* was absolutely correct in his judgment that in the *Communia naturalium* Bacon was discussing individuation from the standpoint of the natural philosopher.[5] Because of this approach, Baeumker argued that Bacon was quite justified in holding that because individual matter and individual form constitute the individual, they may be regarded as the causes of individuation. In other words, Bacon was limiting his approach to the problem of individuation to the process of individuation in the context of natural agency. It is clear from Bacon's texts that the problems of universals, matter and form, nature and agency are not just external appendages to the issue of individuation. They are so closely tied to the issue of individuation in Bacon that it is necessary to present a review of these topics.

I will treat these topics and the problem of individuation in the following order: (1) matter and form, (2) the doctrine of real (as distinct from mental) universals and singulars, (3) the doctrine of individuation in the Parisian Commentaries, (4) the doctrine of universals: *Communia naturalium*, (5) the cause of individuation in *Communia naturalium*.

I. Matter and Form

In the *Communia naturalium*, Bacon lists six uses of the word 'matter' among his contemporaries: (1) Matter is that which is the subject of action, just as wood is called matter in reference to the action of the carpenter. (2) Matter, in its most proper sense, is the essence that with form constitutes the composite, and thus it exists in every created substance. (3) Matter is the subject of generation and corruption and has the property of being an incomplete and imperfect thing in potency to specific being. (4) Matter is the subject of alteration because it receives contrary accidents. (5) Matter may be regarded as *an individual* in relation to the universal, the universal being founded in its individual as in a material principle. (6) Matter is the name for that which is gross and vile, in which sense earth is said to have more matter than fire.[6]

In the *Communia naturalium,* Roger Bacon, using material from the *Summa sapientialis* of Thomas of York, argues that form is that which gives being.[7] Form has a priority to matter as the *finis,* the end of generation and that to which the diversity of composites is due. Form is that which perfects the material principle, is the end that moves the efficient cause, is that through which the composite acts.[8] Form, therefore, is the principle of action and of knowledge. In general, then, for Bacon, matter and form are two incomplete substances, two principles of being, that integrate the individual substance.

In his later works, and especially in the *Opus tertium* (1267–1268), Bacon seems to have been preoccupied with the problem of the homogeneity of matter in all things. That is, he denies the principal view of the *vulgus philosophantium* at Paris, which holds that matter is one in number in all things *(quod materia sit una numero in omnibus rebus).*[9] Throughout his later works (1266–1292), Bacon explicitly holds that matter is "not numerically one, but *per se* and *ex se* numerically distinct in numerically distinct beings." Does Bacon believe that matter is in no sense one? In his early works, he does define matter as pure possibility.[10] This is the matter or potentiality that is at the base of all contingent being. Matter is the original source of this potentiality. In this sense, one can talk about an essential unity of matter. Matter as potentiality is alike in all contingent beings. This is the nonbeing of creatures in contrast with the being of the creator. For Bacon, one can therefore speak of the matter of all creatures, corporal and spiritual. While all creatures exist as numerically distinct finite beings, they share in a common unity, the unity of matter.

In his later works, Bacon abandons this distinction, and argues that matter differs from matter as form differs from form.[11] In this, he is arguing against those who hold that form alone divides, and that matter is one in number in all things. By matter in this latter sense, we mean definition 2: matter as a simple essence that is opposed to form as the other part of the composite.

Bacon in many places does talk about the common matter and common form, especially in regard to universals. One can speak of a common matter, namely, the genus that is common to two species. The essential unity of matter, however conceived, does not imply numerical unity. The principles of numerically distinct things must be numerically distinct.

Bacon's distrust of the numerical unity of matter finds a parallel in Albertus Magnus's distrust of the numerical unity of matter. Both thinkers believed that such a view of matter led willy-nilly to a facile identification of matter with God. Bacon makes this clear in the *Opus tertium*. And Albertus Magnus also holds a similar view.[12] Perhaps, the most important aspect of this common position on Bacon's and Albertus Magnus's part, is their marked opposition to the *Fons vitae* of Avicebron (Ibn Gabirol) in respect of the theory of numerical unity of matter.

The main issue in Bacon is that of the relation of matter to form. It is best exemplified in two later works, the *Communia naturalium* and the *De multiplicatione specierum*.[13] In his view of *Natura* as active generating agent, Bacon presents a theory of the multiplication of species, which is found in both the earlier and later works. The form or species, which is the first effect of a natural agent, brings about the emergence of the thing from the potency of matter. Bacon states firmly that the forms do not come from outside the matter. Yet, he also holds that the forms are not totally from inside the matter. Matter has *an active potency* and this potency is actualized due to the action of the natural external agent.[14] Bacon holds, therefore, that the active potency or incomplete form in matter receives from the external agent a complement or power (*virtus, species, forma*). The incomplete form is not matter or an accident of matter; rather, it is the substantial form, essentially the same as the complete form.

II. The Doctrine of Real (as opposed to mental) Universals and Singulars in the Parisian Commentaries

In the *Opus maius,* Bacon makes it clear that when he is speaking of universals: "I am speaking of universals in respect of their true being, as a metaphysician must consider them, and not merely in respect of the elementary teaching of Porphyry and the method of logic."[15]

Bacon's account of universals and singulars is explicitly linked to the discussion of individuation in the *Communia naturalium*.[16] But already in the *Parisian Questions* of the 1240s, one finds important elements of Bacon's position. At the outset, it should be noted that some disagreement exists among modern scholars concerning the status of individuals and universals in Roger Bacon. The issue hinges on whether it is correct to call Bacon's position on universals a form of *realism* and if so, what kind of realism? Theodore Crowley argued that some of Bacon's texts, if benignly interpreted, could yield a moderate realist position on universals.[17] More recently, Thomas S. Maloney argues strongly in favor of Bacon as an extreme realist in regard to the problem of universals. Maloney presents a very thorough analysis of Bacon's views on universals in *Questiones supra libros prime philosophie Aristotelis,* the *Questiones altere supra libros prime philosophie Aristotelis,* and the *Communia naturalium.*[18] He acknowledges a marked change of emphasis in the *Communia naturalium,* especially in regard to the state of the individual. Yet, he maintains that there is a continuity in Bacon's position on universals and individuals between the earlier and later works. Crowley, on the other hand, argues that the position or individuals in the *Communia naturalium* proves that Bacon's views on individuals changed radically in the 1260s and that this change proves that Bacon was not an extreme realist.

Briefly, Bacon's account of universals in his early works is as follows: The universal is predicated of many individual things, but mental intention is not so predicated, thus, the universal is not a species or intention in the mind. This position, with some partial modification, is Bacon's constant position. Universals in the strict and primary sense, as the foundation of the objectivity of knowledge, are found outside the mind in things. Bacon offers many reasons for this view.[19]

The crucial question, then, is, What is the status of the universal as it is found to exist outside the mind? And what is the relation of the individual to the universal outside the mind? Bacon tackles the matter explicitly in questions 3 to 8 of the *Questiones prime* and again in the *Questiones altere.*[20] One thing is clear: For Bacon, there are no universals that exist in themselves as individual things. Insofar as genera and species have a reality as objective correlates to the logical order, they have reality for the sake of individuals. In many texts, Bacon rules out the views of Plato on universals. In question 3 of the *Questiones prime,* Bacon meets the objection that a universal has immaterial being, and further, "form is individuated through its matter, but whatever exists in things exists in such matter, therefore, whatever is there is individuated, but a universal is not individuated. . . ."[21] Against this, Bacon argues as follows: A universal is either in the mind or in things. If it is not in the former, therefore it has to be in the latter. To the second objection, he answers that something is in matter in two ways: "either immediately in determinate and particular matter (*in materia signata et particulari*), and such a thing is individuated, *or* it exists immediately in common matter."[22] A universal, therefore, has no need of being immediately individuated since it arises from common matter and common form. "And because the common matter and common form exist along with the proper matter and form of individuals, the universal is in this way in singulars."[23] Thus, for Bacon, one cannot split up the common matter and particular matter or the common form and the form of the particular individual. The two go together in the structure of individual beings.

In question 4, in answer to the view that a universal is only fully constituted with reference to the mind, Bacon answers that the universal in and of itself is prior to all knowledge. He remarks: "This follows because a universal is nothing other than a nature in which singulars of the same [nature] agree; but particulars agree in this way in a common nature predicable of them, without any act of the mind.[24] For Bacon, there are no Platonic universals existing as individual things outside of the mind. Real universals do exist, but these universals, common natures, or essences are only found in particulars. They are already individuated due to form and matter. Thus, in the real concrete thing, the mutual interrelation of common matter and proper matter, and of common form and proper form, is such that *in re* there is just one individual. There is not a singular individual somehow tied to a common nature. The real common nature is realized in this or that particular individual.

At this point, Bacon asks, are there universals in singulars? He states a number of objections to a universal being present in a singular. In answer to these objections, Bacon states:

> Only three kinds of being are imaginable: either [being] in and of itself, [being] in the mind, or [being] in things; but a universal is not something that has being in and of itself and stands on its own, because then it would be a Platonic idea; neither [does it have being] in the mind, as we have seen. . . . Again, a universal is a common nature in which particulars agree; but Socrates and Plato and [others] of this sort cannot agree in a common nature which is in them unless the nature [be] in some way duplicated in them, because a universal is nothing other than a common nature extended into particulars and existing in them as duplicated, in which all things truly exist. And thus, without them [the particulars] there can be no universals . . . [25]

In the response, Bacon argues that there are two kinds of particulars: the determinate here and now particular, and the indeterminate particular (*particulare vagum*). This latter kind exists with "an indeterminate here and now without precision."[26]

In question 6, Bacon, following Aristotle, distinguished "the perfecting form of a singular thing which is not common to many" from "the universal which is common to many." At this point, Bacon meets an issue head on, which will recur in the 1260s. The objection states that since the division of men into individuals is not a division through form, but through matter, and since no new perfecting form other than a common, universal form is added beyond the specific form, *the species* will be the perfecting form of individuals. Bacon, anxious to defend the priority of individuals over species, responds, "it should be said that a species is a form because all parts of a definition are forms that are generative." The division of things in nature, that is, animals into rational/irrational, is not a division through form into individuals. Bacon states:

> This, however, is a division through matter. Of men, one is Socrates, another Plato. And he [Aristotle] is talking there of matter, that is, of individuals, and there is no formal division through form, that is, through universals, whether differences or species. Yet, individuals have their own proper form and matter.[27]

Much of what follows this text belongs more appropriately to a study on universals in Bacon.[28] In passing, one should note one important remark by Bacon. He argues in the expanded *Questiones altere* that a nature is a universal in a very specific sense. A nature is said to be "the state and complement of natural things, and also [something] inclusive of them due to its very breadth. . . . Hence, it is not a nature properly speaking but is something belonging to a nature."[29]

III. The Doctrine of Individuation in the Parisian Commentaries

In the *Questiones supra libros prime philosophie Aristotelis* from which the preceding discussion of universals and singulars is taken, one also finds a brief discussion of individuation.[30] The discussion begins and ends with a consideration of the nature of definitions. The issue is concerned with the individuality of that which is definable. This is twofold, universal and particular. Bacon sets out to deal with the total individual: What makes this individual to be an individual? The division of the questions is as follows:

1. On the parts that enter a definition.
2. Whether, concerning these causes, the principles of things ought to be the efficient cause of individuation of this kind?
3. Whether matter alone or form alone or both matter and form together are the cause of individuation?
4. On the supposition that matter is the cause of individuation, is it alone the cause of individuation?
5. Which of these (matter and form) is the more important cause of individuation?
6. Is it possible to posit the nature of individuation in separated forms, for example, in Platonic ideas?
7. Whether an individual has a definition?

8.   Concerning that which is defined *apud nos,* is it the genus or the species ?

9.   Whether a *particulare sive individuum* such as Socrates and Plato should have a definition?

10.   Whether that in itself which is to be defined is the matter or form (*materia vel forma*), pure or composed?

a. On the Parts That Enter a Definition

In the first question, Bacon argues that it appears to be the case that accidents are not the cause that makes this individual to be this individual. Bacon's account involves a number of arguments, a *sed contra,* and a *solutio.* The following is a brief summary.

No accident is a perfection of substance. An individual is a substance. Thus, the accident is not its perfection. The major stands, since every perfection is no more noble than that of which it is a perfection. Again, if accidents were the cause of individuation, it would involve either one or many accidents. It does not involve one accident, since this one accident would be the accident either of a species or of an individual. It is not an accident of the former, since it would have to be either an *accidens per se* or *ejus accidens per accidens.* The *accidens per se* is convertible with species, and this latter cannot draw anything with it, since nothing convertible draws things with it. Nor is it an *accidens commune per accidens.* This also does not draw anything with it, for it is not the *accidens* of an *accidens* of species. Nor is it an accident of an individual. The proof of this is that, if it were, it would have to be a *per se* accident. And it is not such a thing since according to Porphyry, a *per se* accident does not come together in an individual. Nor is it a common accident. Nor does an aggregate of accidents such as fatherland, parents, and so forth make an individual. In fact, matter and form constitute a thing sufficiently, and hence, they are the causes of individuation.

However, the contrary view is expressed by many. For Porphyry, "individuals differ solely according to number" and as a result, both numerical unity and individuation come from accident. Boethius in *De trinitate* argues that the distinction of three persons is brought about not by species or genus but by accident. He says the same thing in his *Commentary on Porphyry.* In his *Metaphysics,* Algazel argues that in composite being, which is different from the simplicity of the first cause, the cause of individuation is not species or form but accident. Or rather, the individual is caused through the composition of accidents. Again, according to the definition of a name, the name 'individual' is that of an accident. This is so because the individual and the indivisible signify the same thing. But 'individual', 'one', 'indivisible', and such names are accidental in nature since they are made from accidents.

Bacon's *solutio* to these objections is as follows. When one speaks of any individual substance, it is both a substance and an individual; and insofar as it is a substance, accident is not its cause, insofar as it is an individual or one or many or anything of this sort, "accident is formally its perfection". For this name 'individual' is accidental by reason of its definition. Whence one according to number is an individual and an individual is one in number. But insofar as things are individuals, they are so in a twofold manner: either according to the formal cause, and therefore accident is the formal cause of the individual; or according to the efficient cause of individuation, and therefore the principles of the substance are the efficient causes of individuation such as unity when I say that this substance is one. Because insofar as it is a substance, substance is its cause. Insofar as it is one, it is so in a twofold manner: either according to the formal cause and therefore by accident, or according to the efficient cause and therefore the principles of substance and the unity of the principles are the cause. This is a sufficient answer. In the case of Algazel difference is taken to cover all substantial forms, and commonly insofar as it precedes species and what follows from it in an indifferent manner.[31]

b. Concerning these Causes, Ought the Principles of Things Be the Efficient Cause of Individuation of this Kind?

We have seen that the individual in the definition of an individual has accident as its formal cause, as names like 'one', and 'individual', and the like demonstrate. Should the principles of things be regarded as the efficient causes of individuation of this kind? It appears that they should. After all, that which is the prior cause is the cause of the effect to which it is ordered. But matter and form are the causes of the composite substance that is individuated. Thus, it seems that the principles of substance are the efficient cause of the individuation that is the accident of individual substance. Again, all that through which something comes into existence is the efficient cause of that thing. The efficient cause is that through which (*per quod*) something occurs. But matter and form are that through which accident enters a particular thing, therefore, they are the efficient causes. Against this, there is the objection from *Physics,* Book Two. Matter and form do not coincide. But the principles of the subject are the principles of the matter in which it exists and to which adhere accidents of one kind or another. The resolution of this difficulty is as follows. I say that the principles of substance are the efficient causes of individuation *a quibus et per quem* individuation is caused and has being. To the objection he answers that, while the material principle *ex quo* and the efficient cause do not coincide, yet, the material principle *in quo* coincides well with the efficient cause.[32]

c. Is Matter Alone or Form Alone the Cause of Individuation? Or Is the Combination of Matter and Form the Cause of Individuation?

Now it seems that matter is not the cause. Matter is something that is received, but form moves and acts as is said in *De generatione*. An accident of this kind lacks an efficient cause, and thus, matter is not an efficient cause. Again, on the same point, nothing that is a cause of confusion is a cause of distinction and individuation, but matter is a cause of confusion. To the contrary, one can argue according to the beginning of *On the Heavens and the World*. Every sensible thing is sensible through its matter, and the sensible and singular are convertible, thus, the singular or (*sive*) the individual is an individual through matter. Again, in *Physics*, Book Two, matter is the cause of accidents like a mother. Now apart from this definition of matter, there is matter as the reason for the production of things, whence matter is the radical efficient cause of this individuation. He concedes this by expanding the name 'efficiency'. After all, matter is not just a mere nothing. Indeed, it is a certain definite nature and essence. And so it has an actuality by reason of essence whose actuality in a certain manner can be the cause for the occurrence of certain *passiones*. And so, matter can be the original efficient cause of natural *passiones* in a certain manner. To the objection, he responds that the definition of efficiency in relation to the composite and to the form, which is consequent on the *passiones*, ought not to be called ''matter'' in the strict sense. However, the definition of the purely material *passiones* that are for the sake of productivity and efficiency, such as pure materials like mathematics and the like, are to be attributed to matter. And this is implied in the proposition. For individuation, and material property and unity and the like, draw their essence and origin from matter. Whence, matter is able to be the sole cause of individuation or at least the greatest cause or possibly the co-cause. Again, one must note that 'matter' is used in two senses. In the first, it is a cause of confusion, disorder and break-up in things. In the second, it is there as substance and essence and, in this manner, it is a distinct cause, a finite substance, and a distinct substance. Thus, it can be an efficient cause of individuation.[33]

d. On the Supposition That Matter Is the Cause of Individuation, Is It the Only Cause of Individuation?

For the answer to this question and the remaining ones, I will be brief. In this case, Bacon takes the text from Aristotle "*generans non generat aliud a se nisi propter materiam*". This is so because matter alone is sufficient for ''otherness''. It is the cause of otherness and individuation, because two things are divided according to number. From a series of arguments based on the receptivity of things in and through matter, Bacon supposes that matter is the sole and sufficient cause of individuation. Even substantial form is individuated according to the individuation of matter. And yet, to the contrary, in the text of Aristotle, one finds that "act divides and distinguishes, and act and form are the same". Bacon concludes that form is a cause of individuation and that matter is a cocause of individuation with form. The "*propter materiam*" is analyzed in detail by Bacon. Again, he spells out the nature of receptivity in matter in and through the nature of the receiver as well as in substantial forms. The substantial form has a certain power above its nature. The accidental cause generally depends on the connection of its matter and so it is proper for it to receive the cause of its individuation from its matter. Yet, the substantial form is not received in this way. The substantial form is a cause just like the matter. It is not, however, the principal cause. Rather, it is the instrumental or formal cause.[34]

In answer to question 5 (which of these, the matter or the form, is the more important cause?), Bacon concludes that "antonomastically and for the greatest part, the matter is the cause or individuation. But form is an original and principal cause of individuation and so it is an efficient cause in a certain way."[35] In brief, form gives unity, definiteness and individuality to matter. But it gives matter such characteristics only in an instrumental way. The original cause, however, has these characteristics. To question 6 (whether it is possible to place the principle of individuation in separated substances such as Platonic forms?), Bacon replies that in separated substances there is no individuation according to number. There is, however, individuation according to species. In answer to the last four questions on definition, Bacon argues that definition is concerned with universal knowledge—that is, demonstrative knowledge through causes.[36] From its nature and by definition, a particular has no definition. Yet, an *individuum* has a *verissimam entitatem*, and there is a corresponding most truthful knowledge of this entity. But it is denied to us in this life. In this life, we depend on demonstrative, causal knowledge based on universals. Again, Bacon emphasizes the fact that individual being and universal being cannot be artificially separated. We saw this earlier concerning universals. And it is apparent from a later work from the 1260s that Bacon held strongly to this position.

IV. The Doctrine of Universals: *Communia naturalium*

To appreciate Bacon's account of the cause of individuation, it is necessary to review the brief account of universals that precedes the account of individuation in the *Communia naturalium*.[37] It shows beyond a doubt that Bacon is speaking explicitly as a natural philosopher. Again, it is clear that this account of universal, nature, and species has a close relation to the doctrine of species and natural agency in the *De multiplicatione specierum*.[38] Above all, it spells out the complex connection between universal and individual in Bacon's natural philosophy. It is possible only to summarize the main points of Bacon's account here.

The reader of *Communia naturalium* will note the polemical tone. And he or she will also note the different context. Bacon is concerned with theological matters. In brief, Bacon is presenting a study of natural philosophy as an aid to the solution of problems in theology. Much reference made to the sophists who are influenced by some authorities who speak about Aristotle. Above all, these sophists have an inadequate understanding of both Aristotle and of the authorities who interpret Aristotle.[39]

One aspect of the treatment of universals and individuals stands out. Bacon is no longer concerned with a broad analysis of universals and singulars. He has a definite polemical purpose in mind: He aims to prove that, in the intention and execution of nature, the individual has definite ontological priority over genera and species. His account of universals and the cause of individuation is a sustained attack on any contemporary position that would subordinate the individual to the species. Rather, species and genera are there for the sake of the individual.[40]

Chapter [1] 7 of *Distinctio tercia* in *Communia naturalium,* Book One, Part II, is concerned with universals (*de universalibus*).[41] With the following chapter, which is a review of authorities on universals, it sets the context for the discussion of the causes of individuation and universality that follows in the two final chapters of this *distinctio*. According to Bacon, one great difficulty is concerned with the natural priority of a universal over a particular. "In no other field," he says, "are the authorities in so much disagreement." The Stagirite himself seems to contradict himself. Yet, in the sixth book of the *Metaphysics* of Avicenna, the way to the correct answer is indicated. "There are two kinds of Nature, universal and particular, Avicenna teaches in the sixth book of [his] *Metaphysica*."[42] Bacon adds:

> Universal [nature] is the governing force of the universe [and is] diffused among the substances of the heavens [and] throughout all the bodies in the world; it is [that] in which all bodies agree and through which all are maintained at a certain general level of perfection and well being. This universal nature is the corporeal nature that is designated in the second genus, which is [that of] "body", and this nature excludes all incompatible things which are abhorrent to the whole universe, such as a vacuum.[43]

There also exists a "particular nature" that is the directing power of species (*virtus regitiva speciei*) with its individuals. This in turn is twofold,

"the directing power of species and the directing power of an individual, because in every [act of] generation there arises one species and likewise one
individual, because an individual does not exist without a species, nor the
converse."[44] Bacon illustrates the influence of generative nature with the example of the embryo. The *virtus informativa* that informs the embryo is twofold and is complementary. One, the directing power of the species, intends
the production of man [in general], but in a secondary manner, it intends the
production of the individual man. The other, the directing power of the individual, primarily intends the production of the determinate man, and secondarily, the production of man [in general].

In the process of generation, there is a double track of influence. First,
there is the development of universal to inferiors like substance to body to
animal to man. And there is that of a singular line of influence from determinate substance to determinate body to determinate animal to determinate
man. In the first line of influence, "the universal is prior to a particular in
[both] the work and execution of nature, but is posterior in intent."[45] That is,
universal nature does not just intend animality, but rather this particular animal. In the line of singular influence, one proceeds from "a more confused
and more universal individual that is first in the operation and execution of
nature, but is second in intent, because the end intended by nature is the most
complete one."[46] The universal is prior according to the kind of nature that
is the directing power of a species, which is universal in the intent and operation of nature. This is so, since it mainly brings about a universal. Yet in
the operation and intent of nature that is the governing power of an individual, the individual is wholly prior.[47]

In what follows in *Communia naturalium,* Bacon forcefully argues that
all of nature's operation is essentially directed toward the production of the
individual. Moreover, he explicitly argues for the ontological priority of the
individual over universals and species. He says:

> But if we would speak about the universal nature that is the directing
> power of the universe, [we should say that] it intends and brings about
> *an individual first and principally,* about which there is mention in the
> *Book of the Six Principles.* Nature operates in a hidden manner in
> things: once a determinate man is generated, man is generated. And *the
> cause of this is that one individual excells all universals in the world,
> for a universal is nothing but the agreement of many individuals.*[48]

In what follows in this account of universals, Bacon explains what he
means by 'an individual'. And once again, he returns to a defense of the absolute priority of the individual over the universal. He begins by making a
distinction between the individual in itself and the individual in relation to

other individuals. There is the individual as something absolute in itself;
namely, "that which constitutes it and enters its essence." This *absolute nature of an individual* is infinitely more important than that by which one individual agrees with another individual. By its *universal,* one individual
agrees with or disagrees with other individuals. The individual itself has,
however, a being that is limited through itself and is absolute. "Thus, it is
more noble than its universal."[49]

Theological reasons, also, influence Bacon, in his view that a "universal is not favorably compared to singulars. For God did not make the world
for the sake of universal man, but for singular persons." He continues: "It is
clear, therefore, that a singular is incomparably better than a universal."
Thus, universal nature, even though it directs both the universal and the
individual,

> primarily brings about and intends an individual, because it is better.
> And thus, the two natures [that] of a universal and the directing power
> of an individual, will principally intend and will bring about an indi-
> vidual. And these two [universal nature and the individual] are more
> effective than the directing force of a universal on the level of species.
> Therefore, speaking plainly and absolutely, we must say that an indi-
> vidual is prior in nature [to a universal] both in operation and in
> intent.[50]

In the light of all of this, Bacon insists that "it is necessary that the
ranking according to prior and posterior be denominated absolutely and simply from the governing nature of an individual. . ."[51] Thus, the governing
nature of an individual and therefore an individual as such is prior [in nature]
according to operation and intent. And "an individual is prior in nature to its
universal." In the end, a universal is nothing but the comparison or agreement of one individual with another, and this is nothing by comparison with
the absolute nature of the individual as such. Bacon ends the chapter with a
reference to Avicenna and Aristotle. According to Avicenna, "there is a similar, but stronger, comparison of a universal to a particular, namely, [that] of
an accident to [its] subject." That is, the relation of universal to individual is
analogous to that of accident to subject. The former is external to the latter.
One should note in all of this that Bacon uses the words 'individual' and 'singular' interchangeably. Bacon cites Aristotle in the *Metaphysics* to argue that
in generation all acts and operations belong primarily to the individual.

"Since the whole *vulgus* [at Paris] holds the contrary position, because
of certain authorities, the views of the latter must be presented."[52] Bacon, in
effect, turns to the texts of Aristotle and, by means of a literal cross-reference
of Aristotle's texts, argues that "an individual is first in the operation of na-

ture and second in intent, if we would speak simply and absolutely."[53] This consideration of texts from Aristotle shows clearly that Bacon is opposed to any interpreter of Aristotle who would subordinate individuals to species and universals. And in the context of the University of Paris in the early 1260s, it is not idle to argue that he aimed his polemic at the "new" interpretations of Aristotle that took the notion of species so seriously.[54]

IV. The Cause of Individuation: *Communia naturalium*

Roger Bacon's answer to the question of the cause of individuation will no doubt be lacking in satisfaction for many people. Taken in it bare bones as presented in chapter [31] 9 of *Communia naturalium*, vol. 1, Part II, it simply reflects Bacon's personal annoyance at the wide range of doubt on the question in his time. Bacon, after a consideration of objections, returns to the distinction we saw previously: There is the individual as an absolute nature, that is, something incomparable with other things; and there is the individual in its universal aspects as comparable with other things. He says:

> And when they ask what the cause of individuation will be if neither species nor anything added to species causes it, one should first inquire of them what the cause of universality is if neither an individual nor anything added to it would make a universal? This [whole] question is foolish because it supposes that nothing else can be found that causes an individual except species and something in addition to species. For [an individual] has its own singular principles entering its essence, just as a universal has [its own] universal [principles].[55]

Bacon proceeds to argue that if one tries to push back the question of individuation into the nature of the principles governing singulars and universals, one has to ask what is the cause of individuation of matter and form. For example, in the case of the first individual, namely, the determinate substance that is an individual of the most general genus, its components are individuals, made up of first form and first matter. In turn, how are these individuated? He continues: "And what makes them to be individual, since they are not anything except their own universals, namely, first universal form and first universal matter."[56] Bacon's answer is brief: The Creator makes each and everything in accord with what its property requires. Thus, he makes the nature in which individuals agree (the universal) to be universal; and he makes the nature that is peculiar to each individual as such to be individual. And that is that. In desperation, he ends the brief section on the cause of individuation with the remark: "And thus, there is much foolishness in a question of this sort which they raise about individuation."[57]

The reader will have noted that Bacon refers to "the vulgus", "they", those concerned with "species" and the priority of species. It is evident from the preceding that Bacon is responding polemically to a number of distinct positions that give priority to species in the explanation of individuation. Therefore, a brief review of the positions listed by Bacon is in order.

In Bacon's view, this important question about individuation is as yet unresolved and is corrupted by many false responses.[58] Some say (1) that species is the whole essence of individuals and [that] species has different being only in the individuals. Others (2) say that matter added to universal form makes an individual. Still others (3) hold that potency is added to species as a designation and thus is designated in different things. Bacon's answer to these positions is that neither man nor something added to the species man makes a determinate man. Rather, one has need of the line of influence of singulars, like the line of influence of universals, so that it is clear that just as animal stands to man, so a determinate animal stand to this determinate man. And in the light of what was said about universals, "a determinate man is prior to man in the operation and intent of nature. And [that] man attaches [to an individual] outside the essence of the individual after the manner in which an accident [does], and like that in which it should be compared to another individual."[59] Bacon is adamant about the ontological priority of the individual as such:

> Therefore, an individual, in as much as it is an individual, naturally has [its own] true being and its essence first, before, its universal arises. And thus neither a universal nor anything added to it makes an individual. And hence the proper principles entering the essence of an individual constitute it, just as a determinate soul and a determinate body make a determinate man [and] just as soul and body constitute man. And this is what Aristotle says in the seventh book of the *Metaphysics* . . .[60]

Even in the line of influence in nature, the line of universals is subordinated to the line of singulars. The reason "the sophists" take "form", "species", and "universal" to be the determining factor in individuation is that they misunderstand Aristotle in the seventh book of the *Metaphysics*. When it says that man consists of form in matter, and when it says that "one who generates does not generate anything other than himself except because of matter," the sophist misunderstands these words. The sophist thinks that these words mean that "matter added to specific form makes an individual, just as there is a solemn opinion that species in diverse matters would become diverse individuals, just as an image in a mirror becomes many when the mirror is broken into different pieces."[61]

The real issue here is the precise sense in which the word 'matter' is being used. For Bacon, 'matter' is not being used here to refer to the other part of the composite or as a subject in generation, but as a foundation of something in which that thing would consist. Thus, numerical difference does not exist because of the specific nature, but because of the individual nature. This latter nature is called 'matter' because it stands beneath a specific nature. And it is called 'form' because it accrues later and exists in it. Again, the vulgus is wrong when it interprets Boethius to say that species is the whole being of the individual. It fails to distinguish the individual in its specific nature as this individual from the individual as comparable to another individual. In the latter case, the agreement is allowed by the presence of universals. One further position on individuation is mentioned by Bacon in his account in *Communia naturalium*. He argues that "the sophists" are involved in another absurd position on universals and singulars, one that is worse than those listed previously. Some, he says, believe that a "universal is nothing; it neither in the mind nor in things. And they believe in fantasies of the sort; namely, that whatever is in a singular is singular, because beyond a singular there is [only] a subject. So, there will exist only that which is singular and individual, whatever would be in it."[62] For example, Socrates is singular, so too is soul, knowledge, whiteness, and body in Socrates. Even the thing received in the mind is singular. Those who hold this view say: "That a universal is nothing in reality and that singulars do not agree in something through *participation,* but only through *imitation,* and they are similar, as two men agree through imitation and are similar. But an ass is similar to them neither through imitation nor through participation. But that theory destroys the foundations of things and of philosophy."[63]

This is, indeed, a radically, singularist view of reality. The external imitation of things mentioned here is quite different from the participated similitude that Bacon allows to the universal that is instantiated or multiplied in the singular. In effect, it implies an evacuation of all universality. All realities, things and ideas, are radically singular.

The remainder of Bacon's account has to do with an attack on this position. In the first place, according to Bacon, this position contradicts Aristotle's account of the presence of the singular in the universal and of the universal in the singular. In the second place, Bacon introduces his well-worn distinction of individual being: absolute and relative. He explains the latter as follows. One individual agrees with another in regard to a specific nature, "like [when two things agree in] humanity, which is whole and wholly in both, as Boethius says in the third book of his *Commentary on the Predic-*

aments of Aristotle.''[64] Now, one can say that "what is in a singular is singular" if one means the unique and absolute being of the individual as such. But such a view does not make sense in regard to "the specific nature" or universal through which individuals are compared. In the third place, every predication would be equivocal, were this position of "the sophists" to be accepted. As Bacon puts it: "If one says, 'Socrates is a man' and 'Plato is a man', and if nothing is common to them by participation, but only by imitation, then, the same thing is being predicated of itself".[65]

In Bacon's view, this breaks down the notion that in logic species is truly predicated of individuals. This view would evacuate species completely. Thus, it would also remove "one of the famous universals, which cannot be done." Again, if this view were true, the most general [category] would be the most specific. And if the sophists view were true, property and accident would be the lowest species.

Bacon concludes his account of the cause of universality by arguing a position that he also presents in *Opus maius:* the universal that is treated in the natural philosophy and metaphysics of Avicenna is different from and superior to the universal as treated in the logic of Porphyry.

VI. Conclusion

In the first two parts of this chapter, we saw that the problem of individuation in Roger Bacon is intimately related to the problems of matter and form, universals and natural agency. Bacon held strictly to a theory of the universal as existing in reality outside the mind. This universal, however, is not an independent Platonic form. It is a state and complement of any natural thing.

In our third section, we examined Bacon's first explicit treatment of individuation in the Parisian Commentaries dating from the 1240s. This school exercise enables us to see Bacon as a master in arts as he works out the principles of individuation. Accidents are not strictly speaking the cause of individuation. In this Bacon argues explicitly against Porphyry, Boethius, and Algazel. His solution to the issue is as follows. Accidents can be said to be "the formal perfection of an individual." But matter and form are strictly speaking the cause of the individuation of the individual substance. In this analysis, Bacon explicitly points out that he is speaking of a combination of matter *in quo* and form. He rules out a combination of matter *ex quo* and form. For Bacon, matter is not just a mere nothing: It has positive characteristics; it is in some sense an existent. Is it therefore the sole cause of individuation? Bacon concludes that, while it is the major cause of individuation of the individual substance, it is, with form, a cocause of individuation.

In the fourth section, dealing with the treatment of universals in the *Communia naturalium,* we noted two new factors. We saw that Bacon introduces a new polemical tone that is inspired by theological concerns. And we saw that he defines the universal agency of Nature in such a way that all species and genera are subordinated to individuals. That is, species and genera are ontologically subordinated to the individual as such. Nature brings about the individual primarily and principally. In this account, we noticed Bacon's distinction between the absolute nature of the individual as such and the nature of the individual in so far as one individual can be compared with another. It is clear from Bacon's own statements that he is consciously opposing the whole *vulgus philosophantium* at Paris in the 1260s which in his view simply worshipped species and universals. In Section V we examined Bacon's account of the cause of individuation in the *Communia naturalium.* Bacon's analysis here is less satisfactory than his presentation in the *Parisian Commentaries.* He points once again to his distinction of the two natures of the individual, the absolute nature in itself and the nature that can be compared with other individuals. In answer to the question of what causes the absolute nature of the individual as such, he argues that God is the cause of such a nature. This, of course, does not negate his view from the Parisian Commentaries. He would still wish to argue that matter and form are co-causes of the individuation of any natural substance. The most significant change from the 1240s to the 1260s is as follows. In the Parisian Commentaries, Bacon barely mentions in passing that the individual as such has a *"verissimam entitatem".* Unlike the principles of individuation, namely, matter and form, we cannot have adequate and full knowledge of "the individual as such" in this life. Therefore, we have to depend on causal-demonstrative scientific knowledge by means of the universal. In the *Communia naturalium,* Bacon argues on the basis of natural philosophy that all the powers of nature are directed to the production of the individual as such. Thus, species, genera, and universals, while having an essential role in the generation of natures, are ultimately and ontologically subordinated to the being of the individual. If one asks Bacon what is the cause of the absolute being of the individual, as distinct from that being by which one individual can be compared with another, he answers that it is obviously the Creator. While this answer does not identify the inner principles of individuation in individual substances, it is understandable in a context where the Latin Averroists placed such a strong emphasis on species.

In terms of influence, Bacon's emphasis on the absolute nature of the individual as such and its distinction from the comparative nature of the individual, introduces a problem that would become central in Scotus and Ockham. Bacon's analysis of individuation and of universals is a most significant marker on the road to the analysis of these topics in the fourteenth century.

Notes

1. Roger Bacon was born in England, master of arts at the University of Paris (ca. 1240–1247), independent scholar (ca. 1247–1255), and Franciscan friar in Paris from at least 1256 to 1276 or thereafter. He ended his days at Greyfriars in Oxford. Died 1292.

2. Robert Steele, ed., *Opera hactenus inedita Rogeri Baconi*, fasc. 10 (Oxford: Clarendon Press, 1930), pp. 239–246. I will refer to this work as *Questiones;* fasc. 11 (Oxford: Clarendon Press, 1932), pp. 137–170. I will refer to this work as *Questiones altere*.

3. Bacon composed *De multiplicatione specierum, Opus maius, Opus minus, Opus tertium, Communia mathematica* and *Communia naturalium* in the 1260s. Although there is considerable uncertainty about the precise dating of these works, it is agreed that there is much cross-reference among them. The doctrine of species, with its evident implications for a doctrine of individuation, is found in all of these works. There is, therefore, much repetition.

4. Robert Steele, ed., *Opera hactenus inedita Rogeri Baconi*, fasc. 2 *Liber primus Communium naturalium Fratris Rogeri* (Oxford: Clarendon Press, 1905 [?]), pp. 92–107. I will refer to this work as *Communia naturalium*.

5. Clemens Baeumker, "Roger Bacons Naturphilosophie, inbesondere seine lehre von Materie und Form", *Franziskanische Studien* 3 (1916): 1–40.

6. *Communia naturalium*, vol. 1, Part II, p. 62; for an account of Bacon's theory of matter and form, see Dorothy E. Sharp. *Franciscan Philosophy at Oxford in the Thirteenth Century* (Oxford: University Press; London: Humphrey Milford, 1930), pp. 127–151. See also Theodore Crowley, *Roger Bacon: The Problem of the Soul in His Philosophical Commentaries* (Louvain: Editions de l'Institut Supérieur de Philosophie; Dublin: James Duffy & Co., 1950), pp. 81–119.

7. *Communia naturalium*, vol. 1, Part II, pp. 123–124.

8. For a collection of the texts from *Communia naturalium* that characterize form as a principle of action and knowledge, see Dorothy E. Sharp, *Franciscan Philosophy*, pp. 142–143.

9. *Opus tertium*, ed. J. S. Brewer, in *Fr. Rogeri Bacon opera inedita* (*Rerum Britannicarum Medii Aevi Scriptores*, London, 1859), pp. 120–131.

10. *Questiones altere*, pp. 57–58.

11. *Opus tertium*, pp. 125–126.

12. For an account of Albertus Magnus's view on this question, see James A. Weisheipl, O.P., "Albertus Magnus and Universal Hylomorphism", in Francis J. Kovach and Robert W. Shahan, eds., *Albert the Great Commemorative Essays* (Norman: University of Oklahoma Press, 1980), pp. 239–260.

13. For *Communia naturalium*, see notes 5 and 6. For the topic in *De multiplicatione specierum*, see David C. Lindberg, ed., *Roger Bacon's Philosophy of Nature: A Critical Edition, with English Translation, Introduction, and Notes, of De multiplicatione specierum and De speculis comburentibus* (Oxford: Clarendon Press, 1983), esp. pp. 14–21 on matter, form and individuals.

14. *De multiplicatione specierum*, pp. 12–13, 30–31.

15. John Henry Bridges, ed., *The Opus maius of Roger Bacon*, Part II, vol. 3, (London, 1890; reprinted Frankfurt-am-Main: Minerva, 1964), p. 150: "Loquor de universalibus secundum eorum esse verum, sicut metaphysicus habet considerare, non solum secundum puerilem doctrinam Porphyrii et secundum logicae rationem."

16. See *Communia naturalium*, p. 107. Since *Communia naturalium*, Book 1, Part II, up to at least *distinctio quarta* was used in the writing of *De multiplicatione specierum*, a work written by 1267, it is to be assumed that this part of *Communia naturalium* was either written before or concurrently with *Opus maius*. It is most likely that it was written before the *Opus maius*.

17. Theodore Crowley, "Roger Bacon: The Problem of Universals in His Philosophical Commentaries", *Bulletin of the John Ryland's Library* 34 (1951–1952): 264–275. See Thomas S. Maloney, *Three Treatments of Universals by Roger Bacon— A Translation with Introduction and Notes* (Binghamton, NY: *Medieval and Renaissance Texts and Studies*, 1989).

18. Thomas S. Maloney, "The Extreme Realism of Roger Bacon", *The Review of Metaphysics* 38, no. 4 (June 1985): 807–837. The merit of this study is that it gives an analytic outline of the contents of Bacon's *Questiones, Questiones altere,* and *Communia naturalium* on the nature of universals. Although the author differs considerably from Crowley in the evaluation of Bacon's position on the theory of universals and individuation, the account is thorough and accurate. I do not attempt to adjudicate between the accounts given by Crowley and Maloney on the status of the *realism* that is to be attributed to Bacon's theory of the universal. I do, however, give more weight to the view that Bacon in *Communia naturalium* does, at least polemically, place greater emphasis on the unique status of the individual as such than he does in his early philosophical commentaries. Due to limitation of space, I do not reproduce this breakdown of the contents of these tracts. The reader is referred to Thomas S. Maloney, "The Extreme Realism of Roger Bacon", pp. 809, 816–817, 823. I am indebted to Maloney for the discussion and use of his studies and translations on the problem of universals in Roger Bacon.

19. The extent to which Bacon emphasizes the universal outside the mind is clearly stressed throughout Maloney's study. This is a teaching that is constant, though with some change of emphasis, from the early *Questiones* through the *Questiones altere* up to the *Communia naturalium*.

20. In the numbering of these questions, I follow the method provided by Thomas S. Maloney. One does not find these divisions in Steele's edition.

21. *Questiones*, p. 242: "Item: forma individuatur per suam materiam; sed in rebus omne quod est, est in tali materia, ergo omne quod est ibi individuatur; set universale non individuatur, quare etc."

22. *Questiones*, p. 242.

23. *Questiones*, pp. 242–243.

24. *Questiones*, p. 243: "Contra: prius est aliquid scibile quam sciatur secundum actum, ergo cum de universali sit scientia, ipsum precedit omnem cognitionem secundum se et in se. *Quod patet, quia universale nichil est nisi natura aliqua in qua conveniunt singularia ejusdem; set particularia sic conveniunt in natura communi predicabili de eis, sine omni operatione anime".*

25. *Questiones*, pp. 243–244: "Contra: non contingit imaginari nisi triplex esse; aut in se, aut in anima, aut in rebus, etc."

26. *Questiones*, p. 244.

27. *Questiones*, p. 245.

28. See Thomas S. Maloney, "The Extreme Realism of Roger Bacon", notes 4, 19, for a discussion of the relation of the *Questiones altere* to the *Questiones*. See also pp. 816–817 for a complete table of contents of the *Questiones altere*.

29. *Questiones altere*, (series A), pp. 143–144: ".4. *modo dicitur natura nomine communi et extenso, illud scilicet quod est status et complementum rerum naturalium, et etiam ipsarum per sui latitudinem comprehensivum, et hoc modo dicitur natura universale, unde non est natura set aliquid nature proprie loquendo.*"

30. *Questiones supra libros prime philosophie Aristotelis*, pp. 226–239. See also Mara Huber-Legnani, *Roger Bacon, Lehrer der Anschaulichkeit: Der franziskanische gedanke und die Philosophie des Einzelnen*, Freiburg Hochschul-Sammnlung Philosophie, vol. 4 (Freiburg: Hochschul, 1984).

31. *Questiones*, pp. 226–227.

32. *Questiones*, p. 228.

33. *Questiones*, pp. 228–229.

34. *Questiones*, pp. 228–230.

35. *Questiones*, p. 231: "Quod concedo quod antonomastice et maxime est materia causa individuationis; set forma est causa originalis principalis individuationis, et est causa efficiens aliquo modo. Unde illa propositio omne generans generat aliud etc. intelligendum est quod materia est cause principalis et maxime et antonomastice, unde materia est cause individuationis secundum numerum, unde materia est causa originalis et completissima magis individuationis quam forma, quia omnis causa primaria plus influit etc. et ideo est."

36. *Questiones*, pp. 232–237.

37. *Communia naturalium*, pp. 92–96.

38. *De multiplicatione specierum*, Part I, pp. 1–91.

39. *Communia naturalium*, vol. 1, Part II, ch. 7.

40. *Communia naturalium*, vol. 1, Part II, ch. 7, p. 95.

41. Bacon's new interest in the priority of the individual over universals is reflected in his attempt to qualify the nature of demonstrative science in *Opus maius*, part VI, *de scientia experimentali*. Here, he evidently changes Aristotle's account of demonstrative science, and gives priority to "an *intuition* of the truth."

42. The importance of this distinction from the *Metaphysica* of Avicenna for the discussion of universals in Bacon has been noted by Thomas S. Maloney in "The Extreme Realism of Roger Bacon", see pp. 825–836. The notion of universal nature as a generative force of the substances of the universe, of nature as a principle of motion and rest, can also find its source in Aristotle's *Physica*. Bacon without doubt is using Avicenna to interpret Aristotle.

43. *Communia naturalium*, vol. 1, Part II, ch. 7, p. 92: "Natura dupliciter est universalis et particularis, ut Avicenna docet sexto *Metaphisice*. Universalis est virtus regitiva universi diffusa in substancias celorum per omnia corpora mundi, et est in quo omni corpora conveniunt, et per quam omnia salvantur quadam generali perfeccione et salute, et hec natura universalis est natura corporalis que per secundum genus, quod est corpus, designature, et hec natura excludit omnia inconveniencia que toti universo repugnant ut est vacuum." See E. M. Macierowski & R. F. Hassing, "John Philoponus on Aristotle's Definition of Nature: A Translation from the Greek with Notes," *Ancient Philosophy* 8 (Spring, 1988), 73–100, for the argument that Avicenna draws on John Philoponus for this idea of nature.

44. *Ibid.*, p. 93: "Natura particularis est virtus regitiva speciei cum suis individuis et ideo hec est duplex, scilicet, virtus regitiva speciei et virtus regitiva individui, quia in omni generacione quidem fit una species et similiter unum individuum quia individuum non est sine specie, nec e converso."

45. *Communia naturalium*, vol. 1, Part II, ch. 7, p. 93: "Si ergo comparemus universale ad sua inferiora in linea predicamentali, ut substanciam ad corpus, et corpus ad animal, et animal ad hominem, tunc secundum operacionem nature et execucionem, prius est universale quam particulare, set posterius est secundum intencionem."

46. *Ibid.*, pp. 93–94: "Primo enim fit hec substancia quam hoc corpus et hoc corpus quam hoc animal, et hoc animal quam hic homo, et ideo individuum magis confusum et magis universale prius est secundum operacionem nature et execucionem. Set posterius est secundum intencionem, et patet quod non quiescit natura

quando in embrione fit hoc animal, sed operatur donec veniat ad hunc hominem. Et ideo individuum magis signatum et magis particulatum est prius intencione nature.''

47. *Communia naturalium*, vol. 1, Part II, ch. 7, p. 94.

48. *Ibid.*, p. 94.

49. *Communia naturalium*, vol. 1, Part II, ch. 7, pp. 94–95.

50. *Ibid.*, p. 95.

51. *Communia naturalium*, vol. 1, Part II, ch. 7, pp. 95–96: "Ergo tunc oportet quod a natura regitiva individui denominetur ordo secundum prius et posterius absolute et simpliciter.''

52. *Communia naturalium*, vol. 1, Part II, ch. 8, p. 96: "Quoniam tamen totum vulgus est in contrarium propter quasdam auctoritates, ideo exponende sunt.''

53. *Ibid.*, pp. 96–97.

54. For further evidence that Bacon, in his writings in the 1260s, was preoccupied with Latin Aristotelianism (and with Latin Averroism), see Jeremiah Hackett, ''Practical Wisdom and Happiness in the Moral Philosophy of Roger Bacon'', *Medioevo* 12 (1986): 55–109.

55. *Communia naturalium*, vol. 1, Part II, ch. 9, p. 100.

56. *Ibid.*, p. 100–101.

57. *Ibid.*, p. 101.

58. *Ibid.*, pp. 98–99.

59. *Ibid.*, p. 99.

60. *Ibid.*, p. 99.

61. *Ibid.*, pp. 99–100.

62. *Communia naturalium*, vol. 1, Part II, ch. 10, pp. 105–106 (see note 62).

63. *Ibid.*, p. 106.

64. *Ibid.*, p. 106.

65. *Ibid.*, p. 106.

7

BONAVENTURE
(B. CA. 1216; D. 1274)

PETER O. KING

I. Introduction

Bonaventure[1] does not give an isolated treatment of individuation, addressing it only in the context of largely theological concerns; nevertheless, a clear and coherent general theory of individuation can be extracted from his scattered remarks. Bonaventure identifies the metaphysical principles of matter and form intrinsic to a thing as jointly necessary to account for the individuality of the individual and, when such principles produce a substantial unity, to entail the distinctness of the individual from all else. His detailed explanation of how these principles concur in the metaphysical constitution of the individual is subtle and complex, crucially depending on an alignment of the form/matter distinction with the act/potency distinction. Since Bonaventure explicitly denies that there is any single principle or cause of individuation, maintaining instead that the minimal unit of analysis is a pair of jointly necessary principles, his theory is strikingly different from other theories put forward in this period; it is similar in some respects to the theory advanced much later by Suárez (see J. Gracia's contribution to this volume). It is not clear that Bonaventure's alternative approach can ultimately be successful. Nevertheless, an examination of his treatment of individuation proves to be rewarding, because his approach calls into question several assumptions that are uncritically adopted in more traditional approaches to the problem of individuation.

The discussion will proceed as follows. In Section II, the criteria Bonaventure adopts for individuality and associated notions such as singularity and incommunicability will be examined. In Section III, Bonaventure's rejection of alternative solutions to the problem of individuation, and his own proposed solution, will be put forward. In Section IV, the alignment of form/ matter with act/potency will be explored. In Section V, the contrast between "local" and "global" accounts of individuation will be put forward as a way of making sense of Bonaventure's solution to the problem of individuation. In Section VI, the remaining problems of distinctness and discernibility will be taken up.

Two remarks about the following investigation are in order. First, the account of individuation studied here will be that which Bonaventure offers for *created* beings, creatures. As customary with medieval philosophers, Bonaventure offers an entirely different account of individuality and distinctness in the case of the divine: God's individuality and distinctness, the individuality and distinctness of the divine persons in the Trinity, and the distinctness of the human and divine natures in the Incarnation. These topics will be addressed only when they have a bearing on the individuation of creatures. Second, most of the investigation will focus on questions of sameness and difference at a time, rather than over an interval of time—"synchronic" versus "diachronic" identity. Medieval philosophers often treated diachronic identity as secondary, deriving it from the account given for synchronic identity; whether this holds true for Bonaventure or not, the problem of identity over time will not be taken up here.

II. Criteria of Individuality

Although Bonaventure's terminology is not completely stable, he seems to identify three criteria that constitute individuality, that is, that make something to be an individual rather than any other kind of entity. An individual is that which (1) is undivided in itself; (2) subsists *in se* and *per se;* and (3) is distinct or divided from others.[2] Each of these deserves further comment. As for (1), the connection between 'individual' and 'undivided' is suggested by the form and etymology of *individuum*. Bonaventure does not explain the nature of the "division" in question, but his discussion makes it clear that he endorses the standard medieval account, described later by Duns Scotus (for example) as follows: An individual is incapable of being divided into "subjective" parts, that is, of being divided into many parts each of which is of the same nature or kind as the whole of which they are parts.[3] The standard contrast is with the universal, which is capable of being divided into such subjective parts; thus the species "man" may be "divided" into many men, but Socrates cannot be so divided. Therefore, individuality is at least in part a modal feature, involving the impossibility of a division into subjective parts.

As for (2), for present purposes, we can take "subsistence" as a generalization of "existence"; only actual beings can be said to exist, but possible beings may be said to "subsist", and some possible beings—say, the twin brother of Socrates—may correctly be characterized as individuals.[4] Whether they are in fact individuals depends on whether they are *in se* and *per se*. For an entity to be *in se* is for it not to be "in" another, for example by inherence, as accidents are in substance. (Note that this entails that accidents, strictly speaking, are not individuals, although we may certainly speak of accidents being individualized by their presence in an individual substance while in themselves they are nonindividual; Bonaventure draws this consequence explicitly in *III Sent.*, d. 10, art. 1, q. 2, resp.) For an entity to be *per se* is for it to require nothing else in order to be. It is notoriously difficult to spell out this criterion.[5] Bonaventure seems to mean no more by it than that no further essential factors are required for the entity to exist, although nonessential factors may be required. Hence the twin brother of Socrates is a *per se* being, since no additional essential factors would be required for his existence, despite the fact that he needs determinate size, shape, color, location, and the like, as well as existence, to be an actual being. Bonaventure, in common with other philosophers, held that in the case of creatures being *in se* and being *per se* are either jointly present or absent: "every creature is either a being *per se* and *in se,* and so composed out of others, or is a being *cum alio* and *in alio,* and so composed with another" (*I Sent.*, d. 8, art. 2, q. unica, resp.).

As for (3), an individual must have internal unity and independence, as spelled out in (1) and (2), respectively, and also must be distinct or "divided" from other beings. Note that this may be the result of a distinct principle or cause: That which makes a thing either the very thing that it is, or the kind of thing that it is, need not be the same as that which makes a thing different from others, either of the same kind or of different kinds.

These criteria determine what it is to be individual. If there are individuals—and Bonaventure certainly holds that there are—they must satisfy these criteria, which in turn means that each individual possesses determinate metaphysical features in virtue of which it can satisfy these criteria. Therefore, Bonaventure's general theory of individuation must identify these determinate features, which explain the individual's inability to be divided into subjective parts, how the individual requires no further essential factors, and the differentiation of the individual from all else. As we shall see in Section III, Bonaventure identifies the principles of matter and form that are intrinsic to the individual as jointly necessary to account for its unity and independence, entailing its differentiation from others.

There is close parallel between individuality and singularity: to be singular is "to be predicable of only one"; namely, in an identity statement such as "This is Socrates".[6] Hence singularity is a linguistic property, not a metaphysical one. Yet Bonaventure understands the linguistic properties of terms to be grounded in real features of their referents, so that it is precisely because something is individual that a term directly referring to it can be predicated of it alone. Thus no separate account of the logic of singular terms is required.

Another notion closely related to individuality is incommunicability: To be incommunicable, in Bonaventure's view, is "not to be part of another or entering into the composition of a third [thing]" (*III Sent.*, d. 5, art. 2, q. 2, resp.). Individuality need not entail incommunicability; Bonaventure specifically describes the separated human soul as singular, and hence individual, but as communicable since it is apt to be united with a body as an essential feature (*III Sent.*, d. 5, art. 2, q. 3, resp.). However, incommunicability marks out a kind of "unshareability" in common with individuality and in fact is the generalization of individuality appropriate to the case of the Trinity; many, if not most, of Bonaventure's remarks on individuation occur in discussions of incommunicability.

Armed with these notions, then, we can turn to an examination of Bonaventure's general theory of individuation and in particular to making sense of his claim that "in the case of creatures individuation arises from a double principle" (*II Sent.*, d. 3, pars. 1, art. 2, q. 3, resp.), namely form and matter.

III. The "Double Principle" of Individuation

In *II Sent.*, d. 3, pars. 1, art. 2, Bonaventure addresses the question of "personal discreteness" in angels, that is, whether some angels are distinct persons of the same species; since Bonaventure takes personhood to entail individuality, much of his discussion is devoted to an analysis of 'individual discreteness': the problem of individuation.[7]

In, q. 2 Bonaventure asks whether personhood in angels is substantial or accidental. He rejects the reply that individual discreteness comes from accidents, arguing first that accidents depend on individual substances for their being and hence are consequent to the individuality[8] of the essence (fund. 3), and second that accidents cannot be the source of numerical distinctness since diverse accidents are numerically one in the substance (fund. 6).[9] (The other arguments offered are specific to personal discreteness.) Bonaventure directly asserts his rejection of accidental individuation: "nor can it be true that individual distinctness is by accidents, since individuals differ according to substance, not only according to accidents" (resp.). However, Bonaventure tries to accommodate the merits of the intuition that accidents are involved in individuation in his response to the question (resp.):

'Individual discreteness' expresses two things, namely individuation and, consequently, distinctness. Individuation is from the indivision and appropriation of principles; the principles of a thing, when they are conjoined, appropriate each other and produce the individual. But being discrete or being distinct from another is consequent upon this, and from this there arises number, and so an accidental property consequent upon substance. Thus 'individual discreteness' expresses something accidental and something substantial; therefore, it should be stated that any individual discreteness whatever comes from the existence of a natural form in matter.[10]

The last sentence gives the key to interpreting the ''indivision'' and ''appropriation'' of principles: These terms describe the metaphysical union of the principles of form and matter, which jointly constitute the individual. There is an appropriation of form to matter when the form is or becomes the form of this matter, and there is an appropriation of matter to form when the matter is or becomes the matter of this form. The indivision of matter and form is for these two ''appropriated'' principles to be unified with each other. So understood, there is a serious difficulty: How can form be appropriated to matter unless matter is already individuated, so as to be *this* matter, and how can matter be appropriated to form unless form is already individuated, so as to be *this* form? If matter were prior to form, or form prior to matter, there would be an obvious solution: The prior principle would be responsible for the individuation of the other principle, and a more fundamental account would have to be given of the individuality of the prior principle. And, in fact, priority is the issue in the Bonaventure's next question.

In q. 3 Bonaventure asks whether individual discreteness is due to the formal principle or to the material principle, noting that there has been a debate over the proper response (although without identifying the participants in the debate). He describes the traditional alternatives (resp.): Some philosophers have said ''that individuation comes from matter, since 'individual' does not add anything beyond the species but matter'', although ''others saw the issue otherwise, namely that individuation would be from the form, and said that beyond the form of the *species specialissima* there is an individual form''. Yet Bonaventure rejects each of these positions as involving something implausible. He says: ''it is quite difficult to see how matter, which is common to everything, would be the main principle and cause of distinctness; again, it is difficult to grasp how form is the entire and special cause of numerical distinctness . . . how shall we say that two fires differ formally (or even any other way), [fires] which are made many and numerically distinguished only by the division of a [single] continuous [fire], where there is no induction of a new form?'' Matter is unsuited for individuation because in itself it is common; form, because there are intuitive counterexamples, such as the division of a continuous whole into parts of the same kind, when no new form seems to be induced. Bonaventure therefore embraces a third position:

Hence there is a third position which is much clearer, namely that individuation arises from the actual conjunction of matter with form, from which conjunction each appropriates the other to itself—just as it is clear that when an impression or stamping of many seals on wax which previously was one takes place, neither the seals can be made many without the wax, nor is the wax enumerated except because diverse seals come about in [the wax]. Still, if you were to ask from which [individuation] comes principally, it should be stated that an individual is a this-something (*hoc aliquid*). That it is a *this,* it has more principally from the matter, by reason of which the form has a location in space and time. That it is *something,* it has from the form. An individual has being (*esse*) and also has existence (*exsistere*). Matter gives existence to the form, but form gives actual being (*actum essendi*) to the matter. Therefore, in the case of creatures, individuation arises from a double principle.[11]

In short, Bonaventure rejects the suggestion that either principle might be prior to the other; each provides a necessary component of individuality: Matter locates the form in space and time, form actualizes the potencies latent in matter. Yet this account seems vulnerable to the difficulty outlined previously: How can matter "locate" the form if the form is not already individualized, and how can form "actualize" the matter if the matter is not already individualized? By identifying a double principle of individuation, Bonaventure seems to inherit all the problems associated with each traditional solution without receiving any explanatory advantages.

The key to understanding Bonaventure's attempt to resolve this difficulty is provided in the wax analogy. The composite entity that is the seal has intrinsic principles of matter and form: The matter of the seal is wax, and the form of the seal is the shape embossed on the signet ring.[12] The matter "exists" prior to the seal, at least as a lump of wax; the form 'exists' prior to the seal, at least on the ring. When the signet ring is pressed on the wax, the abstract geometrical shape has been given existence, namely, in the wax, and determinate potencies of the wax are actualized, namely, the power to acquire a given shape. The result is the individual composite entity, the seal. Hence three factors in the analogy must be clarified: first, how matter can give existence to the form without itself being individualized; second, how form can actualize the potencies of matter without itself being individualized; third, how the actual conjunction of nonindividualized matter and nonindividualized form produces a determinate individual. Bonaventure provides subtle and sophisticated accounts of the first and second factors, and the third factor can be accounted for, at least in part, by drawing a distinction between local and global explanations of individuality. This will be examined in Section V. To begin with, then, we shall have to examine Bonaventure's understanding of form and matter more closely and in particular the close relationship between form and matter, on the one hand, and act and potency, on the other hand.

IV. Form and Matter as Act and Potency

Bonaventure does not explicitly argue for the alignment of form/matter with act/potency; it is assumed rather than explored. However, we can identify two general contexts in which this alignment takes place; namely, in analyzing the composition of created beings and in identifying the factors involved in change. The first context may be illustrated by Bonaventure's remark in *II Sent.*, d. 3, pars. 1, art. 1, q. 1, resp.: "I see neither cause nor reason how it can be denied that the substance of the angel be a composite of diverse natures, as is the essence of every creature that is a *per se* being (*ens*); and if it is a composite of diverse natures, those two natures are related in the manner of the actual and the possible, and so as form and matter."[13] The conclusion Bonaventure draws here—that all created beings are composites of matter and form—is explicitly restated in the next question: "the metaphysician considers the nature of every creature, and especially the substance of *per se* being, in which there is to consider its actual being (*actum essendi*), and form gives this, as well as the stability of *per se* existing, and matter gives this and is what form requires."[14]

The second context in which Bonaventure aligns form and matter with act and potency can be illustrated by Bonaventure's arguing from the fact of change in the rational soul, which entails act and potency, to the presence in the soul of form and matter (*II Sent.*, d. 17, art. 1, q. 2, resp.): "The rational soul, since it is a this-something (*hoc aliquid*) and apt to subsist *per se*, to act and be acted on, to move and be moved, thus has within itself a foundation of its existence: both a material principle from which it has existence (*exsistere*) and a formal [principle] from which it has being (*esse*)."[15] All created beings are composites of form and matter and, as such, composites of act and potency.[16] Therefore, a proper analysis of the nature of matter and form will have to be concerned with the respects in which matter is aligned with potency and form aligned with act. However, before we can turn to this analysis, some preliminary remarks about *esse* and *exsistere* are in order.

Although Bonaventure does not offer a systematic account of *esse* and *exsistere*, their main characteristics (in the case of creatures) are clear.[17] First, *esse* and *exsistere* are themselves neither essential nor accidental features. They are not any sort of form at all. Bonaventure accepts the traditional axiom *forma dat esse* and adds to it the axiom *materia dat exsistere*, but the former takes *esse* to be consequent upon the form, not a form itself, and the latter takes *exsistere* to be consequent upon matter, not matter itself. Second, *exsistere* is a feature of actual beings, as opposed to merely possible beings, above and beyond the subsistence or manner of subsistence that such possible beings have. Third, *esse* refers to the actuality that which is informed by a form possesses.[18] The actuality conferred by the form is therefore correlative to potency and might be described more accurately as "actualizedness". Hence '*actum essendi*' refers to the actualizing of that which is informed by the form. Everything that has *exsistere* must have *esse,* but the converse need not hold; not every actualization will produce a genuine existent. For example, Socrates's twin brother is in one sense "actualized" by the forms he possesses, but he is a mere "being in potency" (*ens in potentia*). It is equally true that something may be actualized by a form and yet lack features that are necessary to be a concrete existent; other forms may be required, since something may be actualized with respect to a given set of potencies and yet possess further potencies that must be actualized to exist, or to exist as the thing in question.[19] An acorn is an actual acorn but only potentially an oak tree, although in some sense it possesses the form of the oak tree within itself.

Matter, according to Bonaventure, is in itself "a mere being in potency" (*II Sent.*, d. 3, part 1, art. 1, q. 3, resp.); it is "in potency in every way" and " 'informed' by every possibility" (*II Sent.*, d. 12, art. 1, q. 1, resp.), that is, with possibility for all forms (*II Sent.*, d. 3, pars. 1, art. 1, q. 2 ad 3). Bonaventure draws some consequences of this view in an argument that matter, in whatever it is, is numerically one: "since matter is a being wholly in potency, it thus has no act by its essence, no form, and therefore no distinctness; if it has no distinctness and is not nothing, it is thus necessary that it be one without multitude, and so numerically one" (*II Sent.*, d. 3, part 1, art. 1, q. 3, resp.). Matter by definition is free of all forms, so no distinctness or differentiation is possible. The "numerical unity" that matter possesses in virtue of being numerically one by its nature is a special kind of unity; Bonaventure calls it the "unity of homogeneity":

> If [matter] has unity, it has the unity of homogeneity. Clearly, this unity can remain at once in diverse things: if many dishes come from the same gold, they are of the same gold by homogeneity. But the gold which is in one differs from the gold which is in another, so they are not one by continuity. If, therefore, matter is not one by actual simplicity, like the angel, nor by continuity, like a mountain or a chunk of gold, but only by homogeneity, and this is not removed by the advent of forms, then matter is one under all forms, as [it is one] with all forms abstracted. But with all forms abstracted, there is no distinctness in matter; rather, it is understood as simply one. Therefore, matter is now numerically one in all things [that have been] made material, since it is a being wholly in potency.[20]

Matter in itself is a homogeneous unity, and questions of individuation do not arise. Bonaventure's view of "numerical unity" is quite different from the more standard view. In the same discussion, Bonaventure explicitly cautions us against confusing the essence of matter with any kind of corporeal matter (ad 6): "If anyone wants to understand the unity of matter, it is necessary for the soul to abstract from individual unity and to climb up beyond the act of the imagination and to think of a being wholly in potency by privation, and so one will somehow be able to grasp it. So long as matter is thought of as an extended mass (*moles*), in no way will one reach the considered unity of essence."[21] Since "matter considered in itself is neither spiritual nor corporeal" (*II Sent.*, d. 3, pars. 1, art. 1, q. 2 ad 3), and is a homogeneous unity in spiritual and corporeal beings, it has neither extension nor volume. Matter is essentially pure passive potency, the capacity to be informed—the infamous *materia prima* of the scholastics.

However, these remarks pertain only to the essence of matter. Bonaventure is clear on this point: "any capacity consequent upon the essence of matter is indifferently related to spiritual and corporeal form, but since matter is never deprived of all *esse*, matter consequent upon *esse* is one thing in spiritual beings and another in corporeal beings" (*II Sent.*, d. 3, part 1, art. 1, q. 2 ad 3; see also d. 12, art. 1, q. 1, resp.). Matter can exist only as informed, that is, along with some form that gives it *esse*. For reasons that are partly theological, Bonaventure considers the case of corporeal matter at length. The existence of corporeal matter is directly ascribed to God's creative activity, who informs matter with a single form (*II Sent.*, d. 12, art. 1, q. 3, resp.):

> [Corporeal] matter is produced under some form, but it was not a complete form nor one giving complete *esse* to matter. Hence [this form] did not so inform the matter such that it might be called 'informed'; nor was the appetite of matter as yet appeased, and thus matter could still desire other forms. Hence there was a disposition for further forms, not complete perfection. And since unformed matter had an appetite and inclination for many forms, hence, although the form did not have in itself diverse natures, nevertheless matter in its diverse parts had a certain imperfect diversity—not from diverse complete acts, but more from appetites for diverse [forms]—and hence is called a mixture and confused.[22]

The form that initially informed matter to produce corporeal matter gave it the basic characteristics of mass and extension, as Bonaventure remarks: "Matter was not corporeal in such a way that it was complete in the genus 'body', but in the way in which it had extension and corporeality, since it did not have a perfect actuality of form, as stated before."[23] Given that corporeal

matter has mass and extension, it thereby has spatial location, as noted in
II Sent., d. 12, art. 2, q. 3, resp.: "Since [corporeal] matter was a mass having extension, and the empyrean heaven had rotational motion, it was in a
place, and since it was bodily (*corpulenta*) substance, it filled place. Again,
since it had a certain distinction in its parts according to thinness and thick-
ness, but as a quasi-plenum, it had position according to higher and lower, but
only imperfectly."[24] Therefore, corporeal matter originally had the characteristics of a plenum, filling space.[25] There is as yet no real issue regarding
individuation, that is, the source of the individuality of corporeal matter,
which in its existence still has only a unity of homogeneity; the material
quasi-plenum (*semiplenam*) is a quantitative whole, whose parts are only relatively distinguished, and its informing form is as yet unique.[26]

The succeeding stages in the organization of corporeal matter into material substances are clearly outlined by Bonaventure. First, the elemental
forms of earth, air, fire, and water advene on corporeal matter, presumably
through direct divine agency.[27] Second, the elemental forms enter into the
"mixed form" (*forma mixtionis*), which are most likely familiar stufflike
compounds, for example copper and gold.[28] Third, the mixed forms enter
into the "complex form" (*forma complexionis*) of organic bodies, for example flesh and cellulose. At some point in the process, direct divine agency
is no longer required for the production of distinct composites of form and
matter, and natural agency can take its place. Since the elemental forms of
earth, air, fire, and water inform matter already possessed of mass and extension, the resulting composites may be said to have place, they may also
have local physical properties such as motion or a tendency to move in a
given direction. Such collisions and combinations of the elementary compounds could then naturally produce mixtures. Organic bodies present a more
interesting case. Bonaventure holds that the production and behavior of
organic bodies cannot be understood without postulating what he calls, following Augustine, "*rationes seminales*"—principles of growth and development. A *ratio seminalis* is a potency for a given form, a potency that in some
sense already "virtually contains" the form in question. Moreover, this potency is active: In standard circumstances, it will be actualized unless prevented. Bonaventure offers two homely examples by way of clarifying the
nature of the *ratio seminalis.*[29] The form of the rose is already present in the
rosebud; the rosebud "virtually" possesses the form of the rose. So long as
sufficient sunlight, moisture, and the like are present, the rosebud will develop into a rose, unless prevented from so doing (say, by being cut). Similarly, an embryo virtually possesses the form of that into which it will
develop in standard conditions, unless prevented from so developing. This is
how matter, which is in itself pure passive potency, can also have "an appe-
tite and inclination for many forms", as Bonaventure says in *II Sent.*, d. 12,

art. 1, q. 3, resp. (cited previously). Natural agents do not literally create forms, but actualize or permit the actualization of the potencies for form latent within matter (*II Sent.*, d. 7, part 2, art. 2, q. 1, ad 4).

Forms are universal. In *II Sent.*, d. 18, art. 1, q. 3, Bonaventure asks whether the *ratio seminalis* can be called a universal or singular form (by 'singular' here he obviously means ''individualized''). There are essentially two reasons for postulating universals (resp.):

> It is necessary to postulate universal forms due to (1) cognition and (2) the univocity of predication. Thus if there is only a complete cognition when the whole *esse* of the thing is cognized, and there is no cognition except through form, then there must be some form which includes the whole *esse*. Moreover, we call this [form] the 'essence', and it is a universal form, as Avicenna says. (He says that the essence is nothing but the quiddity of a universal thing.) Similarly, there is no genuine univocity except when some things are similar to each other in one common form, which is essentially predicated of them. Moreover, the form in which many are similar to one another can be only a universal form, and what is essentially predicated of them can be only a form including the whole. Hence the universal form is nothing other than the form of the whole, which is universal, since it is of itself apt to be in many.[30]

True predication and accurate cognition are grounded on metaphysical facts, as Bonaventure recognizes in his reply to an objection (ad 3): ''the similarity between Peter and Paul is true and real; and so it is necessary to posit some third [factor] in which they are similar to each other; and in like manner there is a real similarity between a man and an ass, and hence the philosophical consideration [of species and genera] is not empty.''[31] The ''form of the whole'' (*forma totius*) is contrasted with the ''form of the part'' (*forma partis*) slightly earlier (resp.):

> Form is universal. But not any form whatsoever is strictly universal; there is the form of the part and the form of the whole, and the universal is not the form of the part but rather the form of the whole. Soul is not said to be universal in respect of one man, but rather man. Moreover, those [who hold this position] say that the form of the whole is that which gives *esse* to the whole, and this is called the 'essence' of the thing since it includes the whole *esse;* and the metaphysician considers this form. But the form of the part, which has no *esse* in a genus except by reduction, is not strictly called 'universal'; still, it can be called in a way 'universal' by its root (*radicatione*), since it is indiffer-

ent to many, which can come about from it, just as a cause is said to be universal because it can [be] in many.[32]

The distinction between these two classes of forms is clarified by Bonaventure's remarks in *III Sent.*, d. 2, art. 2, q. 3, resp.:

> It should be said the 'species' expresses form—but not any [form] whatsoever, but the form of the whole, i.e., the form including the whole *esse*. It is according to this that Boethius says that "the species is the whole *esse* of its individuals", and Avicenna and other philosophers agree with this. Therefore, the 'specific common form' can be understood in two ways: either (1) according to predication, or (2) according to constitution. According to predication, 'man' expresses a form common to Peter and Paul. According to constitution, 'man' expresses a form that is simultaneously related to soul and body, and that results from the conjunction of the soul with the body. The soul and the body concur in constituting one essence. Thence it is that what is constituted from soul and body has one specific form, common by predication to it and to others so constituted, and nonetheless common to the constituting parts by a definite informing and completeness.[33]

In a composite substance such as Socrates, the form of the part is his individual soul and the form of the whole is the species "man".[34] The species gives *esse* to the entire composite and does so in virtue of the *esse* given to the body by the soul and the fixed *exsistere* given to the soul by the body. Only the species is, strictly speaking, universal, since it alone falls under a genus and thereby may be common to many; the form of the part is classed under a genus only by reduction, as a constituent of the form of the whole. In modern terms, the form only of the whole is instantiated. The form of the part is not instantiated, since it is contrasted with the matter that it informs to produce the composite. The form of the whole, on the other hand, may be said to "include" matter, since it is the form of the entire composite of matter and the form of the part. The form of the whole may for the same reason be said to "include" the form of the part as a constituent. (Put another way, the actuality of the composite is distinct from the actuality of its constituent parts, though dependent on it: The composite can be actualized only through the actuality of its constituent parts.) Unlike the form of the whole, the *ratio seminalis* is not instantiated. Like the form of the part, the *ratio seminalis* is actualized only in something that instantiates a form of the whole. Since the form of the whole may be construed as a further actuality of the form of the part, it makes little difference whether we say that the form which is virtually contained in the *ratio seminalis* is the form of the whole or only the form of the part.

In *II Sent.*, d. 18, art. 1, q. 3, resp., Bonaventure describes a common position that maintains that in addition to universal forms there are also individual forms, where an individual form is formally different from its corresponding universal form as more "complete", such that in addition to the form "man" in Socrates there would also be the form "Socrateity". Bonaventure says that "this position is not to be dismissed; it is that of great men and seems to concur with authority, reason, and sense". However, Bonaventure opts for another position, which rejects the existence of individual forms, saying that this position too "is the position of many great men, and indeed the majority approves it more [than the other position]; nor is it without merit, since it too agrees with reason, authority, and sense" and in fact is "more common and more intelligible and closer to sense". Bonaventure describes his position as follows:

> Moreover, [the universal form] is particularized[35] not through the addition of a further form, but through its conjunction with matter; from this conjunction, matter appropriates a form to itself, and form [appropriates] matter [to itself], as stated previously. And since this form is never separated from matter, there is never a universal form without a particular. Although the one is not without the other, still the one differs from the other. Although there cannot be whiteness without body, it still differs from body. Hence inseparability does not entail complete identity.[36]

Forms are universal in themselves, as Bonaventure says in *II Sent.*, d. 3, part 1, art. 2, q. 3, ad (1)–(3): "no form is individual except according to its conjunction with matter." Forms may be individualized without being individual or thereby becoming individual—no formal difference is introduced through the conjunction of form and matter, which individualizes the form. The form of the whole becomes concretely realized as the form of the part, but its nature is not altered.

Bonaventure's rejection of individual forms seems to render his solution to the problem of individuation highly suspect: If forms are not individual, how then can the individuality possessed by individuals be accounted for? Even the combination of form with matter does not seem able to avoid this difficulty, since—whether Bonaventure's identification of a double principle of individuation is question begging or not—form is universal of itself. How can indeterminate matter combine with universal form to produce individuality? How can the form of the whole, universal of itself, become actualized as the (individual) form of the part? To see how Bonaventure can respond to these difficulties and to address the issue of question begging, we need to put together his accounts of form and matter in their alignment with act and potency, and draw a distinction between local and global explanations of individuation.

V. Local and Global Explanations of Individuation

The scattered threads of Bonaventure's solution to the problem of individuation can now be drawn together and systematized. The key is found in the common mediaeval understanding of modality, shared by Bonaventure, which treats modality as a feature of subjects rather than as characterizing alternative states of affairs. In this sense, modal features may be possessed by subjects: the ability to sing, actually singing, the power to be shaped into a statue. Such modal features are unlike other properties, which fall under genera and species, and indeed unlike anything else that exists: Following Aristotle's lead (*Metaphysics* V, 7, 1017a8–1017b9), medieval philosophers generally held that potency and act are divisions of being, just as the ten categories are an alternate division of being, and so is a basic metaphysical aspect of created beings. Thus the actualization of a potency does not constitute any sort of formal difference, since form is specific to the categorial division of being while potency and act are a distinct division of being. Therefore the internal articulation of potency and act will differ from that of categorial being, and it is to this articulation that we now turn.

There are two main types of potency, passive potency and active potency. Passive potency is the power to undergo or receive some act or action, as for example to be informed by a form. Active potency, in contrast, is the power to do or perform some act or action. The content of each potency, whether passive or active, specifies the "act" or actualization that is an actualization of the potency. Potencies are individuated by their corresponding acts, that is, by what counts as a determinate actualization of the potency. Distinct acts can be actualizations of one and the same potency, as the distinct activities of walking and running exercise the same more basic abilities involved in moving one's legs; one and the same act can be an actualization of different levels of potency, as the activity of singing a baritone aria is simultaneously an actualization of the potency to sing that aria, an actualization of the potency to sing, and an actualization of the potency to produce vocal sounds. (The two cases are not all that distinct: It may be that a set of basic powers, such as the ability to move one's legs and the capacity to produce vocal sound, are involved in all other activities.) With these distinctions in mind, we can recast some of Bonaventure's claims canvassed in Section IV.

Matter is in its essence a purely passive potency, that is, the bare potency to be informed by any form whatsoever: Any form at all would count as an actualization of matter. As purely passive potency, matter cannot be actual, since this would imply some determinate actualization. However, this essential characteristic of matter as purely passive potency does not exclude or preclude matter actually existing; matter is not destroyed when its potencies are actualized, just as a singer does not lose his or her ability to sing when actually singing. In this sense, matter or potency is a principle of all created being, since every created being is and must be an actualization of such essentially passive indeterminate potency.[37] For the very same reason, namely, that every created being is and must be a determinate actualization of potency, form or act must equally be a principle of all created being. Neither can be ultimately prior to the other in creatures, since they are interdefined.

The individuality of an individual is due to the appropriation and indivision of the intrinsic principles of form and matter: when the form is or becomes the form of this matter and when the matter is or becomes the matter for this form, and the "appropriated" form and matter are unified. The initial difficulty, posed in Section III, was that this account seems to be question begging, since it requires the individuality of the form and the individuality of the matter prior to explaining the individuality of the composite. The wax example suggested that the problem of individuation should be treated as having three component parts: how form can actualize the potencies of matter without itself being individualized, how matter can give existence to the form without itself being individualized, how the actual conjunction of nonindividualized matter and nonindividualized form produces a determinate individual. The first two depend on the relation of form and matter understood as act and potency; the last, the ultimate ground of the preceding two, on the difference between local and global explanations of individuation.[38]

Form is that which actualizes the potencies latent in matter, whether active or passive. Put another way, the matter that is to be the matter for the form must already possess a potency for the form. This requirement is nontrivial; not all matter is immediately equipped to be the matter for a given form—the matter of Socrates is not immediately fit to be informed by the form of a wine glass, for example, although his matter could be broken down far enough into its constituents so that this might be possible. Thus the matter that is to be the matter of the form is already structured as required by the form, and hence must in some sense already contain the form, at least in potency. In the case of living creatures, the form is contained virtually by way of a *ratio seminalis*.[39] That is, the organic matter that is to be the matter of Socrates possesses the active potency to develop into a body informed by rationality (and hence a composite informed by the species "man"), and in standard conditions it will do so unless prevented. The active potency of organic matter is not a potency for an individual form, since there are no individual forms, but is rather a potency for specific form; it is not the potency for "Socrateity", but for "man". Yet just as the generic active potency to sing that is present in a singer may be actualized by singing a baritone aria, so too the generic active potency for man present in some organic matter is actualized by vivifying the organic matter with rational life, and this is precisely what it is for Socrates to exist. Socrates is no more than the actualization of the generic or specific active potency of given organic matter; since actualization does not constitute any formal difference, there need be no individual form "Socrateity".[40] This actualization is due either to the operation of natural agency, which reduces the potencies to act, or by the presence of standard conditions and the absence of impediments, which is sufficient for a *ratio seminalis* to be actualized. Form gives *esse* to matter by being the actualization of its latent potencies. Therefore, form may actualize the determinate specific potencies that are latent in matter without itself being individualized.

So stated, there seems to be an obvious objection: the actualization brought about by the generic or specific form seems to presuppose the individuality of the matter—a determinate subject with certain latent potencies—and so the individuality of the matter itself stands in need of further explanation. Yet while the objection has some force, it is too strong: Bonaventure will argue that the actualization carried out by the form does not require the individuality of the matter, but only its capacity to be informed, as a being in potency or "stuff". Let us examine the details of his account more closely.

The matter entering into the composite, before it is informed, retains the characteristics of a being in potency, not possessing determinate actuality. More accurately, it does not possess the determinate actuality given it by that form which is to inform it. This need not preclude the matter possessing actuality from other forms, imperfect or incomplete *esse,* which is nonetheless sufficient for spatio-temporal location. If we imagine organic matter that is organized into the structure of a human body, although not yet informed, then there is as yet no "individuality" to the matter: it is not a *per se* being, but a mere accidental unity, a collection of organic parts. That such an uninformed body is not a unity is shown by its speedy dissolution. The parts may have local unity, as shown by the fact that they are distinguished into blood, bones, flesh, organs, and the like, which allow the "body" to have determinate spatio-temporal location, but in the absence of the soul these are temporary and partial unities. Put another way, there is something arbitrary about singling out any matter as the matter of the form in the absence of that form that gives the matter complete *esse.* The same point emerges with more clarity if we consider a lump of wax that is shaped into not one but two distinct seals. Prior to being informed, the wax is no more one than two, and there is no way to distinguish its parts, since the potency to be shaped into a seal is homogeneously present throughout. If the lump of wax is first divided so that there are two lumps distinct by spatio-temporal location, and then each lump receives the form of a different seal, the two lumps of wax are still one by the unity of homogeneity or continuity. This example shows that the individuality or unity of matter is relative to form and that with respect to a given form matter functions as a "stuff" rather than as an individual, even if the same matter possesses other forms with respect to which it is a concrete unity.[41] Matter is a "stuff" by its nature since it is in potency, awaiting the determinate actualization given by the form. Hence when form actualizes the potencies latent with the matter, that matter is a "stuff" with respect to the form rather than an individual. Thus form does not presuppose the individuality of matter (quite the opposite), and the nonindividuality of matter with respect to the form does not preclude the matter giving spatio-temporal location to the form.[42]

Therefore, generic form and stufflike matter account for the individuality of a composite of form and matter. Form is not individual, but possessed generically (and perhaps virtually) in the potencies of matter, and the actualization of such potencies gives *esse* to the matter. Equally, the matter is not individual as regards the form in question, but an indeterminate stuff that may nevertheless have spatio-temporal location (and other characteristics as well) such that its potencies can be actualized and the form given existence and location.

Bonaventure's solution to the problem of individuation, then, is a 'local' explanation of individuality: It explains the individuality of any given individual by recourse to potency and act. It is possible, in the case of any given individual, locally to explain the individuality of that individual. The explanation, citing the intrinsic principles of matter and form, will have recourse to logically and perhaps temporally prior entities that themselves may be individual composites of matter and form. The individuality of Socrates is due to Socrates being a composite of *this* form in *this* matter. That Socrates has *this* form is a consequence of the determinate generic potencies possessed by a lump of extrinsically individuated matter that localizes the form; that Socrates has *this* matter is a consequence of the *esse* given to a lump of matter by the actualization of its potencies. The possession of a determinate generic potency, such as the potency to be informed by "man" rather than "ass", and the localization of one form rather than the other in space and time, depends on the characteristics already possessed by the "lump" of matter: to have the potency for "man" rather than "ass" the "lump" must be an organized and structured collection of legs, arms, hands, and the like, or at least the nutritive and developmental collection of abilities possessed by the zygote or embryo; the possession of the given potencies will determine which forms can be put into act. Hence the individuality of Socrates depends on the characteristics of an individual complex composite of form and matter, one that is in potency to further actualization. Bonaventure's explanation of individuality is therefore local: the individuality of any composite of form and matter is explained through the characteristics of prior individual composites of form and matter. The individuality of these prior composites is itself not explained but assumed for the purposes of the explanation. And given that the same question can be raised with regard to these prior composites, can Bonaventure's account be extended to explain the individuality of all individuals at once—that is, can it serve as a 'global' or general explanation of individuation?

The answer is that it cannot: There is no global explanation of individuality. Bonaventure's account of individuality, when applied to particular cases, will identify the particular principles involved in that case; the unity of the individual can be explained by reference to other individuals and the mechanism of potency and act. If we ask why this individual exists rather than another, or indeed why any individual exists at all, a local explanation in terms of natural agency is possible: Socrates exists because of the potencies and forms latent in organic matter, which themselves are the result of his parents' causal activity, and so forth. This kind of response can be extremely detailed, as the sketch of Bonaventure's account of the physical world in Section IV has shown. Yet ultimately the reason for the existence of any individual depends on direct divine agency: God created corporeal matter and informed it with certain potencies. Equally, the individuality of any individual is ultimately the result of direct divine agency: God initially structured being through potency and act. The individuality of any individual can be explained only in terms of the individuality of other individuals that are prior to it. The explanation given for this is a matter of the detailed causal relations of generation. The classical problem of individuation *is* the problem of existence—at least, insofar as the problem of individuation can be given sense at all and is not simply confused.[43]

Therefore, Bonaventure takes the classical problem of individuation to depend on deeper metaphysical and theological truths about potency and act. His denial of the possibility of what I have called a "global" explanation does not vitiate any of the local explanations that may be given. If we ask what makes Socrates to be the very thing he is, the answer is that it is his intrinsic principles of matter and form. If we ask what makes Socrates to be the kind of thing he is, the answer is that it is his form, an answer that does not commit Bonaventure to the existence of universal forms (other than as individualized actualizations of material potencies)—and to be "his" form, the form "man" is actualized in matter, so matter is and must be part of this answer. If we ask what makes Socrates distinct from others of the same kind, the answer is that it is his matter—and to be "his" matter, the stufflike matter has to be actualized by form, and so form is and must be part of this answer. Bonaventure's insistence on the necessity of both of the principles of form and matter in explaining individuation reveals the limitations of other accounts that identify only one factor as responsible for individuality.

To put the point sharply, Bonaventure denies that the "problem of individuation", understood as the quest for a single principle or cause that explains the individuality of every individual, has a solution. But his denial goes deeper than that. Bonaventure holds that there *could not be* any principle or cause that accounts for the individuality of every individual and that to search for one is a sign of confusion—a conflation of distinct problems, each of which has an answer, into a single confused problem that could not have any answer. There cannot be any "global" or general account of individuation, because individuality is a metaphysically *relative* feature of the world: What it is to be individual depends on the relative position a thing occupies in the series of potencies and their correlative actualizations, how a given parcel of "stuff" has a sufficiently high degree of local organization relative to other stuffs that it may be called "individual".

An analogy will clarify these points. Consider the difference between an absolute theory of space, in which a position in terms of an independent framework can be specified for any or all beings, and a relative theory of space, in which the position of any being depends on the position of all other beings. The relative theory of space allows only a local account of the position of any being; namely, how the given being is related to other beings. There is no independent framework in terms of which the position of all beings could be specified. The general request for the position of a being independent of its relations to other beings makes no sense on a relative theory of space; to demand an account of the position of a being independent of all other beings is simply confused. There is no "absolute" or "global" answer to this question, since the kind of explanation generated by the relative theory of space does not permit the question to be formulated. (Other than as a question receiving the somewhat trivial answer that spatial position exists because God created beings with relative situation, that is.) The lack of an answer to such a question is not an epistemic fact, but a metaphysical one—if the world is such that space is constituted only relatively, then no "global" account of position in terms of an independent framework is possible.

So too with Bonaventure's theory of individuation. The demand for an independent framework of principles or causes in terms of which the individuality of the individual can be explained without reference to other individuals is simply confused; Bonaventure holds a local or "relative" rather than a global or "absolute" theory of individuation, and the question cannot be formulated. (Other than as a question receiving the somewhat trivial answer that individuals exist because God created beings structured by potency and act, that is.) The lack of any answer is not epistemic but metaphysical:

Individuality is constituted by the relative degree of actualization of the potencies of a being. All beings are combinations of potency and act, but the relevance of this fact to the problem of individuation has been obscured by the misleading character of the statement of the problem.

In its general form there can be no solution to the problem of individuation. However, Bonaventure does not dismiss it as a pseudo-problem, because it includes three genuine subproblems, each of which is capable of solution: how to explain the unity of the individual, which is a result of the conjunction of form and matter; how an individual comes to be out of what is nonindividual, which is initially given a local natural explanation but ultimately rests on supernatural agency; and how the individual is distinct from all else and known to be distinct—which is the subject of the next section.

VI. Distinctness and Discernibility

When describing individuality as the result of the intrinsic principles of form and matter, Bonaventure says that "being discrete or being distinct from another is consequent upon this [conjunction of form and matter], and from this there arises number, and so an accidental property consequent upon substance" (*II Sent.*, d. 3, part 1, art. 2, q. 2 resp.). The same point is made somewhat earlier: "it is possible [for matter] to be completed by form with regard to *esse,* by the advent of which there is constituted an individual numerically one by actual and complete unity, from the advent of which there comes about distinctness, and multitude arises in things" (*II Sent.*, d. 3, part 1, art. 1, q. 3, ad 2). Distinctness or discreteness is derived from the unity of the individual. Bonaventure gives us a clue how to interpret this rather cryptic claim in *II Sent.*, d. 3, part 1, art. 2, q. 2, ad 6: "Just as accidental unity unavoidably follows from substantial unity, which is not a principle of indivision but consequent to it, so too number unavoidably follows from substantial diversity. Still, according to the thing and its nature, the distinction is from a substantial principle, not an accidental [principle]."[44]

In Sections IV and V we have seen how the substantial unity of the individual is produced by the intrinsic principles of matter and form. Now it might be thought that 'unity' is an accidental property, falling under the category of Quality. But Bonaventure here draws a distinction: Since 'one' is a transcendental term, like 'truth' and 'good', each of which is on a par with the transcendental divisions of being like potency and act or the categorial division, it may correctly be applied across all the Aristotelian categories. When applied to items in the category of Substance, it denotes the unity of a *per se* being, and in particular cases the individuality of the individual.[45] The substantial unity that is produced by the conjunction of matter and form, then, is the foundation for the distinctness or discreteness of the individual, since in the appropriation of principles the form is or becomes the form of this matter and the matter is or becomes the matter for this form. The form and the matter are individualized through each other and appropriated to one another through their indivision; no other individual could have or possess these principles, since they are unique to their possessor. Therefore, substantial unity entails the distinctness or discreteness of the individual.

Substantial unity also brings in its train accidental unity, and thereby unity in the category of Quantity. The former claim, that substantial unity entails accidental unity, is Bonaventure's way of saying that accidents are individuated by the individual substances that possess them and that they characterize. He chooses this indirect way of stating his claim for two reasons. First, as noted in Section II, accidents by definition cannot be "individuals" in the strict sense. Second, because numerically distinct accidents do not produce any numerical diversity in that in which they are present (*III Sent.*, d. 6, art. 1, q. 1, resp.): "It is plain that those things of which one is predicated of the other are not distinguished from each other in number, although they are formally distinguished. For example, if 'Peter is a musician' were stated, *Peter* and *musician* are not two, although there is a distinction between Peter and his music."[46] (To be 'distinguished in number' is for things to be numerically distinct, capable of being counted.) Accidents are formally distinguished but really identical in that in which they are present. Hence accidents have a kind of unity that is derivative from the unity of the substance in which they are present. The latter claim, that substantial unity thereby entails unity in the category of Quantity, is of special interest, because such unity is the principle of number (or of enumeration). Corporeal substances, which all have physical matter, have this sort of unity. Thus numerical identity and distinctness follows directly from the combination of matter and form. As Bonaventure says, being one and being distinct are derived from the same source.[47]

The individualization of accidents by the substance in which they are present also explains how distinct individuals are discernible. As Bonaventure says in *III Sent.*, d. 10, art. 1, q. 2, resp., "it should be said that, putting aside all accidents and properties (which do not produce individuation but only display it), individuation is from intrinsic principles in that [such principles] constitute one supposit in which the whole *esse* of a thing is stabilized." The distinctness of accidents is a guide to the distinctness of that in which the accidents are present: the accidents "display individuation". Typically, individuals are distinguished by sensing their distinct accidents (as recounted at length in the *Itinerarium mentis ad Deum*), but this does not exclude a grasp of the principles from which such accidental differences flow. As Bonaventure says in *II Sent.*, d. 3, part 1, art. 2, q. 2, ad 5, replying to an objection that his account is unworkable since we could never have knowledge of the principles of matter and form, by the Aristotelian slogan that "sensing is of particulars and understanding of universals":

> It should be said that although sense is only of singulars in a certain way, still, the understanding can be not only of universals but also of singulars. Accordingly, the difference [between sense and intellect] should not be understood with precision. This is clear, since only the intellect comprehends the intrinsic principles of Peter and of Plato. Putting aside all accidents, [the intellect] bespeaks them to be discrete and distinct.[48]

The understanding can grasp the intrinsic principles of an individual, that is, the understanding can directly grasp the individuality of the individual. The mechanics of how the understanding is capable of so doing are extremely complex, but we need not enter on them here; it is sufficient to note that for Bonaventure the discernibility of individuals is due to their intrinsic individuality.

VII. Conclusion

Bonaventure's insight into the dependence of questions about individuation on the more basic metaphysical division of being into potency and act gives his answer a depth that puts it far beyond other accounts of individuation and reveals their limitations. Whether in the last analysis Bonaventure's account of individuation is satisfactory is another issue altogether. The crucial theological premises are not acceptable, or no longer as accepted as they once were, and it is not clear how much of his account could survive their rejection. Quite independent of theology, the medieval understanding of modality as primarily a feature of subjects as well as the view that individuals are composites of form and matter are not in currency any longer. Bonaventure's account of individuation is so entwined in its theological and Aristotelian roots that it would be difficult, if not impossible, to produce a modernized version of his theory that retained any fidelity in details. However, the philosophical merit of Bonaventure's account of individuation does not reside solely in a wholesale translation into modern jargon. Neither is it only of antiquarian interest. Its real merit lies in the penetrating insights Bonaventure offers into how the traditional "problem of individuation" involves and obscures more basic philosophical questions, and his suggestion that an account of a fundamentally different kind should be offered. The central intuition Bonaventure has to offer is that the world is composed of various kinds of "stuffs" that occasionally have a sufficiently high degree of local organization such that some parcel of stuff can be called "individual".

We may not accept his analysis, but the sophistication and complexity with which he develops this intuition challenge alternative medieval and modern approaches alike. And that is, perhaps, Bonaventure's true philosophical legacy.

Notes

1. References to Bonaventure, unless stated otherwise, are taken from *Sanctae Bonaventurae opera omnia,* edita studio et cura pp. Colegii S. Bonaventurae; 10 vols. (Florence: Ad Claras Aquas (Quaracchi), ex typographia Colegii SS. Bonaventurae, (1882–1902), and are largely drawn from his *Commentaria in quatuor libros Sententiarum Magistri Petri Lombardi* (hereafter abbreviated as *Sent.*) in vols. 1–4 of this work. All translations are my own; in citations of the Latin text, the punctuation of the original has been retained. References to the latter are given in standard form: book, distinction, part (if any), article, question, section of the question.

2. In *III Sent.*, d. 5, art. 2, q. 2, resp., Bonaventure says that an individual is that which is "undivided in itself and distinct from others" (*in se indivisum et ab aliis distinctum*). Somewhat later, in *III Sent.*, d. 10, art. 1, q. 3, resp., he says that something may be called 'individual' in two ways: as that which is "undivided in itself" (*indivisum in se*), and as that which is "divided from others and subsists *in se* and *per se*" (*ab aliis divisum et subsistit in se et per se*). Three points should be noted. First, since Bonaventure's concern in the latter question is to distinguish the senses in which it can be said that Christ, as man, is an individual, it seems reasonable to take these two "ways" in which something can be called "individual" as component elements of a single sense rather than as two distinct senses associated with a single word, which would render 'individual' ambiguous; this interpretation may be supported by Bonaventure's claim, discussed in Section VI, that being distinct or divided from others is consequent upon being undivided. Second, I propose to treat the formulations 'distinct from others' and 'divided from others' as equivalent; the choice of words is otherwise similar, and there is no support in the texts for a distinction between 'distinct' and 'divided'. Third, it is not clear whether Bonaventure intended the characterization "subsists *in se* and *per se*" to be an additional factor or to be an explanation of 'divided from others'; the former seems to me the more plausible view, since this characterization alone allows Bonaventure to maintain that the human nature of Christ is not an individual (since it subsists through the uncreated Word and not in and through itself).

3. Duns Scotus, *Ordinatio* II, d. 3, part 1, q. 2, n. 48, in vol. 7 of *Opera omnia,* studio et cura Commissionis Scotisticae (ad fidem codicum edita), praeside P. Carolo Balić (Vatican City: Typis Polyglottis Vaticanis, 1950–); see also A. Wolter's contribution to this volume. Note that this characterization presupposes rather than explains the "division", and clearly does not exclude forms of division into nonsubjective parts: Socrates's foot is a genuine part of him, but not a subjective part. It seems clear that "inability to be divided into subjective parts" is the medieval cor-

relate to our contemporary notion of "uninstantiability", with the added virtue that it is not taken as primitive but rather as a consequence of more fundamental metaphysical characteristics.

4. The term 'subsist' (*subsistere*) carries much more philosophical and theological baggage than this. The philosophical baggage largely stems from the remarks of Boethius in *Contra Eutychen*, III, 44–50, where he says that "that which does not require accidents in order that it might be 'subsists' . . . individuals also subsist" (*The Consolation of Philosophy and the Theological Tractates*, edited and translated by E. K. Rand and revised by H. F. Stewart, revised by S. J. Tester, Loeb Classical Library, (Cambridge, MA: Harvard University Press; and London: Heinemann, 1978), 2nd printing. The individual 'supports' accidents, but does not require them. Bonaventure seems to incorporate this sense in the additional clause that the being is *per se*. The theological baggage derives from the attempt to find Latin equivalents for the Greek trinitarian vocabulary of the Church Fathers and early Councils; however, since Bonaventure's characterization is intended to cover the case of creatures as well, we shall not pursue its theological import here. This interpretation is at best a first approximation; it will be modified in Sections IV and V with the discussion of the relation between the medieval *ens in potentia* and possible beings.

5. There are special theological difficulties. Interpreted strictly, it seems to entail that only God is a *per se* being, since only God literally requires nothing else to be (a conclusion later explicitly drawn by Spinoza); furthermore, each creature is created or sustained by God, which suggests a kind of existential dependence, and each creature is composite, which suggests the need for an external agent to combine its constituent elements. There are also philosophical difficulties: Even if primary substances can be loosely considered "independent" entities, a being such as Socrates, who is at least in part a corporeal substance, must have some color, some weight, some position, and the like, which suggests some kind of "dependence" of a substance upon its accidents.

6. This characterization of singularity derives from Porphyry by way of Boethius: see Boethius's translation of Porphyry's *Isagoge*, ed. L. Minio-Paluello in the series *Aristoteles latinus* I. 6–7, (Paris: Desclée de Brouwer, 1966), p. 7. However, neither Porphyry nor Boethius draws a strict distinction between individuality and singularity—see Jorge J. E. Gracia's discussion of the legacy of the early Middle Ages in this volume. Bonaventure cites this characterization in *III Sent.*, d. 5, art. 2, q. 2, resp., explicitly as a definition of singularity. In *III Sent.*, d. 10, art. 1, q. 2, resp., he says that something may be loosely called "individual" if it is said of only one, although in this sense even an accident may be called "individual" (ruled out by the second criterion of individuality); such a usage is obviously transferred to the level of reality from the linguistic level where it strictly belongs. It should be noted that in Porphyry and Boethius, as indeed in Bonaventure, the characterization is given as "what is predicated of only one", but Bonaventure is clear that predicability is at issue, not actual predication: in *III Sent.*, d. 2, art. 2, q. 2, resp., he posits the case that there is only one man, but even then the term 'man' would not thereby be singular, since it is a matter of what a term is 'apt' to be predicated of, i.e., its predicability.

7. Bonaventure does not in general distinguish between the principle of multiplication of individuals within a species and the problem of individuation, other than in the special case of the divine; since everything else falls into a species, there is no pressing need to distinguish sharply the two questions.

8. Reading *individualitatem* for *individuitatem* in the text.

9. Each argument assumes something a defender of accidental individuation might not be prepared to grant. Bonaventure supports the antecedent of the first argument by Aristotle's dictum in the *Categories* that "no accident exists except in an individual substance", but this need not entail that accidents essentially depend on the individuality of the substance—only that accidents cannot exist unless an individual substance exists, which is compatible with the claim that the inherence of the accident in the species brings about the individual, that is, that the individuality of the substance depends on accidents. The second argument assumes that the numerical identity of distinct accidents in an individual prevents any accident from being the cause of the individuality of the substance, which certainly need not be the case. For example, someone might hold that one particular accident causes the individuality of the substance, which then is responsible for the numerical identity of all other accidents.

10. *II Sent.*, d. 3 part 1, art. 2, q. 2, resp. (vol. 2, p. 160a–b): "Discretio autem individualis duo dicit, scilicet individuationem et consequenter distinctionem. Individuatio autem est ex principiorum indivisione et appropriatione; ipsa enim rei principia, dum coniunguntur, invicem se appropriant et faciunt individuum. Sed ad hoc consequitur esse discretum sive esse distinctum ab alio, et surgit ex hoc numerus, et ita accidentalis proprietas, consequens ad substantiam.—Et sic individualis discretio dicit aliquid accidentale, et aliquid substantiale. . . . Dicendum igitur, quod quemadmodum individualis discretio ex exsistentia formae naturalis in materia."

11. *II Sent.*, d. 3, part 1, art. 2, q. 3, resp. (vol. 2, pp. 109b–110a): "Ideo est tertia positio satis planior, quod individuatio consurgit ex actuali coniunctione materiae cum forma, ex qua coniunctione unum sibi appropriat alterum; sicut patet, cum impressio vel expressio fit multorum sigillorum in cera, quae prius est una, nec sigilla plurificari possunt sine cera, nec cera numeratur nisi quia fiunt in ea diversa sigilla. Si tamen quaeras, a quo veniat principaliter; dicendum, quod individuum est hoc aliquid. Quod sit hoc, principalius habet a materia, ratione cuius forma habet positionem in loco et tempore. Quod sit aliquid, habet a forma. Individuum enim habet esse, habet etiam exsistere. Exsistere dat materia formae, sed essendi actum dat forma materiae—Individuatio igitur in creaturis consurgit ex duplici principio." Bonaventure apparently considered this passage to be his most complete statement about individuation; he later refers to it as providing necessary details about individuation, e.g., in *III Sent.*, d. 10, art. 1, q. 2 (where the theory is applied to the case of Christ's individuality).

12. Technically it is the mirror image in relief of the shape embossed on the signet ring, but this is a needless complication for our purposes; nothing hangs on this point.

13. *II Sent.*, d. 3, part 1, art. 1, q. 1, resp. (vol. 2, p. 91a): "Non video causam nec rationem quomodo defendi potest quin substantia angeli sit composita ex diversis naturis, et essentia omnis creaturae per se entis; et si composita ex diversis naturis, illae duae naturae se habent per modum actualis et possibilis, et ita materiae et formae."

14. *II Sent.*, d. 3, part 1, art. 1, q. 2, resp. (vol. 2, p. 97b): "Metaphysicus considerat naturam omnis creaturae, et maxime substantiae per se entis, in qua est considerare et actum essendi, et hunc dat forma; et stabilitatem per se exsistendi, et hanc dat et praestat illud cui innititur forma, hoc est materia."

15. *II Sent.*, d. 17, art. 1, q. 2, resp. (vol. 2, pp. 414b–415a): "Anima rationalis, cum sit hoc aliquid et per se nata subsistere et agere et pati, movere et moveri, quod habet intra se fundamentum suae exsistentiae: et principium materiale a quo habet exsistere, et formale a quo habet esse."

16. The passages cited are representative; many such are scattered throughout Bonaventure's works. Note that potency and act need not be identified with matter and form, as P. Robert maintained in *Hylémorphisme et devenir chez saint Bonaventure* (Montreal: Librarie St. Françoise, 1936), pp. 28–45 and pp. 143–148, since there may well be potency and act that are not assimilated to matter and form (e.g., the species containing the genus potentially). Although Bonaventure's analysis of compositeness in created beings, as well as his statement and defense of hylomorphism, are more complex than is indicated here, none of the complexity affects the fundamental alignment of act and potency with form and matter. Some details will be considered in Section V. The 'matter' present in the rational soul is spiritual matter, not corporeal matter, as will be made clear later.

17. The qualification 'in the case of creatures' is important: In God, *esse* is an essential feature and is not conferred by any form. More work needs to be done toward understanding Bonaventure's complex doctrines of *esse* and *exsistere*. The classic modern study is that of J. Bittremieux, "Distinctio inter essentiam et esse apud S. Bonaventuram", *Ephemerides Theologicae Lovanienses* 14 (1937): 302–307. For developments see especially G. Klubertanz, "*Esse* and *Exsistere* in St. Bonaventure", *Mediaeval Studies* 8 (1946): 169–188; L. de Mercin, "Notes sur le probléme de l'étre selon saint Bonaventure," *Études Franciscaines,* new series, 11 (1961): 2–16; C. Bigi, "La struttura dell'essere secondo s. Bonaventura", *Collectanea Franciscana* 32 (1962): 209–229; J. F. Quinn, *The Historical Constitution of St. Bonaventure's Philosophy,* (Toronto: Pontifical Institute of Mediaeval Studies, 1973), in particular Ch. 2.

18. Bonaventure does not clearly distinguish two interpretations of the phrase 'that which is informed': (1) *esse* is the actuality given by the form to the subject or substrate in which the form inheres; (2) *esse* is the actuality given by the form to the entire composite of matter and form. The same ambiguity affects his understanding of *actum essendi.* The distinction of the form of the whole and the form of the part discussed later does not clarify the ambiguity. This point is overlooked by Corrado da

Altari in "Individuo e principio di individuazione in S. Bonaventura," *Studi Frances-cani* 58 (1961): 264–286.

19. The two cases are not so disparate as might at first seem. The view that possible existence is concrete existence in a possible world is alien to the medieval framework of potency and act; an *ens in potentia* need not possess all of the features required for concrete existence—it may be what is sometimes called an "incomplete" entity. Indeed, Bonaventure himself talks of "completive" forms (*formae completi-vae*), that is, forms whose *esse* renders something capable of concrete existence, and at times he underscores this point by saying that forms that are not completive only offer "incomplete" *esse*. Furthermore, in *II Sent.*, d. 12, art. 1, q. 1, ad 6, Bon-aventure says that an *ens in potentia* is "not entirely something and not entirely noth-ing, but a medium between non-being and actual being."

20. *II Sent.*, d. 3, part 1, art. 1, q. 3, resp. (vol. 2, p. 100b): "Sed si habet unitatem, unitatem homogeneitatis habet. Haec autem unitas simul manet in diversis, sicut patet: si de eodem auro fiant multa vasa, illa sunt de eodem auro per homoge-neitatem. Sed aurum quod est in uno differt ab auro quod est in alio, adeo ut non sint unum per continuitatem. Si igitur materia non est una actuali simplicitate, ut angelus, nec continuitate, ut mons vel auri frustrum, sed sola homogeneitate, et haec non tol-litur per adventum formarum, ita est materia una sub omnibus formis, sicut omnibus formis abstractis. Sed abstractis omnibus formis, nulla est distinctio in materia; immo intelligitur ut simpliciter una. Nunc igitur materia est in omnibus materiatis numero una, quia est ens omnino in potentia."

21. *II Sent.*, d. 3, part 1, art. 1, q. 3, ad 6 (vol. 2, p. 101b): "Si quis enim vult unitatem materiae intelligere, oportet ab unitate individuali animum abstrahere et su-per actum imaginationis conscendere et omnino ens in potentia per privationem cog-itare, et sic poterit aliqualiter capere. Quamdiu enim materia ut moles extensa cogitatur, ad unitatem essentiae consideratam nullo modo pertingitur." To think of matter "by privation" is only one of the two ways of knowing matter, as Bonaventure explains in *II Sent.*, d. 3 pars. 1, art. 1, q. 1, resp.: "Matter is knowable in a twofold way, namely by privation and by analogy. Knowledge by privation is firstly by re-moving the form, thence removing the [disposition]* to the form, and considering that essence bare in itself and, as it were, intelligible only in a dark way. Knowledge by analogy is by a consimilar disposition (*habitudinem*); the disposition of matter is by potency, and so this knowledge is by the comparison of matter to form by the medi-ating potency." [*Reading *dispositionem* with codices bb, cc, and 1, rather than *dis-ponens* with the text.]

22. *II Sent.*, d. 12, art. 1, q. 3, resp. (vol. 2, p. 300a): "Materia illa producta est sub aliqua forma, sed illa non erat forma completa nec dans materiae esse com-pletum, et ideo non sic formabat quin adhuc materia diceretur informis; nec appetitum materiae adeo finiebat quin materia adhuc alias formas appeteret. Et ideo dispositio erat ad formas ulteriores, non completa perfectio. Et quoniam ad multas formas ma-teria informis appetitum et inclinationem habebat, ideo, quamvis illa forma non haberet in se naturas diversas, tamen materia in diversis suis partibus quandam di-

versitatem habebat—non ex diversis actibus completis, sed magis ex appetibus ad diversa—et ideo permixta dicitur et confusa." See also Bonaventure's remarks in *II Sent.*, d. 3, part 1, art. 1, q. 2, ad 4: "When it is claimed that extension is from matter, it should not be understood that it is from matter according to its essence, but according to its *esse*, insofar as it sustains a corporeal form which is not apt to be in matter unless with extension, although in itself [matter] consists in a simple essence."

23. *II Sent.*, d. 12, art. 1, q. 3, ad 5 (vol. 2, p. 301a–b): "Materia illa non sic erat corporea quod esset completa in genere corporum, sed sic habebat extensionem et corporeitatem, quia* non habebat perfectam formae actualitatem, sicut praedictum est prius." [*Reading *quia* for *quod* in the text.]

24. *II Sent.*, d. 12, art. 2, q. 3, resp. (vol. 2, p. 306a): "Dicendum quod cum materia illa esset moles habens extensionem, et caelum empyreum haberet ambiens, quod ipsa in loco erat, et cum esset substantia corpulenta, locum replebat. Rursus, cum in partibus distinctionem quandam haberet secundum subtilitatem et grossitatem, sed semiplenam, positiones secundum sursum et deorsum quodammodo sed imperfecte habebat."

25. The Aristotelian volumetric definition of 'place' as "the innermost unmoving boundary which contains" a substance (*Physics* IV, 4 212a20) entails that spatial location, as an accident of individual substances, is not defined by the extended mass that is the initial state of corporeal substance, although Bonaventure's comments about restricted directionality suggest that position may be defined.

26. Bonaventure is not completely consistent, but it seems plausible that he took the initial form that produces corporeal matter to be light (*lux*) rather than the traditional, and unanalyzeable, "form of corporeity" (*forma corporeitatis*). The remark in *II Sent.*, d. 12, art. 1, q. 3, ad 5, cited earlier, is one of the few places he mentions corporeity, and here it is specifically a consequence of the form rather than the form itself. Further, Bonaventure's discussion in *II Sent.*, d. 12, art. 2, q. 2, is inconclusive; there Bonaventure maintains that matter was produced before any of the days of creation in the order of nature, and that the creation of the earth preceded the creation of light. But the "order of nature" is a nontemporal ordering of logical priority, and it is consistent to suppose that matter is logically prior to its informing, while temporally simultaneous with it. On the positive side, in *II Sent.*, d. 3, part 1, art. 1, q. 2, ad 5, Bonaventure holds that matter is called 'dark' (*tenebra*) by the privation of its form, "which form is light (*lumen*)". In *II Sent.*, d. 13, art. 2, q. 2, resp., he supports the position that "light is the substantial form of all bodies", and in ad 5 he notes that "the form of light, although it is posited in the same body with other forms, is not posited as an imperfect disposition that is apt to be perfected by a later form, but rather it is posited as a form and nature that goes along with every other corporeal form, giving [to such a corporeal form] an efficiency in acting"—a description that would explain how corporeal matter can be homogeneously one in all corporeal bodies and yet give *exsistere* through spatio-temporal location to corporeal beings.

27. The elemental forms are logically posterior to corporeal matter, although it is not clear that their informing corporeal matter is a distinct temporal stage. In *II Sent.*, d. 12, art. 1, q. 3, ad 3, Bonaventure says: "as for when it is objected that the elemental forms are the first in corporeal matter, it should be said that this is true as regards forms that give complete *esse* to matter, but that [initial] form which unformed (*informis*) matter had did not give complete *esse* to it, and so preceded or could precede simple forms as well as composite forms (which attribute complete *esse* to [matter])." It is not clear whether the elemental forms are required for *exsistere,* or whether the initial form that produces corporeal matter is sufficient.

28. Whether the latter is reducible to the former or is a supervenient form is a difficult question. In *II Sent.*, d. 18, art. 1, q. 3, resp., Bonaventure says that the former "mediates" or "acts as a medium" for the latter, which suggests genuine supervenience; in *III Sent.*, d. 6, art. 2, q. 1, resp., he says "there is a certain union in which there is an alteration of each unifiable [factor] and the production of a third nature, and this is because there is here an incompatibility and no excelling predominance [of either factor], as the elements are united to constitute mixed bodies". The same holds true for the relation of mixed forms to complex forms. In *II Sent.*, d. 15, art. 1, q. 2, Bonaventure takes up the production of organic bodies, but the discussion is inconclusive; he says that the body of an animal "exists (*constans*) from the four elements". A satisfactory answer to the question would depend on a more exact analysis of the sense in which Bonaventure can be said to endorse what has come to be known as the doctrine of the "plurality of forms"; that is, to maintain that there may exist distinct substantial forms simultaneously within the individual.

29. Bonaventure discusses *rationes seminales* at length in *II Sent.*, d. 7, part 2, art. 2, q. 1, the source of the rose example (resp.). The 'virtual containment' described in the text abbreviates Bonaventure's complex and subtle doctrine (*ibid.*): Bonaventure is careful to point out that the form does not, properly speaking, come from the natural agent or from the essence of the matter in which the *ratio seminalis* is found. Rather, *rationes seminales* are created as active potencies inhering in matter (the technical term is that they are 'concreated'), functioning as the principles "in which, from which, and by which" natural agents may bring about new composites of matter and form. The embryo example is set forth in *II Sent.*, d. 12, art. 1, q. 3, resp.

30. *II Sent.*, d. 18, art. 1, q. 3, resp. (vol. 2, p. 441a–b): "Necesse est ponere universales formas propter cognitionem et praedicationis univocationem. Si igitur non est integra cognitio nisi totum esse rei cognoscatur, et non est cognitio nisi per formam, necesse est aliquam formam esse quae complectatur totum esse. Hanc autem dicimus essentiam, et haec est universalis forma, ut dicit Avicenna. (Dicit enim quod essentia nihil aliud est quam quidditas rei universalis.) Similiter, non est vera univocatio nisi quando aliqua in ina forma communi realiter assimilantur, quae de ipsis essentialiter praedicatur. Forma autem in qua plura assimilantur non potest esse nisi forma universalis, quae vero essentialiter praedicatur de illis non potest esse nisi forma totum complectens. Forma igitur universalis non est aliud quam forma totius, quae, cum de se nata sit esse in multis, universalis est."

31. Bonaventure makes the same point in his *Collationes in Hexaemeron*, col. 4, n. 9: "It is plain that two men are similar to each other [in something], but a man and an ass are not; thus the likeness must be grounded and stabilized in some stable form, and not [a form] which is in another since that would be particular—hence in some universal [form]." The passage continues in the Delorme edition as follows: "Note that the form by which one man agrees with another is a real agreement (*convenientia*) stabilized in a universal form" [Collationes in Hexaemeron et Bonaventuriana quaedam selecta, ad fidem codicum mss. ed. F. M. Delorme, *Bibliotheca franciscana scholastica medii aevii,* vol. 7; (Florence: Ad Claras Aquas (Quaracchi), 1934), p. 52].

32. *II Sent.*, d. 18, art. 1, q. 3, resp. (vol. 2, p. 441a): "Universale forma est. Sed non quaelibet forma proprie universale est; est enim forma partis et forma totius, et universale non est forma partis sed forma totius. Anima non dicitur esse universale respectu unius hominis, sed homo. Illam autem dicunt esse formam totius quae quidem dat esse toti, et haec dicitur essentia rei quia totum esse complectitur, and hanc formam considerat metaphysicus. Formam vero partis, quae in genere non habet esse nisi per reductionem, non est dicere proprie universalem; potest tamen aliquo modo dici universalis per radicatione, cum illa est indifferens ad multa, quae possunt fieri ex ipsa, sicut causa dicitur esse universalis quia potest in multa."

33. *III Sent.*, d. 2, art. 2, q. 3, resp. (vol. 2, p. 48b): "Dicendum quod species dicit formam—et non quaecumque, sed formam totius, hoc est formam complectentem totum esse. Iuxta quod dicit Boethius quod 'species est totum esse individuorum', et Avicenna et alii etiam philosophi in hoc concordant. Forma ergo specifica communis dupliciter potest intelligi: aut secundum praedicationem aut secundum constitutionem. Secundum praedicationem 'homo' dicit formam communem Petro et Paulo. Secundum constitutioinem 'homo' dicit formam quae respicit animam et corpus, et quae resultat ex coniunctione animae cum corpore. Anima enim et corpus concurrunt ad unam essentiam constituendam. Et hinc est quod constitutus ex anima et corpore habet unam formam specificam, communem sibi et aliis sic constitutis per praedicationem; communem nihilominus partibus constituentibus per quandam informationem et completionem."

34. Although the terminology of "form of the whole" and "form of the part" is common to all scholastics, Bonaventure is explicit that in Socrates the form of the part is his individual soul; the common view held that in Socrates the form of the part is his humanity. For Bonaventure, 'humanity' is simply an abstract denomination of "man", not corresponding to any distinct metaphysical entity.

35. The term translated 'particularized' is *particularizatur,* which I take as equivalent to 'individualized'. Bonaventure does not seem to distinguish between them.

36. *II Sent.*, d. 18, art. 1, q. 3, resp. (vol. 2, p. 441b): "Particularizatur autem non per additionem ulterioris formae, sed per coniunctionem sui cum materia; ex qua coniunctione, materia appropriat sibi formam, et forma materiam, sicut dictum est supra. Et quia nunquam est forma haec separata a materia, nunquam est forma uni-

versalis sine particulari. Quamvis autem unum non sit sine altero, differt tamen unum ab altero. Quamvis enim albedo non possit esse sine corpore, differt tamen a corpore. Unde inseparabilitas non ponit identitatem omnimodam.''

37. God's initial creation, then, must have been to establish the existence of a new metaphysical feature of being, namely potency. (It is ''new'' since there is no potency in God, only act.) God's next creation was to establish the relation between potency and act. It is only at this point that God could create matter as a metaphysically basic form of potency, namely, passive potency for any actualization, and so establish the metaphysical principles of all created being. Note that by 'created being' I do not mean only the beings actually created by God, but such possible beings as Socrates's twin brother. Once these principles are in place, then the more ordinary process of creating actual beings structured by these principles can occur. Of course, these ''stages'' are logical rather than temporal; to say that God creates ex nihilo is simply to maintain that all these stages occur simultaneously, though some are logically prior to others.

38. By a ''local'' explanation of individuation I mean an explanation of the individuality of an individual in terms of proximate principles or causes of that individuality. These principles or causes may also require individuation. A ''global'' explanation of individuality identifies principles or causes (either proximate or remote) that do *not* require individuation. Global explanations entail local explanations, but the converse does not hold.

39. This is true for all living creatures except man, whose soul is directly created by God rather than educed from a *ratio seminalis* in the way in which, say, the soul of Brunellus the Ass is virtually contained in the *ratio seminalis;* see *II Sent.*, d. 19, art. 1, q. 2, ad 3 (Bonaventure discusses nonrational animate creatures in *II Sent.*, d. 15, art. 1, q. 1). Aside from recognizing the nobility of man, this provides a philosophical basis for distinguishing the mortal souls of irrational creatures and the immortal souls of rational creatures: The former have souls that are only the actualization of the determinate matter of the animal's body, and so perish with the dissolution of the body, but the latter have souls that are not as closely tied to matter, being directly created by God, and so are capable of having some act that is not the act of any bodily organ which can therefore survive bodily dissolution. (The nonbodily ''act'' in question is the act of understanding, and the powers of the rational soul, as distinguished from the vegetative or nutritive soul, in particular.) I will simply ignore this theological complication, and treat Socrates and Brunellus in the same fashion.

40. Note that this claim depends on the proviso expressed in the preceding note, since it entails that the difference of souls is a corollary of the difference of the matter that they actualize. This is true for nonrational animate creatures, though not for humans. Note also that, while this claim is true of the relation between the species and the individual, it may also be applied to the relation between the genus and the species in like manner: the actualization of the species also counts as the determinate actualization of the genus. The genus and the species do differ formally, so the converse need not hold for a particular species.

41. In *II Sent.*, d. 15, art. 1, q. 2, ad 4, Bonaventure writes that "the later and more posterior the form, the more noble it is, for those [composites] that are anterior to it are material with respect to the posterior" (*anteriora sunt materialia respectu posteriorum*).

42. Note that individuality cannot derive from the spatial location of the composite or of the matter itself, for, as noted previously, 'place' is defined only relative to an existent individual according to Aristotelian doctrine. The consequences of this doctrine for Bonaventure's theory will be explored in the rest of this section.

43. So stated, there seems to be an obvious counterexample: nonactual possible individuals, such as Socrates's merely possible twin brother. But it is not clear that this is a genuine counterexample, for even merely possible beings are described as having some degree of relative actualization of material potencies. Socrates's merely possible twin brother *would be* an actuality of the potencies latent in given bones, flesh, and so on, and his individuality may be explained in terms of such. This example shows that, strictly speaking, real existence is not required for individuality. Alternatively, Bonaventure might deny that there are any merely possible individuals; his discussion of the status of that which God conceives before creation suggests this.

44. *II Sent.*, d. 3, part 1, art. 2, q. 2, ad 6 (vol. 2, p. 107b): "Dicendum quod sicut unitatem substantialem consequitur unitas accidentalis inseparabiliter, quae non est principium indivisionis sed consequens ad illam, sic diversitatem substantialem consequitur numerus inseparabiliter. Tamen secundum rem et naturam distinctio illa est a substantiali principio, non accidentali."

45. The qualification "in particular cases" is important, since nonindividuals such as species and genera also have unity and can be described as beings per se.

46. *III Sent.*, d. 6, art. 1, q. 1, resp. (vol. 2, p. 149b): "Planum enim est quod illa quorum unum de altero praedicatur invicem non numerantur, quamvis formaliter distinguantur. Utpote si dicatur 'Petrus est musicus', musicus et Petrus non sunt duo, quamvis inter Petrum et [musicam]* suam sit distinctio." [*The text reads *musicum,* which makes no sense; given the context, it is likely a corruption of *musicam.*]

47. In *II Sent.*, d. 18, art. 2, q. 1, resp., Bonaventure explicitly grants arguments proving that souls are diverse; the third argument is "ab eodem esse et esse unum sive esse distinctum; sed unumquodque habet esse a sua perfectione: ergo distinctionem."

48. *II Sent.*, d. 3, part 1, art. 2, q. 2, ad 5 (vol. 2, p. 107b): "Dicendum quod etsi sensus solummodo sit singularium, intellectus tamen potest esse non solum universalium sed etiam singularium. Unde non est intelligenda illa differentia cum praecisione. Et hoc patet quia solus intellectus comprehendit intrinseca principia Petri et Platonis. Circumscriptis omnibus accidentibus, dicit eos esse discretos et distinctos." To 'understand with precision' is a technical phrase, meaning that the understanding in question is taken to exclude the addition of further characteristics. Here, Bonaventure is making the point that to say, e.g., that understanding is of universals does not positively exclude that it may be of singulars as well.

8

THOMAS AQUINAS
(B. CA. 1225; D. 1274)

JOSEPH OWENS

I

Individuation is a topic encountered frequently by St. Thomas Aquinas in the course of his varied writings. Yet it is not made the express subject of any of his uncontestedly authentic works. It is dealt with as a main item in two doubtfully authentic treatises, the *De principio individuationis* and the *De natura materiae*.[1] But in the undoubtedly genuine writings it is given sustained consideration only in the commentary on Boethius's *De trinitate,* on the occasion of dealing with the Boethian problem of numerical differentiation by accidents.[2] It is met with quite frequently in short passages in the course of the *Scriptum* on the *Sentences* of Peter Lombard and in scattered texts here and there in the rest of the Thomistic corpus. The fact remains, however, that individuation is treated in these genuine works only on the occasion of some other topic. It is not discussed broadly as a theme just in its own right. The result is that the topic as a whole comes into focus only after comprehensive study of the texts and with the expenditure of perhaps unexpected effort on the part of the reader.

The background against which Aquinas discusses individuation is extensive but clear. It is partly logical, namely, in the Porphyrian tree in which the predicates descend from the most universal down to the most specific in relation to the individual subject of which they are asserted or denied. It is partly in the realm of natural philosophy, in which the substantial form is received into matter and multiplied numerically by that reception. It is also metaphysical, insofar as individuation means the unity of a thing in itself and thereby its differentiation from others, for unity is a transcendental property that follows upon being. In all three phases of the background, Aristotle looms large in his logic, natural philosophy, and metaphysics. But development considerably beyond Aristotle is to be expected in Aquinas, mainly on account of the intervening centuries of Islamic and Christian philosophical speculation.

There are difficulties in that background concerning the problems of individuation. In the Porphyrian tree, being seems placed both at the top and at the bottom. With the Aristotelian explanation, the individual Socrates or Callias is seen first. Then the narrower specific natures are observed, and in rising scale the widest predicates of all are finally reached. Being is the most universal of all these, with unity either accompanying it or following upon it.[3] But with Aquinas the existential actuality of being is what is encountered in absolute fashion in any observed thing.[4] The existence of the thing is immediately known through an operation of the mind that may technically be termed "judgment", in which a thing is immediately seen to exist. The thing is thereby immediately known as a being, for the existential actuality is what constitutes it a being either in reality or in the mind.[5] The result is that being is directly attained in a highly individualized manner through judgment, yet is conceptualized as the widest of all universal objects. As directly attained through the synthesizing act of judgment, it is forging all the varied elements of the thing into a unit.[6] It is thereby making them what we understand to be an individual.

A little reflection will show at once what this existential synthesizing effects. In the accidental order it makes into a single unit a human person and the qualities of tallness and musical accomplishment. They become one real existent; namely, the tall musician. There is no reason in human nature as an essence why that particular person should be a musician, or be tall. Human nature is found in other persons without those qualities. There is no essential bond uniting them. The bond is existential, insofar as they are brought together by real existence in the one person. Correspondingly there is no reason in the essence of a person why his or her form (the soul) should be actuating the particular matter of which the body is constituted at the moment. Different matter keeps coming and going with the anabolism and catabolism of nutrition, yet the soul remains the same. There is no essential reason, either in the form or the matter, why this particular form should be in this particular matter at the given instant. The reason is existential. The two are united in the existence they are actually enjoying at the time. The existence makes them a unit.

This unifying feature of existence becomes even more striking when existence itself is what subsists, that is, in God. From the existence that comes and goes in sensible things, existence that is accidental even though it is the basic actuality of those existents, one can reason to existence that is a nature.[7] Where existence is regarded as a nature, the reasoning of Parmenides applies.

It contains and unites everything within its own unity. It is the existence of all things, and all things have their primary existence in it.[8] It necessarily individualizes itself. Subsistent existence is its own individuation.[9]

This unifying and individuating feature follows upon existence wherever it is shared. It is truly a transcendental property. In one place Aquinas notes that unity, unlike the other transcendental properties of being, may follow upon essence as well as upon existence.[10] But with essence the one instance given for it is primary matter that is pure potentiality. Primary matter cannot exist as such. There is no question here of an existent. There is merely lack of any actuality that could give rise to distinction in primary matter conceived just in itself. No positive unity is involved. Unity has a negative feature, namely, lack of division. The negative feature can be present where nothing formally positive is there, as holds in the case of primary matter. But as far as the unifying feature of existential actuality is concerned, unity follows upon being as a genuine transcendental property, in spite of the phase in which it differs from the status of the other transcendental aspects. This individuating function of existence may be expressed tersely: "For everything in accordance with the way it has existence has unity and individuation."[11] Whether as subsistent in God or as accidental in creatures, existence is, in the order of being, the basic "cause of individuation". Aquinas can repeatedly insist that existence is what makes one thing differ from another: "As existents, however, they differ, for a horse's existence is not a man's, and this man's existence is not that man's."[12] In the language of the *Liber de causis,* God's individuation is his own pure goodness.[13] In all other things their existential actuality is the basic synthesis that makes each a unit in itself and renders it distinct from all others.

The notion of an individual that emerges from these texts is the one regularly referred to by Aquinas; namely, that of an actual existent divided off from others but undivided in itself. It is expressed clearly in his early work, the *Scriptum* on the *Sentences* of Peter Lombard: "two features belong to the notion of an individual, namely that it be actually existent either in itself or in something else; and that it be divided from other things that are or can be in the same species, existing undivided in itself."[14] Those two features, existence as a unit in itself and its division from all other things, remain the hallmark of individuality throughout the writings of Aquinas. But existence itself is the actuality that brings this about. Existence can accordingly be called the basic 'cause of individuality' in his philosophical thinking.[15]

II

Yet there are complications in the notion that existence is the primary cause of individuation in the real world. Existence just in virtue of its own notion cannot give rise to any diversity.[16] Plurality of beings requires grounding in natures other than that of being. To impart existence outside its own self, subsistent existence has to produce it as the existence of something else. Existence is God's nature, and his action follows upon it. Existence is accordingly his proper or characteristic effect, and everything that proceeds from him does so under that aspect of existence. But precisely "in giving being he produces that which receives the being."[17] Only as the existence of something other than itself can existence be at all imparted. The result is that the new existential actuality gives being to the nature that determines and limits it. Any existential actuality other than subsistent existence necessarily involves its own limitation. But this limiting nature requires no prior actuality to exercise that function. It brings about the limitation and determination only in its role as potentiality.[18]

As in Michelangelo's superb fresco in the Sistine Chapel, the finger tip of the Creator reaches out to the creature at a single point only. From that one point the creature comes into being in its full panoply. Its existence is basic to it, yet it remains really other than the existence that actuates it. In the real otherness it has its own essential meaning that is different from the nature of its cause. But this makes its essence or nature the cause of its distinction from subsistent existence. In the distinctive form that determines and characterizes the finite nature, then, should not one look for the cause of its otherness and thereby the real cause of its individuation?

This consideration introduces a new and important viewpoint for the problem of individuation. Individuation is brought about by something that functions only in a potential, not actual, manner. Within a finite essence, the form exercises an actual role in regard to the determination and characterization of the matter. As actual it makes this matter human, this matter equine, this matter bovine. It thereby gives rise to the different types of natures. But in making the existence human or equine or bovine, it functions only as a potentiality antecedent to existential actuation. This brings into bearing upon the question the general norm that, outside subsistent existence, the explanation for individuality is to be sought not in something actual, but rather in what is potential.

What role, then, is left to form in the causing individuation? In the Aristotelian background of Aquinas, form is the cause of being.[19] For Aristotle, this meant that the form gives being to both the matter and the composite body. For Aquinas, it meant the same, but with the proviso that an efficient cause was furnishing the influx of existence.[20] It meant that for him form was functioning as cause in its own realm of formal causality, shaping and determining the existence appropriate to the nature of the thing brought into being. From that viewpoint only was the form the cause of the thing's existence for Aquinas. What gave it existence, simply speaking, was its efficient cause. Yet in its own order the form was genuinely the cause of the finite thing's existence, insofar as it was the potentiality that gave the existence its formal determination. Aquinas can maintain that "the whole determination of being follows upon the form".[21]

This background helps explain a well-known and important statement of Aquinas in regard to existence and individuation: "Each being possesses its act of existing and its individuation in accordance with the same factor."[22] Scholars have recognized that in contexts like this the expression 'in accordance with' (*secundum*) means for Aquinas that some kind of causality is being exercised. Here the causality is meant to bear on both the thing's existence and the thing's individuation. The same cause is assigned to them both. Against the preceding background, accordingly, the form that is the cause of the existence will thereby be the cause of the individuation. The meaning is not exactly the same as that of the text from the *Reply to John of Vercelli* (see note 11). There the point was that everything had unity and individuation in accordance with its having existence. Here the thing has both its existence and its individuation in accordance with some other cause that is the same for both. Against the background just sketched, that cause should be the form. But there is no clash in the nuancing of the two passages. According to the one, existence is the cause of individuation. According to the other, the form is the cause of being and, as in the first passage, would through the existence be the cause of the individuation. The form, by determining the existence, would thereby determine the individuation. This metaphysical order of form and existence is stated explicitly in the *De spiritualibus creaturis:* "Now everything is actually a being through a form, whether in accordance with substantial existence or accidental existence. Hence every form is an actuality; and in consequence it is the reason for the unity by which anything is one."[23]

The reasoning here is thoroughly consistent. Existence cannot be imparted unless limited and determined by an essence other than itself. Though determining as a potentiality, the essence is thereby made actual. Every existent form is accordingly an actuality and as cause of being is making the thing one. Much difficulty in this question, however, arises from the way the human mind originally gets its notion of form. The notion of form is first attained in a concept and is thereby universalized. It is what characterizes and distinguishes the respective natures of man, animal, plant, metal, and the accidental modifications of size, weight, color, and the like. To pinpoint the notion of form to an individual, one has to add the ultimately particular and unrepeatable circumstances of place and time, for instance the form or soul of the historical Socrates. But the notion just in itself remains universal. With Aristotle, the same word *eidos* was used for both the physical form that is individual in Socrates, and the universal species that is studied in logic. This made the transition from one to the other meaning easier. But it leaves the way open to confusion, and today there is fairly wide acceptance of the view that the notions of form and universal coincide.

Against the Aristotelian background, then, one need not be surprised to find Aquinas introducing form as something universal of itself. Yet for him it is something that can be individual in real existence: "For every form as such is universal, unless it happens to be a subsistent form, which, from the very fact of its being subsistent, is incommunicable."[24] Where a substantial form exists in itself, as in the case of pure spirits, it is individual of itself. Here form and species coincide in reality. There can be only one individual in such a species, for the one individual is the whole species: "That is why among these substances we do not find a multitude of individuals in the same species, as has been said, except in the case of the human soul because of the body to which it is united."[25]

This doctrine allows form to be something that is individualized by itself in the case of angels. Form is obviously the cause of that individuation, since the determining form distinguishes one angel from another. But the same criterion holds in the case of the human soul, despite the difference in the two types of spirit. There are many souls in the one human species, each individuated one apart from the others. Though the occasion of the individuation with them is matter or body, the individuation remains the same even after separation from the body. The human soul thereby continues in its individuation just by itself:

> And even though the individuation of the soul depends on the body as for the occasion of its beginning, because it acquires its individuated being only in the body of which it is the actuality, it is not necessary that the individuation cease when the body is removed. Because the soul has a separate being, once the soul has acquired its individuated being by having been made the form of a particular body, that being always remains individuated.[26]

In cases of both angel and human soul, therefore, what determines the existential actuality is what determines the individuality. Even without the body the soul continues to be an individual. The individuality stays with the form, and in that way can be seen to come from the form. The form causes the individuality, even though in the case of human beings it allows a plurality of different individuals within the one species. This further problem in regard to the human soul can be left for consideration in the treatment of the way matter individuates bodily form.

The difficulty in regarding form as the cause of individuality stems accordingly from the origin of our notion of form in something universal. In all the direct objects of our cognition, whether minerals, plants, animals, or human beings, the form is the principle of universality. But our way of thinking must learn to adapt itself to its own paradoxes. Even the word 'individual' is a term of universal bearing. 'Socrates is a man' and 'Socrates is an individual' both predicate something universal of Socrates. Callias, Socrates, Plato, and Aristotle are all individuals, just as they are all humans. In the one case the predication is made in first intention, in the other case it is made in the second intention: "But the individual can be signified in a twofold way, either by a noun of the second intention, like the noun 'individual' or 'singular', which does not signify the singular thing but the intention of singularity; or by a noun of the first intention, which signifies the thing to which the intention of particularity belongs."[27] As a second intention predicate, 'individual' bears upon the relation of the singular instance to its logical species. That is the connotation we naturally give to this second intention term. There is difficulty in applying it to a case in which that connotation does not exist. To say "Gabriel is an individual" would tend to imply that there are other individuals of the same specific nature, just as the assertion "Socrates is an individual" implies that he shares one specific nature with Callias and Xenophon and every other human person who has lived or could live. So, in our way of thinking, even a universal term 'individual' has to be used to describe the here and now instance. In the first intention, only the proper name 'Socrates', strictly so used, can limit the signification to the one real object. In speaking of the Platonic Socrates, the Socrates of Xenophon, or the Socrates of Aristophanes, one is already using the name to denote a type. Only when it indicates the real Socrates of the particular place and time in history is it pointing out a single and unrepeatable instance in actual reality. That is why the technique of pointing to something with the finger was meant in the use of the term *demonstratio* to indicate the individual.[28]

Even the notion of individuality, then, does not serve to individuate. It merely ranges Socrates under a second-intention class; namely, the class of individuals. It is attained by precisive abstraction, corresponding to the way "humanity" is conceived by the precisive abstraction of human nature from the instances in which it is found. One text in Aquinas can speak of "Socrateity", giving it a formal sense.[29] But though functioning after the manner of a form it does not individuate by way of a further form added to the specific nature. Aquinas can therefore make the blanket statement: "Now every form is of itself common: hence the addition of a form to a form cannot be the cause of individuation."[30] For Aquinas there is no possibility of a form of haecceity.

But that is a far cry from saying that a form cannot provide its own individuation. It cannot individuate any other form. In the angels it individuates itself. In virtue of its form each angel is an individual. The difference of each from the others is taken "from the whole quiddity".[31] The form, in the case of the purely spiritual substances, is the whole quiddity. With them the substantial form is the cause of individuation. With human beings, the situation is somewhat different. Though spiritual, they are not pure spirits. Their nature, or quiddity, is composed of form and matter. Yet even with them the form is in its own way the cause of their individuation, since they retain that individuation after separation from matter. But that is a further problem and has to be considered in the framework of the general roles that form and matter play respectively in the individuation of materials things.

In materials things, in fact, form can hardly be denied some role in the individuation. The two substantial principles of a material thing are form and matter. But the matter just in itself is not the cause of any differentiation. It is subjected to the requirements of form. It "is attributed to each species according to the suitability of its form"[32] and is received "in accordance with the exigency of the form".[33] Its particular determination, then, will be prescribed by the form. Somewhat as existence is of such a nature that it requires limitation by something other than itself if it is to be multiplied, so a form that shows itself to be repeatable in different instances does not attain its entire perfection in any one of them. Multiplication in different instances is what is suitable to its nature. It has the exigency for existence in different individuals. The form also prescribes the amount of matter it requires. The amount is different in an elephant and in a mouse. Even the same physical form prescribes different amounts and structures of matter for the same individual in course of its growth. It guarantees the same individuation from zygote through embryo, fetus, child, adult, and senior citizen, despite all changes in matter, in size, and in other appearances. Certainly it is in an outstanding manner the cause of individuation, since it keeps the individuation the same throughout all changes in matter and accidents. It is in this way the cause of the thing's being one, as well as of the thing's being, in accord with the Aristotelian formula. The form has in consequence full right to be regarded as cause of individuation in material things. In immaterial substances, of course, it has no competitor in the order of essence. But even where it has a coprinciple in constituting the essence of a thing, as it has in any material substance, the determining role of the form seems to reach down to the individuation.

This is a problem, however, that remains to be considered when the role of matter in individuation is investigated. For the present, it is sufficient to keep in mind that the role of form in causing universality is no impediment to its influence in shaping individuality. The resemblances seen in a number of sensible things ground our universal conceptions of them. In this way form is the basis of universality. But that same form, which on account of its nature as material form requires existence in matter, likewise requires existence in a particular section of matter. In this way it is truly a cause of the material thing's individuality. It preserves that same individuality throughout all changes in growth, and in the case of the human soul keeps it intact despite the change undergone in bodily death.

III

Although individuation is a problem that extends to both the divine nature and the angelic natures, with different answers respectively in those two cases, the scholastic controversies have historically focused on the individuation of material things. Aristotle had emphasized that these things may be specifically the same in form, but that they are different from one another in virtue of their matter.[34] The earlier medieval writers, it has been pointed out, did not use the expressions 'cause of individuation' or 'principle of individuation'.[35] These phrases, however, became standard in the thirteenth century. 'Cause of individuation' could be used in regard to the individuation of God or the angels (e.g., note 11). But 'principle of individuation' came in general usage to mean the cause of individuation for corporeal things that belonged to the same species.

This is the situation in which Suárez, with his wide experience in summing up the state of the question in scholastic controversies, introduced the Thomistic position as "There is therefore the famous opinion asserting that the principle of individuation is designated matter. This is the opinion of D. Thomas. . . . And this is considered to be the opinion of Aristotle . . ."[36] A slight suspicion or doubt could well be attached to the claim of its Aristotelian origin, for Aristotle does not expressly mention the notion of "designation". Still further, Thomistic tradition had come to add the kind of designation, in the full-blown phrase 'matter designated by quantity'.[37]

Though this exact expression is not found in writings of Aquinas its content is undoubtedly present. From the works of the earliest period of his literary activity in his *Scriptum* on the *Sentences* to the Aristotelian commentaries of the latest period, Aquinas insisted on the designation of matter by quantitative dimensions so that it be able to exercise the function of individuating bodies. The reason was stated very clearly. Matter itself provides no distinguishing feature. Taken just alone, it cannot individuate anything. It is something common to all bodies. It is what makes them all be material things. There is nothing in it, just by itself, that would explain the division of one body from another or any kind of distinction of one from the other. It has first to be conceived as spread out and parceled off as it were into different units by the accident of quantity. Only in that way can matter function as the principle of individuation for bodies. Designated dimensions, consequently, are required in matter when it is regarded as the principle of individuation.

The notion of somehow determined dimensions has to be included in the definition of the principle of individuation for material things. Matter may be
accepted as the primary principle of individuation, for it is in the order of
substance and the substance is what is being individuated basically. But with
it quantity, though accidental in being, has to function as the ultimate reason
for the individuation. Though in it the root of the individuation is located, it
can be ranked only secondary as a principle, on account of its accidental status in being.[38]

A number of difficult problems confront this notion of individuation.
Despite its formal ranking of matter as primary and quantity as secondary in
the functioning of individuation, it would seem at first sight to make the individuation of a substance depend basically upon something accidental.
Quantity, though an accident, is explicitly the root or ultimate reason for the
individuation. Only quantity of its own nature means the spreading of something in parts outside parts, in continuous quantity, and by the dividing of
those parts the establishing of discrete corporeal beings. Its very nature is to
place part outside part in a thing that remains formally the same. Iron remains iron, wood remains wood, a horse remains equine through all the parts
contained in a three-dimensional compass. Matter, of course, is extended in
space without the addition of any new formal characteristic. But it is only
through quantity that it is so extended. That is enough to make matter function as a principle, indeed the primary principle, of individuation. Yet not its
own nature, but only the nature of quantity, is what enables it to fill that role.
It is extended not by itself, but by the accident of quantity. Quantity is the
only feature that is individual of itself and thereby functions as the principle
of individuation for all else in the corporeal thing. The whole individuation
of a body, both in its substance and in all its other accidents, is made to depend upon quantity. But quantity, as a accident, has to presuppose for its existence the individual substance upon which it depends for its being.

Another difficulty arises from the manner in which the quantitative dimensions cause the individuation. Throughout his writings from early to late,
Aquinas maintains that the individuating dimensions need to be designated
(*signatae*), indicated (*demonstratae*) and determined (*determinatae*). But as
far back as the second book of the *Scriptum* he had noted that undefined (*interminatae*) dimensions suffice for this individuation. The reason given is that
in growth the same individual continues to exist throughout all the changes in
size and shape from birth to maturity, decline and death.[39] The dimensions
have to be definite (*terminatae*) at any given moment. But the individuation
does not depend precisely upon the size and contour of any one given instant.
If the individuation depended in that way upon the dimensions, it would keep
changing incessantly at every moment of the thing's existence. The thing
would become a new and different individual with every change in place and

time. The philosophy of substance would give way to a panphenominalism. But in a philosophy that upholds the continuance of the same substance throughout all accidental changes, the individuation cannot change with every spatial or temporal variation. The dimensions therefore individuate in indefinite fashion, insofar as they are the dimensions required by a human being, a lion, an elephant, a tree, or the individual unit in any chemical compound. Within the limits and contours allowed by the thing's nature, the dimensions may be regarded indefinitely as the determining factor in the individuality. In their undefined status they designate or demonstrate or determine the matter in its functioning as the primary principle of the individuation. But they *really* individuate, in their potential fashion. This is not at all a merely logical quantification through the application of the notion "particular", itself a universal notion.

So much is this the case that in the third book of the *Scriptum* it is taken for granted that definite dimensions are only "in some way"[40] the principle of individuation. The undefined dimensions are generic in character. In their widest genus they mean dimensions taken merely as such, in general. In narrower scope, but still generic, they would be those required by human nature or any other nature indefinitely for all its stages of growth. As definite, they would be those of a specific shape, say a cube or a sphere, and of a definite measurement, such as four inches square. But the only dimensions that ever exist in reality are the specific ones. They are "terminated" or definite in their natures and ready to actuate the real substance. A generic shape that is neither square nor circular nor of any other specific type exists only in the abstraction of the mind. It is but a specific shape taken in nonprecise abstraction. So regarded by the mind, the undefined dimensions can be seen as really identified at the moment with the definite dimension here and now, and in that way these latter can be looked upon as the principle of individuation.

The explanation of individuation by undefined dimensions goes on to the end of the fourth book of the *Scriptum*.[41] The contemporary treatise *De ente et essentia* mentions only designated or determined dimensions, without notice as to whether they are definite or undefined. The *De veritate* and the ninth *Quodlibet* mention undefined dimensions, and the commentary on Boethius's *De trinitate* deals with them in considerable detail.[42] The latter expresses even more strongly than the fourth book of the *Scriptum* (note 41) the difficulty of attributing the individuation to dimensions in their definite status. It asserts bluntly that as definite the dimensions cannot individuate. But in the context and with the explanation given, it does not clash in meaning with the text from the *Scriptum*. The passage in the commentary on Boethius is noting that the dimensions can be considered in two ways. They are the same dimensions, but they can be looked upon from two different viewpoints. If they are regarded as "terminated" or completed in accordance with a determined measure and figure, they are completed beings in the category of quantity. So regarded, they cannot be the principle of individuation. The reason is that this "termination" or completion of the dimensions varies frequently with the same individual, with the result that the individual would not remain numerically the same. This reason is the same as the one given in the *Scriptum* for individuation by undefined dimensions. The overall meaning, then, is that the same dimensions have to be viewed in their generic or undefined status if they are to serve as the principle of individuation. That merely makes explicit the meaning in the statement of the *Scriptum* that matter "in some way" under definite dimensions is the individuating principle. It specifies what the "some way" is.

There is hardly room to object that the definite dimensions as such could individuate the corporeal thing in the initial moment of its existence, and then leave that thing itself to take care of its own individuality throughout all succeeding variations of size and shape. The individuation still needs a cause. If the cause were the exact contours and measurements of the first moment of the thing's existence, as soon as those exact dimensions ceased to exist the individuation would perish. If the same individuation is to persist, the same cause must continue to function. That cause can be only the dimensions in their undefined status.

In the uncontested works of Aquinas from 1260 on, the undefined dimensions are not brought forward. He is content to speak only in terms of designated or determined dimensions, without specifying whether they are definite or undefined. No satisfactory reason seems apparent for this silence about them. The doubtfully authentic treatise *De natura materiae* seeks to refute both the way Averroes explained them and a less objectionable attempt found in other writers at the time.[43] This might suggest fear of the Averroistic understanding of the undefined dimensions as the cause for unwillingness on the part of Aquinas to use that terminology any further.[44] But in the late period of his life he can refer to the Averroistic doctrine without showing any signs of worry. More likely the problem seems to have lost interest for him. The requirement of undefined dimensions would seem so evident that no further discussion of it would be necessary. In the *De natura materia*, moreover, the interest of the author was not focused on showing how the same individual substance could be safeguarded, but rather how the same dimensions of a person who had just died could be continued in the corpse.[45]

The way the undefined dimensions function as principle of individuation brings to the fore the problem how as accidents they could function in any priority at all to the substance and the existence. The language regularly used by Aquinas is that they are understood in advance in the notion of the thing.[46] They are understood not as existing in incomplete fashion in reality, but as a goal required by the nature of a material thing. To come into being, a material form requires existence in matter. Otherwise it would be a pure spirit. But of its nature it is meant to inform not matter in general, but a particular portion of matter in the shape and size suitable for a stone, a plant, or an animal. Likewise in the case of living things that grow or decrease in size and contours and in the case of substances that expand or contract with temperature, the individuation is directed toward the whole range of measurements and shapes that the substance can take on. The dimensions individuate as undefined. All that determination springs from the nature itself and is prescribed by its form.[47] *Real* individuation is what is caused.

Even in regard to existence in matter, then, and in regard to the undefined dimensions that individuate, the form of the material thing is the cause of the individuation. It causes the individuation not insofar as it is simply a form, but insofar as it is a form meant by its own nature to actuate a particular portion of matter. That orientation is not something accidentally added to it, but is contained in its inmost nature. Quite as created existence has to actuate a finite essence really other than itself, so the form of a material thing can exist only in matter other than itself in the real world and under dimensions that determine its size and shape. Matter and dimensions function indeed as principle of individuation, but only on account of the "exigency" that the form has for them. Not only in spiritual substances, but also throughout the realm of material things, the doctrine of Aquinas shows clearly enough that the form functions in this individuating manner and especially in regard to the problem of undefined dimensions. This causality of the form in its bearing upon individuation has not been emphasized in the Thomistic tradition, but it is a requirement of the texts and has not gone entirely without notice.[48]

Understanding the undefined dimensions in terms of an exigency of the form for their task is of great help in assessing the comparatively recent controversy about them. On the one side, commentators have regarded the notion of undefined dimensions in Aquinas as an aberration springing from a passing influence of Averroistic doctrine and definitely abandoned by him at the end of the middle period of his writing. In this way they see either really complete abandonment of the undefined dimensions or development of the doctrine on individuation in a way that rendered them unnecessary. Other recent commentators maintain on the contrary that they represent the genuine thinking of Aquinas on the topic and that he never abandoned or changed it.[49] The understanding of the form as the cause of the undefined dimensions seems to meet satisfactorily all the doctrinal objections brought against them. But the historical objection that Aquinas does not mention them in the final period of his writings remains to be met in the manner of an argument from silence. Nowhere is there any hint that he is deliberately rejecting them, and there seems to be no adequate ground for showing that relevant passages in the later works required repetition of the doctrine of undefined dimensions on the occasions on which designated or determined dimensions were asserted as the principle of individuation. Rather, if there was intent to reject them, explicit mention of the denial might be expected, with a careful explanation of how without them the persistence of the same individual under all dimensional changes in growth and location and time and the theological problems of the Eucharistic species and the resurrected body could be understood. The requirement for undefined dimensions had been carefully thought out and defended. It could hardly be dropped without detailed and equally careful explanation.

IV

The foregoing investigation shows how Aquinas makes use of two different sequences in explaining individuation.[50] One sequence is the order in being. First comes existence, the thing's most basic actuality. Then comes substance, with its components in material things of form and matter. Of these two, form is prior. Then come the accidents of material things, of which the first is quantity. Existence gives the thing its thoroughgoing individuation by synthesizing everything in the thing into a single unit, both on the essential and accidentals levels. In God it individuates just by itself. In purely spiritual beings it itself is determined by the form as a potentiality, a potentiality that thereby determines the angel's individuality without further help. In material things the form remains prior to the matter it actuates, as well as to the dimensive quantity that marks the matter off into separate portions in the three dimensions required by the thing's nature. Finally, the other accidents, such as exact measurements and shape, situation and sensible qualities, follow upon the thing's quantity.[51]

On the other hand, a reverse order holds in our understanding of the notion (*ratio*) of individuation. This understanding has to start from the concept of what in itself alone exhibits individuality. Our understanding of things is always conceptual, no matter what our factual knowledge about them is. Our understanding even of existence is conceptual, even though we originally know existence through judgment.[52] Our concept of existence is most general, applying to everything that exists. Our concepts of substance and form are correspondingly universal. Likewise our concept of matter is of something common and just in itself shows no division or even distinction into parts. Only quantity in its own nature means part outside part. It exhibits the distinction of parts and thereby the possibility of their real division into separate units. It is in that way the "root" of individuality, as far as the notion is concerned.[53] The other factors, as we represent them in our concepts, depend upon quantity to individuate them. Matter is rendered the individuating principle through quantity, form is individualized by reception into designated matter, and existence is conceived as the existence of this individual body because of its determination by the essence of the material thing. In our concepts quantity alone individuates by itself, the rest individuate by means of quantity. We reason to a different state of things in God and angels, but the basis of our *concept* of individuation remains quantitative.

These considerations throw light upon several apparent anomalies encountered in the course of the foregoing discussion. They show how existence always individualizes as an actuality, while the concept to which it gives rise when it actuates an essence is the most universal concept of all; namely, a being. Hence being is at both top and bottom of the Porphyrian tree and contains all its *differentiae*. Likewise they give a reason why the phrase 'principle of individuation' could come to be restricted to the individuation of material things. By the very nature of our thinking we envisage an individual in quantitative terms. We continue to do so even after we have reasoned to the very different orders of individuation in God and in the pure spirits. Also made clear is the way the notion of a "principle" has to be taken in this context. It is not a principle in the Cartesian sense of an eternal truth that is intuited either in itself or in the nature of things or in the mind of God. On the contrary, it is a conclusion carefully reasoned to from what we see in sensible things. Far from being something immediately evident, it is reached only after intricate and difficult reasoning from what is observed in the sensible world. Finally, the role of the accidents in individuation, the problem faced by Aquinas in the Boethian context, comes to the fore. Through the accidents that we immediately see we reason to basic individuality behind them. We may be deceived at times, as when the figure of a robot on the stage goes through its act in stiff mechanical fashion and only at the end relaxes into a deeply human smile to receive the applause of the surprised audience. Appearances may be deceptive as to where the individuality lies, but they are our means of coming to know it through careful and, where necessary, prolonged scientific investigation.[54]

It is crucial, then, to keep in mind the twofold sequence when reading Aquinas on individuation. In the notion of individuation undefined quantitative dimensions have to be given the basic place. They have to be "understood in advance" of all the other factors.[55] But they have no priority in existence. They are not regarded as already existing in an incomplete way when they exercise their individuating function. When they exist they are always definite. But as purely potential, just like primary matter, they are at the basis of our conceptual explanation of real individuality.

V

A dominating conclusion emerges from the *ensemble* of the texts in Aquinas on individuation. It is that in the real order the basic cause of individuality for him is existence. Existence is what most of all makes a thing a unit in itself and marks it off as distinct from all others. That is the hallmark recognized by him first and foremost for individuation. The hallmark extends throughout all orders of being. It applies to God, to angels, to material substances and to all accidents. Even in the area of what came to be covered in tradition by "the principle of individuation", namely, material things, the first requirement was that the thing be an actual existent. Only after that fundamental condition came matter and quantity.[56] What real existence brought about was always an individual, whether it was a substance or an accident. What is universal could have existence in cognition, but even there the real operation of the mind in which it had cognitional existence was something particular.[57] In the real order existence was for Aquinas the foremost and all-pervading cause of individuality.

Form was likewise a cause of individuation for him, but in the order of essence only. In purely spiritual creatures it was the sole essential cause of the individuality of a substance, insofar as just by itself it was the potentiality that determined the existential actuality of the thing. Though always in potential fashion, it gave not only specific but also individual determination to the existence. In material things it was but one of the two substantial principles involved. But it was the principle that demanded existence in matter and in matter under designated dimensions. In accordance with its generic and specific requirements it prescribed the appropriate dimensions and the accidents that went with the thing's nature.

As principle of individuation, matter under dimensions is concerned in immediate fashion with the bodily aspects of the thing, in that generic abstraction. But form as the cause of individuation bears on the full accompaniment of qualities and endowments that fill out the richness of individuality, on the vital, sentient and rational levels as well as on the corporeal. Though Aquinas did not have the means to draw out these possibilities in the way they have been developed by the explorations of modern phenomenology, anthropology, and psychology, his doctrine on individuation need not at all be restricted to the drab and uninspiring region of the quantitative. Rather, in the way it bases individuation on the exigencies of the real form, it leaves itself open to expansion in all the qualitative fields. Dimensions follow upon form as corporeal. But from that same form as living and sentient and rational, indefinitely variegated individual characteristics flow forth on each of those three higher levels. There is no limit to the richness of individuation, just as there in fact is no Liebnizian limit to the goodness of a created universe. The dimensions of individuality itself are undefined.

Notes

1. *De principio individuationis*, in *Divi Thomae Aquinatis: Opuscula philosophica*, ed. Raymund M. Spiazzi (Rome: Marietti, 1954), pp. 149–151. A survey of the differing views on its authenticity is given in Ingbert Klinger, *Das Prinzip der Individuation bei Thomas von Aquin* (Münsterschwarzach: Vier-Türme-Verlag, 1964), pp. 103–105. For the other work, there is a critical edition by Joseph M. Wyss, *"De natura materiae" Attributed to St. Thomas Aquinas* (Louvain: Nauwelaerts, 1953).

2. See *Sancti Thomae de Aquino Expositio super libri Boethii de Trinitate*, ed. Bruno Decker (Leiden: E. J. Brill, 1955), 4, 2; pp. 137–145.

3. See Aristotle, *Metaph.*, I, 1, 981a5–b29, and the rout simile at *Post. Analyt.* II, 19, 100a6–b3, for the ascent to the most universal. On the inseparability of being and unity, see *Metaph.*, IV, 2, 1003b22–32, and for a discussion of the question, Karl Bärthlein, *Die Transzendentalienlehre der alten Ontologie*, Vol. 1 (Berlin: De Gruyter, 1972), pp. 109–370. On the general background of the problem of individuality for a thirteenth century writer, see Jorge J. E. Gracia, *Introduction to the Problem of Individuation in the Early Middle Ages* (Washington, DC: Catholic University of America Press, 1984), esp. pp. 18–54.

4. ". . . illud quod cadit in intellectu per modum actualitatis absolute: . . ." *In Peri hermeneias* I, 5, 22; Leonine ed., Vol. 1, p. 28. See textual variants listed and discussed in footnote, *ibid.*

5. Cf. Thomas Aquinas, *Scriptum super libros sententiarum magistri Petri Lombardi*, ed. P. Mandonnet (Paris: Lethielleux, 1929), I, 33, 1, 1, ad 1m; I, p. 766. *De ente et essentia* 3, 26–70; Leonine ed., 433, p. 374. In regard to the functioning of judgment, cf. infra, n. 52.

6. ". . . esse rei ex materia et forma compositae, a qua cognitionem accipit, consistit in quadam compositione formae ad materiam, vel accidentis ad subjectum." *Sent.* I, 38, 1, 3, Solut.; I, p. 903. Cf. "Sed intellectus noster, cujus cognitio a rebus oritur, quae esse compositum habent, non apprehendit illud esse nisi componendo et dividendo . . ." *Ibid.*, ad 2m; p. 904. So, ". . . esse simpliciter non est nisi individuorum; . . ." *Sent.* I, 23, 1, ad 2m; I, 557.

7. See *Sent.*, I, 8, 1, 1, Solut.; I, p. 195. *De ente* 4, pp. 94–146; Leonine ed., pp. 376–377.

8. *Sent.*, I, 8, 1, 2, Solut.; I, p. 198. *Contra gentiles* I, p. 26, shows that this patristic conception is not to be understood in a formal sense, as though it referred to common being. Cf., ". . . creaturae, secundum hoc quod in Deo sunt, non sunt aliud a Deo: quia creaturae in Deo sunt causatrix essentia, ut dixit Anselmus." *Sent.* I, 36, 1, 2, ad 1m; I, p. 836. See also *Quodlibeta* 8, 1c, ed. Raymund Spiazzi (Turin: Marietti, 1956), pp. 158–159.

9. "Ita etiam divinum esse est determinatum in se et ab omnibus aliis divisum. . ." *Sent.* I, 8, 4, 1, ad 1m; I, p. 219. "Deus enim per essentiam suam est aliquid in se indivisum, et ab omnibus quae non sunt Deus, distinctum." *De potentia*,

8, 3c, ed. Paul M. Pession, S. Thomae Aquinatis, *Quaestiones disputatae,* 9th ed. (Rome: Marietti, 1953), II, 220a. See also *De ente* 5, 23–24; XLIII, p. 378. Undivided in itself and divided from others is Aquinas's regular description of an individual, e.g. "Individuum autem est quod est in se indistinctum, ab aliis vero distinctum." *Summa theologiae* I, 29, 4c; Leonine ed., IV, p. 333.

10. ". . . unum indifferenter se habet ad hoc quod respiciat essentiam vel esse. Unde essentia rei est una per se ipsam, non propter esse suum; et ita non est una per aliquam participationem, sicut accidit de ente et bono." *De veritate* 21, 5, ad 8m.227–231; Leonine ed., XXII, p. 607. In this way primary matter considered just in itself can be said to be one—see *De ente* 2, 237–238; XLIII, p. 373. On the two ways in which something may be called numerically one, se *De principiis naturae,* c. 2; ed. John J. Pauson (Louvain: E. Nauwelaerts, 1950), p. 86.4–11. See also *Summa theol.* I, 11, 1, ad 1m; IV, 107.

11. ". . . unumquodque enim secundum quod habet esse, habet unitatem et individuationem." *Responsio ad Fr. Joannem Vercellensem de articulis XLII,* q. 108; in *Opuscula theologica,* ed. Raymund A. Verardo (Rome: Marietti, 1954), I, p. 240 (no. 935). The context is the "causa individuationis animarum" (*ibid.*). The point is that bodies are only in a way (*aliqualiter*) the cause of individuation of souls. Also, "Secundum quod res habent esse, ita habent pluralitatem et unitatem, nam unumquodque secundum quod est ens, est etiam unum." *Compendium theologiae,* 71; in *Opuscula theologica,* I, pp. 34–35 (no. 124). Cf. infra, n. 23.

12. "Differunt autem secundum esse; non enim idem est esse hominis et equi, nec huius hominis et illius hominis." *ST* I, 3, 5; IV, p. 44. For other references, see David Winiewicz, "A Note on *alteritas* and Numerical Diversity in St. Thomas Aquinas, "*Dialogue* 16 (1977): 697, n. 14.

13. See *Sent.* II, 3, 1, 2, Solut.; II, pp. 90–91. *De ente* 5, 23–24; XLIII, p. 378.

14. ". . . de ratione individui duo sunt: scilicet *quod sit ens actu* vel in se vel in alio; *et quod sit divisium ab aliis quae sunt vel possunt esse in eadem specie, in se indivisum existens.*" *Sent.* IV, 12, 1, 1, ad 3m; ed. M. Fabianus Moos (Paris: Lethielleux, 1947), IV, p. 503 (no. 49).

15. See , note 11. In this context 'cause' and 'principle' have the same meaning, as with Aristotle at *Metaph.* IV, 2, 1003b24, though 'principle of individuation' came to be restricted conventionally to the order of material things; cf. infra, nn. 35–37. On the general scholastic understanding of the two terms at the time, see Gracia, *Introduction,* p. 37.

16. "Esse autem, inquantum est esse, non potest esse diversum: . . . *Contra gentiles* II, 52,Si enim, Leonine ed., XIII, p. 387a21–22.

17. ". . . Deus simul dans esse, producit id quod esse recipit: . . ." *De pot.* III, 1, ad 17m; II, p. 41. Also: ". . . ex hoc ipso quod quidditati esse attribuitur, non solum esse, sed ipsa quidditas creari dicitur . . ." *Ibid.,* III, 5, ad 2m; p. 49.

18. "Unde non sic determinatur *esse* per aliud sicut potentia per actum, sed magis sicut actus per potentiam." *De pot.* 7,2, ad 9m; II, p. 192.

19. See Aristotle, *Metaph.* VII, 17, 1041a9–b28; VIII, 2, 1043a2–26.

20. ". . . esse per se consequitur formam creaturae, supposito tamen influxu Dei; sicut lumen sequitur diaphanum aeris, supposito influxu solis." *Summa theol.*, I, 104, 1, ad 1m; V, p. 464.

21. "Cum . . . tota determinatio essendi consequatur formam . . ." *Sent.* I, 23, 1, 1, Solut.; I, p. 556.

22. *St. Thomas Aquinas, O.P.: Questions on the Soul,* trans. James H. Robb (Milwaukee: Marquette University Press, 1984), 1, ad 2m; p. 49. The Latin is, ". . . unumquodque secundum idem habet esse et individuationem." Robb text, *Quaest. de an.* (Toronto: Pontifical Institute of Mediaeval Studies, 1968), p. 61. Robb lists one variant in which *unum* is added to *esse* in the sentence.

23. "Est autem unumquoduque ens actu per formam, sive secundum esse substantiale, sive secundum esse accidentale: unde omnis forma est actus; et per consequens est ratio unitatis, qua aliquid est unum." *De spiritualibus creaturis,* 3c; in *S. Thomae Aquinatis Quaestiones disputatae,* ed. M. Calcaterra and T. S. Centi (Rome: Marietti, 1953), II, p. 380. Cf., "Unumquodque enim secundum hoc est unum, secundum quod est ens" Ibid. ". . . cum unitas rei sequatur formam, sicut et esse, oportet quod illa sint unum numero quorum est forma numero una" *Contra gent.* II, 83; XIII, p. 524, 8–10. In this way form continues to be the source of all determination: ". . . ce que saint Thomas lui-même qualifie de principe de toute détermination, la forme." A. Krempel, *La doctrine de la relation chez saint Thomas* (Paris: Vrin, 1952), p. 587.

24. *De ver.* 2, 6, 53–56; XXII, pp. 65–66. *Truth,* trans. Robert W. Mulligan, (Chicago: Henry Regnery, 1952), I, p. 92. The Latin is: ". . . omnis enim forma inquantum huiusmodi universalis est nisi forte sit forma subsistens, quae ex hoc quod ipsa subsistit incommunicabilis est."

25. *De ente,* 5, 56–59; XLIII, p. 378. *On Being and Essence,* trans. A. Maurer, 2d ed. (Toronto: Pontifical Institute of Mediaeval Studies, 1968), pp. 62–63. The Latin is, "Et ideo in talibus substantiis non inuenitur multitudo indiuiduorum in una specie, ut dictum est, nisi in anima humana propter corpus cui unitur."

26. *De ente* 5, 59–68; XLIII, pp. 378–379, trans. Maurer. The Latin is, "Et licet indiuiduatio eius ex corpore occasionaliter dependeat quantum ad sui inchoationem, quia non acquiritur sibi esse indiuiduatum nisi in corpore cuius est actus: Non tamen oportet ut subtracto corpore induiuiduation pereat, quia cum habeat esse absolutum ex quo acquisitum est sibi esse indiuiduatum ex hoc quod facta est forma huius corporis, illud esse semper remanet indiuiduatum."

27. *Sent.* I, 23, 1, 3, Solut.; I, p. 563. The Latin is, "Sed individuum dupliciter potest significari vel per nomen secundae intentionis, sicut hoc nomen 'individuum'

vel 'singulare', quod non significat rem singularem, sed intentionem singularitatis; vel per nomen primae intentionis, quod significat rem, cui convenit intentio particularitatis." Cf. I, 26, 1, 1, ad 3m; I, pp. 623–624. Also III, 6,1,1, Solut.1; III, p. 225 (no. 23).

28. See M.-D. Roland Gosselin, *Le "De ente et essentia" de S. Thomas d'Aquin* (Paris: Vrin, 1948), p. 11, n. 1; 58.

29. "*Uno modo* quo distinguitur et constituitur formaliter, sicut homo humanitate, et Socrates Socrateitate." *De pot.* 8, 3c; II, p. 220.

30. "Omnis autem forma de se communis est: unde additio formae ad formam non potest esse cause individuationis." *Quodl.* 7, 1, 3c; p. 136. This refers to individuation of one form by another form, and not to individuation of the angelic form by itself.

31. *De ente* 5, 101; XLIII, p. 379; trans. Maurer, p. 64.

32. *Saint Thomas Aquinas: Treatise on Separate Substances*, 19, 108; trans. Francis J. Lescoe (West Hartford, CT: Saint Joseph College, 1963), p. 154. The Latin is, "Cum enim unicuique speciei sit attributa materia secundum convenientiam suae formae, . . ." *ibid.*

33. ". . . secundum exigentiam formae . . ." *Sent.* II, 30, 2, 1, Solut.; II, p. 781. Cf.: ". . . *forma substantialis materialis aliquo modo habet ordinem ad dimensiones,* cum dimensiones interminatae praeintelligantur in materia ante formam substantialem, . . ." *Sent.* IV, 12, 1, 3, Resp. 1; IV, p. 520 (no. 137).

34. Aristotle, *Metaph.* VII, 8, 1034a6–8; XII, 8, 1074a33–35. In Jonathan Barnes ed., *The Complete Works of Aristotle* (Princeton, NJ: Princeton University Press, 1984), II, 1632 and 1697.

35. See Gracia, *Introduction*, p. 266: ". . . they asked about what 'made' things individual."

36. "Est ergo celebris sententia, affirmans principium individuationis esse materiam signatam. Haec est sententia D. Thomae. . . . Et existimatur haec sententia Aristotelis." F. Suárez, *Disputationes metaphysicae* V, 3, 3; in *Opera omnia* (Paris: Vivès, 1856–1877), XXV, p. 162.

37. For example, "Secundum Thomistas principium individuationis est materia *signata quantitate,* i.e. distincta seu divisa per quantitatem." Josef Gredt, *Elementa philosophiae aristotelico-thomisticae,* 7th ed. (Freiburg: Herder, 1937), I, p. 296 (no. 386). On the historical origin of the standard Thomistic expression, see J. Bobik, "La doctrine de saint Thomas sur l'individuation des substances corporelles", *Revue Philosophique de Louvain* 51 (1953): 40, n. 54.

38. "Et ideo *primum individuationis principium est materia,* qua acquiritur esse in actu cuilibet tali formae sive substantiali sive accidentali. *Et secundarium prin-*

cipium individuationis est dimensio, quia ex ipsa habet materia quod dividatur.'' *Sent.* IV, 12, 1, 1, ad 3m; IV, p. 503 (no. 49).

39. See *Sent.* II, 3, 1, 4, Solut.; II, p. 97. II, 30, 2, 1, Solut.; I, pp. 781–782. On the preoccupation with the phenomena of nutrition, see *ibid.*, pp. 776–787. Theological considerations regarding the partition of the Eucharistic species and the disposition of the resurrected body and similar topics are his more frequent concerns. The Latin *'terminatae'* and *'interminatae'* are not easy to translate. *'Terminatate'* is use synonymously with 'completed' and means completion by specific perfection in contrast to the incomplete status of the generic perfections just in themselves. It is best rendered by 'definite', in the way for instance that human nature is a definite type of animal and vegetative nature. *'Interminatae'*, in contrast, may be expressed by 'undefined', in the sense that the generic natures are taken as undefined by their specific difference. 'Indefinite' would not convey the right sense, because in this case the dimensions always are definite in fact, but are being considered without their defining characteristic, and accordingly as 'undefined'. The English 'indefinite' would tend to leave the impression that the dimensions were in reality that way. 'Determined' or 'determinate', 'undetermined' or 'indeterminate', may without hesitation be used to translate *'determinatae'* or *'indeterminatae'*, since a determination may be either generic or specific. The undefined dimensions, in consequence, are always determinate just as they are always "designated", with 'determinate' understood as involving the determination proper to the particular type of plant or animal. The exact measurements and the precise shape at any given moment express the specific quantitative *differentiae* that pertain to the definite dimensions.

40. ''Unde cum principium individuationis sit materia aliquo modo sub dimensionibus terminatis considerata, ex ejus divisione natura humana dividitur et multiplicatur.'' *Sent.* III, 1, 2, 5, ad 1m; III, p. 45 (no. 145).

41. See *Sent.* IV, 12, 1, 2; IV, pp. 504–517 (nos. 54–125). Also IV, 44, 1, 1, 3, Solut. 1; Vivès ed., XI, p. 297. IV, 44, 1, 2, Solut. 5, ad 3m; XI, p. 307. A study of the texts of Aquinas on this topic may be found in my article ''Thomas Aquinas: Dimensive Quantity as Individuating Principle'', *Mediaeval Studies* 50 (1988): 279–310.

42. *De ver.* 5, 9, arg. 6; XXII, p. 161.49–52. *Quodl.* 9, 6, 1c; p. 191b. *In Boeth. de trin.* 4, 2, Resp. 6–7; pp. 143.2–21; and ad 3m; p. 144.16–27.

43. *De nat. mat.* (see note 1) 3, 34–4.33; pp. 104–111.

44. E.g., M. -D. Roland Gosselin, *Le "De ente essentia"*, pp. 109–112; Bruno Decker (see note 2), p. 143, n. 1. But see Aquinas, *De spirit creat.* 3, ad 18m; II, p. 383. In that comparatively late work the doctrine did not cause trouble.

45. *De nat. mat.* 4, 102–142; pp. 115–116.

46. See ''cum dimensiones interminatae praeintelligantur in materia ante formam substantialem . . .'' *Sent.* IV, 12, 1, 3, 3, ad 3m; IV, p. 520 (no. 137). Cf. texts

previously cited from *De veritate* and *In Boeth. De Trin.* in note 42, and those cited from the *Scriptum* on the *Sentences* in note 41.

47. See previous text, note 24, on the universality of form insofar as it is form.

48. E.g., Krempel, *La doctrine,* pp. 587–589.

49. For the theory of change in opinion on the part of Aquinas, see Jean R. Rosenberg, *The Principle of Individuation: A Comparative Study of St. Thomas, Scotus, and Suárez* (Washington, DC: Catholic University of American Press, 1950), pp. 25–40. Against change in his doctrine, see Umberto degl'Innocenti, "Il pensiero di San Tommaso sul principio d'individuazione", *Divus Thomas* (Piacenza) 45 (1942): 35–81; J. Bobik, "La doctrine", 37–38, and "Dimensions in the Individuation of Bodily Substance", *Philosophical Studies* (Maynooth), 4 (1954): 66–79.

50. Cf.: ". . . quantitas dimensiva secundum suam rationem non dependet a materia sensibili, quamvis dependeat secundum suum esse; . . . ." *Sent.* IV, 12, 1, 1, 3, ad 2m; IV, p. 503 (no. 48).

51. In this regard, continuous quantity is basic. In answer to the argument that number as discrete quantity is prior because simpler and more abstract, Aquinas answers: "Ad sextum dicendum quod numerus formaliter loquendo est prius quam quantitas continua, sed materialiter quantitas continua est prior, cum numerus ex divisione continui relinquatur, ut dicitur in *III Physicorum.*" *In Boeth. de. trin.* 4, 2, ad 6m; p. 145.8–11.

52. A discussion of this topic may be found in an exchange between Barry Miller and myself in articles in *The New Scholasticism* 53 (1979): 475–485, and 56 (1982), 371–380. On the role of sense judgment in the grasp of existence for Aquinas, see my article "Judgment and Truth in Aquinas", *Mediaeval Studies* 32 (1970): 138–158.

53. ". . . prima radix huiusmodi multiplicationis ex dimensione esse videtur." *Contra gent.* IV, 65, Habet; XV, p. 209b17–18.

54. "Alia vero accidentia non sunt principium individuationis, sed sunt principium congnoscendi distinctionem individuorum." *In Boeth. de trin.* 4, 2, Resp.; p. 144.1–3.

55. See texts listed in note 46.

56. ". . . de ratione individui duo sunt: scilicet *quod sit ens actu* vel in se vel in alio; *et quod sit divisum ab aliis.. . . ." Sent.* IV, 12, 1, 1, 3, ad 3m; IV, p. 503 (no. 49).

57. "Et quamuis hec natura intellecta habeat rationem uniuersalis secundum quod comparatur ad res quae sunt extra animam, quia est una similitudo omnium, tamen secundum quod habet esse in hoc intellectu uel in illo est quedam species intellecta particularis." *De ente* 3, 103–107; XLIII, p. 375.

9

HENRY OF GHENT
(B. CA. 1217; D. 1293)

STEPHEN F. BROWN

I. Introduction

Henry of Ghent conducted his Quodlibet II shortly before Christmas 1277, a number of months after the Paris condemnations.[1] Henry had been one of the sixteen theologians who formed the commission examining the suspect positions that Bishop Tempier condemned.[2] In q. 8 of this 1277 Quodlibet Henry asked, Can two angels be made distinct by God by reason of substantial principles alone?[3] In his answer, formulated principally in opposition to those who claimed that matter alone can be the cause of individuation, Henry was quick to remind his audience that this position was one found recently among those articles condemned by the Parisian bishop.[4] One of those condemned articles says, "That God cannot multiply many individuals in any given species without matter." Another states, "That forms do not admit division except by reason of matter." A third one declares, "That, because intelligences do not contain matter, God could not produce many intelligences belonging to the same species."[5]

At the first approach, Henry's question (Can two angels be made distinct by God by reason of substantial principles alone?) might seem a very limited question about individuation: It appears to focus only on a particular class of beings, angels. To interpret the question in this limited way, however, would be just as wrong, in the view of Henry, as to interpret the condemned positions as limited theses, positions concerned only with particular instances of individuation. In fact, for Henry, a study of this particular question brings us to the heart of the issue: that neither matter nor form taken in itself can be the ultimate cause of individuation in any created being. The precise and proximate cause of individuation must be located at an even deeper metaphysical stratum of reality than these substantial principles of matter and form.[6] Philosophers, Henry argued, for all the subtlety of their arguments and the acceptability of much of what they might say about individuation in regard to particular types of beings, fail to get to the problem at its most profound level.

II. The Philosophers on Individuation

Aristotle, in Book XII of his *Metaphysics,* tells us that "all things that are many in number have matter".[7] This declaration suggests, according to Henry, that in material beings alone is it possible to have many individuals within the same species.[8] Spiritual substances such as the moving principles of the heavenly bodies, thus cannot be many in number. Each is its own "species", or better, its own essence, since we are not properly dealing with a species when we speak of such spiritual substances or immaterial forms.[9] Most important of all, as Henry indicated in his earlier *Summa,* for Aristotle such spiritual substances are gods: "Doubtlessly, then, Aristotle posited many gods, existing naturally (i.e. necessarily) of themselves; and he linked all these gods to some one first god, not in a way that the others would receive from this first god their existence after not existing, but rather that this first god preceded the others in the order of dignity and in the order of being a prior moving principle."[10]

We should not be suprised, Henry contends, that each separated form or substance is a unique individual for the Philosopher. It follows necessarily, not so much from his position that individuation takes place through matter, but rather from Aristotle's thesis that each of these spiritual substances is a god and a necessary being.[11]

Henry, throughout his career, held that this was the chief issue to be considered when searching for the cause of individuation. In Quodlibet V (1280) he tells us that for Aristotle and his followers each of these separated substances is a god and refers us back to his treatment in Quodlibet II.[12] In 1287 he opens Quodlibet XI with a summary of the philosophers' opinions: The essence of a separated substance exists in only one supposit; there is no distinction between its essential being and its existential being, but its essence would of itself be a certain necessary existence; and each of these subsisting separated substances would be a certain god, although among these there would be a certain one and highest god.[13]

Although the principal issue for Henry, as he examines over the years the cause of individuation, surrounds the divine character of immaterial substances, there are other positions of the philosophers, even dealing with material forms, that Henry sees the need to examine more carefully. When we look into the cases of material things, we see that some special cases involved

in our search raise some difficulties. In Quodlibet II Henry looks at Book I
of Aristotle's *De caelo*. There the Philosopher studies the possibility of a plurality of worlds. He argues that there can be only one world in these words:
"Such a plurality is in fact impossible if this world contains the entirety of
matter, as in fact it does."[14] Likewise, in Quodlibet XII, Henry notes that for
Aristotle the sun and the earth's moon also are not capable of being plurified,
since each of them contains all its appropriate matter.[15] In these instances,
then, of material forms, as well as in the cases of immaterial forms or substances, Aristotle does not posit that there are many individuals under the
same form or essence. In regard to material forms, like the world, the sun,
and our moon, which did not admit of plurification, the difficulties Henry
found were that the Philosopher's view set a limit to God's power and considered only what was possible in the present order of nature.[16]

In material substances where an infinite number of individuals can be
found in different species, Henry is willing to admit a role to matter and
quantity. He knows the position of Aristotle in this area in detailed fashion
and likewise the theory of Averroes concerning determined dimensions. After
reviewing their positions, he concludes in Quodlibet II of 1277: "It is evident
in a most clear manner that matter and quantity cannot be called the exact
reason and cause of the individuation and distinction of individuals belonging
to the same species, although they are a cause of individuation in material
and corporeal things, in which alone the Philosopher admitted that a nature
may be multiplied in many supposits, for it was only such beings that he admitted to be created. . . ."[17]

III. Henry's Critiques of the Philosophers

Henry contends that the positions of Aristotle and his followers have no
necessity about them. If we look at immaterial forms or substances apart
from God, they are creatures, not gods or necessary beings. Now the essence
of any creature whatsoever, no matter to what degree it might be immaterial,
still is a creaturely essence that does not have existence of itself. In the language of Henry's famous intentional distinction, the intention of existence or
subsistence is distinct from the intention of the creature's essence. The conjunction of a creature's essence and its existence or subsistence in a supposit
does not take place by the creature's essence making itself to be subsistent.
As Augustine declares in the opening chapter of the *De trinitate:* "There is
nothing whatsoever that begets itself that it may exist."[18] If a creature's essence is to come into existence, then, this must be through the causality of
another being. No creature is of itself a singular being, nor is its essence formally identical with its existence. Using the language of Avicenna, Henry
claims that such an essence holds itself indifferently to singular existence, by

which he means that the essence would subsist in just one supposit, or universal existence, which means that it could subsist in many supposits. There is no creaturely essence that may not be, on its part, multiplied in many individuals.[19]

Henry even insists that Aristotle would have been forced to admit this to be the case if he were going to be consistent with his argument in Book I of the *De caelo,* where he argued against many worlds. The master of theology who served on Tempier's theological committee sets up a parallel between the shape in itself and the shape in combination with matter and the creature's essence in itself and the essence existing in a supposit.[20] Aristotle declares in regard to the first couple of the parallel:

> For instance, the form of the sphere is one thing and the gold and bronze sphere another; the shape of the circle again is one thing, the bronze or wooden circle another. For when we state the essential nature of the sphere or circle we do not include in the formula gold or bronze, because they do not belong to the essence, but if we are speaking of the copper or gold sphere we do include them.[21]

Arguing *a pari ratione,* Henry concludes that just as Aristotle would have to concede this distinction in the case of forms or shapes in regard to matter, so he would have to admit it in considering a created essence in respect to a supposit in which it exists: that it is capable of being present in many supposits, since from its part it is determined neither to one thing nor to many things. It is, therefore, either numerically many or else it is able to be many. The parallel holds in both cases.[22]

After setting up this parallel, Henry notes that Aristotle held that every absolute form, considered apart from its matter or from its supposit, is a material form, and so he would necessarily have had to admit that every form of a creature insofar as it is a creature has to be distinct from its supposit. So, every form of a creature is a universal form and is multiplied or multipliable. If in fact it is not found in many supposits, the reason is because one of them contains all the matter available to that species.[23]

Now the Philosopher himself took a different route: He defended the position that an immaterial substance, by the very fact that it has no link with matter, is numerically one, and that it is not a creature but a certain divine nature. He declares that each of them is a certain kind of god and that each in itself is a certain kind of singularity and a certain kind of necessary being. By admitting that there are many spiritual substances, he therefore admitted that there were many gods and many necessary beings. Now this is totally impossible, as Avicenna has shown in Book VIII of his *Metaphysics.*[24]

To avoid this impossible consequence, that there are many gods that are single and unique, Aristotle would have to view these many spiritual substances, distinct from God, as creatures and then explain how they are multiplied after the manner of what he described as a material form. Strictly speaking, these spiritual substances are not material forms, but they, like material forms, are multipliable. Henry, at his own turn, will have to explain what must be added to these spiritual forms or essences to individuate them.

If there is no necessity of admitting Aristotle's position in regard to immaterial forms, namely, that they are divine beings that exist necessarily and that they have a certain singularity, the same could be said for his teaching concerning material forms that have only one supposit in the species. It is true that forms such as the world, the sun, and our moon each contain all the matter now existing that is possible to their forms within the nature of things. But there is a need to distinguish between what is impossible according to the laws of nature (*secundum naturam*) and what is absolutely impossible (*simpliciter*); and this distinction is unacceptable to Aristotle. Aristotle, however, failed to realize that what is impossible according to the laws of nature can be possible to God, the ruler of nature. For Henry, therefore, there is the possibility that God could create new matter, so that these forms, which in fact are limited to one supposit, are not absolutely so limited on their part to one supposit. These material forms could have many individual supposits, if God created new matter.[25] These material forms on their part are indifferent, as Avicenna would say. They could enjoy singular existence, that is, subsist in just one supposits; or they could enjoy universal existence, that is, subsist in many supposits. Such material forms, on their part may be multiplied in many individuals, even if de facto they are found only in one. Like immaterial forms, they are on their part multipliable. Henry, at his turn once again, will have to explain what precisely must be added to these material forms or essences to individuate them.

IV. Henry's Contemporary Opponents

Aristotle and his Commentator were not Henry's only opponents. He also faced in Quodlibet II, those whom he called *"nostri philosophantes"*, quite likely the same people as the *"nonnulli Parisius studentes in artibus"* mentioned in the prologue of the 1277 condemnations.[26] Henry speaks of them as those who wish to follow the Philosopher in holding that in separated forms there can be only a unique individual in each species (or essence).[27]

His primary opponents seem to be Boethius of Dacia and Siger of Brabant. Boethius, in his commentary on the *Topics* asks: "Cannot God make two separated substances belong to the same species?" He argues that, since a separated substance is its own species and another one is its species, then if there are two of them, they are distinct from one another and each is its own species. Therefore, they are specifically distinct. Those things, however, that are specifically distinct cannot be in the same species. God, then, cannot make them two separated substances belonging to the same species, because such a thing cannot happen.[28] He allows himself, however, an escape from the difficulties this might present for the faith, by saying that perhaps God has some way of doing what does not seem possible, even though the secret of divine wisdom is unknown to us.[29]

Siger took up the same issue many times. In chapter 7 of his *De anima intellectiva* he declares: "In forms that are separated from matter the individual is the very species itself, and therefore for another individual to be in the same species is for it also to be contained under another individual, and this is impossible."[30] He, likewise, left himself an opening in this treatise for escaping doctrinal difficulties by offering a profession of faith.

Siger studied the same issue in his commentary on Book III of the *Metaphysics* and judged that it was foolish to ask if a form that is free of matter has many individuals belonging to the same species. And he continues with the comparison that, since the being of forms separated from matter are like the being of Socrates (an individual), then it is not possible that there be many individuals in the same species.[31]

Finally, in his *Questions on the 'De causis'*, he argues that to produce two immaterial substances in the same species is to make contradictories at the same time.[32]

In addition to Boethius of Dacia and Siger of Brabant, an anonymous author of the same period even more explicitly indicates the philosophic impossibility of an immaterial form being able to be multiplied numerically in the same species: "It is true that according to faith there can be numerically many separated forms in the same species; yet according to Aristotle and all the philosophers this is impossible."[33]

All three of these authors stress the philosophic impossibility of numerically many separated forms in the same species. Does Henry provide a response to their claim?

V. Henry's Answer to the Contemporary Followers of Aristotle

Henry gives these members of the arts faculty who want to follow Aristotle in saying that in the case of separated forms there can be only a unique individual in each species (essence), two options. Either they should accept Aristotle's teaching that each of these separated forms is a god and a necessary being in whom there is no distinction of essence and existence. This option would make them most faithful to Aristotle, but would place them in a position contrary to the faith and vulnerable to the argument of Avicenna against a multiplicity of gods and necessary beings. Their other option is to admit that the separated forms are like the essences of all creatures: They are essences existing from all eternity in the divine mind that can be created. They do not exist of themselves, and the intention of their essence is distinct from the intention of their supposit and subsistence. In this case they would have to admit the *a pari ratione* argument Henry gave before and say that each of these essences on its part is multipliable in many supposits. If these essences are not actually multiplied or cannot be actually multiplied, then it is not because they on their part are not multipliable. Rather, it is because for Aristotle and his followers they lack matter.[34]

Let us make a supposition. If Aristotle had admitted that there was an immaterial essence that belonged to the realm of creatures, he would have approached the problem in the following way: Although such immaterial creatable essences on their part were multipliable in many supposits, nonetheless they never would be actually mutiplied in many supposits; nor could they ever be actually multiplied. The reason why they could not be so multiplied is because that which is necessary for a multiplication to take place is missing. For, according to Aristotle, that by which multiplication could take place is only matter and material quantity, because he did not see anything else by means of which one and the same specific (essential) form could be different in one supposit and also in another. It is for this reason that he never admitted that any form separable from matter could have existence after nonexistence except by matter (or if we use the *a pari ratione* argument—by the subject) in which it would be received.[35]

But if you follow this second option, you run into a number of difficulties. The first difficulty is a philosophic one. It is this: There would be something in a basic element of nature, namely, the possibility of a multiplication in many supposits belonging to an essence, and yet it could never be brought to act by any agent. Thus there would be something vain and useless in the natural potency of the essence. Likewise, nature would act uselessly if it would make that which in itself is multipliable such that it could nonetheless never by multiplied by any agent. Now in fact Aristotle and Averroes never posited such a potency in the basic makeup of a created nature. For they never posited anything that could be multiplied without at the same time positing an agent by which it could be multiplied in act. Therefore, since Aristotle held, on the one hand, that a form could be multiplied only by matter, and, on the other, that by positing a created separated form it was necessary to posit this separated form or essence to be multipliable, it is most evidently clear that the Philosopher did not admit any created form separated from matter but rather admitted that every form belonging to a creature is material and that every separated form is a certain divine nature.[36]

This second option also presents another difficulty: It sets up a situation in which some fundamental aspect of a creature could be possible and yet it could not be brought actually to happen by the infinite power of the Creator.[37]

Given, then, the impossibility of admitting either of these two options, are there any other ways of explaining the character of a created separated form that would truly allow it to be multiplied in many individuals?

VI. Henry's Explanation of the Individuation of Created Immaterial Substances

Henry could think of two actual alternatives for explaining how a created spiritual being, which because it is created is capable of being multiplied, could in fact be multiplied. According to him, both the Christian faith and Aristotle's philosophy identify divinity and singularity: A divine being is singular; a singular being is divine. For Aristotle a spiritual or separated substance is divine and singular. Multiplicity, for him, can come only at the level of matter. One could easily expect that some, in answer to Aristotle and his contemporary followers in the arts faculty, might tend to agree with the Aristotelian principle that individuation or plurification comes through matter and attempt to apply this principle to created spiritual being. The result would be an extension of the Aristotelian concept of matter to make it include a principle of individuation that could be called spiritual matter. The concept of "spiritual matter" was not a new one fabricated in Henry's time. It was employed by Avicebron and became characteristic in many earlier thirteenth century authors.[38] The chief defender of spiritual matter who employs it as the principle of individuation for spiritual creatures in Henry's own era was William de la Mare.[39]

Henry, however, interprets this position as excluded by one of the condemned propositions ("That, because intelligences do not contain matter, God could not produce many intelligences belonging to the same species"). For the positing of a spiritual matter implies that "without matter neither individuation nor distinction could take place".[40]

Henry himself reaches for another alternative to explain the individuation or plurification of created spiritual essences:

> It is necessary to posit in them another mode of individuation. Since those beings which do not depend on matter do not receive their existence except through the agent alone, so also do these things have existence and exist as individuals in distinct supposits through the same agent. Likewise from the same agent do they receive their individuation and plurification. We should realize that in the case of spiritual forms that their individuation and establishment in a supposit have to be brought about by an agent [not matter]. Now this takes place in so far as a spiritual essence serves as the *terminus* of the action of the agent. This action has as its *terminus* an individual, since something universal

and common comes into existence only in a singular. Thus, although spiritual forms are simple, they subsist in supposits in an individual way, so that in these supposits the form of itself expresses something absolute considered in itself, whereas the supposit expresses something as a limited being, having in itself a participation of the determined form. It is this principle of determination or limitation which principally and from within makes the establishment of the supposit, and this is the case whether they are individualized by matter [in regared to material forms] or by the agent [in regard to spiritual forms].[41]

Applying this to the case of the two angels in the same species, Henry claims that the two angels are individually distinct by this fact alone: they actually subsist in reality. For, in actual reality, outside the community of essence that is found in both angels, the subsistence of one is not the subsistence of the other, for one of them could exist without the other. Thus, it is by the intention of subsistence that they differ from one another, that this angel is not the other angel. The principle of subsistence of actual existence differs in each of the two, and it is intentionally distinct from the common essence found in both.[42]

The analogy Henry provides to make us see his point is the following: A continuum of itself is capable of being divided into a number of quantitative parts that it actually contains as undivided parts, and it is divided into these quantitative parts by the very fact that they are separated from one another (no other thing being added to the essence of each multiplied continuum[43]). The result of this separation is that each new continuum has in itself the perfect essence of a continuum but only in a partial way the full quantity of the original continuum. In a parallel way, the essence of the angelic species is capable of being divided into a number of essential parts which it as an absolute essence virtually contains as undivided parts. It is divided into these essential parts by the very fact alone that through the actual subsistence which is joined to the essence the individual angels are separated from one another, each having in itself the perfect essence of an angel but only in a partial way the full quantity of "angelness", because it is not present to any of them after the manner of an absolute divisible essence but rather it is in each of them as an individual diminishing of this absolute angelic essence.[44]

It is at this point in Quodlibet II's statement of his position that Henry reminds us of the details of his original question (Can two angels be made distinct by God by reason of substantial principles alone?). For the most part he has attacked the position which claimed that matter was the principle of individuation. This, however, is not the full extent of Henry's thesis. Considering both substantial principles, Henry argues that neither form nor matter can be the ultimate principle of individuation. He has taken care of matter as an ultimate principle of individuation. He now shows in what way form cannot of itself serve as the ultimate principle of individuation:

> So it must not be said that the two angels differ because the nature of one is not the nature of the other. . . . . But because the subsistence of one is not the subsistence of the other, and it is this subsistence which makes the essence as found in one differ from it as it is found in the other, and, it also makes that which is one and simple in essence to be many in existence. This subsistence itself in a supposit is altogether necessary for the actual existence of the essence, in one as in the other, not in a way that would make them numerically one, but rather making them different in number, though they may be alike according to species. The reason why it is by two distinct principles that each of the angels may be said to be an angel pure and simple and that each may also be said to be "this angel" or "that angel" is because the intention of the essence considered absolutely, by which each is called an angel, is distinct from the intention of this and that subsistence, by which they are said to be "this angel" and "that angel." It is thus clear how it is by the intentions of subsistence of the two angels that the individuation of the common essence takes place in them.[45]

Yet, the conjunction of these two principles, of essence and subsistence, in the one and the other angel cannot be brought about by these principles themselves, because on their part they do not have what it takes to make themselves subsist in actual reality. So, it is necessary that the conjunction of these principles take place in them by the action of another cause, making each of them to be distinct through the essence existing in act and making this angel not to be that angel and that angel not to be this one. The first efficient cause of their individuation, then, must be said to be God, who gives to each of these angels its subsistence in actual reality and separately.[46]

When Henry goes beyond considering the efficient cause and asks what besides the form is in the supposit, by means of which it has individual existence and by means of which the form has individual existence of this particular species, he, following Avicenna, answers that it is an "*accidens adventitium tantum*", that is, a concomitant or connatural accident.[47] It is, for Henry, in a very broad sense of the term 'disposition', a special kind of disposition (*quasi dispositio*) of the supposit in so far as it is a supposit, making the supposit to be a supposit of a specific kind and making it to be a supposit having a determined or limited form of this species.[48]

When he pushes the issue further and wonders what the supposit brings about formally in creatures, the master from Ghent tells us it is not something positive, since this would lead to an infinite regress, as we would have to explain how this positive principle is individualized.[49] The proximate cause of the supposit and of individuation is something negative. It is a negation by which the form itself, which of itself is specific, is made, as a *terminus* of God's creative action, completely undivided in a supposit and individual and singular by a privation of all divisibility; and it is divided from every other being. As is evident, for Henry a twofold negation is involved. One negation removes from within all multipliability and diversity. Through subsistence the supposit no longer has the possibility to be one thing or another, the way the form of a species has a capability of existing in diverse supposits. The other negation gives it a concrete specific identity that separates it from all the other members of that species. The subsistence by which a supposit becomes a supposit renders it incapable of being multiplied and separates it from every other individual in the same species.[50] In brief, Henry has returned to the classical definition of an individual: *indivisum in se, divisum a quolibet alio.*

VII. Henry and the Critics

Henry's claim that *subsistentia* or *existentia* is the proximate principle of individuation is not a new position. St. Bonaventure,[51] William of Auvergne,[52] Praepositinus,[53] and quite likely a long list of other writers preceded him. Certainly, what was novel in Henry's treatment was the 1270s context within which he developed his thesis and so strongly criticized the members of the arts faculty at Paris who wished to follow Aristotle on this issue. This context stimulated him to a much more thorough metaphysical treatment of the existence position than that given by his predecessors.

No criticism of Henry's thesis follows the full lines of his position. Peter Olivi[54] and John Duns Scotus[55] attacked Henry for holding that subsistence only adds a twofold negation to the essence it individualizes and nothing positive. There is no doubt that this stress on the negative effects of subsistence is present in Henry's Quodlibet V.[56] Henry's Quodlibet II makes no mention of these negations, and in Quodlibet XI Henry tries to put them in a more precise framework. There he clearly distinguishes between positive individuation and the individuation that takes place negatively.[57] The positive character of individuation is that subsistence adds to a particular essence a real relation to the Creator as the efficient cause of the individual's actual existence. For Henry, the proximate principle of individuation is not the absolute essence (e.g., humanity), nor the particular essence (this humanity), for these as such do not exist.[58] The created existence or subsistence of this man or of this angel is the key. Without subsistence, received from God, "this humanity" does not exist. But speaking negatively, "this humanity," from the fact that it *is* and is *this* humanity, holds itself negatively toward those members we could imagine as being under this individual if it were a divisible species. "This man" similarly has a negative consideration in relation to all the other things surrounding it: It separates or distinguishes itself from every other individual.[59]

Focusing on another aspect of Henry's position, Scotus likewise attacks those who hold that existence is the principle of individuation. This objection might not be aimed primarily at Henry, but the description of *esse essentiae* and *esse existentiae* give it some link to Henry. The difficulty Scotus has regarding this position is that "existence" is indeterminate. How can it be a principle of determination or individuation? Henry does not answer this type of objection, but quite likely, if he had had the occasion, he would have admitted an individualizing role is played by the *ratio determinati* that limits the absolute essence, for example, humanity, to one of its subjective parts—this humanity. Yet, Henry would insist that this determining *ratio* that allegedly "makes" the absolute essence (humanity) to be particular (this humanity) actually does nothing. It plays its role only when "this man", this particular subsistent, exists. The determination takes effect only when the Creator gives it subsistence.[60]

Godfrey of Fontaines seemed to have Henry in mind when he noted in Quodlibet II, q. 5 that the problem of subsistence is different than the problem of individuation.[61] Henry's likely answer would be that the "confusion" of these two problems was not an oversight. Aristotle himself did not distinguish them.[62] If Godfrey, or anyone else wanted to distinguish them, Henry would judge that they would fall victim to his arguments against Boethius of Dacia, Siger of Brabant, and the other members of the arts faculty.[63]

Giles of Rome in Quodlibet II, q. 7 of 1287 did not precisely attack Henry, but he did manifest a certain hesitancy in regard to the articles relating to individuation, expressing regret that more mature deliberation had not been given them and hoping that a more sound consideration might be used in their regard sometime in the future. Henry reports Giles's attempt to skirt the condemned propositions and provides a refutation of Giles' arguments in Quodlibet XI, qq. 1–2. He responds to Giles's charge that the condemned articles need more mature deliberation by twice introducing judgments concerning the condemned propositions, judgments that are not found in Quodlibeta II or IV: (1) "But, because this was condemned *reasonably* . . ." and (2) "But his whole position is false and erroneous and was condemned at Paris, and the condemnation was made *reasonably*...."[64]

VIII. Conclusion

Henry, in his treatment of individuation throughout his career, kept very close to the Philosopher's texts, stressing strongly the divine status

Aristotle gave to the separated substances. A Christian thinker, in Henry's view, could not accept this position. Perhaps Aristotle's thesis could be adapted, but Henry judged that such an adaptation had both philosophical and theological problems. The condemnations of 1277, in which he participated as a member of Tempier's commission, might have been in helter-skelter order from a logical viewpoint, and Tempier might have overstepped his mandate from Pope John XXI,[65] but Henry's *Summa quaestionum* and Quodlibeta II, V, and XI show that a great deal of preparatory and follow-up deliberation was given to the condemned propositions concerning individuation. There is little doubt that Henry provided the commission with strong arguments against the individuation propositions which were condemned. It would be well worth the effort to examine his corpus on the issues related to the other 216 propositions. Such a search could provide us with many of the arguments presented to the commission against the condemned articles and give us stronger grounds for judging not only Henry's claim in Quodlibet XI that the propositions concerning individuation were reasonably condemned, but also for evaluating the reasonableness of the condemnation of many of the other articles.

Notes

1. Henry of Ghent, *Quodlibet II*, ed. R. Wielockx (Leuven: University Press, 1983), p. 5. I would like to thank the Lynde and Harry Bradley Foundation for the support of the research for this article.

2. *Ibid.*, q. 9, p. 63: "In hoc enim concordabant omnes magistri theologiae congregati super hoc, quorum ego eram unus,. . ."

3. *Ibid.*, q. 8, p. 35: "Utrum possint fieri a Deo duo angeli solis substantialibus distincti."

4. *Ibid.*, q. 8, p. 45: "Unde et inter erroneos articulos nuper ab episcopo parisiensi damnatos damnata est illa positio."

5. *Ibid.:* "Unus enim illorum articulorum dicit sic: 'Quod Deus non possit multiplicare plura individua sub una specie sine materia.—Error.' Alius vero dicit sic: 'Quod formae non recipiunt divisionem nisi secundum materiam.—Error, nisi intelligatur de formis eductis de potentia materiae.' Tertius dicit sic: 'Quod, quia intelligentiae non habent materiam, Deus non posset plures eiusdem speciei facere.—Error.' "

6. Henry of Ghent, *Quodlibet V*, q. 8 (Paris, 1518), vol. 1, f. 165vL: "Haec ergo est opinio sua de causa individuationis et determinationis formae ad suppositum in formis materialibus plurificabilibus per supposita quantum est ex parte formae, et

est vera in talibus formis ut secundum cursum naturae; sed non explicat praecisam et proximam causam individuationis.''

    7. Aristoteles', *Metaph.* XII, ch. 8 (1074a 33–34).

    8. Henry of Ghent, *Quodlibet II*, q. 8, p. 36: ''Aristoteles enim in XII *Metaphysicae* ponit causam eius fuisse materiam, ubi dicit: 'Quaecumque sunt multa numero, habent materiam.' In quo sistit, et nihil plus dicit. Per quod dat intelligere quod in solis materialibus possibile est sub eadem specie et natura simplici per essentiam esse plura individua.''

    9. *Ibid.*, q. 8, p. 42: ''. . . sub una specie—id est essentia, quia proprie non habet ibi esse ratio speciei. . . .''

    10. Henry of Ghent, *Summa quaestionum*, art. 25, q. 3 (Paris, 1520), vol. 1, f. 154rH: ''Proculdubio ergo Aristoteles posuit plures deos naturaliter ex seipsis existentes, reducendo omnes ad unum primum, non sicut a quo alii haberent esse post non esse, sed sicut praecedens eos in ordine dignitatis et principii motivi.''

    11. Henry of Ghent, *Quodlibet II*, q. 8, pp. 41–42: ''Quid mirum ergo, si Philosophus dicit quod in formis separatis in una specie, id est essentia, non est nisi unicum individuum? Hoc enim de necessitate sequitur, non tam ex illo quod falso posuit, non esse scilicet plura individua sub eadem specie nisi per materiam, quam ex alio sacrilegio quod tamquam sacrilegus posuit, quod scilicet quaelibet earum deus quidam sit et quoddam necesse esse.''

    12. Henry of Ghent, *Quodlibet V,* q. 8, f. 165vM: ''Non enim posuit differentiam inter deum et alias formas separatas nisi quia posuit eum primum principium in genere formarum separatarum. Quamlibet enim illarum deum posuit, quemadmodum alibi exposuimus. . . .''

    13. Henry of Ghent, *Quodlibet XI,* q. 1 (Paris, 1518), vol. 2, f. 438rO: ''Oportet scire quod sententia philosophorum fuit quod in separatis non esset aliud esse speciei et suppositi; et sic quod essentia non subsisteret nisi in unico supposito; et quod ulterius non esset illius aliud esse essentiae et aliud existentiae; sed quod ipsa essentia esset ex se quoddam necesse esse et quaedam existentia; et sic quod quodlibet suppositum subsistens in essentia separata esset deus quidam, licet in diis est unus primus et summus.''

    14. Aristoteles', *De caelo* I, ch. 9 (278a 25–28). Cf. Henry of Ghent, *Quodlibet II,* q. 8, pp. 37–38: ''Unde dicit in I *Caeli et mundi:* 'Omne cuius forma est in materia, res illa habet multas partes infinitas.' Quod dicit ex sermone illorum qui volebant ostendere quod mundi possent esse multi arguendo sic: 'Omnis res quae ex natura sua absoluta est forma sola praeter dispositionem suam cum materia (sicut est forma orbis, quando est per se, praeter dispositionem qua est cum aere et auro, nam non ingreditur in sermone suo aurum aut aes), quantum est de se, possibile est ut ipsa sit in materiis multis; aut ergo est multa, aut possibile est ut sit multa. Cum ergo caelum sive mundus est huiusmodi, ergo etc.' Ubi dicit Commentator: 'Bene potest concedere inductionem ex omni habente formam in materia, quod in essentia inveniuntur

plura individua aut infinita. Ideo enim dicitur in definitione universalis quod est natum dici de pluribus. Forma enim est subiectum universalitatis.' Et re vera bene concedit istud Philosophus quod verum sit, quantum est ex parte formae. Unde dicit quod 'istud est rectum ex sermone cui non est contradicere.' Vult tamen quod, quantum est ex parte materiae, potest esse impedimentum. Unde dicit ibi Commentator: 'Et est contradictio quia hoc forte possibile est secundum formam, impossibile autem secundum materiam, cum possibile sit quod materia toto (tota?) sit inclusa in hac forma.' Unde Philosophus, respondendo illorum rationi, dicit: 'Verumtamen caeli non sunt multi propter hunc sermonem, nec possible est ut sint multi, quoniam caelum est factum ex materia tota.' In formis ergo materialibus continentibus in se totam suam materiam possibilem ad suam formam et in formis immaterialibus patet quod Philosophus plura individua non posuit sub eadem forma et essentia.''

15. Henry of Ghent, *Quodlibet XI*, q. 1, f. 438vS: ''Sed aliter in formis caelestium corporum et aliter in formis separatis immaterialibus. In primis enim dicunt quod etsi forma speciei quantum est ex se sit plurificabilis, ut forma solis et lunae, quia tamen continet in se totam materiam possibilem ad ipsam secundum unicam determinationem, et hoc quia, ut dictum est, forma substantialis in talibus praecedit omnem rationem dimensionum et est materia subiectum eius sub ratione indivisibilis. Idcirco, ut dicunt, secundum Philosophum, in II *De caelo et mundo*, impossibile est formas talium plurificari, et impossibile est omnino plures esse soles aut plures lunas, et quod Deus non posset facere solem alium ab isto, neque lunam aliam ab ista.''

16. Henry of Ghent, *Quodlibet II*, q. 8, p. 38: ''Licet enim aliqua forma materialis, ut huius caeli, contineat totam materiam iam existentem quae possibilis est ad suam formam possibilitate naturae, non tamen continet simpliciter omnem materiam possibilem ad ipsam. Posset enim Deus illi consimilem creare. Quod tamen multum abhorreret Philosophus, qui nihil poneret possibile fore in rerum natura, nisi quod actu et formaliter vel materialiter et in potentia materiae esset iam in universo, nec Deum posse facere alia in naturis et essentiis rerum quam fecit, neque nova aliqua convenientia in natura et essentia cum eis quae sunt, nisi ex materia per motum caeli, ut alibi debet ostendi.''

17. Henry of Ghent, *Quodlibet II*, q. 8, p. 47: ''Patet igitur clarissime quod materia et quantitas non possunt dici praecisa ratio et causa individuationis et distinctionis individuorum eiusdem speciei, licet sunt causa eius in rebus materialibus et corporalibus, in quibus Philosophus solum posuit unam naturam multiplicari in plura supposita, quia solummodo talia posuit esse creata . . .'' Cf. *Quodlibet V*, q. 8, vol. 1, f. 165vL.

18. August., *De trinitate*, I, c. 1, n. 1 (*PL* 42, 820).

19. Henry of Ghent, *Quodlibet II*, q. 8, pp. 38–39: '' 'Quoniam essentia creaturae cuiuslibet, quantumcumque immaterialis, neque est existens neque subsistens neque habet rationem suppositi ex hoc quod in natura sua absoluta essentia quaedam est, quia de se non habet esse nisi in conceptu mentis et intellectus divini vel angelici et humani si fuerint homo aut angelus in esse. Ita quod extra intentionem essentiae creaturae ut essentia est, sit intentio existentiae, subsistentiae et suppositi. Et sunt

quaedam duo: essentia scilicet et in supposito subsistentia. Quorum coniunctio si fu-
erit, ut quod ipsa essentia sit in supposito subsistens per existentiam, quia non potest
hoc esse per ipsam essentiam facientem se ipsam subsistentem in supposito per existentiam (tunc enim quidlibet ex eo quod est aliquid per essentiam, esset aliquid per
existentiam, quod est impossibile, quia 'nihil se ipsum producit ad esse ut sit,' secundum Augustinum in principio *De trinitate*), necesse est igitur ut coniunctio illorum sit
per aliam causam facientem ipsam essentiam fore subsistentem in existentia actualis
suppositi. Nulla ergo essentia creaturae, ratione ea qua essentia est, habet rationem
suppositi aut actualiter subsistentis. Ita quod nulla earum, quantum est ex se, de se sit
singularitas quaedam, nullaque earum, sicut nec effective, sic nec formaliter est suum
esse sive sua existentia, sed hoc est privilegium solius essentiae divinae quod ipsa ex
se formaliter sit singularitas quaedam et idem in eo sunt essentia et existentia. Quod
autem non ex se sed solum ab alio agente singulare est in supposito subsistens, quia
ex se nulli appropriatur et est essentia tantum, quantum est ex se, indifferenter natum
est esse singulare, subsistendo in unico supposito, vel universale, subsistendo in pluribus. Quod etiam bene dicit Avicenna et determinat in V *Metaphysicae* suae. Ex quo
sequitur apertissime quod necesse est ut non sit essentia creaturae, in quantum creatura est, quin possit quantum est ex se, in plura individua multiplicari, quantumcumque sit abstracta a materia.''

20. *Ibid.*, q. 8, p. 40: ''Quod necesse etiam concedere habebat Philosophus.
Sicut enim, ut iam dictum est, omnis res quae ex natura sua absoluta est forma solum
praeter dispositionem suam cum materia, considerata secundum se absque dispositione cum materia, quantum est de se, possibile est ut sit in multis materiis—et ita aut
est multa numero in materia, aut possibile est ut sit multa—, sic omnis res quae ex sua
natura absoluta est forma solum praeter dispositionem suam in supposito, considerata
secundum se absque dispositione quam habet in supposito, quantum est de se, non
magis determinatur ad unum quam ad multa. Aut ergo est multa numero in suppositis,
aut possibile est ut sit multa.''

21. Aristoteles, *De caelo*, I, ch. 9 (278a1–6).

22. Henry of Ghent, *Quodlibet II*, q. 8, p. 40: ''Sicut enim illud necesse habet
concedere in formis respectu materiae, ita et hoc respectu suppositi. Consimilis enim
est ratio utrobique.''

23. *Ibid.*, q. 8, pp. 40–41: ''Quia ergo omnem huiusmodi formam, quae ex
natura sua absoluta est aliquid praeter dispositionem suam cum materia aut cum supposito, posuit esse formam materialem, et etiam omnem formam creaturae, in quantum creatura est, necesse habuit ponere esse talem, ut dictum est, ideo etiam necesse
habuit ponere omnem formam creaturae esse materialem, et sic omnem esse universalem, vel multiplicatam vel multiplicabilem per plura supposita, et si non esset multiplicabilis, non esse impedimentum ex parte sui sed ex parte materiae, ut dictum est.
Et sic posuit causam quare in formis quandoque non est nisi unicum individuum sub
una specie et quandoque sunt plura individua sub ea—licet semper possint esse plura,
quantum est ex parte formae—, non esse nisi materiam. Ut, quod non sit neque potest
esse sub specie nisi unicum individuum, hoc sit solum ex parte materiae, quando

forma continet totam suam materiam in unico individuo, et quod aut sint aut possint esse plura, quantum est ex parte materiae, quando forma non continet totam materiam possibilem ad suam speciem in unico individuo.''

24. *Ibid.*, q. 8, p. 41: ''Et sic Philosophus unumquodque eo solo quod separatum est a materia, posuit esse unum numero, et cum hoc etiam non esse creaturam sed quandam divinam naturam, ut alibi ostensum est. Et ex hoc quod ponit quodlibet eorum esse deum quemdam, ponit quodlibet eorum esse ex se singularitatem quandam et quoddam necesse esse, tam propter separationem a materia, quam propter indifferentiam essentiae a supposito et existentia sua, ut alibi declaratum est. Ponendo enim plura esse separata a materia, ipse plures deos et plura necesse esse posuit. Quod omnino est impossibile, ut bene probat Avicenna, VIII *Metaphysicae,* et alibi expositum est.''

25. *Ibid.*, q. 8, p. 38: ''Quod primo patet ex parte materialium. Licet enim aliqua forma materialis, ut huius caeli, contineat totam materiam iam existentem quae possibilis est ad suam formam possibilitate naturae, non tamen continet simpliciter omnem materiam possibilem ad ipsam. Posset enim Deus illi consimilem creare. Quod tamen multum abhorreret Philosophus, qui nihil poneret possibile fore in rerum natura, nisi quod actu et formaliter vel materialiter et in potentia materiae esset iam in universo, nec Deum posse facere alia in naturis et essentiis rerum quam fecit, neque nova aliqua convenientia in natura et essentia cum eis quae sunt, nisi ex materia per motum caeli, ut alibi debet ostendi. Nulla est ergo forma materialis, quin simpliciter, quantum est ex se, possit sub se habere plura individua, materia non impediente.'' On the distinction between *impossibilitas secundum naturam et impossibilitas simpliciter,* see R. Hissette, *Enquête sur les 219 articles condamnés à Paris le 7 mars 1277* (Louvain: Publications Universitaires, 1977), pp. 43–49.

26. Henry of Ghent, *ibid.*, q. 8, p. 42: ''Nostri ergo philosophantes, si velint sequi Philosophum in hoc consequente. . . .'' Cf. R. Hissette, *ibid.*, p. 13, for the prologue to the condemnations. For Aquinas's inclusion in the condemnations, see pp. 83–84.

27. Henry of Ghent, *ibid.*, q. 8, p. 42. ''Nostri ergo philosophantes, si velint sequi Philosophum in hoc consequente, quod scilicet in formis separatis sub una specie—id est essentia, quia proprie non habet ibi esse ratio speciei—non potest esse nisi unicum individuum. . . .''

28. Boethius de Dacia, *Quaestiones super librum Topicorum,* ed. N. G. Green-Pedersen and J. Pinborg (Copenhagen: Librarium G. E. C. Gad, 1976), IV, q. 3, pp. 203–204: ''Cum enim substantia separata sit sua species, et alia etiam sit sua species, si sint duae, se ipsis distinguuntur, et quaelibet illarum est sua species. Ergo specie distinguuntur. Quae autem specie distinguuntur, non possunt esse sub una specie. Hoc ergo non potest esse, ergo nec fieri.'' Cf. R. Hissette, *Enquête,* p. 84.

29. Boethius de Dacia, *ibid.*, p. 204: ''Unde rem aliquam potest Deus totaliter auferre, sed rei aliquid incompossibile facere non videtur posse. Et hoc dico salvo secreto divinae sapientiae quam nemo novit.''

30. Siger of Brabant, *De anima intellectiva,* ed. B. C. Bazán (Louvain: Publications Universitaires, 1972), ch. 7, p. 103: "In separatis enim a materia, individuum est ipsa sua species, et ideo aliud individuum esse sub specie est etiam ipsum contineri sub alio individuo, quod est impossibile." Cf. R. Hissette, *Enquête,* p. 85.

31. Siger of Brabant, *Quaestiones super librum Metaphysicae,* ed. C. Graiff (Louvain: Publications Universitaires, 1948), III, q. 13: "Unde in separatis a materia cum esse eorum sit quasi esse Socratis, non est possibile quod sint ibi plura individua in eadem specie." Cf. R. Hissette, *Enquête,* p. 85.

32. Siger of Brabant, *Quaestiones super librum De causis,* ed. A. Marlasca (Louvain: Publications Universitaires 1972), q. 24: "Producta autem intelligentia aliqua a causa prima, aliam producere eamdem secundum speciem esset aliam producere secundum individuum et nihilominus eamdem producere secundum individuum. . . ." Cf. R. Hissette, *Enquête,* p. 86.

33. Auctor incognitus, *Quaestiones super librum De anima,* ed. F. Van Steenberghen (Louvain: Publications Universitaires, 1971), III, q. 6, p. 312: "Verum est quod secundum fidem possunt esse plures formae numero separatae in specie una; tamen secundum Aristotelem et omnes philosophos hoc est impossibile." Cf. R. Hissette, *Enquête,* p. 86.

34. Henry of Ghent, *Quodlibet II,* q. 8, p. 42: "Aut si negant hoc primum antecedens et ponant secundum, quod scilicet formae separatae sunt essentiae creabiles et nihil de se nisi solum essentiae in intellectu divino existentes ab aeterno, sicut erant essentiae aliarum creaturarum, et quod extra intentionem essentiae earum ut essentiae sunt absolutae, sit intentio suppositi, subsistentiae et existentiae, necesse habent ponere quod quaelibet earum, quantum est de se, multiplicabilis sit per plura supposita, ut patet ex iam declaratis, et, si non multiplicentur actu, nec actu multiplicari poterint, quod in hoc non est defectus nisi ex parte materiae, quia nullam habent."

35. *Ibid.,* q. 8, pp. 42–43: "Unde et Philosophus, si posuisset aliquam essentiam creaturae immaterialem, hoc posuisset per hunc modum videlicet quod, etsi essent aliquae formae creaturarum immateriales omnino separatae a materia, licet, quantum est ex parte ipsius formae, essent multiplicabiles per plura supposita, quod tamen numquam essent actu multiplicatae nec umquam possent esse actu multipicatae, et hoc propter defectus eius quo habet fieri huiusmodi multiplicatio, quod, secundum ipsum, non potuit esse nisi materia et quantitas materialis, quia non vidit aliud quo una et eadem forma specifica in sua essentia esset diversa in hoc supposito et in illo. Unde nec posuisset aliquam formam separabilem habere esse post non esse, nisi per materiam et subiectum in quo reciperetur. . . ."

36. *Ibid.,* q. 8, pp. 43–44: "Quorum unum est quod aliquid esset in potentia in fundamento naturae et creaturae, scilicet possibilitas multiplicationis per plura supposita, quae esset in eius essentia, et numquam per quodcumque agens posset deduci ad actum, et ita esset ibi frustra et otiosum, iuxta illud quod dicit Commentator super principium *Metaphysicae,* quod 'si essent aliqua intelligibilia abstracta et non posset esse aliquis intellectus qui ea posset intelligere, tunc natura in hoc otiose egisset, quia

scilicet fecit illud quod in se est naturaliter intelligibile, quod tamen a nullo intellectu posset intelligi'. Similiter otiose egisset, si fecisset quod in se naturaliter est multiplicabile, quod tamen nullo agente posset aliquando esse multiplicatum. Sed hoc falsum est, quoniam, ut dicit ibidem Commentator, 'concessum est ab omnibus quod nulla res est otiosa in fundamento naturae et creaturae'. Sed re vera talem potentiam numquam posuit in fundamento naturae et essentiae creaturae. Numquam enim posuisset aliquid posse multiplicari, quin simul posuisset per aliquod agens potuisse actu fore multiplicatum. Et ideo, cum non posuit formam omnino posse multiplicari nisi per materiam, et tamen, ponendo essentiam creaturae separatam, necesse erat ponere ipsam multiplicabilem, ut dictum est, planissime patet quod Philosophus nullam formam creaturae posuit separatam a materia, sed omnem formam creaturae posuit esse materialem et omnem formam separatam esse quandam divinam naturam, ut dictum est.''

37. *Ibid.*, q. 8, p. 44: "Secundum vero inconveniens est quod aliquid esset possibile in fundamento creaturae, quod non esset reducibile in actum per virtutem infinitam Creatoris. Ut sic sequeretur quod non esset vere omnipotens, quia non posset agere quidquid ex parte rei possibile esset fieri.''

38. *Ibid.*, q. 8, vol. 1, f. 165rL: "Ideo erat opinio Philosophi et sequacium eius quod eadem est formae individuatio quae est eius plurificatio, ita quod in formis separatis quibus non potest contingere plurificatio, nulla contingit omnino individuatio; immo quaelibet earum ex se et natura sua singularis est, nullo modo individuata, neque multiplicata, neque individuabilis, neque plurificabilis.'' Cf. *ibid.*, q. 8, pp. 45, lin. 52–46, lin. 66 et *Summa quaestionum,* art. 25, q. 3, vol. I, ff. 155rO–156rT. For the earlier authors (Alexander of Hales, St. Bonaventure, Roger Bacon, Robert Kilwardly, cf. M.-D. Roland-Gosselin, *Le "De ente et essentia" de S. Thomas d'Aquin* (Paris: Vrin, 1948), p. 30, n. 2. For Avicebron, cf. Avencebrolis (Ibn Gebirol), *Fons vitae,* tr. IV, ed. C. Baeumker (Münster: Aschendorff 1895), pp. 211–256.

39. Cf. F. Pelster, *Declarationes magistri Guilelmi de la Mare O.F.M. de variis sententiis S. Thomae Aquinatis,* art. 10 et 12 (Melle: Aschendorff 1956), pp. 14–16.

40. Henry of Ghent, *Quodlibet II,* q. 8, p. 45: "Quod si hoc error est, patet re vera quod illi multum errant, qui ponunt in angelis esse materiam ut per ipsam materiam unusquisque habeat suam individuationem, et per multiplicationem sive per materiae divisionem ponant angelorum ab invicem distinctionem sub eadem specie, quasi sine materia illa nec individuatio nec distinctio huiusmodi fieri posset, cuius contrarium sententiant iam dicti articuli.''

41. Henry of Ghent, *Quodlibet V,* q. 8, vol. 1, ff. 165vM–166rM: "Oportet igitur in eis ponere alium modum individuationis. Quare cum illa quae non dependent a materia esse non recipiant nisi per solum agens, et ab eodem habent res esse et esse hoc aliquid in supposito distincto et ab eodem similiter habent multiplicari sive plurificari. In talibus ergo simpliciter sciendum est quod eorum individuatio et ratio suppositi habet fieri per agens, in quantum scilicet terminat actionem agentis, quae non habet determinari nisi ad hoc aliquid, quia universale et commune non fit nisi in sin-

gulari, ita quod licet huiusmodi formae sint simplices in eisdem tamen individualiter subsistunt, ita quod in eis forma ex se dici aliquid ut simpliciter et absolutum. Suppositum vero dicit aliquid ut determinatum, habens in se formae determinatae participationem. Quae quidem ratio determinationis facit principaliter et ab intra rationem suppositi et hoc sive sit per materiam sive per agens.''

42. Henry of Ghent, *Quodlibet II*, q. 8, p. 50: "Quantum ergo ad distinctionem unius essentiae secundum individua per tale accidens, quod sic appellat Avicenna 'adventitium tantum', dicendum est, descendendo ad nostram quaestionem, quod duo angeli in solis substantialibus existentes, posito etiam quod nullum accidens reale differens re ab eorum essentia in se habeant, neque scilicet potentiam neque habitum neque aliquid huiusmodi, sunt individualiter distincti hoc solo quod subsistunt in effectu. Ubi extra communitatem essentiae in ambobus subsistere unius non est subsistere alterius cum unus eorum subsistere posset sine altero. Et sic per hoc ab invicem differunt, quod iste non est ille, duplicata scilicet natura speciei sive essentiae angelicae in eis per rationem subsistendi sive existendi in actu aliam in uno et aliam in altero, quae est praeter intellectum essentiae communis in utroque.''

43. *Ibid.*, q. 8, pp. 49–50: "Nulla enim re alia addita essentiae rei, ipsamet fit suppositum subsistens in existentia actuali, hac sola intentione adiecta qua ipsa habet esse effectus Dei, et hoc in natura et essentia, ipsam de non esse in esse producendo.''

44. *Ibid.*, q. 8, pp. 50–51: "Et ita, sicut continuum ex se est divisibile in partes quantitativas quas continet in se indivisas, et eo solo dividitur secundum eas quod ab invicem separantur, utraque partium recipiente in se perfectam rationem continui sed partialiter quantitatem molis, sic essentia speciei angelicae ex se est divisibilis in partes essentiales quas virtute continet in se indivisas, et eo solo dividitur secundum eas quod per subsistentiam actualem appositam separatur ab invicem, utroque eorum recipiente in se perfecte rationem essentiae sed partialiter quantitatem virtutis eius, quia non est in aliquo illorum ad modum essentiae absolutae divisibilis sed est in utroque eorum ut aliqua decisio eius indivisibilis.''

45. *Ibid.*, q. 8, p. 51: "Et sic non est dicendum quod hoc solo differunt quia natura unius eorum non est natura alterius—eadem, dico, secundum numerum—, sed quia subsistentia unius non est subsistentia alterius, quae facit differre essentiam ut est in uno, ab ipsa ut est in altero, et eam quae una est et simplex in essentia, facit esse plures in existentia. Ipsa enim subsistentia in supposito omnio necessaria est ad essentiae existentiam actualem, tam in uno quam in altero, non secundum idem numero, sed secundum aliud et aliud numero, consimile tamen specie. Ut sic sit per aliud et aliud, quod uterque illorum dicatur esse angelus simpliciter et quod dicatur esse iste vel ille, quia intentio essentiae simpliciter, qua uterque dicitur angelus, est alia ab intentione subsistentiae huius et illius, qua dicuntur iste angelus et ille. Patet ergo quomodo per intentiones subsistentiae duorum angelorum fit essentiae communis individuatio in eis.'' Cf. *Quodlibet V*, q. 8, f. 166rM: "Unde angelitas non ex eo quod est angelitas, neque ex eo quod est haec angelitas, habet rationem suppositi ab intra sed angelus iste habens determinate hanc angelitatem quia ex se, non est hic nisi quia est huius. Ratio enim determinationis super formam adveniens est ratio constituendi

suppositum determinatum in quo designatur forma quae proprie non est determinata, neque individuata, nisi quia est suppositi determinati et individuati tam in materialibus quam in spiritualibus.''

46. Henry of Ghent, *Quodlibet II*, q. 8, p. 50: ''Sed quia coniunctio istorum duorum, scilicet essentiae et subsistentiae in uno et in altero, non potest esse ex se ipsis—quia ex se non habent quod subsistunt in effectu, ut dictum est—, sed oportet quod fiat in eis per aliam causam, facientem utrumque eorum esse alterum per essentiam existentem in actu, et hunc non esse illum et e converso—ut sit totum causatum quod est in utroque—, ideo causa individuationis eorum prima et efficiens dicendus est Deus, qui dat utrique eorum subsistentiam in effectu et seorsum.''

47. Henry of Ghent, *Quodlibet XI*, q. 1, vol. 27, f. 418vQR: ''Quare cum forma quae ex se communis est et indeterminata non potest descendere in suppositum nisi aliquo modo determinetur in illud, quia aliter non esset suppositum quid determinatum sub specie, quod tamen omnis ratio suppositi requirit: ita quod si ponatur suppositum subsistere in re extra sine omni determinatione implicantur contradictoria, scilicet quod esset determinatum et indeterminatum, et illa determinatio fit per aliquod esse non aliud ab ipso esse indeterminato. *Quod quidem esse determinatum non est vere accidens, licet sit extra rationem speciei.* Determinatio necessario fit per aliquid. Si enim illud esset vere accidens, tunc suppositum sub specie non esset unum nisi per accidens, et nullum per se, quod falsum est. Unde secundum diversum modum ponendi esse indeterminatum speciei determinari in supposito, secundum hoc diversimode ponitur species descendere in suppositum aut in supposita. Sed hoc alio et alio modo dicunt fieri in formis materialibus et in formis separatis a materia. In materialibus enim dicunt quod verum est quod forma determinatur per materiam in qua habet esse et recipi, non ut consideratur ipsa materia in sua essentia simplici, sed ut est sub dimensionibus. Et hoc dupliciter, quoniam in quibusdam formam substantialem in materia naturaliter praecedent dimensiones interminatae, ut in generabilibus et corruptibilibus. In quibusdam vero forma substantialis in materia naturaliter praecedit omnem rationem dimensionum, ut in corporibus caelestibus, secundum quod hoc plane dicit Averroes in libello *De substantia orbis.* In primis autem quia dimensiones quodammodo praecedunt formam substantialem in materia, materia sub ratione divisibilis est subiectum suae formae, ita quod secundum quod unam partem sui potest esse subiecta formae specificae secundum unam determinationem quam habet ab illa, et non secundum aliam. Sed secundum illam aliam potest esse aequaliter subiectum eiusdem formae specificae secundum aliam determinationem quam habet ab illa. Et ideo in talibus quia forma secundum unam determinationem non necessario continet sub se totam suam materiam possibilem ad sui susceptionem, per materiam fit individuorum plurificatio sub una specie specialissima et recipit ipsa forma per hoc diversa esse in diversis suppositis.'' Cf. *Quodlibet II*, q. 8, p. 49: ''Quae quidem accidentia Avicenna distinguit in tria genera, qui et secundum hoc tangit tres modos diversos quibus diversa diversimode individuantur, cum dicit immediate post illud quod iam dictum est de V *Metaphysicae:* 'Ipsae vero proprietates et accidentia aut erunt adventitia tantum, ita ut non sint de essentia ullo modo, et haec sunt accidentia, quae accidunt individuis rerum simplicium, aut erant dispositiones superadditae; ex

quibus quaedam sunt, quibus intellectis remotis ab hoc signato, necesse est ut habeat esse hoc signatum quod est praeter alia, quia continget destrui veritatem suae alietatis comitantis, et quaedam sunt, quibus intellectis remotis, non est necesse provenire destructionem sui esse postquam habuit esse vel corruptionem suae essentiae post eius appropriationem, sed destruetur alietas et eius diversitas ad alia, secundum quod diversum est ab aliis absque destructione singularis. Fortassis autem hoc obscurum est penes nos et non determinatur. Noster autem sermo non est de hoc quod scitur, sed secundum quod res est in se.' "

48. Henry of Ghent, *Quodlibet V,* q. 8, f. 166rM: "Sed quid est in supposito super formam quo habet esse hoc et quo per ipsum forma habet esse hoc quia est huius? Dico aliquid praeter materiam et praeter agens quod est quasi dispositio suppositi in quantum suppositum est, quod non potest esse materia nec agens. Haec enim dispositio derelicta est circa formam in supposito, et facit suppositum esse suppositum, ut habens formam et rationem compositionis ex forma et ratione determinationis in ipsa."

49. *Ibid.,* q. 8, f. 166rM: "Hoc enim viso videbitur ratio suppositi et individuationis proxima, et quid est quod suppositum formaliter faciat in creaturis. Et est dicendum quod est aliquid extra intentionem formae concomitans eius productionem, vel per agens vel per materiam, vel per utrunque. Quare cum super naturam rei factae concomitans ipsam ex sua producti non potest esse aliquid positivum et absolutum, quia illud oporteret esse factum, et similiter in sua natura esset determinabile, sicut et ipsa forma, necessario faceret compositionem realem cum ipsa forma tanquam aliquid aliud secundum formam ab ipso appositum ipsi, quemadmodum forma differentiae est aliud a forma generis nisi ponamus in forma substantiali intentionem et remissionem sicut est in accidentali, ut in uno supposito subsistat sub gradu intensiori, in alio vero sub gradu remissiori. Sed tamen adhuc restat difficultas quaestionis, supposito quod subsistat in duobus suppositis eiusdem gradus. Oportet ergo quod sit aliquid negativum aut positivum respectivum. Non positivum respectivum, quia respectus ille necessario fundaretur in ipsa re ut facta est, et ita ut determinata in supposito."

50. *Ibid.,* q. 8, f. 166rM: "Oportet igitur quod sit aliqua conditio negativa. Est igitur dicendum quod in formis creatis specificis ut specificae sunt, ratio individuationis ipsarum qua determinatur in suppositis et quae est ratio constitutiva suppositi, est negatio qua forma ipsa quae ex se est specifica in esse rationis, ut est terminus factionis, facta est indivisa omnino in supposito et individualis et singularis privatione omnis divisibilitatis per se et per accidens et a quolibet alio divisa, ut sic sit processus in formis creatis, quia forma generis habens solam unitatem rationis in se est per formas divisa, quae ipsam determinant ad speciem. Forma vero speciei determinata est in forma specifica non divisibilis neque determinabilis per formas diversas nec quantum est de se per formas easdem specie, sed solum per aliquid aliud a se, non solum ut per agens formam in esse producens, ut in formis separatis, aut per materiam, ut in rebus materialibus, ut dictum est. Sed cum hoc quod habet esse per agens aut per materiam habet etiam esse per aliquid aliud et completive, quia agens aut materia non est ultimum et completivum quo quasi formaliter fit individuatio et ratio suppositi, immo

per hoc quod forma ab agente producente eam, aut per materiam in se habet esse indivisum omnino, et a qualibet alia forma divisum, cum qua in specie communicat. Quae quidem negatio non est simplex sed duplex, quia est removens ab intra omnem plurificabilitatem et diversitatem, et ab extra omnem identitatem, ut dicatur ita haec quod tantum haec, non habendo, scilicet, intra se possibilitatem ad esse aliud et aliud sicut habet forma speciei, et iterum tantum haec quod non sit aliqua aliarum suae speciei. Et haec duplex negatio omnino formaliter rationem formae determinat qua determinatione supra essentiam formae constituitur suppositum absolutum, quod vere dicitur hoc aliquid quasi tantum hoc et non aliud nec intra se nec extra, et sic nullo modo aliud quid.''

51. See the article on St. Bonaventure in this volume, pp. 141–172.

52. Guillelmus Alvernus, *De universo,* I, 2, ch. 9 (*Opera omnia* I; Aureliae 1674), p. 852. Cf. M.-D. Roland-Gosselin, *Le "De ente"* , pp. 72–74.

53. Praepositinus, *Summa,* III (cod. Vat. lat. 1174), f. 52ra: "Unde non sequitur 'secundum quod est homo est aliquid [quod est] Pater vel quod non est Pater, vel substantia quae est Pater [vel quae non est Pater]. Sicut si dicam 'Petrus humanitate est homo, ergo humanitate est hic homo vel alius homo, vel homo qui est Socrates vel qui non est Socrates.' Non enim Petrus humanitate est hic homo sed tantum homo, sed sua propria existentia est hic homo. . . .''

54. Peter Ioannis Olivi, *Quaestiones in II Sent.*, q. 15, ed. B. Jansen and Claras Aquas (Quaracchi: Typographia Collegii S. Bonaventorae, 1922), p. 277.

55. John Duns Scotus, *Ordinatio,* in *Opera omnia,* II, d. 3, p. 1, q. 2, nn. 47–56, (ed. Vaticana, 1976), t. VII, pp. 412–416. Cf. *Reportatio Parisiensis,* II, d. 12, q. 6, ed. L. Vivès (Paris, 1894), t. 23, pp. 33–34.

56. Henry of Ghent, *Quodlibet V,* q. 8, f. 166rM. Cf. *Summa quaestionum,* a. 53, q. 3, vol II, f. 63rT.

57. Henry of Ghent, *Quodlibet XI,* q. 1, f. 419rT: "Similiter forma angeli ita habet rationem universalis secundum rationem speciei specialissimae, sicut est forma hominis aut asini, et ita rationem communis et abstracti per intellectum et indeterminati atque determinabilis, etsi non per materiam, tamen per esse in supposito, quia, ut dictum est, non est suppositum nisi per determinationem aliquam, ut impossibile sit dicere quod non sit aliud esse essentiae angeli simpliciter et huius angeli. Immo oportet quod sint differentia secundum rationem determinati et indeterminati, quam quidem determinationem effective non habet forma nisi a producente ipsa in existentia actuali, quia non terminatur actus productionis ad essentiam rei simpliciter ut est essentia sub ratione indeterminati sed solummodo ut est haec essentia, quia omnis actus et operatio est circa singularia. Formaliter autem habet determinationem in hoc supposito, quia in ipso est secundum hoc esse proprium huic supposito; et sic positiva eius individuatio non fit effective nisi per producentem, et formaliter non nisi per hoc esse. Qualiter autem habeat fieri individuatio negative, alibi sufficienter exposuimus.''

58. Cf. *ibid.* See also Richard of Mediavilla, *Quaestiones super II Sent.*, d. 3, q. 4, a. 1 (Brescia, 1591), vol II, f. 59ra and the article on Richard of Mediavilla and Hervaeus Natalis in this volume, pp. 000–000.

59. Henry of Ghent, *Summa quaestionum,* a. 53, q. 3, f. 63rS: "Quamquam enim secundum Ambrosium, I *De trinitate,* omnis creatura certis limitibus suis contenta est, humanitas tamen ampliorem habet latitudinem spiritualem sive rationis essentiae suae quam haec humanitas. Et ideo haec humanitas respectu humanitatis simpliciter est determinata, limitata et significata, in qua significatione consistit primo ratio singularis formae subiectivae, sicut et individuatio ipsius formae communis. Ex consequenti autem fit utrumque eorum per negationem consequentem illam determinationem et annexam ei non per unicam sed per duplicem, per quam scilicet separatur ab eo quod est sub se, et ab eo quod est iuxta se: humanitas enim divisa est in hanc humanitatem et illam. Etiam si non esset divisa, esset tamen quantum est ex se divisibilis, etsi non separatur ab eo quod est sub se per ullam negationem. Sed haec humanitas ex eo quod est haec, nec est divisa, nec divisibilis in aliqua sub se suae naturae, et ideo negative se habet ad ea quae imaginari possent sub se; negative etiam se habet ad ea quae sunt iuxta se, et ex opposito divisa sub specie."

60. John Duns Scotus, *Ordinatio,* II, d. 3, p. 1, q. 3, nn. 60–64 (ed. Vaticana), t. VII, pp. 418–420 and *Reportatio parisiensis,* II d. 12, q. 7, pp. 35–36. See Henry, ibid: "Fit autem illa eius individuatio in parte subiectiva, ut humanitas in hac humanitate, immo in hoc homine effective, non nisi per agens dans ei esse, nec per materiam etsi habeat materiam, nec per aliquod accidens ei inhaerens, sed primo per suam significationem et determinationem quam habet ab agente illam." Cf. *Quodlibet XI,* q. 1 (f. 419rV:) "Immo oportet quod sint differentia secundum rationem determinati et indeterminati, quam quidem determinationem effective non habet forma nisi a producente ipsa in existentia actuali, quia non terminatur actus productionis ad essentiam rei simpliciter ut est essentia sub ratione indeterminati sed solummodo ut est haec essentia, quia omnis actus et operatio est circa singularia."

61. Godfrey of Fontaines, *Quodlibet VII,* q. 5 (ed. Philosophes Belges 3: 299–301). Cf. J. F. Wippel, *The Metaphysical Thought of Godfrey of Fontaines* (Washington, DC: Catholic University of America Press, 1981), pp. 227–228 and 349. Cf. his paper on Godfrey in the present volume, pp. 000–000. Cf. J. Paulus, *Henri de Gand* (Paris: Vrin, 1938), p. 365. On Godfrey's position concerning separated substances, see Wippel, *The Metaphysical Thought,* p. 366. Later, after Henry's death, in *Quodlibet XII,* q. 10, Godfrey holds that the condemned articles were sustained by many Catholic theologians and were theologically defensible. See Wippel, *ibid.,* p. 369.

62. Cf. J. Paulus, *Ibid.,* p. 365: "Contrairement à S. Thomas qui fait dans l'aristotélisme un choix, et rejette la thèse de la subsistance soit par soi, soit par la matière, pour conserver celle de l'individuation par soi ou par la matière, Henri veut, comme Aristote, que l'individuation et la subsistance marchent de pair et solidaires l'une de l'autre."

63. See Section V.

64. Cf. Giles of Rome, *Quodlibet II,* q. 8. (Lovain, 1646), p. 65: "Optandum vero foret quod maturiori consilio tales articuli fuissent ordinati; et adhuc sperandum quod forte de iis in posterum sit habendum consilium sanius. Hinc in praesenti, quantum possumus et ut possimus, articulum sustinemus." Ed. Venetiis 1503, f. 15v: "Vellemus autem quod maturiori consilio articuli illi ordinati essent, et adhuc forte de eis in posterum habebitur consilium sanius. Ad praesens, autem, quantum possumus et ut possimus, articulum sustinemus." See Henry of Ghent, *Quodlibet XI,* q. 1, f. 418vQ: "Sed quia hoc damnatum est *rationabiliter.* . . ." and f. 418vT: Sed hoc totum falsum est et erroneum atque damnatum Parisii, et hoc *rationabiliter,* ut iam tactum est circa formam separatam principaliter."

65. F. Van Steenberghen, *Maître Siger de Brabant* (Louvain: Publications Universitaires, 1977), pp. 146–155.

10

GODFREY OF FONTAINES (B. CA. 1250; D. 1306/09), PETER OF AUVERGNE (D. 1303), AND JOHN BACONTHORPE (D. 1345/48)

JOHN F. WIPPEL

Twentieth-century students of Thomas Aquinas are familiar with his views concerning the individuation of material substances. Many are also aware that there has been some disagreement among late nineteenth and early twentieth century scholars concerning the proper interpretation of Thomas's position. According to one reading, for Aquinas the principle of individuation falls on the side of matter as related in some way to quantity. According to another reading, Aquinas also makes quantity the principle of individuation along with matter.[1] In addition, there is some difficulty in deciding whether it is to determined or to undetermined dimensions that Thomas appeals in his development of quantity's role in individuation.[2]

Thomas's views were known to late thirteenth and early fourteenth century thinkers as well. At the same time, other theories of individuation were proposed by a number of them. In the present study I have singled out for special consideration the particular solution developed by Godfrey of Fontaines, and subsequent discussion of this same approach by Peter of Auvergne and John Baconthorpe. Godfrey's position has been interpreted differently by the few twentieth century specialists who have examined his texts concerning this.[3] But some fifty years ago E. Hocedez edited an important text taken from Peter of Auvergne's Quodlibet II, and in the course of discussing Peter's position, he noted its similarity with that advanced by Godfrey.[4]

This in itself is quite interesting since in Peter we have a leading master from the arts faculty at Paris whose career as a master in arts apparently goes back to the earlier 1270s. As is well known, Peter himself completed some works (commentaries on Aristotle) left unfinished by Thomas Aquinas.[5] Godfrey's career as a student in the arts faculty must have come to an end in the early 1270s, and at least by 1274.[6] One wonders whether Godfrey might possibly have assisted at some of Peter's lectures. On the other side of the coin, Godfrey served as regent master in the theology faculty from 1285 until ca. 1303–1304. Since Peter did not take up the formal study of theology until late in the century, he must have been a student in that faculty during Godfrey's regency. In fact, it is generally admitted that Peter himself studied theology under Godfrey (and under Henry of Ghent).[7] In Peter, therefore, we encounter a master who was quite familiar with the work of Aquinas, on the one side, and of Godfrey of Fontaines, on the other.

Some decades after Godfrey's and Peter's discussion of individuation in their respective Quodlibets (dating from the early to late 1290s), John Baconthorpe considered this same problem in his Commentary on the *Sentences.* He represents Godfrey and Peter as defending the same position and then accepts this as his own view as well. At the same time, he makes some interesting comments concerning the position that was frequently ascribed to Thomas Aquinas and contrasts this with what he regards as Thomas's actual thought on the matter.[8]

In the present chapter I propose to set forth Godfrey's views concerning individuation, Peter's theory as found in his Quodlibet II, and John Baconthorpe's discussion of the same. This will cast some light on the historical accuracy of Peter's and John's understanding and usage of Godfrey's position and will offer one important illustration of Godfrey's influence on other late thirteenth and early fourteenth century thinkers. John's precisions concerning the proper interpretation of Aquinas's position will also be noted.

I. Godfrey of Fontaines

On another occasion I have examined in some detail Godfrey's views concerning individuation.[9] For my present purposes, therefore, it will be enough for me to summarize my earlier findings. Roland-Gosselin has suggested that Godfrey distinguishes between a substantial principle of "individuality" and an accidental one and that for Godfrey the substantial form of a composite entity serves as its substantial principle of individuation. He questions whether Godfrey himself fully appreciated the difference between substantial unity and numerical unity. According to Hocedez, it was this precise distinction that Peter of Auvergne clarified, though Hocedez also acknowledges that Godfrey's discussion of the general issue is more complete and more profound than that offered by Peter.[10] As M. De Wulf reads him,

Godfrey identifies substantial form as the principle of individuation. But according to a more recent writer, R. Arway, De Wulf himself has failed to distinguish adequately between the problem of individuality and that of individuation. Like Thomas Aquinas, Godfrey would have proposed matter as signed by dimensive quantity as the principle of individuation.[11]

In an effort to clarify this situation, I have found it helpful not to turn immediately to Godfrey's explicit discussion of individuation in Quodlibet VII, qu. 5, but to his earlier Quodlibet VI, qu. 16. (While Quodlibet VII seems to have been disputed in the 1290/1291 or the 1291/1292 academic year, Quodlibet VI seems to date from 1289.[12]) In his earlier discussion Godfrey distinguishes between the kind of unity that is convertible with being and the kind that serves as a principle of number. Godfrey acknowledges that in a sense every unity may be regarded as a principle of number, since multitude itself implies some kind of number. But in distinguishing the kind of unity that serves as a principle of number, Godfrey has in mind the number that is based on discrete quantity and therefore falls under the genus quantity. To avoid confusion and at the same time remain faithful to Godfrey's text, I proposed distinguishing between numerical unity in the broad sense (the kind that is convertible with being) and numerical unity in the strict sense (the kind based on quantity).[13] The first kind of unity is often known as "transcendental unity" or "ontological unity" within the scholastic tradition. Important for our immediate purposes is Godfrey's claim within this same context that by reason of its form any being enjoys this last-mentioned kind of unity—transcendental unity (numerical unity in the broad sense). In support of this Godfrey comments that by reason of its form a given being is what it is, undivided from itself, and divided from all else.[14]

Numerical unity taken in the strict sense, of course, is not convertible with being and hence is not transcendental. It is found only in things that enjoy continuous quantity. And, comments Godfrey, it is only because of the division of such continuous quantity that different members of the same class or species can be realized and, therefore, distinct substances within the same class or species.[15] If substance depends on quantity to have numerical unity in the strict sense and therefore to be multiplied numerically, quantity itself does not depend on anything else in order to enjoy such strict numerical unity. As Godfrey himself describes this, in the case of quantity, numerical unity taken broadly (transcendental or ontological unity) and numerical unity taken strictly do not differ from one another really but only by a distinction of reason. By its very nature quantity is continuous and divisible and therefore undivided in itself and divided from all else. Given this, of its very nature quantity enjoys transcendental unity, or what Godfrey here refers to as "essential unity". A material substance can participate in the unity given by quantity only as in something superadded to that substance. Hence this kind of unity, numerical unity taken strictly, is accidental to the material substance considered as such.[16]

Godfrey maintains this position to avoid an infinite regress. If quantity itself depended on something else for its unity, then that added factor would itself have to depend on something else again, ad infinitum.[17] In sum, there-fore, in this discussion Godfrey has distinguished between numerical unity taken broadly (transcendental unity) and numerical unity taken strictly. If he has appealed to the substantial form of a given substance to account for its transcendental unity, he has proposed quantity as that upon which such a sub-stance depends for its numerical unity in the strict sense.

With this background in mind we are now in position to turn to God-frey's Quodlibet VII, qu. 5. There he addresses himself to the following is-sue: "Does supposit (*suppositum*) add any reality (*res*) to essence or nature?"[18] Before presenting his lengthy reply he introduces an important distinction. Nature and supposit may be contrasted with one another in two different ways. On the one hand, by 'nature' one may understand that which is signified by an abstract term, in the manner of a simple form to which it belongs to be participated in by something else. So understood nature in-cludes only those things which belong to a thing's essence—for instance, that which is signified by terms such as 'humanity' or 'whiteness'. All that does not pertain to a thing's essence is not only not included in the meaning of nature when it is so used, but is excluded from its meaning. Contrasted with nature when it is so understood is the supposit, taken as that which is signi-fied concretely and as something composed. By reason of its concrete way of signifying (or connotation) though not its primary meaning (or denotation), more is included in the meaning of supposit than is included in the meaning of nature taken abstractly. To illustrate this Godfrey cites that which is sig-nified by terms such as a 'man' or a 'white thing'. To ask about the rela-tionship between nature and supposit when they are so understood is to investigate the relationship between an essence or quiddity, on the one hand, and that which has such a quiddity or essence, on the other. In other words, it is to raise the metaphysical issue of subsistence.[19]

Nature and supposit may also be contrasted in another way. By 'nature' one may understand that which is signified by a general or universal term and that, while being one in definition, can be participated in by many individ-uals. To nature so understood one may contrast 'supposit', understood this time as a singular or as an individual thing—that is, as something undivided in itself and divided from all other individuals. To ask what supposit when taken in this way adds to nature is to seek for the principle of individuation. It is to ask what the individual adds to the universal, or what this man adds to man (or this human to humanity).[20] While Godfrey considers each of these ways of comparing nature and supposit in considerable detail in Quodlibet VII, qu. 5, here we shall be concerned only with the second of these, that is, with his discussion of the problem of individuation.[21]

Godfrey begins his examination of the problem of individuation by observing that because the different individuals within a given species share in the same common nature, they cannot be distinguished from one another by that which they have in common. If this is true, it would seem that in addition to the nature implied by their membership in the same species, something else must be found in each of them that will individuate that nature as it is realized there. But if something must be added to the specific nature in each individual to account for its individuation, it seems to follow that any such superadded thing can be only something accidental. Thus something accidental would itself be the principle of individuation. Godfrey notes that various authorities may be cited in support of this—Porphyry, Boethius, John Damascene, and Avicenna.[22]

But then he argues forcefully against the view that something accidental could be the principle of individuation. For instance, an individual or first substance is no more an accidental aggregate than is the species or second substance. Otherwise, second substance could not be predicated essentially of first substance. Hence something accidental cannot be the principle of individuation. Again, individual accidents seem to be posterior to and superadded to substance. Hence they presuppose the individuation of the substance in which they inhere, rather than vice versa. Finally, any such theory would reduce the distinction between different substances within the same species to the purely accidental level.[23]

Godfrey comments that if any accident could serve as the principle of individuation, it would be quantity. He recalls a point we have already seen from his discussion in Quodlibet VI, qu. 16. Only insofar as a substantial form is received in quantified matter can such a form enjoy numerical unity in the strict sense and hence be multiplied numerically. Hence it would seem that the numerical multiplication and the individuation of material substances depend on quantity.[24]

Godfrey considers this suggestion carefully, but ends by rejecting it. If quantity were to serve as the principle of individuation, it could do so only by functioning as the efficient or final or material or formal cause of individuation. Godfrey sees no reason for holding that quantity is either the efficient or the final cause of individuation. Quantity can hardly serve as the material cause of individuation, since rather the substance composed of matter and substantial form is the material cause or subject of quantity. Quantity must be rejected as a formal cause of individuation because admission of this would imply that two substances within the same species differ from one another only in accidental fashion, not substantially. In short, they would not be two different substances but one and the same substantial reality. When two substances differ from one another substantially, the substantial form of one cannot be formally identical with the substantial form of the other.[25]

To extricate himself from this seeming impasse, Godfrey notes that there are individual immaterial substances as well as individual material substances. One cannot appeal to quantity to account for the fact that there are individual immaterial substances. Hence the cause of their individuation can be only the indivision of their substantial forms into other forms of the same kind. In like fashion, reasons Godfrey, even in material things the form whereby an individual is what it is and subsists is also its principle of individuation. As he puts it, something is undivided in itself and one through that whereby it is what it is. Even in material substances this is their substantial form.[26]

As already noted, in Quodlibet VI, qu. 16 Godfrey had proposed substantial form as the principle of numerical unity taken broadly, or of transcendental unity. In the present discussion he has now concluded that the same substantial form is also the formal principle of individuation. The undividedness from itself or ontological unity enjoyed by any substance by reason of its substantial form is prior in nature to any of its accidents, including quantity. Hence it is also prior in the order of nature to any division that might belong to such a substance by reason of an accident. At the same time, Godfrey notes that matter is in potency to its appropriate substantial form. Hence it is also in potency to the undividedness given to the composite by the form. To this extent, concludes Godfrey, matter may also be regarded as a principle of individuation insofar as it is a kind of principle, that is, a subject, for its substantial form.[28]

At the same time, Godfrey acknowledges that material substances may be multiplied within their species. Any such substance, insofar as it is simply considered in itself, is not divided into many individuals of the same kind. It is capable of such division insofar as it is in potency to quantity. Hence if it is quantified by means of the accident quantity, it is also divided into many such substances by means of this same accident.[29] One might immediately object that Godfrey has in effect made quantity the formal principle of individuation. Against this he can counter that he has distinguished between the principle of strict numerical unity, on the one hand, and the formal principle of individuation, on the other. If he proposes quantity as the principle of strict numerical unity, he denies that it is the formal principle of individuation. Only the substantial form of any such substance can be its formal principle of individuation. As regards spiritual substances, their substantial forms are also their principles of individuation. But since they do not enjoy strictly numerical unity, there is no principle of such numerical unity within them. Not being material, they are obviously not subject to quantity.

While Godfrey denies that quantity is the formal principle of individuation, he finds it necessary to assign some role to quantity in the individuation of material substances. For numerically distinct substantial forms of the same kind to be received into matter, matter itself must be divided. Matter is rendered divisible by quantity. Because of this, material substances enjoy strictly numerical unity. And insofar as such strictly numerical unity is multiplied because of quantity, such substances differ numerically from one another. Hence Godfrey proposes that, while it is not the formal cause of individuation, quantity does prepare and dispose matter so that it can be divided into different parts. In other words, quantity serves as a kind of material and disposing cause of individuation.[30]

This should not be taken as implying that quantity itself is the material cause of individuation, but only that it disposes matter so as to render it extended, divisible, and capable of receiving numerically distinct forms within the same species. Godfrey finds support for his position in Averroes's *De substantia orbis*.[31]

At this point in his discussion Godfrey introduces the issue of dimensions. If one thinks of matter as being prior (not in time but in nature) to its substantial form in the order of material causality, one may also think of matter when so viewed as being subject to *undetermined* dimensions. One should not regard undetermined dimensions as being prior in nature to matter when matter is considered in terms of its proper entity. Nor should one think of these undetermined dimensions as being prior to the substantial form viewed in terms of its entity. But matter does depend upon quantity and hence upon such dimensions to be divided into different parts of the same kind. And substantial form likewise depends on matter to be so divided, as we have already seen. Hence Godfrey concludes that undetermined dimensions may be regarded as prior to matter (and hence to form) in this respect, that the presence of such dimensions is necessary to render matter divisible into different parts of the same kind, and hence to account for matter's reception of different forms of the same kind.[32]

Godfrey also comments that the same may be said of a given substantial composite when it is considered as actualized by its given substantial form. Its matter will now depend on dimensions, but *determined* dimensions this time, in order to be rendered divisible and receive different substantial forms of the same kind. Given this, while he continues to deny that quantity itself is the formal cause of individuation—the substantial form is—Godfrey concludes that quantity may be described as formally causing the division of matter into different parts of the same kind.[33]

In concluding this section, we should recall the following points from Godfrey's position. First, as already indicated, Godfrey insists that his theory does not reduce the difference between individual material substances within the same species to the purely accidental level. He states that such substances will differ from all others both *formally* and *substantially*. One such substance will differ from another because it has its own form and its own matter.[34] Second, in answer to the question originally raised in this disputation, Godfrey denies that supposit when taken as the individual adds anything real to nature taken as the universal in terms of its (supposit's) primary meaning or denotation.[35] Third, according to Godfrey the substantial form of a material substance is its formal principle of individuation. Quantity, on the other hand, plays an important role in individuation by rendering matter divisible into different parts of the same kind. Finally, Godfrey has distinguished between numerical unity taken broadly (transcendental unity) and numerical unity taken strictly. Corresponding to this he has proposed substantial form as the principle of transcendental unity, and quantity as the principle of strictly numerical unity.[36]

II. Peter of Auvergne

Peter of Auvergne examined this problem on at least two different occasions, that is, in his *Quaestiones in Metaphysicam* and in his Quodlibet II, qu. 5. Both of these texts have been edited by Hocedez.[37] While it is difficult to date precisely Peter's *Quaestiones*, his Quodlibet II seems to have been disputed ca. 1297 and is clearly the later treatment.[38] Hocedez originally felt that, in spite of some verbal dissimilarities between Peter's two discussions of individuation, they were in fundamental agreement. But in his subsequent, more detailed study of this issue in Peter, he came to the opposite conclusion. The position defended by Peter in Quodlibet II departs considerably from that developed in his earlier *Quaestiones*.[39] Since here I am especially interested in Godfrey's influence on Peter's presentation, and since it is only Peter's discussion in Quodlibet II that could have been influenced by Godfrey's Quodlibet VII, qu. 5, I shall concentrate on that text in Peter.

Peter's Quodlibet II, qu. 5 is directed to this issue: Is the principle of individuation for a composite substance identical with its principle of numerical unity?[40] The opening argument offered against this assertion is interesting. The principle of individuation in the case of a composite substance is the quantity by which it is rendered divisible (from others within the same species); but the principle of its numerical unity is not quantity. In proof of the last point the objection contends that someone who rises from the dead will be numerically one and the same as he was before, even if he does not have the same quantity.[41] One is reminded of the question posed for Godfrey in his Quodlibet VI, qu. 16: If a human body should rise without quantity, would it still be numerically one and the same as it was before?[42] In attempting to resolve this question, Peter indicates that he will proceed according to three steps. He will determine first what are the principles of individuation; second, what are the principles of numerical unity; and third, from this the answer to the general question.[43]

As regards the first point, Peter begins by noting that individuation is a kind of privation, since individuation is a negation of division. But, he continues, there is no per se active (efficient) principle for a privation, but only a 'privative' principle. And if there is no active principle, there is no final cause either, since the end and the agent correspond. Given this, there will likewise be no formal principle for the individual insofar as it is an individual since, to repeat, individuation is a privation.[44] But a privation does have a material principle, for it must have a subject in which it is realized. Therefore there must be a per se material principle for individuation considered precisely as individuation. And this material principle can be realized only in something else, since the individual as such bespeaks the negation of division (from itself). Hence Peter's immediate task is to determine what accounts for the fact that an individual within the genus of composite substance enjoys indivision.[45]

Peter then considers a number of solutions that have already been proposed. He recalls that there was an ancient view that held that the principle of individuation is a collection of accidental properties. He cites texts from Porphyry and from Avicenna in connection with this, but then rejects this position out of hand. That which is common to many things in terms of its definition (*ratio*) cannot be their principle of individuation. But a collection of accidents simply considered as such can be common to many. Thus if 'white' can be predicated of many things, so can the combination of 'white' and 'cultured' be said of many, granted that these will be fewer in number. Moreover, a combination of 'white' and 'cultured' and 'walking' can also be predicated of many things, granted that these will be still fewer in number.[46]

Again, reasons Peter, something numerically one does not result from many things that differ in species except by reason of something else that makes them one in number. And this factor itself will have to be one in number. No mere accident or combination of accidents can serve this function, since all of these are still common.[47]

Peter then considers another approach according to which quantity would be the principle of individuation. He notes that texts are cited from John Damascene and from Boethius in support of this position. This theory rests upon the claim that that by which an individual is first distinguished from others of the same species is its principle of individuation and that through that by which it is first distinguished from others it is also undivided in itself. But it is by reason of quantity that one thing is first distinguished from another within the same species. Therefore quantity is the principle of individuation.[48]

Against this view Peter counters that it seems to be even less reasonable. First of all, if a composite substance were first individuated by means of quantity, an individual instance of that substance would therefore be determined by quantity. (Implied in Peter's argument is the view that such a substance would therefore be defined in terms of quantity.) If this were so, such an individual substance would be something accidental in the formal sense and not a substance. This, in turn, runs counter to Aristotle's remark in the *Categories* where he states that first substance is said to be substance in the primary sense and most fully. Consequently, an individual composite substance would not be an *unum per se* but an *unum per accidens*.[49]

Moreover, since an individual composite substance is the *per se terminus* of the process of generation, it would follow that the *per se terminus* of generation would be only an accidental aggregate (*unum per accidens*). Since generation may be defined in terms of the form of that which is thereby generated, it would also follow that generation itself would belong to the genus of quantity (rather than really being substantial) and that generation would be only a motion that terminates in quantity.[50]

In still another argument against the claim that quantity is the principle of individuation, and one that reminds the reader of Godfrey's criticism of this same theory, Peter notes that that which is posterior in nature to an individual substance cannot be its principle of individuation. A cause is prior in nature to its effect; but quantity is posterior in nature to the individual substance. This follows from the fact that quantity is an accident and its being presupposes the being of its substance. Accidents, Peter comments, are and are said to be beings because they happen to an existing substance. But if quantity is posterior to the being of a substance, it is also posterior to that substance's individuation. Therefore the individuation of quantity presupposes the individuation of a given substance just as the being of quantity presupposes the being of its substance.[51]

At this point Peter returns to the opening argument mentioned earlier. That argument had assumed that the very thing by reason of which a substance is first distinguished from others within the same species is identical with that substance's *per se* principle of individuation. Against this Peter offers the example of the sun. The sun is an individual substance within the genus substance, and yet it is not distinguished from any other member of its own species by quantity. The same holds for the heaven and for the moon. In like fashion, if among things that are subject to generation and corruption one should be found that is unique within its species, it too would be an individual; and yet it would not be actually distinguished from others within the same species by reason of its quantity. Therefore, argues Peter, one need not identify that by reason of which something is an individual with that whereby it is distinguished from something else.[52]

This point will be crucial for Peter's eventual solution, and he proceeds to develop it more fully. It is of its own nature that an individual substance is undivided as a substance. But to be divided from something else is something that "happens" to such a thing that is undivided in itself. Therefore, insists Peter, it is not through that whereby something is first undivided in itself that it is necessarily divided from others of the same species. To be divided from others of the same species is accidental to such a thing.[53] Peter immediately connects this with the ancients' distinction between two kinds of one or unity. There is a one that is simply undivided of itself—an essential one; and there is one that is divided from something else—by reason of accidental unity. We have already seen how central this distinction is to Godfrey's theory of individuation. However, there is an added precision in Peter's presentation. He connects indivision from itself with the first kind of unity (unity of being or transcendental unity), and division from everything else only with the second type (accidental or strictly numerical unity). Godfrey holds that it is in terms of the first kind of unity that a substance is both undivided in itself and divided in the order of substance from everything else.[54]

Given this distinction between the two kinds of unity, Peter rejects as irrational that "axiom" (*dignitas*) generally assumed by defenders of this position—that one should identify that by which something is distinguished from others within the same species with that by which it is an individual in itself. (Peter does acknowledge in the case of quantity that by means of that whereby something is distinguished from others of the same species, it is also undivided from itself. In each case this is by reason of quantity itself. But, he quickly points out, this is not individuation in the order of substance, but something accidental to that.)[55]

Having rejected the view that quantity is the principle of individuation, Peter turns to another position. Some hold that prime matter serves in this capacity, since it is the first receiving principle (*receptaculum*); and the first receiving principle is undivided and not multiplied of itself. Against this Peter counters that an actual effect must have a principle that is actual, just as an effect in potency must have a principle in potency. But an individual within the genus of composite substance is something in actuality. Therefore its principle of individuation must also be something that is undivided in actuality. Prime matter, however, is not something that is either divisible or indivisible in actuality, but only in potentiality. Therefore prime matter as such cannot be the immediate and actual principle of individuation.[56]

Moreover, since prime matter simply viewed in itself is one, if it were the principle of individuation, things that have one and the same prime matter would themselves be only one individual. But one and the same prime matter belongs to that which is generated and that which is corrupted. Hence that which is generated and that which is corrupted would also be only one individual. Consequently, prime matter cannot be the *per se* principle of individuation.[57]

None of these candidates, therefore, will serve as the *per se* principle of individuation—neither a collection of accidents, nor quantity, nor any other single accident, nor prime matter. Give this, Peter concludes by process of elimination that only the substantial form whereby an individual substance subsists can fulfill this function. In support he first argues that through that whereby something enjoys being either in a particular fashion (*secundum quid*) or without qualification (*simpliciter*), it is also undivided and one either in a particular fashion or else without qualification. In other words, transcendental unity or the undividedness of a thing from itself follows upon being. For instance, Peter continues, it is through whiteness that something is in a given way—white; and it is also through whiteness that it is undivided in terms of whiteness. So too it is by reason of that whereby something is a man that it is one and undivided as a man. But a composite substance subsists by reason of its form, as Peter notes he has shown in the previous question (Quodlibet II, qu. 4); for actual being belongs to a thing in the formal sense by reason of its form. Therefore it is also by reason of its form that a composite substance is not divided into many other things of the same kind. But this—for it not to be divided into others of the same kind—is for it to be an individual substance. Consequently, in the case of a composite substance, its *per se* principle of individuation is its substantial form.[58]

In addition, continues Peter in words that in large measure are taken literally from Godfrey's Quodlibet VIII, qu. 5, a composite substance exists in reality through its form before, in the order of nature, any of its accidents do. The actual existence of any such accident presupposes the existence of its substantial subject. But something is undivided in actuality by means of that whereby it exists in actuality. Therefore, the indivision of a composite substance as this substance is realized in actuality is prior in nature to the existence of any of its accidents. Consequently, it is also prior to any indivision that might belong to that substance by reason of an accident. If therefore the individuation of such a substance is identical with its indivision from itself, individuation by form is prior in nature to any indivision it may have by reason of quantity. Peter comments that this argument is more indirect in nature than direct.[59]

Peter then offers another argument that will also remind the reader of Godfrey's reasoning. Individuation in the case of a composite substance takes place by something that is similar or proportional to that whereby it occurs in separate substances. Each separate substance is an individual because its form is not divided into others of the same kind. Therefore a lower and material substance is individuated because its form is not divided into many others of the same kind.[60]

In support of this argumentation Peter comments that, just as the form is the principle of being for material substances, so is it their *per se* principle of indivision. Such a form is undivided in terms of its definition (*ratio*) into forms that differ in genus, and hence generic unity derives from that form. It is also undivided into forms that differ in species, and therefore specific unity derives from it. In like manner it is undivided of itself into many individuals of the same kind, and hence to be an individual material substance also derives from this same substantial form.[61] Then, in another text taken literally from Godfrey, Peter comments that because matter is in potency to the form by which it actually exists, so is it in potency to the indivision that comes to it through its form. With this in mind, Peter acknowledges that matter may be regarded as a principle of individuation in some sense, that is, to the extent that it is a kind of principle or subject for its form.[62]

Peter concludes this first part of his discussion by commenting that it is now evident that the *per se* principle of individuation for a composite substance is the form by means of which that substance subsists. From this he also concludes that it is now clear that to be an individual is to enjoy undividedness in terms of being. This in turn comes through form.[63]

One rather puzzling aspect remains in Peter's account. In beginning his discussion he had described individuation as a kind of privation and commented that privation lacks efficient, final, and formal causes, while granting that it needs a material cause. In the course of working out his personal solution he has defended Godfrey's view according to which the substantial form of a composite substance is its principle of individuation. Like Godfrey he also notes that matter enters into individuation only as a subject for the substantial form and hence, presumably, for individuation. But to appeal to substantial form as the principle of individuation is hardly to identify it as a material cause of individuation. On the contrary, he has acknowledged that matter itself, insofar as it is a subject for substantial form, may be described as the subject of individuation. Substantial form, on the other hand, which Peter has identified as the *per se* principle of individuation, rather seems to be a formal cause or principle of individuation. In fact, Godfrey has so described it. While Peter has not explicitly named substantial form the 'formal principle' of individuation, his presentation of its role seems to amount to regarding it as such. One wonders how all of this can be reconciled with Peter's opening denial that there is a formal principle for individuation and whether that denial may not be a carry over from Peter's earlier views, one that he has not successfully integrated into the theory he is now accepting—that form is the *per se* principle of individuation.[64]

With this Peter turns to his second task—to determine what are the principles of numerical unity. In words that repeat Godfrey's text almost verbatim he comments that, while a material substance of itself is not divided

into many of the same kind or species, it is in potency to such division insofar
as it is in potency to the quantity whereby something is first so divided in the
formal sense. Therefore, just as such a substance is quantified by reason of an
accident that is added to it, so is it divided into many of the same kind or
species by something superadded, that is, by quantity. With Godfrey, Peter
now notes that number taken strictly is caused by division in terms of quantity. Therefore that is said to be numerically one in the strict sense that is
undivided in terms of that nature by which it is distinguished from others
within the same species. This, he comments, is quantity. Therefore quantity
is the *per se* principle of numerical unity taken strictly, while the substantial
form by which something exists in reality is its principle of individuation.[65]

Peter comments that one may refer to something as being undivided in
itself rather than as enjoying numerical unity and distinction from others
within the same species. In this sense and improperly speaking, one may refer
to numerical unity within the genus substance. When so taken, to be numerically one (or to enjoy transcendental unity) is really the same as to be an
individual within that genus. To put this another way, Peter is accepting Godfrey's account of the distinction between numerical unity taken broadly (transcendental unity) and numerical unity taken strictly. To enjoy the first kind of
unity is to be an individual within the genus of substance, presumably because each of these—to be an individual and to enjoy transcendental unity—
is due to the same principle, the substantial form. Strict numerical unity, on
the other hand, is based on quantity.[66]

Peter now takes up his third point: Can one identify the principle of
individuation for a composite substance with its principle of numerical unity?
One cannot identify the principle of numerical unity taken strictly with the
principle of individuation. The principle of individuation for a composite
substance is its substantial form, while the principle of strict numerical unity
is quantity. On the other hand, if one takes numerical unity in a substance in
the broader and improper sense, meaning thereby that such a substance is
not divided into others of the same kind, in this case the principles of individuation and such numerical unity are one and the same, that is, the substantial form.[67]

From all of this, Peter's dependency upon Godfrey for his theory of individuation is clear enough. Both hold that the substantial form of a material
substance is its principle of individuation. Godfrey has specified that the substantial form is its *formal* principle, while Peter leaves this unsaid. Both hold
that quantity is the principle of numerical unity taken strictly, although Godfrey has spelled out in greater detail quantity's contribution to individuation
as well. Both assign some role to matter, insofar as it is the subject of its
substantial form. Central to both presentations is the distinction between nu-

merical unity taken strictly (based on quantity) and numerical unity taken broadly (transcendental unity). As I have already indicated, Peter's presentation of substantial form as the principle of individuation is difficult to reconcile with his earlier denial that the individual (or individuation) as such has a formal cause and his claim that it can have only a material cause. On this point there seems to be some tension and even some inconsistency in his position. Finally, it does not seem to me that Peter has spelled out the distinction between numerical unity taken broadly (transcendental unity) and numerical unity taken strictly any more clearly than Godfrey had done. To appreciate this in Godfrey, however, one must consult his Quodlibet VI, qu. 16, as well as his discussion in Quodlibet VII, qu. 5.[68]

III. John Baconthorpe

With this we come to John Baconthorpe's discussion of individuation in dist. 11, qu. 2, of his Commentary on Book III of the *Sentences*. It is interesting to note that in qu. 1 of this same distinction 11, John had considered the general question raised by Godfrey in his Quodlibet VII, qu. 5 ("What supposit adds to nature"), but in its application to the problem of subsistence. There John had noted and repeated many of Godfrey's criticisms of Giles of Rome's theory of subsistence, but he had also criticized Godfrey's personal solution to the same issue.[69] In qu. 2 John attempts to identify the formal principle of individuation and the principle that accounts for the multiplication of individuals within the same species.[70]

John begins by noting that this amounts to determining whether that principle whereby the individual is constituted as such is to be identified with that whereby individuals are distinguished and multiplied (within their species) and with that whereby the supposit adds something to nature.[71] (In qu. 1 John had maintained that the supposit does add something to nature—the formal act of subsisting.)[72] John now proposes to establish three points: (1) to show that the principle whereby the individual is constituted as such is not to be identified with that whereby individuals are distinguished and multiplied or with that whereby the supposit adds something to nature; (2) to establish the formal principle of individuation; (3) to identify the formal principle for the multiplication of individuals within the same species.[73]

As regards the first point, John immediately attempts to show that the principle of individuation is not to be identified with that whereby individuals are distinguished from one another and multiplied within the same species. In support he points to the case of the form of heaven. As Aristotle states in Book I of the *De caelo* and as Averroes explains in his Commentary on the same, because the form of heaven actualizes all of its matter, there cannot be many heavens. Nonetheless, it is certain that heaven is a given individual. Hence something can be a principle of individuation without being a principle of multiplication within a species.[74] In other words, heaven is an individual and must have a principle of individuation. Yet, since it is unique or since it is not multiplied within its kind or species, it does not have a principle of multiplicity within its species. Given this, something can serve as a principle of individuation without at the same time functioning as a principle of multiplication. Peter, it will be recalled, had developed a similar argument by appealing to the cases of the sun, the moon, and heaven.[75]

John draws a second argument from the case of Intelligences.[76] But his text then immediately goes on to offer an argument to show that the principle which accounts for the individuation and for the multiplication of individuals is not to be identified with that which supposit adds to nature. It would seem that these two arguments should be separated. Unfortunately, John does not explain his reference to the Intelligences. It will be recalled, however, that like Godfrey, Peter had argued that in the case of separate substances each is a separate substance precisely because its form is not divided into others of the same kind or species. Or as Godfrey had put it, there are individual immaterial substances. Since they lack quantity, their individuation cannot be due to quantity.[77] In short, John's reference to the case of the Intelligences seems to be an anticipation of his ultimate answer to the issue of individuation. As we shall see, with explicit reference to Godfrey and Peter, he will identify the principle of individuation with substantial form.

John's text immediately develops the other argument—to show that the principle of individuation and the principle of multiplication for individuals within the same species are not to be identified with that which supposit adds to nature. He reasons that when an individual nature is constituted in terms of its essential being (*in esse naturae*) by its intrinsic principles, it acquires existence per se. Hence its existence per se (which is for it to be a supposit) presupposes in the order of nature though not in the order of time that its nature is 'already' individuated. If this is so, that which the supposit adds to nature cannot be identified with the principle of individuation or with the principle that accounts for the multiplication of such a nature.[78]

With this John turns to his second task—to identify the formal principle of individuation.[79] The reader will note that John does refer to the "formal" principle of individuation even as Godfrey (in contrast with Peter of Auvergne) had done. John immediately states, and in apodictic fashion, that form is the principle of individuation.[80] He draws what appears to be one of his strongest arguments from Averroes's Commentary on Book II of the *De anima*. There the Commentator writes that an individual is an individual only by reason of its form; for something is an individual only by means of that whereby it is realized in actuality. And it is realized in actuality only by its form, not by its matter. John finds support for this final point in Aristotle's identification of the soul with actuality.[81]

John develops other arguments from Averroes's Commentary on the same Book II of the *De anima*. For instance, Averroes reasons that something is an individual through that by means of which it enjoys unity. But it enjoys unity by reason of its form, not by reason of its matter.[82] Or again, argues John, natural things differ from artifacts in this: that a natural thing is described as an individual by reason of its form, whereas artifacts enjoy unity by reason of their matter.[83] Or still again, reasons John, Averroes's remarks suggest the following argument. One way of identifying that which makes something an individual and a "this" is to note that when that factor is removed, the thing in question is no longer an individual and a "this". But in the case of natural things, when their forms are removed, they cease to be the "this" and the individual they were previously. In the case of artifacts, however, the same thing happens when their matter is removed. Hence, in the case of natural things form serves as their principle of individuation.[84] In still another argument John comments that something is animated by reason of the fact that it has a soul. But the soul has been described by Aristotle as the first perfection of a natural body, and as form. Therefore, it is through its form that such an animated or living thing is this being, or an individual.[85]

Then, of particular interest to us in the present study, John notes that Godfrey defends the very same position in his Quodlibet VII, qu. 5, and that Peter of Auvergne also does in his Quodlibet II, qu. 5. John comments that both were strongly moved by Averroes's argumentation in his Commentary on Book II of the *De anima* and especially by the first two arguments mentioned in the preceding paragraphs.[86] After presenting some other arguments offered by Peter, John repeats the point that this view—that form is the principle of individuation—was held by Godfrey and Peter, and above all because of the first of the arguments from Averroes just mentioned.[87]

John notes that Godfrey and Peter offer another argument and in large measure repeats a text found in both of them. A composite substance enjoys being in actuality before (in the order of nature) any accident comes to it. In support he cites (as Peter had done) Averroes's *De substantia orbis:* The subjects for all accidents are individual instances of substance that exist in actuality. But it is through that whereby something exists in actuality that it is undivided in actuality. Therefore the undividedness of a composite substance as it exists in actuality is prior to the being of any of its accidents. But for any such substance its individuation is its very undividedness.[88]

Before turning to his third main point—his effort to identify the formal principle for multiplication of individuals within the same species—John devotes considerable attention to the position of Thomas Aquinas. He begins by noting that Thomas had mistakenly been interpreted as holding that quantity is the principle of individuation. Against this John argues that Thomas does not identify quantity as the principle of individuation, but rather as the principle of multiplication for individuals within the same species. For instance, Thomas holds that quantity is the principle of division. But division causes multitude, as Aristotle states in *Metaphysics* X. Therefore, reasons John, Thomas wants to maintain that quantity is the principle that accounts only for the multiplication of individuals; it is not the principle of individuation.[89]

John then offers a series of arguments, apparently drawn from Aquinas, which conclude that quantity is the principle for numerical multiplicity of individuals.[90] Here it will be enough for me to mention the fourth argument. A form does not differ from other forms except insofar as its matter is different. And matter is not different except by reason of quantity. Therefore quantity accounts for the otherness or difference of form.[91]

It may be that John regards this and like arguments as originally intended by Thomas to show that quantity is the principle of numerical multiplicity within species but that, in John's view, they have been misinterpreted as implying that quantity is the principle of individuation. In any event, John then offers another series of arguments to show that quantity is not the principle of individuation but that substantial form is. His fourth and fifth arguments are worth mentioning. According to the fourth, substantial generation has its proper terminus, just as do alteration and increase in quantity. But the terminus of substantial generation can be only a substantial form, since generation in general terminates in something individual. Therefore the substantial form makes something an individual. The reader will recall a similar argument from Peter.[92] The fifth argument reasons that so long as the formal principle of individuation remains, the same individual remains. But if God should decide to unite the soul of Peter with the body of Paul at the general resurrection, Paul's proper quantity would remain in its proper matter. If quantity were the principle of individuation, one and the same Paul would remain just as before, which, comments John, is obviously false.[93]

John also replies to each of the arguments drawn from Thomas to show that quantity is the principle of numerical multiplicity.[94] Thus against the fourth argument's claim that form is diversified only by reason of matter John defends the exact opposite. Matter is rendered other by reason of diversity of form. Here he finds support from Averroes's Commentary on Book II of the *De anima*—the members of a lion differ from those of a deer only because the soul of one differs from the soul of the other.[95]

John now takes up his third main point—to identify the formal principle that accounts for multiplicity of individuals within species. He begins by considering in greater detail the view he has attributed to Aquinas—that this principle is quantity. After presenting some other arguments in support of this position, John cites an interesting text from Thomas's Commentary on the *De Trinitate* of Boethius. There, as John reports, Thomas reasons that no material form insofar as it is a form can be multiplied of itself. He comments that Thomas adds the restriction ''insofar as it is a form'' to allow for the case of an Intelligence that is *this* Intelligence or an individual of itself even though it cannot be multiplied in kind. (John adds that one could also argue that a form is not capable of being multiplied insofar as it is a form for another reason—if it were received in the totality of its matter, it could not then be multiplied. John's point seems to be that if form qua form could be multiplied, then even this kind of form—a form received in the totality of its matter—could be multiplied.) But if a material form is not multiplied of itself insofar as it is a form, it is multiplied only insofar as it is received in matter. Matter itself is not divided and multiplied except by means of quantity. Therefore quantity is the principle that accounts for numerical multiplicity of individuals within species.[96]

As John correctly observes, in this same text Thomas adds that the quantity in question is not determined quantity. Determined quantity can vary, while the individual retains its numerical identity. Only undetermined quantity can account for the numerical multiplication of individuals within a species. Such undetermined quantity, continues John, is in matter prior to the reception of its form and divides the matter into different parts so that it can receive different forms.[97]

After briefly noting that authorities such as Porphyry, Boethius, John Damascene, and Aristotle may also be cited in support of the view that quantity is the principle of multiplication for individuals, John argues at length against this claim. For instance, those things distinguished quantitatively are distinguished by quantity. Therefore those things distinguished substantially must be distinguished by means of substance. Since Socrates and Plato are clearly distinct substantially, they must be distinguished in substance. Hence multiplicity within the genus substance cannot be accounted for by appealing to quantity.[98]

In another argument John reasons that if Socrates and Plato are distinguished from one another only by accidents, then they will not differ in substance. Therefore, if by any power (divine power, presumably), all of Socrates's accidents were changed and numerically different accidents substituted for them, even though his original prime matter and his original substantial form would remain, it would follow from this theory that he would be numerically different from his former self.[99]

Again, if quantity is the cause or principle of multiplicity, the quantity in question must either be determined or undetermined. Neither will do, argues John, since determined quantity presupposes an actually existing individual substance; and undetermined quantity, being common both to that which is generated and to that which is corrupted, cannot distinguish them numerically.[100]

If therefore, as interpreted by John, Thomas Aquinas does not regard quantity as the principle of individuation, he does view it as the principle that accounts for numerical multiplicity of individuals within the same species. And this, as we have now seen, is no more acceptable to John than is the claim that quantity itself is the principle of individuation. Hence, even though he has made this interesting distinction concerning Thomas's position, he ends by rejecting both readings of Aquinas. Quantity is not the formal principle of individuation; substantial form is. In saying this, John is in agreement with Godfrey of Fontaines and Peter of Auvergne. But in denying that quantity is the principle that accounts for numerical multiplicity in the strict sense and, therefore, for numerically distinct individuals within the same species, he differs from them as well as from Thomas.[101]

John next considers and rejects another view according to which prime matter would serve as the formal principle for the multiplication of individuals within the same species. Against this claim he reasons, for instance, that just as a being that exists in actuality requires an actual principle to constitute it in actuality, so do things that are distinct in actuality require actually distinct principles to account for their distinction. Distinct individual substances are actual beings and must therefore be distinguished by actual principles. But the distinct matters in which they are realized are always beings in potency insofar as such matters are simply viewed in themselves. Hence matter cannot account for the actual distinction of individual substances from one another within the same species.[102]

After rejecting some arguments based on various texts of Aristotle that would seem to favor matter as the principle of multiplication for individuals within a species, John attempts to establish his own position—that substantial form fulfills this function. He begins by developing some remarks made by Averroes in his Commentary on *Metaphysics* XII and in his *De substantia orbis*. According to Averroes matter is distinguished with respect to different forms by means of different aptitudes (*habilitates*). Since a determined form requires a determined quantity, the dimensions proper to that form must in the order of nature already be present in the matter determined to that form. But these dimensions are realized in matter only in potency and, therefore, Averroes refers to them as "undetermined".[103]

John develops these indications in the following way. The distinction in matters and dimensions presupposed for distinct substantial forms in constituting distinct individual substances is a distinction of beings in potency. When numerically distinct substantial forms are introduced into such distinct matters and dimensions so as to constitute actually distinct substances, the substantial forms themselves are acts. Mere being in potency is not of itself sufficient to establish either natural beings or artificial beings or to enable us to define them (except perhaps in some extremely diminished sense). Being in

actuality enables us to identify something as such in the proper sense. Therefore the actual distinction and multiplication of individual substances within
a species is completed and perfected by their substantial forms; for these
forms are beings in actuality.[104]

John offers many other arguments in support of this same position, only
a few of which can be mentioned here. For instance, that whereby something
first exists in the full sense (*simpliciter*) is that whereby it is distinguished
from everything else. But it is by its substantial form that every supposit first
exists in this way. Therefore it is through its form that a supposit is distinguished from every other and multiplied.[105] Another argument reminds the
reader of John's earlier refutation of one of the arguments offered in support
of quantity as the principle of numerical multiplicity. Diversity in matter and
diversity in dimensions are required because of distinct substantial forms, and
not vice versa, John reasons. Again he appeals to Averroes's Commentary on
the *De anima* for support. Hence the most fundamental (and formal) principle
for the distinction and multiplication of individual substances is substantial
form, not prime matter or quantitative dimensions.[106]

In replying to one of the arguments attributed to Aquinas in support of
quantity as the principle of multiplication, John sums up the essentials of his
own position. This argument reasons that division and multiplicity first follow upon quantity. John distinguishes between determined and undetermined
quantity. Determined quantity cannot account for such division and multiplicity, since it simply makes the distinction of individuals evident to the senses
without causing such division. In fact, distinction in terms of determined
quantity presupposes the distinction and multiplication of individual substances. Undetermined quantity fares no better, continues John. Matter is first
distinguished by the different aptitudes (*habilitates*) for distinct forms that are
realized in it; only as a result of these distinct aptitudes are distinct dimensions realized in matter, and then only as potential or as undetermined. Indeed, even if one admits that undetermined quantity itself accounts for this
first distinction within matter, it will follow from this that quantity is only the
first potential principle for such multiplicity of individuals, not its first actual
principle. Actual distinction and multiplication of such individuals within a
given species requires actual distinguishing principles, and these can be only
distinct substantial forms.[107]

IV. Conclusion

In sum, therefore, John has rejected quantity as the formal principle of
individuation and, along with Godfrey and Peter, has opted for substantial
form. He has suggested that Thomas Aquinas did not really intend to say that
quantity is the formal principle of individuation, but only that it is the formal

principle for multiplicity and distinction of individuals within a species. Even so, John has also seen fit to reject this position and, in doing so, has not only distanced himself from Aquinas but has rejected the second part of the solutions proposed by Godfrey and Peter. Crucial to both of their discussions was the distinction between the formal principle of individuation—substantial form—and the formal principle for numerical multiplication of individuals within the same species—quantity.

Moreover, in identifying substantial form as the formal principle for such multiplication and distinction within a species, John seems to have created a problem for himself. As already noted, he had introduced his discussion by arguing that the principle of individuation is not to be identified with that principle whereby individuals within a species are distinguished from one another and multiplied. To that extent he seemed to be opening the way for full agreement with Godfrey and Peter. If the *formal* principle of individuation is substantial form, as it is for all three writers (if only by implication in Peter), then the principle that accounts for multiplicity and distinction of individuals within the same species should be something else. But instead of drawing this conclusion, John seems to have fallen into inconsistency by identifying both the formal principle of individuation and the formal principle for multiplicity and distinction with the same species with the substantial form. Not only does he differ with Godfrey and Peter concerning this last-mentioned point; he seems to differ with himself!

As regards this seeming tension within John's personal position, I can offer no better solution than that proposed by one of the *Conciliationes* published along with the 1618 Cremona edition of John's Commentary on the *Sentences* and his Quodlibets. *Conciliatio* XLV notes the seeming contradiction and then proposes this solution. In distinguishing between the principle of individuation and the principle of multiplication of individuals within the same species at the beginning of his discussion, John did not wish to deny in the absolute sense that they are one and the same; for then he would have fallen into contradiction. He simply wanted to make the point that it is possible in some cases for the formal principle of individuation to constitute an individual as such, but without at the same time distinguishing and multiplying individuals within a given species.[108] It is true that John had cited just such a case in defending the distinction between the formal principle of individuation and the principle of multiplicity for individuals within a species—that is, heaven. And it may well be that this is the only way of saving him from self-contradiction. If so, it is unfortunate that John himself did not clarify his position on this particular point.

One of John's great virtues for the modern reader is the care with which he cites and presents the views of other medieval thinkers—in this case,

Thomas, Godfrey, and Peter. As regards the philosophical value of his particular solution to the problem of individuation and numerical multiplicity of individuals within species, his position seems to take a step backward rather than a step forward. Godfrey's (and Peter's) distinction between the solutions to the problem of individuation and the problem of numerical distinction and multiplication of individuals within a species is an interesting development both historically and philosophically. John's initial recognition of that distinction is clouded by his apparent repudiation of it in his proposed solution.[109]

Notes

1. For a good survey of this see I. Klinger, *Das Prinzip der Individuation bei Thomas von Aquin* (Münsterschwarzach, 1964), pp. 2–9. He correctly calls attention to the importance of the historical and chronological approach to Thomas's discussions of this proposed by M.-D. Roland-Gosselin in his *Le "De ente et essentia" de S. Thomas d'Aquin* (Paris, 1926, 1948), pp. 104–134, and is attentive to questions of chronology and development in his own study.

2. For a good overview of this see Klinger, *Das Prinzip,* pp. 9–10.

3. For references see notes 9, 10, and 11.

4. See his "Une question inédite de Pierre d'Auvergne sur l'individuation", *Revue Néoscolastique de Philosophie* 36 (1934): 355–386.

5. On his life and works see in particular Hocedez, "La vie et les oeuvres de Pierre d'Auvergne", *Gregorianum* 14 (1933): 3–36; F. J. Roensch, *Early Thomistic School* (Dubuque, 1964), pp. 92–98; A. Monahan, "Peter of Auvergne," *New Catholic Encyclopedia* (New York, 1967), vol. 11, pp. 211–212; P. Glorieux, *La littérature quodlibétique de 1260 à 1320,* vol. 1 (Kain, 1925), pp. 257–263; vol. 2 (Paris, 1935), p. 219; *Répertoire des maîtres en théologie de Paris au XIIIe siècle,* 2 vols. (Paris, 1933), vol. 1, pp. 412–417; *La faculté des arts et ses maîtres au XIIIe siècle* (Paris, 1971), pp. 275–278. That he was already a well-known master in arts by 1275 is implied by the fact that he was then appointed as rector of the university in the hope of introducing some peace into a divided faculty. See Roensch, p. 92 and references. Hocedez, following Denifle, expressed some hesitation about identifying the rector of 1275 with the Quodilibetal master of the 1290s ("La vie", pp. 7, 10), but the identity of the two is generally accepted. For some interesting indications concerning Peter's development from his original closer fidelity to the views of Aquinas, through a period of growing independence (as evidenced in his Questions on the *Metaphysics*), to his much more independent and non-Thomistic period (as reflected in his Quodlibets in Theology, dating from 1296–1301), see B. Bazán's remarks in *Trois commentaires anonymes sur le Traité de l'âme d'Aristote* (Louvain and Paris, 1971), pp. 383–385.

6. See my *The Metaphysical Thought of Godfrey of Fontaines* (Washington, DC, 1981), pp. xvi–xviii, and the references given there.

7. *Ibid.*, pp. xix–xxviii (on Godfrey's later career and his writings as a master in the theology faculty). For the view that Peter studied theology under Godfrey (and under Henry of Ghent), see Hocedez, "La vie", p. 14; "La théologie de Pierre d'Auvergne", *Gregorianum* 11 (1930): 525; Roensch, *Early Thomistic School*, p. 107; Monahan, "Peter of Auvergne", p. 211; M. De Wulf, *Histoire de la philosophie médiévale*, 6th ed., vol. 2 (Louvain, 1936), p. 269. Bazán (*Trois commentaires*, p. 383) suggests that Peter's eventual move toward an increasing independence in thought from Aquinas was influenced by masters such as Henry and Godfrey. For the same view see F. Van Steenberghen, *La philosophie au XIIIe siècle* (Louvain, 1966), p. 506. On the question of individuation, Hocedez has clearly established Godfrey's influence on Peter. This will be illustrated later.

8. On Baconthorpe, see B. M. Xiberta y Roqueta, *De scriptoribus scholasticis saeculi XIV ex ordine Carmelitarum* (Louvain, 1931), pp. 167–240; A. Maurer, "John Baconthorp", *New Catholic Encyclopedia*, vol. 7, pp. 1029–1030; Chrysogone du Saint-Sacrement, "Maître Jean Baconthorp. Les sources, la doctrine, les disciples", *Revue Néoscolastique de Philosophie* 34 (1932): 341–365; De Wulf, *Histoire*, vol. 3 (Louvain, 1947), pp. 110–111; N. di S. Brocardo, "Il profilo storico di Giovanni Baconthorp", *Ephemerides carmeliticae* 2 (1948): 431–543. Baconthorpe seems to have lectured on the *Sentences* at Paris before 1318 and became a master in theology there before 1324 (De Wulf, *Ibid.*, p. 110; di S. Brocardo, "Il profilo", pp. 471–484). His three Quodlibetal Disputations and his Commentary on the *Sentences* have been printed several times. Here, because of its availability, I shall follow the Cremona edition, 2 vols. (1618/repr. Gregg, 1969). For his discussion of individuation see *In III Sent.*, dist. 11, qu. 2, art. 1–3 (vol. 2, pp. 72–77). John evidently reworked his Commentary for publication some years later. See Xiberta, *De scriptoribus*, pp. 181–182, for evidence that the Commentary on Book I dates from 1325. Also see the remark in *In III Sent.*, dist. 20, qu. 3, art. 1 (p. 131): ". . . quia a principio mundi ipsi computant quinque millia. 70 annos usque ad annum Domini 1339 in quo praesens opus fuit scriptum." On Baconthorpe's alleged "Averroism", see J. P. Etzwiler, "Baconthorpe and Latin Averroism", *Carmelus* 18 (1971): 235–292; and his "John Baconthorpe, 'Prince of the Averroists'?" *Franciscan Studies* 36 (1976): 148–176.

9. *Metaphysical Thought*, pp. 349–369.

10. For Roland-Gosselin see his *Le "De ente et essentia"*, p. 129. For Hocedez see his "Une question inédite", p. 358. Note his comment: "Il y a donc accord parfait entre le maître et le disciple: remarquons cependant que le maître est plus complet et plus profond."

11. For De Wulf see *Un théologien-philosophe du XIIIe siècle. Étude sur la vie, les oeuvres et l'influence de Godefroid de Fontaines* (Brussels, 1904), pp. 119–120; *Histoire*, vol. 2, pp. 294–295. For R. Arway see his "A Half Century of Research on Godfrey of Fontaines", *The New Scholasticism* 36 (1962): 205–206 and note 36.

12. For discussion of the dating of Godfrey's Quodlibets, see J. Wippel, *Metaphysical Thought*, pp. xxiii–xxviii.

13. On this see J. Wippel, *ibid.*, pp. 25–26, 353–355. For Godfrey's Quodlibet VI, qu. 16, see *Les Quodlibets Cinq, Six, et Sept de Godefroid de Fontaines*, ed. M. De Wulf and J. Hoffmans, Les Philosophes Belges, vol. 3 (Louvain, 1914), pp. 254–260 (cited hereafter as PB 3.254–260). Quodlibet VI, qu. 16 is directed to this issue: "Utrum si corpus humanum resurgeret sine quantitate esset idem numero quod prius." Note in particular: "Est enim quoddam unum quod convertitur cum ente et quoddam quod dicitur principium numeri; intelligendum tamen quod quaelibet unitas est principium alicuius numeri, quia omnis multitudo est aliquis numerus; sed cum dicitur quod est quoddam unum quod est principium numeri intelligitur specialiter de numero qui est quantitas discreta sive de genere accidentis quod est quantitas." (PB 3.256).

14. PB 3.256–257. Note in particular, "Quod autem existens non existit nisi individualiter et sic unumquodque existens est quoddam individuum, hoc, inquam, formaliter inest ei per suam formam qua est id quod est et in se indivisum et ab alio divisum."

15. PB 3.258. "Unum autem quod est principium numeri proprie dicti ut est aliquid de genere quantitatis non convertitur cum ente nec reperitur nisi in his in quibus est quantitas continua, quia nec est nisi in talibus diversitas secundum numerum talem et distinctio aliquorum secundum talem numerum ex divisione quantitatis continuae, cuius est per se habere partes eiusdem rationis. . . ."

16. PB 3.258–259. Note in particular, "Sed in quantitate non differunt realiter, sed solum secundum rationem, unum quod convertitur cum ente et quod est principium numeri, quia ipsum quod est essentialiter continuitas et partibilitas quaedam secundum se indivisum quid et divisum ab aliis et sic est unum sua tali unitate essentiali ut participatur ab alio, scilicet a substantia cui accidit, est unitas accidentalis illi; unde, quod est unitas essentialis in quantitate secundum se est unitas accidentalis in substantia cui accidit."

17. See PB 3.258: "Et, quia non est in rebus processus in infinitum, unitas et multitudo talis est in substantiis per aliquid additum, scilicet per huiusmodi quantitatem, et, cum quaelibet quantitas sit una tali unitate . . . tales partes ipsius quantitatis, ut scilicet sunt partes quantitatis, non sunt unum vel plura dicto modo per aliquam rem additam. . . ." Also see the text cited in note 16.

18. For Quodlibet VII, qu. 5 see PB 3.299–336. Qu. 5 is addressed to this question: "Utrum suppositum addat aliquam rem supra essentiam vel naturam."

19. PB 3.300–301.

20. PB 3.301. Note in particular, "Quaerere autem quid addit suppositum sic acceptum ad naturam sic acceptam est quaerere de causa individuationis sive quid addit singulare super commune, scilicet haec humanitas super humanitatem, hic homo super hominem, haec albedo super albedinem, hoc album super album."

21. For Godfrey's discussion of the first way of contrasting nature and supposit see PB 3.301–318. On this see J. Wippel, *Metaphysical Thought*, ch. 6 ("Subsistence, Supposit, and Nature"), pp. 227–246.

22. PB 3.319–320. For his citation of Porphyry, see the editors' suggestion that he is here referring to Porphyry's *Commentary on the Categories (In Categorias scholia in Aristotelem)*, ed. C. Brandis (Berlin, 1836), pp. 2a–3. Godfrey's citation does not name the work of Porphyry. The editors also cite Boethius's Commentary on this same work (PL 64.105–106), since Godfrey does refer to "Boetius in commento. . ." On the other hand, Henry of Ghent cites these same passages in connection with the view according to which individuals within the same species would differ only by reason of their accidents. See his Quodlibet V, qu. 8 (*Quodlibeta* [Paris, 1518; repr. Louvain, 1961]), fol. 165r. In discussing this same general view—individuation by accidents—J. Paulus gives some references to Porphyry's *Isagoge* and to the Boethian translation and Commentary on the same (*Henri de Gand. Essai sur les tendances de sa métaphysique* [Paris, 1938], pp. 333–334). For a similar reference to Boethius in Peter of Auvergne's discussion see Hocedez, "Une question inédite", p. 371. Like Paulus, Hocedez refers to Porphyry's *Isagoge* (Busse ed., [Berlin, 1887], pp. 7:23–24 [text], 33:4–7 [Boethian translation]. Godfrey and Henry also cite Boethius's *De trinitate*, for which see ch. 1 in *The Theological Tractates*, Stewart-Rand-Tester ed. (Cambridge, MA, 1978), p. 6:24–25. Both Godfrey and Henry also refer to John Damascene's *De duabus naturis et una persona Christi*, for which see *De duabus in Christo voluntatibus* (PG 95:130), and to Avicenna's *Metaphysics* V, for which see *Liber de philosophia prima sive scientia divina V–X*, ed. S. Van Riet (Louvain, 1980), Bk. V. ch. 4, p. 264:45–47.

23. Underlying the first of the arguments mentioned in my text is Godfrey's conviction that the individual does not add to the species that which is no more included in the designation of the individual than it is in the designation of the species. But accidents are no more included in the designation or definition of the individual in the genus substance than they are within that of the species. "Per speciem autem intelligimus substantiam secundam quae de prima dicitur et in illa est non sicut in subiecto, sed sicut in supposito, cuius essentiam totam dicit, sicut se habet hic homo sive Sortes ad hominem; sed quicquid est de significato et intellectu vel ratione huius hominis vel Sortis determinate est de significato et intellectu vel ratione hominis simpliciter et indeterminate et nihil amplius." For this and other arguments see PB 3.320–321.

24. PB 3.322. Note in particular, "Videtur ergo quod haec individuatio et divisio vel distinctio secundum numerum et individuum habet esse in omnibus aliis tam accidentibus quam substantiis per solam quantitatem; et ideo tota difficultas praesentis inquisitionis quantum ad entia materialia videtur versari circa quantitatem. Nam, si aliquod accidens sit causa individuationis, hoc videtur quantitati tribuendum."

25. PB 3.323. Note in particular, "Ergo, cum in Sorte et Platone sit substantia et quantitas, oportet quod differant et secundum quantitatem ut plura quanta et secundum substantiam ut plures substantiae. Sicut enim oportet quod ad hoc quod

accidentaliter distinguantur quod formaliter secundum formas accidentales distinguantur ita quod haec non est illa, ita ad hoc quod substantialiter sive ut plures substantiae ab invicem distinguantur, oportet quod formaliter per formas substantiales
sint distincta ita quod haec forma substantialis huius individui formaliter non est illa,
sed est alia ab ipsa.'' Otherwise, Godfrey argues in the immediately preceding context, just as in the case of the Trinity the single divine essence is essentially undivided
in the three divine persons but rather is divided in terms of three relative properties,
so in the case of material substances all individuals of the same species would be completely undivided in terms of their substantial nature, but would exist under different
parts of quantity.

26. PB 3.323: ''. . . ergo etiam in materialibus forma per quam individuum est
id quod est et subsistit in natura est etiam principium individuationis; quia per illud
per quod aliquid est id quod est est indivisum et unum; sed substantia materialis per
formam subsistit in esse.''

27. PB 3.324.

28. *Ibid.*

29. PB 3.324–325. See in particular, ''Quare quantitas est per se principium
unius secundum numerum, sicut forma per quam aliquid existit in natura est principium [with Paris BN 14.311 and instead of proprium in PB] individuationis et sic proprie loquendo non est idem principium per se individuationis in genere substantiae
materialis et unius secundum numerum, quia principium unius secundum numerum
est quantitas in quantum secundum quantitatem est indivisum in se et divisum ab alio
eiusdem rationis cum quo facit numerum. Principium autem per se individuationis est
forma secundum quam divisa est substantia in plura eiusdem rationis.''

30. PB 3.325; 328–329.

31. PB 3.325–326. Godfrey cites Averroes's *De substantia orbis* as follows:
''. . . quia materia de se est indivisibilis, non potest plures formas simul recipere nisi
habeat esse divisibile per aliquid divisibile per se quod est ratio qua aliquid dividitur,
quod est quantitas de cuius ratione est habere partes eiusdem rationis propter quod
materia participans eam per ipsam habet partes eiusdem rationis'' (p. 326). For Averroes see c. 1 (Venice, 1562), vol. 9, ff. 3vb–4ra. Godfrey's citation is not literal. In
this same general context Godfrey has also cited Aristotle (*Met.* XII, c. 8[1047a33–
34]; *Met.* VII, c. 8[1034a6–8][instead of *Metaphysics* V as Godfrey's text reads]), and
Averroes's Commentary on the passage from *Metaphysics* VII (*In VII Met.* [1034a6–
8], c.8, text 28 [Venice, 1562], vol. 8, f. 178v).

32. PB 3.327, 335.

33. PB 3.327, 336. Note in particular, ''Ex hoc etiam non sequitur quod quantitas cedat in rationem causae formalis in ratione individuationis, immo ipsa forma
substantialis, licet habeat quantitas rationem causae formalis in substantiam esse divisibilem et extensam; quia, licet id entitatis quod habet quantitas sit posterius natura
quam id entitatis quod habet substantia singularis, tamen, ut dictum est, id divisibil-

itatis quod habet quantitas in partes eiusdem rationis est prius naturaliter quam dividi
et extendi substantiae, ut dictum est; et sic quantitas dicto modo est prius natura quam
substantia, licet etiam id entitatis quod habet quantitas sit posterius natura tota substantia composita'' (336).

34. PB 3.328, 332–333. For discussion, see J. Wippel, *Metaphysical Thought*,
p. 363.

35. PB 3.329–330. See J. Wippel, *ibid.*, pp. 363–364.

36. For references and discussion of Godfrey's views concerning the individuation of the separated soul and the possibility of multiplying angels within the same
species see J. Wippel, *ibid.*, pp. 364–369.

37. See his "Une question inédite", pp. 370–379 (Quodlibet II, qu. 5), 379–
386 (*Quaestiones metaphysicae*, L. VIII, qu. 25).

38. See Glorieux, *La littérature quodlibétique*, vol. 1, pp. 257–258; Hocedez,
"La vie", p. 15.

39. Hocedez, "Une question inédite", p. 363 and n. 19. To be precise, Hocedez here concludes that it seems more probable that owing to the influence of Godfrey of Fontaines Peter had completely abandoned his first account of individuation.

40. "Postmodum querebatur de substantia composita quantum ad eius indivisionem, utrum scilicet eadem sint principia individuationis substantie composite et
unitatis secundum numerum ipsius" (*ibid.*, p. 370).

41. *Ibid.*

42. Cited in note 13. There is a difference between the two questions, however.
Godfrey's questioner considers the theoretical possibility of a body's being raised
from the dead without *any* quantity, while the argument in Peter's text rather suggests
that the quantity in the risen body might be greater or lesser than was true of that body
when living. In commenting on this, Godfrey points out his difficulty in understanding how such could be possible—that the resurrected body could lack all quantity—
but indicates his unwillingness to deny that such might be possible for the divine
power (PB 3.255–256).

43. Hocedez, "Une question inédite", p. 371.

44. *Ibid.* Note in particular, "Propter quod individui, secundum quod individuum, non est formale principium, cum sit privatio, nec principium activum, nec
etiam finale."

45. "Privationis autem est principium materiale: privatio enim vult habere naturam subiectam, et ideo individuationis, secundum quod huiusmodi, principium est
materiale per se; et tantum in alio, secundum quod individuum dicit indivisionem"
(*ibid.*). By the expression '*in alio*' in the last part of this text Peter seems to mean that

individuation, being a privation, must be in a subject or in something that is other than the individuation or privation itself; hence *in alio.*

46. For the references to Porphyry's *Isagoge* and to Avicenna's *Metaphysics* see note 22. For Peter, see Hocedez, "Une question inédite," p. 371.

47. Hocedez, *ibid.*, pp. 371–372.

48. P. 372. For John Damascene see his *De fide orthodoxa*, ed. E. M. Buytaert (St. Bonaventure, NY, 1955), ch. 50 (Bk. III, ch. 6), pp. 186:12–187:15. For the thought if not the words, see Boethius, *In Isagogen Porphyrii Commenta* (CSEL 48), ed. secunda, Bk. III, chs. 2 and 9 (pp. 200:10ff.; 205:4–7; 228), also cited by Hocedez, "Une question inédite", p. 372, n. 7.

49. Hocedez, *ibid.*, p. 372. For Aristotle see his *Cat.*, ch. 5 (2a11).

50. *Ibid.*

51. P. 373. Note in particular, "Individuatio igitur quantitatis supponit individuationem substantie, sicut esse huius supponit esse illius, secundum ordinem naturae." For Godfrey's argument see p. 225 above.

52. For the opening argument see p. 370, especially lines 6 and following, and in my text above p. 228. For Peter's criticism of the argument's assumption see p. 373. Note in particular, "Igitur non est necesse quod per illud sit aliquid individuum, per quod ab alio distinguitur."

53. Note in particular, ". . . indiviso autem secundum quod huiusmodi accidit divisio ab alio quod est aliquid positivum" (p. 373). Although one may wonder about the antecedent for the final '*quod*' in this text, Peter seems to mean that the *fact* of being divided from something else (rather than the mere *division*) is something positive. One would, therefore, expect him to propose a positive principle to account for this fact.

54. P. 373. For Godfrey see, for instance, the text from Quodlibet VI, qu. 16 cited in note 14. For that same general context, see PB 3.256–257, and my discussion in *Metaphysical Thought*, pp. 25–26.

55. Pp. 373–374.

56. P. 374.

57. *Ibid.*

58. Pp. 374–375: "Primo quia per illud, per quod aliquid est secundum quid vel simpliciter, est indivisum et unum simpliciter vel secundum quid; sicut per quod aliquid est album, puta per albedinem, per illud est indivisum in albedine . . . et per hoc quod aliquid est homo, est unum et indivisum in eo quod homo. . . . Sed substantia composita in actu extra animam per formam subsistit in esse, sicut ostensum est in questione precedenti, quia esse in effectu convenit formaliter substantie per for-

mam. Igitur per formam est indivisum in esse in plura eiusdem rationis: hoc autem est individuum in genere substantie. Igitur per se principium individuationis est forma in substantia composita''. Hocedez has reproduced the section of Quodlibet II, qu. 4, where Peter argues that actual being belongs to a thing by reason of its form (p. 375, n. 13). For the full text of this same question see A. Monahan, ''Quaestiones in Metaphysicam Petri de Alvernia'', in *Nine Mediaeval Thinkers: A Collection of Hitherto Unedited Texts*, ed. J. Reginald O'Donnell (Toronto, 1955), pp. 177–181. In this text, Peter rejects real distinction and intentional distinction between essence and *esse* (in the case of composite creatures), as does Godfrey. See pp. 178–180. For fuller discussion of Godfrey's views concerning this see my *Metaphysical Thought*, ch. 2. Limitations of space will not permit further examination here of the similarities between Peter's positive views concerning the essence/*esse* relationship and the position defended by Godfrey.

59. Compare Peter (pp. 375:63–376:73) with Godfrey (PB 3.323–324). As Hocedez observes (p. 376, n. 15), all of the words in Godfrey's presentation of this argument are found in Peter's text. There is one interesting exception, however. Peter's text reads: ''Igitur indivisio substantie composite extra animam in esse nature naturaliter precedit esse cuiuscumque accidentis eius; quare et *indivisionem* que competit ei per accidens quodcumque'' (p. 376:70–73). In Godfrey's text one rather reads for the final part of this passage: ''. . . quare et *divisionem* quae competit sibi per quodcumque accidens'' (PB 3.324, line 3).

60. See p. 376:77–84, and compare with Godfrey, PB 3.323.

61. See pp. 376:84–377:92.

62. For Peter see p. 377:92–96. As Hocedez indicates, here he literally cites Godfrey (see PB 3.324, lines 3–6).

63. See p. 377:96–99.

64. Thus in his *Quaestiones in Metaphysicam* Peter had denied that a privation can have of itself an efficient cause, or a formal cause, or a final cause; it can have only a material cause. See Hocedez, ''Une question inédite'', pp. 359–360. For Peter's text—q. 25 of his Commentary on Bk VIII (Bk VII according to Monahan)—see Hocedez, *ibid.*, pp. 382–383, and Monahan, ''Quaestiones in Metaphysicam'', pp. 170–171. Note in particular, ''Individuatio ergo, cum sit quaedam privatio, causam efficientem non habet per se, nec formalem nec finalem, sed causam materialem solum habet per se. Et haec est natura substantiae quae subest individuationi''.

65. For Peter, see p. 377:100–114. Here he is literally citing Godfrey's text. For which see PB 3.324.

66. See p. 378:14–17.

67. For Peter, see p. 377:19–32. Here again Peter reproduces portions of Godfrey's text. For these see Hocedez, ''Une question inédite'', p. 378, n. 19.

68. Here I have in mind Hocedez's remark concerning this distinction in Godfrey and in Peter: "'. . . mais ce que le philosophe liégois exposait d'une façon souvent confuse, le chanoine de Paris le précise avec une netteté remarquable" ("Une question inédite", p. 358). Had Hocedez also consulted Godfrey's Quodlibet VI, qu. 16 in studying this issue, he would have found a precise exposition of this same distinction.

69. See John Baconthorpe, *Quaestiones in quatuor librum sententiarum et quodlibetales*, III Sent. 11, 2 (Cremona, 1618), 72–77. For qu. 1 ("Quid addat suppositum supra naturam?"), see pp. 68–71. For discussion of Godfrey's theory and his critique of Giles of Rome's position, see *Metaphysical Thought*, pp. 232–242.

70. III *Sent.* 11, 2, 72–77.

71. "Utrum unum et idem sit principium quo constituitur individuum, et quo distinguuntur seu multiplicantur individua, et quo suppositum aliquid addit super naturam" (p. 72).

72. III *Sent.* 11, 1, 3, p. 71. Note in particular, "Dico ergo ad articulum quod suppositum addit super naturam actum formalem subsistendi ad se praevium omni connotationi Godofredi respectivae, et omni inhaerentiae accidentium et modis positis ab Aegidio."

73. See III *Sent.* 11, 2, Intr., p. 72.

74. III *Sent.* 11, 2, 1, p. 72. Note in particular, "Igitur aliquid (sicut patet de caelo) est principium individuationis, quod non est principium multiplicationis." For Aristotle, see *De caelo* I, 9 (278a25ff.) For Averroes, see *In I De caelo* (278a25), ch. 9, text 93 (Venice, 1562) 5.62rF–62vH. Note especially, "Quod autem fit ex tota materia, impossibile est reperire duo individua in actu. . . .''

75. For Peter's text, see Hocedez, "Une question inédite", p. 373, as well as my note 52 and the corresponding text.

76. For John, see III *Sent.* 11, 2, 1, p. 72: "Item patet in Intelligentiis."

77. For Peter and Godfrey, see the references given in note 60.

78. "Etiam illud quod est principium individuationis et multiplicationis individuorum non est illud quod suppositum addit super naturam. Quia quando natura individua constituitur in esse naturae per sua principia intrinseca, tunc consequitur ipsum suum esse per se, ita quod suum per se esse, quod est esse suppositum, praesupponit ordine naturae etsi non durationis ipsam naturam individuam. Principium autem formale individuationis et distinctionis seu multiplicationis non consequitur ipsam naturam individui sed praecedit ipsam sicut principium principiatum. Ergo non sunt idem" (p. 72).

79. "Secundus articulus. Quodnam sit principium formale individuationis?" (III *Sent.* 11, 2, 2, p. 72).

80. "Ubi dico quod forma est principium individuationis; nec de hoc debet esse opinio aliqua" (*ibid.*).

81. For John, *ibid.* For Averroes, see *In II De anima,* commen. 9 (ed. F. Stuart Crawford [Cambridge, MA, 1953]), p. 144:13–15. For Aristotle, see his attempt to develop a definition of the soul in *De anima* II, ch. 1. John himself refers specifically to the part of Aristotle's *De anima* II, ch. 1 falling under comment. 6 (in Averroes's Commentary). For which see the Stuart Crawford ed., p. 136 (412a26ff.). For some interesting remarks concerning whether Aristotle's remark in *De anima* II, ch. 1 (412a6–9), should be taken to imply that for him form individuates, see M. De Corte, *La doctrine de l'intelligence chez Aristote* (Paris, 1934), p. 199, note 5.

82. "Item, comm. 7, arguit sic: per illud est individuum, per quod aliquid est unum; sed non est unum per materiam sed per formam" (p. 72). For Averroes see *In II De an.* (412b6), ch. 1, text 7, pp. 138–139. While Averroes here makes the point that the form of a thing deserves the names '*unum*' and '*ens*' in the primary sense, John has inserted the assumption that, through that whereby something is one, it is an individual. Perhaps he sees some justification for this in the following text from Averroes: "Congregatum enim non dicitur unum nisi per unitatem existentem in forma; materia enim non est *hoc* nisi per formam" (p. 139:36–38). Here, however, the '*hoc*' that I have italicized seems to refer directly to '*unum*' rather than to being an individual.

83. "Item, comment. 8: In hoc est differentia inter artificialia et naturalia, quia naturale individuum non dicitur hoc nisi per formam suam, sed in artificialibus est hoc per materiam suam, non per formam suam. Sed illo, quo est hoc, illo est individuum (III *Sent.* 11, 2, 2, p. 72). For Averroes, see *In II De an.* (412b11–15), ch. 1, text 8, pp. 142-143, especially p. 143:96–103.

84. III *Sent.* 11, 2, 2, p. 72. Here John is developing some remarks made by Averroes in the text cited in the preceding note.

85. "Item, commento septimo, arguit sic: Animatum non est hoc esse nisi ex hoc, quod habet animam. Sed declaratum est quod anima est prima perfectio corporis naturalis, et forma. Igitur per formam est animatum hoc esse seu individuum" (*ibid.*). For Averroes, see *In II De an.* (412b6), ch. 1, text 7, p. 138:25–28.

86. "Hanc viam tenet Godofredus, Quodlibet 7, q. 5, et Petrus de Alvernia, Quodlibet 2, quaest. 5, propter argumentum Commentatoris, commento nono et septimo" (III *Sent.* 11, 2, 2, p. 72).

87. "Haec ergo est opinio Godofredi et Petri de Alvernia, quorum utrorumque ratio principalis est ratio Commentatoris supra dicta secundi *De anima,* commento 9" (III *Sent.* 11, 2, 2, p. 73).

88. "Et uterque addit aliam rationem, et est haec. Substantia composita prius est in actu naturaliter per formam existens quam quodcumque accidens adveniat ei. Unde Commentator, *De substantia orbis,* primo capitulo: Subiecta omnium accidentium sunt individua substantiae, quae sunt in actu. Sed per illud per quod aliquid ex-

istit in actu, est indivisum in actu. Ergo indivisio substantiae compositae extra animam praecedit esse cuiuslibet accidentis. Sed individuatio est indivisio naturaliter. Ergo.'' *Ibid.* Compare with Peter's text, Hocedez, ''Une question inédite'' (375:63–376:75), and with Godfrey's Quodlibet VII, qu. 5 (PB 3.323–324). Also see my remarks in note 59. For Averroes, see his *De substantia orbis,* ch. 1 (Venice, 1562), vol. 9, fol. 4ra.

89. For John, see p. 73 (''§Secundus''). Note in particular, ''Igitur volebat solum arguere quod quantitas est principium multitudinis individuorum; imponitur tamen illi quod posuit quod quantitas est principium individuationis.'' For Thomas's usage of Aristotle's notion that division causes multitude, see, for instance, his Commentary on the *De Trinitate,* qu. 4, art. 1 (*Sancti Thomae de Aquino Expositio super librum Boethii De trinitate,* ed. B. Decker [Leiden, 1959]), p. 134:9–11. For Aristotle, see *Met.* X, ch. 3(1054a22ff.).

90. For John, see p. 73. Though the parallel is not perfect, one may compare the first argument with Thomas's *In De trinitate,* qu. 4, art. 2, ad 3 (Decker ed., p. 144:14–16).

91. ''Item, forma non est alia nisi quia alia est materia. Sed materia non est alia, nisi propter quantitatem. Ergo, etc.'' (*ibid.*). Compare with Thomas, *In De trin.,* qu. 4, art. 2, ad 4 (pp. 144:28–145:2).

92. ''Item, Philosophus, 5. *Physic,* . . . vult quod generatio substantialis habet proprium terminum, sicut alteratio et augmentatio. Sed hoc non est nisi forma substantialis. Sed generatio communis terminatur ad hoc aliquid. . . . Ergo forma substantialis facit hoc aliquid'' (*ibid.*). For Peter of Auvergne, see note 50 and the corresponding text.

93. ''Item, remanente formali principio individuationis in propria natura videtur idem individuum. Sed si Deus uniret animam Petri corpori Pauli in resurrectione, ibi esset propria quantitas in propria materia. Ergo idem Paulus, qui primo. Hoc est manifeste falsum'' (*ibid.*). For fuller discussion of this particular point, John refers to his Commentary on Book II of the *Sentences,* dist. 11, art. 2. For this see in the 1618 Cremona edition, vol. 1, p. 537b (arg. 7). For a similar case as proposed by John of Paris in his Commentary on Book IV of the *Sentences* see J.-P. Müller, ''Un cas d'éclectisme métaphysique: Jean de Paris (Quidort) O.P.'', *Miscellanea Mediaevalia* 2 (Berlin, 1963): 655–656. There John rather reasons that if the soul of Peter should be united with the ashes of Paul at the resurrection, we would still have numerically one and the same Peter *propter identitatem formae.* As Müller also points out, this follows from John's distinction between the cause or principle of individuation, on the one hand, and the cause or explanation for multiplication of individuals within the same species, on the other. While John holds that form is the principle of individuation, he concludes that quantity serves as the principle of multiplicity for individuals within a species. Müller suggests that John of Paris owes his distinction to Godfrey's Quodlibet VI, qu. 16, though he thinks that the application of this to the question of the identity of the bodies of the resurrected is probably due to John himself (p. 656). This, therefore, would be one more instance in which John of Paris came under the

influence of Godfrey of Fontaines. For another see my "Godfrey of Fontaines: Disputed Questions 9, 10, and 12", *Franciscan Studies* 33 (1973): 353–354. (The text on p. 354, third line from the bottom, should read: "Compare p. 370, line 22—p. 371, 1. 5. . ."). For more on John of Paris's views concerning individuation see Müller, "Eine Quästion über das Individuationsprinzip des Johannes von Paris O.P. (Quidort)", in *Virtus Politica. Festgabe zum 75. Geburtstag von A. Hufnagel,* ed. J. Möller and H. Hohlenberger (Stuttgart, 1974), pp. 335–356. In this question John does not make form the principle of individuation. As Müller also indicates, in his *Correctorium corruptorii 'Circa',* John of Paris had pointed out that for Aquinas the cause of multiplication of individuals within a species is quantitative dimension, whatever may be the cause of individuation. John suggests, but in tentative fashion, that for Thomas the principle of individuation is not the same as the principle of multiplication of individuals: "Quia forte materia pertinet ad principium individuationis, sed quantitas per se divisibilis est causa multiplicationis individuorum sub una specie. See *Le Correctorium corruptorii 'Circa' de Jean Quidort de Paris,* ed. J.-P. Müller (Rome, 1941), a. 28, pp. 160–161.

94. III *Sent.* 11, 2, 2, p. 73.

95. *Ibid.* For Averroes see *In II De an.* (417b29), ch. 5, text 60, p. 221:47–50; *In I De an.* (407b23–224), ch. 3, text 53, p. 75:17–19.

96. For John's text, see art. III (*ed. cit.,* p. 74). "Declarat se alibi Thomas super primo Boetii *De trinitate* sic. Quia nulla forma materialis inquantum est forma est de se multiplicabilis. Et dicit 'inquantum est forma' pro Intelligentia quae de se est haec et non multiplicabilis. Sed hoc non est inquantum est forma sed inquantum quaedam Intelligentia. . . . Ergo forma non est multiplicabilis de se inquantum est forma. Ergo est multiplicata secundum quod recipitur in materia. Sed materia non est divisa et multiplicata nisi per quantitates. Ergo quantitas est principium etc." For Thomas, see *In De trinitate,* qu. 4, art. 2 (Decker, pp. 142:20–143:5). Note that in explaining why no form insofar as it is a form is "this" or an individual, he focuses on the case of the rational soul. In a certain way it is this individual (*hoc aliquid*) of itself, but not insofar as it is a form. John rather applies this to the case of a separate Intelligence and notes that of itself it is both "this" (or an individual) and not capable of being multiplied. This is not because it is a form, but because it is a given kind of form.

97. "Addit tamen quod illa quantitas non est quantitas terminata, quia talis quantitas variatur eodem remanente individuo in numero, sed quantitas interminata, quae in materia praecedit formam, et distinguit in eas diversas partes ad diversas formas . . ." (p. 74). For Thomas's discussion of the distinction between determined and undetermined dimensions and his denial that determined dimensions can serve as the principle of individuation, see *In De trinitate,* qu. 4, art. 2 (Decker, p. 143:9–15). For his appeal to undetermined dimensions see p. 143:15–21. Note in particular, "Et ex his dimensionibus interminatis materia efficitur haec materia signata, et sic individuat formam, et sic ex materia causatur diversitas secundum numerum in eadem specie." For discussion of Thomas's apparent shift concerning the role of determined vs. un-

determined dimensions in accounting for individuation, see Klinger as cited in notes 1 and 2.

98. In addition to the references to Porphyry, Boethius, and John Damascene (for which see notes 22, 46, 48, where they were cited in connection with the principle of individuation), John refers to Aristotle's *Metaphysics* V, ch. 13 (1020a13ff.). For John's argument, see p. 74 (marginal heading: "Contra S. Thomam Arg. 1").

99. *Ibid.* See arg. 4. For a similar argument in John see the text cited in note 93, and the remarks about the line of reasoning used by John of Paris.

100. *Ibid.* See arg. 5.

101. It is unlikely that John did not realize that he was differing with Godfrey and Peter on the last-mentioned point. Still, he does not explicitly direct his attack against them in rejecting quantity as the principle of numerical multiplication of individuals.

102. See p. 75, arg. 1, against the view that matter is the principle of numerical multiplication within a species.

103. "Dico ergo quod forma est principium distinctionis et multitudinis individuorum. Quod declaratur: Verum est enim secundum Commentatorem, 12 *Metaphy.* com. 2, quod materia est distincta respectu distinctarum formarum per distinctas habilitates. Etiam secundum Commentatorem *De substantia orbis,* tract. 1. Cum forma determinata determinatam quantitatem requirat, oportet in materia determinata respectu determinatae formae quod praecedant dimensiones propriae illi formae in materia. Sed illae dimensiones sunt in potentia in materia, ut dicit, et ideo vocat illas interminatis" (p. 75, "Tertius"). For Averroes, see *In XII Met.* (1069b26–32), ch. 2, text 11, vol. 8, p. 297rDF; *De substantia orbis,* ch. 1, 9, 4r–4v.

104. See p. 75 ("Tertius"). Note in particular, "Sed ens in potentia non dat denominationem rebus naturalibus, nec artificialibus, nisi forte aliquam valde diminutam, ens autem in actu dat denominationem completam. Ergo. . . ."

105. See p. 76, arg. 2.

106. *Ibid.* See the third "Item". Cf. the references given in note 95.

107. *Ibid.*, "Ad primum".

108. *Ibid.*, vol. 2, p. 791.

109. For another early fourteenth century thinker who seems to have been heavily influenced by Godfrey's Quodlibet VI, qu. 16 and Quodlibet VII, qu. 5, one may consult T. W. Köhler's recent study of James of Metz and his views concerning unity: *Der Begriff der Einheit und ihr ontologisches Prinzip nach dem Sentenzenkommentar des Jakob von Metz O.P.* (Rome, 1971). See, for instance, pp. 157–160 (on the distinction between the two kinds of unity); pp. 271–294 (on James's knowledge of Godfrey's Quodlibet VII, qu. 5 in discussing the relationship between nature and sup-

posit and the problem of individuation; and James and Godfrey's Quodlibet VI, qu. 16); pp. 314–318 (some parallels between James, Peter of Auvergne, and Godfrey). Köhler also points out certain differences between Godfrey and James in these same sections. It is interesting to observe that Baconthorpe has not named James of Metz along with Godfrey and Peter as a defender of substantial form as the principle of individuation, even though James did defend that position (see, for instance, p. 287).

11

JAMES OF VITERBO
(B. CA. 1255; D. 1308)

JOHN F. WIPPEL

This Augustinian master of theology's four Quodlibetal Questions were delivered at Paris in the 1290s, from 1293–1296 according to their editor, E. Ypma.[1] Lottin had proposed an earlier dating for Quodlibets I and II; that is, 1291 and 1292, respectively.[2] My own research has confirmed the claim by Lottin that Godfrey's Quodlibet VIII, q. 3, manifests knowledge of James's Quodlibet I, q. 5.[3] This being so, it is quite likely that James was aware of Godfrey's Quodlibet VII, q. 5, when he conducted his own Quodlibet I and even more so that James was familiar with Godfrey's discussion of numerical unity in the latter's Quodlibet VI of 1289. At the same time, as will be shown later, James knows of Thomas Aquinas's discussion in his *Expositio* on Boethius's *De trinitate*, q. 4, art. 2.

James takes up the issue of numerical unity and individuation in Quodlibet I, q. 21. The following question had been put to him: If the soul should reassume other ashes at the resurrection, would a man be numerically the same as he formerly was?[4] In proposing his own solution to this question, James comments that one must first consider the issue of numerical unity in things composed of matter and form or, as he puts it, the cause of such numerical unity. He also remarks that just as there are different ways of explaining the cause of individuation, so the cause of numerical unity may be assigned in different ways.[5]

James remarks that according to the generally accepted way of speaking, an individual and that which is numerically one are identified. But he notes that closer investigation, in accord with the practice of more ancient writers, shows that something is not said to be an individual for the same reason that it is said to be numerically one. Nonetheless, he grants that what is an individual is also numerically one. For his present purposes, therefore, he is willing to take the cause of individuation and the cause of numerical unity as one and the same. By doing this he will be able to show that, just as there are different views about the cause of individuation, so are there different positions concerning the cause of numerical unity.[6]

According to one approach, continues James, the agent is the cause of a thing's numerical unity. This is so because what causes a thing's being must also cause its unity. And an agent is the cause of a thing's being, since it actualizes what was previously only in potency. Therefore, it follows that an agent is also the cause of that thing's unity. Moreover, support for this view seems to be afforded by a remark made by Aristotle in *Metaphysics* VIII.[7]

James finds this account insufficient, however; for an agent is only an extrinsic cause of a thing's being and of its being one. In addition to such an extrinsic cause there must also be an intrinsic cause of its entity and its unity. And as he goes on to remark, there is much doubt concerning the identity of this intrinsic cause.[8] As the reader will notice, so far in this discussion there has been no effort on James's part to distinguish between unity of being (ontological unity) and strictly numerical unity.

According to a second approach, accidents that exist within a composite serve as the intrinsic cause of that composite's numerical unity. Among such accidents, quantity especially fulfills this function; for it belongs to quantity of itself to be a "this" and to be individual. Support for this view is drawn from Boethius's *De trinitate,* where he writes that variety of accidents produces numerical difference.[9] Defenders of this position also cite another text from this same Boethian work, where he comments about place that pertains to quantity: "If in our mind we separate all accidents from these, still place is diverse for each; and this in no way can we imagine to be one; for two bodies will not occupy one and the same place."[10]

James remarks that if diversity of accidents results in numerical diversity, unity of accidents will cause numerical unity. That by which a thing is distinguished from others is the cause of its unity.[11]

Nonetheless, James also has difficulties with this approach. First of all, since accidents are not the cause of the being of a composite entity, they cannot cause its numerical unity. This is especially so because unity in terms of number seems to be unity in essence or substance. Presupposed by James is the view that whatever causes a thing's unity must also cause its being. Accidents do not cause a composite thing's being. Therefore they do not cause its unity. Again we wonder why James does not see fit to distinguish between unity in number and unity in being. Instead he identifies them. Such a distinction might, of course, weaken his argument.[12]

Moreover, objects James, what is received in something else cannot be the cause of the individuation of that which receives it. And if this is so, neither can it be the cause of the receiver's numerical unity. But all accidents are received in something else, that is to say, in substance. Therefore they cannot be the cause of the numerical unity of a composite entity. As for Boethius's remark that variety of accidents produces numerical difference, James would have us interpret this as Gilbert of Poitiers had done. By this Boethius does not intend to say that such accidents are the cause but only a sign or indication of the unity or diversity in question. In other words, they enable us to recognize that such unity is present and exercise an epistemological rather than an ontological function as regards this unity.[13]

With this background in mind, James turns to another theory. Matter is the cause of a thing's numerical unity. Even so, defenders of this general position are divided. Some hold that matter taken without qualification is the cause of numerical unity. They point out that a form cannot be such a cause because form, simply considered in itself, can be communicated to others and received in others. This shows that form as such is not a "this" or an individual of itself. Form derives this characteristic from matter. Defenders of this position also hold that accidents cannot be the cause of a thing's numerical unity; for they are received in something else.[14] Moreover, suppose that matter could be freed from all its accidents but still informed by its substantial form. In that eventuality, the composite would still be an individual and numerically one. This would be so, even though there could not be many such individuals at the same time, if there were no quantity in such an entity; for it is through quantity that matter is divided. Hence defenders of this view admit that an accident—quantity—does contribute to the multiplication of individuals because division belongs to quantity of itself and to matter by reason of quantity. But the cause both of individuation and of numerical unity is matter, not quantity.[15]

Others use a different approach in holding that matter is the cause of numerical unity. Matter simply taken as such and without qualification cannot cause numerical unity. If it were to do so, all things subject to generation and corruption would be numerically one since their matter is one. But matter is a cause of numerical unity insofar as it is subject to dimensions, not to determined dimensions, which frequently vary in the same individual, but to undetermined dimensions. Undetermined dimensions render matter designated (*signata*), and this in turn serves as the principle of individuation and of numerical unity.[16]

Here James appears to have in mind Thomas Aquinas's position and, in fact, q. 4, art. 2 of the latter's Commentary on the *De trinitate* of Boethius. There Thomas writes: "And it is from these undetermined dimensions that matter is rendered this designated matter, and thus individuates form, and thus from matter there is caused numerical diversity within the same species."[17] In fact, in the next lines James cites almost literally from Thomas's treatise.

James: Et quia huiusmodi dimensiones sunt de genere accidentium, ideo
          diversitas secundum numerum, quandoque reducitur in diversi-
          tatem materiae, quandoque in diversitatem accidentium. Et hoc
          ratione dimensionum praedictarum.[18]
Thomas: Et ideo cum hae dimensiones sint de genere accidentium, quan-
          doque diversitas secundum numerum reducitur in diversitatem
          materiae, quandoque in diversitatem accidentis, et hoc ratione di-
          mensionum praedictarum.[19]

Hence, in basing himself on this particular text, James counts Thomas
among those who regard matter as designated by undetermined dimensions as
the principle both of numerical unity and of individuation. He does this without ever mentioning Thomas by name.

At the same time, James rejects this position as insufficient. If the
cause of a thing's being is the same as the cause of its unity, form—the primary cause of its being—must also be the cause of its unity. Therefore, continues James, some conclude that form is the cause of numerical unity.[20]

Given so many different ways of accounting for numerical unity, James
now sets down the view that appears to him to be more probable. It seems
reaasonable to hold that both form and matter are the cause in primary fashion of numerical unity in a composite being, though differently. Quantity
must also contribute something to this kind of unity, but in still another way.
Other accidents do not cause such unity, but only attest to it by serving as a
sign or indicator.[21]

In developing this position James appeals to Aristotle's *Metaphysics* V
to support the claim that matter serves as a cause of a thing's numerical unity:
"Those things are one in number whose matter is one."[22] But in *Metaphysics* X Aristotle seems to attribute the causation of such unity to form.[23]
James finds confirmation for the latter reading both in Averroes's Commentary on the passage from Book X, and in his Commentary on *De anima* II,
ch. 1.[24] Farther on in his commentary on this chapter in the *De anima* Averroes writes that an individual is not a "this" except through its form, not
through its matter. And again he writes: "An individual does not become an
individual except through its form; for it is not an individual except insofar as
it is a being in actuality, and it is a being in actuality through its form, not
through its matter."[25]

From these passages James concludes that according to Aristotle and
Averroes both matter and form are the cause of numerical unity. This is reasonable, he remarks, since these are the principles which essentially constitute a composite substance. Yet each causes numerical unity in its own way.
To explain this, James notes that something is said to be one in number in two
ways: (1) in terms of its singularity only, in that it is a "this" and an indi-

vidual; (2) in terms of its perfection and totality in that it is not merely a "this" but something whole and complete within its species.[26]

If we take numerical unity in the first way (as implying singularity and a "this"), matter is its cause. What causes numerical unity of this kind must be a "this" through itself; through it other things will become "this". But this cause can be only matter. Because matter receives all else in the composite and is not itself received by anything else, of itself matter is a "this" and numerically one in the sense of being singular.[27]

Even so, while matter is the primary and principal cause of this kind of numerical unity, quantity as subject to dimensions also contributes something. Just as a special and proper kind of division and undividedness pertains to quantity, so does a special and proper kind of unity.[28] This is why Aristotle says in both *Metaphysics* V and *Metaphysics* X that in one sense the one is that which is continuous; and the more truly it is continuous, the more truly it is one. But the kind of unity based on a thing's being continuous belongs to numerical unity and especially to the first kind of numerical unity James has distinguished. And as he has just indicated, the cause of this unity is matter. Just as quantity among all accidents follows most greatly from matter, so does the unity pertaining to quantity follow from the unity that belongs both to matter and by reason of matter to the composite.[29]

Accordingly, in matter-form composites a twofold unity contributes to the first kind of numerical unity (singularity or being a "this"). One is the substantial or essential unity of the thing, and its cause is matter. The other is an accidental unity, and its cause is quantity as subject to dimensions. The first is more fundamental than the second.[30]

From all of this, continues James, it seems to follow both that matter is the cause of the numerical unity enjoyed by quantity itself (since quantity is received in matter) and conversely that quantity is the cause of matter's numerical unity (since matter is extended by quantity and rendered divided or undivided). Given this, James thinks it reasonable to agree with those who say that matter, insofar as it is subject to undetermined dimensions, is the cause of individuation or of numerical unity. In sum, matter is the primary cause of numerical unity taken in the first sense (as singularity), and quantity is its cause in some secondary fashion. Other accidents do not cause such unity, but simply serve as signs or indicators that this unity is present.[31]

When numerical unity is taken in the second way—as perfection and completeness—its cause is not matter but form. Nothing else in the composite can cause such unity, except by way of consequence and as related to form. This is so because a composite enjoys perfection and actuality by reason of its form.[32]

James also comments that in immaterial substances their very essence or nature, insofar as it is realized in actuality, causes their numerical unity in

both of the senses he has distinguished. By reason of the fact that such a nature is not received in something else and is fitted by nature to exist in itself,
it is of itself a "this" and singular. In other words, the essence or nature is the
cause of the numerical unity (singularity) of the subject (*suppositum*) that enjoys such a nature. At the same time, because the essence or nature is a substantial actuality, through its nature the suppositum is something perfected
and complete within its species. Hence it enjoys numerical unity of the second type.[33]

In human beings, the cause of unity taken in the second sense (as perfection and totality) is the rational soul, that is, the form of the human body.
But the cause of unity taken in the first sense (singularity) is not only matter
together with quantity, as in other composite entities, but the human form or
soul as well. Because this form is an immaterial substance and can subsist in
itself, it has its own unity (singularity) just as it has its own existence.[34]

During the following academic year James returned to the issue of
quantity and individuation in Quodlibet II, q. 1, while responding to this
question: Can God produce any accident without a subject?[35] In the course of
discussing this general issue, James notes that some maintain that if by divine
power quantity can exist without a subject, quality cannot. Among the accidents quantity alone can exist without its subject because everything that exists in actuality must be a "this" and an individual. That which cannot be
"this" and an individual without something else cannot exist without that
other thing. But all accidents other than quantity are individuated through
their subjects. Therefore they cannot exist without such subjects. Because
quantity is a "this" and an individual of itself, it does not need a subject to
be individuated. This is so even though it does need a subject to exist just as
do other accidents. Insofar as an accident needs a subject only in order to
exist, it can be kept in existence by divine power without that subject. This
follows from the fact that a subject contributes to the existence of a (proper)
accident in the manner of an efficient cause.[36]

According to this position, insofar as an accident needs a subject to be
individuated, it cannot be made or kept in being by God without its subject.
For an accident is individuated by a subject insofar as it is received in that
subject as form in matter. But God is the subject for nothing else in the way
matter is the subject of form. Therefore quantity and only quantity can be
kept in being by divine power without its subject. This is so because in the
natural course of events quantity needs a subject to exist, but not to be individuated. Because it is individuated of itself, it will still be an individual
"this" if it is kept in being by God without its subject.[37]

Central to this position is the claim that quantity is individuated of itself
and not by its subject. James finds defenders of this view offering two arguments in support of this claim. First of all, that which is by itself something

designated (*significatum*) and subject to the here and now, and by which other things are designated and subject to the here and now, is individuated of itself. For it is of the nature of an individual to be subject to the here and now and to be designated. But quantity is subject to the here and now of itself; hence it is something designated of itself, and other things are designated, that is, individuated, through quantity. This is so because it is through quantity that a substance is determined to its given place.[38]

Second, what is divisible and capable of being multiplied of itself, and through which other things are multiplied, is individuated of itself. This follows because to be multiplied pertains to individuals. But quantity is divisible and capable of being multiplied of itself. Other things are multiplied through quantity. Once again, therefore, it follows that quantity is individuated of itself.[39]

Consistent with views we have already seen from his Quodlibet I, James expresses serious reservations about the claim that quantity is individuated of itself and not by its subject. He finds this open to question in itself, and also challenges the arguments offered in its support. As regards the position as such, he counters by noting that philosophers distinguish two ways in which an individual may be understood: (1) as a singular, for instance, in the way this humanity or this whiteness are individuals; (2) as something that is a whole in itself and not capable of being conformed to anything else.[40]

Understood in the second way, James now explains, the individual adds something to the singular. That which is an individual only in the sense of being singular can be like something else, as this whiteness can be like that whiteness. But that which is an individual in the second way cannot be conformed to or like something else in all respects. An individual taken in this second sense is not some one and simple thing, but a collection of many forms. James indicates that this second understanding of an individual is taken from Porphyry, who states that an individual is said [to be] that which consists of characteristics (literally, properties) of this particular kind; and this particular set of characteristics will never be found in anything else.[41]

This twofold division of ways in which something may be regarded as an individual more or less conforms to the two ways James has proposed in Quodlibet I in which something may be numerically one. Thus an individual taken in the first sense within the present context corresponds to what James there describes as that which is numerically one in the first way, that is, this singular or individual thing.[42] An individual taken in the second sense within the present context seems to correspond roughly to the second way in which something may enjoy numerical unity according to Quodlibet I; that is, as being whole and perfect. However, in the present discussion this second usage has been developed. What enables us to regard something as an individual in this second sense, that is, as being whole and complete within itself, is the fact that it includes all of its given characteristics (properties) and that this set or combination of characteristics is unique.[43]

In any event, James now denies that quantity is individuated of itself whether we take an individual in the first or second sense as he has just distinguished them. Quantity is not individuated of itself when we understand the individual in the first sense—as a singular and a "this". This is so because what is an individual either cannot be received in something else and is therefore an individual and singular of itself, or else it can be received in something else and is therefore individuated by that which receives it. Because quantity, like other accidents, can be received in something else, it seems that it is an individual and a "this" through that which receives it and not of itself. (This is hardly an argument on James's part, but a simple assertion of his position.) Moreover, if we take an individual in the second sense, neither quantity nor any singular form may be regarded as an individual in and of itself, for such an individual is a collection of many forms (properties).[44]

In addition, James questions the two arguments offered in support of the claim that quantity is self-individuating. According to the first of these, quantity is of itself something designated. To this James responds that, if by this designated thing we have in mind something singular, quantity is not rendered designated of itself but rather through the singular character of the subject in which it is received.[45] And when it is argued that something is in place through its quantity, James counters that quantity is not the ultimate and unqualified reason for a thing's being in place. Quantity rather accounts for the fact that it is in place in this given way, that is, circumscriptively and as measured by that place. Some other cause must be found to account for the fact that is determined to place as such.[46]

As for the second argument based on the claim that quantity is divisible of itself, James counters that individuation is one thing and divisibility or capacity to be multiplied another. While a certain divisibility does belong to quantity of itself, individuation comes to it through something else, that is, the subject in which it is received. As for the broader question at issue in Quodlibet II, q. 1, James observes that from the standpoint of individuation no greater impossibility seems to be involved in quality's existing without a subject than in quantity's doing so.[47]

In sum, James seems to be defending a compromise position. This is not all that unusual for him, as may be seen from his discussion of the relationship between essence and existence in created entities.[48] As regards what he has referred to as numerical unity in the first sense (according to Quodlibet I) and also as regards individuation in the first sense (according to Quodlibet II), that is, singularity, matter is the primary cause of this. But it is not matter in the unqualified sense that serves as such a cause, but only insofar as it is subject to undetermined dimensions and therefore to quantity. Hence quantity also plays an important if auxiliary role in accounting for such numerical unity and individuation; for quantity renders matter divisible. To this extent, as has been noted previously, James seems to be indebted to Thomas Aquinas.[49]

When it comes to numerical unity in the second sense—whereby something is a complete or perfected whole and unique—in Quodlibet I James assigns the primary causality of this to form. In doing this he may be making a nod in the direction of Godfrey of Fontaines.[50] But James's remarks in Quodlibet II reveal that he does not account for this by appealing only to substantial form. It is rather the total set of characteristics (forms or properties) to which he now turns. On this point he differs from Godfrey and appears, in fact, to hark back to a much earlier approach that was foreshadowed, at least, by Porphyry and Boethius.[51] Finally, nowhere in either of these discussions is there clear recognition of the distinction between numerical unity taken in the strict sense and numerical unity taken broadly, that is, unity of being, as Godfrey had distinguished these in his account. In this respect, therefore, James's position appears to mark a step backward rather than a step forward.[52]

Notes

1. *Jacobi de Viterbio O.E.S.A. disputatio prima de quolibet*, ed. E. Ypma (Wurzburg, 1969), p. VI and n. 10. Cf. Ypma, *La formation des professeurs chez les Ermites de Saint-Augustin de 1256 à 1354* (Paris, 1956), pp. 92–96. In the first reference (note 10) Ypma cites D. Gutiérrez, "De vita et scriptis Beati Jacobi de Viterbio", *Analecta Augustiana* 16 (1937–1938): 290–294. Gutiérrez's study also appeared with slight modification as an independent monograph, *De B. Iacobi Viterbiensis O.E.S.A. vita, operibus et doctrina theologica* (Rome, 1939). See pp. 15, 33. Also see P. Glorieux, *La littérature quodlibétique*, 2 vols. (Kain [Belgium], 1925; Paris, 1935), vol. 1, pp. 214–217, vol. 2, pp. 144–146.

2. *Psychologie et morale aux XIIe et XIIIe siècles*, vol. 3, 2 (Louvain, 1949), p. 731, n. 2; vol. 4, 2 (Louvain, 1954), p. 869, n. 2.

3. Wippel, "The Dating of James of Viterbo's Quodlibet I and Godfrey of Fontaines' Quodlibet VIII", *Augustiniana* 24 (1974): 348–386, especially 365–372. Also cf. note 35.

4. *Jacobi de Viterbio . . . disputatio prima de quolibet*, p. 223: "Utrum, si anima in resurrectione resumeret alios cineres, esset idem homo numero qui prius fuit." See the similarity between this question and that considered by Godfrey in his Quodlibet VI, q. 16 (as cited in note 13 of the preceding chapter). Also see p. 228 and n. 41 for a similar argument in Peter of Auvergne's Quodlibet II, q. 5; and n. 93 for a similar discussion in John of Paris.

5. *Disputatio prima*, p. 223.

6. *Ibid.*

7. *Ibid.*, pp. 223–224. For Aristotle, see *Metaph.* VIII, ch. 6 (1045b19–22). In James's version this text reads: "Simile est quaerere unius quae causa et quae causa essendi. Unum enim aliquid unumquodque et quod potentia et quod actu unum aliqualiter est. Quare causa nulla alia, nisi id quod ut movens ex potentia ad actum."

8. *Disputatio prima*, p. 224.

9. *Ibid.* For Boethius see his *De trinitate* 1, in *Boethius. The Theological Tractates. The Consolation of Philosophy*, ed. H. F. Stewart, E. K. Rand, S. J. Tester (Cambridge, MA, 1978), p. 6: "Sed numero differentiam accidentium varietas facit."

10. *Disputatio prima*, p. 224, where James cites Boethius's *De trinitate*. For which see pp. 6–8: ". . . nam vel si animo cuncta ab his accidentia separemus, tamen locus cunctis diversus est quem unum fingere nullo modo possumus; duo enim corpora unum locum non obtinebunt. . . ."

11. *Disputatio prima*, p. 224.

12. "Cum enim accidentia non sint causa essendi composito, nec etiam esse possunt causa unitatis numeralis, et maxime quia unitas secundum numerum videtur esse unitas in essentia vel substantia. . . ."

13. *Disputatio prima*, p. 225. For Gilbert, see *The Commentaries on Boethius by Gilbert of Poitiers*, ed. N. A. Häring (Toronto, 1966), p. 77. For helpful discussion see Jorge J. E. Gracia, *Introduction to the Problem of Individuation in the Early Middle Ages* (Munich and Vienna, 1984), pp. 170–173. On the original passage in Boethius, see pp. 100–103.

14. *Disputatio prima*, p. 225.

15. *Ibid.*

16. *Ibid.* Note especially, "Sed est causa prout subest dimensionibus, non quidem terminatis, quae variantur frequenter circa idem individuum, quod permutari convenit secundum mensuram ipsius et figuram, sed interminatis quae manent. Ex huiusmodi enim dimensionibus efficitur materia signata, quae principium est individuationis et unitatis secundum numerum."

17. *Expositio super librum Boethii De trinitate*, ed. B. Decker (Leiden, 1959), qu. 4. a. 2, pp. 142–143. For the distinction between determined and undetermined dimensions see p. 143:9–21. Note the final sentence and its similarity with the text from James cited in the preceding note: "Et ex his dimensionibus interminatis materia efficitur haec materia signata, et sic individuat formam, et sic ex materia causatur diversitas secundum numerum in eadem specie."

18. *Disputatio prima*, p. 225. James's text is followed by this remark: "Et similiter dicendum est de unitate secundum numerum."

19. *Expositio super librum Boethii*, pp. 143–144.

20. *Disputatio prima*, p. 226. Again we find no indication that James will distinguish between numerical unity and unity of being (ontological or transcendental unity) or between the causes of these two kinds of unity.

21. *Ibid.* Since this is a good statement of the position James is preparing to defend, it merits quotation: "Videtur autem rationabiliter esse ponendum, quod tam forma quam materia sunt causa unitatis numeralis in composito principaliter, diversimode tamen. Quantitas autem secundum aliquem modum facit ad unitatem huiusmodi. Cetera vero accidentia hanc unitatem non faciunt sicut causa, sed probant sicut signum."

22. *Ibid.* For Aristotle see *Metaphysics* V, ch. 6 (1016b32–33).

23. *Disputatio prima*, p. 226. For Aristotle see *Metaphysics* X, ch. 1 (1052a22–25). As James presents this text: "Ait enim sic: quod unum dicitur aliquid maxime, non solum si sit continuum, sed si sit 'totum, et habens aliquam formam et speciem', et hoc naturaliter. Et subdit quod id quod est tale, habet in se quod est causa sibi, ut sit continuum et unum."

24. For Averroes's Commentary on the passage from *Metaphysics* X, see *Aristotelis opera cum Averrois commentariis* (Venice, 1562–1574) = *In X Metaph.* (1052a22–25), ch. 1, text 1 (Venice, 1562–1574), vol. 8, p. 250rBC. For the text from Aristotle's *De anima*, see *De anima* II, ch. 1 (412b8–9). In James's own text this reads: "Hoc enim unum et esse cum multipliciter dicatur quod proprie est actus est." For Averroes, see *Commentarium magnum in Aristotelis De anima libros*, ed. F. Stuart Crawford (Cambridge, MA, 1953) = *In II De anima* (412b8–9), ch. 1, text 7, p. 139.

25. *Disputatio prima*, p. 226: " 'Individuum non est hoc, nisi per suam formam, non per suam materiam.' Et iterum infra dicit: 'Individuum non fit individuum nisi per formam. Quia non est individuum nisi secundum quod est ens actu et est in actu per suam formam, non per suam materiam.' " For the first citation in Averroes, see *In II De anima* (412b10–17), ch. 1, text 8, Crawford 143; for the second see *In II De anima* (412b17), ch. 1, text 9, Crawford 144. My translation is of the text as quoted by James.

26. *Disputatio prima*, p. 227. Note especially, "Unum enim numero dupliciter dicitur. Uno modo ratione singularitatis tantum, ut quia est hoc et singulare. Alio modo ratione perfectionis et totalitatis, ut quia non solum est hoc, sed est aliquod totum et perfectum in aliqua specie."

27. *Ibid.* Note in particular, "Materia autem est huiusmodi. Cum enim ipsa sit receptaculum omnium aliorum et in alio non recipitur, se ipsa est hoc et unum numero singularitate."

28. *Ibid.* ". . . tamen ad huiusmodi unitatem etiam dimensiva quantitas facit aliquo modo."

29. *Ibid.* For Aristotle see *Metaphysics* V, ch. 6 (1015b36–1016a17); *Metaphysics* X, ch. 1 (1052a19–21).

30. *Disputatio prima,* p. 227.

31. *Ibid.,* pp. 227–228.

32. *Ibid.,* p. 228. "Accipiendo vero unum numero secundo modo, scilicet ratione perfectionis et totalitatis, forma est causa unitatis numeralis, et non materia; nec aliquid aliud quod sit in composito, nisi ex consequenti et ut comparatur ad formam. . . . Quia perfectio et actus est in composito per formam."

33. *Ibid.*

34. *Ibid.*

35. If, as we have proposed on another occasion, James's Quodlibet I dates from Lent 1293, his Quodlibet II would more than likely fall into the following academic year, i.e., 1293/1294. On the other hand, if Quodlibet I itself dates from December 1293, and hence from the 1293/1294 academic year, Quodlibet II should then be placed in the 1294/1295 academic year. See Wippel, "The Dating of James of Viterbo's Quodlibet I", pp. 383–385. For Quodlibet II, qu. 1, see *Jacobi de Viterbo O.E.S.A. disputatio secunda de quolibet,* p. 5: "Primo igitur quaeritur: Utrum Deus possit facere quodcumque accidens sine subiecto."

36. *Disputatio secunda,* pp. 14–15. It should be noted that this discussion is preceded by a detailed introduction including a distinction between absolute accidents and relative accidents. Among absolute accidents James has first examined quantity in its various subdivisions (pp. 10–14). He finds general agreement (among Christian thinkers) that continuous quantities, i.e., lines, surfaces, and body, can be kept in existence by divine power without their substantial subject because of Christian belief that such happens in the case of the Eucharist (p. 11). As for those who deny that quality can exist without a subject, he clarifies that by this they have in mind a proximate subject; for they do admit that it can exist without its remote subject, or substance, as in the case of sensible qualities which remain in the Eucharist (p. 14).

37. *Ibid.,* p. 15. James summarizes this position's view concerning other accidents: "Cetera vero accidentia, quae non solum ad existentiam, sed etiam ad individuationem subiecto indigent, nec naturaliter nec miraculose fieri aut conservari possunt sine subiecto; quia implicaretur contradictio, si ponerentur existere sine subiecto. Nam essent individua in quantum sine subiecto existerent actu, et non essent individua in quantum sine subiecto individuationem habere non possunt."

38. *Ibid.*

39. *Ibid.*

40. *Ibid.* "Uno modo sumitur individuum pro singulari; et sic dicitur quod haec humanitas et haec albedo est individua. Alio modo dicitur individuum quod secundum se totum nulli alii potest esse conforme. . . ."

41. *Disputatio secunda*, p. 16. "Illud autem quod hoc secundo modo dicitur individuum, non potest esse alii per omnia conforme. Unde individuum hoc modo sumptum non est aliqua res una et simplex, sed est multarum formarum collectio. Sic autem sumitur individuum a Porphyrio, qui dicit quod individuum dicitur quod ex huiusmodi proprietatibus constat, quarum collectio numquam in alio eadem erit." For Porphyry, see *Porphyrii Isagoge et in Aristotelis Categorias commentarium*, ed. A. Busse (Berlin, 1887), p. 33. For this in Boethius's Latin translation see *In Isagogen Porphyrii commentorum editio secunda*, ed. S. Brandt (Vienna, 1906), pp. 234–235. For discussion, see Jorge J. E. Gracia, *Introduction to the Problem of Individuation*, pp. 67–70. On Boethius's discussion in the second edition of his Commentary, see pp. 74–81.

42. See earlier, p. 265.

43. See earlier, p. 265.

44. *Disputatio secunda*, p. 16.

45. *ibid.* Again James seems to be content merely to assert this without offering any additional evidence or argumentation.

46. *Ibid.*

47. *Ibid.*, pp. 16–17.

48. See James's discussion of this in Quodlibet I, qu. 4. On this see Wippel, "The Relationship Between Essence and Existence in Late Thirteenth-Century Thought: Giles of Rome, Henry of Ghent, Godfrey of Fontaines, and James of Viterbo", in *Philosophies of Existence: Ancient and Medieval*, ed. P. Morewedge (New York, 1982), pp. 131–164, especially 132–134 and 147–148.

49. See page 259.

50. As will be recalled from our discussion of Godfrey in the preceding chapter, he appeals to substantial form as the principle of transcendental or ontological unity (numerical unity taken broadly) and to quantity as the principle of numerical unity taken strictly. He also regards substantial form as the formal principle of individuation. See pp. 222–228.

51. See note 41.

52. See the similar remark we have made about John Baconthorpe (p. 243).

12

JOHN DUNS SCOTUS
(B. CA. 1265; D. 1308)

ALLAN B. WOLTER

Though Scotus in most of his major works refers to his theory of individuation, his ideas on this subject seemed to have undergone little change or substantial development in the course of his academic life.[1] Already in *Lectura* we find a very systematic and extensive presentation of his position, one that he felt required only minor revisions to stand in the *Ordinatio* as an expresssion of his mature thought about this matter. In this present article we follow this early *Lectura* account with occasional references to some clarifications gleaned from other works, especially from the revision of these first lectures in the *Ordinatio*.

Scotus tells us a dispute about "the personality of the angels" occasioned the series of questions he devoted to this topic in each of these two commentaries on the *Sentences*. If this strikes us as strange, recall, that Book II of Peter Lombard's *Sentences*, which Alexander of Hales had introduced as the textbook for bachelors in theology, began with the creation, nature, and properties of the angels. With the Boethian definition of 'person' as "an individual substance of a rational nature" in mind, Peter declared that each angel represents a distinct person, for each is a rational individual substance. However, based on certain remarks of Aristotle, a number of the scholastics in the latter half of the thirteenth century insisted that "all individuation stems completely from matter" and hence it is questionable whether angels are technically "individuals" and therefore "persons". So controversial had the question become by 1277 that we find several of the "errors" condemned by Stephen Tempier, Bishop of Paris, on the advice of the theological faculty of the university, referring to this opinion.[2] Though in his *Quodlibet* Scotus seems to think it still worth while to mention these condemnations as relevant to the question of angelic individuation, he qualifies his claim with the words "videntur istum articulum prima facie reprobare".[3] Perhaps he had in mind the fact that no less an authority than Godfrey of Fontaines had declared these matters were still open to theological discussion.[4] At any rate in his *Lectura* and *Ordinatio* he discusses the question of individuation of material substances, and in particular Godfrey's theory, on purely philosophical grounds with no reference to any theological implications.

Various Views on the Individuation of Material Substances

"Concerning the third distinction (which treats of the personality of the angels)", he writes, "the first question is raised about the singularity in material substances. For it is on the basis of the divergent views about the cause of individuation in material substances that their proponents think differently about the personality of the angels, and about their personality or unity in one species."[5]

As we read on, it soon becomes clear Scotus's treatment of the subject of individuation is intimately connected with his views on the objective nature of our intellectual knowledge. The problem arose because the human intellect with its gift of generalization always grasps some common or potentially universal characteristic of the objects it perceives through the senses, and yet it discovers no reason why the nature or quiddity of what it abstracts should not be multiplied indefinitely. In this sense, what is known about a thing is not what is uniquely individual, but some property or feature it has in common with other things. Granted that formal universality arises only when the concept in the intellect is perceived as common to many individuals and predicable of them, there still seems to be something in the nature of each thing that is isomorphic with the sort of thing we think it to be. Scotus called this its sortal aspect its "*natura communis*" and he felt that unless one admitted its reality prior to any actual intellection, the whole objectivity of our intellectual enterprise was threatened.

This "Scotistic realism", as Charles Sanders Peirce was later to call it, surfaces in his initial question on individuation. "Hence, it is asked first whether a material substance by its very nature is a 'this', that is a singular and individual. And here 'singularity' is not understood as a second intention [i.e., a concept of a concept] corresponding to 'universality' as its opposite, but the question concerns the material substance itself. Is a material substance of its very nature numerically one, incapable of division into several individuals?"[6] His prefatory arguments pro and con also contrast the so-called nominalistic versus the realistic theories as to whether an isomorphism exists between the universal concept and the natures to which it refers.

First Theory: No Special Cause Is Needed to Individuate What Is Real

Exposition of the Theory

In the "corpus" of this first question, Scotus as usual presents in some detail the contemporary view he is opposing. "Some say to this question that there is no intervening cause between the nature of a thing and its singularity. One should not look for any further reason . . . for those causes that give a nature its existence also account for its singularity."[7] The "causes" he has in mind are the four Aristotle mentions, namely, the efficient, material, formal, and final causes. As the editors of the *Lectura* indicate, Scotus may have had in mind Roger Marston or Peter de Falco, who had proposed such views a decade or so earlier.[8] The primary reason proponents of this view claim the whole individuation question is a pseudo-problem is that everything about a thing as it exists in the real world is singular. It takes on a universal character only because of the way we think and hence speak about it. When something pertains to a thing simply (such as its singularity) whereas another (like universality) does so only in qualified sense, then the former pertains to it as such by its very nature. Consequently, singularity is characteristic of a real thing by the very fact that it is what it is.

Refutation of the Theory: Scotistic Realism

Scotus presents two arguments against this, both stemming from his realistic notions of knowledge. His first argument seizes upon the admittedly different way in which the intellect conceives the real object. If the real is by its essence and nature individual, then knowing it only in terms of what is not individual but universal is no knowledge of it at all, for such so-called knowledge is radically opposed to a thing's singularity.[9]

This suggests a second argument wherein Scotus elaborates in some detail what he considers to be the realistic prerequisites for intellectual knowledge of singulars. Simply put, some form of isomorphism between intellect and the known object is needed. According to Aristotle what is known is the essence or form, which is not of itself individual. Hence, Aristotle claimed something more than the form is required, and he identifies the more with "matter". Matter, however, as Scotus conceived of it—and as he discusses in a later question in detail—will not do the job, since it is really distinct and hence extrinsic to the individuated form. However, Aristotle was right in assuming it to be something more than what formally and essentially constitutes the nature of a real thing. Scotus's wording here is somewhat involved and has led to some misinterpretation of his view. If something more is required, then the nature or quiddity is something less than the singular. And this is what Scotus means when he argues secondly: "Anything whose proper unity is less than numerical unity, is not numerically one; but the unity of a stone's nature is less than numerical unity; therefore the unity that the stone's nature has of itself is not numerical."[10]

The major, he says, is evident, because a lesser unity is consistent with the opposite of a greater unity; that is, plurality is the opposite of singularity. Singularity represents a greater unity than specific or generic or any other sort of unity. If something is singular, there cannot be another instance of it; but if our notions tell us only the sort of thing the object is, nothing about this sortal quality as such is opposed to that quality being found in more than one singular or individual.

The minor is also true, for there are many sorts of real unity that are less or not as great as numerical unity; specific, generic, analogical unity come to mind, and these unities are not simply fictions of the mind. Indeed, as Peirce was later to point out, the very reality of the laws of nature are based on these "lesser unities" Scotus refers to here.[11]

If one denies the validity of this argument, then this is equivalent to the claim that there is no real unity among things other than numerical unity. This is clearly false, Scotus insists, and he gives six detailed arguments why it is so.

Not all are of equal merit, since they reflect antiquated Aristotelian notions that might well be questioned today. The first is an argument for generic unity based on the implications of Aristotle's statement that "in every genus there is a first unity that is the measure of all that follows in that genus".[12]

A second argument is based on Aristotle's distinction of specific and generic unities—a distinction that cannot be justified simply in terms of how we think of the two, for though we form but a single concept of each, one notion has greater reference than the other. The difference in reference, however, stems from some sort of real difference in the nature of what we conceive.[13]

A third argument is based on Aristotle's claim that some sortal relationships are based on similarity. Similarity, however, is a real, not just a conceptual, relation and it requires some real basis in the object. This cannot be numerical unity or singularity, for then all things would be equally similar, which is nonsense.[14]

Scotus's fourth argument is in some respects an anticipation of Peirce's observation about the laws of nature requiring a real foundation. He writes: "The opposition [read 'interrelation'] between two real extremes, is real. . . . Now heat destroys cold apart from any thinking about it. Each of the opposite extremes, therefore, is something real and their opposition [read 'interrelation'] is really one by a real unity."

The way in which certain things like heat and cold are united or form a functional unit, however, is not numerical unity, for then all physical things would be interrelated in the same way, since they are all individuals.[15]

Scotus's fifth argument is based on the fact that when we see a white object we actually do not discern it as just this white object but rather *a* white object. Indeed, if God were, unknown to us, to make two such distinct objects each with its own unique singularity and present them to our vision sequentially, but uninterruptedly, then apart from any other clues we would be unable to distinguish one from the other. In his revised *Ordinatio* Scotus suggests that if God miraculously presented the two distinct white objects of identical shape and form in one and the same place, we would see the twin objects as one. One might add that if God miraculously bilocated one such object, we would see the one individual as twins. To Scotus this "Gedanken experiment" indicates that we do not perceive the individuating difference of singulars, but only their sortal nature. He sees an actual instance of such a situation in the case of the sunrays. According to the medieval theory current in his day, as the sun moves, its rays are continually changed so that one individual ray replaces the other without interruption, yet we perceive this numerical diversity as a simple continuity.[16]

Scotus's sixth and final argument is based on the fact that there are various degree of diversity among real things that cannot be accounted for if the only real diversity is based on their individuality. Socrates differs less from Plato than he differs from something purely quantitative such as a line, yet everything should be equally different from everything else, if the only basis for real difference is the fact that each thing is singular.[17] Some contemporary critics of nominalism have constructed an analogous argument based on degrees of resemblance rather than difference.[18]

Using the nature of stone as an example, Scotus draws the following conclusion:

> We must say that it is not a unity of singularity that characterizes stone as stone, for then it could not be thought of under the aspect of universality except by conceiving it under an aspect opposed to what is proper to it, as the first argument proves. What is more, if it were singular of itself, there would be no real unity other than numerical unity, which is false as the second argument shows. I say then, according to Avicenna (V *Metaphysics*) that: "Equinity is just equinity; of itself it is neither one nor many, universal nor singular."[19]

Scotistic Realism

In the *Ordinatio* version he spells out more fully how he understands this dictum of Avicenna.

I understand 'it is not of itself one' of numerical unity, and 'it is not several' of the plurality opposed to that unity; and that it is not actually "universal" (viz. in the sense that, as an object of the intellect, something is universal), nor is it of itself "singular". For though it is never in reality without some one of these features, of itself it is not any one of them, but it is something naturally prior to all of these—and according to this natural priority the "what it is" is the *per se* object of the intellect, and as such it is considered by the metaphysician and is expressed by an [essential] definition; and propositions in the first mode of *per se* predication are true of it under this aspect, for nothing is asserted *per se* in the first mode of the quiddity as abstracted from everything that is naturally posterior to it unless included in the quiddity essentially.[20]

He goes on to say that not only is this nature indifferent of itself to being in the intellect or being in a particular, and thus is indifferent to existence as a universal or existence as a particular or singular, but also as it first exists in the intellect, it does not have of itself universality. Upon reflection we may see it can be understood as being universal, since it is divested of singularity, but "universality is not included as a part of the first concept we have of it".[21] Our initial concept is that of the metaphysician, a first intention that refers to the extramental nature; only upon reflection do we perceive that this nature, though abstracted from a singular thing, as indifferently conceived, is predicable of many and as such it is conceived formally as a universal. But this concept that includes universality is a second intention, that is, a concept of a concept, and it is the logician, not the metaphysician, who deals with "second intentions applied to first intentions".[22] In short, the indifferent nature is an isomorph that can exist either in the thing, associated there with a unique individuality, or in the intellect, as divested of such.[23]

He explains this "picture theory" of concept and reality further.

And just as according to its existence in the intellect the nature is not of itself universal, but universality accrues incidentally to the first notion we have of it, so too insofar as that nature is an object—that is also insofar as it is extramental, where the nature is together with singularity, that nature is not of itself determined to singularity, but is naturally prior to that feature which contracts it to that singularity. And insofar as it is naturally prior to what contracts it, it is not repugnant to that nature to be without it. And just as it had true intelligible being as an object in the intellect . . . so also in the thing according to that entity it has true real being extramentally,—and according to that entity it has a proportional unity that is indifferent to singularity, so that it is not repugnant to the unity it has as such that it be associated with any unity of singularity (hence it is in this way that I understand the expression 'nature has a real unity, less than numerical unity'). And although it may not have this [lesser] unity of itself, so that it lies within the essential notion of the nature (for ''equinity is only equinity'', according to Avicenna, V *Metaphysics*), nevertheless that unity is a proper attribute of that nature according to the primary entity it possesses, and hence ''this'' is neither of itself intrinsic to that nature, nor is ''this'' properly included necessarily in that nature according to the primary entity it possesses.[24]

This is what gives intellectual knowledge of extramental things its reality, for ''there is in things something common, which is not of itself 'this' and therefore is not of itself repugnant to 'not-this'. But this common something is not actually universal, because it lacks that indifference according to which a universal is completely universal, namely, according to which this thing that is the same by some identity is predicable of every individual, such that it is each of these.''[25]

Second Theory: Individuation as a Double Negation

The cash value of these arguments for realism so far as individuation is concerned is to give a negative answer to the original question as to whether a material substance is of itself or by its nature individual or singular. Something more is required. But is this positive or negative? Scotus presents this as his second question,[26] for Henry of Ghent, who so frequently provides him with the springboard for a discussion, claimed all that is needed is a double negation.

Exposition of the Theory

Unity or oneness, after all, is defined, first, as the indivision of a thing in itself (i.e., it is not divided into 'subjective parts'), and second, as its division from all else (i.e., it is something apart or distinct from any other such thing). The double negation refers to these two aspects. Note that scholastics contrasted subjective parts with essential parts; the former refers to the order of extension, the latter to that of comprehension or intension. Thus all the genera, species, or individuals that can be grouped together under one class or category are said to be the subjective parts of that class.[27]

Refutation of the Theory

Scotus points out that to say something is numerically one or individual, does not refer to the simple fact that the individual is undivided subjectively. Henry's double negation theory might account for such factual indivision, but it cannot explain why it is logically repugnant that an individualized nature should be further instantiated. Only some positive feature of a thing can explain such repugnance. This is clear, for individual uniqueness is a perfection, and it cannot stem from a mere privation or negation. Furthermore, according to Aristotle, every negation stems from and presupposes something positive that is naturally prior to what is negative. It remains, therefore, to discuss what such a positive feature might be.[28] And the subsequent questions take up some suggested possibilities.

Third Theory: Existence Individuates

The first suggestion is that actual existence, as involving something positive over and above the essence or nature, might be the reason why a material substance is one or singular?[29]

Exposition of the Theory

The reason cited for this view is that, according to Aristotle, it is the function of act to distinguish and of the ultimate act to make the final or ultimate distinction, which is that based on individuation.[30] The editors suggest Peter de Falco, a Franciscan master who flourished around 1280, as the possible proponent Scotus may have had in mind.

Refutation of the Theory

Scotus's main objection is that existence seems to be as common as the nature itself it is supposed to differentiate. Each individual is unique and hence each should have its own proper principle of individuation that is not identical but primarily diverse and unlike that of any other individual.[31]

He also adds the idea that the actuality that existence gives is quite different from the relationship of potency and act that operates between the determinable and determining perfections that constitute the various substantial differences of things. Both the varying degrees of specific difference (the actuating factor) as well as the respective generic perfections (the potential factor) express substantial characteristics of a nature or essence. The sense in which existence gives actuality to a potential essence is quite different.[32] This argument anticipates the point Scotus will make in his last question, namely, that the relationship of the individuating difference to the specific nature it individuates is analogous to the way in which the specific difference is related to the genus it specifies.[33]

Fourth Theory: Quantity Individuates

In question four he asks, ''Is quantity that positive thing whereby a material substance is a 'this' and singular and indivisible in many subjective parts?''[34] Since many of the late scholastics espoused some view of this kind on the authority of Aristotle, Scotus devotes more space and care to its refutation than he gave to any of the preceding opinions.

Exposition of the Theory

In his explanation of the theory, Scotus indicates that the view is based on Aristotle's definition of 'quantity'.[35] " 'Quantum' means that which is divisible into what is in it, each of which is by nature a 'one' and a 'this.' " Proponents of this theory, he says, take this to mean that function of dividing things into parts of the same sort pertains primarily to quantity. Now the division of a species into individuals is just such a division into parts of the same sort, since this is what distinguishes the division of a species into individuals from the division of a genus into species; therefore, individuals of the same species are distinguished by quantity, and as a consequence, material substance becomes singular through quantity.[36]

Before taking up a refutation of this opinion, Scotus in the *Lectura* prefaces some clarifying remarks. He tells us he is not asking about the "vague" cause of individuation, that is, in the general sense that we speak of all individuals having a principle of individuation, for since every individual is numerically one, we can abstract the notion of it being a "this" or "this one". What he wishes to indicate is that each individual has its own proper and unique haecceity. Language as descriptive is by its nature general or universal. What we need is something that is proper to only one individual. Linguistic philosophers, like Russell and others, have tried create indexical terms to express what Scotus calls "determinate singularity".[37] Thus, if 'this' indicates the proper haecceity of one individual, then we have to refer to the second by a different index term such as 'that', and a third as 'thet' or 'thit' or 'thot', and so forth.

Scotus could also have added another preliminary observation; namely, that he understands by 'quantity' here the accident of quantity. He also assumes that quantity has its own thisness.

Refutation of the Theory

Scotus marshals his several arguments against this theory of individuation under four main headings.

a. The First Is Based on What Is Meant by Singularity or Numerical Unity. As long as a material substance remains such, that is, as long as it is, does not perish, or is annihilated or changed substantially, it retains its unique singularity or "thisness", and yet God could miraculously make material substance exist in a form where it would no longer have its initial quantity, but some other quantity or no quantity whatsoever. And if you object that one cannot appeal to miracles, this is no argument because God cannot do anything miraculously that involves a contradiction, and if he can make this substance exist without the quantity that initially individuated it, it implies that it is no contradiction that the material substance be separated from its individuality.[38]

Furthermore, it is not necessary to appeal to any miracle, for when one material substance is rarefied, its quantity is altered. And according to one doctor, who proposes this theory more coherently than others do, says Scotus—the editors of the Vatican edition think he apparently had in mind Godfrey of Fontaines[39]—in rarefaction the same numerical quantity does not remain, but the prior quantity perishes completely. Or at least, when the substance is condensed, everyone admits the entire quantity does not remain. Nevertheless, numerically the same substance is rarefied or condensed. Now if its singularity stems from sameness of quantity, how can matter be rarefied or condensed and remain the same numerical substance, if it does not retain the same singularity? Furthermore, if the rarefied quantity afterward is condensed, it will return as the same numerical quantity. Therefore in this theory it would seem that a material substance can thus lose its singularity and regain it without undergoing a substantial change—which is impossible.[40]

Scotus appeals also to a theological argument based on how the scholastics of his day commonly explained the Eucharistic transubstantiation.[41]

b. Scotus's Second Approach Is on the Basis of How Substance and Accident Are Related. According to Aristotle, substance is prior by nature to any accident.[42] This priority is based on the nature of substance and holds good for all the subdivisions of substance that are included in the "Porphyrian tree". Scotus's term for this hierarchical arrangement is 'predicamental coordination'. The division of a species into its individuals pertains to the same predicamental order as does the division of a genus into various species, according to Scotus. In favor of this one might cite Aristotle's view that the individual is substance in a primary sense, whereas genus and species are such only secondarily. Aristotle in the *Categories*, where he makes this distinction, is speaking of substance as the subject of predication. Hence, one could accept Scotus's contention that the division of species into its subjective parts (i.e., individuals) is as much a substantial subdivision as is that of a genus into its species, and hence this subdivision pertains to same orderly hierarchy as do the other divisions of substance. Anything accidental is by nature posterior to what a thing is substantially, and hence quantity as an accident cannot account for the division of a species into individuals any more than an accidental difference can account for a division of a genus into its species.[43]

Scotus reprimands Averroes for misinterpreting the priority relationship between quantity and substance and also argues extensively against two contemporary theories (seemingly those of Godfrey and Giles) that attempt to circumvent his basic argument. In the interests of brevity, however, we omit his interesting discussion of these matters.

   c. *Scotus's Third Approach Again Appeals to "the Predicamental Co-ordination", Which Considers Division of Substances into their Subjective Parts.* As we noted previously, the substantial divisions of this sort extend to the individuals that fall under the most special species as well as to species that fall under genera.

   Scotus argues equivalently as follows. Wherever we have precise or strict orderly hierarchy, the principles that determine the order must be somehow intrinsic to the things ordered. Put another way, we can say that all that pertains to the ordering can be found there apart from any other ordered arrangement. Furthermore, each item in the one ordered set is different from any other item of another ordered set. What Scotus has in mind, it seems, is this. The way substances are ordered in the Porphyrian tree is on the basis of what they are and presuppose essentially. Every well-ordered set of categories requires not only a highest but a lowest term and eventually an ultimate one. Scotus sees the latter as the individual. Likewise in a well-ordered hierarchy, such as this is assumed to be, the entire substantial coordination is independent of any item from another hierarchical order. This would be the case where the orders refer to different categories, since such are by definition, mutually exclusive. Hence, no item from an accidental order, such as quantity, can be the reason why a particular sort or individual substances has the place it has in the hierarchy of substances.[44]

   Scotus presents several variants on this basic theme, all based on the analogy that exists between an individuating difference and a specific difference. The first two variants are much the same. One argues that the ultimate in any ordered series requires that some member of the order above it be predicated of it *per se*. For instance, if individuals are the ultimate or lowest in the order, they should have something predicated of them substantially. But if the individual is individuated by something accidental to its substance, such as quantity, one cannot predicate the species of it essentially or *per se*. The other argues conversely that what is predicated (i.e., the higher) is predicated according to the sort of thing it is. For instance, genus is predicated substantially of the species below it *per se*. In a similar way, the most special species, which is next to last in the substantial order, is predicated essentially or *per se* of something substantial beneath it; but again if the individual is individuated by reason of something accidental, then what falls under the ultimate species is not anything substantial.[45]

   Scotus's third variant is rather involved. In the preceding two, he argued from the way the higher or more general notion is predicable of the lower; here he argues from what is required to limit or determine that higher notion to something less universal. The limiting factor must be something that falls under that category, not under some other category. Take the specific notion of man; it is a substantial notion and as such is universal. It cannot not be limited substantially or *per se* by a qualification or determination that pertains to some accidental category. One does not specify Socrates or Plato by adding some accidental qualification such as "white" or "black" to the universal notion "man", though "man" is in potency to either accidental specification. Now Socrates is an individual or primary substance, and one does not specify the universal notion of man substantially by some accidental qualification. What this implies and is made clear in the corpus of Scotus's last and sixth question is that the individuating difference is something substantial and is predicated of the individual in the first *per se* mode. Putting this another way, we can say that Socrates's haecceity, together with what makes him human, constitutes a *per se* or substantial union, as contrasted with "white man" or "black man", each of which represents an *"ens per accidens"*, not an *"ens per se"*.[46]

   d. Scotus's Fourth and Final Attack on the Theory of Quantitative Individuation Is Based on the Notion of Quantity as Such. The three preceding arguments (a–c) are valid against any sort of accidental individuation. The present argument is specifically against quantitative individuation. For, if quantity is the reason why a material substance is singular, it is quantity either as having or not having determined dimensions or boundaries. It is not bounded quantity, because boundaries presuppose the substance has some substantial form, hence, since it follows as the effect of form, it cannot be the cause of that form's singularity. If one claims it is unbounded quantity, since such remains the same in what is generated and what perishes according to those who propose this, hence if such quantity were the cause of singularity, what is generated and what perishes would be the same singular and the same "this", because each would have the same basis or reason for its particular singularity.[47]

   Furthermore, no nature as such is of itself a "this"—as the first question on individuation makes clear. But quantity by its nature, just as "flesh" qua flesh is not of itself "this flesh" so quantity qua quantity is not of itself "this quantity". If this be so, then quantity cannot be the primary reason why anything is just "this".[48]

Refutation of Reasons in Favor of the Theory

   After attacking the theory on these four grounds, he turns to the reasons advanced in favor of the opinion; namely, that quantity gives us a formal reason why something can be divided into parts of the same sort and hence it is the reason why a specific material substance can be divided into individuals that are specifically the same. The main objection he has to this is that whatever the formal reason for divisibility is, it must be something that is formally present in whatever is divided by that division. But quantity is not formally in the specific nature of a material substance.[49]

Furthermore, underlying the whole argument is the false impression that by dividing some quantity into its integral parts one divides a specific nature into its subjective parts. Never is any integral part the whole quantity, yet a "subjective part" is always a whole or entire nature and it is the sort of nature that one is "dividing".[50]

What is more, he argues, the text of Aristotle the proponents of this view appeal to is misinterpreted. In explaining how quantity is divided, Aristotle's very way of speaking indicates that the parts are in the quantity before the division occurs; hence, he does not refer to new parts that are produced by the division. Furthermore, by dividing some quantum into "the parts that are in it", one does not get parts of the same sort. Assume some quantum has six parts; one can divide this into two triads or three pairs or into one section having four parts and another having two. Here we have a division of quantity into parts that are in it, but these parts are not of the same sort. The parts that are in the quantum, when integrated give us the whole. But this is not the way a specific nature is divided into individuals, as if the specific nature were a sort of integration of their individual natures. Hence, to appeal to quantity to explain division into parts of the same sort is wholly irrelevant.[51]

Fifth Theory: Matter Individuates

Scotus concludes that quantity will not provide the additional positive factor one needs to explain individuation. Hence, he raises a fifth question: "Is material substance individuated through its matter?"

Exposition of the Theory

There are those, he says, who are wont to say that the reason a material substance is a "this" and a "that", and so on is because its form is received into this matter or that matter, and thus the whole singularity of a material substance stems from its matter. Various texts from Aristotle are appealed to in favor of this opinion.[52]

Refutation of the Theory

This theory also will not do. The peculiarity of the individuating principle is that it is unique and primarily diverse; this means there is nothing in two such haeceities that is "common" and provides a basis for abstraction.

Another way of putting this is to say that the only "common" feature is the relationship each unique haecceity bears to the same sort of nature, but if the two haecceities differ, so too does the relationship to these two different terms. Hence, there is no way in which one can abstract something common from what individuates. If one chooses to call this "matter"—and there is a sense, Scotus admits, that Aristotle calls "matter" whatever lies outside the essence or form[53]—then one should say the same of matter as of haecceity. Scotus seems to have this in mind when he writes: "If, from this matter and that matter one cannot abstract matter, and from this man and that man one can abstract man, then matter does not pertain to the essence of man; but this is clearly false", for matter does pertain to the essence or quiddity of man. Hence, he insists, one can abstract "matter" from this matter and that matter, and consequently, matter is indifferent to being in this or that. But what is indifferent with respect to several things of the same sort cannot be the reason they are unique, or individual, or several. Consequently, one must seek a reason why any matter itself is individual or singular.[54]

Scotus gives an additional argument based on the physical theory of how one element changes into another. "If matter is the cause of individuation and singularity, since matter remains the same when fire perishes and changes to water, the singularity will remain the same, and therefore the same singular will exist." If you say it is no longer the same singular, since it no longer is the same species, this will not do either. For if fire can perish and become water, so too water can perish and become fire again and then since the original fire and the second fire have both the same matter and species, they are numerically the same—which no one admits.[55]

Sixth Theory: Scotus's Theory of Haecceity

Scotus's sixth and final question is one to which he will give a positive answer: "Is a material substance individual through something positive determining the nature to be just this individual substance?"[56]

The View of Godfrey of Fontaines

Scotus begins by giving what seems to be the opinion of Godfrey of Fontaines as he understands it. "To this question some say that the specific nature is of itself this or one,—nevertheless, since this nature that is of itself this, is in several only through quantity, it follows that a material substance though it is this of itself, owes it presence in several individuals to its quantity."[57]

Several authorities are cited to prove this point, but the rational argument is that if the nature of stone could be divided such that through the division it would be this or that singular, then the nature would not express the entire essence or quiddity of the individual, but there would be something in the individual in addition to the specific nature that would contract and divide it.[58]

Furthermore, it is admitted that, although the division of a *quantum* is not into subjective parts, nevertheless the *quantum* is divided only where the nature is divided and what suffices to divide the *quantum* into quantitative parts also suffices to divide the nature into subjective parts. Since quantity is the primary basis for the first division, it is also the primary basis for the second as well. But that by which the whole is divided is that which really distinguishes the parts, and therefore they are subjective parts of a specific nature and nevertheless they are distinguished through quantity.[59]

Godfrey gives an example of how these two notions are compatible. According to Aristotle (*Physics* I, 2 185b2–5) substance is of itself indivisible, yet it is able to be divided insofar as it receives extension through quantity. He sees in this a situation analogous to what he is claiming; namely, that though quantity is not the formal reason why a material substance is one, nevertheless it is a dispositional cause why one could divide it.

Exposition of the Theory

Scotus sees two ways in which one might interpret this distinction. One is that there is but one specific nature (for instance that of a stone), and it is of itself a "this". While remaining such it receives this or that quantity, but still retains in itself its own singularity as distinct from that of quantity. For Godfrey argues that quantity is not the formal cause of individuation, since then one individual of this species would differ from another only numerically and not substantially. Now Scotus sees this as saying in plain words that the same material substance undivided and indistinct in itself is informed by many quantities, and for this reason there are many individuals of that species.

The other interpretation would be that, when the nature receives this or that quantity, that nature becomes several distinct entities, thus taking on several singularities in the category of substance, although quantity is a "sine qua non" condition for its doing so.[60]

Refutation of the Theory

Scotus sees the first interpretation, as a form of extreme realism, running afoul of many of the theological, metaphysical and physical theories commonly accepted in his day.[61]

The other interpretation he regards as internally inconsistent. If the material substance is of itself just "this" prior by its nature to any relationship to quantity, how can it be divided by being informed by quantity? For to say it is substantially just "this" is to deny that it can be "not-this". The example cited does not prove the point, for there is actually a fallacy of consequent involved in the way it is used. For they argue that although substance is not of itself such (i.e., divisible into subjective parts), it is of itself nonsuch (i.e. "nondivisible"). Therefore, something other than substance, namely, quantity, is required. Scotus will argue, to the contrary, that even though a most specific nature is not of itself divisible into many individuals, it is not indivisible of itself; for if it were, it could never be divided into individuals. In the theory he will propose, one need not go outside the substantial nature of the individual to something accidental to divide it; though not divided qua nature, it is divisible qua nature, and by an individuating difference that is as intrinsic to the individuated substance as the specific difference is intrinsic to a specific nature.[62]

Scotus's Personal View

After this lengthy discussion, Scotus is prepared to present his own opinion. "I reply therefore to the question that material substance is determined to this singularity by some positive entity and to other diverse singularities by other diverse positive entities".[63] First, he says, I will give arguments for this conclusion and afterward explain the nature of this positive individuating entity and how it functions.

Arguments for the Theory

His basic argument is that unity logically is always attributed to some positive entity. If this is true of being in general, then it should also be true of that unity of singularity opposed to any further division into subjective parts. This sort of unity is not a property of the entity that constitutes the nature or quiddity of the individual, for as he stressed in his initial question, this is less than numerical unity, and this unity of the nature is consistent with the idea of there being more than one individual of that sort, hence it is not of itself an adequate explanation of why this individual is just this individual and not another. This positive entity to which we attribute singularity, therefore, must be formally other than the entity constitutive of the specific nature. Now this positive individuating entity, though formally distinct from that of the specific nature, forms with it a *per se* unity; that is to say, it is not something accidental to the individual.[64]

His second argument is based on the idea that, where two things differ, each difference must in the last analysis be reduced to something that is primarily diverse, that is, having nothing in common with the difference of the other. Now individuals (of the same species) differ in the proper sense of the term; that is, they have something in common (their specific nature) and something that is different. This difference must in the last analysis be reduced to something that is primarily diverse, for it is unique to the individual in question and other than what is unique about the other individual. Now the nature in this individual and the nature in that individual is not the primary reason why they differ, but rather why they resemble or agree with one another. For though the nature in the one is really not the nature in the other, they do not differ in their specific or formal character from one another; otherwise there would be no real resemblance or agreement between the two individuals (of the same species); therefore, there must be something else in each whereby they differ. Now this is not quantity, nor existence, nor something negative, as was shown in the preceding questions, therefore it must be something positive, pertaining to the very substance of each. Consequently, Scotus concludes, there is something positive in the category of substance in this individual that contracts or limits its specific nature to just this individual and something else in that individual that contracts or limits its specific nature to just that individual. And it is the "thisness" in the one and the "thatness" in the other that make the two individuals of the same species or nature, primarily diverse or individual.[65]

Reply to an Objection

In the *Ordinatio* Scotus poses an objection that someone may have raised to his claim that a specific nature as it exists in the individual has some real unity less than numerical unity. "If there is any such real unity, it is either in the same numerical subject or in some other subject as well. Now it is not in the same numerical subject, for whatever is in that one subject is numerically one; neither is it in two or more subjects, since in two distinct subjects (or persons) there is nothing that is really one, for this is a property of divine subjects or persons (as Damascene points out)."[66]

Earlier in the *Ordinatio* Scotus had admitted that the sense in which the three divine persons share the same nature is quite different from the way individuals of the same species share a common nature. For the divine nature by reason of its infinity is unique or individual, it needs no special principle of individuation.[67]

He gives this answer:

As was stated in the solution to the first question on this matter [of individuation], nature is prior naturally to "this nature", and the unity proper—that follows nature qua nature—is prior naturally to its unity qua this nature. And under this prior aspect there is a metaphysical consideration of the nature, and its definition is assigned and propositions are true in the first *per se* mode. And therefore in the same thing that is numerically one there is some entity that has a unity less than numerical unity and it is real; and that to which such unity pertains is formally "*de se*" one by numerical unity. Therefore, I concede that this real unity is not something existing in two individuals but in one.—And if you object: "Whatever is in the same numerical individual is the same numerically", I reply, first, with another similar situation that is even more evident, that whatever is in one species is one specifically; "therefore color in whiteness is one specifically," "therefore it [i.e., color] does not have a unity that is less than specific unity" does not follow. For just as has been stated elsewhere (viz., in Book I, in the question "about attributes" . . . [68]) that "something can be said to be animated denominatively, as body,—or *per se* in the first mode, as man" (and just as a surface is said to be 'white' denominatively, as a white-surface is said to be "white" *per se* in the first mode, because the subject includes the predicate),—so I say that the potential [e.g., the color in whiteness or the specific nature in the individual] that is contracted by the actual is informed by that actual, and thereby it is informed by that unity that follows upon that actuality or that act [e.g., the color difference or the individuating difference]; and so it [e.g., color or the nature] is "one" by the proper unity [i.e., specific or individual unity] of that actual, but denominatively it is thus [i.e., specifically or numerically] one (it is not thus one of itself, nor in the first mode [*per se*] nor as an essential part).—Color then in whiteness is one specifically, but not of itself nor *per se* nor primarily, but denominatively; the specific difference however is one primarily, because it is repugnant to it primarily to be divided into several species; whiteness is specifically one *per se,* but not primarily, because it is specifically one through something intrinsic to it (viz. through that difference).[69]

Hence, his conclusion:

Thus I concede that whatever is in this stone is one numerically,— either primarily or *per se* or denominatively. [The individuating difference or] that through which such unity pertains to this composite, perhaps would be such primarily; this stone would be such *"per se"* [for] that which is primarily one by this unity [i.e., the individuating difference] is a *per se* part of this; that potential [i.e., the stone nature, in itself less than numerically one] perfected by this actual [individuating difference] is only "denominatively" numerically one. . .[70]

Exposition of the Theory

After this digression, Scotus returns to the explanation he gave earlier in the *Lectura* as to just how this positive individuating difference is related to the nature it individuates—namely, by analogy with the way a specific difference is related to its proximate genus.

He compares an individual to a species in terms of the latter's triple relationship to what is below it, and to what is above it, and to what is side by side with it.[71] Consider what is below a species. Every species can be divided into subjective parts; if it is not an ultimate or most special species, those parts can be specifically different; if it is ultimate or atomic, those parts can be quantitative or numerically different, that is, there can be more than one individual of that same sort. The unity of a species, then, is less than numerical unity, and all it excludes is "division into essential parts",[72] that is to say, the species has a "*per se*" or essential unity. An individual on the contrary, he says, "defies division into any sort of subjective parts",[73] or as he puts it in the *Lectura,* "it is completely opposed to being divided".[74] That is to say, the individual is atomic in an even more radical sense, for it cannot be divided further into individuals of the same sort. "Of the same sort" has to be added, for an individual substance obviously need not be entirely indivisible; if it is a material substance, consisting of essential parts such as matter and form or different integral or organic parts, however, any attempt to separate or dissect those parts destroys its unity and integrity as an individual substance of that sort.

If we compare a species or individual to what is above each, that is, to the generic or specific nature, respectively, again there is similarity as well as difference. "Not only is the concept of the genus determined by the concept of the individual", says Scotus,[75] "but the reality from which the notion of genus is taken is naturally prior to that reality from which the notion of the difference is taken, and that reality from which the genus is taken is determinable and able to be contracted by the reality of the difference. Similarly, in the individual, the specific nature is determinable and able to be contracted by the reality from which the individual difference is taken. Hence, just as in the same real thing (such as whiteness) there are diverse formal perfections or formal entities, from one of which the notion of the genus (such as that of color) is taken, and another formal entity from which the notion of the difference (that of whiteness) is taken, . . . so there is a positive entity in the same real thing from which the specific nature is taken, and an entity formally other from which the ultimate individual difference is taken, an entity that is totally "this", and is opposed to any division whatsoever. And as the reality of the genus is in potency to the differential reality, so the reality of the nature, qua nature is in potency to the reality from which the individual difference is taken. But still there is a dissimilarity, for the difference with the generic nature constitutes what sort of being it is, also called its 'quidditative' or 'formal' being, whereas the individual difference together with the nature is not constitutive of what sort of thing the individual is, for this difference lies outside the notion of what it is (i.e., of its quiddity or essence) and therefore does not constitute it in its constitutive or formal being, but rather in its material being, insofar as 'material' is opposed to 'formal' being, in the sense of 'formal being' just mentioned and in the sense that the Philosopher calls form the 'what-the-something-was-to-be.' "[76]

If we compare the specific difference to what is side by side with it, namely, another specific difference, though not everything we conceive of as a specific difference is primarily diverse from every other such, if each of our concepts of two such formal differences is primitive or irreducible, that is, if each is technically "simply simple", then the formal entities or formalities from which such real concepts are derived are themselves primarily diverse. And in this latter case, such formal or specific differences resemble the individual or individuating differences, for each formality or entity that individuates a singular nature is primarily diverse from every other such entity.[77]

If you ask Scotus, "What is this 'individuating entity' in a material substance? of what does it consist? is it something identical or derived from its matter, or form, or the composite of both?" he gives this answer in the *Ordinatio:*

> This entity therefore is not matter or form or the composite insofar as each of these is a "nature",—but it is the ultimate reality of the being which is matter or which is form or which is the composite; so that wherever something is common and nevertheless determinable, even though it involves one real thing, we can still distinguish further several formally distinct realities, of which this formally is not that; and this is formally the entity of singularity and that is formally the entity of a nature. Nor can these two realities ever be two distinct real things, in the way the two realities might be that from which the genus is taken and that from which the difference is taken (from which two realities the specific reality is taken),—but in the same real thing there are always formally distinct realities (be they in the same real part or the same real whole).[78]

There are two further points I would like to mention before concluding this chapter. The first concerns the term 'haecceity'. On several occasions we used this to refer to Scotus's individuating difference. Actually, in subsequent decades, this designation was widely used, both by those who accepted and those who rejected his theory.[79] Since Scotus never used the term in his *Lectura, Ordinatio,* or *Quodlibet,* however, some attributed its usage exclusively to his disciples. As P. Minges pointed out,[80] however, Scotus does seem to have used the term a few times, for instance, in his Paris lectures and in the question he devotes to individuation in his *Questions on Aristotle's Meta-*

physics.[81] However, if numbers are any indication, Scotus seems to have preferred '*differentia individualis*' to '*haecceitas*' as the proper name of what he
was talking about.

The second point concerns the question of the intelligibility of "haecceity". What he says in question one, about our inability to differentiate two
white objects or two individual sunrays on the basis of their respective
"haecceities", indicates that we do not know the individuating difference
"*per se*". In fact if we could, there would have been no need of this long
discussion as to what individuates a material substance. Scotus is perfectly
willing to accept this conclusion as a small price to pay for what seemed even
more important to him, the fact that our generalizations about the real world
and the individuals in it have an objective foundation. He is also willing to
accept the idea that what first motivates our intellect, in this life at least, is
what can be abstracted from sense images.[82] But it is the accidental features
of objects in the real world that impinge upon our senses, and it is these we
must use to identify and differentiate individuals.[83] How we know singulars,
however, is irrelevant to the question of angelic individuation, which—as we
recall—was the problem that triggered Scotus's lengthy metaphysical discussion of individuation.[84] The intelligibility question, however, surfaces briefly
in one of the initial arguments used to introduce question six.[85] If haecceity
is a positive entity formally distinct from but really identical with the specific
nature of a substance, it should be as intelligible as the specific difference
itself, particularly if it forms a *per se* unity with the nature in the same way
as the specific difference forms a *per se* unity with the generic nature. Obviously, the objector argues, this is not the case, for if haecceity were intelligible, the singular nature would be known qua singular, not qua nature.
Aristotle recognized this difference between intellectual and sense knowledge, when he pointed out that the intellect has to do with universals, the
senses with singulars.[86] Scotus's answer acknowledges the problem but
solves it succinctly with a distinction. Just because our intellect cannot ap-
prehend haecceity intellectually, does not mean it is *per se* unintelligible.
God and the angel can know it directly and *per se*. The reason we cannot
grasp it intellectually is due not to any lack of intelligibility on the part of the
individuating entity, but to the imperfection of our intellect and the way it
functions in our present life.[87] And he appeals to Aristotle's famous distinction: "As the eyes of the owl are to the blazing sun, so is the reason in our
soul to the things which are by nature most evident of all".[88]

As I have dealt elsewhere extensively with his theory of what our intellect can know in both its present state and the afterlife and how he believes
we know the singular at present, I refer the interested reader to these
studies.[89]

Notes

1. Apart from passing references to his theory, Scotus deals with it in detail in the second book of his several commentaries on the *Sentences*. In *Lectura* and *Ordinatio* the treatment occurs in distinction 3; for these works we use the as yet incomplete Vatican edition (*Ioannis Duns Scoti O.F.M. opera omnia.* (Vatican City: Typis Polyglottis Vaticanis, 1950–1982); for the other works we use the Vivès edition (*Joannis Duns Scoti, O.M. opera omnia.* 26 vols. Paris: Vivès, 1891–1893). In the Paris *Reportatio,* basically the same set of questions are raised in distinction 12, (qq. 3–8; Vivès ed., XXI, 20–41); he also devotes one question in Bk. VII of *Quaestiones subtilissimae super libros Metaphysicorum Aristotelis* (q. 13) to this topic: "Utrum natura lapidis de se sit haec, vel per aliquid extrinsecum?" (Vivès ed., VII, pp. 402–426); and the subject of whether matter is necessary for individuation surfaces briefly in his magisterial *Quodlibet,* (q. 2, art. 1, nn. 3–4, 20–21; Vivès ed., XXV, 61–62, 90–91).

2. Cf, *Chartularium Universitatis Parisiensis* I, p. 549, art. 96: "Quod Deus non potest multiplicare individua sub una specie sine materia"; also art. 81: "Quod, quia intelligentiae non habent materiam, Deus non posset facere plures eiusdem speciei" (p. 548); art. 191: "Quod formae non recipiunt divisionem, nisi per materiam.— Error, nisi intelligatur de formis eductis de potentia materiae." (p. 554)

3. *Quaestiones quodlibetales,* q. 2, n. 4; Vivès ed., XXV, 61.

4. Godfrey of Fontaines, in question 5 of his twelfth *Quodlibet,* written around 1296 or 1297, asks: "Does the Bishop of Paris sin because he fails to correct certain articles condemned by his predecessor?" and, pointing specifically to articles 96 and 81 according to which God cannot multiply individuals within a species without matter, and God cannot produce many intelligences (or angels) in the same species because they lack matter, declares these matters are still open to discussion for they have been defended by many Catholic teachers. See J. F. Wippel, *The Metaphysical Thought of Godfrey of Fontaines* (Washington, DC: Catholic University of America Press, 1981), pp. 382–383.

5. Duns Scotus, *Lectura in librum secundum Sententiarum,* dist. 3, pars 1, q. 1, n. 1; Vatican ed., XVIII, 229. For an English translation of these questions see my *Duns Scotus' Early Oxford Lecture on Individuation* (Santa Barbara, CA: Old Mission Santa Barbara, 1992).

6. *Ibid.*

7. *Ibid.,* nn. 5–7, 230–231; see also *Ordinatio* II, dist. 3, pars 1, q. 1, nn. 5–6; Vatican ed., VII, pp. 393–394.

8. Roger Marston writes: "The aforesaid opinion speaks as if all individuation stemmed completely from matter, which is false. For individuation is from the efficient cause that generates or gives it being, from the matter as providing the occasion, from the form however as formally constituting; for this gives being formally and con-

sequently makes it distinct and one. I concede therefore that God could make several forms of the same species, apart from any matter." (*Quodlibet* I, q. 3, ed. G. F. Etzkorn and I. C. Brady; Quaracchi Florence: Typographia Collegi S. Bonaventurae, 1968), p. 13.

9. *Lect.*, n. 8; XVIII, 231; *Ord.*, n. 7; VII, 394.

10. *Lect.*, n. 9, p. 231; *Ord.*, nn. 7–8, 394–395.

11. *Lect.*, nn. 10–11; XVIII, 232; *Ord.*, nn. 9–10; VII, 395.

12. *Lect.*, nn. 13–16; XVIII, 232–233; cf, Aristotle, *Metaphysics* X, ch. 1 1052b18; see also *Ord.*, nn. 11–15; VII, 396–397.

13. *Lect.*, nn. 18–20, XVIII, 233–234; *Ord.*, nn. 16–17, VII, 397–398.

14. *Lect.*, n. 21; XVII, 234–235; *Ord.*, n. 18; VII, 398.

15. *Lect.*, n. 22; XVIII, 235; *Ord.*, n. 19; VII, 398–399.

16. *Lect.*, nn. 23–24; XVIII, 235–236; *Ord.*, nn. 20–22; VII, 399–400.

17. *Lect.*, nn. 25–27; XVIII, 236; *Ord.*, nn. 23–28; VII, 400–402.

18. See D. M. Armstrong, *Universals and Scientific Realism*, vol. 2, *A Theory of Universals* (Cambridge: Cambridge University Press, 1978), pp. 105ff.

19. *Lect.*, nn. 28–30; XVIII, 236–237.

20. *Ord.*, nn. 31–32; VII, 403.

21. *Ibid.*, n. 33; VII, 403–404: "Non solum autem ipsa natura de se est indifferens ad esse in intellectu et in particulari, ac per hoc et ad esse universale et particulare (sive singulare),—sed etiam ipsa, habens esse in intellectu, non habet primo ex se universalitatem. Licet enim ipsa intelligatur sub universalitate ut sub modo intlligendi ipsam, tamen universalitas non est pars eius conceptus primi, quia non conceptus metaphysici, sed logici (logicus enim considerat secundas intentiones, applicatas primis secundum ipsum). Prima ergo intellectio est 'naturae' ut non cointelligitur aliquis modus, neque qui est eius in intellectu, neque qui est eius extra intellectum; licet illius intellecti modum intelligendi sit universalitas, sed non modus intellectus!"

22. *Ibid.*

23. *Ibid.*

24. *Ibid.*, n. 34, 404–405.

25. *Ibid.*, n. 38; 407–408.

26. *Lect.*, n. 39; XVIII, 240.

27. *Ibid.*, n. 43, 241.

28. *Ibid.*, nn. 45–51, 242–243; *Ord.*, n. 49–56; VII, 413–416.

29. *Lect.*, n. 54; XVIII, 244: "Propter tertiam opinionem circa individuationem substantiae materialis, quaeritur si substantia materialis sit haec et singularis
per existentiam actualem"; see also *Ord.*, n. 59; VII, 418.

30. *Lect.*, n. 55; XVIII, 244: "Et dicunt quidam sic. quia 'ipsius actus est dis-
tinguere,' ex VII *Metaphysicae* [c. 13 1039a3–7],—ergo ultima distinctio est per ultimum actuale; ultimum autem actuale est ipsum esse exsistentiae, quia totum aliud
quod praecedit est quasi in potentia ad esse; ergo supposita eiusdem speciei, quibus
competit ultimata distinctio, habent distingui hypostatice et sic constitui per esse
exsistentiae."

31. *Ibid.*, nn. 55–57, 245: "Exsistentia actualis non habet differentias per
se . . . ; ergo non est de se distinctivum, et per conseuqens non potest esse prima
causa alicuius distinctionis. Praeterea, actualis exsistentia est eiuusdem rationis in hoc
et in illo, sicut natura in hoc et in illo; ergo sicut natura non est de se haec." See also
Ord., nn. 61–62; VII, 418–419.

32. *Lect.*, n. 58; XVIII, 245: "Praeterea, in omni coordinatione praedicamen-
tali [sicut arbor porphyriana] potest inveniri quodlibet quod est illius coordinationis,
excepto et excluso quolibet quod non est illius coordinationis; sed esse exsistentiae
non pertinet ad coordinationem substantiarum nec sicut species nec sicut differentia
nec sicut genus; ergo in coordinatione praedicamemntali antequam intelligatur exsistentia actuali, ita et individua illius generis erunt in illa coordinatioe antequam intelligatur exsistentia actualis"; see also *Ord.*, n. 63; VII, 419–420.

33. *Lect.*, nn. 169–173; XVIII, 281–284.

34. *Lect.*, n. 61; XVIII, 246; see also *Ord.*, n. 66; VII, 421.

35. Aristotle, *Metaphysics* V, ch. 13 1020a7–8.

36. *Lect.*, n. 67; XVIII, 248; see also *Ord.*, nn. 71–74; VII, 423.

37. *Lect.*, n. 71; XVIII, 249–250: "Ad videndum de ista opinione, praemitto
unum de intellectu quaestionis, quod non quaeritur de causa individuationis vage, secundum quod unum numero potest abstrahi ab 'hoc uno' numero et illo ratione unitatis numeralis, quae communis est,—sed quaeritur propter quid substantia materialis
est singularis hac singularitate determinata, ut propter quid est 'hic lapis' ita quod 'hic
lapis' non potest esse alius."

38. *Lect.*, nn. 73–76; XVIII, 250–51; see also *Ord.*, nn. 77–80; VII, 427–428.

39. See XVIII, 251, n. 1. For an excellent account of Godfrey's theory of individuation, see J. F. Wippel, *Metaphysical Thought*, ch. 9, pp. 349–369.

40. *Lect.*, n. 77; XVIII, 251.

41. *Ibid.*, n. 78; 251–252; see also *Ord.*, n. 81; VII, 428–429.

42. Aristotle, *Metaphysics* VII, ch. 1 1028a10–1028b2.

43. *Lect.*, n. 79; XVIII, 252–253; see also *Ord.*, nn. 82–83; VII, 429–431.

44. *Lect.*, nn. 91–94; XVIII, 258–259; see also *Ord.*, nn. 89–92; VII, 433–436.

45. *Lect.*, nn. 92–93; XVIII, 258: "Praeterea, ultimum cuiuslibet coordinatione requirit predicationem superiorem in illo ordine, per se; sed 'ens per accidens' non recipit 'praedicationem essentialiter' superiorum per se, in genere; ergo ultimum in nulla coordinatione praedicmentali includit res diversarum coordinationum.— Praeterea, species in quocumque genere est species secundum rationem illius generis; sed de ratione speciei est quod sit praedicabilis, et hoc est singulare: ergo est singulare in genere substantiae, circumscripto omni accidente.''

46. *Ibid.*, n. 93: "Praeterea, quando aliquid convenit alicui secundum aliquam rationem praecisam,—cui covenit essentialiter illa ratio praecisa et illud quod convenit secundum illam rationem; . . . sed in coordinatione substantiae convenit 'esse universale,' et hoc ratione naturae generis huius absolutae; ergo cui convenit illa natura absoluta (et non contracta), illud erit universale illius coordinationis. Sed in quantum ponitur contractum aliquid per rem alterius generis, nihil omnino ponitur contractum in illo genere,—sicut per hoc quod ponitur contractus per albedinem Socrates, non magis contractus est in genere substantiae quam erat prius; igitur si poneretur aliquid contractum in natura substantiae per rem alterius generis, simul esset singulare et universale.'' See also *Ord.*, n. 92; VII, 435–436.

47. *Lect.*, n. 95, XVIII, 259.

48. *Ibid.*, n. 98, 260.

49. *Ibid.*, n. 102, 261.

50. *Ibid.*, n. 103, 261–261.

51. *Ibid.*, nn. 104–105, 262.

52. *Ibid.*, nn. 128–132, 269–271.

53. See F. Alluntis and A. B. Wolter, *God and Creatures: The Quodlibetal Questions,* n. 2.59 (Princeton, NJ, and London: Princeton University Press, 1975), pp. 48–49.

54. *Lect.*, n. 133, 271–272.

55. *Ibid.*, nn. 135–136, 272.

56. *Ibid.*, n. 139, 273.

57. *Ibid.*, n. 146, 275; see J. F. Wippel, *Metaphysical Thought*, ch. 9, for a more detailed account of Godfrey's view.

58. *Lect.*, n. 150, XVIII, 276.

59. *Ibid.*, n. 151.

60. *Ibid.*, n. 153, 277; see also *Ord.*, nn. 155–156; VII, 468–469.

61. *Lect.*, n. 161; XVIII, 279; see also *Ord.*, n. 165; VII, 473.

62. *Lect.*, n. 162; XVIII, 279–280; see also *Ord.*, nn. 166–167; VII, 473–474.

63. *Lect.*, n. 164; XVIII, 280.

64. *Ibid.*, n. 166, 279–280; see also *Ord.*, n. 169; VII, 474–475.

65. *Lect.*, n. 162; XVIII, 279–280; see also *Ord.*, n. 170, VII, 475.

66. *Ibid.*, n. 171, 476.

67. *Ibid.*, n. 39, 408; see also his proof that there can be only numerically one infinite being in *Ordinatio* I, dist. 2, pars 1, q. 3; II, 222–243 and the parallel passages in the *Lectura* (XVI, 146–157) and *Reportatio* I A (A. B. Wolter and M. M. Adams, "Duns Scotus' Parisian Proof for the Existence of God," *Franciscan Studies* 42 [1982]): 307–316).

68. *Ord.*, I, dist. 8, n. 214; IV, p. 271.

69. *Ord.* II, dist. 3, pars 1, q. 6, nn. 172–174; VII, 476–477.

70. *Ibid.*, n. 175, 477–478: "Ita concedo quod quidquid est in hoc lapide, est unum numero,—vel primo, vel per se, vel denominative: 'primo' forte, ut illud per quod unitas talis convenit huic composito; 'per se' hic lapis, cuius illud quod est primo unum hac unitate, est per se pars; 'denominative' tantum, illud potentiale quod perficitur isto actuali, quod quasi denominative respicit actualitatem eius."

71. *Ibid.*, nn. 176–183, 478–481; see *Lect.*, nn. 170–172; XVIII, 282–284.

72. *Ibid.*, n. 177; VII, 478: "Illa unitas naturae specificae minor est ista unitate, et propter hoc non excludit omnen divisionem . . . sed tantum illam divisionem quae est partium essentialium; ista [i.e., individualis] excludit onmem."

73. *Ibid.*, "Huic entitati individuali primo repugnat dividi in quascumque partes subiectivas, et per ipsam repugnat talis divisio per se toti cuius illa entitas est pars."

74. *Lect.*, n. 170; XVIII, 282: "Sic proportionaliter est in individuo, quod ibi est entitas quaedam, a qua—secundum unam perfectionem—accipitur ratio differentiae individualis, cui omnino repugnat dividi."

75. *Lect.*, n. 171; XVIII, 282–283.

76. Quod-quid-erat-esse" was the literal translation of Aristotle's τὸ τί ἦν εἶναι; "forma" here is the Latin translation of Aristotle's εἶδος, not μορφή; cf. *Metaphysica* V, c. 2 1013a26–28.

77. *Lect.*, n. 172; XVIII, 283–284: "Nam licet differentiae specificae quae accipiuntur a tota natura possint habere aliquid commune 'in quid' dictum de eis, tamen differentiae quae accipiuntur ab ultimis perfectionibus, non habent aliquid commune

in 'quid' dictum de eis . . . ita in proposito differentiae individuales accipiuntur ab ultima perfectione quae est in re et in natura, et ideo differentiae individuales sunt primo diversae non habendo aliquid in quid dictum de eis (nec ens nec aliquid aliud), ut dictum est in I [scil. in *Lectura* I, d. 3, n. 122; XVI 271–272]; per huiusmodi igitur differentiae individuales primo diversas, ad quas naturae sunt in potestate et contrahibiles, individuantur et fiunt singulares''; *Ord.*, n. 183; VII, 481: ''Comparando vero tertiam differentiam specificam ad illud quod iuxta se est, scilicet ad aliam differentiam specificam,—licet quandoque posset esse non primo diversa ab alia sicut est illa entitas quae sumitur a forma, tamen ultima differentia specifica est primo diversa ab alia, illa scilicet quae habet conceptum 'simpliciter simplicem.' Et quoad hoc dico quod differentia individualis assimilatur specificae universaliter sumptae, quia omnis entitas individualis est primo diversa a quocumque alio.''

78. *Ibid.*, n. 187, 483–484. Though the formal distinction between the haecceity and the nature is never based on two distinct real things that could be separated, the reality from which the genus is taken could at times be really distinct from the reality from which the specific difference is taken, e.g. in a living body, Scotus believes the specific difference ''living'' derives from the some life principle that is really distinct or separable from the body, which has its own ''forma corporeitatis''.

79. It is used frequently by Antonius Andreas, e.g ''Individuum addit super naturam speciei, puta proprietatem sive differentiam individualem, quae est individuationis praecisa causa, et vocatur haecceitas.'' (*Expositio textuali librorum Metaphysicorum*, lib. 1, *summa* 2, cap. 4, n. 61 in *Joannis Duns Scoti opera omnia*, (Vivès ed., V, 506); see also pseudo-Scotus, *Super lib. I Posteriorum*, q. 36, n. 4 in the same edition (II, 298–299). By Suarez's time the name seems to have become customary, for he says ''solet vocari haecceitas vel differentia individualis''. (*Disputationes metaphysicae*, disp. 5, sectio 2, n. 5).

80. Parthenius Minges, O.F.M., *Ioannis Duns Scoti doctrina philosophica et theologica*, tom. I (Ad Claras Aquas: Ex typographia Collegii S. Bonaventurae, 1930), pp. 66–67.

81. See *Reportata parisiensia* II, dist. 12, q. 5; Vivès ed., XXIII, 25, 29, 31, and 32; *Quaestiones subtilissimae super libros Metaphysicorum Aristotelis* lib. 7, q. 13, nn. 9 and 26; VII, 410 and 426.

82. He deals with this limitation of our intellect as compared with that of the angels later in part 2, question 1 of this same distinction, both in the *Lectura* (cf. n. 254, XIII, 309–310), and in even more detail in the *Ordinatio*. See nn. 289–93; VII, 535–93: ''Sed quod est istud impedimentum?—Respondeo: intellectus pro statu isto non est natus movere vel moveri immediate nisi ab aliquod imaginabili vel 'sensibili extra' prius moveatur . . . Et secundum istum modum expositionis movetur intellectus ab obiectis imaginabilibus,—et eis cognitis, potest ex eis cognoscere rationes communes et immaterialibus et materialibus.'' See also Book I, dist. 3 of either the *Lectura* (n. 300; XVI, 345–346) or the Ordinatio (n. 187; III, 113–114), where Scotus points out the difference between how our intellect operates at present and how its optimum operation will differ in the afterlife.

83. In Book VII of his *Quaestiones subtilissimae super libros Metaphysicorum Aristotelis,* he has not only a question on the individuation of a material substance (q. 13; Vivès ed., VII, 402–426) but an important one, the question of whether the singular is *per se* intelligible to us. (q. 15; VII, 434–440). I have analyzed this latter question in some detail, see note 89.

84. "Seventh and finally in this matter," says Scotus "I ask whether it is possible for several angels to be in the same species?" (*Ord.*, n. 212; VII, 495); in the earlier version, he centered his query even more specifically on the question of personality: "Can there be several persons in the same species of angels?" *Lect.* II, dist. 3, pars 1, q. 7, n. 196; XVIII, 293.

85. *Lect.*, n. 142; p. 274; *Ord.*, n. 144, VII, 464: "Tunc singulare, compositum ex natura et illo per se determinante, esset per se unum; ergo per se intelligibile,— quod videtur contra Philosophum II *De anima* et VII *Metaphysicae,* ubi videtur aperte velle quod intellectio est 'universalis' et sensus et sensatio est 'ipsius singularis' ".

86. Aristotle, *De anima* II, c. 5: 417b22–23; *Metaphysica* VII, c. 10 1035b33–1036a8.

87. *Lect.*, n. 180; XVIII, 286: "Ad aliud quando arguitur quod tunc singulare erit per se intelligibile alia specie quam natura speciei, sicut species alia similitudine quam genus, quia sicut tunc species addit super genus, ita singulare super speciem,— dico quod singulare non intelligitur intellecta specie, et quod singulare intlligitur per se ab intellectu qui potest omnia intelligere intelligibilia (sicut Deus et similiter angelus). Unde quod non intelligatur per se ab intellectu nostro, hoc non est ex parte singularis, sed ex imperfectione intellectus nostri,—sicut noctua non videat solem, non est ex parte solis sed ex parte noctuae." In the *Ord.*, n. 191, VII, 486: "Concedo quod 'singulare' est per se intelligibile, quantum est ex parte sui (si autem alicui intellectui non sit per se intelligibile, puta nostra, de hoc alias); saltem non est ex parte eius impossibilitas quin possit intelligi, sicut nec ex parte solis est impossibilitas videndi et visionis in noctua, sed ex parte noctua."

88. Aristotle, *Metaphysics* II, ch. 1 (993b9–11).

89. A. B. Wolter, "Duns Scotus on the Natural Desire for the Supernatural," *New Scholasticism,* 23 (1940): 281–317; "Duns Scotus on Intuition, Memory and Our Knowledge of Individuals", in *History of Philosophy in the Making,* ed. L. J. Thro (Washington, DC: University Press of America, 1982), pp. 88–89.

13

HERVAEUS NATALIS (B. 1250/60; D. 1323) AND RICHARD OF MEDIAVILLA (B. 1245/49; D. 1302/07)

MARK G. HENNINGER

One of the most distinguished and energetic champions of Thomas Aquinas in the first quarter of the fourteenth century was Hervaeus Natalis, who defended Thomas's doctrine from the criticisms of John Duns Scotus, James of Metz, Henry of Ghent, Peter Aureoli, and Durand of Saint Pourçain.[1] As far as can be determined, Hervaeus Natalis lectured on the *Sentences* around 1303 in Paris. He became master of theology there in 1307, and from then until 1309 he held three quodlibetal sessions. We have Hervaeus's determinations of these sessions in his *Quodlibets* I–III.

In 1309 he was elected head of the Dominican province of France and, among many other activities, presided over the commission that investigated the *Sentences* commentary of Durand of Saint Pourçain in 1314, censuring over ninety propositions of his fellow Dominican.[2] Hervaeus was a prolific writer but unfortunately most of his works are still unedited. Hence on many points it is difficult to know how his teaching is related to the doctrine of Aquinas, for whose canonization Hervaeus worked so long and hard after being elected unanimously master general of the Dominican Order in 1318.[3]

In two of his quodlibetal questions, Hervaeus discusses the principle of individuation in material things.[4] The earlier, *Quodl.* VIII, q. 11, dates from 1304/05. L. Hödl has established the authenticity of *Quodl.* VIII, along with the other "minor quodlibets," that is, *Quodl.* V–X.[5] Hödl is convinced, rightly I believe, that Hervaeus disputed *Quodl.* VIII while a bachelor of theology, taking the part of "responder" in a session directed by the then regent-master of theology, Jean Quidort. By comparison with texts in Hervaeus's *Sentences* commentary, Hödl has shown the doctrine of *Quodl.* VIII to be that of Hervaeus.

This conclusion is confirmed by my research, for Hervaeus's authentic *Quodl.* III, q. 9 of 1309 reproduces parts of *Quodl.* VIII, q. 11, almost verbatim, and the doctrine is substantially the same. As we will see, the primary role of quantity in individuation is found in both. But in the later *Quodl.* III, Hervaeus expands his discussion: He treats other opinions at length and situates the nucleus of his solution having to do with quantity in a larger context with other "extrinsic" and "intrinsic" principles of individuation. To show this development, I first present his doctrine of the earlier *Quodl.* VIII, q. 11, and then that of *Quodl.* III, q. 9.

Hervaeus's Doctrine in *Quodlibet* VIII, q. 11

In *Quodl.* VIII, q. 11, Hervaeus states, "I say that individuation is in part through quantity and in part through others".[6] This succinctly states an idea that remains throughout his writing on individuation: the central but nonexclusive role of quantity.

He begins[7] by defining an individual as what is undivided in itself and divided from all else and proceeds to explicate indivision and division in turn. Treating indivision, he claims that it is twofold: there is (1) an indivision by which something is undivided from itself, and (2) another by which one part of a continuum is undivided from other parts. Regarding (1), such indivision is a property of each thing from itself and no further principle need be sought. For each thing from itself is self-identical and as a consequence is, from itself, undivided from itself. He states further that each thing is identical with itself through itself formally speaking, though it may have individual being from another as from an efficient cause. This last short reference to an efficient cause becomes developed only later in *Quodl.* III, q. 9. He does state in *Quodl.* VIII, q. 11, however, that this first type of indivision is had from the individual itself, not through quantity.

Regarding (2),[8] this indivision is not that of one whole thing being self-identical with itself and so undivided from itself, but is the indivision of one part of a continuum from another. This indivision of parts of a continuum pertains first and *per se* to quantity and to other things through quantity. This type of analysis—properties proper to quantity accruing to substances and other accidents—is another constant of his theory of individuation.

Division from others is also twofold, specific and numerical. (3) Individuals are distinct in species from other individuals of different species through "the absolute *ratio* of the specific form". Part of the absolute *ratio* of the specific form of man is to have a rational soul, and man differs specifically from all individuals that do not have this type of soul.

Another type of division is (4) that of many things of the same species distinguished from each other numerically. The ultimate principle of numerical distinction of this type is quantity:

But with respect to this—that whatever individual be divided and distinct from another of the same species—the principle of individuation of material substances is quantity, with respect to those things that are simultaneous. For one individual is distinguished from another of the same species through that to which it pertains firstly and *per se* to be divided into similar existing parts of the same species. But this pertains first and *per se* to quantity, because matter is not able to be divided into similar parts except through quantity. Nor are there able be many forms of the same species except in diverse parts of matter (at least in material things.) But to quantity, all else aside, firstly and *per se* it pertains to have similar parts. And therefore, with respect to such individuation, as said, a substance must be individuated through quantity.[9]

This view of quantity's primary role is repeatedly found in Hervaeus's discussions, not only in various replies to objections in this question 11,[10] but also in question 10 of the same *Quodlibet,* whether the dimensions of matter are other than the dimensions of quantity.[11] Hervaeus holds that they are the same: Dimensions (as height, breadth and depth) and divisibility into parts pertain first and *per se* to quantity and to matter *per accidens* by being joined to quantity.[12] With quantity "joined" to matter, the division and indivision of parts that pertains *per se* and firstly to quantity "redounds" to quantified matter.[13] In another formulation he states that having parts pertains to quantity as the *ratio* of having parts; but having parts pertains to matter as the subject of the *ratio* of having parts.[14] He denies[15] that quantity imparts these properties to matter "effectively", as if quantity extended matter putting into it a certain extension other than that of quantity. Rather, as the quality of, say, whiteness, formally by itself makes something white without making another quality diverse from itself, so quantity formally by itself makes matter quantified with dimensions and parts.

In *Quodl.* VIII, q. 10 and q. 11, then, Hervaeus accords to permanent continuous quantity the primary role in distinguishing individuals within a species. In addition, he uses successive continuous quantity in his theory to account for the numerical diversity of accidents existing successively in the same subject, as when what is hot is cooled and becomes hot again. Hervaeus states that this successive quantity is time to which first and *per se* it pertains to be divided into successive parts.[16] In a summary statement, he compares simultaneous and successive numerical diversity:

For as the diversity of simultaneously existing material things of the same species comes from the diversity of parts of permanent continuous quantity according to position (since to it [quantity] such division firstly pertains), so also the numerical diversity of [accidents] succeeding one another in the same subject comes from the diversity of parts of successive continuous quantity that is time to which firstly and *per se* it pertains to be divided into successive parts.[17]

He seems to hold that the two instances of heat are numerically diverse, and the cause of this diversity cannot be the permanent quantity that remains numerically the same throughout the qualitative change. The numerical diversity of heat has its principle in time to which a numerical diversity of successive parts pertains firstly and *per se*. It seems that this property—diversity of successive parts—accrues to the two heats, so that the quality of heat at t_1 is numerically diverse from the heat at t_2 simply by virtue of the successively diverse "parts" or instances of time that "designate" the heats.

In summary, two points should be noted about Hervaeus's early discussion. First, he finds no problem in accounting for the indivision of a thing from itself; no other principle other than the thing itself as self-identical need be sought. For Hervaeus, the problem of individuation is primarily that of the distinction of individuals within the same species. Second, his theory almost exclusively rests upon the role of quantity that is "joined" to matter communicating to it the properties of having dimensions and being divisible into parts. He succinctly summarizes both points: "it seems that the principle of individuation and plurification of many in the same species is that to which firstly it pertains to have parts; but this is quantity, ergo etc."[18]

Still, there are certain inadequacies and unresolved problems in this early account. For example, there is the classic objection that will trouble all who accord quantity a central role in their theories: what is posterior, as the accident of quantity, cannot have a role individuating the prior, the substance.[19] The priority and posteriority involved is not temporal but "natural". One way of taking this last is "If any two distinguishable elements are so related in virtue of what they are that the very notion or existence of one, call it *B*, entails the notion or existence of the other, call it *A*, but not vice versa, then *A* is prior by nature to *B* even if neither is temporally prior to the other."[20] Since the existence of an accident depends on its subject, but not vice versa, the accident is posterior in nature to the subject. And it seems that what is posterior in this sense cannot individuate the prior on which it depends for existence.

Hervaeus replies briefly[21] that, although a substance as substance is prior to quantity, its being distinct from others is not prior to quantity, as substances that are located are prior to quantity, but that they are located or in a place is not prior to quantity, but vice versa. Hervaeus is aware that in his theory substance and quantity depend on each other in different ways and in different ways each can be said to be prior and posterior to the other. But in this question he does not give a more precise explanation and formulation of this difference; this is had only later in *Quodl.* III, q. 9.

In another reply[22] he states that quantity is not the only principle accounting for numerical distinction of members of the same species. The members also differ "through their essential principles", as Socrates differs from Plato in that Socrates's matter and form are (numerically) distinct from Plato's. Hervaeus says that this diversity of matters and forms is ultimately due to quantity. (Similarly, he argues that it is not precisely because angels are lacking matter that they are not multiplied in a species, but it is the lack of matter with quantity.)[23] This accords with his emphasis on the role of quantity, but leaves unexplained the relations between quantity and these "essential principles"; for example, do these essential principles have any role in individuating the accident of quantity? He does tentatively attempt to clarify the relations between these various types of principles. For example, he states that the formal reason (*ratio formalis*) for numerical distinction is the accident of quantity, and the passive and material reason is matter that is apt to be extended through quantity.[24] This accords with his remarks in *Quodl.* VIII, q. 10, that quantity formally and not effectively extends matter.

In summary, Hervaeus is aware that the role of quantity in individuation needs to be supplemented by a number of other principles; that is, matter, form, and the efficient cause of the individual. But he does not pursue these problems in *Quodl.* VIII, q. 11. Hervaeus the bachelor did, after all, play the role of "responder" only on the day of the disputation. Only later, in his own *Quodl.* III, q. 9, did he attempt a more balanced synthesis of the principles of individuation.

Hervaeus Natalis's Doctrine in *Quodlibet* III, q. 9

Three or four years later in 1309 in *Quodl.* III, q. 9, he begins his discussion by following almost verbatim his earlier treatment. Once again, regarding the cause of a thing's indivision from itself he sees no reason to seek another principle other than the thing itself as self-identical. He then discusses an individual's division from others, and continues, as in his earlier treatment, with various types of indistinction and distinction.[25] He does, however, introduce a further distinction, that between integral and subjective parts.[26] When there are parts of the same type and that which is divided is one in extra mental reality, the parts are integral, as a single piece of wood is cut into two parts. When parts are of the same type and that which is divided is not one in extra mental reality but only in reason (*ratio*), the parts are subjective, as man is divided into the subjective parts Socrates and Plato.

With this distinction, he can formulate the problem of individuation: "And concerning such subjective parts is the whole doubt; namely, through what are subjective parts of the same type multiplied and distinguished from

each other?''[27] Hervaeus's construal of the problem of individuation as that
of distinction remains.

Hervaeus's Discussion of Two Theories

a. Richard of Mediavilla

One of the opinions Hervaeus examines before presenting his own
states that ''each thing is formally distinct from all others only through itself'', that is, through its essence.[28] As one reads through this position as
presented by Hervaeus, one becomes aware that it is not only division from
others that depends on essence, also indivision from self depends solely on
essence. Only one principle of a thing's indistinction from self and distinction from others need be posited, the thing's essence. Although Hervaeus
does not name the proponents of this theory, Richard of Mediavilla taught a
version of it.

We know that Richard of Mediavilla was a bachelor of theology at Paris
in 1283 and incepted the following year as a master of theology.[29] From this
period, 1284–1287, are to be dated his three quodlibets. He was called ''doctor clarissimus'' for his clear and orderly presentation and had an interest in
physical science, often using arguments drawn from experience.[30] Although
solidly of the old school of Augustine and Bonaventure, he at times departs
from it adopting opinions of Thomas Aquinas. For example, Richard holds
that intellectual knowledge comes through the abstractive activity of the
agent intellect with no need of special divine illumination.[31] But, against
Thomas, he accords some small degree of actuality to matter, so that God
could preserve it without a form.[32]

Richard treats the problem of individuation in one of his forty-five
early disputed questions that date from the end of 1284. He also discusses
individuation in various places in his *Sentences* commentary, but his most
extensive treatment is in Book II, distinction 3, articles 3–5.[33] His doctrine
in his *Sentences* commentary is substantially the same as that in the disputed
question: The principle of individuation is a thing's own essence as indivisible. For clarity through contrast, I first treat briefly his notion of a universal
that is ''divisible''.

In distinguishing various senses of the term 'universal', Richard asserts
that a ''true universal'' is an essence as understood in such a way that it is
predicable of many.[34] The way in which it is understood is by prescinding
from the numerical unity and multiplicity that the essence enjoys in extramental reality. The property of an essence called ''universality'' is constituted by the mind and befalls (*accidit*) the essence only as it is thought.[35]
Hence a universal cannot exist extramentally. Further, because the universal

is predicable of many and represents many, Richard talks of the universal as "divisible" in many numerically distinct members of the same species.[36]

In contrast to a universal, Richard says that an individual is not predicable of many, and it is that concerning which it can be truly said, "This is that signed thing in act existing in extramental reality and not another."[37] Further and important, in contrast to a universal an individual is not divisible.

It could be objected that as a matter of fact the individual Socrates is divisible, can be divided into parts. But if so, he would no longer be a human being. Hence, Richard adds that an individual is indivisible "saving the integrity of the essence". It is not a question of indivisibility *tout court,* but a certain type: a lack of divisibility into other members of the same species.[38]

The question of individuation becomes that of accounting for this indivisibility that characterizes individuals. For Richard, this is had through a thing's essence. His repeatedly used formula is, *a* is an individual through its essence insofar as the essence is indivisible "saving its integrity".[39] Because a thing is indivisible through its essence, it is an individual through its essence.

So also for distinction. Richard holds that *a* is divided from others through that by which it is undivided from itself. Hence it is through a thing's essence that it is divided from many.[40] With this view of individuation he approaches the question of whether there can be numerically many angels of the same species. "I respond that God was able to create many angels of the same species. . . . A thing is formally numerically one through its essence insofar as it is indivisible saving its integrity. But by what a thing is numerically one is it distinguished from another thing. So if God can make whatever does not include a contradiction, it is to be held that He was able to make many angels in one species."[41]

Richard is careful when speaking about this indivision or numerical unity of the thing's essence. In his treatment in the second book of the *Sentences,* he claims that to say a thing's essence is numerically one is not to posit something positive superadded to the essence.[42]

Here he is in full agreement with Averroes against Avicenna.[43] According to Averroes, Avicenna taught that being and one add something to essence. But if so, according to Averroes and Richard, an infinite regress would result. For it could always be asked through what is that superadded thing a being or one.

For Richard, then, what is the difference between "The essence is an essence" and "The essence is numerically one"? "Hence the Commentator . . . speaking of being and one says that they signify the same essence but in diverse modes, not diverse dispositions added to the essence. . ."[44] Richard concludes that the "numerical unity of an angel and its essence differ only by reason such that unity adds to essence only the said indivisibility."[45]

Richard teaches, then, that an essence and numerical unity differ only "by reason", that is, both 'unity' and 'essence' signify the same thing but in different ways (*modi significandi*). To assert that the essence is numerically one is only to assert that it is indivisible "saving the integrity of the essence".

It is objected that to be one implies being, and that the being of a creature adds something to the essence, at least a real relation to the creator.[46] Hence, also unity must add something positive to the essence. Henry of Ghent had held that actual existence (*esse existentiae*) did not add anything absolute to the essence, but added a real relation to the creator only as efficient cause. He held that this real relation was "intentionally distinct" from the essence of the creature.[47]

Richard's reply is ambiguous, for he states two positions without himself deciding for either one.[48] According to the first, unity only adds a negation of divisibility to the essence; it does not add anything positive. According to the second, unity inheres in the essence by means of existence, and so unity does add to the essence a real relation to the creator along with the negation of divisibility.

In the first book of the *Sentence's* commentary he also grapples with this issue.[49] There he asks if God's unity adds something to His essence. According to one position, if actual existence and the essence of God do not really differ and do not differ even by distinct concepts (*intentiones, rationes*), then unity posits nothing positive differing from essence either really or intentionally. But if the being of God does differ from His essence by intention, then unity does posit something positive in God, differing from the essence by intention.

In sum, in the passages treating individuation Richard teaches that to predicate numerical unity of an essence does not add anything positive to the essence, but only denies that the essence is divisible saving its integrity. But if one holds that actual existence differs intentionally from essence, then when asserting that the essence is numerically one, one presupposes that the essence actually exists and hence adds something differing intentionally from the essence, that is, actual existence.

When Hervaeus Natalis presents this position in *Quodl.* III, q. 9, he does not treat the ontological commitments attendant upon the denial of divisibility to the essence. Instead Hervaeus marshalls various arguments for the claim that nothing extrinsic to the essence can serve as the principle of individuation, for example, quantity.[50] It is argued, again, that the prior does not have numerical unity through the posterior. But a substance is prior to an accident as quantity; therefore a substance does not have numerical unity through quantity. Or, that which remains numerically the same with numerically diverse quantities is not numerically one through quantity. Prime matter remains numerically the same with numerically diverse quantities, however, since in the generated and the corrupted the numerically same quantity does not remain nor anything else numerically the same except prime matter. Hence, prime matter is not numerically one through quantity.

Further, it would seem that accidents that follow upon quantity, as qualities and relations, would have their numerical unity and plurality through quantity. But this is not always the case. For what is plurified while there remains the numerical unity of quantity does not have plurality from quantity. This happens with some accidents, as the hot can be cooled and heated; the same quantity remains with numerically two qualities of heat.[51]

This position also rules out that in composites matter is the principle of numerical unity and distinction of form or vice versa; that is, form is the principle of numerical unity and distinction of matter.[52] It is argued that *a* and *b* cannot have numerical unity through each other if one can be "plurified" and not the other. But this is the case with matter and form. For matter stands under numerically and specifically diverse forms, as in generation and corruption; and by divine power it is possible that the same soul inform many and diverse parts of matter.

Also it is argued that human souls remain numerically distinct when separated from the body after death. But this would not happen if souls (the forms) were individuated through matter, for without the formal principle the formal effect does not remain. Hence if matter were formally that by which souls are "plurified", without matter there would be no plurality of souls in the afterlife, which is contrary to the faith.

Hervaeus agrees with this position and incorporates into his own theory elements from it. But in itself, the position is inadequate, for Hervaeus believes that it fails to give an account of other principles extrinsic to the essence that have a role as principles of distinction.

b. Duns Scotus

A second opinion that Hervaeus discusses is that of Duns Scotus, and from it Hervaeus takes nothing in constructing his own theory. Hervaeus's presentation of the opinion is brief:[53] according to this opinion, (1) that by which something is a determinate this cannot be anything that it has in common with another. But (2) each thing has matter and form in common with others; hence (3) neither matter nor form can be that by which something is a determinate this and hence an individual. The principle of individuation can only be *haecceitas*, for something is a determinate this through that which is proper to it alone; and this can only be *haecceitas*.

Hervaeus replies that when in (1) it is said that the principle of individuation cannot be what is "common to many" this can be understood as being common in extramental existence or common according to reason. If the former, then what is common is numerically one and common to many.

But then matter and form are not "common in many" in this sense and (2) is false. And if it is understood that something is common according to reason, then haecceity is as common in this sense as matter and form. For in the propositions, 'This haecceity (of Socrates) is a haecceity', and 'That haecceity (of Plato) is a haecceity', the same predicate is said of many and is "common to many according to reason".

In response one could claim that it is not haecceity in this sense of 'common' that is the principle of individuation, but "designated haecceity"; that is, this haecceity of Socrates and this haecceity of Plato. Hervaeus replies that just as "designated haecceity" is not common to many but proper to an individual, so also signed matter and form are not common to many but proper to an individual.

Further, is that haecceity something that is the same or diverse from the matter and form designated by it? If the same, then the position is asserting the same principle of individuation as others have suggested, namely, matter (for, presumably, form is individuated through matter). On the other hand, if haecceity is diverse from matter and form, then the haecceity is either a substance, an accident, or nothing. If it is a substance, then it is either (a) a substance composed of matter and form, or (b) only matter or only form. (In the alternative (b) that the haecceity is not a composed substance, I can see the alternative of a separated form, but I find it odd talking about matter alone as a substance.) Hervaeus believes (b) leads to the opinion of those who hold that the principle of individuation is matter, for again presumably form is individuated through matter. And he believes that (a) leads to those who hold that the composed substance is individuated by itself. Alternatively, if the haecceity is an accident, it cannot be formally relative and so be a relation or be of any of the final six categories, for these are always posterior to and dependent upon absolute accidents and substance. Finally, no one would posit quality to be the principle of individuation; and so if haecceity is an accident it must be quantity, an opinion already proposed by others. For these reasons, Hervaeus believes Scotus's proposal of haecceity adds nothing to the discussion, being ultimately reducible to one of the alternatives already suggested.[54]

Hervaeus Natalis's Own Doctrine in *Quodlibet* III, q. 9.

Having examined these views, Hervaeus takes what truth he finds in the first and tries to synthesize it with his earlier emphasis on quantity. There is a certain tentativeness about his discussion. He claims to give the "more probable opinion",[55] and he seems to be struggling with the complexity and number of principles.

He states that something is plurified and distinct from others in two basic ways, intrinsically and extrinsically.[56] Regarding the first, "each individual formally and intrinsically is distinguished from another through its essence". It is clear that he means the individual's essence existing in extramental reality that is not common to many. He agrees, then, with the first opinion that each thing is distinguished by number from others through its essence as an intrinsic principle.[57] But other causes extrinsic to the essence are required to account for numerical distinction. For Hervaeus, what are these extrinsic causes of plurality?

Something is distinguished extrinsically, that is, through something other than its essence, in four ways: effectively, finally, subjectively, and dispositively.[58]

He explains that the efficient and final causes of a thing's being are also the efficient and final causes of a thing's numerical plurality. Imagine ten red Greek vases of the same type displayed on the shelves of a souvenir shop in Athens. The artisan who made them is the efficient cause of their being and plurality, and the final cause of their being and plurality is the artisan's intention to sell vases to many customers. Note that, although the efficient and final cause is each one, the effects are numerically many.

But with a subjective or a dispositive cause, it is precisely plurality in the cause that brings about plurality in the effect. Regarding the subjective cause of plurality, this quality of red is numerically diverse from that quality of red because the former inheres in a vase, a subject, numerically diverse from that in which inheres the latter quality. The numerical plurality of substances is the subjective cause of the numerical plurality of accidents.

Hervaeus says that all accidents that exist simultaneously have their plurality subjectively from the plurality of subjects in which they inhere.[59] The plurification of these accidents is possible only through the plurification of subjects. This is also true of the accident of quantity: It is plurified through the plurification of subjects.

There is, however, a difference between quantity and the other accidents.[60] For, although the other accidents are in no way the cause of plurality of their subjects, quantity is a dispositive cause of the plurality of quantified subjects. Thomas Aquinas had also spoken of quantity as a dispositive cause.[61] Aquinas's champion, Hervaeus, in *Quodl.* III, q. 9, states clearly that quantity is a dispositive cause of the plurality of integral parts. He is more tentative in claiming that quantity is the dispositive cause of subjective parts, although he does finally affirm it and for the same reason as in the earlier discussion.[62] Division and indivision of parts pertain first and *per se* to continuous quantity; they are passions of continuous quantity. They pertain *per se* to quantity and to other things through quantity as a dispositive cause.

There is a certain order in a composite by which these properties proper to quantity are communicated to it: "comparing however matter to substantial form it seems to me more that form is plurified through matter than the converse, with respect to forms existing simultaneously in matter, because it seems to me that quantity accompanies the composite by reason of matter more than by reason of form and this by receiving; and so quantity plurifies dispositively substance."[63]

Also in his discussion, Hervaeus attempts to work through the problems he had in his earlier treatment. The subjective and dispositive causes are related to each other in a number of ways. Hervaeus explains[64] that a subject and its dispositive cause, permanent quantity, cause each other's plurality but in different ways. Subjectively, the plurality of subjects causes the plurality of quantity, as many numerically distinct subjects cause many numerically distinct accidents of quantity. Conversely, quantity is a dispositive cause of the plurality of a subject and this in two ways. First, quantity is the dispositive cause of integral parts, so that what is numerically one can be divided into many parts of the same type. Second, quantity is the dispositive cause of subjective parts: That a man numerically distinct from others can come into being there must be matter existing under a part of quantity other than another part of quantity.

With this clarification of the mutual dependence relations between a subject and its accident of quantity, he attempts to reply to the objection that the posterior cannot individuate the prior.[65] In his reply,[66] he not only distinguishes between priority taken simply and relatively (*secundum quid*) but also between subjective and dispositive causes. Although individual substances may be simply prior to quantity (as subjects are prior to accidents), still an individual substance is posterior to quantity relatively, for with respect to its individuation a substance depends on quantity as a dispositive cause. It seems to me that some such distinction will have to be made by those who accord quantity the primary role as a principle of individuation of substances. But a critic would ask Hervaeus to be more explicit about the nature of the dependence relations: Can *a* be dependent on *b* for its existence and *b* be dependent on *a* for its numerical distinction?

Another key relation among causes, both intrinsic and extrinsic, is seen in his reply to an objection.[67] If as Hervaeus holds each thing through its own essence is distinguished in number from all others, then two accidents differing only in number could exist in the same subject, which is not to be admitted. He replies that in some cases the intrinsic principle of distinction is insufficient to distinguish something from others of the same species without the concurrent subjective and dispositive principles. It seems, he says, that it is impossible that accidents specifically the same be "plurified" in one subject, since there is lacking that which is needed subjectively for plurification, that is, a plurality of subjects. Hence for Hervaeus, in certain cases one of the causes may be a necessary but not a sufficient condition for numerical plurality.

Finally, Hervaeus sharpens and extends his early remarks about successive quantity (time) as the principle of plurification of successive accidents.[68] Successive quantity is now the *dispositive* cause of numerical diversity of successive accidents and also the dispositive cause of numerical diversity of successive substantial forms in the same matter. "However as to forms succeeding one another in the same matter, the dispositive cause of numerical plurality is diversity in successive quantity, as if from some matter an ox is generated and afterwards corrupts, and from the same matter again through circulation an ox is generated."[69]

Conclusion

In his article on Hervaeus's notion of being, Elliott Allen concludes that, while Hervaeus does make explicit reference to St. Thomas, "there is little or no evidence of any firm grasp of the latter's doctrine of being".[70] Although our knowledge of Hervaeus's thought remains sketchy, Allen's conclusion is a good working hypothesis for explaining some peculiarities of Hervaeus's teaching on individuation.

To be sure, Hervaeus does follow Thomas on a number of points. Like Aquinas, he construes the problem of individuation primarily in terms of the "division" of many individuals within the same species. With regard to a thing's indivision from itself, Hervaeus believes that no principle need be sought other than the thing itself as self-identical. But he makes no mention of Thomas's doctrine of the act of existence that, as Joseph Owens argues, brings about both indivision from self as well as division from others.[71]

Hervaeus follows Aquinas in according to quantity a primary (though nonexclusive) role in individuation. The property of being divisible into parts pertains first and *per se* to quantity and pertains to matter *per accidens* by being joined to quantity. This is a constant in both Hervaeus's discussions of individuation. Furthermore, he believes that there is a certain order in individuating principles by which substantial form is individuated more by matter than vice versa, since quantity is a property of the composite more by reason of matter than by reason of form. This accords with Thomas's doctrine that matter designated by quantity is, in one sense, the ultimate reason for individuation.[72]

However, one does not find in Hervaeus's teaching the corresponding role of substantial form as a Thomistic principle of individuation. The closest he comes to admitting a role to substantial form is his belief that the essence of an individual is an intrinsic principle of individuation. But there is no hint here of the way Thomas understands the substantial form as the formal cause of a thing's existence; that is, as a limiting principle determining the act of existence and so functioning as a principle of individuation. If Owens is right that the role of form in individuation has not been emphasized in the Thomistic tradition,[73] this oversight can be traced back to one of Thomas's most vigorous and vociferous champions, Hervaeus Natalis. Ironically, Durand of Saint Pourçain—who for years drew criticism from Hervaeus for deviating from the doctrine of Thomas—accords the primacy to form over matter in individuation precisely because form gives actual existence.[74]

Finally, because Hervaeus fails to appreciate and use Thomas's notion of existence, Hervaeus's theory of individuation lacks a certain unity characteristic of Thomas's doctrine. In this latter's doctrine, the various roles of substantial form and matter are understood within the context of the act of existence as shared in various degrees and ways by a multiplicity of individuals differing both specifically and numerically. Without this unifying principle in Hervaeus's thought, it is not surprising to find him struggling with the complexity and number of principles, intrinsic and extrinsic. For Thomas, to explain individuation was difficult enough with his doctrine of existence; for some Thomists like Hervaeus (though not Suárez), to explain it without such a notion became almost impossible.

Notes

1. For Hervaeus Natalis's life, see Ag. de Guimarães, "Hervé Noël (d. 1323) Étude Biographique", *Archivum Fratrum Praedicatorum* 8 (1938): 5–81; Frederick J. Roensch, *Early Thomistic School* (Dubuque, 1964), pp. 106–117; see pp. 110–117 for a listing of his works. Also for his works, see P. Glorieux, *Répertoire des maîtres en théologie de Paris au XIII siècle*, 2 vols. (Paris, 1933), vol. 1, pp. 199–206; *La littérature quodlibétique*, 2 vols. (Kain and Paris, 1925–35), vol. 1, pp. 200–08.

2. For Hervaeus's criticisms of Durand, see Josef Koch's *Durandus de S. Porciano O.P.: Forschungen zum Streit um Thomas von Aquin zu Beginn des 14. Jahrhunderts* (Beiträge zur Geschichte der Philosophie des Mittelalters 26, (Münster, 1927), pp. 211–271. I have found no work in which Hervaeus criticizes Durand on the problem of individuation.

3. For the relation of Hervaeus and Thomas on one particular problem, see Elliott B. Allen, "Hervaeus Natalis: An Early 'Thomist' on the Notion of Being", *Mediaeval Studies* 22 (1960): 1–14.

4. *Subtilissima Hervei Natalis britonis theologi acutissimi quolibeta undecim* (Venice, 1513). *Quodl.* III, 9: "Postea querebatur unum generaliter pertinens ad com-

positionem ex materia et forma, et est utrum in talibus materia sit principium individuationis'' (fol. 80vb); *Quodl.* VIII, 11: ''. . . quid sit principium individuationis in
rebus materialibus'' (fol. 152ra). In a related problem, Hervaeus holds that numerically distinct rational human souls could have been created by God before being
united to bodies; the principle of their numerical distinction would be the aptitude for
being united to different bodies; this aptitude depends on their form insofar as it has
a certain degree of being with a potentiality for being united to matter. Since angels
are of a higher degree of being, they are not able to be so united, do not have this
aptitude and are not able to be multiplied in a species; see *Quodl.* III, 9, fol. 82rb;
Quodl. VIII, 4: ''[Utrum] Deus possit facere duas animas solo numero differentes non
infundendo eas corporibus'', fol. 149va–b; *Quodl.* VIII, 11, fol. 152vb–53ra; II *Sent.*
3, 2, fol. 209a–211a (Paris, 1647).

5. L. Hödl, ''Die Quodlibeta minora des Herveus Natalis O.P. (d. 1323)'',
Münchener Theologische Zeitschrift 6 (1955): 215–229.

6. *Quodl.* VIII, 11: ''. . . dico quod individuatio est per quantitatem partim,
partim per alia. . . .'' (fol. 152va)

7. *Ibid.,* 11, fol. 152vb.

8. *Ibid.*

9. *Ibid.,* 11: ''Quantum autem ad hoc, quod quodlibet individuum divisum
sive distinctum sit ab alio eiusdem speciei, principium individuationis substantiarum
materialium est quantitas quantum ad ea quae sunt simul; quia per illud distinguitur
unum individuum ab alio in eadem specie cui primo et per se convenit dividi in partes
similes eiusdem speciei existentes; sed hoc convenit primo et per se quantitati, quia
materia non potest dividi in partes similes nisi per quantitatem; nec possunt etiam esse
plures formae eiusdem speciei nisi in diversis partibus materiae saltem in rebus materialibus. Quantitati autem per se et primo circumscripto quocumque convenit habere
partes similes. Et ideo quantum ad talem individuationem ut praedictum est substantia
habet individuari per quantitatem.'' (fol. 152vb)

10. *Ibid.,* 11, ad 2, fol. 153ra.

11. *Ibid.,* 10: ''Utrum alia sit dimensio materiae et dimensio quantitatis. . . .''
(fol. 152ra–b)

12. *Ibid.,* 10, fol. 152rb.

13. *Ibid.,* 11, fol. 153ra.

14. *Ibid.,* 10, fol. 152rb. See similar remarks a few years later (1307) in *Quodl.*
I, 15: ''Utrum materia sit divisibilis per quantitatem. . . .'' (fol. 30ra–vb)

15. *Quodl.* VIII, 10, fol. 152ra–b.

16. *Ibid.,* 11, fol. 152vb.

17. *Ibid.*, 11: "Sicut enim diversitas rerum materialium eiusdem speciei et simul existentium provenit ex diversitate partium quantitatis continuae permanentis secundum situm, quia ei primo convenit talis divisio, ita etiam diversitas numeralis in eodem subiecto sibi succedentium provenit ex diversitate partium quantitatis continuae successivae quae est tempus cui primo et per se convenit dividi in partes successivas." (fol. 152vb)

18. *Ibid.*, 11: "Contra: illud videtur esse principium individuationis et plurificationis multorum in eadem specie cui primo convenit habere partes; sed hoc est quantitas, ergo etc." (fol. 152va)

19. *Ibid.*, 11, fol. 152va.

20. From Wolter's glossary in John Duns Scotus, *God and Creatures: The Quodlibetal Questions*, ed. Félix Alluntis and Allan B. Wolter (Princeton, NJ, 1975), p. 529.

21. *Quodl.* VIII, 11, ad 4, fol. 153ra.

22. *Ibid.*, ad 5.

23. *Ibid.*, 11, ad 1, fol. 152vb–153ra.

24. *Ibid.*, 11, ad 5, fol. 153ra.

25. *Quodl.* III, 9, fol. 80vb–81ra.

26. *Ibid.*, fol. 81ra.

27. *Ibid.*, 9: "Et de talibus partibus subiectivis est totum dubium, scilicet, per quid partes subiectivae eiusdem rationis multiplicantur et distinguuntur ab invicem." (fol. 81ra); *Quodl.* VIII, 11: ". . . et arguitur quod materia sit principium individuationis quia illud cuius defectu convenit non esse plura individua eiusdem speciei est principium individuationis in eis in quibus inveniuntur plura individua in eadem specie; sed materia est huiusmodi . . . ergo materia est principium individuationis." (fol. 152rb–52va).

28. *Ibid.*, 9, fol. 81ra.

29. For Richard's life and works, see E. Hocedez, *Richard de Middleton, sa vie, ses oeuvres, sa doctrine* (Louvain, 1925); Roberto Zavalloni, *Richard de Mediavilla et la controverse sur la pluralité des formes*, Philosophes médiévaux 2 (Louvain, 1951); F. A. Cunningham, "Richard of Middleton, O.F.M. on *esse* and Essence", *Franciscan Studies* 30 (1970): 49–76, esp. 49–56.

30. P. Duhem, *Études sur Léonard de Vinci. Ceux qu'il a lus et ceux qui l'ont lu*, 3 vols. (Paris, 1906–1913), vol. 2, p. 371.

31. P. Palmaz Rucker, *Der Ursprung Unserer Begriffe nach Richard von Mediavilla. Ein Beitrag zur Erkenntnislehre des Doctor Solidus*, (Beiträge zur Geschichte der Philosophie und Theologie des Mittelalters 31, no. 1; (Münster, 1934).

32. *Clarissimi theologi magistri Ricardi de Mediavilla super quatuor libros Sententiarum Petri Lombardi Quaestiones subtilissimae*, 4 vols. (Brescia, 1591); at the end of vol. 4 is his *Quodlibeta Doctoris Eximii Ricardi de Mediavilla Ordinis Minorum*. For matter having some actuality, see II *Sent.* 3, 2, 1, 2m, vol. 2, p. 54a.

33. The disputed question is, "Utrum in eadem specie possint esse plures angeli inequales in naturalibus." I have used Vatican City, Vat. lat. 868, fols. 16va–19vb. For a list of Richard's disputed questions and a brief description, see E. Hocedez, "Les 'Quaestiones Disputatae' de Richard de Middleton", *Recherches de Sciences Religieuse* 6 (1916): 493–513. For Richard's works, see Glorieux, *Répertoire des maîtres*, vol. 2, pp. 120–123 and for a list of the questions in Richard's Quodlibets, see P. Glorieux, *La Littérature Quodlibétique*, vol. 1, pp. 267–273.

34. II *Sent.*, 3, 3, 1, vol. 2, 56a; *Q. disp.* VIII, Vat. lat. 868, fol. 17va.

35. *Ibid.*, 3, 3, 1, vol. 2, p. 56a–b; II *Sent.*, 3, 3, 2, vol. 2, p. 56b.

36. *Q. disp.* VIII: "Cum enim intelligo naturam humanam sub tali modo quod sibi competit specialitas haec—praedicabilitas de pluribus differentibus numero in quid—non intelligo ipsam ut divisam tamen bene intelligo ipsam ut divisibilem et in plura talia in quorum quolibet salvetur tota." Vat. lat. 868, fol. 17vb. Also, *ibid.:* "Sed constat quod vera natura humana praedicatur de Sorte et Platone inquantum apprehensa ut supra dictum est praeter unitatem et multitudinem. Unde esse naturae humanae sub ratione tali est suum repraesentari intellectui vel suum apprehendi ab intellectu. Unde ut sub ratione tali non debetur sibi esse reale extra quia quicquid est in re extra unum est." Vat. lat. 868, fol. 18ra.

37. *Ibid.:* "Tertio modo dicitur singulare per significationem et per praedicationem de uno solo et huiusmodi potest dici singulare vel individuum omne illud de quo potest dici hoc est ista res signata actu existens in re extra et non alia." Vat. lat. 868, fol. 17va. II *Sent.*, 3, 4, 1, vol. 2, p. 58a.

38. I *Sent.*, 26, 1, 2, *ad* 1: "Dico quod si individuum dicatur quod non dividitur in plura talia, ut individuis homo qui non dividitur in plures homines. . . ." vol. 1, p. 236a. Also II *Sent.*, 3, 4, 1, *ad* 4: "Unitas enim individualis est ipsa essentia inquantum indivisibilis salva integritate sua, seu inquantum indivisibilis in plures essentias tales." Vol. 2, p. 59a.

39. *Q. disp.* VIII: "Dico ergo quod loquendo de hac singularitate vel individuatione substantiae, substantia est singularis vel individua per id quo est haec signata substantia et non alia. Illud autem quo est haec substantia signata et non alia est essentia sua inquantum indivisibilis in plures substantias in quarum qualibet salvetur tota." Vat. lat. 868, fol. 17vb. Also II *Sent.*, 3, 3, 2, vol. 2, p. 57a; II *Sent.*, 3, 4, 1, vol. 2, p. 58b; II *Sent.*, 3, 4, 2, vol., 2, p. 59b; II *Sent.*, 3, 5, 1, 2, p. 60b.

40. II *Sent.*, 3, 3, 2: ". . . unum singulare significatum substantialiter differat ab alio non oportet quod addat differentiam essentialem super speciem, quia per illud per quod singulare significatum est in se substantialiter indistinctum, est ab alio substantialiter distinctum: per suam autem unitatem individualem est in se substantialiter

indistinctum. Unde, et per eam est ab alio substantialiter distinctum. Unitas autem individualis non addit super naturam speciei essentialem differentiam, sed tantum negationem divisibilitatis salva integritate sua: unde natura humana sub ratione qua indivisibilis salva integritate sua est humanae naturae quoddam singulare determinatum seu significatum." Vol. 2, p. 57b; II *Sent.*, 3, 5, 1, vol. 2, p. 60b.

41. *Ibid.*, 3, 5, 1: "Respondeo quod Deus potuit creare plures angelos in eadem specie. . . . Esse autem plures angelos tales, nullam contradictionem includit, sive habeant materiam sive non. Quia quamvis supradicto modo sint similes, ad haec se ipsis formaliter possunt distingui, quia . . . res est una numero formaliter per essentiam suam, inquantum indivisibilis, salva integritate sua. Sed per quod res est una numero, distinguitur a re alia. Cum ergo Deus possit facere quicquid non includit contradictionem, tenendum est, quod potuit facere plures angelos in specie una. Unde et Dominus Stephanus Parisiensis Episcopus et Magister in Theologia excommunicavit istum articulum quo exprimitur, quod Deus non potest multiplicare individua sub una specie sine materia." Vol. 2, p. 60b; *Q. disp.* VIII, Vat. lat. 868, fol. 18rb.

42. II *Sent.*, 3, 4, 2: ". . . substantia est una numero per essentiam suam ita, quod unitas non addit super ipsam, nisi indivisibilitatem, quae non dicit super essentiam substantiae aliquid positivum." Vol. 2, p. 59b.

43. *Ibid.*, 3, 4, 1, vol. 2, p. 58b.

44. *Ibid.*: "Unde Commentator super 4 metha. loquens de ente et uno dicit quod significant eandem essentiam, sed modis diversis, non dispositiones diversas additas essentiae et aliquibus interpositis: postea dicit quod substantia cuiuslibet rei est una essentialiter non per rem addita illi."

45. *Ibid.*: "Indivisibilitas autem non dicit aliquam rem positivam, et sic unitas numberalis ipsius angeli et sua essentia non differunt nisi ratione eo quod unitas super essentiam non addit nisi indivisibilitatem praedictam."

46. *Ibid.*: "Item esse unum numero praesupponit esse. Sed esse creaturae dicit aliquod superadditum essentiae, quia saltem includit relationem ad Creatorem; ergo multo fortius sua unitas," Vol. 2, p. 58a.

47. One formulation of Henry's intentional distinction is: if *a* and *b* are really the same, and neither the concept of *a* includes that of *b*, nor vice versa, then *a* and *b* are intentionally distinct. See his *Quodlibet* V, 6, 2 vols. (Paris 1518; reprint Louvain, 1961), vol. 1, fol. 161r–vL. On the intentional distinction between essence and existence, see *Summa: (Quaestiones ordinariae)* 28, 4, 2 vols. (Paris, 1520; reprint St. Bonaventure, NY, 1953), vol. 1, fols. 167S–68Z). For much of what more could be said on Henry's intentional distinction, see Jean Paulus, *Henri de Gand. Essai sur les tendances de sa métaphysique* (Paris, 1938), pp. 220–237; J. Gómez Caffarena, *Ser participado y ser subsistente en la metafísica de Enrique de Gante*, Analecta Gregoriana 93 (Rome, 1958), pp 88–92; John Wippel, *The Metaphysical Thought of Godfrey of Fontaines* (Washington, DC, 1981), pp. 80–85. For Henry's doctrine of real relation, see Mark Henninger, *Relations: Medieval Theories 1250–1325* (Oxford, 1989), pp. 40–58.

48. II *Sent.*, 3, 4, 1, *ad* 4: "Dicunt aliqui quod unitas immediator est essentiae creaturae quam suum esse in effectu, quia unitas ultra essentiam non addit aliquid positivum, sed tantum negationem divisibilitatis. Unitas enim individualis est ipsa essentia inquantum indivisibilis salva integritate sua, seu inquantum indivisibilis in plures essentias tales." Vol. 2, p. 59a. And *ibid.*: "Alii dicunt quod unitas individualis inest essentiae mediante eius esse, et quod ultra essentiam addit relationem ad datorem ipsius esse et negationem supradictae divisibilitatis."

49. I *Sent.*, 24, 1, 2, vol. 2, p. 217a–19a.

50. Hervaeus Natalis, *Quodl.* III, 9, fol. 81rb.

51. For other arguments against quantity as the principle of individuation along with Hervaeus's replies, see *Quodl.* VIII, 11, fol. 152va and 153ra–b.

52. *Quodl.* III, 9, fol. 81rb.

53. *Ibid.*, 9, fol. 81va–b.

54. In *Quodl.* VIII, 11, fol. 152va, he mentions briefly and then rejects three other candidates for the principle of individuation: being (*esse*), matter, and form.

55. *Quodl.* III, 9, fol. 80vb.

56. *Ibid.*, 9, fol. 81vb–82ra.

57. *Ibid.*, 9, fol. 82rb–va.

58. *Ibid.*, 9, fol. 81vb–82ra.

59. *Ibid.*, 9: "Loquendo autem de principio distinctivo subiective videtur mihi quod omnia accidentia simul existentia actu, et praecipue hoc apparet de aliis accidentibus a quantitate, quod habent pluralitatem et distinctionem numeralem a suis subiectis." (fol. 82ra)

60. *Ibid.*: "Sed videtur mihi quod differt de quantitate et aliis accidentibus in hoc, quod alia accidentia non sunt causa pluralitatis suorum subiectorum ita quod pluralitas in eis plurificet subiecta, licet non possit esse sine pluribus subiectis. Sed quantitas est causa dispositiva pluralitatis existentis in subiectis quantitatis prout ex eodem habet ortum divisio in partes integrales et divisio in partes subiectivas ut supradictum est."

61. For example, *Summa theol.* III, 77, 2, corp.

62. *Quodl.* III, 9, fol. 81ra.

63. *Ibid.*, 9: "Comparando autem materiam ad formam substantialem magis videtur mihi quod forma plurificetur per materiam quam econverso, quantum ad formas simul existentes in materia; quia magis videtur mihi quod quantitas consequitur compositum ratione materiae quam ratione formae et hoc susceptive, quare quantitas plurificat dispositive substantiam ut dictum est." (fol. 82ra–b)

64. *Ibid.*, 9, fol. 82ra.

65. For other replies of Hervaeus to objections against quantity's being a principle of individuation, see *ibid.*, 9, fol. 82va–b and *Quodl. VIII, 11, fol. 153ra–b.*

66. *Quodl.*, III, 9, fol. 82va.

67. *Ibid.*, 9, fol. 82rb.

68. *Ibid.*, 9, fol. 82ra.

69. *Ibid.*, 9: "Quantum autem ad formas succedentes sibi invicem circa eandem materiam, causa pluralitatis numeralis dispositiva est diversitas in quantitate successiva, ut si ex aliqua materia generetur bos et postea corrumpatur, et ex eadem materia iterato per circulationem generetur bos." (fol. 82rb)

70. See Allen, "Hervaeus Natalis", p. 3 in note 3.

71. See Joseph Owens's contribution on Aquinas, p. 175.

72. *Ibid.*, p. 188.

73. *Ibid.*, p. 187.

74. See note 29 in Chapter 14 dealing with Durand of Saint Pourçain's theory of individuation in this volume.

14

DURAND OF SAINT POURÇAIN
(B. CA., 1270; D. 1334)

MARK G. HENNINGER

Durand of Saint Pourçain was one of a group of innovative thinkers—
along with Henry of Harclay and Peter Aureoli—who emerged in the second
decade of the fourteenth century. As Henry of Harclay was an early critic of
Duns Scotus, so Durand criticized Thomas Aquinas. Throughout his long career, Durand's questioning provoked from his fellow Dominicans, particularly Hervaeus Natalis, sharp reactions in defense of the Angelic Doctor.[1]

The controversy surrounding Durand began around 1307/8 when the
first redaction (A) of his *Sentences* commentary appeared. In reply to criticisms, Durand wrote a second redaction (B) around 1310/11 in which many
of the offending opinions were left out. This was deemed insufficient and a
commission was set up that in 1314 issued a list of over ninety errors found
in Durand's commentary, most of the offending opinions dealing with matters
of faith and morals. Durand's reaction to this list and the repeated criticisms
of Hervaeus Natalis is recorded in his three quodlibets from Avignon and the
second redaction of his first Paris quodlibet.

The second phase of Durand's stormy career began around 1317, the
year in which there began the process for Aquinas's canonization, which
eventually took place in 1323. Around 1317 a second list of errors was drawn
up consisting of 235 articles on which Durand's teaching deviated from that
of Aquinas. But in 1317 Durand's situation changed dramatically. He was
named bishop of Limoux and so was freed from the Dominican duty to follow
and teach the doctrine of Aquinas. It was during this period (1317–1327) that
Durand finished his third, fullest, and most mature redaction (C). It is this
redaction that is found in the early printed editions. In it he often returns to
his teaching of the first redaction (A), though on other points he modifies his
position in the wake of many objections raised against his teaching since his

first redaction appeared some twenty years before. But controversy continued. Around 1330 a still unidentified Dominican theologian, "Durandellus", published his *Evidentiae contra Durandum*. He was a very good Thomistic critic of Durand, and in this work he provides a detailed reference work examining many points on which Durand (mostly in (A)) violates principles of Thomas. After presenting Thomas's teaching and that of Durand, Durandellus then offers his own criticism of Durand's position.[2]

How did this long and stormy career affect Durand's teaching on the principle of individuation? Durand treats the principle of individuation in only one place, Book II of his *Sentences* commentary, distinction 3, question 2. Surprisingly, in answering this question in (C) he has simply copied verbatim almost the whole of his answer in (A).[3] This is all the more striking since (at least in the first and second books, with which we are interested) Durand's rewriting of (A) is seen on almost every page of (C). Although he changed on other points, he did not on individuation.[4]

There is, however, one clear discrepancy between the two versions. Durand has dropped from (C) an opinion that in (A) was the only one explicitly attributed to Thomas. But the "opinion of Thomas" is presented in such a truncated way as to be positively misleading: (1) substance is individuated through itself and (2) accidents are individuated through substance.[5] Furthermore, Durand does not at all criticize (1) but only (2).[6] It is probable that this was dropped from (C) because of the summary and unsatisfactory presentation and criticism of this opinion in (A).

Not only did Durand's position on the principle of individuation remain unchanged throughout his long career, but, as we will see in Section II, it is quite different from that of Thomas Aquinas. Given this divergence from Thomas's doctrine, one expects that Durand's teaching on individuation would provoke controversy. No mention is made of Durand's teaching on individuation in the first list of errors in 1314. But his doctrine that many angels can be in one species is cited in the second list of 1317,[7] and Durandellus also argues against this thesis in his *Evidentiae*.[8]

In this short study, I present his theory as found in Book II, distinction 3, question 2 of his *Sentences* commentary.[9] Here he asks whether personality or individuation belongs to angels. But this is only a frame surrounding the real problem he treats: What is the principle of individuation both in material and immaterial things? He examines in turn two strong candidates, matter and quantity, before presenting his own theory.

I. Durand's Criticism of Other Theories

I.1 Matter as the Principle of Individuation

According to this opinion, matter is the first and *per se* principle of individuation in material creatures. For this opinion he offers the following argument. (The formulations of this and all succeeding arguments are the result of my reconstruction.)

A.i.   What is individual from itself (*de se*) is the cause of individuation in others.
A.ii.   But in material things, matter is individual from itself.
A.iii. Therefore, matter is the cause of individuation in material things.[10]

It is maintained that the major is true, since what is some quality through itself seems to be the cause of that quality in others, as fire with respect to what is hot.

It is the minor that causes problems. Apparently based on Aquinas, *Summa theol.* I, q. 3. a. 2, *ad* 3, it is argued that

B.i.   Just as the universal is that which is apt by nature to be in many, so the individual is that which is not apt by nature to be in many.
B.ii.   But in material things only matter has this property of not being in others, while other things are in it.
B.iii. Hence only matter is individual from itself, and other things are individuated as they are received in it, as substantial and accidental forms.[11]

Durand begins his response by pointing out an equivocation regarding the sense of 'in'.[12] One thing can be or not be in another in two different ways, and in either way the argument fails. In the first way, by 'in' is meant inherence, as with an accidental form. But then (B.i) is false, for a universal is not in many by inherence. To be or not to be in one or many by inherence does not determine of itself whether something is individual or universal.

But taken in another, second sense of 'in', (B.i) is true, for in this sense a universal is in many and an individual is not. In this sense, Durand explains, one thing is in another through identity and through essential predication. In this sense, man is said to be "in" Socrates and "man" is said of Socrates by essential predication. But the questions immediately arise: What is the ontological status of the universal "man" here, and in what way does it exist "in" the individuals of which it is predicated essentially?

These questions regarding universals are discussed more fully in Section II, where Durand's own theory of individuation is examined. To anticipate, Durand holds that in extramental reality only individuals exist.[13] If in some sense it is true that the universal is "in many through real identity," it is only because the individual and universal nature are identical in extramental reality. They differ only according to reason: What the concept of a species ("man") bespeaks indeterminately, an individual term ('Socrates') bespeaks determinately. The unity characteristic of the universal is only conceptual; the unity characteristic of the individual is real.

On such a theory, (B.ii) is false, for matter is in many things in the way a universal is. Matter is as universal as form, that is, there is a unity characteristic of the universal "matter" just as there is a unity characteristic of the universal "form". In both cases, the unity is a product of the intellect. On the other hand, in extramental reality all is individual: This form is as individual as this matter. "But in this way to be only in one no more pertains to matter [than to form] and to be in many and be said of many is no more inconsistent with it [matter] than with form. For as a form such as whiteness is said of this and of that and is in them in the way in which a universal is in singulars, so also matter is said of this and of that and is in them in the way in which a universal is in singulars."[14]

I.2 Quantity as the Principle of Individuation

The second opinion holds that in material things quantity is the principle of individuation, while immaterial things as angels are individuated through themselves.

Regarding material things it is argued[15]

C.i.   Something is constituted in being as an individual through the same thing that distinguishes it from another individual of the same species.

C.ii.   But one individual differs from another of the same species first through quantity.

C.iii. Therefore quantity is the first principle of individuation.

In the statement of the position, (C.i) is said to be evident. The minor (C.ii) is proved since:

D.i.   Two individuals of the same species do not differ but agree in quiddity or common nature.

D.ii.   Matter and form, taken absolutely, are parts of the common quiddity.

D.iii. Hence, individuals of the same species do not differ by virtue of matter and form taken absolutely.

D.iv.   Individuals of the same species differ through this form and this matter.

D.v.   But a form is not this unless it is received in designated matter.

D.vi.   Matter is designated only through quantity.

D.vii. Therefore individuals of the same species differ first through quantity.

This conclusion is "confirmed" by the fact that a form is individuated through that by which it is rendered incommunicable to many, and this is had through being received in matter designated by determined dimensions. And finally, regarding angels, as material things have the property of being incommunicable through matter designated by quantity, so immaterial substances have this property from themselves and so from themselves are singular and individual.

Durand replies[16] with a standard objection against positing quantity as the principle of individuation, embedding the objection in his own ontology in which only individuals exist in extramental reality. He claims that the subject of an accident is prior by nature to the accident. This doctrine can be traced back to Aristotle's reference to an accident not as a being, but of a being. A composite of matter and form, however, is the subject of quantity; and this is true in extramental reality where, according to Durand's ontology, all things are singular and numerically one. The composite, then, is singular and numerically one prior (at least by nature) to its receiving quantity; hence quantity is not the first principle of individuation. Quantity, in fact, has no role in individuation at all since it comes to a substance already existing as individual.

Furthermore,[17] do the proponents of this theory understand quantity as being an intrinsic and *per se* principle of individuation? If so, part of the very meaning (*ratio*) of 'individual' is quantity. But Durand denies that quantity can be the principle of individuation in this way. For if quantity were part of the very meaning of 'individual', then any supposit (an individual in the category of substance)[18] would necessarily include a thing of a category other than substance, that is, an accidental form of the category of quantity. But then no individual substance would exist through itself (*per se*) or be one through itself. Here Durand seems to be assuming that if anything can be said to exist through itself and be one through itself it should be substance. In addition, other absurdities would follow. Socrates would not be a being through himself or one through himself, but only accidentally, that is, through the accident of quantity. Nor would Socrates be a member of only one category but of two, substance and quantity.

But perhaps these absurdities can be avoided if the proponents of the theory take quantity as the principle of individuation in another way.[19] In this way quantity is not part of the very meaning of 'individual', but the individuation of a substance always accompanies the designation by quantity. Quantity is the "concomitant" principle of individuation. In this account, there is an individuation by quantity that precedes and causes the individuation of the material substance. Durand considers this alternative in two versions, but ends up rejecting both of them. In the first, he considers a material substance statically, without involving any change; in the second, he considers the material substance as being changed substantially.

Regarding the first, Durand argues as he did before: Every accident presupposes an already subsisting subject.[20] And if quantity is an accident of a substance, it presupposes the existence of a subsisting substance—and these in Durand's ontology are always individual and singular. Hence quantity cannot be the principle of individuation of a material substance taken in this first way.

Taking a material substance in the second way at first seems more promising.[21] Here the individuation by quantity precedes and causes the individuation of a material substance involved in substantial change. The argument presented is that if *a* and *b* are individual material substances of the same species, then

E.i.   Something is constituted in being as an individual through the same thing that distinguishes it from another individual of the same species.

E.ii.   *a* does not differ from *b* unless it happens that they be plural.

E.iii.   [For material substances *a* and *b* to be plural, matter must be able to take on numerically diverse forms of the same species.]

E.iv.   Matter cannot take on diverse forms of the same species, either simultaneously or successively, except by quantity.

E.v.   Hence, quantity is that by which *a* and *b* are plural.

E.vi.   Hence, quantity is that by which *a* and *b* differ.

E.vii.   Hence, quantity is the principle of individuation.

With regard to (E.iv), in a substantial change the matter that previously existed with one substantial form loses it and acquires another. Matter does not of itself have this potency to be under many forms; quantity gives matter this potency. "For as to be under the form of blood gives [to matter] the special potency to be changed with respect to a special form, so to be under quantity gives [to matter] the general potency with respect to receiving simultaneously or successively many forms".[22]

Durand replies by denying (E.i). Instead he holds that "what is the principle of individuation is other than the cause and principle for matter being able to be under many forms".[23] He clearly distinguishes here between distinction and individuation, between the principles of multiplication of individuals within a species and the principle of individuation. He states that even if some matter did not have the potency to be under many forms and so could exist under only one form (and so there would not be many individuals of the same species), still there would be one individual. Hence, even if (E.iv) were true in cases of natural generation,[24] it cannot be used to argue for quantity being the principle of individuation. For there to be many individuals of the same species, some principle of multiplication is needed, but even without this principle there can exist an individual.

Before examining Durand's own theory of the principle of individuation, note that his criticism of the quantitative theory of individuation follows the line first taken by Peter Abailard. Durand returns time and again to the accidental nature of quantity and its being posterior, at least in nature, to substance. He uses this principle in his criticism of (D) and in one of his replies to the suggestion that quantity is a concomitant cause of individuation. In addition, he clearly distinguishes between the question of individuation and that of multiplication within a species. This clear distinction is reflected in his own separate discussions of these problems. Consequently, I first examine in Section II.1 his position on the problem of individuation, found in the question we have been discussing. Then I investigate in Section II.2 his question 3 in which he discusses the problem of multiplication within a species.

II. Durand's Theory

II.1 Durand's Theory of the Principles of Individuation

The foundation of his position is that that which is the principle of individuation is the principle of the nature and quiddity. As is clear immediately, his ontology that only singulars exist extramentally is the guiding thread through his whole discussion.

He argues first that those things which are the same in a certain way have the same principles. "But a universal nature and an individual or singular [nature] are the same in extramental reality, but differ according to reason, because what the species bespeaks indeterminately the individual bespeaks determinately. This determination and indetermination are according to being and understanding. For a universal is one only according to concept, but a singular is one according to real being."[25] Hence, with respect to extramental reality a universal and an individual have the same principles, for they are identical in extramental reality.

His ontology, in which only singulars exist extramentally, is also evident in his second reason for his position. That which is convertible with being and predicable of certain things does not add something to those of which it is predicated. "But to be an individual is convertible with real being. For only what is individual or singular exists in extramental being: hence to be an individual does not pertain to anything through something added to it, but through that which it is."[26] If only individuals exist extramentally, there is no need for anything, as Scotus's haecceity, to be added to a common nature.

Durand, however, does not dismiss the problem of individuation as a pseudo-problem. He does ask, "Through what is Socrates an individual?" And his answer makes sense given his ontology: Socrates is an individual through that by which he exists, and these principles are four, two extrinsic and two intrinsic.[27]

The two extrinsic principles are the end and the agent who produced the singular thing, for as Durand repeatedly states, actions are of singulars and terminate in singulars. The two intrinsic principles are this form and this matter. If it is asked through what is a form this form, Durand replies sensibly that extrinsically it is through that which brought it into extramental existence, the agent, for actions terminate in singulars. In addition to the agent, however, matter is a "concomitant" principle of form's individuation insofar as an individual material substance cannot exist without matter.

So also, the extrinsic principle of matter being this matter is the agent; the intrinsic principle is form. His early training with James of Metz is seen in the relation between form and matter.[28] Durand believes that matter's individuation depends more on form than vice versa, for form is more the reason for the being (and so individual being) of matter than vice versa.[29]

Although the use of a comparison to the Trinity is normally a risky way to illuminate one's position, Durand succeeds very well. If a nature common to many supposits were to be one in extramental reality and not just one in concept, then it would be necessary to seek, beyond the nature and its principles, for principles constituting the individual supposits. This is the case in the Trinity, for there are three divine persons, all of whom share in the one divine nature. This one nature is one in reality and is communicated to each of the divine persons equally. Hence what constitutes each person as that person, Father, Son, or Holy Spirit, must be something other than the divine nature that they share. And this traditionally is a relation of origin, paternity, filiation, or passive spiration.

But in Durand's ontology, apart from this one special case, the nature common to many individuals is one only in the intellect and diverse in reality. Hence there is no need to seek for a special principle of individuation other than the principles of the nature; since the individual and nature are the same in reality, so also are their principles the same.

II.2. Durand on the Question of the Possibility of Multiplication of Angels in a Species

In question 2 just investigated, Durand states in passing that angels are individuated intrinsically through themselves.[30] Since Durand believes angels are not composed of matter and form,[31] the one intrinsic principle of individuation of an angel is its form. And as he stated previously, if it is asked through what is the form an individual form, he replies it is through the agent who brought it into being, in this case God. The role of the agent in bringing about an individual form becomes central to his solution to another problem he treats in the following question 3, whether it is possible that many angels be under one species.

Durand's method of treating this problem is significant. According to Durand, the first thing to be understood is that when an effect depends solely on one cause, the effect's "total possibility or impossibility depends on the condition and possibility of the cause."[32] I take Durand to mean that when an effect depends completely on only one cause, whether the effect can or cannot come to exist is solely dependent on the nature and power of its cause. But the angels, along with their unity and plurality, immediately and solely depend on the first cause. Hence the question of the possibility of a plurality of angels in one species is to be argued from the nature of divine power. And for Durand, the divine power extends to all that does not include a contradiction. Hence the whole question of whether angels are able to be multiplied in one species is reduced to finding if there is a contradiction involved in this possibility.

Durand argues that no contradiction is involved, and he uses reason and authorities in his proofs. According to reason he argues[33] that (F.i) every nature that is produced by an agent in a repeatable action is able to be plurified according to number; but (F.ii) every creature is of this type. Therefore (F.iii) angels, as all creatures, are able to be plurified according to number and so also within the same species.

In support of the major argument (F.i), he argues that (G.i) an agent through one action produces one thing; but (G.ii) if an action is repeatable so also is the term of the action. Hence, (G.iii) that agent through many actions produces many things. To support (G.ii) he argues that every action that can be voluntarily interrupted while there remains the active power (which is the principle of the action) can be repeated. As long as the active power remains that produced the first effect, that active power can be used again to produce a second instance of that effect. And this is most true when the action and the effect depend solely on the power of the agent, for in these cases the total potentiality, unity, and plurality of the action and the effect are from the power of the producer. Durand holds that this is the case in creation, for the total action and effect depend only on the power of God.

For Durand, then, God as creator is the type of agent described in (G), for the action by which God produces any creature can be voluntarily interrupted while the active power remains; therefore such an action is repeatable. Hence every creature, including separated substances as angels, can be multiplied in their species through God's repeated action.

This argument is interesting in stressing the role of God's divine power. Durand does not use the term '*potentia absoluta*', but it is clear that he shares the early fourteenth century disposition to appeal to God's power in widely differing contexts. This was prompted in part by the condemnation of 1277 and the general reaction against Greek necessitarianism in its many forms. In this question of Durand, these broader currents are evidenced in a number of

ways: in his formulation of the question ("Whether *it is possible* that many
angels exist under one species?"), in his method, as noted at the beginning
of this discussion, in his solution through God's omnipotence, and finally
in Durand's repeated references to the voluntary and iterable quality of
God's actions.[34]

There are two other examples of these broader currents. Durand uses
authority to support his position, quoting verbatim three articles from the
Paris condemnation of 7 March 1277:[35] It is an error to hold (1) that because intelligences do not have matter God is not able to make many of the
same species (art. 81); (2) that God is not able to multiply individuals under
one species without matter (art. 96); and that forms do not receive division
except by matter (art. 191).

Finally, having decided that it is possible that angels be multiplied in
one species, he asks in the following question 4 whether angels in fact are
numerically many. He replies that from Scripture we know that there is
a great number. And Durand sees no reason why they may not all be of
one species or at least many of them. But in any case, the great number of
angels depends totally on the good will of God who produces as many as
he wishes.[36]

III. Conclusion

For such a strong critic of Thomas Aquinas as Durand of Saint
Pourçain, his discussion of Thomas on individuation is disappointing and al-
lusive. In the first redaction (A) of his *Sentences* commentary, he presents a
very truncated version of Thomas's theory and rightly drops it from his later
redaction (C). One opinion he does criticize in (C)—that the first and *per se*
principle of individuation is only matter—also cannot be correctly attributed
to Aquinas. The closest we have to a criticism of Thomas's opinion is that
concerning quantity as the principle of individuation in material things, as I
have presented it in Section I.2.

Here Durand's criticisms—if indeed directed against Thomas's doctrine—are a strange mixture of perception and blindness. I think he is right to
object to premise (E.i) that something is constituted in being as an individual
through the same thing that distinguishes it from another individual of the
same species. Thomas, again and again, treats the problem of individuation
in terms of multiplication within a species or in terms of division. Instead
Durand explicitly rejects this assumption and literally distinguishes two questions: What was often treated in one *quaestio,* Durand breaks into two,
one dealing with individuation, the other with "plurification" of angels in
one species.

At the same time, throughout Durand's discussion, he makes no attempt to understand Thomas's doctrine of individuation within the broader

context of Thomas's metaphysics of existence. The role of the act of existence and that of substantial form are entirely passed over. Durand moves in a metaphysical world quite different from that of Thomas.

In this he is similar to another thinker in the second decade of the fourteenth century, Henry of Harclay, who, in his own way, moves in another metaphysical world from his teacher Duns Scotus. Both Durand and Henry believed that only individuals exist extramentally; the unity of a universal is ultimately constituted by the mind. But while Henry feels no need to give a positive account of individuation, Durand does. Socrates is an individual through that by which he exists. And for Durand, there are only four "concomitant" principles of a thing's existence as well as of its individuation: matter, form, agent, and end.

Notes

1. The pioneering and still classic work on Durand of Saint Pourçain is Josef Koch's *Durandus de S. Porciano O.P.: Forschungen zum Streit um Thomas von Aquin zu Beginn des 14. Jahrhunderts*, Beiträge zur Geschichte der Philosophie des Mittelalters 26 (Münster, 1927). In addition, see his articles collected in his *Kleine Schriften* 2, Storia e Letteratura 128 (Rome, 1973): "Die Magister-Jahre des Durandus de S. Porciano O.P. und der Konflict mit seinem Orden", pp. 7–118; "Ein neuer Zeuge für die gegen Durandus de S. Porciano Gerichtete Thomistische Irrtumsliste", pp. 119–125; "Die Verteidigung der Theologie des Hl. Thomas von Aquin durch den Dominikanerorden gegenüber Durandus de S. Porciano, O.P.", pp, 127–168.

2. For Durand's opponents, including Hervaeus Natalis and Durandellus, see Koch, *Durandus*, pp. 197–394.

3. For (C) I use *Durandi a Sancto Porciano . . . Petri Lombardi Sententias theologicas commentariorum libri IV* (Venice, 1571). The second book of Durand's first redaction (A) of his commentary is contained in Peter Palude's commentary (c. 1310) of this book, preserved in Vatican City, Biblioteca Vaticana, Vat. lat. 1073; see Koch, *Durandus*, pp. 22–31. I have consulted this codex for Durand's doctrine on individuation in (A).

4. I have not been able to consult codices containing (B), his second redaction. Koch, however, states that this is an embarrassing work, written under pressure from Durand's superiors and with little value for assessing the actual development of his thought; see Koch, *Durandus*, pp. 74, 82, 195.

5. The complete presentation of this "opinion of Thomas" is as follows: "Opinio secunda est Thomae in prima parte, q. 29, art. primo in corpore solutionis ubi dicit quod substantia individuatur per se ipsam, accidentia vero per substantiam; et idem dicit in quaestionibus disputatis in quaestione quid sit prima in corpore solutionis. Prima pars probatur per diffinitionem quam dat Philosophus: prima substan-

tia est per se et maxime subsistat; quod autem est maxime tale ipsum est per se et primo tale et causa aliis. Secunda pars probatur quia accidentia non sunt entia nisi quia entis, et per consequens non sunt unum nisi quia unius, nec duo nisi quia duorum. Et inde est quod duo accidentia solo numero differentia non se compatiuntur in subiecto uno secundum idem." Vat. lat. 1073, fol. 14v. There follow Durand's criticisms.

6. Two arguments of Durand are these: "Contra hoc est quia in eodem subiecto successive et interpollate possunt esse divisi motus solo numero differentes, sicut potest aliquis currere eri et hodie. Ergo aliquo alio quam subiecto hii duo motus distinguuntur. Praeterea in eodem subiecto secundum idem sunt divisa accidentia specie et genere differentia, et e contrario in duobus subiectis specie et genere differentibus sunt accidentia solo numero differentia. A quo autem habet aliquid maiorem differentiam ab eo potest haberi minorem; [differentiam] specie et generis non habeat a subiecto, sed aliude; ergo numeralem." Vat. lat. 1073, fol. 14v.

7. Koch has presented the two lists of errors in "Die Magister-Jahre", pp. 52–118; see 84, n. 56 for the citing in the 1317 list of Durand's opinion that "plures angeli possunt esse in una specie".

8. For Durandellus's *Evidentiae contra Durandum*, I have consulted Vatican City, Biblioteca Vaticana, Vat. Ross. 161, fols. 22vb–29ra, especially fols. 23ra–24ra. For more on Durandellus, see Koch, *Durandus*, pp. 340–369.

9. Since in what follows the two redactions (A) and (C) follow each other almost verbatim, in the notes I cite first the later (C) using the Venice 1571 edition giving numbers of folios and paragraphs, followed by (A) as found in Vat. lat. 1073.

10. II *Sent.*, 3, 2, fol. 136va, n. 6; Vat. lat. 1073, fol. 14v.

11. It is briefly stated that according to this opinion a form not received in matter, as an angel, is individual from itself. This is also found in the passage from Aquinas.

12. II *Sent.*, 3, 2, fol. 136va–b, n. 7; Vat. lat. 1073, fol. 14v.

13. See note 25.

14. II *Sent.*, 3, 2: "Isto autem modo non plus convenit materiae esse in uno solo, nec plus repugnat ei esse in pluribus et dici de pluribus quam formae, sicut enim forma ut albedo dicitur de hac et de illa, et est in illis per modum quo universale est in singularibus, sic etiam materia dicitur de hac et de illa, et est in illis per modum quo universale est in singularibus, patet ergo quod haec opinio procedit aequivoce." fol. 136vb, n. 7; Vat. lat. 1073, 14v.

15. *Ibid.*, fol. 136vb, n. 8; Vat. lat 1073, fol. 15r.

16. *Ibid.*, fol. 136vb, n. 9; Vat. lat. 1073, fol. 15r.

17. *Ibid.*, fols, 136vb–37ra, n. 10; Vat. lat. 1073, fol. 15r.

18. See Durand's definition of 'individual', 'supposit', and 'person' in (C), fol. 136va, n. 5.

19. *Ibid.*, fol. 137ra, n. 11; Vat. lat. 1073, fol. 15r.

20. *Ibid.*

21. *Ibid.*, fol. 137ra, n. 12; Vat. lat. 1073, fol. 15r.

22. *Ibid.*: "Nam sicut esse sub forma sanguinis dat sibi specialem potentiam ad formam specialem in transmutari, ita esse sub quantitate dat sibi generalem potentiam respectu plurium formarum recipiendarum simul vel successive." (fol. 137ra, n. 12; Vat. lat. 1073, fol. 15r)

23. *Ibid.*: "Sed istud non videtur, quia aliud est principium individuationis et aliud est causa et principium quare materia potest esse sub pluribus formis. Esto enim quod materia non posset esse nisi sub una forma nec simul, nec successive, nihilominus adhuc esset dare individuum in illa natura, non enim existeret universaliter sed singulariter." (fol. 137ra, n. 13; Vat. lat. 1073, fol. 15r).

24. In *Ibid.*, 3, 3, fols. 137vb–138ra, nn. 9–13, Durand argues against quantity being the principle of multiplication within a species.

25. *Ibid.*, 3, 2: ". . . sed natura universalis et individua seu singularis sunt idem secundum rem, differunt autem secundum rationem, quia quod dicit species indeterminate individuum dicit determinate, quae determinatio et indeterminatio sunt secundum esse et intelligi, universale enim est unum solum secundum conceptum. Singulare vero est unum secundum esse reale." (fol. 137ra, n. 14; Vat. lat. 1073, fol. 15v) See also II *Sent.*, 6, 7, fol. 140rb, n. 7; fol. 140va, n. 12; I *Sent.*, 35, 3, fol. 95va, nn. 3 and 5.

26. *Ibid.*: "Sed esse individuum convertitur cum ente accepto secundum esse reale. Nihil enim existit in re extra nisi individuum, vel singulare, ergo esse individuum non convenit alicui per aliquid sibi additum. Sed per illud quod est." (fol. 137ra, n. 15; Vat. lat. 1073, fol. 15v).

27. *Ibid.*

28. See J. Koch, "Jacob von Metz, O.P., der Lehrer des Durandus de S. Porciano, O.P.", in *Kleine Schriften*, 1, Storia e Letteratura 127 (Rome, 1973), pp. 133–200.

29. For another expression of the relation of form and matter, see II *Sent.*, 3, 3: "Quaelibet enim res composita ex materia et forma per materiam quidem habet, quod possit esse vel non esse, per solam autem formam habet quod sit actu. . ." (fol. 137va, n. 7).

30. *Ibid.*, 3, 2: "Substantiae autem separatae nullo modo intrinsece individuantur nisi seipsis." (fol. 137rb, n. 15; Vat. lat. 1073, fol. 15v).

31. *Ibid.*, 3, 1, fol. 135vb–36va.

32. *Ibid.,* 3, 3, fol. 137va, n. 5.

33. *Ibid.,* fol. 138ra, n. 14.

34. *Ibid.,* fol. 1. 1. 137rb–va, n. 4; fol. 138ra–b, nn. 14, 16.

35. *Ibid.,* fol. 138ra–b, n. 15. See *Chartularium Universitatis Parisiensis* 1, ed. H. Denifle (Paris, 1889, pp. 548–549; 554.

36. II *Sent.,* 3, 4, fol. 138vb, n. 11.

15

Henry of Harclay
(b. ca. 1270; d. 1317)

Mark G. Henninger

Henry of Harclay can perhaps rightly be called the first Scotist.[1] He had read the *Sentences* in Paris around 1300 when Duns Scotus was teaching there, and this early influence is seen in Harclay's own, as yet unedited, commentary on the first book of the *Sentences*.[2] He became master of theology at Oxford around 1310 and about thirty questions that he disputed at this time have been preserved; in them he shows more independence and maturity than in the first book of the *Sentences*.[3] In 1312 he became chancellor of the University of Oxford and, among other activities, was involved in various administrative disputes with the Dominicans. He died at Avignon in 1317.

Since Pelster's pioneering work in the 1920s, historians often write of Harclay as a "transition figure" between Scotus and Ockham. But from his disputed questions that have been slowly edited over the last thirty years,[4] it has become clear that his relationship to both is quite complex. The pattern of early dependence on Scotus and later independence is evidenced in his changing position on divine prescience and predestination. His ontology of relations and doctrine that only individuals exist outside the mind, along with his use of confused and distinct concepts in dealing with the problem of universals, all show him active and aware of the issues and options in the generation before Ockham. Harclay did not follow a school but was an independent and critical thinker, like Peter Aureoli and Durand of Saint Pourçain. He was one of the few, for example, who defended the anti-Aristotelian "indivisibilist" or atomist theory of the continuum;[5] he also taught the minority view that God is as really related to creatures as they are to Him. At the same time he was sharply critical of Thomas Aquinas and the latter's attempt to reconcile certain doctrines of Aristotle with the Catholic faith. Harclay's conservatism is manifest in these attacks on Aquinas and in his reliance on the Augustinian/Franciscan tradition he embibed from his teacher Duns Scotus.

Since in his early *Sentences* commentary Harclay shares many of Scotus's teachings, it would be interesting to discover if Harclay adopted a version of Scotus's doctrine of haecceity. But as far as I have been able to ascertain from examining this commentary, Harclay has left us no treatment of the problem of individuation. Nor in his later series of questions does he specifically treat the problem of individuation. In these later questions, however, Harclay teaches that any thing existing extramentally by that very fact is singular, that is, incommunicable. This contrasts sharply with Scotus's doctrine of common nature as communicable to many.[6] Given this ontology, it is understandable that Harclay gives no positive account of individuation as Scotus and many others had done. We must cull his doctrine from a number of his disputed questions. In this brief study, then, I first present Harclay's criticism of other theories, namely, that of Thomas Aquinas and a position in some respects similar to that of Duns Scotus. I then examine Harclay's own ontology of singular extramental things as presented in the question on universals. Finally, for a deeper understanding of the extramental foundation for universal concepts I use his question on relations.

I. Harclay's Criticism of Other Theories

I.1 Harclay's Criticism of Thomas Aquinas

In Harclay's question on the immortality of the human soul, he maintains that the soul is naturally corruptible and mortal.[7] Like the angels, our soul tends to revert to nothingness, but it will in fact live forever by the grace and good will of God. Harclay argues against those, like Thomas, who maintain that the human soul is naturally immortal, and in the course of his discussion Harclay treats briefly Thomas's doctrine that the soul is individuated by matter.[8] Harclay's criticisms of Thomas, made in passing, are neither elaborate nor profound, but they do illustrate why the Thomistic solution to individuation was so foreign to Harclay.

Henry believes Thomas is wrong in maintaining both that the human intellective soul is the substantial form of humans and is naturally incorruptible.[9] For if so, then after death there should be as many souls as humans. But there cannot be many numerically distinct souls, since there is only one subsistent form per species separated from matter. Harclay brings forward a number of texts of Aristotle to prove that the Stagirite held there are many individuals in a species through matter.[10] Hence, those enamored of Aristotle who hold that matter is the principle of individuation cannot maintain the plurality of souls after death.

Harclay offers a response in defense of the Thomist position that makes a distinction between angelic and human souls.[11] The former are apt by nature to exist through themselves and not to perfect matter; the latter, however, are apt by nature to perfect matter. Separated human souls are distinguished numerically by their aptitudes for matter, and the angelic souls, lacking such aptitudes, are multiplied only by species.

Hervaeus Natalis, the distinguished early fourteenth century champion of Thomas, held such a position, albeit as probable. He believed that, if God has the power to conserve individual human souls after death without bodies, there is no reason why He could not create them ''from the beginning'' without bodies.[12] Hence, they are distinguished from each other, not by actually being (or having been) united to matter nor by a relation to matter, but by an aptitude for being united to matter. In Hervaeus's statement of the position, it seems that a soul's aptitude for being united to a particular body is the principle of its distinction from other human souls, even if this aptitude were never to be realized. Further, the aptitude is part of the essence of a human soul that has a certain degree of being. As Harclay explains the position, human souls are on the border between bodily substances and purely spiritual substances. Angels, having a higher degree of being, do not have such aptitudes to be united to matter and are not multiplied in a species.[13]

In his reply, Harclay, like Hervaeus,[14] dismisses the suggestion that this aptitude is a real relation. A necessary condition for a real relation is a really distinct term. But the term, the particular body, has been corrupted (or in the hypothesis of preexistence of souls, the body does not yet exist). Nor can the aptitude be a relation of reason, for no being of reason can be the cause of real distinction. Hence the aptitude must be part of the nature of the soul itself. This is, in fact, Hervaeus's position: The aptitude is part of the essence of the soul. But then, Harclay maintains, the distinction of human bodies is caused more by the prior distinction of these forms than the converse. For a distinction in the prior is the cause of a distinction in the posterior. But in Harclay's view of the human person, the soul in ''its absolute nature'' is prior to its being the form of the body, because to be the form of the body is contingent to its nature. Hence, two souls are distinguished more by their nature than by being united to bodies.

These last remarks in Harclay's argument are true only in a view of the human soul quite different from Thomas's; Harclay's view of the human soul is inspired more by Augustine than Aristotle. For Harclay, the human soul's union with the body befalls (*accidit*) it and is contingent to its nature. In its ''absolute nature'' a human soul is not related to a body. In support of his position, Harclay maintains that Augustine seems to have taught that the first human soul was created on the first day of creation and only on the sixth day was infused into a body.[15] Hence, Harclay exploits Hervaeus's hypothesis that God could have created the soul "from the beginning" without being united to the body. Harclay, with his Augustinian view of the human person, takes this possibility seriously in his dismissal of the role of the body and matter in individuation. Hervaeus Natalis, as also Aquinas, would certainly object to such an Augustinian characterization of the human person. For them, as Hervaeus maintains previously, being capable of union with a body is part of the nature of a human soul.

Harclay is strongly critical of Thomas's doctrine that the soul is "designated" by its union with matter.[16] For if a soul can be designated and so individuated only through its union with a body, then God would be unable to make a soul previous to its union with the body. Again, Harclay exploits Hervaeus's hypothesis, turning it against the Thomist doctrine. The dangerous implication of this doctrine is clearly that it limits God's omnipotence. Elsewhere Henry criticizes Thomas's doctrine for just this implication.[17] Here, Harclay loses patience: such a doctrine ought to be harshly rubbed out as plain heresy.

Harclay also argues against matter's "designating" in another way.[18] According to my reconstruction of the argument:

i.   The sign made on the soul by the body is either (a) identical with the soul or (b) really distinct from the soul.
ii. If (i.a), the total substance of the soul is caused by the body—which is heretical.
iii. Hence, (i.b), the designation made by the body is really distinct from the soul.
iv. It is false that this soul is indifferent to this body or that body.
v.   This soul "appropriates" to itself this sign made by this body (iv).
vi. This soul appropriates to itself this sign either (a) through the general *ratio* of soul common to many, or (b) through some *ratio* more contracted and limited than the nature of the species common to many.
vii. But the general *ratio* of a soul common to many cannot be the cause of a soul appropriating this sign from this body rather than that sign from that body.
viii. Hence, not (vi.a).
ix. So, (vi.b) the soul appropriates to itself this sign through some *ratio* more contracted and limited than the nature of the species common to many.
x.   But this type of *ratio* in (ix) is a necessary condition for singularity.
xi. So, the soul in itself is singular without that sign.
xii. So, for individuation of a soul such designation is in vain.

In premises i–iii, Harclay views the intellective soul hardly in an Aristotelian manner as a form of matter, but more as a preexistent entity that receives a really distinct sign from a really distinct body. In premises iv and v, he betrays further Augustinian influences in his emphasis on the activity of the soul over anything "lower", as matter. Henry is offended by Thomas's "rude image" of a seal stamping a passive piece of wax.[19] He passes over the role of quantity and its relation to matter, simply talking of the body giving the sign to the soul. In short, Harclay's view of the human composite, his real antipathy to Aquinas, and as we will see, his ontology of individuals, all prevent him from taking seriously the Thomist alternative to the problem of individuation.

I.2 Harclay's Criticism of a Realist Theory of Universals and Individuation

In another disputed question Harclay asks whether a universal signifies anything outside the soul other than the singular or the supposit and answers clearly in the negative. He submits a doctrine of universals that seems to be that of Scotus to a lengthy series of criticisms. While the many arguments presented for the position are often taken from Scotus, the many counter-arguments are directed against a position held by Walter Burley.[20] The criticisms attack a position according to which the common nature is numerically one in many and the common nature and haecceity are really distinct from one another, differing numerically.[21]

One argument shows the type of criticism that is leveled against this position. Harclay claims that its proponents had used a formulation of the argument against Thomas's contention that quantity is the principle of individuation of, say, the substance of Socrates. Harclay believes if it works against Thomas it works against this theory of a common nature with its "less than numerical unity" being contracted by haecceity, as the human nature of Socrates is contracted by Socrateity.[22]

i.   As the substance of Socrates is a thing other than its quantity, so the humanity of Socrates is a thing differing from Socrateity.

ii.   It is impossible that the humanity of Socrates be with Platoneity.

iii. So, the humanity of Socrates determines to itself this and only this haecceity, that is, Socrateity (ii).

iv.   The humanity of Socrates determines to itself Socrateity either (a) through a nature more common than a singular nature or (b) through a nature less common than the nature of a species.

v.   But nothing is determined to one supposit more than another through a nature more common and indifferent than a singular nature.

vi.   Hence, not (iv.a).

vii. So, (iv.b).

viii. But a nature less common than the nature of a species is a singular nature.

ix.   Hence, the humanity of Socrates in itself is singular.

First,[40] Harclay holds not only that every extramental thing is singular, but the confused concept is also singular. For the concept as a quality in the soul is just as singular and incommunicable to many as any extramental thing. In addition, Harclay teaches that both the confused concept and, surprisingly, the singular extramental thing are universal. The concept is universal because it represents many confusedly so that through it the intellect cannot distinguish one singular from another of the same kind. And because the singular can be conceived in a confused manner, Harclay claims that it is universal. Ockham and Burley later criticize Harclay's view that one and the same thing can be both singular and universal.[41]

Second, Harclay insists that these confused concepts are not mere poetic figments with no foundation in reality.[42] The foundation for these "philosophical figments" is the real relation of similarity between individuals. His question on real relations helps us understand better this extramental foundation for universal concepts.[43]

In his early *Sentences* commentary Harclay had followed Duns Scotus in adopting a strongly realist position on real relations, but in a lengthy later question he argues against this view and devotes much energy to defending his own position, one closer to that of William of Ockham. Harclay's later theory of relation can be contrasted with Scotus's in the following way.[44] According to Scotus, if R is a real relation, then sentences of the form 'aRb' ('a is really related to b') are true if and only if (1) a and b are really distinct extramental things, (2) there is a real foundation in a for R to b, and (3) there exists an extramental relative thing R inhering in a that is really distinct from its foundation. And, sentences of the form 'R-ness exists' as 'Similarity exists' are true if and only if there exists an extramental relative thing really distinct from, but inhering in, its foundation.[45]

As mentioned, Harclay had held this ontology in his *Sentences* commentary, though even there he voices reservations. But in his later question he develops his own theory holding that if R is a real relation, then sentences of the form 'aRb' are true if and only if (1) a and b are really distinct extramental things, (2) there is a real foundation in a for R to b, and (3) there exists a real relation R, a noninhering condition of a toward b. And sentences of the form 'R-ness exists' are true if and only if there exists a mind-independent condition "in" (noninherence) one thing toward another. Two points should be noted: There is no need to posit a third thing really distinct from, but inhering in a, and the condition of a's being related to b is mind independent.

Betraying his realist Scotist background, Harclay claims that when something becomes really related to another, some "thing" comes to the former. He explains the nature of this thing, however, in his own way: "Therefore, in extending 'thing' to all that which does not depend on the intellect, it is necessary that some new thing be able to come to something and be verified of it, which thing does not inform that to which it comes, but only affirms a condition (*habitudo*) or the fact of being associated (*societas*) or a concurrence together (*simultas*) or coexistence (*coexistentia*) or in whatever way we wished to call [it]."[46] This mind-independent noninhering condition Harclay calls a "real relation".

We can also ask, What are the truth conditions for sentences of the form '*R*-ness exists'? On the one hand, he has rejected an ontology of relations by which substitutions for '*R*-ness' name some extramental relative thing that inheres in a foundation. On the other hand, he does not have an ontology like Peter Aureoli in which sentences of this form are true only if there exists some being of reason.[47] Harclay insists repeatedly that real relations exist independent of the mind. Neither of these ontologies is his: "So a relation posits nothing in its foundation, and yet it is a thing not made by the intellect."[48]

Harclay explains his own view on the being of relation:

Now I say that 'relation' signifies only such conditions or concurrences and association. So a relation posits nothing in a foundation and, however, is a thing not made by the intellect. So I say that when a quality is alone, I call it "whiteness". When, however, there is another [quality of] whiteness with it in reality, the same is called "similarity". And whiteness no more differs from similarity than whiteness absolutely said differs from whiteness when it has a partner. And so that association is the relation.[49]

Here, Harclay is struggling to express the way relations exist. For Harclay, statements of the form '*R*-ness exist' are true if and only if there exists a mind-independent condition "in" (noninherence) one thing toward another. But although a real relation is not an extramental relative thing that inheres in its foundation, neither is it identical with its foundation.

Whiteness and similarity, however, are not the same, but rather radically different. For that condition of association and concurrence is of a nature different from whiteness. And I say that a relation has no stronger being than has that concurrence or association. And that association posits nothing in it [i.e., the subject], but only affirms a condition of it with respect to another.[50]

The foundation is of a nature different from the relation. For example, the former may be an inherent absolute accident, as whiteness, but the latter, the relation of color similarity, is only a condition of the white thing. Despite the difficulty in expression, Harclay's intuition is that a real relation has an extramental ontological status that is not reducible to that of absolute things. On the reality of relations, then, Harclay is representative of a broad middle way, adopting neither a strongly realist ontology like Duns Scotus nor a conceptualist ontology of relations as Peter Aureoli. And this theory of real relation provides an explanation of the extramental foundation for his confused and so universal concepts. "For from those things that are most distinct in reality and that are not one in any thing, still something common to them can be abstracted, for such things can be similar or agreeing; therefore one common concept on the part of the intellect is able to correspond to both."[51]

III. Conclusion

Harclay's conceptualism and his "relational account" of the unity of a universal allow him to posit an extramental world of only singular things, that is, things that are incommunicable—logically incapable of existing in, as constituents of, numerically many simultaneously. With such an ontology, one sees why Harclay felt no constraint to give a positive account of individuation. Having banished Scotus's common nature from his ontology along with any real unity less than numerical, he maintains that each thing posited extramentally by that fact is singular.

But it would be rash to see Harclay as positing a world of "radical individuals", ontological blocks devoid of further ontological distinction or composition. Harclay's treatment of the singular as "really one" or numerically identical in his question on universals is one side of a more complex doctrine that is emerging as more questions of Harclay are edited.

This is clear from two other questions: Harclay's fine-grained discussion of various types of formal identity and distinction when treating the Trinity, and his question on plurality of forms. In the first,[52] he distinguishes (at least in the Trinity) various grades of formal nonidentity within what is really numerically one, and so the profound influence of Scotus is seen even in Harclay's later teaching. In the second,[53] Harclay posits within "one singular thing", like a human, a plurality of substantial forms. Hence, in one way a human is made up of several beings; he even calls these substantial forms "individuals."[54] In another way the final form received completes the composite substance, giving it a certain unity, making it "one" and not many entities. As more of Harclay's questions are edited and compared, we find his teaching is more complex than expected. It is hoped that all of his questions will soon be edited so we can appreciate this complexity and discover more sides of this wide-ranging and surprising thinker.

Notes

1. For Henry of Harclay's life, works and an overview of his philosophy in his later Questions, see F. Pelster, "Heinrich von Harclay, Kanzler von Oxford und seine

Quästionen'', in *Miscellanea Francesco Ehrle* Im Studi e Testi 37 (Rome, 1924), pp. 307–356; A. B. Emden, *A Biographical Register of the University of Oxford to* A.D. *1500*, 3 vols. (Oxford, 1957–1959), vol. 2, pp. 874–875; and references to Harclay in ed. J. I. Catto, *The Early Oxford Schools* (Oxford, 1984).

2. The commentary is found in two codices: Vatican City, Vatican Library lat. 13687, fols. 13v–97v; and Casale Monferrato, Biblioteca del Seminario Vescovile b 2, fols. 1r–84r. See C. Balić, ''Henricus de Harcley et Ioannes Duns Scotus'', in *Mélanges offerts à Étienne Gilson* (Toronto and Paris, 1959), pp. 93–121, 701–702.

3. Most of these Questions are found in three codices: Vatican City, Vatican Library Borghese 171, fols. 1r–32v; Worcester, Cathedral Library F. 3, fols. 181v–215v; Assisi, Biblioteca Comunale 172, fols. 125r–31v, 133r–36r, 149r–53r.

4. Armand Maurer has edited a number of Harclay's later Questions and has helped uncover Harclay's doctrine on a number of issues; see Henry of Harclay, ''Henry of Harclay's Question on the Univocity of Being'', *Mediaeval Studies* 16 (1954): 1–18; ''Henry of Harclay's Questions on Immortality'', *ibid.* 19 (1957): 79–107; ''Henry of Harclay's Questions on the Divine Ideas'', *ibid.* 23 (1961): 163–193; and ''Henry of Harclay's Disputed Question on the Plurality of Forms'', in *Essays in Honor of Anton Charles Pegis*, ed. J. Reginald O'Donnell (Toronto, 1974), pp. 125–159. I have edited three Questions: ''Henry of Harclay's Questions on Divine Prescience and Predestination'', *Franciscan Studies* 40 (1980): 167–243; ''Henry of Harclay on the Formal Distinction in the Trinity'', *Franciscan Studies* 41 (1981): 250–335; ''Henry of Harclay's Question on Relations: An Edition'', *Medieval Studies* 49 (1987): 76–123. See also Harclay's question on universals edited by G. Gál, ''Henricus de Harclay: Quaestio de significato conceptus universalis'', *Franciscan Studies* 31 (1971): 178–234.

5. See John E. Murdoch, ''Henry of Harclay and the Infinite'', *Studi sul XIV secolo in memoria di Anneliese Maier,* ed. A. Maierù and A. Paravicini Bagliani, Storia e Letteratura 151 (Rome, 1981), pp. 219–261; Richard C. Dales, ''Henricus de Harclay. Quaestio 'Utrum mundus potuit fuisse ab eterno' '', *Archives d'histoire doctrinale et littéraire du Moyen Age* 50 (1983): 223–255; ''Henry of Harclay and the Infinite'', *Journal of the History of Ideas* 45 (1984): 295–301.

6. Henry of Harclay, ''Conceptus Universalis'', p. 211, n. 68.

7. Henry of Harclay, ''Immortality'', pp. 85 and 94, n. 3.

8. *Ibid.*, pp. 99–103, nn. 33–49.

9. *Ibid.*, p. 99, n. 33.

10. *Ibid.*, pp. 99–100, nn. 33–34.

11. *Ibid.*, p. 100, n. 35.

12. Hervaeus Natalis, *Quodl.* VIII, q. 4: "[Utrum] Deus possit facere duas a-nimas solo numero differentes non infundendo eas corporibus" (Venice, 1513), fols. 149va–b; *Quodl.* III, q. 9, fol. 82rb.

13. As also Hervaeus, *Quodl.* III, q. 9, fol. 82rb.

14. Harclay, "Immortality", p. 100, n. 36; Hervaeus *Quodl.* III, q. 9, fol. 82rb.

15. Harclay, "Immortality", pp. 102–103, nn. 46–49.

16. *Ibid.*, p. 101, n. 41.

17. *Ibid.*, pp. 79–85, 89–94, nn. 1–24.

18. *Ibid.*, p. 101, n. 41.

19. *Ibid.*

20. See Marilyn McCord Adams, "Universals in the Early Fourteenth Century", in *The Cambridge History of Later Medieval Philosophy,* ed. Norman Kretzmann, Anthony Kenny, and Jan Pinborg (Cambridge, 1982), pp. 411–439; see n. 43, p. 423.

21. Harclay, "Conceptus Universalis", 197–201, nn. 41–49.

22. *Ibid.*, pp. 196–197, n. 40.

23. *Ibid.*, p. 196, n. 40.

24. For more on Burley and Harclay, along with Ockham, see Adams, "Universals", pp. 422–434.

25. Harclay, "Conceptus Universalis", p. 211, n. 67. For a study of Harclay's theory of universals, see J. Kraus, "Die Universalienlehre des Oxforder Kanzlers Heinrich von Harclay und ihre Mittelstellung zwischen skotistischem Realismus und ockhamistischem Nominalismus", *Divus Thomas* (Freiburg) 10 (1932): 36–58, 475–508; 11 (1933): 76–96, 288–314.

26. Harclay, "Conceptus Universalis", p. 211, n. 67: "Tamen ego [dico] quod singularitas [et] etiam incommunicabilitas est proprietas rei exsistentis extra, eam necessario consequens, sive posterius natura sive simul vel prius, non curo."

27. *Ibid.*, n. 68.

28. *Ibid.*, p. 214, n. 73.

29. *Ibid.*, n. 74.

30. *Ibid.*, n. 73.

31. *Ibid.*, p. 212, n. 70.

32. *Ibid.*, p. 212–215, nn. 71–77.

33. *Ibid.*, p. 215–216, n. 78.

34. William of Ockham, *Ordinatio* I, 31, in *Opera theologica,* vol. 4 (St. Bonaventure, NY, 1979), pp. 400:4–402:19.

35. Henry of Harclay, "Conceptus Universalis", p. 216, n. 78; also pp. 221–222, nn. 92–93.

36. Henry of Harclay, "Utrum Deo et creaturis aliquid sit commune univocum": "dico quod necesse est quod sit convenientia ex natura rei inter illa a quibus formatur unus conceptus, sed non est necesse quod sint magis unum ex natura rei quam alia, immo nec aliquo modo unum nec minus nec magis. Ratio istius est: nam convenientia et unitas sunt primo diversa; ideo maior convenientia numquam facit maiorem unitatem, etiamsi convenientia cresceret in infinitum; nam semper convenientia supponit distinctionem, sed unitas contrariatur distinctioni." (Vat. Borgh. 171, fol. 2vb).

37. Harclay, "Conceptus Universalis", p. 227, n. 103. See also his "Utrum Deo et creaturis": "Dico ad illud quod communitati conceptus non necessario correspondet communitas in re, sed ab eadem re simplici omnino accipitur conceptus communis et confusus vel non differens et conceptus distinctivus et magis particularis. . . . non sequitur quod distinctis conceptibus distinctae res correspondeant, quia distinctio in posteriori non arguit distinctionem in priori, nec distinctio in effectu arguit distinctionem in causa aequivoca. Ideo non sequitur quod aliqua sit communis res." (Vat. Borgh. 171, fol. 2ra).

38. "Utrum Deo et creaturis": "quando aliquis effectus essentialiter dependet ex duabus causis, facta variatione in altera illarum causarum etiam alia non variata, sequitur tamen variatio effectus. Sed conceptus noster dependet ab obiecto similiter et ab intellectu. . . . Ergo altera causa, puta obiecto, omnino non variato, propter variam dispositionem in intellectu cognoscente, erit conceptus alius causatus." (Vat. Borgh. 171, fol. 2rb).

39. Harclay, "Conceptus Universalis", p. 216, n. 79.

40. *Ibid.*, p. 218, n. 83.

41. For criticisms of Harclay on this point by Ockham and Burley, see note 24.

42. Harclay, "Conceptus Universalis", pp. 225–227, nn. 101–103.

43. References to Harclay's question on relation are according to paragraph numbers used in my edition, "Henry of Harclay's Question on Relation: An Edition", pp. 76–123. For more on medieval theories of relation, see my *Relations: Medieval Theories 1250–1325* (Oxford, 1989).

44. In what follows, I confine my remarks to a comparison of Scotus and Harclay regarding categorical relations, not transcendental relations.

45. For John Duns Scotus's teaching on relation, see *Ordinatio* II, 1, 4–5, in *Opera omnia,* vol. 7 (Vatican City, 1973), pp. 91–146; *Ordinatio* I, 30, 1–2, in *Opera omnia,* vol. 6 (Vatican City, 1963), pp. 169–202.

46. Harclay, "Relation", n. 51.

47. For Peter Aureoli's doctrine of relations, see the first book of his *Sentences* commentary (Vatican City, Borghese 329, fols. 317v–345v); I *Sent.*, 30–31 (Rome, 1596), fols. 659–718. Also see Mark Henninger, "Peter Aureoli and William of Ockham on Relations", *Franciscan Studies* 45 (1985): 231–243.

48. Harclay, "Relation", n. 52: "Ideo relatio in fundamento nihil ponit, et tamen est res non facta ab intellectu."

49. *Ibid.*, "Modo ego dico quod 'relatio' tantum significat huiusmodi habitudines vel simultates et societatem. Ideo relatio in fundamento nihil ponit, et tamen est res non facta ab intellectu. Tunc dico quod cum qualitate est sola, voco eam 'albedinem'; cum autem alia albedo est secum in rerum natura, eadem vocatur 'similitudo'. Et non plus differt albedo a similitudine quam differt albedo absolute dicta ab albedine quando habet sociam. Unde societas illa relatio est."

50. *Ibid.*, "Non tamen [sunt] albedo et similitudo eadem, immo primo diversa. Nam illa conditio societatis et simultatis est alterius naturae ab albedine. Et dico quod relatio non habet fortius esse quam habet illa simultas vel societas. Et societas illa nihil ponit in eo, sed tantum dicit habitudinem eius ad alterum."

51. Harclay, "Conceptus Universalis": "Ab illis [enim] quae sunt ultima distinctiva in re, [et] quae non sunt unum in aliqua re, nihilominus potest abstrahi aliquod commune eis, quia talia possunt esse similia vel convenientia, ideo unus conceptus communis potest correspondere utrique a parte intellectus." p. 221, n. 92.

52. Henry of Harclay, "Formal Distinction".

53. Henry of Harclay, "Plurality of Forms".

54. *Ibid.*, p. 153, n. 5. See also Armand Maurer, "St. Thomas and Henry of Harclay on Created Nature", in *III Congresso internazionale de filosofia medievale* (Milano, 1966), pp. 542–549.

16

WALTER BURLEY
(B. CA. 1275; D. 1344 OR LATER)

IVAN BOH

Known to the schoolmen as *"doctor amoenus"* or *"doctor planus et perspicuus,"* Walter Burley is recognized as one of the central philosophical figures of the first half of the fourteenth century.[1] His studies and his philosophical activities took place in Oxford and Paris, he conducted disputed questions in Toulouse and Bologna, and he performed diplomatic duties at the papal court in Avignon on behalf of King Edward III. He wrote extensively on logic and natural philosophy as well as on theology, ethics, and political theory. He is also remembered for his *De vita et moribus philosophorum*.

Burley has been characterized variously as a Thomist, as a Scotist and as an Averroist. However, such characterizations are mostly not useful and may indeed be misleading. Strains of his thought could be so characterized, but his philosophical corpus is too varied and the length of his philosophic activity so stretched out that one is not always able to determine what his own position is when he comments on Aristotle or on the Commentator; and it is not impossible that some of his views on a given problem changed or that in the course of time even his general philosophical outlook was modified. He finds himself among the upholders of basic traditional positions as one of the *antiqui*, he argues vigorously for his own views and at the same time attacks both the positions and the arguments of the opponents to whom he sometimes refers as *"moderni"*, and sometimes simply as *"aliqui"*.

The prime sources for the discussion of Burley's basic ontology in general and Burley's notion of individual in particular are the following: *Tractatus de formis*, *Tractatus de materia et forma*, the first book of *In physicam*, and the first two books of the *Super artem veterem*, that is, the commentaries on Porphyry's *Isagoge* and Aristotle's *Predicamenta*. Although Burley must have written a *Sentence Commentary* for his masters degree in theology, it is generally thought by biographers and historians that the work has definitely been lost, and we are thus deprived of discussions of the nature of the individual peculiar to such a context. Moreover, although Burley wrote many *opuscula* and *notulae* on various philosophical topics, he did not leave us with any special tract dealing specifically with the individual or individuation. Yet, in the major works, all of them philosophical, Burley said enough on the subject to enable us to make a historically reliable reconstruction of his notion of "individual" within the framework of his general ontology.[2]

There are six sections to my chapter. In Section I, I present the central ideas of Burley's metaphysics and Burley's defense of an ontological realism. Section II examines the contrasting features of Burley's individuals and universals. Section III offers a discussion of the inner components of Burley's individual and suggests a complex principle of individuation. In Section IV, Burley's examination of an alternative conception of individual is given. Section V raises the question of our intellectual cognition of individuals. Finally, Section VI is a fairly detailed summary of the findings.

I. Act-Potentiality and Form-Matter Dichotomies

There are two leading ideas in Burley's thought on what-there-is. One is the idea that everything other than God falls within the dichotomy of actual and potential being. The form-matter dichotomy is a specific case most readily encountered in our world of generation and corruption of the act-potentiality dichotomy. Because of its direct application in our philosophical accounts of the world of our experience, Burley is preoccupied with the form-matter composition of things, keeping the all-pervasive distinction between act and potency in the background and bringing it into play primarily when reference is made to pure substances.

The other leading idea in Burley's ontology is expressed by the claim that reality consists of two radically different kinds of things (*res*) really distinct from, and irreducible to, one another; that is, particulars, individuals, or singulars (Burley uses the three terms interchangeably) and universals.

Let us look briefly at the two leading ideas. With regard to the first one, Burley takes it for granted that the things present in our experience are composed of matter and form(s) and that they can change, that is, they can assume different forms. Things are always of a given kind, but given suitable causes, they *can* be different in some respect or other. To ensure an adequate conceptual apparatus for dealing properly with potentiality and for avoiding conceptual confusion Burley points out that there are two kinds of potency or potentiality: the subjective potency (*potentia subiectiva*) "which is a potentiality to form," and the objective potency (*potentia obiectiva*) "which is potentiality to existence (*potentia ad existere*)''. He says that the former is ''a principle of being'' whereas he conceives of the latter as a pure possibility. He illustrates the distinction as follows:

> We should beware that potentiality . . . is of two sorts, namely, the potentiality which is the principle of being, and this is called subjective potentiality; the other is the objective . . . potentiality. The way in which the Antichrist is in potentiality is different from the way in which silver is in potentiality to the form of money-coin. For the Antichrist is in potentiality in that he does not exist but could exist. Silver, on the other hand, exists in act and is only in potentiality to receive [forms]. And so the Antichrist is in objective potentiality and silver is in subjective potentiality. Hence, the objective potentiality is a potentiality to existence, and the subjective potentiality is a potentiality to form.[3]

With regard to the matter-form dichotomy, he is especially interested in explaining the difference between primary and secondary matter. In the *De formis* he describes primary matter as ''the matter most remote in any thing composed of it'', and he offers a very instructive argument for the necessity of such pure matter in any hylomorphic composite:

> Primary matter is that matter which is not reducible into matter and form, but is completely simple because it lacks all forms by its own nature and by its own substance, so that it, in its intrinsic nature, does not include any form, even though it is never without some form or other. Now in every composite of matter and form one must arrive at such matter that is completely simple and not reducible into matter and form, as can be illustrated by examining any thing. For example, money is something composed of artificial form and of silver as its matter. I then inquire: Either silver is simple matter or else it is a composite of matter and form. If it were completely simple, then it would be primary matter, and this is false. If it be composed of matter and form, then I inquire about its matter: whether it is completely simple in its nature or is a composite. If it be completely simple, then it is primary matter, and we have what was claimed, namely, that in money there is a matter that is absolutely first. But if the matter of silver is composed of matter and form, we must inquire about its matter in the same manner as before, and thus fall into an infinite regress as in the first case, which is troublesome; or else one finally arrives at a matter which is completely simple and which is not reducible in matter and form, and this is the primary matter. And in this manner one may argue about any other

thing which is composed of matter and form and thus prove that there is primary matter in it.[4]

Burley's acceptance of a hylomorphic composition in things may have been motivated by the search for an explanation of change in natural things; but his present argument for the reality of prime matter is independent of any consideration of change and depends basically on the presumed experiential datum that things of our experience are as a matter of fact not simple but composite.

For purposes of this chapter it is worthwhile to note that Burley explicitly characterizes matter as being-in-subjective potentiality (*ens in potentia subiectiva*). This is true of all matter, be it simple or composite. But "prime matter", he says, "is pure subjective potentiality, because it has no form in its nature, while composite matter is not a pure subjective potentiality, because it contains in its nature a form, as is clear from silver and wood."[5]

We will see that matter, or the material side of composite things, also serves as a principle, or a coprinciple, of the *numerical diversity* of things that are specifically the same. To understand the role of the "material side" of composite things in individuation or in grounding of numerical diversity, we should observe a few further claims about "prime matter". One claim about such matter is that it is "numerically one in all generable and corruptible things". Burley does not deny this, but he adds a caveat to this characterization, saying that "it should not be understood to mean that numerically the same matter is simultaneously in all generable and corruptible things". For if it were understood literally in that sense, then the same matter would be under contrary forms, such as the form of fire and water at the same time, and this is inadmissible.[6]

Burley also has a positive understanding of how one could legitimately say that matter is one and numerically the same in all things. The sense in which this is true is "that numerically the same matter is *successively* in all generable and corruptible things according to the species". Thus numerically the same matter that now is under the form of man will be, successively, under the forms, say, of cadaver, earth, herb, or water, and so on, "in a circle". But, although prime matter is in different places and at different moments of time, it is "of the same nature in all such things because it is simple and in no way reducible into matter and form".[7]

The correlative of matter is form, and this is either substantial or accidental. The former is immediately perfective of prime matter, the latter is immditaly perfective of composite matter. That is, in the language of act and potentiality, the substantial form comes to pure subjective potentiality, which is a principle of being, while the accidental form comes to composite subjective potentiality which is the potential subject of further actualization.

Burley does not hesitate to use figurative language to bring out the difference between the substantial and accidental "informing". He creates a picture of a man dressed in a shirt, with tunic and other pieces of clothing added, suggesting a comparison between the first piece of clothing, the shirt, to the substantial form informing the primary matter, and the additional pieces of clothing to accidental form. However, he is careful to point out that the comparison is very imperfect, because the primary matter receives *simultaneously* all three, the substantial form, the quantity, and the quality, whereas the pieces of clothing are envisioned to be added *successively*.[8]

II. Individuals and Universals

The intelligible structure of reality and the basic bifurcation of things (*res*) into individuals and universals is reflected in the Porphyrian Tree. Burley's view of this intelligible structure is laid out in his commentary on Porphyry's *Isagoge*, and he implicitly presupposes Porphyry's scheme in his commentaries on Aristotle's *Predicaments* (or *Categories*) and on *Physics*, as well as in his *De formis, De materia et forma*, and other works. The tree in question is of course the division of the supreme genus of substance by way of *differentiae* down to the species ("man") and then proceeding without any special warning to individuals ("Socrates", "Plato") under the species ("man"). The impression is thereby created that individuals are related to the species much in the way in which species are related to their genera, that is, by way of difference. The name for this relation frequently mentioned by Burley is "containment", but Porphyry's own statement of the difference between individuals on the one hand and the species and genera on the other, is in terms of predication. "A species", Porphyry says, "is predicated (*predicatur*) of the individual, whereas a genus is predicated of both the species as well as of individuals. . . . The individual, however, is predicated (*dicitur*) of only one particular thing (*de uno particulari*). Now things that are said to be individuals are Socrates and this white thing and this approaching person, and the son of Sophroniscus, provided that Socrates is the only son".[9]

Burley does not seem to dispute Porphyry's characterization. He "interprets" Porphyry as claiming that "an individual is predicated (*predicatur*) of one thing only, namely, of himself, because it does not have anything inferior to itself of which it could be predicated".[10] At least verbally, he still thinks of 'Socrates' as a predicate rather than as a proper name or, at any rate, as a referring expression. But, whereas Porphyry's text, in which '*predicatur*' is used in connection with general terms and '*dicitur*' is used in connection with individual terms, still leaves a possibility of interpreting that Porphyry wished thereby to distinguish the radical difference between predicating a general term of something and using a singular term (*individuum*) for naming or referring to a thing; Burley's passage, in which *'predicatur'* is explicitly used in conjunction with singular terms, would seem to preclude such a possibility. However, Burley goes on to explain the ambiguity of the word 'individual', showing his effort to keep straight various language levels:

> We must know that this name 'individual' can be taken for that which it *signifies* (*significat*), and in this sense it is predicated of many; for Socrates is an individual, and Plato is an individual; or else it could be taken for that which it *names* (*denominat*), and it is in this sense that the author [Porphyry] speaks here. For it is "Socrates" that this name 'individual' names (*denominat*) as 'individual' is taken for what it names, and 'Socrates' is predicated properly of only one thing, namely, of himself.[11]

Burley's clarification of Porphyry's text is helpful, but the characterization of the relationship between individual and general categorial terms is still misleading. What the text just quoted seems to be saying is this. The term 'individual' has two functions, a significative function and a naming (or denominative) function. That is, we can take 'individual' to signify many things—individuals such as Socrates, this man, and so on— and in this sense it is predicated of many, so that 'Socrates is an individual', 'Plato is an individual', and so forth, are perfectly significant sentences. But we can also take 'individual' for what it names (*denominat*), that is, for proper names and other referring expressions of things: for 'Socrates', 'this man', and so on. It is these that are predicated on one thing only; that is, individuals (e.g., 'Socrates') are predicated of one thing only (in this case, of Socrates). The idea of singular terms such as 'Socrates' being predicated seems inappropriate to us, but what we eventually find in subsequent discussions by Burley may make his position less offensive than it looks.

As already mentioned, the relation between species and their genera and of these to higher genera all the way to the *genus specialissimum* was characterized by Burley in one place as one of "containment":

> Individuals are contained (*continentur*) in a species, and species in a genus. This is clear from the ordering in the predicamental line, and it is proved thus. Every part is contained in its whole; but an individual is a part of the species, and a species is a part of the genus, therefore an individual is contained in a species and the species in a genus. The author [Porphyry] adds that an individual is a part and the species is a part and a whole, but this is so in relation to different things. For species is a part with respect to a genus and it is a whole with respect to an individual.[12]

The idea of "containment" employed here seems to be based on the extensional interpretation of general terms. We may indeed find it plausible to say that (the class of) man is a part of (the class of) animal, but we do not normally say that Socrates is a part of (the class of) man. Burley, it seems, while not objecting to the way of speaking about individuals being parts of wholes, finds it necessary to clarify his position as follows:

> We must understand that *an individual is a subjective part of the species,* because species is predicated of an individual directly (*in recto*). And for the same reason a species is a subjective part of the genus, because genus is predicated directly of the species. Now there is this difference between an integral part and a subjective part, namely that of an integral part it is inappropriate to predicate its whole (*suum totum*) directly, but only obliquely. For a hand or a head are integral parts of man because they make up (*integrant*) a man, and therefore this proposition is false, 'A hand or a head is a man'.[13]

We are still troubled with the analysis that claims the species to be a part of the genus. For it seems that Burley had just offered the following analysis: '(The individual) Socrates is a part of (species) man' means "Socrates $\in$ man", and, if this is so, then '(The species) man is (genus) animal' ought to mean "Man $\in$ animal". However, although the genus "animal" is of a greater extension than the species "man", it is not on a higher language level and thus 'Man $\in$ animal' is not a well-formed sentence at all.

Perhaps we should look at his position on this problem differently and say that the second-intentional predicate 'genus' has as its extension members that are species; and in this sense a genus is of a higher language level than the species. However, if we take this route of interpretation, then the argument (A) 'Socrates is a man, man is an animal, therefore Socrates is an animal' [$s \in M, M \in \alpha \therefore s \in \alpha$] fails to hold. But if we envisage an explication of the species-genus hierarchy in terms of class inclusion only, saying that the relationship between, say, man and animal is properly depicted by Man $\subset$ Animal, then the argument (A) becomes a valid argument, given the fact that Man $\subset$ Animal and all species-genus relations are analyzable without residue into universally quantified structures of the form $\forall x \, (x \in M \supset x \in A)$.

Should we suggest that Burley was right when he employed only one relation, that is, either that of *being a part of* or that of *being contained in*, going from individuals through species and genera to the supreme genus? Or that he needed not to worry about the peculiar relation between individuals and species?

Perhaps if we were not concerned with ontology but with pure logic, we might borrow some formal relation from mereology, divest it of any connection with ontology, and safeguard the inferences such as (A) previously without distinguishing radically between individuals and universals. However, Burley is just too much concerned with an ontology that takes both individuals and universals seriously, and we would do him injustice if we tried to oversimplify the problem. Burley obviously recognized the need for an ontological grounding of both, numerical diversity and specific sameness. One does get the impression that he is more concerned with establishing the reality of universals than with elucidating the singular, but this is so only because he was on the offensive against the "*moderni*", who claimed that only singulars exist and that, therefore, the whole question of individuation is simply misplaced.

Burley was no less impressed than Ockham with *the fact* of the world of individual substances, and as a philosopher he does not start with ontological entities, universals, trying to "contract" them to individuals. Of course, he also does not start with some metaphysical bare particular, trying to dress it up with natures and properties. Both universals and prime matter are entities inferred to "account for" what is given to us in experience, although Burley could conceivably argue that there is a sense in which we are *presented with* universals in which we are never presented with primary matter. Burley exhibits a robust sense of reality, and in the course of the critique of a view that he found incoherent or otherwise defective he comes to offer several interesting arguments for the reality of nonsingular entities. Let us take a look at one of them for the sake of illustration:

> Even if no intellect existed, two stones would nevertheless agree (*convenirent*) more with one another than a stone and a donkey. But all agreement is in virtue of some one thing (*aliquo uno*). . . . Therefore there is some one common thing outside the soul in which two stones agree and in which a stone and a donkey do not agree. This is confirmed, for whatever things are really compared in some one thing, they are compared according to *more* or *less,* or according to *equal.* For if *a* and *b* are compared one with the other according to more or less, they are not compared in virtue of that which belongs to *a* only, nor in virtue of that which belongs to *b* only, but in virtue of something which belongs to both. For example, if *a* is whiter than *b,* then *a* and *b* are not compared by the whiteness of *a* itself, nor of *b* itself. For this [proposition] is false, '*a* is whiter by the whiteness of *a* itself than *b* by the whiteness of *a* itself'. This [proposition] is likewise false, '*b* is less white by the whiteness of *a* itself than *b* by the whiteness of *b*'; it is therefore necessary that that by which they are compared belong to both. But nothing singular belongs to both; therefore there is some universal in which those things are really compared one with the other.[14]

In view of Section III, to follow, it may be observed that Burley uses 'individual' and 'singular' interchangeably, almost as a mere stylistic device. Nor does he here speculate on the *nature* of the universal or on its relation to singulars within the species. All that we learn about it is that it is an entity that belongs to all singulars that agree (*conveniunt*) in a certain respect with one another. The universal is precisely the "material" foundation for this "respect" in which singulars agree with one another. The argument is reductive in that it tells us what kinds of constituents there must be in the nature of things independent of our minds if we are to understand that which we commonsensically take for granted.

Although we are not directly concerned here with universals, we can learn some very important facts about individuals from Burley's characterization of the relation between universals and individuals. Consider the following objection to Burley's realism and then his reply:

> Let Socrates be *a* and the universal man *b;* then *a* and *b* agree (*conveniunt*) in that *a* and *b* are two men; therefore *a* and *b* agree in human nature with them, and this nature common to them is a thing other than the things to which it is common. . . . Let therefore that third nature be *c,* and then *a, b,* and *c* are three men, and therefore they really agree in a common human nature. Let that nature be *d.* And thus there is a progression *in infinitum* in the realm of *in-quid* predicates, and also there will be an infinite number of men.[15]

Burley's reply to this objection rests on the most basic feature of his universals and particulars, which the objector seems not to have understood, since he says of universals the same sorts of things as he says of particulars, and conversely. Burley insists that "if it be posited that the universal is a thing other than singulars, then we must say that if *a* signifies an individual, say Socrates, and *b* signifies the species man, then this proposition '*a* and *b* are two men' is false". Adopting the language of Gilbert Ryle and his twentieth century Oxford colleagues, the fourteenth century Oxford philosopher Burley might have charged the objector with having commited a categorial fallacy, that is, a mistake of misplaced predicates, saying of species (or of universals) the sorts of things that can properly be said of individuals only or conversely. Medievals were generally aware of the problem and adopted the rule expressed by the motto *'Talia sunt subiecta qualia sunt predicata'* and its variants.

But Burley says something else that throws light on his conception of fundamental ontological ties, such as the one holding between a singular and a universal:

It is not true that *a* and *b* agree in human nature as a third entity different from those two; rather, one of those is contained under the other, as *a* under *b*, as an individual under a species. But *a* and *b* do not agree in virtue of some third, most specialized species, common to the two of them, because then one of them would be the most specialized species of the other.[16]

Reflecting on this passage we can certainly say that Burley does not consider the relation between an individual, *a*, and a species, *F*, to be a predicamental or descriptive relation represented by *R(a,F)*. This is so because of the radically different ontological status of *a* and *F*. One might wish that Burley had chosen some technical term such as 'exemplification' to stress the difference between such ontological relations and the empirical ones. We might also wish that he had used two sorts of variables and not just one; that is, the lower-case letters *a* and *b* to represent singulars and universals. In any case, we will use both the capital letters and the lower-case letters to represent universals and particulars, respectively. The word he uses to express the relation between *a* and *F* is 'containment'. The idea suggests asymmetry, so that the order counts: It is *a* that is contained under *F* and not the converse. Interestingly, Burley cashes out the idea of this ontological containment in terms of the logical idea of "an individual being under a species". This works quite well for sortal or substantival universals, that is, for cases such as '*a* is a man', but less so for cases such as '*a* is white'.

From another objection to Burley's ontological realism we can learn that although each of Burley's individuals has a specific nature, that nature is not literally a part of individuals: For Burley, there is a real distinction between an individual and its nature.

The objection is as follows: God could not annihilate Socrates without annihilating all men. For "annihilation is a destruction of something with respect to all things that are in it". Therefore, to destroy Socrates God would have to destroy the specific nature of man that is in Socrates; but he could not destroy the specific nature of man without destroying all men along with Socrates.

Burley's denial of this inference rests on his insistence that an individual's species (or nature) is not a *part* of the individual. For particular effects, he says, have particular causes, while universal effects have universal causes, and Socrates is "a particular effect that is composed of none but particular causes, that is, out of *this* matter and *this* form".[17]

This is perhaps an interesting reply to the objection, but we would now like to make sense of it. It is time to attempt to find those few texts that relate more directly to the question of the nature of individual and the ontological ground of individuality. Our next section serves precisely that purpose.

III. The Structure of Individuals

For Burley, individuals are primary substances. These are structured of matter and form. It seems safe to say that Burley acknowledges only one specific or substantial form in any given individual, even though he seems to have been very impressed with the Averroistic plurality-of-form doctrine and went occasionally to such length in his presentation of that view that we could legitimately wonder whether he is speaking only as an impartial historian of philosophy or as a convert to the doctrine, finding it better than its chief competitor, the unicity-of-form view.[18] This is true especially of some passages in his *De formis.* Only the form of corporeity still hovers in the air when he briefly considers the theological case of death and resurrection of Christ.

As was already observed in Section I, the initial motivation for the dichotomy between matter and form probably came from considerations of radical change in material substances, especially of organic substances. Burley himself, of course, took the doctrine from the ancient tradition and did not find it necessary to argue for the dichotomy on the level of physics. He is concerned with the metaphysical issues regarding the essential structure of individuals on the level at which we recognize that we may not equate the particular substantial form with the essence of the hylomorphic composite as a whole.

As a good dialectician, Burley first makes a useful distinction when he considers a difficulty raised by an objector against Boethius's claim that "the species expresses the whole essence of the individual". The objection, briefly, is this: The essence of the individual is the matter and form of the individual, while the most specialized species expresses neither matter nor form; therefore the most specialized species does not express the whole essence of the individual. To meet this objection, Burley points out that by 'essence' we may understand two things, viz., *the form expressing the essence,* or *the form perfecting matter,* and then goes on to explain that every essential predicate is a form expressing the essence of the individual. And, if we understand by 'essence' the essential predicate, then the most specialized species expresses the whole essence of its individual, for species is an essential predicate with respect to the individual that includes all other essential predicates. But if essence is taken from the form that perfects matter, then species does not express the whole essence of the individual.[19]

When Burley says that "every essential predicate is a form expressing the essence of the individual", he has in mind all the substantial genera above the species; for all of them can be predicated *in quid* of any individual falling under that species. By insisting that only essential predication expresses a part or the whole of the essence of an individual, Burley definitely does not intend to equate "individual essence" with "quiddity" of the sort that absorbs both substantial constituents as well as the objects of the *in quale* predications. An individual is not simply a collection of essential and accidental properties.

It is important to note both, Burley's statement that "second substances are universals" and also that "universals are *in* their singulars". This is quite in line with his conviction that universals are entities of their own kind, *really* distinct from singulars; but they are *in* singulars, they are not separate. We could put it succinctly thus: *For every universal (or form) F, there is some individual x, such that F informs x (or such that x has F)*, or more briefly in a symbolic formula: $(\forall F)(\exists x)Fx$. We could agree to call this the "First Principle of Exemplification." The second, related principle could also be formulated in the spirit of Burley's texts; that is, *For every particular or individual x, there is some form F, such that x is informed by F (or such that x has F)*, or more briefly, $(\forall x)(\exists F)Fx$. Again, we might agree to call this the "Second Principle of Exemplification." This latter specifically ensures that every singular is "natured"; there are no "bare particulars" in Burley's ontology. The range of variables extends to universals (i.e., things that can be literally simultaneously in many numerically distinct things; second substances) and individuals (normally, hylomorphically structured first substances). Of course, the range of x may be things (*res*) in the transcendental sense. But if these are to be principles, Burley must have thought of them as universal, necessary, and informative of the structure of our world.

Burley's idea on the basic composition of singulars comes out quite clearly in his commentary on *Predicamenta*, where he says:

> It must be pointed out that only singular substance is not composed of universals but only of singulars; for Socrates is composed only of *this* matter and *this* form, and he is not composed of genera and the difference that are predicable *in quid* of him. On the other hand, the genus substance is composed of the genus and difference and of all genera superior to it. The reason for this is that of a particular effect there are particular causes, and of a universal effect there are universal causes.[20]

Since a singular substance is not composed of universals, Burley was able—as we already saw in Section II—quickly to refute the objection that God could not destroy Socrates without destroying the whole human species, indeed, everything under the supreme genus of substance. He points out that "annihilation is a destruction of a thing with respect to all things that are proper to it, not of all things that are common to itself and to other things". To destroy Socrates, God needs to destroy this matter and this form (intellective soul) making up the individual, that is, Socrates; and no destruction of the human race is entailed by that act.[21]

There is, however, a great difficulty, perhaps insurmountable, with Burley's claim that an individual is composed out of *this* matter and *this* form. For we are interested precisely in the ontological grounding of individuality, in the ground for numerical diversity of specifically same things, and thus in the principle of individuation. We can, of course, appreciate Burley's argument (encountered in Section II) for the insurmountable difference between two ontological kinds of things, universals (which can be-in-many) and particulars (which cannot be-in-many). But the argument for that distinction was relevant to cases such as grounding numerical diversity of the specifically same individuals, Socrates and Plato, each of which is a man. Now we seem to go to the internal structure itself of Socrates and individuals in the familiar sense of Aristotelian primary substances. We have a mention of "individualized" matter and form in the description of the composition of Socrates; that is, Socrates is said to be composed of "this matter" and "this form". What could be meant by 'this' here? If 'this' is a numerical diversifier with the same function as it has in 'this man', then we have not advanced at all: We are left with the same question as we had before when we inquired into the grounds of the numerical diversity of two men, Socrates and Plato, except that we have now a further complication; namely, that the general terms 'matter' and 'form' are no longer terms from the category of substance but terms from the categories of quantity and quality, or possibly terms that are beyond categories and are in some sense transcendental inasmuch as they are closely linked with potentiality and actuality respectively.

If the use of 'this' in 'this matter' is not the same as in 'this man', then what is its function? Burley is not unaware that using numbers can be a sensitive issue,[22] and he does attempt in several places to distinguish between saying that Socrates and Plato are two things and saying that Socrates and man, or an individual and a universal, are two things. But, whereas there can be two instances of man, there can not be two universals *man* (*communis homo*). Can there be two instances of matter? The question becomes blurred when we lose sight of the fact that we are not asking whether there can be two pieces of matter (of a given kind), but rather two pieces of matter as such, unmixed with any form. What makes matter as such numerically distinct in Socrates so as to be *this* matter?

If we reflect on the long quotation in Section I on the nature of primary matter, we may try to reconstruct Burley's thought on such rock-bottom questions in the following way. Primary matter as such does not exist, that is, it has no subjective being; it is a thing, an entity, to which we come by logical analysis when we reflect on any hylomorphic composite we wish. Burley claims that this simple matter to which we are led by a method of intellectual resolution is in fact never without some form or other, even though it does not by its nature claim any particular form. Let the present form be that of man. But what makes the form *man* this form? It is the conjunction of the universal form *man* with matter that individualizes the universal. Strictly speaking, matter itself, in this basic sense of matter, need not be individualized, since without form it cannot exist and with form it automatically "contracts" form and thus receives its reality as mixed matter by way of form.

If this speculative interpretation suggests that in Burley's ontology forms are individuators, since without them matter simply does not exist, neither as primary (by definition) nor as secondary (which again by definition is informed matter), the suggestion is, I think, not completely out of order. But it would be much more accurate to say that *numerical differences are from both, form and matter;* for in the *De formis* Burley himself writes:

> Matter under one form is distinguished *by itself* (*per se*) *and not by form* from the matter which is under another form. The magisterial proposition that says that every distinction is from form is not universally true, but ought to be interpreted thus: Every *specific* distinction is from form. . . . But the distinction of individuals under a species is *as much from matter as it is from form,* and also from accidents. For example, Socrates is distinguished materially by his matter from Plato with an individual distinction, and formally by his form, and accidentally by his accidents.[23]

The last statement is especially revealing of Burley's empirical and holistic approach. He starts with an individual that is fully composed of matter and form and that must have some accidents or others. Accidents themselves can be said to be proper to that individual in the sense that they, as such, are "parts" of this individual and no other: The whiteness of Socrates is not the whiteness of Plato. For this reason one could consider these accidents as being on the side of what cannot be ontologically shared, that is, on the side of individuality. However, if they are "individuators"—and Burley certainly thinks they are, just as much as matter and form—they are so only simultaneously with the form and the matter of the individual of which they are "parts". Moreover, it may be their collection as a whole that becomes important when we raise the question of the discernibility of similars.

IV. An Alternative View of Individuals

At one point in his commentary on Porphyry's *Isagoge*, Burley was considering another conception of individual, that is, the view that "an individual consists of many accidents whose collection cannot be found together in another individual''.[24] Among the properties constituting individuals Burley first lists four—quality, figure, place, and time—but then expands the list to seven. He refers to these as *proprietates individuales,* which we should probably not translate as "individual properties" but rather as "individuating properties". The claim is made that these properties occur in all individuals of a given species and that *as a collection* they are not recurrent. On the other hand, the properties of species are found simultaneously in all individuals of the same species, for example, capable of laughing, capable of learning, and the like, which are properties of the human species.

It is interesting to observe that among the properties of individuals we find two sorts: some seem to be "essential" to individuals, making up *the spatio-temporal framework* for that individual of a given kind to have properties; others are quasi-essential in that they are pervasive to the members of the same species, but seem to be resultant properties of individuals understood as actual things of a given kind. What makes the clusters of individualizing properties *unrepeatable* is the essential individuating set, the spatio-temporal framework.

As a sort of epilogue to this discussion of the individual conceived as a collection of observable qualities and properties Burley makes some remarks on the diversity of individuals that are surprisingly similar to those from the *De formis* which we encountered just two paragraphs earlier:

> We should also understand that one individual substance is not distinguished from another by accidental properties of this sort only; rather, it is distinguished *formally* through its form and matter. Thus, Socrates is distinguished from Plato accidentally by its accidents, formally by its form, and materially by its matter, and it is in reality (*secundum veritatem*) [and not only in our cognition] that an individual substance is distinguished from another by properties of this sort.[25]

I think that this consideration of "individual-as-a-collection" is gnoseological and not ontological, and we might call this pronouncement Burley's "*Principle of Distinguishing Numerical Plurality.*" It is not a simple principle and it mentions the *formal* element first as a principle of distinguishing one individual object from another, although it also mentions the material principle almost in the same breath. Burley's ontology may well be construed as recapitulating his gnoseology, recognizing that the Principle of Individuation invokes a conjunction of two (or more) principles, and not either one of them singly, as grounds of numerical diversity.

V. Intellectual Cognition of Singulars

In the first book of his *Posterior Analytics* (87 b 38–39) Aristotle made the famous pronouncement that the intellect is concerned with universals and that the senses are concerned with singulars. Medieval commentators faithfully reminded themselves of that statement and tried to respect it. Burley is no exception. Having argued for a direct intellectual cognition of singulars, he finds it necessary to square himself with the tradition that held a different view on the matter, basing itself on the authority of the ancients. Burley writes: "But there is a doubt about this, because the Philosopher in the first book of his *Posterior Analytics* says that the intellect is concerned with universals and the sense is concerned with singulars. It thus appears that our intellect does not know anything but universals."[26] He notes that Boethius made a similar remark.

Burley did not want to appear antagonistic to the tradition, but he did need a way out to show that his position was not necessarily at variance with Aristotle's statement. He makes his typical tactical move of introducing a distinction: The statement, 'The intellect is concerned with universals' can be understood either as precising or as making an exclusion. Accordingly,

'Only the intellect is concerned with universals' is certainly true on the ground that no other faculty knows universals. But this statement, 'The intellect is only concerned with universals' is false because the intellect knows singulars also. The sense, likewise, is concerned with singulars either as precising or as excluding. . . . For this statement is true, 'The sense is only concerned with singulars, because the sense can only know singulars'; but this one, 'Only the sense is concerned with singulars' is false, because the intellect is also concerned with singulars.[27]

This distinction enables him to say that at least in one plausible interpretation of Aristotle's statements his own view is not at variance with the tradition. In any case, those who would want to raise an objection to his own position would have to do much more than to cite the criptic remark from the *Posterior Analytics*.

If the preceding account of the Principle of Individuation, the Principles of Exemplification, and the Principle of Distinguishing Numerical Plurality is correct and faithful to Burley's intentions, we can be amazed at the happy absence of intellectual opacity so often insisted upon by those philosophers who stress the unknowability of matter or else allow for only some imperfect or indirect knowability of matter and of singulars. For Burley, individuals are basically intelligible, since they "are contained under the first and adequate object, which is being in its greatest generality".

In Burley's way of thinking, the fact that singulars contain matter does not prevent their intelligibility. He believed that they can in fact be known *distinctly* by the intellect and he produced several arguments for his position. In the *De formis* Burley first attacks the claim that the intellect does not know different individuals of the same species, for example, Plato and Socrates, Brunellus and Favellus, distinctly, although the intellect may know such individuals "indistinctly". (To know two *F*s, *a* and *b*, "indistinctly" is to know them in their universal, that is, in *F*.) He writes: "The intellect [distinctly] knows the difference between the universal and the singular. But one who knows the difference between things distinctly knows the extremes of the difference. . . . Therefore the intellect knows the singular distinctly."[28]

Burley's argument makes certain assumptions. The first premise needs to have 'distinctly' inserted into the statement, as indicated by the addition in the brackets. As for the second premise we must take Burley to mean any intelligent cognitive agent and not only metaphysicians when he says that the one who knows the difference between things distinctly knows the extremes of the difference. That is, he must be claiming that a nonmetaphysician *x*, who apprehends Socrates and Plato, recognizing them to be men, has a distinct knowledge of each, Socrates and Plato, in their discreteness, as well as a distinct knowledge of what it means to be a man, that is, a human being. Burley seems to make an appeal to a prejudgmental and predefinitional encounter of human beings with classes of things of a given kind. In such cognitive situations Burley would reject the claim of a double presentation; that is, that the sense and only the sense, secures a direct contact with singulars, while the intellect knows singulars only as instances of their universals.

From an additional "confirming" argument we get the impression that Burley simply assumes as a fact that we actually have a distinct intellectual presentation of individuals and then speculates as to what must be the case on the side of our cognitive apparatus for such distinct intellectual presentations to occur. He says, "This is confirmed because the intellect in distinguishing the singular and the universal does not distinguish [the singular] from the universal by a universal intention, because by it it assimilates the singular to the universal. It must be, then, that the intellect distinguishes the singular from the universal by a distinct singular intention."[29]

Intentions are mental acts. Each intention is proportionate to its object. Universal intentions are essentially one-many relations, singular intentions are one-one relations. Because Burley and those who spoke of the intuitive cognition of singulars are willing to recognize as a fact that the object of intellectual intention has been reached, he can argue for the two radically (categorically) different kinds of intentions of the intellect. The starting point is based on the phenomenology of experience; the conclusion is reached by a reductive inference.

Another argument starts with the observation that the intellect knows the truth of 'Socrates is not Plato'. The apprehension of any truth is a function of the intellect.

> Now, it must be granted that the intellect knows the singular under the proper concept (*notione*) of the singular and consequently by a proper individual intention. That this is so is evident, because the intellect knows all that is contained under the first and adequate object, which is being in its greatest generality. But the individual under the proper concept of the individual is contained under the being that is the adequate object of the intellect. Therefore the intellect knows the individual under its proper concept.[30]

In his commentary on *Physics* Burley argues that "if our intellect did not understand singulars, he could not make this proposition, namely, 'Socrates is a man'; but this is false". This argument is too weak to undermine Aquinas, who held that the intellect does not know singulars directly but by a reflection on phantasms. A less cryptic argument for the intellectial cognition of singulars is the following:

> If in order for the intellect to understand the singular it must first understand the universal, then it follows that the intellect could never understand the singular. The consequent is false and therefore the antecedent also. I prove the consequence. For the universal is equally indifferent to all its singulars, therefore it does not lead more to a cognition of one singular than another. Thus, either it would lead to the cognition of all of them at the same time, which is impossible, or to the cognition of none of them. It follows that the intellect does not first know the universal in such a way that it would procede from the cognition of the universal to the cognition of the singular.[31]

To establish the first premise Burley produces a plausible reductive reasoning that we could not have intellectual understanding of the singular under the proper aspect (*ratione*) of singular such as we, as a matter of fact, have. An application of *modus tollens* leads to the conclusion that it is not the case that, if our intellect understands the singular, then it must first understand the universal. The 'first' here should be understood as "first in generation", not "first in nature". That is, for us to understand the truth of 'Socrates is not Plato' we need not first subsume "Socrates" under the universal form *man*, since the intellect captures the individual under the *proper* aspect as singular.

But Burley does not tell us what is the ontological counterpart to this proper aspect. Is it proper cause *this* form, or the proper cause *this* matter and *this* form, of Socrates? If so, Burley's notion of intellect must include functions other than those of abstraction, judgment, and reasoning.

VI. Summary

For Burley, there are two radically different ontological kinds irreducible to one another: universals and particulars. Burley understands the nature of these in terms of the traditional metaphysical dichotomies of act-potentiality and of form-matter. Individuality or singularity is associated by him with the "material", localizing and temporalizing, component of being, although he does not endorse the view that matter is of itself the principle of individuation or the ground of numerical diversity. Burley's view seems to be that *beings* are individuated by themselves; and this means, at least for material substances, that they are individual by both matter and form in conjunction. Matter of itself, the primary matter, could not accomplish the task, being a pure subjective potentiality, while matter with quantity or composite matter must be already "informed" and could thus not be invoked as the Principle of Individuation. On the other hand, form itself cannot accomplish the task, being by nature precisely the sort of thing that can be located in many places, be literally shared wholly by many, and provide the foundation for the specific sameness of individuals. Thus, in spite of Burley's recognition of pure or primary matter (which reminds us of bare particulars), we should not identify the two; for bare particulars are understood to have the definite function of accounting for the numerical diversity of the specifically same individuals, while the former by itself, that is, without form, cannot accomplish this task.

Burley's texts themselves strongly suggest that in his understanding of the hylomorphic scheme, the Principle of Individuation is to be construed in terms of a conjunction of this-matter and this-form, and we have attempted to unravel this troublesome idea. Unfortunately, Burley's own treatment of this problem is very short and cryptic.

The importance of the conjunction of the immediate "individual causes" of individuals in Burley's philosophy is bolstered by his idea of the relation of individuals and their natures: While the two are inseparable (although Burley may and could consistently have held that God could separate the two by His *potentia absoluta*), they are nevertheless not identical. Burley emphatically rejected the nominalistic interpretations of Grosseteste's statements such as "the universal is in each of its singulars" and "the universal has being in its singulars". He argued that the famous author did not intend an identification of universals and singulars or that he did not claim that there is only a conceptual distinction between the two.

Burley's own view of the relation between individuals and their natures may be expressed by the two Principles of Exemplification, $(\forall F)(\exists x)Fx$ and $(\forall x)(\exists F)Fx$. What is the logical status of these principles? We might say that they, while not analytically true, are nevertheless synthetic a priori principles. However, the relation of exemplification should not be construed as a descriptive relation. The correct representation of the claim that *a* exemplifies *F* in our improved language is $F(a)$, where exemplification "shows itself" by the juxtaposition of descriptive symbols and by parentheses, given the formation rules of our improved language; it would be utterly incorrect, leading to Bradly's Regress, to represent the relation of exemplification by $E(a,F)$. We should also stress that they are the basic principle of being, the individual variables ranging over first substances and the property variables over forms of any sort. It is because of Burley's clear recognition of these principles that his Principle of Individuation's invocation of both matter and form is plausible within the system.

Individual-as-a-collection of qualities seems to be considered by Burley not on an ontological but rather on a gnoseological level. In any case, any attempt to put an ontological interpretation on this idea within the hylomorphic scheme would seem to result in one of the following: Either matter becomes superfluous and its role as a particularizer is taken over by some second-order relation or structure among qualities or properties that are the irreducible "things" in "cluster" ontologies; or else, matter itself reappears in the guise of spatial or temporal features of singulars-as-collections. In the version of this sort of doctrine of singulars considered by Burley, the second of the two awkward consequences seems to loom prominent. There is no doubt, however, that Burley's own ontological conception construes individuals as Aristotelian first substances. All genuine hylomorphic individuals have natures, albeit inseparable, from them. The distinction between individuals and natures is real, not merely formal. Furthermore, our intellect has a distinct cognition of singulars precisely as singulars and not only as possible instances of a given kind. In this matter, Burley is definitely on the side of the "Franciscan School" and not on the side of those who, like Aquinas, held that our intellectual knowledge of singulars is judgmental and indirect, involving a "reflection" upon phantasms offered by the senses.[32]

VII. Conclusion

The resurgence of the study of medieval philosophy has yet to make progress with respect to many philosophical figures and philosophical topics. The inclusion of Burley in the comprehensive study of the individual and individuation in the high Middle Ages may serve not only as an exposition of Burley's thought on the subject, but also as an incentive to a critical study of Burley's general ontology within which his concept of individual was developed.

Notes

This study was completed during a sabbatical year 1986/7. The author gratefully acknowledges his indebtedness to the Ohio State University as well as to IREX and Fulbright (USEd) Foundations for the research grants to Halle-Wittenberg University, German Democratic Republic, and to Krakow, Poland, during this same academic year.

1. The best comprehensive study of Walter Burley's life and work is Agustín Uña Juárez, *La filosofía del siglo XIV: Contexto cultural de Walter Burley* Biblioteca "La ciudad de Dios" (Madrid: Real Monasterio de El Escorial, 1978). See also James A. Weisheipl, "Ockham and Some Mertonians", *Mediaeval Studies* 30 (1968): 163–213. For a brief biographical note, cf. N. Kretzmann *et al.*, eds., *The Cambridge History of Later Medieval Philosophy* (Cambridge; Cambridge University Press 1982), pp. 888–889. For another detailed study of the life and work of Burley, see C. Martin, "Walter Burley", in *Oxford Studies Presented to Daniel Callus*, Oxford Philosophical Society, new series, 16 (Oxford, 1964), pp. 194–230.

2. The following editions of Walter Burley's writings have been utilized or otherwise consulted: [1] *De formis,* ed. Frederick J. Down Scott (Munich: Verlag der Bayerischen Akademie der Wissenschaften, 1970). [2] *De materia et forma* (Oxford, 1518). [3] *In Physicam Aristotelis expositio et questiones* (Venice, 1501; reprinted New York: George Olms, 1972). [4] *Expositio super artem veterem Porphyrii et Aristotelis* (Venice, 1497; reprinted Frankfurt-am-Main: Minerva, 1967). [5] *De suppositionibus,* in Stephen F. Brown, "Walter Burley's Treatise *De suppositionibus* and Its Influence on William of Ockham", *Franciscan Studies* 32 (1972): 15-64. [6] *De diffinitione,* ed. H. Shapiro and F. Scott, *Mediaeval Studies* 27 (1965): 337–340. [7] *De puritate artis logicae tractatus longior,* ed. P. Boehner (St. Bonaventure, NY: Franciscan Institute Publications, 1955). All the following references to Burley's texts are to these editions.

3. *De formis,* pp. 7f: "Et sciendum est quod potentia . . . est duplex, scilicet, potentia que est principium entis, et hec dicitur potentia subiectiva. Alia est potentia . . . obiectiva. . . . Aliter est Antichristus in potentia et aliter argentum ad formam denarii, quia Antichristus est sic in potentia quod non existit sed potest existere. Sed argentum actu existit et solum est in potentia, quia potest recipere. Unde, Antichristus est in potentia obiectiva et argentum in potentia subiectiva. Unde potentia obiectiva est in potentia ad existere et potentia subiectiva est in potentia ad formam."

4. *Ibid.,* p. 7: "Materia prima est illud quod non est resolubile in materiam et formam sed est omnino simplex propter carentiam omnium formarum de sua natura et

de sua substantia, ita quod ipsa in sui natura intrinseca nullam formam includit, licet numquam sit sine forma. Sed in omni composito ex materia et forma est devenire ad talem materiam omnino simplicem irresolubilem in materiam et formam, quod potest declarari exemplariter in omnibus. Verbi gratia: denarius est quoddam compositum ex forma artificiali et ex argento tamquam ex materia. Quero tunc: aut argentum est materia simplex aut est compositum ex materia et forma. Si sit omnino simplex, tunc esset materia prima, quod falsum est. Si sit compositum ex materia et forma, tunc quero de sua materia: aut est omnino simplex in sua natura aut est compositum. Si sit omnino simplex, tunc est materia prima, et habetur propositum, scilicet, quod in denario est aliqua materia omnino prima. Si autem materia argenti sit composita ex materia et forma, querendum est de sua materia sicut prius, et sic procederetur in infinitum sicut prius, quod est inconveniens, vel tandem deveniretur ad materiam omnino simplicem que non est resolubilis in materiam et formam et illa est materia prima, et ita contingit arguere de quolibet alio composito ex materia et forma probando quod in illo est materia prima."

5. *Ibid.*, p. 8: "Sed materia prima est in pura potentia subiectiva, quia nullam formam in sua natura habet. Sed materia composita non est in pura potentia subjectiva, quia aliquam formam in sua natura includit, ut patet in argento et ligno."

6. *Ibid.*, p. 8: "Materia prima dicitur esse una numero in omnibus generabilibus et corruptibilibus, quod non est sic intelligendum quod eadem materia esset simul in omnibus generabilibus et corruptibilibus. Quia si sic, eadem materia esset simul sub forma terre et ita in eadem materia numero essent simul forme contrarie in summo, scilicet, caliditas in summo et frigiditas in summo, quod est impossibile."

7. *Ibid.*, p. 9: "Illud commune dictum: 'eadem est materia numero omnium' habet sic intelligi: quod eadem materia numero est successive in omnibus generabilibus et corruptibilibus secundum speciem. V.gr.: eadem materia numero que est sub forma hominis, post mortem hominis erit sub forma cadaveris et postmodum sub forma terre et postmodum sub forma rei producte ex illa, ut sub forma herbe vel aque et postea sub forma alterius generati ex illis et sic secundum circulum . . . Cum species rerum generabilium et corruptibilium sunt finite, oportet quod fiat generatio circularis in infinitum, secundum Philosophum secundo *De generatione.*" (336 b 25– 338 b 20).

8. *Ibid.*, pp. 10f.

9. *Super artem veterem,* b3 v A: "Species autem de individuo predicatur. Genus vero et de specie et de individuo predicatur. Generalissimum autem et de genere et de generibus predicatur, si plura sint media subalterna, et de specie et de individuo predicatur; dicitur autem generalissimum quod de omnibus sub se positis generibus et speciebus et de individuis predicatur, genus autem quod ante specialissimum est, et de omnibus specialissimis et de individuis dicitur, solum autem species de omnibus individuis. Individuum autem dicitur de uno solo particulari; individuum autem dicitur Socrates et hoc album et hic veniens et Sophronisci filius, si solus sit Socrates et filius." This is Porphyry's text as quoted by Burley.

10. *Ibid.*, b3 v A: "Individuum predicatur de uno solo, scilicet de seipso, quia non habet inferius eo de quo predicari."

11. *Ibid.*, b3 v A: "Sciendum quod hoc nomen individuum potest accipi pro eo quod significat, et sic predicatur de multis; nam Socrates est individuum, et Plato est individuum. Vel potest accipi pro eo quod denominat, et sic loquitur auctor hic. 'Socrates' enim est id quod hoc nomen 'individuum' denominat, ut individuum sumatur pro eo quod denominat, et 'Socrates' predicatur de uno solo proprie, ut de seipso."

12. *Ibid.*, b3 v B: "Individua *continentur* in specie, et species in genere. Istud patet ex ordinatione in linea predicamentali. Et hoc probatur sic. Omnis pars continetur in suo toto; sed individuum est pars speciei, et species est pars generis, ergo individuum continetur in specie et species in genere. Et addit auctor quod individuum est pars et species est pars et totum, alterius tamen et alterius. Species enim est *pars* generis et totum respectu individui."

13. *Ibid.*, b3 v B: "Intelligendum quod individuum est pars subiectiva speciei, quia species predicatur de individuo in recto. Et propter eandem causam species est pars subiectiva generis, quia genus predicatur in recto de specie et hec est differentia inter partem integralem et partem subiectivam, quia de parte integrali non vere predicatur suum totum in recto sed in obliquo; manus enim et caput sunt partes integrales hominis, quia integrant hominem, et ideo hec est falsa, 'Manus est homo vel caput est homo'."

14. *Ibid.*, a4 v B: "Quia si nullus intellectus esset, adhuc duo lapides magis convenirent quam unus lapis et asinus. Sed omnis convenientia est in aliquo uno. Nam omnis convenientia est unitas fundata supra multitudinem quia quecunque conveniunt, in aliquo conveniunt, ergo est aliqua res communis extra animam in qua duo lapides conveniunt et in qua lapis et asinus non conveniunt. Confirmatur sic. Quia quecunque comparantur realiter in aliquo uno, comparantur secundum magis vel minus, sive secundum equale. Nam si *a* et *b* comparantur adivicem secundum magis et minus, non comparantur in illo quod competit solum *a* nec in illo quod competit solum *b* sed in aliquo quod competit utrique; verbi gratia, si *a* sit magis album quod *b* et *b* non comparatur in albedine ipsius *a* nec in albedine ipsius *b*. Nam hoc est falsum, '*a* est magis album albedine ipsius *a* quam *b* albedine ipsius *a*'. Similiter hec est falsa, '*b* est minus album albedine ipsius *a* quam *b* albedine ipsius *b*'; ergo oportet quod illud in quo comparantur conveniat utrique. Sed nullum singulare competit utrisque, ergo est aliqua res universalis in qua illa comparantur realiter ad invicem."

15. *Ibid.*, a5 r A: "Sit Socrates *a* et homo universalis *b;* tunc *a* et *b* conveniunt quia *a* et *b* sunt duo homines, ergo *a* et *b* conveniunt in natura humana cum eis. Et illa natura communis eis est alia ab *a* et alia a *b* quia per se natura communis est alia res ab ea cuius est communis. Sit ergo illa tertia natura *c* et tunc *a, b, c* sunt tres homines; ergo conveniunt in natura communi hominis realiter. Et sit illa, *d*. Et sic proceditur in infinitum in predicamentis predicatis in-quid, et etiam erunt infiniti homines."

16. *Ibid.*, a5 v A: "Nec verum est quod *a* et *b* conveniunt in natura humana tertia ab illis, immo, unum istorum continetur sub alio ut *a* sub *b* tamquam individ-

uum sub specie. Sed *a* et *b* non conveniunt in tertia specie specialissima communi eis, cum unum illorum sit species specialissima alterius."

17. *Ibid.*, a6 v A: "Et cum dicitur quod si Deus annihilaret Socratem, tunc annihilaret speciem hominis, dico quod non sequitur . . . quia species non est pars individui, ut patet per Philosophum secundo *Physicorum* et quinto *Metaphysice,* qui dicit quod effectus particularis sunt cause particulares, et effectus universalis sunt cause universales. Et ideo Socrates qui est effectus particularis non componitur nisi ex causis particularibus, scilicet ex hac materia et hac forma." Cf. also a passage from the *Predicamenta* (*Super artem veterem,* d3 r B): "Ad illud dicendum quod non oportet quod annihilando individuum annihilatur species hominis, quia species hominis non sit pars Socratis. Unde, annihilata hac materia et hac forma, annihilatur Socrates, quia Socrates non componitur nisi ex hac materia et hac forma."

18. Cf. Anneliese Maier, "Ein Unbeacheter Averroist des 14. Jahrhunderts: Walter Burley", in *Medioevo e Rinascimiento,* Festschrift B. Nardi (Florence, 1955), pp. 477–499. She calls for a recognition of a possible Averroist. Cf. also Zdzislaw Kuksewicz, "The Problem of Walter Burley's Averroism", in *Studi sul XIV Secolo. in Memoriam di Anneliese Maier,* Storia e Letteratura, 151 (Rome, 1981), pp. 341–378. Briefly, Kuksewicz's observation is that Burley's *De potentiis animae* and very likely the *Quaestiones in tertium De anima* are basically anti-Averroistic in outlook; that in Book II of the Commentary on *De anima* Burley tries to understand and even perhaps to interpret and defend Averroes conception in the spirit of the radical Averroistic interpretation; and that Book III of the *De anima* is decidedly Averroistic. It should be added that more recently E. Jung-Palczewska reestablished Burley as a non-Averroist in philosophical psychology. Cf. her "La problème d'Averroïsme de Walter Burley dans son Commentaire sur la *Physique*", *Studia Mediewistyczne* 24 (1986): 101–109.

19. *Super artem veterem Porphyrii et Aristotelis* (Venice, 1497), a3 r A: "Quodlibet predicatum essentiale est forma declarans quidditatem sui individui. Dico ergo quod intelligendo per quidditatem predicatum essentiale, sic species specialissima dicit totam quidditatem individui sui, quia species est unum predicatum essentiale de respectu individui includens omnia alia predicata essentialia . . . Si vero quidditas accipitur pro forma perficiente materiam, sic species non dicit totam quidditatem individui." On Porphyry's views on the subject of individuals and universals, cf. Jorge J. E. Gracia, *Introduction to the Problem of Individuation in the Early Middle Ages* (Munich, Philosophia Verlag, 1984), pp. 67–70.

20. *Super artem veterem,* d2 v B/d3 r A: "Dicendum est quod sola substantia singularis non componitur ex universalibus, sed solum ex singularibus, quia Socrates non componitur nisi ex *hac* materia et *hac* forma et non componitur ex genere et differentia que predicatur de eo in quid; sed de genere substantie componitur ex genere et differentia et ex omnibus superioribus ab ipsum. Et huius ratio est quia effectus particularis sunt cause particulares, et effectus universalis sunt cause universales."

21. Cf. note 17.

22. Cf. *Super artem veterem,* a5 r B.

23. *De formis*, pp. 9f.: "Materia sub una forma per se ipsam et non per formam distinguitur a materia que est sub alia forma. Non est propositio magistralis universaliter vera, scilicet, 'quod omnis distinctio est a forma', sed debet sic intelligi: omnis distinctio specifica est a forma, sicut distinctio hominis ab asino est per formam hominis, scilicet, per animam intellectivam seu per rationabilitatem. Distinctio vero individuorum sub eadem specie est tam per materiam quam per formam quam etiam per accidentia. Verbi gratia: Socrates distinguitur materialiter per materiam suam a Platone distinctione individuali et formaliter per formam suam et accidentaliter per accidentia sua."

24. *Super artem veterem*, b3 v B: "Hic narrat qualiter individuum constat ex multis accidentibus quorum collectio non potest simul reperiri in alio individuo cuiusmodi proprietates sunt, scilicet qualitas, figura, locus, et tempus."

25. *Ibid.*, b3 v B: "Intelligendum etiam quod unum individuum substantie non distinguitur ab alio solum per huius modi proprietates accidentis sed formaliter per suam formam et materiam. Unde Socrates distinguitur a Platone accidentaliter per sua accidentia, formaliter per suam formam et materialiter per suam materiam, et secundum veritatem individuum substantie distinguitur ab alio per huiusmodi proprie tates."

26. *De formis*, pp. 23f.: "Sed tunc est dubium, quia Philosophus dicit primo *Posteriorum* [87 b 38–39] quod intellectus est universalium et sensus est singularium. . . . Ergo videtur quod intellectus non cognoscit nisi universale."

27. *Ibid.*,p. 24: "Dicendum quod intellectus est universalium cum precisione vel exclusione, aliter tamen et aliter, quia intellectus est universalium cum precisione addendo precisionem vel exclusionem intellectus et non universalium. Nam hec est vera: solus intellectus est universalium, quia intellectus et nulla alia virtus cognoscit universalia. Sed hec est falsa: intellectus est solum vel tantum universalium, quia cognoscit singularia, ut predictum est, et sic patet qualiter intellectus est universalium. Sed aliter est sensus singularium cum precisione vel exclusione, quia sensus est singularium cum exclusione addendo exclusionem obiecti et non potentie seu ipsius singularis et non sensus. Hec enim est vera: sensus est tantum singularium, quia sensus non cognoscit nisi singularia et hec est falsa: solus sensus est singularium, quia intellectus est singularium."

28. *Ibid.*, p. 23: ". . . [I]ntellectus cognoscit differentiam inter universale et singulare. Sed cognoscens differentiam inter aliqua distincte cognoscit extremum differentie. . . . Ergo intellectus distincte cognoscit singulare."

29. *Ibid.*, p. 23: "Confirmatur hoc, quia intellectus distinguens singulare ab universali non distinguit ab universali per intentionem universalem, quia per illam convenit singulare universali. Ergo oportet quod intellectus distinguit singulare ab universali per distinctam intentionem singularem."

30. *Ibid.*, p. 23: "Illud est concedendum, scilicet, quod intellectus cognoscit singulare sua propria ratione singularis et per consequens per propriam intentionem

individualem. Quod ita sit patet, quia intellectus cognoscit omne contentum sub suo primo et adequato obiecto quod est ens in maxima sua communitate. Sed individuum sub propria ratione individui est contentum sub ente quod est obiectum adequatum intellectus. Ergo intellectus cognoscit individuum sub propria ratione individui.''

31. *In primo Physicorum,* 10 r B: ''Supposito igitur quod intellectus noster intelligit singulare sub propria ratione singularis, probo quod intellectus via generationis primo intelligit singulare; quia si ad hoc quod intellectus intelligit singulare oportet quod primo intelligat universale, sequitur quod intellectus numquam posset intelligere singulare. Consequens est falsum, ergo et antecedens. Probo consequentiam. Quia universale est equaliter indifferens ad omnia sua singularia, ergo non magis ducit in cognitionem unius singularis quam alterius. Aut igitur duceret in cognitionem omnium simul, quod est impossibile, aut in cognitione nullius. Igitur non intelligit primo universale sic quod a cognitione universalis procedat ad cognitionem singularis.''

32. M. Markowski notices a contrast between philosophers with ''Platonic tendencies'' and Burley: The former supposed that universals were known prior to particulars, while Burley subscribed to the opposite view that the intellect understands first and directly singulars: ''Die Vertreter der philosophischen Tradition, die irgendwie an den Platonismus anknüpften, behaupteten . . . , die menschliche Erkenntnis beginne von dem an, was universaler ist. Burleigh der sich in diesem Fall an den genetischen Empirismus des Aristoteles hielt, war dagegen der Ansicht, der menschliche Verstand erkenne zuerst und unmittelbar das einzelne Seiende (d.h. das Singulare) und erst mittelbar und reflexiv das Universale''. Cf. ''Die Anschauungen des Walter Burleigh über die Universalien'', in *English Logic in Italy in the Fourteenth and Fifteenth Centuries,* ed. A. Maierù (Naples: Bibliopolis-Edizioni di Filosofia e Scienze, 1982), p. 221. Markowski cited from Burley's *De physico auditu,* f. blrb: ''Ad primum horum dico quod intellectus intelligit singulare primo et directe et universale indirecte et quasi per modum linee reflexe et hec est intentio Philosophi tertio *De anima.*''

17

WILLIAM OF OCKHAM
(B. CA. 1285; D. 1347)

ARMAND A. MAURER

The problem of individuation, in the usual sense of the term, does not arise in Ockham's philosophy. The problem occurs when a philosopher maintains that there are natures or essences in individuals, in some way common to the individuals and yet diversified in them. Thus, one who holds that animality exists in all animals, and that it is diversified in them, is pressed to explain what causes the nature of animality to be individuated in all animals. Given the commonness of animality, what makes the individual animal to be the individual it is?

Most philosophers in the Middle Ages had to face this problem because they believed that universals or common natures in some way exist in reality and that they are multiplied in the individuals whose natures they are. Ockham bears witness to the consensus of opinion regarding universals, at the same time distinguishing different schools of thought on the subject. He writes: "All those whom I have seen agree in the solution to this question, saying that there is really in the individual a nature that is in some way universal, at least potentially and incompletely, though some say that it is really distinct [from the individual], some that it is only formally distinct, some that it is in no way distinct in reality but only according to reason or through the consideration of the intellect."[1]

Ockham himself disagreed with all these ways of conceiving the relation between universals and individuals. He contended that individuals do not have natures in some way distinct from individuals. He banished from reality all traces of a realism of universals and adopted the pure position that reality is radically individual and in no sense common or universal. Everything outside the mind, he argued, is a 'this', and it owes its individuality to itself and not to something else. Individuality is a property immediately belonging to a thing; It does not come to it from outside itself.[2]

As a consequence Ockham did not need to search for a principle or cause of individuation. He granted that perhaps one could call the extrinsic and intrinsic causes of a composite thing the cause of its individuation (i.e., its efficient and final causes and its form and matter), for they contribute to its existence. But this does not compromise Ockham's principle that every individual is 'this' of itself, because it does not introduce a special cause or principle between the nature of a thing and its individuality. Even the matter and form that make up a composite individual are individual of themselves and in no need of being individuated by some other principle. The real problem, as Ockham saw it, is not to find the cause of individuation but rather to examine how it is possible for anything to be common or universal.[3]

Though Ockham may give the impression that he is advancing a new doctrine of universals and individuals, its basic tenet, that everything is individual of itself, was already known to Duns Scotus and criticized by him. Since Ockham was well read in Scotus, he cannot have failed to know this. But Ockham does not seem to have read the Franciscans Roger Marston and Peter of Falco, who advanced views on individuality similar to Ockham's in the late thirteenth century and who may have been the objects of Scotus's criticism.[4] Neither was Ockham acquainted with Abailard's position on the individual, which in some respects resembles his own.[5] But these anticipations of Ockham's views on the individual in no way diminish the revolutionary character of his philosophy, for no one before him adopted this position so purely or drew from it all its possible consequences.

Ockham takes up the problem of universals in many works: his treatises on logic, notably the *Summa Logicae;* the first book of his Commentary on the *Sentences,* known as the *Ordinatio;* his *Quodlibets,* and *Questions on the Physics.*[6] His most extensive and penetrating account of the subject is in the *Ordinatio,* distinction 2, questions 4 to 8. These questions are a veritable treatise on universals inserted by Ockham into his Commentary in order to lay the groundwork for the resolution of theological issues, such as the possibility of predicating univocal concepts of God and creatures, and the knowability of the divine essence. The questions present theories of universals arranged according to the degree of reality they ascribe to a universal, beginning in question 4 with the most realistic view of universals, and ending in question 8 with Ockham's own non-realist or nominalist position.

Ockham's Criticism of His Predecessors' Doctrines of Universals

Criticism of the Platonists

The first opinion regarding universals, described in question 4, holds that a univocal universal is a thing (*res*) really existing outside the mind in every individual in a genus or species and belonging to its essence. The universal is really distinct from the individuals and from all other universals. For example, universal humanity is a true reality, really existing outside the mind in all humans, and really distinct from them and from universal animal and universal substance. Moreover, the universal realities existing in each individual of a genus or species are in no way diversified or multiplied in the different individuals.[7]

Ockham does not say who, if anyone, held this opinion. He remarks that it has been falsely attributed to Duns Scotus,[8] perhaps by Henry of Harclay, and he hints at the Platonic basis of the theory, without ascribing it to Plato himself.[9] It bears some resemblance to the doctrine of William of Champeaux, at least as it was interpreted by Abailard.[10]

The theory was devised, according to Ockham, to account for the essential predication of one thing of another and for our definitions and sciences of reality. As Aristotle has shown, the object of a definition is not primarily an individual but a universal substance distinct from the individual and yet intrinsic to it and belonging to its essence. It is this universal substance that is predicated essentially of an individual, as when we say "Socrates is an animal".[11] Moreover, a science of reality (*scientia realis*) must have a universal substance as its object, for science treats primarily of the universal and not of the individual.[12]

This theory of universals receives Ockham's harshest disapproval. It is, he says, absolutely false and absurd.[13] If a universal reality exists in individuals and is really distinct from them, God could by his absolute power create the universal without the individuals or the individuals without the universal; for example, he could create humanity without individual humans or individual humans without humanity. In addition, the theory cannot solve the problem of essential predication. The theory holds that the universal is intrinsic to the individual and yet really distinct from it. It must, then, be a part of the individual. But a part cannot be essentially predicated of a thing; we cannot say, for example, that Socrates is his body or soul or hand. Nevertheless we do say "Socrates is an animal". Hence animal cannot be a part of Socrates. In fact, according to Ockham, in this proposition 'animal' is only a term standing for Socrates. It takes the place of him in our talking and thinking about him. There is no need, then, to suppose that there is a universal reality (*res universalis*) within the individual and predicable of it.[14]

Similarly we do not have to assume that there are universal or common realities as objects of our general definitions. We define 'man' as a rational animal, but this primarily defines the term 'man', not some common reality. Nevertheless the definition may be said to express the individuals in the species or genus, because in a way it can be predicated of them and it stands for them in propositions. Thus we can say that Socrates or Plato is a rational animal (but not simply "rational animal"), and the term 'rational animal' stands for them and other individual men.[15]

As for sciences of reality, Aristotle showed that they have for their primary objects universals and not individuals,[16] but the universals in question are terms and propositions, not common realities. Indeed, according to Ockham, "every science, whether it be a science of reality or rational science [i.e., logic], is concerned only with propositions as with what is known, for propositions alone are known."[17] He is not denying that we know individuals; they are the first objects of the intuitive cognition of the senses and intellect. Neither is he denying that science treats of individuals. The point he is making is that universal propositions are the immediate and direct object of scientific knowledge. Science deals with individuals insofar as the terms of propositions stand for them. In a science of reality (*scientia realis*) the terms of its propositions have personal supposition; that is, they stand for the things they signify, namely, individual realities outside the mind. This is the case with propositions of physics, mathematics, and metaphysics. The terms of scientific propositions may be mental concepts or spoken or written words; the science is said to be a "*scientia realis*" provided that its terms stand for extramental realities. To account for this kind of science, then, it is not necessary to posit universal realities (*res universales*), really distinct from individual things.[18]

Having disposed of this rather crude form of realism of universals, in the next question (5) Ockham turns to a lesser form of realism than the preceding. It agrees with the position described in question 4, that the universal is a reality (*res*) existing outside the mind in individual things and really distinct from them; but the universal is now said to enter into composition with the individual and to be contracted by an individuating difference that renders it individual. Thus the universal is really multiplied and varied in individuals. For example, Plato and Socrates have in common the reality of humanity, but owing to their individual differences Plato's humanity is really not Socrates's.[19]

Ockham notes that this theory of universals, like the preceding, has been erroneously ascribed to Duns Scotus. The editors of Ockham's *Ordinatio* point out that William of Alnwick was likely guilty of this misinterpretation of the Subtle Doctor.[20] In the twelfth century Gilbert of Poitiers defended a theory of universals similar to the present doctrine.[21] Like the preceding, it explains universals and their relation to individuals in terms of things (*res*) and their real distinction. It is a mitigated form of realism, however, for it introduces the notion of an individuating difference that diversifies a universal reality in individuals. For this reason Ockham regards the theory as moving in the right direction but still far from the truth. He argues that if the nature of an individual is really distinct from the individual difference that renders it individual, they are separable, at least by the divine power. There would be no contradiction in a nature's being separated from the various differences it has in individuals. The humanities of Socrates and Plato, being really distinct, could exist in separation from their individuating differences. They would then be really distinct by themselves (*seipsis*) and not through individual differences really distinct from them.[22] This is the position Ockham himself will defend, but first he meets the challenge of several less realistic doctrines of universals.

Criticism of Duns Scotus

In question 6 Ockham describes and criticizes a third, mitigated realistic conception of universals. It is realistic for it maintains that universals really exist outside the mind in individual things; but the universal is now conceived as a nature that is incompletely universal in its real existence and completely universal only as it exists in the mind. In itself a nature is neither universal nor particular. It is universal when it exists in the mind and individual when it exists outside the mind in things. In the latter case it is "contracted" by an individual difference that renders it individual. Unlike the former position the "contracting" difference is held to be really the same as, and only formally distinct from, the nature it individuates.

Ockham identifies this as "the opinion of the Subtle Doctor [i.e., Duns Scotus], who surpassed the others in keenness of judgment".[23]

Scotus's doctrine of universals and individuation is the subject of another chapter of this book, so it will not be necessary to describe it in detail.[24] To ensure that his account of it is accurate, Ockham bases his report on long quotations from Scotus's *Opus Oxoniense*. He gives more attention to the Scotist position on universals than to any other, and it is the only one whose author he identifies by name.

Ockham correctly places the Scotist doctrine between the ultrarealism of question 5, which posits a real distinction between a universal and the individual to which it is "contracted", and the lesser realism of question 7, according to which the distinction between universal and individual is not present in reality but is made by the mind.

The keystone of Scotus's doctrine is rightly identified by Ockham as the notion of a common or "contractible" nature. In Scotus's view a nature is not a 'thing' (*res*), like the universals of questions 4 and 5. Nevertheless it is a real positive entity that of itself has the properties of community and unity that is less than unity in number. Since a nature is common of itself, it needs an additional factor to render it individual. For example, something must be added to humanity to individuate it in this or that human. Scotus argues that the additional factor is not a negation, accident, actual existence, or matter. Rather, it is an entity called an "individual difference," belonging to the category of substance but not to the quidditative or essential order, for it adds no new essential note to the nature but simply renders it individual. Because no one individual difference belongs to the nature of itself, it is possible for the nature to be individuated by several at the same time. A principle of individuation is required not only for the nature as a whole, but for each of its essential parts. For example, the matter and form of a composite material nature need their own individual differences, as the whole composite requires its own. The individual difference is an entity in its own right: it is not matter or form or the composite of the two; rather, it is the ultimate reality (*ultima realitas*) of the being of matter, of the being of form, and of the being of the composite. The entity of the common nature and that of the individual difference are not really distinct, in the sense of being two things (*res et res*). They are, however, two realities or formalities, formally distinct in one and the same thing.

As the common nature of Scotus is not of itself individual, neither is it of itself completely or actually universal. Of itself it is incompletely universal; it takes on complete universality when it is abstracted and conceived by the mind.[25]

The indifferent or common nature of Scotus comes under Ockham's sharp criticism. It is not a real thing (*res realis*) nor a being of reason (*res rationis*), but an entity located somewhere between them. To Ockham, who always looked for explanations in philosophy and theology as simple and uncluttered as possible,[26] the entity of the common nature appeared to be superfluous. If universals and individuals can be accounted for without assuming a common nature, it should be expunged from philosophy.

Scotus argues that because a nature or essence can be defined in itself it must have some being and unity in itself; otherwise, the definition would have no object. Moreover, because a nature can be individual in the real world and universal in the mind it must have a real indifference to these modes of being. But Ockham retorts that a definition is a concept, and like all concepts it signifies individual things. Thus the definition 'rational animal', like the simple concept 'man', signifies all human beings; it does not signify a nature really common to all humans. The alleged indifference of the nature to individual and universal being is in fact a logical indifference to two ways a term can be used in propositions. The proposition 'Humanity of itself is indifferent to being universal or particular' means that 'universal' and 'particular' can be predicated indifferently of humanity. We can say 'Humanity is universal' or 'Humanity is individual'. In the first case 'humanity' stands for the concept ''humanity''; it has what Ockham calls ''simple supposition''. In the second case 'humanity' stands for and signifies all individual humans; it has what Ockham calls ''personal supposition''. Thus, with an adroit use of his theory of *suppositio*, Ockham banishes common natures from the real world.[27]

At the same stroke Ockham eliminates Scotus's formal distinction from philosophy. According to Scotus, the distinction between a nature and its individuating difference is not real, in the strong sense of a distinction between two things (*res*), one of which can exist without the other. Rather, the distinction is formal, in the sense of a distinction between two realities or formalities, one of which is not contained in the definition of the other.[28] Thus, there is a formal distinction or nonidentity between humanity and its individual difference, for the difference is not contained in the definition of humanity.

In rebuttal, Ockham argues against the validity of the formal distinction in philosophy. He contends that the best way to prove distinction between things is by the principle of contradiction. In the world of our experience, if it is true that *a* is and *b* is not, it follows that *b* is not *a*. Now according to Scotus, something can be truly affirmed of a nature and denied of an individual difference. A nature of itself can be common to many individuals whereas an individual difference cannot. Therefore if these are distinct in reality, as Scotus believes, they must be really and not only formally distinct. In short, they must be two "things". The argument is valid:

If every individual difference of itself is proper to an individual, and a nature of itself is not proper to an individual,
Therefore that nature is distinct from the individual difference, and by 'distinct' is here meant "really distinct".[29]

Scotus would insist that this proves only that the nature and individual difference are formally distinct. Contradiction, in Scotus's view, does not always prove a real distinction; sometimes it shows only a formal distinction. If the contradictories are primary and unqualified, as in the example *a* is and *b* is not, one can conclude that the items in question are really distinct. But if a qualification is added, such as 'of itself' or 'formally', then the predication of contradictories proves only a formal distinction. If one can say, for example, that *a* is formally *a* and *b* is not formally *a*, one should conclude that they are formally, and not really, distinct.[30]

Ockham retorts:

It is impossible for some items in creatures to differ formally unless they are really distinct. Consequently, if a nature is in any way distinct from that contracting difference, they must be distinct as two things (*res et res*), or as two beings of reason (*ens rationis et ens rationis*), or as a real being and a being of reason (*ens reale et ens rationis*). But the first is denied by him [i.e., Scotus] and so too is the second. Therefore the third must be granted.[31]

In short, the nature must be distinguished from the individual as a concept from a reality.

In Ockham's views, Scotus's appeal to degrees of contradiction is to no avail, for all contradictories are equally contradictory. It is just as contradictory, for example, to say, "to be formally the divine wisdom and not to be formally the divine wisdom" as it is to say, "to be the divine wisdom and not to be the divine wisdom". The addition of 'formally' does not weaken the contradiction. If this is denied, Ockham contends, there is no way of proving a real distinction among really existing beings. If Scotus should reason that a donkey is not rational and a man is rational, therefore a man and a donkey are really distinct, Ockham could equally well conclude that they are only formally distinct.[32]

In this way, with his rigid and univocal interpretation of the principle of contradiction, Ockham dismisses the formal distinction in philosophy. There remain only the real distinction between things, the mental distinction between beings of reason, and an unnamed distinction between a real being and a being of reason.

Only in theology does Ockham accept the formal distinction, even though it leads to a logical fallacy. The Christian faith teaches that there are three distinct divine Persons who are identical with the one divine essence. Using the principle of contradiction, we should reason:

> The divine essence is the Son,
> The Father is not the Son,
> Therefore the Father is not the divine essence.

The Faith, however, assures us that the Father, like the Son, is identical with the divine essence. But Ockham insists that this is a unique case beyond our comprehension; it should be admitted only because sacred Scripture compels us to. In the created world we never find one reality that is identical with several and with each of them.[33]

Scotus tried to throw some light on the mystery of the Trinity by introducing a formal distinction between the Persons and the divine essence and between the Persons themselves. Though they are really identical, they are formally nonidentical.[34] Eliminating from his ontology formalities or realities as distinct from things (*res*), Ockham was unable to develop a theology of the Trinity with the logical consistency and depth of Scotism. Verbally he agreed with Scotus that the Persons are formally distinct from the divine essence and from each other, but when this is rightly understood, he says, it simply means "that the [divine] essence is three Persons and that a Person is not three Persons", and "that the [divine] essence is Filiation, and Paternity is not Filiation, and nevertheless the essence is Paternity".[35] In other words, the formal distinction, for Ockham, is nothing but a statement of the contradiction he finds in the Trinity. It expresses a mystery held on faith but without logical or ontological justification.

In question 7 Ockham opposes three doctrines that ascribe the least possible reality to universals. They all maintain that the universal and individual are really the same thing and that there is only a distinction of reason between them.[36] In this respect they differ from the theories of universals described in the preceding questions, all of which claim some distinction in reality between the universal and individual. Ockham wants to expunge the last trace of realism from the doctrine of universals, preparing the way for the defense of his own position, that universals exist only in the mind and in no way in reality.

Following the plan of his exposition of doctrines of universals, Ockham has placed the theories in question 7 in an order of decreasing realism, with the last (Henry of Harclay's) closest to his own.

The first theory maintains that both generic and specific forms subsist in individuals but in different ways. A generic form, like animality, in itself has absolutely no real unity but only a unity made by the mind. It exists in individuals only when divided by formal differences, like rational and irrational. However, a specific form, like humanity, has a real and natural unity and individuality just in itself, and as such it is universal. It is individual only when determined (*signata*) to a particular subject, like Socrates.[37]

The author of this opinion is still unknown.[38] It is not Thomas Aquinas, for he denied that a form or essence either generic or specific, considered just in itself, has any unity. It can be one in the mind as a universal, and many in reality in different individuals; but these modes of unity and plurality belong to an essence not in itself but only as it exists. Of itself a nature or essence has no being or concomitant unity.[39]

Ockham's criticism of the first theory is brief. He queries the nature of the distinction between a specific form and its individual determination (*designatio*). If they do not differ in any way, the form by itself is no more universal than the form with its individual determination. If they do differ in some way, they are distinct either in reality (*secundum rem*) or according to reason (*secundum rationem*). The first alternative has been disproved in questions 4–6. The second is also ruled out, because a distinction of reason, in Ockham's view, is present only between beings of reason (*entia rationis*), for example, between concepts.[40] In an earlier question he discussed this type of distinction at length and concluded that it has no bearing on a real thing: No thing is the same as, or distinct from, itself because of a distinction made by the mind.[41] This implies that there is no distinction of reason with a foundation in any one thing—a point to which we shall have occasion to return. The only other possible distinction between a form and an individual is one between a concept (*ratio*) and a real thing. A specific form, then, has no real unity but only the unity of a concept, and as such it cannot be said to subsist in real individuals.

Criticism of Thomas Aquinas

The second doctrine of universals is likely intended to be that of Thomas Aquinas or one of his followers. Ockham describes it as follows: "Others hold that a thing (*res*) is individual according as it actually exists, and the same thing is universal according as it exists in the mind. Thus the same thing is universal with respect to one existence (*esse*) or according to one consideration, and individual with respect to another existence (*esse*) or according to another consideration."[42]

Ockham has couched the Thomistic doctrine in his own language of things (*res*) in place of Thomas's own language of natures or essences. According to Thomas, a nature or essence, considered just in itself, has no being or unity; but it can acquire a twofold being: one in individual things and another in the mind. In individuals the nature has a multiple being (*multiplex esse*) corresponding to the diversity of individuals; as it exists in the mind it takes on the character of a universal, for it is a likeness of many things.[43] A nature is not fully or actually universal in reality but only through an act of the mind that abstracts the nature from the individuals in which it exists. "What is common to many", Thomas writes, "is not anything over and above the many except by the mind alone (*nisi sola ratione*). For example, animal is not something besides Socrates and Plato and other animals except through the intellect that apprehends the form of animal stripped of all its individuating and specifying characteristics."[44]

In criticism of this position Ockham argues that when a thing is given another name because of something extrinsic to it, everything to which that extrinsic factor can belong can receive the name. Consequently, if a thing that is really individual is universal through the existence it has in the mind, we come to the absurd conclusion that every object of the mind can be universal simply by being thought. Thus Socrates, through his existence in thought, can be universal and common to Plato. So too the divine essence can be universal through its existence in thought, though it is at the peak of individuality.[45]

This conclusion is confirmed by a second argument. What is contradictory to the very nature of something cannot belong to it through an extrinsic factor. Now it is contradictory to the nature of one thing to be common to another. Hence universality cannot belong to a thing through an added extrinsic factor such as existence. Hence, whether an individual is thought or not thought, it could not be common or universal through some existence it might have.[46]

These arguments are significant for the light they throw on Ockham's notion of the individual and its relation to existence. His reasoning is dominated by the notion of a thing (*res*) as individual of itself and by essence. For him, a thing is so radically individual that it has nothing in common with any other thing. We have yet to examine Ockham's solution to the problem of universality; given the incommunicability of anything real, how can we account for universals? Ockham takes up this subject in the next question. We are forewarned, however, that existence will not play a role in solving this problem, as it does in the doctrine of Aquinas. In that doctrine the essence of a creature is really distinct from its act of existing (*esse*). The essence of itself has no reality: It is not a thing, but a possibility of existing that is actualized by an act of existing. It can be actualized in reality, and then the essence can exist in many individuals. The same essence can exist in the mind, and then it is universal, being the likeness of many individuals. In Aquinas's view, consequently, the problem of individuality and universality is insoluble without reference to the act of existing (*esse*).[47]

The Thomistic doctrine does not come within Ockham's perspective. In his view, if essence and existence were really distinct, they could only be two things (*res*), one of which God could preserve without the other. An essence could exist without existence—an obvious absurdity! In fact, Ockham contends that there is only a verbal distinction between the terms *res* and *esse*. They signify the same thing, the former as a noun and the latter as a verb.[48] In any case, existence could not account for an individual if it comes to an essence from without, for, as we have seen, individuality for Ockham is a property immediately belonging to a thing, and not something received from outside itself.

Criticism of Henry of Harclay

Though Henry of Harclay's position on universals is closer to Ockham's than the two preceding, Ockham thinks it is likewise open to grave criticism. It holds that the universal and individual are really one and the same thing and differ only by a distinction of reason. Moreover, it agrees with the common opinion that universals in some way exist in real individuals.

Ockham places Harclay among the 'moderns' who maintain that one and the same thing is either individual or universal depending on the way it is conceived by the mind. In a long passage from Harclay's *Disputed Questions,* quoted by Ockham, Harclay contends that an individual is naturally able to stimulate the mind to conceive it in two different ways, either distinctly or confusedly. As a result the mind can form two different concepts of it. One is a distinct concept that represents the individual alone, the other is a confused or vague concept that equally represents several individuals. Thus we can form a distinct concept of Socrates that applies only to him, and a confused concept of man that applies to both Socrates and Plato.[49]

One of the first disciples of Duns Scotus, Harclay initially adopted the Scotist notion of a common nature as the foundation of a universal concept. In his later *Disputed Questions,* however, he abandoned the idea that individuals have essences or natures in common and taught that the only basis of universal concepts is the similarity or agreement among things. For example, because two white things are similar to each other the mind can form a common concept that represents both.

Harclay was on the way to Ockhamism in his conviction that everything outside the mind is by that very fact individual.[50] But in Ockham's view he failed to draw all the implications from this notion of an individual. Had he done so, he would not have written: "Though a thing in itself is individual, *it is universal* insofar as it is passively represented, which is nothing else than that it is confusedly and indistinctly knowable."[51]

Ockham dismisses this as absolutely false and unintelligible. Let us suppose that *a* indistinctly conceived is universal. It follows that *a* indistinctly conceived is common to *b*. We can say, then, that *b* is *a* indistinctly conceived; that Socrates indistinctly conceived is Plato, or that God indistinctly conceived is a creature.[52]

Because Harclay calls an individual in some sense universal, Ockham sees him as making the mistake common to all the philosophers he has discussed: He has attributed contradictories to one and the same thing. To be predicable of many subjects, and not to be predicable of many subjects, are contradictory properties, the first belonging to a universal and the second to an individual. They cannot without contradiction be ascribed to the same thing.[53]

Ockham sums up his criticism of his predecessors' views on universals with these words: "Therefore, I say that a universal does not exist in the thing (*res*) itself, with regard to which it is universal, either really or subjectively, any more than the word 'man', which is a true quality, exists in Socrates or in that which it signifies. Neither is a universal a part of an individual, with regard to which it is universal, any more than a word is part of what it signifies."[54]

Ockham's Own Position on Universals

Having criticized in questions 4–7 doctrines of universals in decreasing degrees of realism, in question 8 Ockham gives his own nonrealist, or nominalist position on the subject. He has consistently defended his stand that everything outside the mind is individual of itself and by essence, and consequently one individual shares nothing with any other. He now raises the question of the nature of a universal: Is it something real, and if so, where is it to be found?

Ockham's *Ordinatio* presents several nonrealist opinions regarding universals, one of which he rejects out of hand and the others he regards as more or less defensible and probable, without choosing any one of them as truer than the others; but he considers any one of them preferable to the opinions disproved in the previous questions. As we shall see, however, in his later works he makes a definite choice among the nonrealist positions.

The opinion rejected by Ockham claims that a universal is not a natural but a conventional sign, like a word (*vox*). It is said to be universal, not by nature but by "voluntary institution". Consequently its meaning could change or be lost "at the pleasure of those who use the language". A natural sign, by contrast, does not depend on the human will for its meaning, and its meaning does not change at anyone's pleasure.[55] According to John of Salisbury, Roscelin proposed a nominalism of this sort, holding that universals are nothing but vocal utterances (*flatus vocis*).[56]

Ockham dismisses this conception of universals with the remark that if it were true, genera and species would not be natural, but only signs whose meaning would be established by convention.[57] He does not deny that spoken and written words are universals; they are indeed signs of many things and they are predicated of them. What he wants to maintain is the essential difference between the universality of words and that of concepts within the mind. Concepts are universal by nature, and they are the primary signs of things; words, both spoken and written, are conventional signs, whose signification is subordinate to that of concepts.[58]

The first opinion Ockham accepts as probable maintains that a universal is a concept of the mind and that it is identical with the act of understanding (*intellectio*). The universal would be an indistinct understanding of something, but not of one thing more than another similar to it. Hence it would be indifferent and common to many individuals. The degree of its universality would depend on its indistinctness: The more universal concepts would be more indistinct. This was the position of the late thirteenth-century philosophers Henry of Ghent and Godfrey of Fontaines.[59]

According to the second probable opinion, a universal is a likeness (*species*) existing as an individual in the mind, but universal in that it equally represents many individuals. This bears some resemblance to the doctrine of 'intelligible species' of Thomas Aquinas and Giles of Rome.[60] Ockham here, and later in his *Sentences,* argues that the mental likeness to which this theory appeals is superfluous and even a hindrance to knowing reality. Ultimately he rejected the theory.[61]

A third probable opinion holds that a universal is a reality existing in the mind, following upon the act of knowing, like the mental *verbum* in the philosophy of Thomas Aquinas.[62] It would be universal as a mental likeness of many individuals. This too is later dismissed by Ockham as superfluous in accounting for universals.[63]

Ockham concludes his explanation of the three doctrines of universals with these words:

> These opinions would agree in the conclusion that the universal would be in itself a true thing, individual and one in number. However, with respect to things outside [the mind] it would be universal and common and indifferent in relation to individual things, and it would be as it were the natural likeness of these things, and so it could stand for a reality outside [the mind]. . . . These opinions cannot be easily disproved, nor are they as improbable or clearly false as the opinions disproved in the other questions [4–7].[64]

After discussing these three theories of universals, Ockham proposes a fourth, which he considers to be equally defensible. According to this theory the universal would not be a real being (*vera res*) existing in the mind. In Ockham's language it would not have "subjective being", but only a nonreal mode of being in the mind called "objective being". To have this type of being things simply need be an object of thought: *eorum esse est eorum cognosci*. Things with subjective being are realities in the categories of Aristotle (but only in the categories of substance and quality, for in Ockham's view these alone are real). Objects with objective being are *ficta*, formed in the mind as likenesses of things actually or possibly existing in reality. When we see something real, like a house, we can fashion an image of it in our mind. A universal may be said to be a *fictum* or *imago* of this sort, indifferently resembling a number of individuals that either are or can be real. In this theory, impossible beings like chimeras and goat stags would also have objective being, but they are *figmenta* rather than *ficta*.[65]

The notion that a universal, or for that matter any concept, has only objective being was widely entertained in Ockham's day, and he himself at first appears to have adopted it. When first commenting on the *Sentences* he gave it most attention and preferred it to the other theories of the concept. In later revisions of the *Ordinatio* he defended several theories, as we have seen, among them the objective being theory. In a final revision he added a long explanation and defense of the alternative theory, that a universal concept is a real entity in the mind in the category of quality. The concept, in this view, is a natural sign of extramental reality as a word is a conventional sign of the same reality. The concept may be thought of as the act of knowing or as a quality different from that act and coming after it. He leaves to the reader's judgment which of these opinions is truer, adding, "I maintain, however, that no universal, unless perchance it be universal by voluntary institution, is something existing in some way outside the soul, but that everything that is by its nature a universal and predicable of many [subjects] exists in the mind either subjectively or objectively, and no universal is of the essence or quiddity of any substance."[66]

In later writings Ockham shows a growing disenchantment with the *fictum* theory of the concept and a favoring of the *intellectio* theory.[67] Even in his *Ordinatio* he raises serious objections to the former theory. The concept functions as a likeness of the thing conceived, but it is difficult to imagine how a *fictum* can be like a real thing. A real accidental being, like a quality, is more like a substance than a *fictum* is, so it is easier to explain the likeness of the mind to reality if the concept is held to be a real quality of the mind.[68] In his *Quodlibets* and *Questions on the Physics*—works postdating the *Ordinatio*—he rallies to the opinion that all concepts and propositions are mental qualities; more specifically they are acts of knowing.[69] A particular concept is an act of knowing whose object is one individual; a universal concept is an indistinct or general act of knowing whose object is a number of individuals with some degree of similarity. For example, the specific concept 'man' is an act of knowing all individual humans, whether actually or only potentially existing. This embraces an infinity of human beings. The generic concept 'animal' is also an act of knowing whose objects extend not only to all humans but also to all animals. When we know nonreal objects like chimeras or gold mountains, we elicit an act of knowing to which nothing corresponds in reality. There is no need to suppose that these objects have a special nonreal mode of existence called "objective being".

Ockham's abandonment of the *fictum* theory of the concept is in line with his fundamental rule that explanations should be as simple as possible. The principle of parsimony, known as Ockham's Razor, is operative throughout his writings. In the present instance—apparently under the influence of his Franciscan confrère Walter of Chatton—Ockham uses it to eliminate *entia ficta* from the mind. Everything that can be explained by them can equally well be accounted for by real acts of knowing. Furthermore, when such entities are thought to be intermediaries between reality and the act of knowing, as Peter Aureol taught, they stand in the way of knowing reality itself.[70]

Ockham's Notion of the Individual

We are now in a position to understand better the nature and importance of the individual in Ockham's philosophy. He assigns two meanings to an individual or singular. In one sense it means whatever is one and not many. So defined, even a universal is really and truly an individual; it is universal insofar as it is the sign of many things and is predicable of them. A spoken or written word is really an individual sound or character, though it can be a conventional sign of many things. A mental concept is also really and truly an individual; its universality is its function of being a natural sign of many things. In another sense an individual is that which is one and not many, and it is not of such a nature as to be the sign of many things. Taken in the latter sense, no universal is individual, for it is the nature of a universal to signify many things and to be predicable of them.[71]

Ontologically, then, every universal is a particular thing: *quodlibet universale est una res singularis.*[72] Functionally, universals are names, either spoken, written, or mental. Ockham calls universals existing in the mind "mental names" (*nomina mentalia*), thereby justifying his traditional title of nominalist.[73]

Though Ockham calls a universal a "singular thing," the adjective 'singular' is redundant, for in his view every thing (*res*) is singular or individual; moreover, it is individual by itself and not through anything extrinsic to it. A nature is individual of itself (*de se haec*).[74] Scotus thought this was a prerogative of the divine nature; a created nature is 'this' (*haec*) through an added haecceity.[75] Ockham extends the notion of a nature's being *de se haec* to the created order.

Individuals, for Ockham, are also primarily diverse (*primo diversa*); that is to say, "There is nothing in [any two individuals] that is one and the same: whatever is in one simply and absolutely of itself is not something that exists in another."[76] We could not wish for a stronger statement of the radical incommunicability of individuals.

An individual, in Ockham's view, is so radically one that it is impervious to any distinction. There is a real distinction between real beings, and, if they are composed, between their parts. For example, two humans are really distinct, and so too are their form and matter. The qualities of whiteness and sweetness in milk are also really distinct individual accidents. A distinction of reason is one made by the mind between several names or concepts. If they are concepts of the same thing, it cannot be said that the thing differs from itself because of the diversity of concepts. A distinction of reason has to do with concepts and not with the real individual. The individual is by nature nondistinguishable.[77]

Ockham limits the range of created individuals to substance and the third species of quality, for example, whiteness and heat.[78] The other accidents are not realities but only terms or names.[79] Relation, for example, is not a thing (*res*) but a term denoting several absolute things.[80] If the relation is made by the mind (like the relation between subject and predicate), it is a relation of reason. If the mind has no role in relating things, they are really related, but they are related by themselves and not by an added relation. For example, things are more or less similar to each other, as all humans bear a close resemblance to each other, more so than humans and brute animals. The specific concept "humanity" and the generic concept "animality" have for their objects individuals in these different degrees of likeness.

The lack of real community among things has repercussions throughout Ockham's philosophy and theology. Thus in his doctrine of knowledge the diversity of things is so profound that the incomplex or simple knowledge of one thing can give us no incomplex knowledge of another. "Everyone experiences in himself", Ockham writes, "that however intuitively or perfectly he knows something, he never knows another thing, unless he had previous knowledge of that other thing."[81] Moreover, the primacy of the individual in being has its counterpart in its primacy in knowledge: Knowledge begins with the intuitive cognition of the individual.[82]

In this chapter we have not been searching for Ockham's principle of individuation, for he assured us at the outset that there is none. Rather, our purpose has been to discover why he believed a principle of this sort to be superfluous. The answer comes to light with his ontology, which reduces all being to things (res), either real or of the mind's own making. Scotism is centered upon the notion of the common nature.[83] Thomism has its focal point in the act of existing (esse).[84] Ockham's originality is shown in his choice of the individual as the capstone of his philosophy and theology. In the world of Ockham the individual is the center of attention, as it would be later in the world of Leibniz, who, incidentally, admired the medieval nominalists, and especially Ockham, as the most profound sholars.[85] For both philosophers, each individual is different from every other, not just in number but in essence. In short, to be an individual is to be perfectly one with itself.[86]

Notes

1. "In conclusione istius quaestionis omnes quos vidi concordant, dicentes quod natura, quae est aliquo modo universalis, saltem in potentia et incomplete, est realiter in individuo, quamvis aliqui dicant quod distinguitur realiter, aliqui quod tantum formaliter, aliqui quod nullo modo ex natura rei sed secundum rationem tantum vel per considerationem intellectus." *Guillelmi de Ockham, Scriptum in librum primum Sententiarum. Ordinatio.* I, d. 2, q. 7; ed. S. Brown and G. Gál. *Opera theologica* 2 (St. Bonaventure, NY: Franciscan Institute, 1970), pp. 225.17–226.3. Ockham's works are cited in the St. Bonaventure edition, which is in two series: *Opera theologica* (cited OTh) and *Opera philosophica* (cited OPh).

2. ". . . quaelibet res singularis se ipsa est singularis. Et hoc persuadeo sic: quia singularitas immediate convenit illi cuius est, igitur non potest sibi convenire per

aliquid aliud; igitur si aliquid sit singulare, se ipso est singulare." *Ordinatio* I, d. 2, q. 6, p. 196.3–6.

3. "Et ita quaelibet res extra animam se ipsa erit haec; nec est quaerenda aliqua causa individuationis nisi forte causae extrinsecae et intrinsecae, quando individuum est compositum, sed magis esset quaerenda causa quomodo possibile est aliquid esse commune et universale." *Ibid.*, p. 197.14–18.

4. See, A. Wolter's chapter on Scotus (p. 273).

5. Jorge J. E. Gracia, *Introduction to the Problem of Individuation in the Early Middle Ages* (Washington, DC: The Catholic University of America Press, 1984), pp. 210–211, 214. M. M. Tweedale, *Abailard on Universals* (Amsterdam: North Holland, 1976).

6. Ockham treats of universals and individuals in the following works: *Expositio in librum Porphyrii de Praedicabilibus,* prooem. 2; ed. E. A. Moody (St. Bonaventure, NY: Franciscan Institute, 1978), OPh 2, pp. 99–292. *Expositio in librum Praedicamentorum Aristotelis,* 8, 1; ed. G. Gál (St. Bonaventure, NY: Franciscan Institute, 1978), OPh 2, pp. 162–171. *Scriptum in librum primum Sententiarum. Ordinatio,* 1, d. 2, qq. 4–8, ed. S. Brown and G. Gál (St. Bonaventure, NY: Franciscan Institute, 1970), OTh 2, pp. 99–292. *Summa logicae,* I, 14–19, ed. P. Boehner, G. Gál, and S. Brown (St. Bonaventure, NY: Franciscan Institute, 1974), OPh 1, pp. 47–67. *Quodlibeta* V, qq. 12–13; ed. J. C. Wey (St. Bonaventure, NY: Franciscan Institute, 1980), OTh 9, pp. 528–536. *Quaestiones in libros Physicorum Aristotelis,* q. 2; ed. S. Brown (St. Bonaventure, NY: Franciscan Institute, 1984), OPh 6, pp. 398–399. For Ockham's treatment of the problems of universals, see M. M. Adams, *William Ockham,* 2 vols. (Notre Dame, IN: University of Notre Dame Press, 1987), vol. 1, pp. 3–141.

7. *Ordinatio* I, d. 2, q. 4, pp. 100.17–101.11. In his *Summa logicae* Ockham criticizes the opinion that a universal is an extramental reality (*res*) or substance composed of several universal *res.* I, 15, pp. 50–54.

8. *Ibid.*, d. 2, q. 5, p. 154.2–4. See I, d. 2, q. 4, p. 100, n. 3.

9. *Ibid.*, d. 2, q. 4, p. 122.12.

10. See *ibid.*, p. 100, n. 3.

11. *Ibid.*, pp. 101.12–103.12.

12. *Ibid.*, 103.13-18.

13. *Ibid.*, p. 108.2.

14. *Ibid.*, pp. 122.7–123.24.

15. *Ibid.*, pp. 127.5–129.20.

16. Aristotle, *Post. Anal.* I, chs. 4–5 (73b26–74a13); *Metaph.* VII, ch. 15 (1039b20–1040a10).

17. ''. . . est sciendum quod scientia quaelibet sive sit realis sive rationalis est tantum de propositionibus tamquam de illis quae sciuntur, quia solae propositiones sciuntur.'' *Ordinatio* I, d, 2, q. 4, p. 134, 7–9.

18. *Ibid.*, pp. 134.3–138.21. For Ockham's doctrine of the supposition of terms, see *Summa logicae* I, 63–77, pp. 193–238.

19. *Ordinatio* I, d. 2, q. 5, p. 154.2–7.

20. *Ibid.*, p. 154, n. 1. Alnwick's question to which the editors refer has been edited by P. T. Stella, ''Illi qui student in Scoto: Guglielmo di Alnwick et la 'haecceitas' scotista'', *Salesianum* 30 (1968): 614–637. For another question of Alnwick on individuation, see *ibid.*, I, 331–387.

21. See Jorge J. E. Gracia, *Introduction to the Problem of Individuation,* pp. 155–193. E. Gilson, *History of Christian Philosophy in the Middle Ages* (New York: Random House, 1955), pp. 140–144.

22. *Ordinatio* I, d. 2, q. 5, p. 154.9–17; p. 159.3–6.

23. ''. . . ista opinio est, ut credo, opinio Subtilis Doctoris, qui alios in subtilitate iudicii excellebat.'' *Ordinatio* I, d. 2, q. 6, p. 161.6–8. Ockham also criticizes the Scotist doctrine in his *Summa logicae* I, 16–17, pp. 54–62.

24. See, Alan Wolter's chapter on Scotus.

25. *Ordinatio* I, d. 2, q. 6, pp. 161–167.

26. This is the principle of parsimony or Ockham's Razor. See A. Maurer, ''Method in Ockham's Nominalism'', *Monist* 61 (1978): 426–443, especially 427–431; ''Ockham's Razor and Chatton's Anti-Razor'', *Mediaeval Studies* 46 (1984): 463–475; M. M. Adams, *William Ockham,* vol. 1, pp. 156–161.

27. *Ordinatio* I, d. 2, q. 6, pp. 171.1–20; 219–220.

28. *Ordinatio, ibid.*, pp. 162.3–163.11. Ockham cites Scotus, *Ordinatio* II, d. 3, q. 6; ed. C. Balić (Vatican, 1973), 7n. 187–188, pp. 483–484.

29. *Ordinatio, ibid.*, pp. 173.11–174.23.

30. *Ibid.*, p. 175.11–17.

31. ''. . . impossibile est in creaturis aliqua differre formaliter nisi distinguantur realiter; igitur si natura aliquo modo distinguitur ab illa differentia contrahente, oportet quod distinguantur sicut res et res, vel sicut ens rationis et ens rationis, vel sicut ens reale et ens rationis. Sed primum negatur ab isto, et similiter secundum, igitur oportet dari tertium.'' *Ibid.*, p. 173.12–17.

32. *Ibid.*, p. 174.8–23. See *Ordinatio* I, d. 2, q. 1, OTh II, pp. 14.8–17.7. See M. M. Adams, "Ockham on Identity and Distinction", *Franciscan Studies* 36 (1976): 44–50.

33. *Ordinatio* I, d. 2, q. 6, p. 175.1–10.

34. Scotus, *Ordinatio* I, d. 2, pars 2, q. 4 (Vatican, 1950), II, pp. 349–361.

35. *Summa logicae* II, 2, p. 254.130–135. See *Ordinatio* I, d. 2, q. 1, pp. 17.9–19.2.

36. *Ordinatio* I, d. 2, q. 7, p. 229.1–6.

37. *Ibid.*, pp. 226.5–227.7.

38. The editors suggest that this was the doctrine of Aquinas and Hervaeus Natalis, while granting that it is not found literally in their works. *Ibid.*, p. 226, n. 1. The *De universalibus*, which they abscribe to Aquinas (p. 225, n. 1), is not authentic. See P. Mandonnet, *Des écrits authentiques de S. Thomas d'Aquin* (Fribourg, Switzerland, 1910), p. 108.

39. St. Thomas, *De ente et essentia* 3; ed. Leonine 43 (Rome, 1976), pp. 374–375.

40. *Ordinatio* I, d. 2, q. 7, p. 240.10–16.

41. ". . . nihil reale potest distingui nec esse idem ratione cum aliquo reali, ita quod sicut distinctio rationis et identitas rationis se habent ad entia rationis, ita differentia realis et identitas realis se habent ad entia realia, et hoc forte non excludendo distinctionem formalem et identitatem ubi debet poni [i.e. in Trinitate]. Ideo dico quod nulla res nec a se ipsa nec a quacumque alia potest distingui vel esse eadem secundum rationem." *Ibid.*, I, d. 2, q. 3, OTh II, p. 75.5–11.

42. "Alii autem ponunt quod res secundum esse suum in effectu est singularis, et eadem res secundum esse suum in intellectu est universalis, ita quod eadem res secundum unum esse vel secundum unam considerationem est universalis, et secundum aliud esse vel secundum aliam considerationem est singularis." *Ibid.*, I, d. 2, q. 7, p. 227.9–13.

43. St. Thomas, *De ente et essentia* 3; ed. Leonine 43, pp. 374–375.

44. "Quod est commune multis non est aliquid praeter multa nisi sola ratione, sicut animal non est aliud praeter Socratem et Platonem et alia animalia nisi intellectu, qui apprehendit formam animalis exspoliatam ab omnibus individuantibus et specificantibus." St. Thomas, *Summa contra Gentiles* I, 26, #5; ed. Leonine 13 (Rome, 1918), p. 81.

45. *Ordinatio* I, d. 2, q. 7, p. 241.2–13.

46. *Ibid.*, p. 241.14–19.

47. For St. Thomas's doctrine of being, see E. Gilson, *Le thomisme,* 6th ed. (Paris: J. Vrin, 1965), pp. 169–189. Translation of the 5th edition: *The Christian Philosophy of St. Thomas Aquinas,* trans. L. K. Shook (New York: Random House, 1956), pp. 29–45.

48. *Summa logicae* III-2, 27; pp. 553–555.

49. *Ordinatio* I, d. 2, q. 7, pp. 227.15–288.20.

50. ". . . dico quod omnis res posita extra animam est singularis eo ipso." Henry of Harclay, "Quaestio de significato conceptus universalis", ed. G. Gál, *Franciscan Studies* 31 (1971). n. 79, p. 216. Quoted by Ockham, *ibid.,* p. 228.4–5.

51. ". . . licet [res] in se sit singularis, quantum ad repraesentationem passivam est universalis. Quod non est aliud nisi quod confuse et [non] distincte est cognoscibilis." Henry of Harclay, *ibid.,* n. 83, p. 218. I have added [non].

52. *Ordinatio* I, d. 2, q. 7, pp. 241.21–242.6. Ockham also criticizes Harclay for holding that a universal always results from indistinct knowledge. In the case of an incomposite or simple object the universal can result from distinct knowledge. "No incomposite reality can be confusedly understood if it is understood, and yet there is truly a universal respecting incomposite items." *Ibid.,* p. 250.10–12. God is an example of an incomposite reality: When known intuitively, he is distinctly known. *Ordinatio* I, d. 3, q. 5, p. 459.9–21.

53. *Ibid.,* d. 2, q. 7, p. 236.9–17.

54. "Ideo dico quod universale non est in re ipsa cui est universale nec realiter nec subiective, non plus quam haec vox 'homo', quae est una vera qualitas, est in Sorte vel in illo quod significat. Nec universale est pars singularis respectu cuius est universale, non plus quam vox est pars sui significati." *Ibid.,* p. 252.1–5.

55. *Ibid.,* p. 271.2–7. On natural and conventional signs, see *Summa logicae* I, 1, pp. 7–9.

56. John of Salisbury, *Metalogicon* II, 17; ed. C. C. I. Webb (Oxford: Clarendon Press, 1929), 2, p. 874. See Abailard, *De generibus et speciebus;* ed. V. Cousin (Paris, 1836), pp. 513, 522sq.

57. *Ordinatio* I, d. 2, q. 8, p. 271.9–12.

58. *Summa logicae* I, 1, pp. 7–9. See A. A. Maurer, "William of Ockham on Language and Reality", *Miscellanea Mediaevalia: Sprache und Erkenntnis im Mittelalter,* 13, 2 (Berlin: Walter De Gruyter, 1981), pp. 795–802.

59. *Ordinatio* I, d. 2, q. 8, pp. 267.7–268.5. See Henry of Ghent, *Quodl.* IV, q. 8, V, q. 14 (Paris, 1518), ff. 98v, 174r–179v. Godfrey of Fontaines, *Quodl.* IX, q. 19; ed. I. Hoffmans, Les philosophes belges, vol. 4 (Louvain: Institut Supérieur de Philosophie, 1914), pp. 270–281.

60. *Ordinatio* I, d. 2, q. 8, p. 269.2–4. See St. Thomas, *Summa theologiae* I, q. 85, a. 2; ed. Leonine 4 (Rome, 1888), pp. 333–334. Giles of Rome, *Sent.* I, d. 19, q. 1, Resp. (Venice, 1521), f. 110va. On the species theory, see Ockham, *Quaestiones in Physicorum* I, q. 4, OPh VI, pp. 404–405; *Expositio in librum Perihermenias* I, prooem. 5, OPh 2, pp. 350–351. For an excellent study of the problem of species, see K. H. Tachau, "The Problem of the *Species in Medio* at Oxford in the Generation after Ockham", *Mediaeval Studies* 44 (1982): 394–443.

61. *Ordinatio* I, d. 2, q. 8, p. 269.6–16; I, d. 27, q. 2, OTh IV, p. 205.8–18; *Sent.* II, q. 12, OTh V, p. 256.5–9.

62. *Ordinatio* I, d. 2, q. 8, p. 269.18–20. See St. Thomas, *De veritate* 4, 1; ed. Leonine 22 (Rome, 1970), pp. 199–120. Ockham criticizes Henry of Ghent's notion of the *verbum* in *Ordinatio* I, d. 27, q. 2, OTh 4, pp. 197–205.

63. *Summa logicae* I, 12, pp. 42.30–43.39.

64. "Istae opiniones concordarent in hac conclusione, quod universale esset in se vera res singularis et una numero; respectu tamen rerum extra esset universalis et communis et indifferens ad res singulares et quasi naturalis similitudo illarum rerum, et propter hoc posset supponere pro re extra. . . . Istae opiniones non possunt faciliter improbari, nec sunt ita improbabiles nec ita evidentem falsitatem continent sicut opiniones improbatae in aliis quaestionibus [i.e., 4–7]." *Ordinatio* I, d. 2, q. 8, p. 270.6–20.

65. *Ibid.*, pp. 271.14–273.22. The distinction between *figmenta* and *ficta* is found in Henry of Harclay, "Quaestio de significato conceptus universalis," p. 225, n. 101.

66. "Hoc tamen teneo, quod nullum universale, nisi forte sit univerale per voluntariam institutionem, est aliquid exsistens quocumque modo extra animam, sed omne illud quod est universale praedicabile de pluribus ex natura sua est in mente vel subiective vel obiective, et quod nullum universale est de essentia seu quidditate cuiuscumque substantiae." *Ibid.*, pp. 291.17–292.1.

67. On this subject see G. Gál, "Gualteri de Chatton et Guillelmi de Ockham controversia de natura conceptus universalis", *Franciscan Studies*, new series, 27 (1967): 191–212. M. M. Adams, *William Ockham* vol. 1, p. 74, n. 10. See *ibid.*, p. 73, n. 9.

68. *Ordinatio* I, d. 2, q. 8, p. 282.1–4. See *Expositio in librum Perihermenias* I, prooem. 7, pp. 360.30–361.60.

69. *Quodlibeta* IV, 35, p. 474.115–120. *Quaestiones in libros Physicorum* I, 6, pp. 406–410. In his *Summa logicae*, however, which is dated c. 132, Ockham does not seem to have made up his mind regarding the nature of the concept. See I, 12, pp. 42–43. He seems to incline to the *intellectio* theory.

70. Ockham criticizes the doctrine of Aureol in *Ordinatio* I, d. 27, q. 3; OTh 4, pp. 238–258. See Peter Aureol, *Scriptum super I Sent.* d. 3, sect. 14, n. 31; ed. E. M. Buytaert (St. Bonaventure, NY: Franciscan Institute, 1952) 2, pp. 690–698. Walter of Chatton, a contemporary of Ockham, argued against the existence of *entia ficta* in his *Reportatio et Lectura super Sententias,* Prologus; ed. J. C. Wey (Toronto: Pontifical Institute of Mediaeval Studies, 1989), p. 198, 260–272.

71. *Summa logicae* I, 14, pp. 48.13–49.64; I, 19, pp. 65–67.

72. *Ibid.*, p. 48.31. See *Quodl.* V, 12, pp. 528–531.

73. *Summa logicae* I, 3, p. 11.27. Some historians prefer to call Ockham a conceptualist, because in his view universals are primarily concepts. See P. Boehner, "The Realistic Conceptualism of William Ockham", *Traditio* 4 (1946): 307–335; repr. in *Collected Articles on Ockham,* ed. E. M. Buytaert (St. Bonaventure, NY: Franciscan Institute, 1958), pp. 156–174.

74. *Ordinatio* I, d. 2, q. 6, p. 224.9–13.

75. Scotus, *Ordinatio* I, d. 1, pars 1, q. 2; ed. C. Balić, 2, pp. 30–31.

76. ". . . dico quod aliqua esse, 'prima diversa' potest intelligi dupliciter: vel quia nihil est unum et idem in utroque, sed quidquid est in uno simpliciter et absolute de se non est aliquid quod est in alio; et isto modo concedo quod omnia individua sunt se ipsis primo diversa, nisi forte aliter sit de individuis ex quorum uno generatur aliud propter identitatem numeralem materiae in utroque." *Ordinatrio* I, d. 2, q. 6, p. 212.18–23.

77. *Ibid.*, I, d. 2, q. 3, pp. 75.4–77.6.

78. *Quodl.* VII, 2, pp. 707–708.

79. *Summa logicae* III-3. 18, p. 666.443–451. Ockham treats successively of the categories of substance and the nine accidents, *ibid.*, I, 42–62, pp. 122–193; also in *Quodl.* VII, 2–7, pp. 706–726.

80. *Ordinatio* I, d. 30, q. 1; OTh 4, pp. 310.20–311.2. Ockham treats extensively of relation in *Summa logicae* I, 49–54, pp. 153–179; also in *Quodl,* VI, 8–30, pp. 611–701.

81. ". . . quilibet experitur in se quod quantumcumque cognoscat intuitive et perfecte aliquam rem, nunquam per hoc cognoscit aliam rem nisi praehabeat notitiam illius alterius rei." *Ordinatio* I, Prol. q. 9; OTh I, p. 241.3–6. See lines 18–21.

82. *Ibid.*, I, d. 3, q. 6, pp. 492.15–496.18.

83. See E. Gilson, *Jean Duns Scot* (Paris: J. Vrin, 1952), p. 451. J. Owens, "Common Nature: A Point of Comparison Between Thomistic and Scotistic Metaphysics", *Mediaeval Studies* 19 (1957): 7–13.

84. See E. Gilson, *Le thomisme*, pp. 169–189; *The Christian Philosophy of St. Thomas Aquinas*, pp. 29–45.

85. W. G. Leibniz, *Dissertatio de stilo philosophico Nizolii*, 28. *Opera philosophica*, ed., J. E. Erdmann (Berlin, 1840), pp. 68–69.

86. See Leibniz, *Selections;* ed. P. P. Wiener (New York: Charles Scribner's Sons, 1951), p. 96. E. Gilson and T. Langan, *Modern Philosophy. Descartes to Kant* (New York: Random House, 1963), pp. 157–158.

18

JEAN BURIDAN
(B. CA.1295/1300; D. AFTER 1358)

PETER O. KING

I. Introduction

Buridan[1] holds that no principle or cause accounts for the individuality of the individual, or at least no principle or cause other than the very individual itself, and thus there is no "metaphysical" problem of individuation at all—individuality, unlike generality, is primitive and needs no explanation. He supports this view in two ways. First, he argues that there are no nonindividual entities, whether existing in their own right or as metaphysical constituents either of things or in things, and hence that no real principle or cause of individuality (other than the individual itself) is required. Second, he offers a "semantic" interpretation of what appear to be metaphysical difficulties about individuality by recasting the issues in the formal mode, as issues within semantics, such as how a referring expression can pick out a single individual. Yet, although there is no "metaphysical" problem of individuation, Buridan discusses two associated problems at some length: the identity of individuals over time and the discernibility of individuals.

The discussion will proceed as follows. In Section II, Buridan's semantic framework, the idiom in which he couches his philosophical analyses, will be described.[2] In Section III, the sense Buridan assigns to 'singular' and 'individual', as well as associated terms and expressions such as 'one' and 'numerically one', will be examined. In Section IV, Buridan's negative arguments in support of his claim that everything that exists is individual will be examined. In Section V, Buridan's "semantic" interpretation of individuation will be discussed, in particular what it is to be a discrete term. In Section VI, general issues regarding Buridan's ontology will be explored. In Section VII, identity over time and the discernibility of individuals will be explored.

II. Buridan's Semantic Framework

For Buridan, as for other philosophers of the fourteenth century, there are three distinct levels of language: written language, spoken language, and mental language, associated respectively with the activities of writing, speaking, and thinking.[3] Each is a fully developed language in its own right, with vocabulary, syntax, formation rules, and the like. They are hierarchically ordered, and the ordering is piecemeal rather than holistic: Particular inscriptions are said to "immediately" signify particular utterances, and particular utterances immediately signify concepts that are mental particulars, "acts of the soul" (QM, V, q. 9). A concept is a natural likeness of that of which it is a concept and signifies what is conceived by the concept. Written and spoken terms are said to "ultimately" signify what is conceived by the concept (TS 3.2.8).

Mental language is a natural language, unlike spoken or written languages which are conventional, and it is perspicuous in rigor. Mental language functions as a canonical or ideal language: It is universal to all thinking beings (other than God), unlike the diversity of merely conventional "natural" languages such as French or Italian and indeed explains the possibility of translation among such "natural" languages; it is expressively adequate, in that it has the resources to express whatever may be expressed; it is unambiguous and nonredundant, in that, respectively, an ambiguous spoken or written term will be correlated with several mental terms each of which has a single signification, while synonymous inscriptions or utterances are correlated with the same mental term. Buridan's distinction between syncategorematic and categorematic terms serves to distinguish logical and nonlogical particles. Categorematic terms have an ultimate signification, while syncategorematic terms have an immediate signification and have ultimate signification only in combination with categorematic terms (TS 2.3.6–7). Syncategorematic terms such as 'and' or 'is' immediately signify simple concepts that combine other concepts, which Buridan calls "complexive concepts"; they are semantic term-forming or sentence-forming functors (TS 2.3.11–143). Sentences of mental language display their logical form in a perspicuous manner. In short, mental language behaves like the semantics for written and spoken language: It is the vehicle through which written and spoken languages are "given meaning" or have an ultimate signification, in the last analysis due to the ways in which a concept may signify that of which it is a concept.

It is one matter to correlate terms with their significates so that a language may be established in the first place; that is accomplished by signification. It is another matter to actually use the terms to talk about their significates, which is a distinct semantic relation between terms and their significates. This latter semantic relation is called "supposition", and accounts for the referential use of categorematic terms. Hence there are two major differences between signification and supposition. First, terms retain their signification at all times, but only in a sentence are terms used referentially, that is, to talk about things and say something about them. Hence a term has supposition only in a sentential context. Second, we do not always use terms to talk about everything those terms ultimately signify; we mention, as well as use, terms, and sometimes we speak only of a subclass of all the significates of a term. Hence a term may have different kinds of supposition depending upon its sentential context. There are two main kinds: personal supposition, which occurs when a term stands for what it ultimately signifies, and material supposition, which occurs when a term does not stand for what it ultimately signifies.[4] Hence in the sentence 'Socrates is human' the term 'Socrates' has personal supposition, referring to Socrates the individual; and in the sentence 'Socrates is a three-syllable word' the term 'Socrates' has material supposition, referring to the utterance 'Socrates'. Note, however, that the term 'Socrates' is one and the same term in each sentence. Much as signification is the medieval correlate to a theory of meaning, supposition is the medieval correlate to a theory of reference—and, like any theory of reference, is the guide to ontology.

Categorematic terms that correspond to simple or incomplex concepts are called "absolute" terms; Buridan argues in QSP, I, q. 4 that there must be such incomplex concepts to avoid the possibility of infinite regress. Categorematic terms that signify something for which they do not personally supposit are called "appellative" or "connotative" terms.[5] Since terms retain their signification at all times, the signification of any string of terms will be the union of the signification of each term: 'white bird' signifies all white things and all birds. The supposition of any string of terms, on the other hand, will be the intersection of the supposition of each term: 'White bird' will supposit only for some white things (those that are birds) and some birds (those that are white). Hence complex phrases are appellative. Now appellative terms do not supposit for, although they may connote, additional entities, and so do not add to the ontology; therefore, ontological commitment is carried only by the individual absolute terms of mental language.[6]

Mental language, and the associated theories of signification and supposition, form the semantic framework for Buridan's analyses of philosophical problems and in particular for his discussion of individuation. As a first step in uncovering Buridan's views, then, his discussion of the signification of the term 'individual' and related terms such as 'singular' and 'numerically one' should be examined. That is the task of the next section.

III. Criteria of Individuality

Buridan describes the principal signification of the terms 'singular' and 'individual' in QM, VII, q. 19 as follows (fol. 53vb):

> The name 'singular' is opposed to the name 'plural', according to grammar, but this is not relevant for us; rather, we shall take it as opposed to the name 'common' or 'universal', and then it seems to me that according to the logician these terms 'singular' and 'individual' are taken as synonymous terms to which [the terms] 'common' and 'universal' are opposed. These are all names of second intention, suppositing for significative terms: 'singular' and 'individual' supposit for discrete terms, and 'universal' supposits for common terms.[7]

A term that ultimately signifies other terms is said to be "a term of second intention", while a term that ultimately signifies something that is not a term is said to be "a term of first intention".[8] Thus the terms 'individual' and 'singular' are on a par with terms such as 'verb,' since each is a general term signifying a kind of linguistic element. In particular, 'singular' and 'individual' signify discrete terms; that is, terms that as a matter of semantics alone are "predicable of only one", namely, in an identity statement such as 'this is Socrates'.[9] Buridan offers us as examples of discrete terms 'Socrates' and 'this man' (TS 3.3.1); presumably proper names, demonstratives, and were Latin to have a definite article, definite descriptions are candidates for discrete terms. (This will be discussed in Section V in more detail.) In the strictest sense, then, individuality and singularity are properties of terms rather than things.

However, Buridan admits a looser sense of 'individual' and 'singular' that applies to nonsemantic objects in the world, and I shall typically follow his dual use of these terms when no confusion can occur. Criteria for individuality as a property of things rather than terms can be inferred from Buridan's discussions of related terms; there seem to be two: (1) absence of division; (2) distinctness from all else.

As regards (1), in QM, IV, q. 7, Buridan raises the general question whether 'being' (ens) and 'one' (unum) convert, that is, are truly predicable of exactly the same things. Buridan argues that they do so convert, but nevertheless they are not synonymous, since "the term 'being' or 'something' (aliquid) is taken according to a simple concept, that is, [a concept that is] free from connotation, and the term 'one' is a connotative term—it connotes the absence of division (carentia divisionis)". Yet they are predicable of exactly the same objects, and despite the fact that 'one' is connotative it does not involve any extra ontological commitment, since "the absence of

division is not a thing that is added on beyond the thing that is the individual, as the privation or the absence of form is not a thing added to the matter''. Now 'absence of division' applies to anything that may be called 'one'
in any way at all, including accidental unities (such as heaps). We are interested in a more particular case, namely, what criteria must be satisfied by
those things that are not just one but that are numerically one. In QM, VII,
q. 19, Buridan points out that 'numerically one' is a name of first intention
and semantically a common term, ''insofar as it is true to say that every being
is one in number'', and it may characterize substances, parts of substances,
and accidents: ''whiteness or matter or the soul is as numerically one as
man.'' Yet Buridan does not specify the kind of division the absence of which
'numerically one' entails. If we restrict our attention to individuals that are
capable of existing *per se,* then the traditional account has it that the divisibility the lack of which is in question is that such beings cannot be instantiated—they cannot be divided either ''into beings [specifically] similar to
themselves'' or ''into subjective parts''—and there is no reason to doubt that
Buridan adopted this traditional view.

As regards (2), Buridan does not address the nature of individual distinctness so much as simply assume it to hold. In QM, VII, q. 17, he asserts
that ''individuals of the same species, such as Socrates and Plato, differ substantially according to their substances, as much by their forms as by their
matter, in that neither is the form of Socrates the form of Plato nor the matter
of Socrates the matter of Plato''. Distinctness from other individuals is an
intrinsic feature of individuality. Note that this claim allows Buridan to offer
a unified account of distinctness: Individuals of different species differ as regards their substantial forms, a claim admitted by all medieval philosophers,
but Buridan holds that individuals of the same species also differ in their
forms. This poses the problem how such individuals are classed together under the same species—indeed, what 'sameness in species' can mean if not
possession of the same form—but Buridan will argue that this is a matter of
a general term suppositing for distinct individuals, not a matter of a metaphysically identical constituent in distinct individuals.

Individuality consists, at least in part, in intrinsic indivisibility and distinctness from all else. They are features of individuality, though they form
no part of its definition—indeed, if individuality is a basic notion then it cannot be defined. Buridan takes indivisibility and distinctness to characterize
everything that exists. It is to the content of this claim that we now turn.

IV. Everything Is Individual

Buridan frequently asserts that every thing that exists is individual:
''every thing exists as singular such that it is diverse from any other thing,

since it is never possible that a term suppositing precisely for one thing be
truly affirmed of a term suppositing precisely for another [thing]." (QSP, I,
q. 7) No principle or cause accounts for the individuality of the individual, or
at least no principle or cause other than the very individual itself. Individuality is a basic feature of the world. Substances and accidents are equally individuals; composites are individuals whose component parts are themselves
individual.[10] Concepts, even general concepts, are individual acts of understanding in individual intellects, spoken and written language so many individual utterances or inscriptions. To support the thesis that every thing that
exists is individual, Buridan argues that there are no nonindividual entities,
whether existing independently or as metaphysical constituents either of
things or in things, and hence that no real principle or cause of individuality
(other than the individual itself) is required.

Buridan argues at length against the existence of universals as nonindividual entities.[11] In QM, VII, q. 15, he asks whether universals are "separated" from singulars, and he notes that, strictly speaking, 'universal' is a
term of second intention, applying to a term that is "predicable of many and
indifferently signifies many and supposits for many, and then its signification
is opposed to the term 'singular' or 'discrete' ''. Universals are trivially
"separable" from singulars in this sense, for one person may have only a
general term in mind and another person only a discrete term in mind. However, Buridan immediately points out that the question is not intended in this
sense, but rather about "the things signified by universal terms", such that
the "separability" at issue is one of independent ontological existence:
Whether universals are things that are distinct from singulars. (In medieval
terminology, whether there is a real distinction between the universal and the
singular.) Buridan takes the claim that there are universals, that is, things signified by universal terms, which are separate from singulars to be Plato's
position, which he stigmatizes as "completely absurd".[12] He offers two arguments against the position characterized in this way. First, the sentence
'Socrates is (a) man' would not be true, since "if *man* is separate from
Socrates then it is diverse from him, and Socrates is not something diverse
from himself". Second, either man is the same in 'Socrates is (a) man' and
'Plato is (a) man' or it is different: If it is the same, then "by an expository
syllogism it follows that Socrates is Plato, for whatever are the same as one
and the same undivided [thing] are the same as each other"; if it is different,
"although separate, then there would be as many separate men as there are
singular men, and this is absurd, and neither has anyone ever held it."[13] Buridan, unaware of the theory of participation, reads the copula in the conceded
sentences of each argument as entailing strict coreferentiality, and so finds the
separation of the forms unintelligible.

Yet Buridan seems aware that this is too shallow an understanding. He
develops an original interpretation of Platonism, based on an analogy with

Averroes's understanding of the active intellect, which severs the formal signification of a term from that for which it (materially) supposits and so might
seem to permit some kind of separation of the universal and the singular
(QM, VII, q. 15, fol. 50vb):

> Yet it is to be believed that [Plato] held [a position] like the position of
> the Commentator on the human intellect. [The Commentator] believed,
> as is apparent from [his commentary on] *De anima* III, that all men
> understand by numerically the same intellect and that this [intellect] is
> separate from all men such that it does not inhere in them but still
> stands to them as present and without any distance (*praesentialiter et
> indistanter*), as we say God stands to the whole world. Therefore, al-
> though there would be many who understand, nevertheless they would
> understand by a unique intellect. The term 'understanding' would cor-
> rectly supposit for men, yet formally signify a thing separate from
> them, namely, the understanding existing in that [unique] intellect, and
> so there is no contradiction that some term supposits for something and
> yet by its formal signification signifies a thing separate from it. Just as
> the term 'agent' supposits for the thing that acts, and yet by its formal
> signification signifies the action by which it is called an 'agent'—
> which nevertheless is not in the agent but in the patient—so too when
> I say ''a stone is seen'' the term 'seen' supposits for the stone and yet
> by its formal signification signifies the seeing by which the stone is
> seen, which is not in the stone but in the eye. Therefore, Plato said in
> this way that humanity or animality is a form separate from these men
> or these animals, which, although [the form] is one and the same, all
> men are nevertheless [men] by that humanity and all animals are ani-
> mals by that animality. Hence Plato would doubtless have granted that
> one man is Socrates and another Plato, and yet Socrates and Plato are
> men by the same humanity. (If the term 'man' were sometimes taken so
> as to supposit for that humanity, then ''Socrates is a man'' would not
> be granted.)[14]

Indeed, we might add that if the term 'seen' were sometimes taken to supposit for what it formally signifies, then ''a stone is seen'' is also false, since
'seen' then supposits for the act of seeing in the eye while 'stone' supposits
for an external object.[15] Universal terms supposit for singulars as the recip-
ients of the metaphysical activity and presence of the associated Form. Hence
universal terms supposit for what they signify, although not for their formal
signification. This interpretation seems to avoid the difficulties with coreferentiality that Buridan found decisive in rejecting the previous crude characterization of Platonism.

Despite the ingenuity of the proposed interpretation, Buridan rejects
"Platonism" of this sort, adopting two of Aristotle's arguments that are
based on the separateness of the Forms: such a position would entail that individuals would be neither knowable nor even entities. The first argument,
that individuals would not be knowable, is a variation of the first argument
given against the previous crude characterization of Platonism (fol. 50vb):

> Those holding this [position] would hold that the humanity by which
> Socrates is a man is the quiddity of Socrates. Now any given thing is
> known properly and simply only in this, that its quiddity is known. But
> in knowing a thing separate and distinct from Socrates, Socrates is not
> known. Therefore, if the quiddity of those sensible things were separate
> and other than them we would not have knowledge of those sensible
> [things]. Yet this is clearly false, since a doctor investigates the science
> of medicine only in order to know how to cure those men regarding
> whom he has scientific knowledge, and still he knows only how to cure
> sensible men.[16]

The objection is ineffective, even without the theory of participation,
since it could be maintained that knowledge of sensible individuals is only
knowledge of them insofar as they are what they are in virtue of a separate
Form. After all, there is no scientific knowledge, strictly speaking, of
Socrates, who is a contingent and mutable particular without a definition.

The second argument is that individuals could not even properly be
counted as entities (fol. 50vb): "Something is not intrinsically a being by a
thing separate [from it], and yet nothing is a being except intrinsically by its
entity; therefore, if the entity of this [individual] were separate from it, it
would not be a being."[17] Yet this objection begs the very point at issue;
namely, whether something can be what it is in virtue of something separate
from it. The defender of Platonism will reply that it is possible, and Buridan's
objection amounts to the mere assertion of the contrary. Buridan also adds an
objection on the grounds of ontological parsimony (fol. 51ra): "It is completely useless to posit such [separate forms] if, leaving them aside, everything can be preserved that could be preserved with them —but everything
can be so preserved, as will be apparent in the resolution of [the principal
arguments]; therefore, etc."[18]

In short, there is no compelling reason to postulate such separate
forms; "everything can be preserved that could be preserved with them",
that is, all the claims admitted by both sides of the dispute can be satisfactorily held as true without postulating separate forms.

In QM, VII, q. 16, Buridan takes up the question whether universals
are distinct from singulars, taking 'universal' and 'singular' as the things that

are signified by universal and singular terms. His answer, again, will be that they are not. Now Buridan does not specify the kind of distinctness involved, but it is clear from his discussion (and especially the principal arguments) that he means any distinction *a parte rei*. In particular, he does not mean to exclude the claim that the universal is distinct from the individual by a pure distinction of reason. Thus his target in this question is any theory that ascribes an ontological status to the universal other than that possessed by the individual. More precisely, Buridan is rejecting any theory that takes the individuality of an individual (anything capable of existing *per se*) to be derived from an extrinsic principle that has independent ontological status; for example, some factor that contracts a common nature, such as matter or haecceity.[19]

Buridan offers several arguments against such theories, the first two of which are the arguments proffered against the crude characterization of Platonism. If 'man' in 'Socrates is (a) man' supposits for something with an independent ontological status, then the terms are not coreferential and hence the sentence is false. Nor can it be maintained that strict coreferentiality is not required, since if, for example, the copula were interpreted along part-whole lines, the sentence 'Socrates is (a) man' would be a denominative rather than an essential predication. Again, if 'man' supposits for something that is the same as Socrates and the same as Plato, then Socrates is Plato, and if it supposits for something distinct in each case, then each of these distinct entities is just as singular as Socrates or Plato himself, "and so it turns out again that there are no universals distinct from singulars."[20] Nor can it be maintained that there are individualized forms but that such forms are what they are in virtue of a distinct universal, since if that distinct universal has an independent ontological status it plays the role played by the Platonist's separate forms, refuted in the previous question. Buridan offers an independent third argument against this position, a dilemma with a subordinate trilemma (QM, VII, q. 16, fol.51va–b):

If humanity is in [Plato] and in Socrates and we posit that Socrates is corrupted, then I ask whether the humanity that was in him is corrupted or remains. If it is corrupted, then it is as singular as Socrates, and a singular distinct from the humanity of Plato, which remains. But if you were to reply that the humanity of Socrates or even the asinity of Brunellus is not corrupted, but remains even when Socrates or Brunellus is corrupted, then it is necessary to hold either (1) that it flies off to another place without a body, which is absurd; or (2) that it at least remains in the cadaver, and then the cadaver would remain either a man or an ass by [the presence of] that humanity or asinity, which is absurd; or (3) that the asinity would remain as separate from the body, and so we return to the separate Ideas of Plato, discussed before.[21]

Therefore, Buridan concludes, "it is vain to hold that there are universals distinct from singulars if everything can be preserved without them—and they can, as will be apparent in the resolution of the principal arguments", where Buridan is largely concerned with contexts in which no individual seems to correspond to the action of the verb: 'I promise you a horse', but no particular horse; 'I desire water', but no particular water; 'fire generates fire', but no particular fire; and the like.[22] His resolution generally consists in pointing out that any given singular will serve the purposes marked out by the main verb (and that a universal would not), and so there is no compelling reason to countenance separate universals.

Buridan is thorough in his semantic reinterpretation of Aristotelianism. In QM, IV, qq. 8–9, he discusses the traditional question whether the essence and the *esse* of a thing are the same and prefaces his discussion with the comment that "I understand by 'essence' the thing itself". The essence of Socrates is not a nonindividual entity, but in fact is simply Socrates himself.[23] Indeed, as regards reality, Socrates is not only his essence but he is also his *esse*. Buridan argues that essence and *esse* only differ in reason, that is, that the terms 'essence' and '*esse*' have distinct connotation, which is not reflected in any difference of supposition.[24] Thus the doctrine of essences poses no problems for Buridan's theory, and with suitable interpretation of claims involving essences, he can adopt the terminology while avoiding its apparent ontological commitments.

Buridan has argued for the negative side of his case, that there are no nonindividual entities, whether existing independently or as metaphysical constituents either of things or in things. Therefore, no real principle or cause of individuality (other than the individual itself) is required. But arguments that are only negative can be only part of the story; Buridan also has to make out a positive case, to show how his semantic interpretation of individuation can provide an adequate explanation of other difficulties.

V. The Semantics of Individuation

The result of Buridan's negative arguments is that universals are not distinct from singulars in any metaphysically interesting way; that is, "the universal is a term or concept in the mind by which we conceive simultaneously and indifferently many things existing as singular outside the soul, and that concept is posterior to those singular things since it is objectively caused by them" (QSP, I, q. 7). Universals are "really" distinct from singulars in the way in which concepts are "really" distinct from that of which they are the concepts. Since the universal term signifies many individuals, it may supposit for those individuals; "individual" and "universal" are alternate ways of conceiving exactly the same things.[25] Since there are no nonindividual real entities, issues such as "whether in substances the spe-cies is contracted[26] to the individual by a substantial or accidental *differen-tia*", which is the subject of QM, VII, q. 17, are simply confused if taken with regard to real entities; they require instead a semantic interpretation (fol. 52va):

> This "contraction" is not with respect to the things signified [by the concept], putting all concepts aside, since then man or animal or body or substance etc. would exist as singular, just as Socrates and Plato [ex-ist as singular], for man is nothing other than Socrates or Plato. There-fore, since man or animal is a thing existing as singular, then if everything else were put aside it is clear that it would not require any contraction such that it would exist as singular. And so it must be said that contractions of this sort have to be understood with respect to con-cepts or terms that are significative of things. . . . A term that is a spe-cies would be said to be contracted to a singular term by the addition of a differentia restricting the specific term to supposit for only that for which the singular term supposits.[27]

The metaphysical question of contraction is interpreted as a semantic ques-tion about the restriction of supposition. The general application of this tech-nique leads to a semantic reformulation of questions regarding individuation. Therefore, the appropriate context in which to raise philosophical problems about individuation is the semantic framework outlined in Section II, with the full apparatus of mental language and concepts at its core. So stated, a closer look at the nature of the concepts that are the terms of mental language is in order.

In QSP, I, q. 7, and in QA, III, q. 8, Buridan inquires about the foun-dations of mental language, addressing the possibility of both universal and singular cognition: "since there are no universals outside the soul distinct from singulars but every thing exists as singular, whence does it come about that things are sometimes understood as universal?" He rejects the traditional response, that this is due to the immateriality and separability of the intellect, instead ascribing it to the internal functioning of the intellect (QSP, I, q. 7, fol. 8vb):

> The reason for this is that things are understood not through this, that they are in the intellect, but through their likeness existing in the in-tellect. Moreover, external things have agreement and likeness among themselves from their nature and from their essence, as I now assume and will later establish. Now if it were the case that there are many [things] similar to each other, anything which is similar to one of them

in that respect in which they are similar [to one another] is similar to every one of them. Hence if all asses in fact have an agreement and likeness with one another, it is necessary that when the intelligible species will represent some ass in the intellect in the manner of a likeness it will indifferently represent any given ass at the same time, unless something prevents it (as will be discussed later). Thus a concept (*intentio*) becomes universal in this way.[28]

The same account is given in QA, III, q. 8. The intelligible species is a likeness, and so objectively similar to all the things that it resembles.[29] Hence things are understood as universal due to the intrinsic "processing features" of the intellect. Yet this response, while grounding universal cognition, seems to make singular cognition impossible: If the intellect always understands through a likeness, then the inherent generality of resemblance seems to preclude singular cognition.

    Buridan avoids the difficulty by pointing out, in essence, that when the thing to be cognized is "within the prospectus of the knower", the direct contact between the knower and the object can supersede the mediating generality of representations. The external senses represent an object to the interior or common sense in a "confused" manner (QSP, I, q. 7, fol. 9ra): "An exterior sense apprehends its object confusedly, with the size and location pertaining to it as well as appearing within its prospectus as either near or far, or to the right or to the left. Hence it perceives its object as singular inasmuch as [it perceives its object] as picked out here or there."[30] This "confusedness" is a matter of the agglomeration of particular circumstances that are fused together (*con-fusa*) in the act of sensing, not the "confusedness" of generality. Now "sense represents a sensible object to the intellect with this sort of confusedness, and just as it primarily represents the object to the understanding, so the intellect primarily understands the thing; therefore, the intellect can primarily know the thing with confusedness of this sort and so as singular". Singular cognition is possible in this way. Thus a singular concept is acquired only by direct contact with the individual, by means of intuitive cognition (QM, VII, q. 20, fol. 54va):

    Nothing is a singular concept unless it is a concept of a thing in the manner of existing in the presence and within the prospectus of the knower, insofar as that thing were to appear to the knower just as by an ostension picking it out, and in that manner of knowing some call "intuitive". It is true that by memory we conceive a thing as singular by this, that we remember it to have been within the prospectus of the knower, and in such a manner it was known.[31]

Mental language is natural, in the sense that the connection between concepts and their significates is nonconventional, and its formal structure is universal to all thinking beings other than God, but its "material" elements—the concepts that make up the nonlogical "vocabulary" of mental language—must be acquired through experience. In effect, Buridan is claiming that the only way to possess concepts that are discrete terms in the vocabulary of mental language is through direct contact with the individual the concept is to signify. Past experiences of direct contact will serve, since the singular concept may be retained in memory. Nevertheless, there must be a direct contact at some point for genuine singular cognition. The actual mechanism by which a new singular concept is acquired, that is, the way a new discrete term is introduced into mental language, is through imposition, a performative act that Buridan describes as akin to baptism (QSP, I, q. 7, fol. 9ra):

> If I were to announce *this* [man] within my prospectus to be picked out by the proper name 'Socrates' (rather than by such-and-so [characteristics]), then the name 'Socrates' would never fit anyone else no matter how similar, unless there were a new imposition and [the name 'Socrates'] were imposed to signify that other person, and hence equivocally.[32]

Singular concepts are related to their significates directly, not through a likeness that would entail a degree of semantic generality.[33] The semantic property of individuality, that is, predicability of only one, is secured through "presence within the prospectus of the knower" as an essential feature in the acquisition of the singular concept.

It follows from this account that there are only two classes of genuinely discrete terms, that is, only two kinds of discrete terms in mental language: the proper names of individuals with which one has come into direct contact, and demonstrative expressions.[34] The names of individuals with which one has never come into direct contact, Buridan holds, are not strictly discrete terms but rather disguised descriptions: "to others who have not seen [Plato or Aristotle], those names are not singular, nor do they have singular concepts corresponding to them simply" (QA, III, q.8); we who have never come into direct contact with Aristotle "do not conceive him as different from other men except by a given circumlocution, such as 'a great philosopher and teacher of Alexander and student of Plato, who wrote books of philosophy that we read, etc.' " (QSP, I, q. 7), which would equally signify and supposit for another individual if there were one having engaged in these activities. Put another way, the fact that 'Aristotle' supposits only for Aristotle is not a matter of semantics but depends on the contingent historical fact that no other individual happens to fit the description, and so it cannot be a discrete term.

The same point may be made about descriptions generally, including definite descriptions: "the expression 'the son of Sophroniscus' is not, strictly speaking, singular, since 'the son of Sophroniscus' is immediately apt to fit more than one if Sophroniscus produces another son" (QA, III, q. 8).[35] However, Buridan isolates a class of expressions closely related to definite descriptions, expressions composed of a demonstrative combined with a common noun (e.g., 'this man'). He calls such an expression a "vague singular" (*singulare vagum*), noting that a genuinely singular concept may correspond to a vague singular due to the indexical force of 'this', although "it is difficult to cognize singularly in this way" (QA, III, q. 8, and QM, VII, q. 17).

Clearly, though, vague singulars do not form a distinct linguistic class in mental language, since they are composed of elements already present. The semantics of mental language, based on the nature of concepts, determine what terms can be properly regarded as discrete. Buridan did not permit natural necessity or even metaphysical necessity to infringe upon the domain of semantics—terms such as 'sun' describe a kind of entity, namely, "the largest and brightest planet", which are naturally unique, but the term 'sun' is nevertheless semantically general—indeed, he is so bold to assert the same for the term 'god', whose referent is not only naturally but metaphysically unique.[36] Truths about the world, even truths about the necessary uniqueness of certain entities, do not secure the semantic individuality of terms. What, then, exists in the world as the correlate to discrete terms? That is, what are the possible individuals that discrete terms might supposit for? This is to ask about Buridan's ontology, at least in its general outlines, and is the subject of the next section.

VI. Buridan's Ontology

What it is to be a being, strictly speaking, is to be capable of existence *per se*. Hence the capability to exist *per se* characterizes all individuals, and conversely.[37] What kinds of individuals are there, that is, what beings can exist *per se*? For Buridan, at least four kinds of beings count as individuals which may exist *per se:* (1) primary substances, that is, the things for which "primary substance" terms supposit; (2) separable substantial forms; (3) prime matter; (4) separable accidents. A closer look at each of these is in order.

First, all beings that Buridan characterizes as "substances subsisting *per se*" will be individuals: God, the Intelligences, primary substances such as Socrates and Brunellus. Anything which, in Aristotelian terminology, can be a "this-something" (*hoc aliquid*) is an individual.[38] Second, at least some substantial forms are separable, namely, the souls of humans, and hence are individuals capable of existing *per se*. So much is obvious and unproblematic.

Third, prime matter, which is of itself a being, may exist *per se*, at least by divine power: In QSP, I, q. 20, Buridan argues that ''[prime] matter is in act, and it would be in act even if it were to exist without either substantial or accidental form inhering [in it]''. However, it naturally exists as informed by some form, and in that condition it is not individual, ''unless God were to conserve it without them''. In its natural condition, prime matter is in act, but only as a component part of some composite substance; it is not of itself a ''this-something'', as Buridan specifically argues. The individuality of prime matter, whether as a component part or as existing independently by divine power, is purely negative, reflecting only the ''absence of division'' described in Section III.

Fourth, Buridan argues in QM, V, q. 8, in consequence of the phenomenon of the Eucharist, that accidents are capable of existing *per se* as separate from any substance: They may exist without inhering in anything at all, at least by divine power.[39] Now if it is not part of the nature of, say, whiteness to inhere in a substance, then a further special kind of metaphysical glue is required for the actual bonding of substance and accident. Buridan terms this glue an ''added disposition'', which is nothing other than an inseparable quality of inherence (inseparable since otherwise there would be an infinite regress of such qualities).[40] This is a clear philosophical break with Aristotle, and Buridan recognizes it to be such, carefully describing Aristotle's position before presenting his alternative view. What makes substances differ from (separable) accidents? Buridan's summary response is that substances are those things that can naturally exist *per se*, while accidents can only exist *per se* through direct divine intervention. Yet this is not an essential difference between substance and accident, and from the metaphysical point of view there is no difference between them.

If there is no metaphysical difference between substance and accident, it follows that a reassessment of the nature of the Aristotelian categories is in order. Buridan regularly insists that the categories are not classifications of things or beings or entities. Nor do they categorize terms, strictly speaking; they are groupings of *modes of predicating* terms of proper names (primary substances). There are many illustrative comments to this effect, but one of the clearest statements is in QC, q. 3 (p.18.96–104):

> But [the categories] are taken from diverse concepts (*intentiones*), according to which terms are connotative (or even nonconnotative) in different ways. From these diverse connotations there arise the diverse modes of predicating terms of primary substances; hence [the categories] are immediately and directly distinguished according to the different modes of predicating with regard to primary substances. If [terms] are predicated *in quid* or essentially of them, then such terms are in the category Substance; if they are predicated denominatively *in*

quale, they are in the category Quality; if [they are predicated] *in quantum,* they are in the category Quantity . . . [41]

This position, taken in isolation, is not atypical; many other medieval philosophers would agree with Buridan's analysis, at least in its general outlines.
The standard analysis, though, builds bridges to ontology by claiming that
such modes of predicating somehow reflect a deep truth about the way the
world is. And this is where Buridan parts company with his Aristotelian her-
itage: He wants to burn all the bridges connecting the categories to ontology.
The modes of predicating terms of primary substances have no privileged
role: Aristotle's list is neither necessary nor sufficient. Buridan frequently refers to *Topics* IV, ch. 3, 124a10–14, in which Aristotle mentions only four
categories, taking this as evidence that they are not necessary; he argues that
they are not sufficient in QC, q. 3 (p.19.137–146):

> Many people labor in vain—those who seek to establish the sufficiency
> of the number of the categories. I believe that the sufficiency of the
> number of the categories could be established or proved only by finding
> [that there are] exactly so many distinct modes of predicating that are
> not reducible to some single more general mode of predicating accord-
> ing to a single general *ratio,* and, hence, there must be so many. But
> just because we do not find more general categories that are not con-
> tained under or reduced to these [ten] modes, we thereby do not posit
> more categories. Accordingly, if we were to discover more general
> modes of predicating beyond the aforementioned ten, it seems to me
> that we should not deny that there are more [than ten] categories. [42]

In QM, IV, q. 6, as elsewhere, Buridan insists that the terms 'action', 'acting', and 'active' pick out diverse most general genera, as do, for example,
qualitas, quale, and *qualitativum.* Indeed, Buridan rejects the name 'substance' as a most general genus, preferring instead the term 'something' (*aliquid*) as the most general genus—motivated by his admission of separable
accidents; substances and separable accidents both fall under 'something'.
What is more, in QC, q. 7, Buridan proves successively that "every substance or divisible quality is quantity"; "every thing, or even every being, is
a relation (*ad aliquid*)"; "every thing and every quantity is quality"; and,
finally, "all things are quantity". [43] In short, Buridan simply discards the traditional Aristotelian categories as a guide to metaphysics. They are semantic
in nature, merely classifying modes of predicating, and one of limited value
at that. Semantics and ontology are distinct enterprises. Only individuals exist, and individuals do not of themselves reflect any categorical features of
the way the world is. [44]

Accidents, then, are just as individual as substances: whiteness is on a par with Socrates. The same analysis that applies to all individuals applies to accidents as well: There is no principle or cause of the individuality of an accident other than the accident itself. Thus accidents do not raise any difficulties with individuation that more standard cases of primary substances do not equally raise. Hence they need not be treated separately.

VII. Identity over Time and the Discernibility of Individuals

Buridan discusses two problems related to individuation; namely, the identity of individuals over time and the discernibility of individuals. While not strictly a matter of the individuality of the individual, each question sheds some light on Buridan's understanding of individuation, and each discussion is noteworthy in its own right.

Buridan devotes QSP, I, q. 10, to the question whether Socrates "is the same today as he was yesterday, positing that today there is added to him something converted into his substance from what he ate, or even positing that some part were removed from him, as if his hand were cut off". He distinguishes three ways in which something is called "numerically the same" as another (fol. 13vb):

> We customarily say that one thing is the same as another in three ways: either (1) *totally,* i.e., because the one is the other and there is nothing in the totality of the one which is not in the totality of the other, and conversely; this is to be numerically the same in the strictest sense . . . (2) *partially,* i.e., because the one is part of the other, and it is especially so-called if it is the greater or more principal [part], or even because the one and the other participate in something which is the greater or more principal part of each . . . (3) according to the continuity of diverse parts, with one [part] succeeding another.[45]

Whether Socrates is numerically the same at different times depends on the sense of 'numerically the same' adopted. According to (1), "it should be said that I am not the same as what I was yesterday, for yesterday something was part of my totality that now is no longer (*resolutum est*), and also something else yesterday was not part of my totality that, after eating, is of my substance". In the strictest sense, then, Socrates is not totally the same yesterday as today. However, according to (2), "a man remains the same throughout his entire life, since his soul, which is the more principal (or indeed the most principal) part, remains totally the same". In this sense Socrates is partially the same yesterday and today, due to the total sameness of his principal part, the soul. According to (3), which is the loosest sense, a being with parts that succeed one another, either completely, such as a river, or partially, such as the organic matter of living bodies, can be called "numerically the same" from one time to the next. In this sense, Socrates is successively the same from day to day, despite the processes of growth and decay.

Identity over time is clearly parasitic on more basic notions of identity, for no matter which of (1)–(3) may be in question, whether a being is numerically the same at one time as another depends on the more basic identity or nonidentity of its parts. Unfortunately, Buridan does not separate the question of individuality from that of identity; it is one matter to grant that every thing is individual, another to ask about the criteria for identity and distinctness for different kinds of things. From his discussion of the various senses of 'numerically the same', it follows that simple beings, or beings without inessential component parts, are strictly numerically the same from one time to the next, so long as they exist. Hence souls and the Intelligences are numerically the same at all times. (The question cannot sensibly be applied to God, who is not in time.) A plausible conjecture would be that the issue of identity over time can be raised only for material beings; this would be the case if the quantitative parts of any object can be only material parts. Buridan's discussions of quantity, e.g., in QC, qq. 8–9, support the conjecture.

There is a separate epistemic question about the discernibility of individuals; namely, what the principle or cause is by which distinct individuals of the same kind are perceived or known to be distinct. In QM, VII, q. 17, Buridan asserts that "we have no way to perceive the difference among individuals of the same species except by accidents or by extraneous [factors]". He supports his claim by a striking example (fol. 52va):

> If there were two stones completely similar in shape, size, color, and so on for the other [accidents], and they were brought into your presence successively, you would have no way to judge whether the second brought to you were the same as the first brought to you or the other one. And so too if there were men completely similar in shape, size, color, and so on for the other accidents.[46]

The impossibility of reidentification shows that there is no privileged knowledge of distinct individuals as distinct. (Note the form of this conclusion: There is certainly knowledge of distinct individuals, but the knowledge of distinct individuals as distinct is in question.) Now this version of the example applies to the limited case of individuals that are substances, but Buridan also offers a variation of the example that applies to discerning individual accidents (*ibid.*):

> Indeed, this is true not only in the case of substances but also for the case of accidents: if there were whitenesses similar to each other in in-

tensity (*gradus*) and they were in subjects similar to each other in shape, size, etc., you would not have any way to know whether it was the same whiteness or the other one which was shown to you previously.[47]

Accidents are metaphysically as individual as substances and present the same epistemic problems of discernibility as substances. Buridan concludes that "the *differentiae* through which individuals of the same species appear to be distinguished by us are accidental *differentiae*, that is, certain accidents or [factors] extraneous to those individual subjects". Thus individuals of the same species are distinct of themselves, and so differ substantially, but their distinctness is known only through accidental or extrinsic factors. Hence "we perceive the contraction of the species to the individual not by substantial *differentiae* but by accidental [*differentiae*], yet the things signified by individual terms are themselves substantially distinguished".

This account raises two difficulties. First, if substances are discernible only through accidental *differentiae*, how can substance terms fail to connote accidents? Buridan takes this problem up in QM, VII, q. 17 ad 2 (fol. 52vb):

It may be said that substantial terms in the category of substance are not completely free from the connotation of accidents; it is necessary to consider accidents at least in the imposing [of the term]. Still, because the intellect can free the concept of the subject from the concept of the accident, in imposing [the term] we intend to free it up so that the term does not connote the accidents, although by them we are led to the notion of the substance.[48]

The direct intuitive contact with an individual is not to be confused with the intuition of an individual as individual; direct intuitive contact allows a singular name to be imposed and a singular concept to be formed, but such concepts do not free one from the possibility of error, either as mistaken identification or being unable to reidentify the individual. Buridan explicitly points this out when discussing the formation of singular concepts (e.g., QSP, I, q. 7). Therefore, substance terms may be absolute, despite the necessity of extrinsic individuating factors in the imposition of the term.

The second difficulty Buridan's account poses is that it seems to threaten an infinite regress. Grant that two substances can be discerned as two only by some accidental or extrinsic factor. How will that accidental or intrinsic factor be perceived as distinct, especially if the two substances each possess it (e.g., if both are white)? Buridan takes this up in QM, VII, q. 17, ad 4 (fol. 52rb):

I grant that it is true in the case of accidents as well as in the case of substances, namely that the diversity of those which are of the same species is perceived only by certain accidents; neither is an infinite regress necessary, since we know how to distinguish the whiteness of a horse and the whiteness of a cow, for we perceive the distinctness of the cow and the horse in which there are these whitenesses. Similarly, we know how to distinguish a cow from [another] cow, since one is white and the other black, and [we know how to distinguish] colors of the same species by substances or shapes or by sizes of diverse species, and so too [we can distinguish] substances by shapes and colors or as being substances of this sort. Thus all these may be perceived in relation to each other without an infinite regress.[49]

There is no principled way in which distinct individuals are discernible. Individual substances of the same species may be discerned by their distinct accidents, and if both are perceived at once then their distinct locations will serve; distinct accidents may be discerned by inhering in discernibly distinct subjects, as for example whitenesses inhering in the specifically distinct subjects of a horse and a cow. As Buridan notes in QM, VII, q. 15, even putting matter aside a man and an ass "have extremely different accidents and extremely different natural operations, which appear sensibly to us and of different kinds". In short, discernibility is a relational property, not an intrinsic feature of individuals or due to some factor in a principled way. Hence there need be no infinite regress, since in practice there is a way to discern distinct individuals.

VIII. Conclusion

Buridan rejects the metaphysical form of the problem of individuation, maintaining instead that the apparently metaphysical difficulties it raises can be understood better as semantic questions—an approach that has some affinities with contemporary philosophical work. The legacy of Buridan's treatment of such problems is the rigorous and careful application of the semantic framework of mental language to metaphysical questions, even to the point of casting doubt on metaphysics as a discipline independent of semantics. What, in the final analysis, makes substances differ from accidents, given that accidents are capable of existing *per se*? I think the correct answer, for Buridan, is that it is a question he does not much care about. Once the bridges from the Aristotelian categories to ontology have been burned, the status of the theoretical vocabulary of substance and accident is left up in the air—which is exactly where, it seems to me, Buridan leaves it. There is a suggestion in his writings that a kind of "functionalist" approach to ontology is the correct one, that we should identify substances as central points of causings and effectings, so that to characterize something as a substance is to say that it is a pattern in the ebb and flow of events distinguishable as a node in the causal nexus such that the work nominally done by metaphysicians should in fact be done by physicists. But it is no more than a suggestion, and Buridan does not work it out. It was left to the philosophers of the next several centuries to complete the break with Aristotle, and eventually to reject the substance-accident terminology Buridan has deprived of theoretical foundations.

Buridan's theory of individuation may be summarized in three claims: Individuality is a basic feature of the world; there are no nonindividual beings; metaphysical problems are, by and large, disguised semantic problems. These deceptively simple claims provide the seeds of a radical break with Aristotle and traditional Aristotelian philosophy. His contribution is to work out some of the implications of these claims in a rigorous manner, leaving the rest for his successors. Contemporary philosophy is again sympathetic to Buridan's claims. Perhaps it has something to learn from his results as well.

Notes

1. References to Buridan are taken from a variety of his works (with abbreviations listed): *Questions on the "Categories"* (*Quaestiones in Praedicamenta*) (QC); *Questions on the "Physics"* (*Quaestiones subtilissimae super octo Physicorum libros Aristotelis*) (QSP); *Questions on the "De caelo et mundo"* (*Quaestiones De caelo et mundo libros Aristotelis*) (QCM); *Questions on the "De anima"* (*Quaestiones in De anima secundum tertiam*) (QA); *Questions on the "Metaphysics"* (*Quaestiones in Metaphysicam Aristotelis*) (QM); *Treatise on Supposition* (*Tractatus de suppositionibys*) (TS); *Sophismata; Treatise on Consequences* (TC). Details about each of these may be found in the Bibliography. References to the *quaestiones* are in the standard book/treatise and question number format; references to TS and TC follow the numbering scheme in King's translation; references to *Sophismata* VIII follow the numbering scheme in Hughes's translation. Translations are mine unless specifically noted otherwise. I would like to thank J. A. Zupko for making his work on Buridan's *Questions on the "De anima"* available to me. It should be noted that, while these include most of Buridan's works available in published form, from incunabula to modern critical editions, many other works remain in manuscript: line-by-line commentaries on Aristotle; independent treatises such as the full *Summulae de dialectica;* other *quaestiones.* All claims made about Buridan can be only tentative until his corpus is fully available. The classic discussion of Buridan's works is given by Edmond Faral, ''Jean Buridan: Maître dès arts de l'Université de Paris,'' in the *Histoire littéraire de France,* vol. 27, deuxième partie (Paris: Imprimerie Nationale, 1949), pp. 462–605.

2. For further discussion of the points raised in the summary of Buridan's semantic framework, see the introduction to Peter King, *Jean Buridan's Logic,* Syn-

these Historical Library vol. 27 (Dordrecht: D. Reidel, 1985). See also Calvin Normore, "Buridan's Ontology", in *How Things Are: Studies in Predication and the History and Philosophy of Science,* ed. James Bogen and James E. McGuire (Dordrecht: D. Reidel, 1984), pp. 187–200, and the introduction to G. E. Hughes, *John Buridan on Self-Reference* (Cambridge: Cambridge University Press, 1982). The description will be specific to Buridan; for example, Buridan, unlike say William of Ockham, does not admit a category of "simple supposition" (TS 3.2.5), and so it is not described in the following.

3. The theory of the three levels of language is given a textual foundation through Aristotle's opening remarks in the *De interpretatione,* 16a3–8, as understood in Boethius's translation. See Norman Kretzmann, "Aristotle on Spoken Sound Significant by Convention", in *Ancient Logic and its Medieval Interpretations,* ed. John Corcoran, Synthese Historical Library, vol. 9 (Dordrecht: D. Reidel, 1979), pp. 3–21, for the importance of this proviso.

4. More exactly: a term *t* has personal supposition in a sentence if and only if either (1) some sentence of the form 'This is *t*' is true, or (2) some clause of the form 'and that is *t*' can be added to an existential sentence, or to a sentence presupposing an existential sentence, to produce a true sentence. The demonstrative pronoun and the copula of (1) and (2) should be taken in the appropriate tense, grammatical number, and mood. This definition is a generalization of the account of personal supposition Buridan sketches in TS 1.2.9. A term has material supposition at all other times, for example, when an inscription such as 'Socrates' supposits for the inscription or for the concept of Socrates rather than for Socrates himself.

5. Strictly speaking, three semantic relations are involved: a term such as 'white' *supposits* for an individual white subject, *connotes* the quality whiteness, and *appellates* the special disposition of inherence in a subject (TS 1.4.8). Buridan seems to call such terms "appellative" and the relation they have to what they do not stand for "connotation", although such terms may also loosely be called "connotative". The characterization given in the text is not strictly accurate; it should be phrased as a conditional: If a term signifies something for which it does not supposit, something "extrinsic" to the referent, then that term is appellative; see TS 1.4.1, 5.1.1., 5.2.5, and *Sophismata* I, Theorem 6. Yet there are also appellative terms that signify something not really distinct from that for which the term supposits, having only "intrinsic" connotation, such as 'creative' when speaking of God (since God's creative power is identical with the divine essence according to QM VII, q. 4) or 'rational' in speaking of humans (since rationality is a constitutive differentia of humanity according to TS 1.4.6). For an alternative view of connotation, see L.M. De Rijk, "On Buridan's Doctrine of Connotation", in *The Logic of John Buridan,* ed. Jan Pinborg (Copenhagen: Museum Tusculanum, 1971)

6. The distinction between terms with intrinsic and extrinsic connotation, combined with Buridan's thesis that accidents may exist while inhering in no subject (as they do in the Eucharist) complicates this claim; more exactly, ontological commitment is carried by individual absolute terms and individual nonabsolute terms with

only intrinsic connotation. It should also be noted that the distinction between intrinsic and extrinsic connotation renders the claim, "complex phrases are appellative", not strictly accurate: Phrases in which the individual terms each signify exactly the same and supposit for what they signify will not be appellative. This applies to trivial examples such as 'man man man', but also to phrases that include an absolute term and an appellative term with only intrinsic connotation, such as 'creative God' (and perhaps 'one being', as discussed in Section III).

7. The text reads: "Dico quod hoc nomen 'singulare' secundum grammaticam opponitur huic nomini 'plurale', sed de hoc nihil ad nos; immo capiamus ipsum prout opponitur huic nomini 'commune' vel 'universale', et tunc videtur mihi quod apud logicum isti termini 'singulare' et 'individuum' verificantur pro terminis synonymis quibus opponitur 'commune' vel 'universale'. Et sunt haec omnia nomina secundarum intentionum supponentia pro terminis significativis: 'singulare' enim et 'individuum' supponunt pro terminis discretis, et 'universale' supponit pro terminibus communis."

8. Any term may materially supposit for a term, since it may materially supposit for itself, but only a term of second intention may personally supposit for terms. Buridan does not endorse the standard account that terms of first intention signify extramental entities while terms of second intention signify mental entities. Rather, terms of second intention signify terms *as* terms, that is, complete with semantic properties; and this applies indifferently to elements of written, spoken, or mental language. For example, the term 'mental act', although it signifies mental entities such as concepts that are terms of mental language, presumably is not a term of second intention, while the term 'verb', which also signifies concepts that are terms of mental language (as well as inscriptions that are terms of written language and utterances that are terms of spoken language), presumably is a term of second intention. There are borderline cases: 'Inscription', 'utterance', and 'concept' are the most obvious.

9. This characterization of singularity derives from Porphyry by way of Boethius; see Boethius's translation of Porphyry's *Isagoge,* edited by Lorenzo Minio-Paluello in the series *Aristoteles latinus,* vol. 1, 6–7 (Paris: Desclée de Brouwer, 1966). In Porphyry and Boethius the characterization is given as "what is predicated of only one", but Buridan is clear that predicability is at issue, not actual predication. The qualification 'as a matter of semantics alone' will be important, as we shall see in Section V.

10. This claim should be stated more precisely, since the individuality of a composite that is an accidental unity may not be basic but rather derivative from the individuality of its component parts, as the individuality of a heap is derivative from the individuality of the pebbles that make it up; Buridan is willing to call any agglomeration of individuals an "individual" in this sense, including the individual made up of Socrates's ear, Rouen Cathedral, and the dark side of the moon. (Equally, Buridan would take the grammatically singular, rather than plural, number of 'every thing' into account, so that there are things that are not individual but rather individuals: See, e.g., QC, q. 7, QM IV, q. 7, and TC 1.8.84–86.) More exactly, every thing capable of existing per se is individual, a proviso that includes primary substance,

separable substantial form, separable accidents, and matter—see Section VI. In QSP I, q. 20 Buridan states: "although many beings (*entia*) have *esse* through extrinsic causes of their entity or essence that are active either finally or subjectively, nevertheless, every *ens*, by its entity or essence alone, is that which is essentially and intrinsically."

11. It should be noted that universals may be only one kind of nonindividual entity; Buridan also argues against the existence of other "abstract" entities, such as the *complexe significabile*. (The status of the connection between "abstractness" and generality or nonindividuality is not clear in Buridan.) However, only universals will be examined here.

12. Buridan notes another sense in which something may be called "universal", namely, "according to causality", the way in which causes may have more or fewer effects or kinds of effect (see, e.g., QM VII, q. 15 and QSP I, q. 7). Plato's theory of Forms was familiar to mediaeval philosophers solely through the characterization, or caricature, given by Aristotle in the *Metaphysics*. Nevertheless, Buridan thought enough of such "Platonism" to offer two formulations of it, and indeed to discuss it at all—it was customarily taken for granted in the scholastic period that Aristotle had said all that needed to be said about "Platonism". For example, neither Duns Scotus nor William of Ockham ever mention it as a live metaphysical option. Finally, it should be noted that Buridan regularly refers to Aristotle's disproof of Platonic Forms in *Metaphysics* VII (e.g., in TS 3.2.5 and in QM VII, q. 15 and q. 16 *contra*), presumably to the discussion in *Metaphysics* VII, ch. 14, 1039a23–1039b18, rather than the more extended treatment in *Metaphysics* XIII and XIV. See Alessandro Ghisalberti, *Giovanni Buridano: dalla metafisica alla fisica,* for a different interpretation of Buridan's discussion of Plato and Platonism.

13. Buridan's statement of the arguments is as follows: "This position is completely absurd, since it follows that the sentences 'Socrates is (a) man' and 'Socrates is (an) animal' would not be true. Surely Plato himself, and all others, would grant that the consequence is false. But the consequence is obvious, since if man is separate from Socrates then it is diverse from him, and Socrates is not something diverse from himself; therefore, Socrates is not (a) man. Again, if Socrates is (a) man and Plato too is (a) man, then by conversion man is Socrates and man is Plato. Therefore, I ask whether it is the same undivided man that is Socrates and that is Plato, or if it is one that is Socrates and another that is Plato. If it were said that it is the same and undivided, then by an expository syllogism it follows that Socrates is Plato, for whatever are the same as one and the same undivided [thing] are the same as each other. Yet if it were said that it is not the same man but one in one and another in the other, although separate, then there would be as many separate men as there are singular men, and this is absurd, and neither has anyone ever held it. It is certainly to be believed that Plato never held that there were things separate from each other but not distinct for which the terms 'Socrates' and 'Plato' supposit and for which the sentence 'Socrates is (a) man'' is verified'." Note that the conversions Buridan uses take '*Socrates est homo*' and convert it to '*Homo est Socrates*'; the lack of an article in Latin renders the translation somewhat obscure.

14. The text reads: "Sed credendum est quod ipse opinabatur sicut commentator opinatur de intellectu humano. Ipse enim credidit, ut apparet III De anima, quod eodem intellectu in numero homines intelligerent et quod ille esset separatus ab omnibus hominibus ita quod non inhaerens illis sed tamen assistens eis praesentialiter et indistanter, sicut diceremus deum assistere toti mundo. Quamvis ergo essent multi intelligentes, tamen unico intellectu essent intelligentes, et iste terminus 'intelligens' bene supponat pro hominibus, tamen significat formaliter rem separatam ab eis, scilicet intellectionem in isto intellectu exsistentem; unde nullum est inconveniens quod terminus aliquis supponat pro aliquo et tamen formali significatione significat rem separatam ab illo. Sicut iste terminus 'agens' supponit pro re quae agit, et tamen formali significatione significat actionem qua ipsum dicitur agens—quae tamen non est in agente sed in passo—ita cum dico 'lapis videtur' vel 'lapis est visus' iste terminus 'visus' supponit pro lapide et tamen formali significatione significat visionem qua lapis videtur, quae non est in lapide sed in oculo. Ita ergo dicebat Plato quod humanitas vel animalitas est forma separata ab istis animalibus vel hominibus, quae licet sit una et eadem tamen illa humanitate omnes homines et omnia animalia illa animalitate sunt animalia. Et ideo indubitanter concessisset Plato quod alius homo est Socrates et alius Plato, et tamen eadem humanitate Socrates et Plato sunt homines. (Si aliquando ille terminus 'homo' sumeretur prout supponeret pro humanitate tunc ista non concederetur 'Socrates est homo'.)"

15. There is an obvious difficulty with Buridan's suggestion; namely, that a term need not supposit for that which it formally signifies, despite the fact that Buridan clearly takes such a term to have personal rather than material supposition. This problem is not local to the proposed interpretation, since, as Buridan correctly points out, it arises with regard to ordinary terms such as 'agent' and 'seen'. I do not know of any discussion in which Buridan tries to work out the details of ordinary signification and formal signification.

16. The text reads: "Sic ponentes ponebant quod humanitas qua Socrates est homo est quiditas Socrates. Et unumquodque non scitur proprie et simpliciter nisi per hoc quod scitur quiditas eius, et tamen in sciendo rem separatam a Socrate non sciretur Socrates. Si igitur quiditas istorum sensibilium esset separata et alia ab eis non haberemus scientiam de istis sensibilibus. Et tamen hoc est manifeste falsum, quoniam medicus non quaerit scientiam medicinalem nisi ut sciat sanare illos de quibus habet scientiam, et tamen non scit sanare nisi homines sensibiles."

17. The text reads: "Aliquid non est ens intrinsice per rem separatam, et tamen nihil est ens nisi per suam entitatem intrinsice; ergo si entitas huius esset ab isto separata non esset ens."

18. The text reads: "Omnino frustra ponuntur talia si praeter ista omnia possint salvari quae cum illis salvantur, sed possunt ut apparebit per solutiones; ergo etc."

19. It is not clear whether Buridan took his arguments to be effective against theories that deny any independent ontological status to the common nature, e.g., theories that maintain that the common nature has no real being or that the common nature is neutral with respect to being (as Aquinas is alleged to have held). Presumably

Buridan would simply ask what theoretical benefit is gained by taking individuality to be derived from a "common nature" that does not and cannot exist rather than holding that individuality is a *per se* characteristic of individuals.

20. Buridan's statement of the arguments is as follows: "I say that there are no universals distinct from singulars, since then it would follow that the predication of a universal term of a singular term would be false, as in saying 'Socrates is (a) man'. But the consequent is false, and the consequence is proved as follows: if there were some thing that the term 'Socrates' signified [other] than that signified by the term 'man', these terms would not supposit for the same thing, and so the affirmative sentence would be false. Yet some reply that terms correctly supposit for the same [thing] even if one of them were to signify something that the other does not signify. Accordingly, 'Man is white' is true, and yet the term 'white' signifies whiteness, which the term 'man' does not signify. But this sort of reply runs into another unacceptable [difficulty], namely that the sentence ['Socrates is (a) man'] would not be quidditative, but rather denominative, just as 'Socrates is white' [is denominative] in that the term 'white' signifies or connotes something other than Socrates, and this would also be so in the case at hand. Again, as was argued in Book VII, q. 15, the universal is predicated of its inferiors as by saying, e.g., 'Socrates is (a) man' and 'Plato is (a) man', and these sentences are converted as 'Man is Socrates' and 'Man is Plato'. Either man is the same and undivided that is Socrates and that is Plato, or it is one in the one and another in the other. If you were to say that it is the same and undivided, then it follows by an expository syllogism that Socrates is Plato: 'Man is Socrates, and the same man is Plato; therefore, Socrates is Plato.' But if you were to say that one man is Socrates and another man is Plato, it then follows that these are singulars just as much as Socrates and Plato, and so it turns out again that there are no universals distinct from singulars." Note that the conclusion of the second argument, contrary to Buridan's claim, is not the same as the conclusion of the second argument against the crude characterization of Platonism.

21. The text reads: "Si humanitas est in ⟨Platone⟩* et in Socrate et ponamus quod Socrates corrumpatur, ego peto utrum humanitas quae erat in eo corrumpitur an manet. Si corrumpitur, ista est singularis sicut Socrates, et singularis distincta ab humanitate Platonis quae manet. Si vero dicas quod humanitas Socratis vel etiam asinitas Brunelli non corrumpitur, sed manet Socrate vel Brunello corrupto, tunc oportet dicere quod fugiat ad alterum locum sine corpore, quid est absurdum, vel quod adhuc manet in cadavere, et tunc in illa humanitate vel asinitate remanet adhuc cadaver homo et asinus, quid est absurdum, vel tu pones tertium membrum quod illa asinitas manebit separata a corpore, et sic reverterentur ideae Platonis separatae de quibus ante dictum fuit." [* = The text reads *in te,* but the remainder of the argument discusses Plato.]

22. Verbs such as 'desire' are "intentional verbs"—verbs that introduce what we now call "opaque contexts". Examples of such intentional verbs are verbs that are (1) cognitive or epistemic, such as 'know', 'understand', 'believe', and the like; (2) conative verbs, such as 'want', 'desire', 'intend', and the like; (3) promissory verbs,

such as 'owe' or 'promise'. The fullest list, though Buridan acknowledges its incompleteness, is found in TC 3.4.7; their characteristics are discussed in *Sophismata* IV, sophisms 7–15, TS 3.8.24–31, TS 5.3.1–8, TC 1.6.12–16, TC 3.7.3–10, QM IV, q. 8 and q. 14, QSP II, q. 12. For a more detailed discussion of intentional verbs, see the introduction to *Jean Buridan's Logic*. Note that the "opacity" introduced by generation in Buridan's example of fire generating fire is a consequence of final causality, which is the fundamental explanation for why these contexts are opaque; the opacity of intentional verbs is a special case of final causality. Whatever the deficiencies of the medieval physics of final causality, they did not take it to presuppose cognitive capacities.

23. Understanding 'essence' as the concrete thing itself is, in fact, an older medieval understanding of the term 'essentia'—it is common in philosophers of the twelfth century, e.g., Peter Abailard. Buridan gives no sign that he sees himself as reviving an older usage, however.

24. Buridan's diagnosis of the difference in connotation between 'essence' and '*esse*' is worth remarking, since he seems to suggest an analysis of existence as presence: "it seems to me that the verb 'to be' (*esse*) connotes presence, which 'essence' does not connote, nor the name 'stone', etc. It does not connote temporal and successive presence, but rather presence as you are present to me. Even if all things were at rest, it is nevertheless true that 'to be going to be' or 'to have been' necessarily connote succession; yet if succession were never apparent, because all the [things] that now are perpetually had been, without any succession or motion, I believe that we would never have judged something to have been or something to be going to be, but we would have judged those [things] to be that are now apparent to us in the aspect of sense. Perhaps we apply the connotation of such presence to the present time for distinguishing between 'to be' and 'to have been' and 'to be going to be', although for understanding a thing to be it would not be necessary to understand some time (*aliquid temporis*) along with it, but only that a thing is apprehended in the mode of presence within the prospectus of the knower, even if there were no succession or it were imagined. Moreover, when we free (*absoluimus*) the concept of a thing from the concept of such presence, and also from the concept of the relation of a thing to such presence, then we impose the names 'essence' and 'man' and 'stone' for signifying things."

25. Put another way, the universal term or concept may be "identified" with any one of its instances as that which the universal term or concept signifies; Buridan admits this usage, although properly speaking the relation is not identity but signification. What precisely a given universal term or concept supposits for is a function of the sentential context in which it appears; the most general case is "distributive supposition", according to which "from a common term there can be inferred any of its supposits individually or even all conjoined together in a conjunctive sentence" (TS 3.6.1). For example, the term 'man' in 'every man is running' distributively supposits for each and every individual man. Buridan offers rules for distributive supposition in TS 3.7, and some rules for contexts that block distributive supposition in TS 3.8.

Note that there is an asymmetry between 'individual' and 'universal': While these terms strictly apply to concepts, every thing capable of existing *per se* may correctly be described as individual, but only misleadingly as universal.

26. "Contraction" is the genus of which "individuation" is the lowest species: It refers to the relation between the more general and the less general. Individuation is precisely the relation between the species and the individual, e.g., between man and Socrates; contraction includes this as well as the relation between the genus and species, e.g., animal and man.

27. The text reads: "Ista contractio non est quantum ad res significatas circumscriptis conceptibus, quia ita singulariter exsistit homo vel animal aut corpus aut substantia et caetera, sicut Socrates vel Plato, quia nihil aliud est homo quam Socrates vel Plato. Cum ergo homo vel animal sit res singulariter exsistens, etiam si omnia alia essent circumscripta manifestum est quod non indiget aliqua contractione ad hoc quod singulariter exsistat. Oportet ergo dicere quod huiusmodi contractiones habent intelligi quantum ad conceptus vel terminos significativos rerum. . . . Ita etiam terminus qui est species diceretur contrahi ad terminum singularem per additionem differentiae restringentis terminum specificum ad supponendum pro illo solo pro quo supponit terminus singularis."

28. The text reads: "Et ratio huius est quia res intelliguntur non per hoc quod sunt apud intellectum sed per suam similitudinem exsistentem apud intellectum. Res autem extra ex natura et ex essentia sua habent inter se convenientiam et similitudinem, ut suppono et postea declarabo. Modo si sit ita quod sint multa invicem similia, omne illud quod est simile uni eorum quantum ad hoc in quo sunt similia est simile unicuique aliorum. Ideo si omnes asini ex natura rei habent adinvicem convenientiam et similitudinem, oportet quod quando species intelligibilis in intellectu repraesentabit per modum similitudinis aliquem asinum ipsa simul indifferenter repraesentabit quemlibet asinum, nisi aliud obstet (de quo postea dicetur). Ideo sic fit universalis intentio."

29. It might be thought that Buridan's account runs into difficulties with the nonindividual status of the objective resemblance (the "agreement and likeness") between individuals of the same species: Is this not to countenance some real similarity, and so to countenance universals? The answer is that it does not. In QM V, q. 6, Buridan argues that "whatever [things] are said to agree or to be diverse of themselves, in those [things] the agreement or disagreement are not things or dispositions added to those things", and that "the diversity of Socrates from Plato is Socrates, and conversely that the difference of Plato from Socrates is Plato, just as the paternity of Socrates to Plato, positing that there is no thing added, would not be Socrates and Plato, but rather would be Socrates, and the filiation of Plato would be Plato". In general, the relation of A to B is just A, and the relation of B to A is just B. (Note that this entails that all relations are, in modern jargon, ordered pairs.) Relations are distinguished by what they connote. Hence "similarity" has no real ontological status, reducible to pairs of similar items in a token-token reduction. Moreover, the degree of similarity required for distinct beings to be counted as the same may vary depending

on context. Inscriptions and utterances are counted as "the same" if they resemble one another strongly enough; Buridan terms this "equiformity". In most cases, distinct occurrences of an inscription, e.g. 'Socrates' and 'Socrates', may be counted as equiform. Self-referential contexts, such as appear in the statement of the liar paradox, force a more fine-grained approach to similarity classes. See Hughes, *John Buridan on Self-Reference,* for more detail on this point.

30. The text reads: "Sensus autem exterior obiectum suum apprehendit confuse, cum magnitudine et situ ad ipsam tamquam apparens in prospectu eius aut longe aut propre aut ad dexteram aut ad sinistram; ideo percipit obiectum suum singulariter tanquam demonstratum hic vel ibi." See also QA III, q. 8: "Exterior sense cognizes the sensible in the manner of existing within its prospect, in a certain location . . . although exterior sense cognizes Socrates, or whiteness, or white, nevertheless this is only in a species represented confusedly, since [it represents] the substance, the whiteness, the magnitude, and the location in accordance with what appears in the prospect of someone cognizing it" (trans. J. A. Zupko). The interior or common sense is no better off as regards this confusedness (QSP I, q. 7): "the interior sense cannot free and abstract the appearance (*speciem*) of the object as color or sound from this kind of confusedness . . . hence the interior sense only perceives singularly." In QSP I, q. 7, Buridan criticizes at length theories that take intellectual knowledge of the singular to be derived from a "reflection on sense" rather than a distinctive and direct capacity of the intellect.

31. The text reads: "Nullus est conceptus singularis nisi sit conceptus rei per modum exsistentis in praesentia et in prospectu cognoscentis tanquam illa res appareat cognoscenti sicut demonstratione signata et istum modum cognoscendi vocant aliqui 'intuitivum'. Verum est quod per memoriam bene concipimus rem singulariter per hoc quod memoramur hoc fuisse in prospectu cognoscentis, et per talem modum illud cognovisse."

32. The text reads: "Si hunc in prospecto meo demonstratum voco 'Socratem' nomine proprio non quia talis vel talis sed quia isti nunquam alii quantumcumque simili conveniret hoc nomen 'Socrates' nisi ex alia impositione esset impositum ad significandum illum alium et sic equivoce." Buridan also describes imposition explicitly as baptism: "the name 'Aristotle' was imposed for signifying him in accordance with a singular concept, because those designating him [while Aristotle was] within their prospectus said 'let this child be called "Aristotle"!' " (QA III, q. 8, modified from Zupko's translation and reading vocetur for vocatur); "the term 'Aristotle' is a singular term . . . and was imposed according to a singular concept, namely, when Aristotle was designated [and] it was proclaimed 'let him be called "Aristotle"!' " (QM VII, q. 20).

33. Note, however, that this account of singular concepts sits uneasily with the basic claim that concepts signify their significates through natural objective similarity, that is, though intrinsic features, rather than through the genetic and causal story suggested by imposition—especially in QM VII, q. 17, in which Buridan offers as a reason for the nondiscernibility of similar individuals that "our intellect understands

things not as they are in it but according to their likenesses''. This tension is not specific to Buridan. William of Ockham, for example, adopts the general line that concepts ''resemble'' their significates, but in *Reportatio* II, qq. 12–13, and *Quodlibeta* I, q. 13, he asserts that intuitive cognition is of one individual rather than another, no matter how similar, due to the causal role played in the genesis of the concept by that very individual.

34. Obviously such ''proper names'' need not be the names of persons, or even animate beings. In QM VII, q. 17, ad 2, Buridan notes that a ''proper name'' (a discrete term) may be imposed upon an accident, as in, e.g., naming this whiteness 'Robert'. For Buridan, demonstratives are a subclass of the general linguistic class of ''identificatory-relative terms'', which may have anaphoric as well as pronominal reference (see TS § 4). Buridan states the point clearly for 'this' in QA III, q. 8: ''the demonstrative pronoun 'this' is not correctly applied according to its mode of signifying unless there is a cognition of the thing in the mode of existing in the prospect of someone cognizing it'' (trans. J. A. Zupko). In QSP I, q. 20, Buridan notes that ''when the pronoun 'this' is taken simply and without addition, it supposits only for a total substance subsisting *per se*''; that is, for an individual. The proper names of individuals with which one has come into direct contact are like constant-valued demonstratives. Buridan also allows demonstrative expressions of the form 'this man' to function as complex singular referring expressions: See the discussion of vague singulars that follows.

35. This is contrary to the assertions in Peter King, *Jean Buridan's Logic,* p. 41, and Alan R. Perreiah, ''Buridan and the Definite Description'', *Journal of the History of Philosophy* 10 (1972): 153–160. Nevertheless, Buridan is clear on this point—or as clear as he can be, given the lack of a definite article in Latin.

36. See QSP I, q. 7, and QM VII, q. 18. Buridan states the point succinctly in QM VII, q. 20: ''there are many terms, each of which supposits for a single (*unica*) thing, and it is not possible (with its signification unchanged) that [each of these terms] supposit for many. For example, the term 'god' can never supposit for many things according to its proper signification, since it is impossible that there be many gods. So too the term 'sun' or the term 'moon' cannot supposit for many unless a miracle were to happen, since it is not possible by nature that there be another sun or another moon or another world, and so on. Yet the aforementioned terms are not singular terms; rather, they are more common terms due to their manner of imposition: it is not repugnant to these terms from the manner of their signification to supposit for many. Indeed, if *per possibile* or *per impossibile* there were another god or another sun or another moon, the aforementioned terms would, without any new imposition, supposit for them just as they supposit for those that now exist. Yet on the part of the things signified, it is repugnant that they supposit for many, although a term is not called 'singular' from such repugnance. Thus it should be said that the aforementioned terms do not correspond to singular concepts, but rather to specific and common concepts, since with regard to the manner of conceiving it is repugnant that such a concept be indifferent to many things.''

37. See QC q. 4A: "It should be noted that 'to exist *per se*' is taken in two ways—rather, in many ways. (1) [It is taken] for that which is not a part of something one *per se* and which depends on or sustains nothing; in this sense only God exists *per se*. (2) It is taken for that which is not a part of something one *per se* nor is in something as in a subject; in this sense separate substances and *per se* composites exist. (3) That is said to be and to exist *per se* which is not in something as in a subject, whether it is a part of something one *per se* or not; in this sense not only perfect substance exists *per se* but also that which is part of something else. And in the case at hand I call all that 'one *per se*' which is one (i) indivisibly, as God and the angels; or (ii) essentially, as bronze and other substantial composites of their [own] essential parts; or (iii) by continuation, as wood and other things whose parts are continuous with each other (*cuius partes ad invicem continuantur*)." In the discussion that follows we shall concentrate on (2); that is, the ability to continue in existence independently, which characterizes primary substances, accidents, separable substantial forms, and matter. A complete understanding of this notion would also involve an analysis of what Buridan understands by 'existing' or 'subsisting', especially in light of his comments in QM IV, q. 9, in which *esse* seems to be equated with the presentiality of an object (see note 24).

38. In QM VII, q. 19, Buridan states that the term 'this-something' (*hoc aliquid*) is "a term of first intention, since it supposits for substance subsisting *per se*." What is more, it supposits for individuals, since "common terms are restricted by the demonstrative pronoun to supposit for only one supposit, namely, only for that which we signify demonstratively." Buridan summarizes: "The term 'this-something' is a discrete term suppositing for only one . . . the term 'this-something' taken simply and strictly only supposits for the total substance subsisting *per se,* and not for some accident, nor for [some] part of a substance subsisting *per se* (i.e., for its matter or for [its] form). For the question simply inquiring 'what is this?' inquires about the total substance subsisting *per se* and not about some part or some accident of it." That this is a feature of 'this-something' due to the presence of the demonstrative is borne out by Buridan's account in QSP I, q. 20: "I say that although [when] the demonstrative pronoun 'this' is taken *secundum quid,* that is, with additions, it correctly supposits for accidents, such as 'this color', 'this whiteness', 'this accident', nevertheless, when the [demonstrative] pronoun 'this' is taken simply and without addition, it only supposits for a total substance subsisting *per se.* Accordingly, although there are many accidents in a stone, nevertheless if we simply ask what this is, we do not say that it is whiteness or magnitude; nor do we say that this is an aggregate [composed] of whiteness and the stone; rather, we precisely answer that this is a stone . . . the term 'this' taken simply supposits for a substance subsisting *per se.*"

39. Buridan establishes this claim as a general result, which is independent of the question concerning which accidents actually exist. Certainly some accidents from the category of quality, such as whiteness, genuinely exist. Motions also exist; see Calvin Normore, "Buridan's Ontology", for a defense of the independent existence of motions. Relations, on the other hand, seem to be no more than the foundation, i.e.,

the principal *relatum*. There is as yet no consensus on the particular kinds of accidents Buridan countenances. However, see the remarks below about how, e.g., every thing is a relation, for some reason to have skepticism about any neat summary of Buridan's views on such matters.

40. See QM V, q. 8, ad 2: "I say that there must be an added disposition for this, that the whiteness inhere in the stone (or even for this, that it depend on the stone), for the reason that it is possible that it persist not inhering or depending on the stone. Further; [if] you say that the disposition inheres in the subject and depends on it, I concede [the point], but this is *inseparably,* just as Aristotle believed that whiteness inhered in the stone. Accordingly, God could not bring it about that there be an inherence of whiteness in the stone and that there not be whiteness, since that would imply a contradiction. It is not possible that there be such modes of relating this to that (*tales enim modos se habendi hoc ad illud*) unless this or that exists. Hence, since they ⟨inseparably⟩* inhere and depend, it should be said that they inhere of themselves and they depend without any further disposition, and hence there is no infinite regress. When it is asked what subject such a disposition inheres in, [my answer is that] I believe that it should be said that the disposition required for this, that man be white, beyond man and whiteness there is the inherence of whiteness in man and it exists subjectively through it, such that whiteness is formally inhering in that man through this inherence and subjectively through itself. And thus I say that the ray [of light] depends on the sun through the added disposition which is the dependence inhering in itself. These dispositions are truly accidents that are inseparably related to their subjects, as Aristotle believed [was the case for] whiteness and hotness." [*For '⟨in⟩separably' the text has *separabiliter,* which makes no sense given the context; it seems obvious that *inseparabiliter* is the correct reading.] Such "added dispositions" are inseparable, but they may, of course, be destroyed, as when God preserves the accident without its inhering in any substance.

41. The text reads: "Sed sumuntur ex diversis intentionibus, secundum quas termini sunt diversimode connotativi vel etiam non connotativi. Ex quibus diversis connotationibus proveniunt diversi modi praedicandi terminorum de primis substantiis; et ita directe et immediate distinguuntur penes diversos modos praedicandi de primis substantiis. Si enim praedicentur in quid sive essentialiter de ipsis, tunc tales termini sunt de praedicamento substantiae; si vero praedicantur in quale, tunc sunt de praedicamento qualitatis; et si in quantum, sunt de praedicamento quantitatis. . ." See also, e.g., QM IV, q. 6; *Sophismata* IV, Remark 3; the beginning of Treatise § 1 of the (as yet unedited) *Summulae de dialectica;* and elsewhere.

42. The text reads: "Et ideo in vanum laboraverunt plures, qui per huiusmodi divisiones voluerunt assignare sufficientiam numeri praedicamentorum. Credo ergo quod non possit aliter assignari vel probari sufficientia numeri praedicamentorum, nisi quia tot modos praedicandi diversos invenimus non reducibiles in aliquem modum praedicandi communiorem acceptum secundum aliquam unam communem rationem, ideo oportet tot esse. Sed etiam quia non invenimus praedicabilia communia, quae sub istis modis non contineantur vel ad eos reducantur, ideo non ponimus plura praedicamenta. Unde si aliqua praedicabilia communia inveniamus habentia alios modos

praedicandi praeter dictos decem, apparet mihi omnino, quod non esset negandum, quin essent plura praedicamenta."

43. The assumptions Buridan makes to establish these theorems are minimal: "I assume that the genus 'quantity' is truly and universally predicated of every abstract term that is strictly in the category of quantity, taking each personally, since the genus should be truly and universally predicated of any of its species. It is also assumed that all the abstract [forms] of concrete [terms] that strictly speaking predicate *in quantum* are strictly in the category of quantity, and so too the abstract [forms] of concrete [terms] that predicate *in quale* are in the category of quality. Otherwise, nobody could appropriately distinguish terms of the categories, nor assign in which category they should be placed" (QC q. 7).

44. Given Buridan's rejection of the Aristotelian categories, what is the status of metaphysics? In QM VI, q. 2, Buridan states that "the distinction [of the speculative sciences] is originally taken from some incomplex principles [i.e., terms], since after all this distinction should be taken from *rationes* or concepts, and not conclusions or principles". The speculative sciences are distinguished by different "incomplex principles", that is, by being concerned with different terms of sentences. Since we are speaking, as always, of mental sentences, these terms are concepts, which are the reasons (*rationes*) for the imposition of the utterance or inscription as a term. Although "it is difficult to say what these terms are", Buridan remarks, they can be specified: Metaphysics is concerned with the term '*ens*' (being); physics with the term '*ens mobile vel quantum*' (mobile being or quantity); mathematics with the term '*ens measurabile*' (measurable being). See also QSP I, q. 3, and QCM I, q. 1, for further discussion of this point.

45. The text reads: "Tripliciter consuevimus dicere aliud alicui esse idem in numero. Primo modo totaliter, scilicet quia hoc est illud et nihil est de integritate huius quod non sit de integritate illius et econverso; et hoc est propriissime esse idem numero . . . sed secundo modo aliud dicitur alicui idem partialiter, scilicet quia hoc est pars illius, et maxime hoc dicitur si sit maior vel principalior, vel etiam quia hoc et illud participant in aliquo quod est pars maior vel principalior utriusque . . . sed adhuc tertio modo et minus proprie dicitur aliquid alicui idem numero secundum continuationem partium diversarum in succedendo alteram alteri."

46. The text reads: "Si essent duo lapides omnino similes in figura, in magnitudine, in color, et sic de aliis, et successive apportarentur in tua praesentia, tu nullam viam haberes ad iudicandum utrum secundus apportatus esset ille idem qui primus apportatus fuit an alter. Et ita etiam de hominibus si omnino essent similes in figura magnitudine et colore et sic de aliis accidentibus." The same example is employed in QSP I, q. 7, and QA III, q. 8.

47. The text reads: "Immo etiam hoc non solum veritatem habet de substantiis immo etiam de accidentibus: si enim essent albedines consimiles in gradu et essent in subiectis consimilibus in figura magnitudine et caetera, tu non haberes viam cognoscendi utrum esset eadem albedo an alia quae tibi prius et posterius praesentaretur."

48. The text reads: "Ad aliam posset dici quod termini substantiales de praedicamento substantiae non sunt omnino absoluti a connotatione accidentium; saltem in imponendo oportet considerare accidentia. Tamen quia intellectus potest absolvere conceptum subiecti a conceptu accidentis, nos imponendo sic intendimus absolvere ut terminus non connotet accidentia, quamvis per illa ducamur ad notitiam substantiae."

49. The text reads: "Ad ultimam concedo quod ita bene verum est in accidentibus sicut in substantiis, scilicet quod eorum quae sunt eiusdem speciei non percipitur diversitas nisi per quaedam accidentia; nec oportet procedere in infintum, quia albedinem equi et albedinem bovis scimus distingui, quia percipimus distinctionem bovis et equi in quibus sunt ille albedines. Similiter, bovem a bove scimus distingui quia ille albus est ille niger et colores eiusdem speciei per substantias vel figuras vel per magnitudines diversarum specierum, et sic etiam substantias per figuras et colores aut substantias huiusmodi. Et sic sine processu in infinitum percipiuntur invicem omnia."

19

Cardinal Cajetan (Thomas De Vio) (b. 1468; d. 1534) and Giles of Rome (b. ca. 1243/47; d. 1316)

Linda Peterson

Cajetan's most sustained discussion of the problem of individuation appears in his commentary on Aquinas's *De ente et essentia*.[1] In that work, he defends a position that he asserts to be consonant with Aquinas's final thinking on the subject of individuation and that, as he acknowledges, differs markedly from the account that Aquinas had advanced early on in his *Sentence* commentary. The *De ente et essentia* commentary, however, does not contain Cajetan's last word on individuation. In a later commentary on the *Summa theologiae*,[2] his earlier position gives way to a new account that, on reflection, he takes to mirror more accurately Aquinas's ultimate position. To provide a framework for analyzing Cajetan's approach to the problem of individuation, it will be useful to begin by briefly surveying the parameters of the problem as they are delineated within the broader Thomistic corpus. This general introduction to the philosophical and exegetical task confronting Cajetan will be followed by a synoptic presentation of the way in which the thirteenth century philosopher Giles of Rome[3] approached the same network of issues with which Cajetan struggled almost two centuries later. Giles's position on individuation emerges as an intermediate theory, midway between Aquinas's *Sentence* commentary account and the positions subsequently advanced by Cajetan. Juxtaposing Giles's views with those of Cajetan will help bring the development of Cajetan's thought more clearly into focus. The remainder of the chapter will then be devoted to an articulation and assessment of Cajetan's own contribution toward a solution to the problem of individuation.

I. Constraints on a Solution to the Problem

In his *In Librum de causis expositio,* Aquinas distinguishes between universals and particulars: "Ad cuius evidentiam considerandum est quod aliquid dicitur individuum ex hoc quod non est natum esse in multis; nam universale est quod est natum esse in multis".[4] Thus, a universal is what is naturally apt to be shared by or communicated to many individuals,[5] and an individual is whatever cannot be so shared, that is, whatever is *incommunicable.* Correspondingly, he remarks elsewhere (*Summa theologiae* III, Q. 77, A. 2, Resp.) that "it is of the very notion of an individual that it cannot be in several".[6] In both passages, he goes on to identify two ways in which incommunicability can be achieved. In the case of corporeal substances, the substantial form is rendered incommunicable by virtue of its inherence in matter. When it is received in matter, it is limited or restricted to being the form of a particular substance so that it cannot be further shared by anything else: "matter is the principle of individuation of all forms that inhere in a subject. Because, since these forms are naturally meant to be received in something as their subject, from the very fact that one of them is received in matter, which itself exists in no subject, it follows that neither can the form itself thus existing be in another [i.e., the form cannot then be communicated to or shared by anything else]."[7] Accordingly, Aquinas maintains that, in general, any form that is of the sort to be received in some subject is limited or individuated by the receiving subject.

Since, in the case of inherent substantial form, the subject of inherence does the individuating rather than the form,[8] a multiplicity of subjects of inherence makes possible multiple instances of the same specific form. Matter, then, makes possible numerically diverse instances of a given nature or essence by providing multiple subjects of inherence in which the form is separately "contracted" (contained, limited, defined), resulting in the existence of numerically many individuals specifically the same.[9] Hence, he maintains that intraspecific individuation (viz., the numerical diversity of individuals under a common nature or species) is possible only where the form is received into matter.

Concomitantly, Aquinas holds that whatever is not of the sort to be received in something else is limited or individuated through itself.[10] He then identifies a second way in which a form can be incommunicable: "immaterial separated forms, subsisting of themselves, are also individuated in themselves".[11] Thus, in the case of immaterial, naturally noninherent forms, the individualizing principles are included in the essence: "where the form does not exist in matter, where it exists simply in itself, there can be nothing except the essence; for then the form is the entire essence. And, in such cases, of course there cannot be a number of individuals sharing the same nature, nor can the individual and its nature be distinguished."[12] Since, for noninherent forms, the form itself, in the absence of any natural subject, does the individuating, these forms can be interspecifically diverse (i.e., there can be numerically many individuals of different species.) But essentially incommunicable forms, in this view, are not subject to intraspecific individuation. Hence, according to Aquinas, in the case of subsistent, self-individuating forms, there can be only one individual per species (e.g., there is a single angel per angelic species).[13]

In the discussion to follow of Giles's and Cajetan's accounts of individuation, the focus of attention will be primarily on their divergent views regarding the individuation of material, naturally inherent forms. Both philosophers, as we will see, straightforwardly accept Aquinas's position concerning the mode of individuation of self-subsistent, immaterial forms. It is with the attempt to provide an account, within the general framework of Thomistic metaphysics, of the role that matter plays in intraspecific individuation that significant problems arise. Three pivotal Thomistic theses combine to generate the difficulties:

T1:   *Prime matter, as the ultimate subject of inherence of specific form, is pure potentiality and so, in and of itself, is completely without form, whether substantial or accidental.*[14]

T2:   *There can be only one substantial form per substance.*[15] (This will be referred to, hereafter, as Aquinas's "unitarian thesis" regarding substantial form.)

T3:   *Accidents are existentially dependent on substance; that is, accidental forms have substances as their natural subjects of inherence so that they are naturally posterior, in the order of existence, to substance.*[16]

If matter is to make possible numerically many instances of the same specific form by providing a multiplicity of subjects of inherence, it seems that it must be divisible to be capable of receiving forms in its various parts. One possible solution to the problem of material individuation rests on the presupposition that the subject of inherence of specific form is matter already under the substantial form corporeity. This is, in fact, the position Aquinas adopts in his *Sentence* commentary, where he maintains that the matter in which any given specific form inheres is already subject to a generic form that produces in it indeterminate accidents of dimensive quantity.[17] The matter so informed is thereby subject to extension and is thus divisible into numerically many subjects of inherence. While this latter position adheres to T3, it violates T1 and T2. Accordingly, in his commentary on Aristotle's *Metaphysics*, Aquinas, concerned to preserve the unitarian thesis regarding substantial form, implicitly rejects the *Sentence* commentary view and faults certain ancient philosophers for holding a similar view. He points out that, in such an account, not only is matter substance (contrary to T1) but, moreover, matter alone is substance (a conclusion that follows from T2).[18]

Since both Giles and Cajetan joined with Aquinas in holding T1 and T2, neither philosopher could accept the view that matter under some generic form receives and individuates specific form. Yet an alternative solution is suggested by Aquinas's claim that dimensive quantity is individuated in and of itself.[19] Supposing that the accidents of dimensive quantity could somehow inhere in matter prior to any substantial form, quantified matter would then have extension and the divisibility prerequisted for numerically many subjects of inherence for substantial form. Neither Giles nor Cajetan could accept this alternative, however, since it stands in diametric opposition to T3, a thesis that both philosophers endorsed.

If prime matter, regarded as undifferentiated potentiality, is incapable of serving as a principle of individuation and given that accounts of individuation involving informed matter (matter under some generic substantial form or an accidental form) are problematic, the problem of material individuation emerges as a kind of Gordian knot. Both Giles and Cajetan struggled to untie this knot, and we will turn now to an examination of the positions resulting from their respective efforts.

II. Giles on Individuation

Though it would be inaccurate to characterize Giles of Rome as being a thoroughly committed Thomist,[20] his views on individuation were significantly influenced by his acceptance of certain basic presuppositions that together form the overarching parameters of a Thomistic approach to the problem of individuation. To begin with, he shares Aquinas's assumption that what is individual is incommunicable. Accordingly, he maintains that separate substances (self-subsisting forms) are "essentially individual" in that each of these naturally noninherent forms or natures is essentially incapable of having many instances, that is, of being shared in or participated by many.[21] He thus follows Aquinas in claiming that such forms are not subject to intraspecific individuation, though they are individuated interspecifically.[22] Correspondingly, he agrees with Aquinas that numerical multiplicity within a single species requires matter-form composition,[23] and he holds that inherent forms are individualized by being "contracted" (or limited) to the conditions of matter.[24] Thus matter, in receiving and limiting inherent form, makes it impossible for the form, as individualized, to be communicated to some further subject of inherence.

As has been noted, we also find, in Giles's works, an explicit endorsement of the conjunction of T1–T3. In his *Theoremata de esse et essentia,* he characterizes uninformed matter as "pure potentiality" that is, in and of itself, "indivisible and unextended".[25] And, in his treatise *De gradibus formarum*, he upheld the unitarian thesis regarding substantial forms and vigorously opposed the pluralist position as being contrary to Catholic doctrine.[26] He further maintained that accidental forms cannot inhere in matter as pure potency but are capable of inhering only in matter already under some substantial form.[27] He thus held that the existence of accidents presupposes some substance as their subject of inherence.[28]

Accordingly, Giles emerges as being faced with the following problem regarding the individuation of inherent material forms. How can matter, qua essentially indivisible and unextended pure potentiality, intraspecifically individuate substantial form by providing diverse subjects of inherence that severally contract or limit the same specific form? Giles's acceptance of the thesis regarding the natural priority of substance to accidents would seem to preclude his claiming, in addition, that the matter which receives and limits substantial form is already under some accidental form that accounts for its divisibility into multiple subjects of inherence. Yet, at first blush, Giles does seem to be making that claim. For he maintains that "indeterminate dimensions precede [i.e., are prior to the inherence of] the substantial form in matter".[29] Initially, this view is reminiscent of Aquinas's *Sentence* commentary position in terms of which matter under indeterminate dimensions receives and individuates specific form. But the *Sentence* commentary account, at least, has the apparent advantage of consistency since it presupposes the falsity of the unitarian thesis (T2) in that the matter subject to indeterminate dimensions is held to be under the generic form corporeity. And it has the further advantage of preserving the thesis concerning the existential dependency of accidents on substance (T3). Giles's view, however, seems to stand in violation of T3, which is paradoxical in light of his explicit endorsement of this thesis. We will turn now to an examination of Giles's attempt to resolve this apparent inconsistency.

Giles holds that, while matter is essentially indivisible and unextended, divisibility is of the essence of quantity.[30] Further, he holds that quantity is capable of modifying matter and of giving it the "existence of extension".[31] He also maintains that the existential union resulting from the modification of matter by quantity is not a third thing (*res*) really distinct from matter, just as the union of any accidental form with its subject does not result in the generation of a new substance.[32] Instead, in his view, the union of matter and quantity is only a "mode of existence" of matter itself.[33] Taken together, the foregoing claims imply that the inherence of indeterminate dimensions in matter prior to substantial form would not be in violation of the unitarian thesis, since the existential union of matter and quantity is not a substantial union. Accordingly, the subject of inherence of indeterminate dimensions in matter prior to substantial form would not be in violation of the unitarian thesis, since the existential union of matter and quantity is not a substantial union. Accordingly, the subject of inherence and the individualizing principle of specific form would not be, in Giles's account, a substance, and the specific form would still be the single substantial form of the resultant matter-form composite. Yet nothing in Giles's account, up to this point, suffices to show that matter under indeterminate dimensions would not constitute a union of subject and accident. Hence, since matter is not a substance on his view, it remains to be shown how his account is not in violation of T3.

One way out of this dilemma would be to hold that the indeterminate dimensions inhering in matter prior to substantial form are *not* accidents of matter. And this appears to be what Giles maintains. For he holds that matter that is actually extended and subject to determinate quantitative dimensions is matter already under some substantial form.[34] Accordingly, in his account, only substances are really extended and capable of having determinate size and shape. Matter, however, that is indeterminate and in potency to those determinate quantitative dimensions that it will receive following the inherence of the substantial form is unextended.[35] Thus, when Giles claims that matter, prior to the inherence of substantial form, is subject to indeterminate dimensions, he is not saying that matter is really extended and indefinitely spread out before it receives substantial form. The view that matter under the generic form corporeity is indefinitely extended and thus capable of receiving forms in its various parts is Aquinas's *Sentence* commentary view. But it is not a position that Giles chose to endorse. Thus, there is only a surface similarity between the *Sentence* commentary position on material individuation and Giles's position given that both accounts specify matter under indeterminate dimensions as the subject of inherence of substantial form. What Aquinas meant when he spoke of matter under "indeterminate dimension", viz., indefinitely extended matter, however, was very different from what Giles had in mind, viz., matter with the potency to be subject to determinate dimensions following the inherence of substantial form. Accordingly, in his *Theoremata de esse et essentia*, Giles remarks:

> . . . God has so endowed the essence of matter that where there is a change in matter there a form is induced, so God has also endowed the essence of matter that the essence of matter has a certain indetermination in itself by reason of which it is subject to the reception of this or that form. Thus, as was has the property that it can be round and four-sided and many other figures, so the essence of matter has the property that it can be subject to this form and the opposite and to many other forms. And just as the essence of wax is diversified because subject to

this or that form, so the essence of matter is diversified because subject to this or that form.[36]

Thus, Giles's claim is that matter under indeterminate dimensions is not a union of subject and accident; instead, the indeterminacy in question is part of the very essence of matter. His account then, read along the lines suggested here, is not inconsistent. Nonetheless, some questions remain. For there is the further difficulty of explaining how matter as the mere indeterminate potency for subsequent determinations (viz., those quantitative and qualitative determinations to be effected by the substantial form) can receive, "contract" and individualize inherent substantial form. The passage just quoted suggests that a diversity, in matter, of specialized receptive potencies for substantial form yields a multiplicity of material subjects of inherence. If that is, indeed, Giles's view, then he can be credited with an insight regarding a possible solution to the problem of material individuation that Cajetan was to exploit much later on. We will turn now to an examination of Cajetan's address to this problem.

III. Cajetan's Initial Position

Cajetan begins his discussion of individuation in the *De ente et essentia* commentary by remarking that the problem of individuation is analyzable into two subproblems: (1) the problem of finding some principle in virtue of which any given specific nature is rendered incommunicable so that it cannot be further shared or participated in by anything else, and (2) the problem of finding some principle that accounts for the numerical distinction of individuals sharing the specific nature.[37] It would seem, prima facie, that finding a solution to the first problem is a precondition for solving the second. For, within the metaphysical framework of Aristotelian hylomorphism, the issue of how the subject of inherence receives and limits specific form resulting in the existence of numerically many instances of the same specific nature is philosophically prior to the issue of how the resultant individuals are empirically distinguished or differentiated. The question regarding distinction, then, might be settled in terms of some feature extrinsic to the individuals themselves, say relative spatial location, whereas the prior question relating to incommunicability is settleable only in terms of some intrinsic feature that is metaphysically constitutive of the particular substance[38] Cajetan, however, offers a single "intrinsic principle of individuation"[39] as a solution to both subproblems. The reason for this is that he is concerned to find the radical origin (the intrinsic causal foundation or ground)[40] of real distinction, rather than with isolating the criteria by which we make intraspecific distinctions at the level of sense experience. His interest, then, is in finding one metaphysical principle, intrinsic to the corporeal composite, which will explain (1) how, e.g., Socrates's humanity (as an instance of human nature in general) is uniquely his (viz., incommunicable, incapable of being common to many), and (2) how Socrates's humanity differs constitutively from Plato's. Accordingly, the subproblems that Cajetan identifies are really two sides of the same coin.

Before reviewing the solution to the problem of material individuation that Cajetan proposes in the *De ente et essentia* commentary, it will be useful to survey briefly his reasons for rejecting Aquinas's *Sentence* commentary account.[41] Initially, he runs through the theses primarily motivating that account:

T4: *The division of matter into multiple subjects of inherence for substantial forms is a prerequisite for intraspecific individuation.*[42]

T5: *Bodily existence (viz., three-dimensional substantial existence) cannot be generated from what is nonbodily.*[43]

He indicates that it was thought to follow from the conjunction of T4 and T5 that matter, prior to receiving specific form, must be really extended and thus divisible into the parts in which it severally receives the subsequently inherent forms. And, as we have already seen, the position was that matter under the generic form corporeity and subject to indeterminate dimension satisfies the conditions expressed in T4 and T5. In responding to this position, Cajetan makes explicit his endorsement of T1–T3;[44] prime matter, as pure potency, receives a single substantial form, and the resultant matter-form composite is then the only proper subject of inherence for accidental forms. Accordingly, he rejects T5, maintaining instead that the matter which receives and individuates specific form is nonsubstantial: ". . . a body is brought forth [generated] from matter which is not a body".[45] Yet he accepts T4 with the following qualification: The division (or distinction) of matter into parts (multiple subjects of inherence) is not made possible by virtue of matter's being really extended and subject to indeterminate dimensions prior to specific form.[46]

Thus far, it is apparent that Cajetan's negative account resembles that of Giles of Rome. For Giles, as we have seen, also rejects T5 and accepts T4 only in a qualified way in that he denies that matter is really extended prior to receiving specific form. Cajetan's positive account of material individuation, however, as presented in the *De ente et essentia* commentary, represents a departure from Giles' view. We will turn now to an examination of Cajetan's position as put forward in that commentary.

In Cajetan's account, the principle of intraspecific individuation (viz., the intrinsic principle of incommunicability and ground of real distinction) is *designated matter* (*materia signata*).[47] 'Designated matter', for Cajetan, signifies matter with the capacity (proximate potentiality) for a determinate quantity and no other.[48] Thus, he maintains that the principle of individuation is not matter actually having quantitative dimensions ("*cum certis dimensionibus*"[49]) and subject to real extension, since such matter, already informed, is incapable of receiving substantial form. Rather, in his view, what enables matter to provide numerically many subjects of inherence for substantial form is its division into multiple "receptive potencies", each of which has a particularized receptivity for those determinate quantitative dimensions to be effected by the subsequently inherent form. Yet, if matter, considered apart from form, is only the bare potentiality for any substantial form whatsoever, Cajetan reasoned that something other than matter itself must account for its having a particularized receptive potency. Accordingly, his claim is that the agent ("*agens particulare*"), for example, human semen prior to the inherence of the intellectual soul, so influences the matter that it is able to receive only certain kinds of subsequent determination.[50] So, for example, the matter that is properly disposed to receive a human soul is capable of subsequently receiving only those quantitative and qualitative determinations that are the natural concomitants of human existence. His position, then, is that the disposed matter has its particularized receptivity, not only in relation to quantitative determinations, but also in relation to the "proper qualities"[51] that will be permanent features of the resultant composite.[52] Thus, the matter that constitutes Socrates, for example, also has a specialized receptivity for those qualitative determinations associated with his particular sex and racial characteristics.[53]

In view of the prior disposition of matter, in Cajetan's account, for qualitative as well as quantitative determinations, one might expect his definition of designated matter to refer to the qualitative determinations as well. But Cajetan holds that quantitative determinations, in corporeal substances, are prior to qualitative determinations.[54] (Being extended, for example, is a prerequisite for having color.) Accordingly, his claim is that, since material distinction has its foundation primarily in quantity, the definition of designated matter, as a principle of individuation, appropriately specifies only the capacity or proximate potentiality for determinate quantity.[55]

Cajetan's position emerges as having certain theoretical and exegetical advantages over alternative views positing actually extended matter as the subject of inherence and individualizing principle for specific form. Perhaps most important, from the point of view of providing a Thomistic analysis of individuation, it accounts for how a specific nature can have numerically many individualized instances in a way that preserves the unitarian thesis regarding substantial form. And, it accommodates the empirically evident fact that the process of generation and corruption has a certain natural order. So, for example, what is now wine, under certain conditions, is naturally apt to become vinegar, whereas the reverse of this process obviously would not be a natural occurrence. Thus, within the context of Aristotelian hylomorphism, the matter that is now predisposed to receive a certain specific form is naturally incapable of receiving any other specific form. Cajetan's position regarding the proximate potentiality of matter for only a specialized range of subsequent quantitative and qualitative determinations supplements the hylomorphic analysis of substantial change so that it better squares with this feature of our experience.

His position also paves the way for a solution to the problem of why certain accidents appear to survive the process of substantial change. For example, Socrates's corpse initially appears to have the exact dimensions, skin color, and so forth, that characterized the living Socrates. But, following the unitarian thesis (T2), the substantial form intellectual soul is the single substantial form of the living human composite. Accordingly, when Socrates dies and his soul ceases to inform matter, a new substantial form (the form of the corpse) begins to inhere in the matter once constitutive of Socrates. Death, in this view, involves the corruption of one substance (the animate composite) and the generation of a new substance (the corpse). And since accidents have only substances as their natural subjects of inherence (T3), determinate accidents (e.g., dimensions, skin color) are said to "follow on" substantial form. This set of assumptions, then, necessitates the conclusion that the accidents of the corpse, appearances to the contrary notwithstanding, cannot be numerically the same as those of the living composite. Thus, Cajetan observes that, "the opinion of the Thomists is: no accident is identical in number in the generated and corrupted thing. For this follows necessarily from our principles. . . . [If] no accident is in matter as its subject [following T3], and if there is only one substantial form in the composite [T2], it is impossible that the same accident remain numerically identical . . ."[56] Still, the problem remains of explaining why the accidents should be qualitatively similar given that they differ numerically. Cajetan's proposed solution to this problem is that dispositions for certain quantitative and qualitative determinations are so "rooted" in the matter that they are capable of surviving substantial change.[57] The accidents, for example, dimensions, that are then effected in the generated composite by virtue of the relation obtaining between the newly inherent form and the disposed matter are qualitatively similar due to their having the same radical foundation or causal origin.

Moreover, Cajetan's construal of "designated matter" clarifies Aquinas's claim, in *De ente et essentia,* Ch. 2, Section 4, that given that a thing's definition signifies its essence, the designated matter of which Socrates, for example, is constituted would be a part of his definition if he could be defined.[58] Accordingly, just as the form and common (undesignated) matter are included in the definition of the species and together make up the nature or essence of the species, so Socrates's individualized essence is constituted by his individualized (designated) matter and the substantial form that is rendered incommunicable and really distinct by virtue of its inherence in that matter.[59] Now matter actually extended and having determinate dimensions (determinate size and shape) could not fit this bill. For if matter with actual dimensions were a part of his individualized essence, Socrates would not remain numerically identical throughout the changes in size and shape accompanying the process of growth.[60] Cajetan, however, is careful to formulate his own analysis of individuation so that identity through change is preserved: "we say that the determinate quantity involved in individuation [i.e., the proximate potentiality for determinate quantity] is not a rigid unit but has some play. For as any natural species determines for itself a maximum and a minimum quantity within a certain latitude, so any individual determines for itself this quantity within certain limits, and not as a rigid unit."[61] His idea, then, is that the designated matter which is included in Socrates's individualized essence is not matter having a mere receptive potency for only those quantitative determinations that immediately follow upon the form's first being introduced into matter. Rather, it is a specialized receptive potency for the whole range of quantitative determinations that the substantial form will subsequently effect, a range peculiar to members of the human species and to Socrates's own growth rate and particular build.

In view of Cajetan's endorsement of the Thomistic thesis that designated matter is partially constitutive of the individualized essence of any given corporeal composite, it is clear that designated matter is a component of his principle of identity for corporeal substances. And, indeed, he remarks that "it is certain that if the designated matter or the proper matter, which is the same thing—of Socrates were eliminated, this one [Socrates] would not remain, nor would his form remain this form."[62] Hence, he holds that designated matter, while both necessary and sufficient for material individuation, is a necessary but not sufficient condition for numerical identity. Material and formal sameness, in his account, are separately necessary and together sufficient for the identity of the composite.

Cajetan's general position on substantial identity figures importantly in his discussion of the survival, in human beings, of the postresurrection composite and the postmortem individuation of the intellectual soul in separation from matter. In the following passage in the *De ente et essentia* commentary, he maintains that, "Two separated human souls are not distinguished formally, or by matter, even though they are pure forms separated from matter. . . . However distinction of forms, since it is present wherever there happens a division between forms, is found in two separated souls, because they are adapted to diverse bodies [i.e., to numerically diverse portions of designated matter.]"[63] And, in a related passage, he remarks that, "The substantial symmetry of this soul to this body does not follow on being this soul; it constitutes precisely this soul."[64] His claim that separated souls are numerically multiplied in virtue of their "substantial symmetries" or "substantial inclinations to diverse bodies"[65] is then combined with his account of identity in terms of both formal and material continuity to yield the following account of postresurrection survival. The soul's reunion with the same designated matter in which it inhered during the lifetime of the composite will result in a human being numerically one with the premortem individual.[66]

It should be noted that Cajetan is careful to distinguish the separated soul's mode of individuation from that of angelic, naturally self-subsisting forms. He follows Aquinas in claiming that angelic forms, though not subject to intraspecific individuation, are interspecifically diverse and are numerically distinct in that each angelic form is essentially incommunicable.[67] Separated souls, on the other hand, are held to be specifically the same and intraspecifically individuated owing to each soul's having a specialized particularizing relation to a determinate portion of designated matter. He further indicates that the difference between the separated soul's mode of individuation and that of an angelic form has the following consequence. While an angelic form could survive an existential gap, a separated intellectual soul could not. For example, suppose that God wished to annihilate Gabriel and then later restore or recreate the numerically identical angel. In Cajetan's view, it is possible for God to do this. since Gabrielhood, as an angelic form, is essentially incommunicable, Gabriel is the only possible instance of his nature. Hence, if God were to annihilate and then restore Gabrielhood, the newly created Gabriel, as the only possible member of his species, would necessarily be numerically one with the previously annihilated Gabriel. But, in view of the separated soul's mode of individuation, Cajetan reasoned that it would not be possible to annihilate and then subsequently restore, say, Socrates's separated soul. For given that (1) human souls are many under a single species, and (2) Socrates's soul remains individuated in its separated state by virtue of its "substantial inclination" to a certain portion of designated matter, numerical identity, or survival, on these assumptions, is ensured only on condition that both relata of the individualizing relation (viz., the soul and its commensurate matter) persist. Accordingly, if Socrates's separated soul were annihilated (i.e., were to cease to exist altogether), the individualizing relation would be destroyed. Hence, no subsequently created soul would be numerically one with Socrates's previously existing soul. Cajetan summarizes all of this in the following passage:

. . . the angel who is restored would necessarily be numerically the same angel, since it is from one and the same principle that Gabriel is an individual and is Gabriel. . . . (However,) if numerically the same soul is not taken up again—which ought not be annihilated if the notion of the resurrection is to be saved,—it would not be numerically the same man as the one who has the possibility of being restored by God numerically the same.[68]

IV. Cajetan's Revised Position

In spite of its many apparent advantages, Cajetan could not rest content with his position on material individuation as presented in the *De ente et essentai* commentary. For, on reflection, he concluded that his earlier position has one significant disadvantage in that it violates the thesis regarding the natural priority of substance to accidents (T3). Cajetan's reasons for reaching this conclusion can be made explicit by briefly reviewing Aquinas's account of the potentiality for quantitative determinations as an inseparable accident (inseparable dispositional property) of the corporeal composite.

In his treatise *De principiis naturae*, Aquinas distinguishes between accidental features that are necessary attributes of their subjects and those that are not: "Sed duplex est accidens scilicet necessarium quod non separatur a re, ut risibile ab homine; et non necessarium quod separatur, ut album ab homine."[69] He thus takes a thing's necessary accidents to be accidental properties that are *inseparable* from the thing to which they belong, while a thing's nonnecessary accidents are its separable features. The distinction between inseparable and separable accidents is further cashed out in terms of a distinction between accidents that have a *permanent cause* in their subject and those that do not. Attributes having to do with particular postures (e.g., sitting, walking) are given as paradigmatic examples of separable accidents that have no permanent cause in the subject.[70] Inseparable accidents, on the other hand, are dispositional properties that have a permanent cause in the subject in which they inhere; and, in Aquinas's account, it is as a consequence of their having a permanent cause in the subject that they are properties that the subject cannot fail to have.[71] He further divides inseparable accidents into two subcategories, and the division is made in terms of differences in the permanent causal principles productive of these properties:

If an accident inheres necessarily and always in a subject, it must have its cause in the subject—in which case the accident cannot but inhere. Now this can occur in two ways: in one way, when it is *caused from the principles of the species*, and such an accident is called a *per se* attribute or property; in another way, when it is *caused from the principles of the individual.* . . . [72] (emphasis mine).

When Aquinas says that certain accidents are "caused by the principles of the species", he means that they proceed from or are caused by the substantial or specific form.[73] He often uses the locution 'proper accidents' to refer to accidents of this sort.[74] And, when he mentions accidents that are caused by the "principles of the individual" he is referring to accidents deriving primarily from the matter of which the composite is constituted and from the matter's relation to the specific form.[75] Examples of proper accidents, in human beings, are dispositional properties or capacities associated with intellective, sensory and nutritive operations.[76] So, for example, the intellectual soul has the tendency to organize matter in such a way that the resultant human being has the capacity of sight. Granted, in some cases, this visual capacity is frustrated owing to bodily deformities. But Aquinas maintains that the soul of a blind person does not lack those dispositional properties associated with sight. Rather, he maintains that the soul "virtually" retains the tendency to exercise the capacity to have visual perceptions even when, due to the "defects of matter", it is prevented from doing so.[77] His claim is then that the relevant dispositional properties (or radical aptitudes) are inseparable features of the composite substance, since these dispositions would cease to exist only on the condition that the form from which they derive ceases to exist, in which case the composite would be corrupted.[78]

Cajetan notes that Aquinas includes dimensive quantity among those accidents caused by the "principles of the individual".[79] And he further remarks that, "when generation is terminated in itself, primarily in the substantial composite, there is generated consequent to this its inseparable accidents, one of which is quantity which follows upon substantial corporeity."[80] Yet Cajetan's position here is not that having certain actual determinate dimensions is an inseparable accident of the composite. Rather, he is referring to the disposition toward a certain range of quantitative determinations characteristic of the size and shape of members of the given species and of the individual's peculiar growth rate and build. Now, as we have seen, Cajetan's claim, in the *De ente et essentai* commentary was that the disposition (or proximate potentiality) for quantitative determinations exists in matter prior to the substantial form and that matter so disposed is the principle of individuation. Yet it follows from this network of assumptions that, just as the disposition for a certain range of quantitative determinations is an inseparable *accident* of the composite, the same disposition present in matter prior to the inherence of substantial form would be, likewise, an accidental modification of matter. This conclusion, however, did not sit well with Cajetan, for he recognized that it stands in clear violation of T3. Further, Aquinas, in the *Summa theologiae*, appeals to T3 in arguing that "it is impossible for any accidental dispositions to preexist in matter prior to the substantial form".[81] Accordingly Cajetan, desiring to preserve T3 and to conform to the views of Aquinas, was compelled to abandon his previous position on material individuation.

In his commentary on the *Summa theologiae*, Cajetan explicity rejects his earlier position,[82] and sets forth his new account. As before, he intends his approach to the problem of material individuation to be circumscribed by the constraints on a solution to the problem specified in T1–T3. Thus, the possibility of numerically many subjects of inherence for substantial form cannot be explained by supposing the material subjects of inherence to be already under some form, whether substantial or accidental. The only remaining possibility is that the numerical distinction of matter has its source and foundation in matter's very nature or essence.[83] And, since quantity is the primary ground of numerical distinction, Cajetan now holds that matter, taken as the root and cause ("*radix et causa*")[84] of quantity, is essentially diversified.[85] Thus, his final position represents an even more radical departure from Aquinas's *Sentence* commentary account presupposes that *one* indefinitely extended matter is capable of receiving diverse specific forms in its various parts by virtue of its being under a generic form. The *De ente et essentia* commentary view subsequently posits *one* matter, now unextended and nonsubstantial, to be divisible into multiple subjects of inherence for substantial form by virtue of its having a diversity of receptive potencies, again owing to formal influences (i.e., of the "*agens particulare*"). Accordingly, Cajetan, in developing his first position on material individuation, was still laboring under the bewitchment of the *Sentence* commentary account. In developing his final position, he sees matter, not as a single undifferentiated principle standing in need of the diversification that can be provided only by form, but rather as being a principle that, by its very nature, is multiple; that is, numerically many *matters* are seen as providing numerically many subjects of inherence for substantial form.

So construed, Cajetan's later position can be read as being consonant with the account Aquinas advances in his *Tractatus de substantiis separatis*, reportedly written shortly before his death:[86]

> Now there cannot be a division according to matter except because the matter is distinguished through itself and not through a diverse disposition or form or quantity; for this would mean that the matter is distinguished according to quantity or form or disposition. Therefore, we must finally reach the conclusion that *there is not one matter for all things but that matters are many and distinct in themselves*. Now it is proper for matter to be in potency. This distinction of matter must

therefore not be understood according as matter contains its diverse forms or dispositions, for this is outside the essence of matter, but according to the distinctions of potency with respect to the diversity of forms.[87]

Cajetan's final address to the problem of material individuation also trades on an intuition, hinted at but not fully spelled out by Giles of Rome: that matter, though by nature indivisible in the sense of being unextended, is nonetheless essentially diversified into a multiplicity of receptive subjects of inherence for substantial form. Ultimately, Aquinas, Giles, and Cajetan appear to agree that, to account for how matter accomplishes intraspecific individuation, it is not necessary to posit a single undifferentiated metaphysical principle that relies on formal effects for its individuating efficacy. Rather, many essentially numerically distinct matters are capable, in and of themselves and independent of the diversifying influences of form, of severally receiving and rendering incommunicable inherent specific forms.

Notes

1. In *De ente et essentia D. Thomae Aquinatis Commentaria,* ed. P. M. H. Laurent (Turin: Marietti, 1934). For biographical information on Cajetan, see "Bio-bibliographie de Cajetan", in *Revue Thomiste* 17 (1934–35): 3–49; Cajetan; *Commentary on Thomas' 'On Being and Essence',* trans. Lottie H. Kendzierski and Francis Wade, S.J. (Milwaukee: Marquette University Press, 1964). See translator's introduction, pp. 1–37; Frederick Copleston, S.J., *A History of Philosophy,* vol 3, *Ockham to Suarez,* Part III, pp. 335–340.

2. *Commentaria in Summa theologiae,* in *S. Thomae Aquinatis Opera omnia,* iussu Leonis XIII edita (Rome, 1882–1948), vols. 4 and 5.

3. For information on the life and works of Giles of Rome (Aegidius Colonna Romanus), see P. Nash, "Giles of Rome", *New Catholic Encyclopedia,* vol. 6 (1967), pp. 414–485. See also *Aegidii Romani Theoremata de esse et essentia,* ed. Edgar Hocedez, S.J. (Louvain, 1930), Editor's Preface and Introduction, pp. v–xiv, and 1–129. For an excellent review of Giles's metaphysics, see John F. Wippel, *The Metaphysical Thought of Godfrey of Fontaines* (Washington DC: The Catholic University Press, 1981).

4. Propositio IX, Lectio IX: 235. (Rome: Marietti, 1955)

5. See also *In Duodecim libros metaphysicorum Atristotelis expositio,* L. VII, I. XIII, 1574, where Aquinas notes that, in Aristotle's account, a universal is properly characterized as "what is naturally apt to exist in many" rather than as "what [actually] exists in many". (Rome: Marietti, 1950), p. 379.

6. "Est enim de ratione individui quod non possit in pluribus ease". Black-friars ed. (London: Eyre & Spottinwoode, 1965), p.132.

7. *Summa theologiae* III, q. 77, a. 2, *Responsio:* ". . . materia est individuationis principium omnibus formis inhaerentibus: quia, cum hujusmodi formae, quantum est de se, sint natae in aliquo esse sicut in subjecto, ex quo aliqua earum recipitur in materia, quae non est in alio, jam nec ipsa forma sic existem potest in alio esse" Blackfriars ed., vol. 50, pp. 132–134.

8. See *De spiritualibus creaturis,* a. 1, ad 9: "whenever . . . many individuals are under one common species, the distinction between many individuals is through individual matter, which has nothing to do with their specific nature". The Latin runs as follows: "Quandocumque igitur sub una specie sunt multa individua, distinctio multorum individuorum est per materiam individualem, quae est praeter naturam speciei" (Rome: Marietti, 1965).

9. See *Summa theologiae* I, q. 7, a. 1, Resp.

10. *In Librum de causis expositio,* Propositio IX, L. IX:235: "Unde oportet deventire ad aliquid quod non est natum recipi in aliquo et ex hoc habet individuationem, sicut materia prima in rebus corporalibus, quae est principium singularitatis. *Unde oportet quod omne illud quod non est natum esse in aliquo, ex hoc ipso sit individuum*" (emphasis mine).

11. *Summa theologiae* III, q. 77, a. 2, *Resp.*: ". . . formae immateriales separatae, per se subsistentes, sunt etiam per seipsas individuae" Blackfriars ed., vol. 58, p. 132.

12. "In his vero quae non habent formam in materia, sicut sunt formae simplices, nihil potest esse praeter essentiam speciei; quia ipsa forma est tota essentia. Et ideo in talibus non possu esse plura individua unius speciei, nec potest in eis differre *mentarium*", ed. tertia, P. F. Angeli M. Pirotta, O.P. (Rome: Marietti, 1948), p. 169. *Aristotle's De anima in the Version of William of Moerbeke and the Commentary of St. Thomas Aquinas,* III: IV, L. 706, trans. K. Foster and S. Humphries (New Haven, CN: Yale University Press, 1951). See also *De spiritualibus creaturis,* a. 8, *ad* 4: ". . . dicendum quod sicut forma quae est in subiecto vel materia, individuatur per hoc quod est esse in hoc; ita forma separata individuatur per hoc quod est nata in aliquo esse" (Rome: Marietti, 1915), p. 348.

13. *De ente et essentia,* ch. 5, Section 5; *De unitate intellectus contra averroistas,* ch. 5, Section 103; *Summa theologiae* I, q. 75, a. 7.

14. For Aquinas's argument (by induction over various modes of change) for the existence of prime matter as pure potentiality for substantial form, see *In Octo libros physicorum Aristotelis expositio* I,L. 12–15.

15. For Aquinas's defense of his unitarian thesis regarding substantial form, see his commentary on Aristotle's *De anima,* Book II, Ch. 1, L. 1, Section 224; *Summa*

contra gentiles II, Ch. 58, Section 6; *De spiritualibus creaturis,* a. 1, ad 9; *Summa theologiae* I, q. 76, a. 4.

16. Regarding the natural priority of substance to accident, see *In Duodecim libros metaphysicorum* VII, L. 2: C. 1291. (An exception to the general rule regarding the existential dependency of accidents on substance is made in Aquinas's account of transsubstantiation. See *Summa theologiae* III, q. 77, a.2. But Aquinas makes it clear that the persistence of the bread and wine apart from their natural subjects is owing to "divine power" and is, thus, outside the order of natural occurrences.)

17. See I *Sent.* d. 8, q. 5, a. 2: "Et propterea materia prima, prout consideratur nuda ab omni forma, non habet aliquam diversitatem, sed efficitur diversa per aliqua accidentia ante adventum formae substantialis cum esse accidentale non praecedat substantiale. Uni autem perfectibilit debetur una perfectio. Ergo oportet quod prima forma substantialis perficiat totam materiam. Sed prima forma quae recipitur in materia, est corporeitas, a qua nunquam denudatur. . . . Ergo forma corporeitatis est in tota materia, et ita materia non erit nisi in corporibus. Si enim diceres, quod quidditas substantiae esset prima forma recepta in materia, adhuc redibit in idem: quia ex quidditate substantiae materia non habet divisionem, sed ex corporeitate, quam consequuntur dimensiones quantitatis in actu; et postea per divisionem materiae, secundum quod disponiture diversis sitibus, acquiruntur in ipsa diversae formae" Mandonnet ed., Paris, 1929. See also M. D. Roland-Gosselin, O.P., *Le "De ente et essentia" de S. Thomas D'Aquin,* VIII (Kain: Le Saulchoir, 1926), ch. 11, pp. 104–117. For an excellent discussion of Aquinas's *Sentence* commentary account of material individuation and its place in the development of late medieval thought on the problem of individuation, see Marilyn McCord Adams, *William Ockham* (Notre Dame, IN: Notre Dame Press, 1986). In particular, see the chapter entitled "Matter, Quantity and Individuation".

18. *In Duodecim libros metaphysicorum* VII, L. 2: C. 1283 and 1284.

19. *Summa contra gentiles* IV, Ch. 65, Section 4019: "Habet autem et hoc proprium quantitatis dimensiva inter accidentia reliqua, quod ipsa secundum se individuatur. Quod ideo est, quia positio, quae est *ordo partium in toto,* in eius ratione includitur: est enim quantitas *positionem habens"* (Turin: Marietti, 1961), p. 368.

20. On the extent to which Giles's philosophical views depart from those of Aquinas, see Frederick Copleston, S.J., *A History of Philosophy,* vol. 2, *Augustine to Scotus,* ch. KLIV (Westminster, MD: The Newman Press, 1950) and P. Nash, "Giles of Rome."

21. Th. XII: "Nam formae separatae se ipsis sunt hoc aliquid. Nam eo ipso quod sunt formae non receptae in alio, ut in materia, se ipsas individuantur", Hocedez ed., pp. 73–73; and Th. III: ". . . quia formae separatae habent totum quod est de ratione illarum formarum; ideo si secundum hunc ordinem quem videmus, in talibus non potest esse plurificatio in eadem forma, propter hoc quod quodlibet habens talem formam, habet quidquid pertinent ad rationem illius formae et non superest quod aliud possit participare illam formam. Non tamen propter hoc concluditur quin

possit esse plurificatio in diversitate formae, ideo in formis separatis potest esse pluri-ficatio etsi non secundum eandem formam sive secundum eandem speciem, tamen secundum diversitatem formae et secundum varietatem speciei,'' ibid., p. 12.

22. *Ibid.*

23. *Ibid.*, Th II: ''Nam non possemus intellegere quod aliquid sint plura nu-mero et eadem specie, nisi sint composita ex materia et forma'', Hocedez ed., p. 6; and ''. . . plurificatio secundum numerum in eadem specie praesupponit composi-tionem ex materia et forma'', p. 9.

24. *Ibid.*, Th. X: ''. . . ratio individualitatis sumitur ex materia, quia in hoc ipsa forma trahitur ad conditiones materiae. . . .'' p. 56.

25. *Ibid.*, Th. X: ''Materia quidem sine forma cum sit pura potentialitas, nec potest intellegi nec existere'', Hocedez ed., p. 50. Th. VI: ''. . . materia dicit poten-tiam puram. . .'' p. 26, and Th. XV: ''. . . materia secundam se quid indivisbile et quid inextensum nominat,'' p. 99.

26. See *De gradibus formarum* (Venice, 1502), and ed. J. S. MaKaay, *Der Traktat des Aegidius Romanus Liber die Einzigheit der Substantiellen Form* (Wurzburg: St. Rita-Druckere, 1924) See also Copleston, *History of Philosophy,* vol. 2, ch. 44.

27. *Theoremata*, Th. XIV: ''. . . forma tamen accidentalis non advenit rei omnino in potentia sed advenit rei iam existenti in actu, quia advenit materiae iam factae in actu per formam substantialem,'' Hocedez ed., p. 89.

28. *Ibid.*, Th. XIV: ''. . . omnis forma accidentalis tanquam subiectum imme-diatum vel saltem mediatum praesupponit substantiam. . .'', p. 91.

29. *Ibid.*, Th. VII: ''Est tamen diligentur advertendum quod dispositiones in-completae praecedunt formam substantialem in materia, sed completae sequuntur si-cut *dimensiones indeterminate praecedunt formam substantialem in materia,* sed determinatae sequuntur'', p. 36, emphasis mine.

30. *Ibid.*, Th. XXII: ''Nam de ratione quantitas est quod sit divisibile. . . .'', p. 157.

31. *Ibid.*, Th. XV: ''. . . nam materia secundum se quid indivisibile et quid inextensum nominat, sed si coniungatur quantitati resultabit in ea quaedam extensio et habebit materia esse extensum'', p. 99.

32. See *Ibid.*, Th XV (pp. 92–100). In particular, see p. 96: ''Ergo materia de se est in potentia ut extendatur et ut determinatur potentia per actum. Cum vero actu coniungitur quantitati, actu extenditur et actu determinatur. Quare materia non ex-tensa et extensa non differt nisi sicut indeterminatum et determinatum, propter quod ipsa extensio quae competit materiae per quantitatem non est res tertia, differens a materia et a quantitate, sed est quaedam determinatio materiae vel est quidam modus se habendi, sive quidam modus essendi, quem habet materia ut est quantitati coni-

uncta. Et sicut esse quod dat quantitas non est res tertia differens a quantitate et suo subiecto, sed illud esse nihil est aliud quam quaedam determinatio materiae per quantitatem, sic esse quod dat quaelibet alia accidentalis forma, non est res tertia differens a forma illa accidentali et suo subiecto, sed est quaedam determinatio subiecti per huiusmodi formam''.

33. *Ibid.*

34. See note 29.

35. See note 32.

36. *Theorems on Existence and Essence*, trans. M. S. Murray. This passage in the Hocedez edition reads as follows: "Dedit ergo Deus hoc essentiae materiae haberet quandam diversitatem in se ipsa secundum quod subicitur alteri et alteri formae. Sicut etiam hoc habet cera quod potest esse rotunda et quadrilatera et mularum figurarum, sic hoc habet essentia materiae quod potest esse sub hac forma et sub opposita et sub multis formis. Et sicut vere ipsa essentia cerae diversificatur secundum quod est sub alia et alia figura, sic ipsa essentia materiae diversificatur secundum quod est sub alia et alia forma'', p. 105.

37. See the Laurent edition, Quaestio 5: "Utrum materia sit principium individuationis", Section 34, p. 50: "Duo ergo quaeruntur concurrentia ad individuationem, scilicet quo, primo, natura specifica reddatur incommunicabilia et quo, primo, realitur distinguatur ab alius ejusdem speciei''.

38. For a very insightful and illuminating discussion of incommunicability (noninstantiability) and distinction (as an extrinsic relation) see Jorge J. E. Gracia, "Individuals as Instances". *The Review of Metaphysics* 37, no. 1, (September 1983): 37–57.

39. See Cajetan's reference to an *"intrinsecum individuationis principium"*, (Laurent ed., p. 53) which is held to account both for incommunicability and for intraspecific numerical distinction.

40. See Q. XVII, Section 150. Regarding his position that incommunicability and real distinction can be accounted for in terms of the same intrinsic principle metaphysically constitutive of the corporeal composite, see Q. 4, Section 37: ". . . quia cum in substantia composita non sunt nisi materia et forma et compositum ex his, et accidentia quaecunque individuo accidunt, nullam aliam intrinsecam causam habent, nisi aliquid horum: et sic investigandum individuationis causam non opertet extra hoc vagari'', Laurent ed., p. 56.

41. Q. 18 (Laurent ed., pp. 223–234). Cajetan notes that this position was advanced by Averroes in *Libro de substantia orbis* as well as by Aquinas in his *Sentence* commentary (see n. 3, Laurent ed., p. 225). The title of *Quaestio* XVII reads "Utrum dimensiones *interminatae* praecedunt formam substantialem in materia" (emphasis mine). I have continued to use indeterminate rather than interminate so that the terminology here will parallel that of earlier sections of this chapter. Nothing of philo-

sophical and exegeticval significance seems to hinge on the usage of one expression rather than the other.

42. Q. 17 Section 139, (Laurent ed., p. 224).

43. ''. . . omnis divisio formae materialis praeexigit diversitatem partium materiae'', Laurent ed., p. 224.

44. He also indicates that his response follows Aquinas's position in *Summa theologiae* I, q. 76, a. 6. (see q. 7, Section 139.)

45. ''. . . corpus enim fit ex materia quae non est corpus . . .'' Laurent ed., p. 225.

46. ''. . . sed talis distinctio partium materiae praeexacta non oportet quod fiat per interminatas dimensiones ipsi materiae inhaerentes sed fit per dimensiones precedentium compositorum'', Laurent ed., p. 226. His reasons for claiming that the distinction of matter into parts is brought about by the dimensions of the preceding composite are made explicit later.

47. Q. 5, Section 37.

48. ''Materia signata nihil aliud est quam materia capax hujus quantitatis, ita quod non illius'', Laurent ed., p. 53.

49. Cajetan maintains that Aquinas, in referring to designated matter, was careful to refer to it as matter ''*sub certias dimensionibus*'', i.e., not as matter *with* dimensions, but rather as matter so influenced that it has a specialized potency for certain determinate dimensions.

50. ''Imaginandum est enim quod agens particulare, puta hoc semen, continue appropriat materiam ad animam humanam, ita hoc semen ad hanc animam. Unde cum in primo instanti generationis Sortis, quod est primum esse Sortis et primum non esse formae praecedentis et accidentium primo ordine naturae fiat particulare compositum particulare terminate per se primo generationem . . .'', Laurent ed., p. 54.

51. ''. . . dicitur quod non solum quantitas tali modo signat materiam sed etiam qualitates propriae. Materia enim Sortis ita est capax harum qualitatum quod no aliarum, sed quia sola quantitas immediate recipitur in substantia et ex sola quantitate oritur radicaliter distinctio materialis, ideo ad propositum, materiam signatam, materiam sub certis dimensionibus et non sub certis qualitatibus dicimus'', Laurent ed., p. 59.

52. Q. 17, Section 139: ''. . . quando generatio terminatur per se primo ad compositum substantiale, generatur consecutive ejus accidentia inseparabilia'', Laurent ed., p. 226.

53. Q. 18, Section 145: ''Accidentium sequentium materiam quaedam sequuntur eam in ordine ad formam generalem quaedam in ordine ad formam specialem. Illa accidenta dicuntur sequi materiam in ordine ad formam generalem, quae individual

generis altioris conveniunt ratione magis suae materiae quam formae, sicut hoc mix-
tum habet cutis nigredinem non ex ratione formae mixti sed quia materia sua talis
passa est, puta in tali climate ubi calor solis abundat. Illa vero dicuntur et consequi
materiam in ordine ad formam specialem, quae individuo inferioris generis vel speciei conveniunt magis ratione materiae quam formae, sicut hoc animal est masculi-
num non ratione animae principaliter, sed quia materiam ad animam dispositam talis
passio comitata est.'', Laurent ed., p. 234.

54. Aquinas expresses this view concerning the natural priority of quantitative
to qualitative determinations in *Summa theologiae* III, q. 77, a. 2, where he remarks
that the accidents of dimensive quantity are a "particular principle of individuation"
for all other accidents. The whiteness of Scorates is numerically other than the whiteness of Plato on account of its being delimited by determinate spatial boundaries; and,
in the same place, he says that likewise, *"omnia alia accidentia* referantur *ad subjectum mediante quantitate dimensiva"*, Blackfriars ed., p. 132.

55. See note 51.

56. See q. 18, Section 148, *Commentary on Thomas' 'On Being and Essence'*,
trans. Kenderzierski and Wade, p. 317. This Latin text runs as follows: ". . . sciendum est Thomistarum esse opinionem: Nullum accidens esse idem numero in genito
et corrupto. Sequitur enim hoc necessario ex nostris principiis. Nam si nullum accidens est subjective in materia et non datur nisi una forma subsantialis in composito,
impossiblile est idem accidens remanere idem numero.'', (Laurent ed., p. 235)

57. ". . . sed multa accidentia sequuntur compositum ex necessitate materiae,
quae sunt licet non incompossibilia: aliqualiter tam opposita ipsi fomae, ut patet de se.
Ed ideo quod figura et similia sequuntur cadaver ex necessitate materiae, quia scili-
cent agens naturale non potest tam cito dispositiones per tot transmutationes radicatas
corrumpere totaliter, et ideo similes dispositiones sequuntur, et quia non sunt facientes
pro forma geniti, ideo ad corruptionem properatur.'', Laurent ed., p. 237.

58. See Cajetan's claim, in q. 5, Section 37: ". . . haec namque materia [ma-
teria signata] est pars intrinseca Sortis de definitione ejus si diffiniretur.'', Laurent
ed., pp. 53 and 54. See also *Summa theologiae* I, q. 119, Resp., where Aquinas maintains that nature can be taken in two ways: viz., in reference to the species and, second, in reference to the individual. Accordingly, whereas the form and the common
matter pertain to the nature of the speciess, individual signate matter and the form
individualized by that matter pertain to the nature of a particular individual.

59. See Capitulum 3. *In de ente et essentia D. Thomae Aquinatis Commentarium*, Laurent ed., pp. 59–79.

60. For Cajetan's discussion of this point, see q. 5, Sections 38 and 39.

61. Trans. Kendzierski and Wade, p. 106. The Latin reads as follows: ". . .
dicitur quod quantitas terminata ad individuationem concurrens non stat in indivisibili
sed latitudinem habet. Sicut enim quaelibet species naturalis determinat sibi quanti-

tatem maximam et minimam infra quamdam latitudinem: ita et quodlibet individuum determinate sibi hanc quantitatem infra tales limites et non in indivisibili.'', Laurent ed., p. 59.

62. Trans. Kendzierski and Wade, Corp. II, q. 5. Section 57, pp. 101–102. ''. . . circumscripta Sortis materia signata, seu materia propria, quod idem est, certum est quod non remanet hic, neque forma ejus remanebit.'', Laurent ed., pp. 55–56.

63. Trans. Kendzierski and Wade, p. 267. The text, in the Laurent edition, reads: ''Duae enim animae humanae separatae non distinquuntur formaliter seu per materiam, licet sint purae formae a materia abstractae. . . . Distinctio autem formarum, cum sit undecumque inter formas divisio accidat, in duas animas separatas invenitur ex hoc quod diversis corporibus coaptatae sunt,'' pp. 193–194.

64. Trans. Kendzierski and Wade, p. 266. (''Ita substantialis commensuratio hujus animae ad hoc corpus non sequitur animam hanc, sed constituit ipsam hanc.'', Laurent ed., p. 192.)

65. See Cap. 6, Section 121: ''Non enim dicimus animam individuari formaliter per actualem unionem ad corpus, sed per coaptationem substantialem ad hoc corpus.'', Laurent ed., p. 194.

66. See Cap. 2 q. 5, Section 37.

67. For his extended discussion of the individuation of angelic substances, see Cap. 5 q. 9 and q. 10.

68. Trans. Kendzierski and Wade, p. 201. (''. . . necessario idem numero angelus, ex eodem enim Gabriel est hic et Gabriel . . . dicamus quod si in resurrectione non resumeratur eadem anima numero, quae non annihilata esse debet: si resurrectionis ratio salvanda est, non esset idem homo numero cum quo stat idem numero posse reparari a Deo.'', Laurent ed., p. 140.

69. Caput Secundum (Pauson ed.), p. 83.

70. *Quaestiones de anima*, q. 12, ad 7.

71. By 'permanent cause', we might understand Aquinas to mean a cause that persists throughout the lifetime of the subject. But construing ''permanent cause'' in this way has the awkward consequence that merely temporal permanence will not yield the required inseparability. On the supposition, for example, that whatever causal principles accounting for Socrates's pallor remain in him throughout his lifetime and are never frustrated, there will be no time at which he is without that feature. But one could argue that the conclusion that being pale is one of his inseparable attributes in unwarranted, since there is no reason to suppose that the relevant causal principles themselves inhere in him necessarily, or that they could not be impeded or frustrated, e.g., by some external agent. Accordingly, some accidents that have an enduring or constant cause would seem to be no less separable than accidents having a merely transitory cause. To see why Aquinas holds necessary accidents to be in-

separable properties of their subjects, it is important to understand that by 'permanent cause' he is referring to those causal principles that are metaphysically constitutive of their subjects, viz., matter and form.

72. *Commentary on the Posterior Analytics of Aristotle* I, L. 14. (75a18–37) trans. F. R. Larcher (New York: Hamilton Printing Co., 1970)

73. See *Quaestiones de anima*, q. 6, obj. 4 and Reply.

74. See his commentary on Aristotle's *Posterior Analytics* I, L. 10: 73a34–b26, and *Quaestiones de anima*, q. 12, ad 7.

75. See *De ente et essentia*, ch. 6, Section 6 and *Summa theologiae I*, q. 54, a. 3, ad 2.

76. See *Quaestiones de anima*, q. 12, and *Summa theologiae* I, q. 77, articles 1–8.

77. See *Summa theologiae* I, q. 78, a. 1 and his commentary on Aristotle's *Metaphysics*, VI, L. 3: C. 1210–1211.

78. For Cajetan's discussion of radical aptitudes, see *De ente et essentia* commentary, q. 18, Sections 150–153.

79. *Ibid.*

80. Q. 17, Section 139, trans. Kendzierski and Wade. (Laurent ed., p. 226: ". . . sed quando generatio terminatur per se primo ad compositum substantiale, generatur consecutive ejus accidentia inseparabilia de quorum numero est quantitas quae substantialem corporeitatem sequitur''.)

81. See *Summa theologiae* I, q. 76, a. 6: "Unde impossibile est quod quaecumque dispositiones accidentales praeexistant in materia ante forma substantialem", Blackfriars ed., p. 76.

82. For a detailed discussion of Cajetan's revised position regarding material individuation, see Joseph Bobik, "The 'Materia Signata' of Cajetan", in *The New Scholasticism* 30, no. 2 (April, 1956). Cajetan's rejection of his first position is made explicit in the following passage: "Per materiam autem sub certis dimensionibus, non intelligo, ut olim exposui in commentariis *De ente et essentia*, materiam cum potentia ad quantitatem: quoniam potentia illa est in genere quantitatis [and is, therefore, an accident]." *Commentaria in Summa theologiae*, q. 29, 1, IX.

83. "Sed intelligo materiam distinctam numero, non ut subiectum quantitatis, sed ut prius natura ipsius fundamentum, radix et causa; ita quod ipsa materia in se est prius sic distincta quam quanta; ut sic effectus proportionetur causae", *ibid.*, q. 29, 1, IX.

84. *Ibid.*

85. "Materia autem, quae radix fundamentumque est quantitatis, non est, etiam in illo priori, extra participantia quantitatis naturam: immo, ut melius loquamur, est quasi praehabens quantitatis naturam.", *ibid.*, q. 29, 1, X.

86. For information regarding the date of this treatise, see Thomas Aquinas, *Treatise on Separate Substances*, ed. Francis J. Lescoe (West Hartford, CN: St. Joseph College, 1963), Introduction, pp. 1–34.

87. Trans. Lescoe, *ibid.*, p. 69 (emphasis mine). The Latin text, in *Tractatus de substantiis separatis*, runs: "Non est autem divisio secundam materiam nisi quia materia secundum se ipsam distinguitur, non propter diversam dispositionem vel formam aut quantitatem, quia hoc esset distingui materiam secundum quantitatem aut formam seu dispositionem. Oportet igitur quod finaliter deveniatur ad hoc quod non sit una omnium materia sed quod materiae sint multae et distinctae secundum seipsas. Materiae autem proprium est esse in potentia. Hanc igitur distinctionem materiae accipere oportet non secundum quod est vestita diversis formis aut dispositionibus, hoc enim est praeter essentiam materiae, sed secundum distinctionem potentiae respectu diversitatis formarum. Cum enim potentia distinguatur secundum id ad quod primo potentia dicitur.", Cap. VI, Section 31, Lescoe ed., p. 68.

20

CHRYSOSTOM JAVELLUS (B. 1472; D. 1538) AND FRANCIS SYLVESTER FERRARA (B. 1474; D. 1526)

MAURICIO BEUCHOT

Javellus and Ferrara, who lived at about the same time, were two Dominican Thomists who adopted different interpretations of the formula used by Thomas for the principle of individuation: *materia signata quantitate*. Javellus follows the same interpretative line of Cajetan, while Ferrara understands the principle of individuation differently.[1]

To study them together may help us see that the doctrine of the individual in Thomism was neither completely unitarian nor homogeneous, perhaps owing to the very difficulty of both the problem and the doctrine. We shall see the reasons each of them gives in support of his interpretation. Javellus, following Cajetan, interprets designated matter as expressing a relation to a determinate quantity, although not in act, but rather in potency; on the other hand, Ferrara says that it is matter under quantity (*sub quantitate*) already in act.

We shall study the views of both in the typical and most significant texts with respect to this theme. For Javellus we shall use question 15 of his *Quaestiones* on Aristotle's *Metaphysics* V and, for Ferrara, his *Commentarium* to chapter 21 of St. Thomas Aquinas's *Summa contra gentiles* I.[2]

We shall use Javellus's text as the basis for structuring our discussion, since it is the most orderly and pointed, and we shall add, in the appropriate places, Ferrara's exegesis and defense. We shall end with Javellus's defense against Scotus and the solution to some doubts.

In his commentary to Aristotle's *Metaphysics* V, in question 15, Javellus asks whether the principle of individuation in material things is either designated matter or thisness (he calls it "*haecceitas*"). He wishes, thus, to compare the Thomistic and Scotic views to determine which counts with more solid foundations and demonstrative arguments. He carries out his task

while commenting on the Aristotelian causes and their effects, particularly in
the discussion of the material cause and its effect. He takes as a cue Aristotle's saying: "Those things are one in number whose matter is one in
number."[3] And, since he finds two interpretations of the principle of individuation—the Thomistic and the Scotistic—and he favors the former, he
will defend it by solving Scotus's objections against it and he will attack
Scotus's own position. But, to follow the order generally favored by scholastics, he begins by explaining the sense of the question by stating its terms.

I. Terms of the Question and Its Formulation

For Javellus and Ferrera, the intension of 'individual' includes two
things: (1) incommunicability and (2) distinction with respect to others.
Hence, to ask for the principle or cause of the individual (i.e., what is known
as the problem of the principle of individuation) is the same as to ask what
is the cause that the specific nature, which is of itself communicable, become
incommunicable in the individual Socrates, and, consequently, be precisely a
this (*'haec'*, the term from which Scotus derived *'haecceitas'*). Moreover, it
also implies asking for the cause of why Socrates, having already that incommunicable nature, is distinguished from any other man with a substantial, and
not just accidental, distinction. Concerning the extension of 'individual',
both Ferrara and Javellus say very little, but they lead one to think that both
substances and accidents are individual, and of substances both corporeal and
incorporeal, although in this text they deal only with corporeal substances.[4]

According to Javellus, the material individual may be considered in two
ways: (1) as thing—*ut res,* and (2) insofar as it is placed in a category under
the lowest species. In (1) it is considered really—physically and metaphysically, although it does not add any distinctions; in (2) it is considered in terms
of reason—that is, logically. He discusses both ways in this text. The real
(that is, physical-metaphysical) concerns, then, the cause of the substantial
distinction among corporeal beings. Javellus makes clear that such a distinction cannot be caused by quantity alone, since quantity is an accident, and,
therefore, posterior to substance. But neither can it be caused by substance
together with quantity, since from them can result only an accidental unity.
What is needed is a cause that yields substantial unity, for when the notion of
one in itself is added to the notion of individual, we then have a real
consideration.[5]

The logical problem (from the point of view of reason) consists in
searching for the reason why the speices is contracted into the individual
placed under a category, so that the principle that effects the contraction expresses the whole nature of the individual, and for that very reason, moreover, is predicated of it *in recto.*[6]

II. St. Thomas's Opinion

Javellus begins by presenting St. Thomas's opinion, to which he naturally and obviously devotes more space and care. Following an ordered procedure, he will speak first about the real consideration of the individual and later of its consideration according to reason.

A. The Real Consideration of the Individual

In the section where Javellus considers the individual in real terms, he provides a literal exposition of the Thomistic texts. He also adds a statement about the profound meaning of those texts and of Thomas's thinking, rejecting other positions, including that of Ferrara. Afterwards he presents and proves his interpretation and resolves some difficulties.

1. Exposition of the Thomistic Doctrine. St. Thomas saw that the individual must have *incommunicability* (which is opposed to the communicability of the universal with respect to its inferiors) and *distinction* with respect to any other individual. For that reason he identified the principle of individuation with matter and quantity, for matter accounts for incommunicability and quantity for distinction.[7]

But St. Thomas's texts themselves have allowed Thomists to interpret the conjunction of matter and quantity differently. Sometimes the texts state that the principle of individuation is matter insofar as it underlies designated dimensions, but at other times they state that it is matter insofar as it is related to this or that quantity; and still at other times that it is matter insofar as it is considered under certain dimensions.[8] Javellus finds difficulties in the interpretation of the Thomistic texts themselves. In general, he concludes that for St. Thomas the principle of individuation can be said to be matter, although not matter taken in just any way, but rather as designated matter, and designated matter is matter considered under certain dimensions. Indeed, what is most difficult is to interpret the formula '*materia signata quantitate*', that is, the kind of designation involved.[9]

Considering the lack of agreement among Thomists concerning the designation of matter, Javellus has to provide his own hermeneutics of the Thomistic formula and reject other interpretations that seem to him inadequate. In fact, he agrees with Cajetan and cites him while defending his interpretation, and he disagrees with Capreolus (whom he also cites) and with two other interpretations of Thomas. He does not identify the last two but one of them corresponds to Ferrara's view and for that reason we will insert it here.

Javellus adds only a few precisions concerning the determined or undetermined quantities or dimensions and begins, then, with an analysis of the mentioned interpretations. According to him, some say that St. Thomas understands the Thomistic formula to mean that matter and quantity form an aggregate. But Javellus believes that to be impossible, "because to what is being and one by itself cannot be assigned a principle that is one accidentally; but the aggregate of matter and quantity is one accidentally, since they belong to different genera and categories; therefore, [the aggregate of matter and quantity is not a principle of what is one being by itself?]"[10]

2. *Ferrara's Interpretation.* In Javellus's list follow others who say that the Thomistic formula signifies matter in act under (*sub*) quantity. That is Ferrara's position, who has a section on how to understand '*materia signata*' in the mentioned commentary to chapter 21. And the interpretative position that appears to Ferrara in more harmony with St. Thomas's thinking is the one that holds that "designated matter is to be understood as matter under quantity" (*materia sub quantitate*), in such a way that both matter and quantity contribute to individuation. He explains:

Certainly matter, as individual, is incommunicable by the exclusion of the communication whereby the universal is communicated to the particular. For, since matter is the first subject, not received in any inferior, the nature received in matter as such cannot be communicated to any inferior. But quantity concurs insofar as the individual is distinct from any other individual of the same species, with a quantitative and material distinction. Hence, just as two [things] come together in the individual, namely, incommunicability and distinction, so designated matter, which is the principle of individuation, includes two [things], namely, incommunicable matter itself and quantity to which pertains primarily the material distinction. So that, neither matter by itself nor quantity by itself [individuate], but rather it is matter, designated and limited by quantity, that individuates, giving incommunicability by reason of matter and distinguishing naturally by reason of its determination by quantity.[11]

Thus Ferrara holds that individuation requires quantity to be in matter. In another place he uses the expression '*materia signata sub quantitate*', which reveals his view in a nutshell. And he argues that that is Thomas's view, referring to *Summa theologiae* III, q. 77, a. 2 and *In IV Sententiarum*, d. 12, q. 1, a. 1.[12] In those texts St. Thomas says that the individual must have two properties: incommunicability and distinction; matter is the principle of the first and quantity of the second. Consequently, the total principle of individuation is *materia signata*, that is, *materia sub quantitate*, since it is designated by quantity, which is a sign because it renders matter sensible and determinate to the *hic et nunc*.

Ferrara himself raises a difficulty (surely expected by Cajetanists) that argues that there can be no quantity in matter before form (in Thomas's system). But Ferrara counterargues that there is never an instant in which form unites to matter without quantity, for a particular form unites only to a particular matter distinct from all others, but matter is distinct from others only through quantity. Hence, incommunicability, distinction, and determination to the *hic et nunc* come to the individual through matter with quantity.[13]

To this must be added that accidents presuppose the form in matter considered as formal cause, but with respect to the material cause and dispositively it is the reverse, in relation to some degree of form? For this reason Ferrara insists on his position and alleges that the form can be in matter and constitute the supposit or individual only if "matter is understood prior to quantity, through which it becomes this and distinct from [any] other part of matter".[14]

3. Javellus's Interpretation. Against the positions adopted by Soncinas and Ferrara, Javellus tries to exclude the opinion that the Thomistic formula, *materia signata quantitate,* signifies matter in act under quantity—for then matter would have quantity in the moment in which it functions as principle of individuation. Javellus criticizes it because in the school of St. Thomas it is not accepted that accidents precede form in matter. And he gives the following argument against the said opinion: In the instant in which the individual, for example Socrates, has its first being through generation, its generation as a singular composite in the genus of substance occurs. But in that very and precise instant there is no quantity in act in the matter, because the form that ceased existing before generation does no longer informs matter, and all the accidents that accompanied it have ceased existing. And the quantity relative to the form that the matter is going to receive through generation does not yet exist, because it is posterior to substantial form; therefore, in that first instant of the generation of Socrates there is no quantity in act in matter. But quantity must be presupposed in matter in some way; and, if not actually, at least potentially or "radically", expressing a relation to the said matter; for in that first instant ends the substantial generation, whose term is the singular substance, since actions come from substantial supposits or individuals; "hence the material singular is singular before any received and permanent quantity in matter; thus it is not necessary that designated matter include quantity in act."[15] Hence, it includes it only in potency, as Javellus will argue in his view. In fact, he is preparing the ground to persuade us to accept a special relation between matter and quantity that would be only potential. This is precisely Cajetan's position, which Javellus adopts immediately after.

This opinion, which originates with Cajetan,[16] interprets the formula '*materia signata quantitate*' as matter that is receptive potency of a quantity and not another, in virtue of a relation or disposition that the particular agent that produces the composite gives to it; such an agent disposes it to this or that form that requires this or that quantity. And thus "*signata*" does not add to "*materia*" something *in recto,* that is, in act, but *in obliquo,* as something potential, that is, the relation to this or that quantity. Even more, since matter is something potential, what is added to it is distinct only through a distinction of reason, for that relation is in reality matter itself; and it is that, before any accident, the distinctive principle of the individual, insofar as it is a substance, can be assigned. Such is the (Cajetanist) sense that satisfies and convinces Javellus, and the one he believes more defensible against attacks from adversaries.[17]

4. *Proof of This Interpretation.* According to Javellus, the designated matter that has potentiality to one quantity and not another is constrained to that individual quantity, that is why it is of itself incommunicable to many individuals. Consequently, it is primarily and by itself incommunicable. And, since it is such primarily and by itself, it renders particular that in which it is; that is, it makes the individual. Moreover, that to be communicated to others is repugnant to it is proven because it becomes proper to the individual and then it ceases to have the nature of common, or communicable, matter. Moreover, that this incommunicability belongs to it primarily and by itself is proven because if it were taken away from the individual, there would be no reason why it could not be communicated; because it would have no incommunicability through the form, since the form is of itself communicable; nor would it have it through matter as such, because matter is common to every material individual; nor would it have it through quantity and the other accidents, because at least in the natural order (although not temporally or chronologically) they follow the substance of the individual. Consequently, it remains only that it be incommunicable through designated matter.[18]

Now, if it is argued that with this is proven only the incommunicability or indistinction in itself, but not distinction with respect to others, Javellus answers that designated matter is a sufficient principle of both. The reason is that matter is incommunicable and indistinct from the fact that it is capable of only a particular quantity, and because matter is distinct from any other matter related to any other quantity from the fact that it is related by the producer to such a quantity and not another. It is because of the distinction produced by the designation in matter that the individual is distinct from any other individual.[19]

5. *Solution to Some Doubts or Difficulties.* It was said that matter's designation causes that it be related to a certain quantity. But Javellus has to examine the following question: Is that quantity supposed to be in act in matter?[20] If it is supposed to be in act, there is a contradiction with what was

said before; if it is supposed to be in potency, then the effect precedes the cause. How can one get out of this dilemma?

Javellus says that "a certain Thomist"[21] answers that in the first instance there is no individual distinct from another with numerical distinction, but rather with a transcendental distinction, that is to say, not with a quantitative, but rather with an essential, distinction. But Javellus objects that in Thomism quantitative union is required (and because of that the quantitative distinction too). Besides, matter by itself is potential, and what distinguishes must be in act; so distinction must result from the addition of form or of quantity. But it cannot be form, because the particular form is received in a matter that is already distinct from the rest, for otherwise that form would inform any other matter or none at all. Therefore, it must be distinguished through quantity. Hence, there is a numerical and not just a transcendental distinction. Moreover, with the transcendental distinction are distinguished only immaterial individuals, but not material ones; and for that reason it has to be a numerical or quantitative distinction. Javellus concludes:

> And because of that I hold that in that first [instance] there is a quantitative distinction in the material individual which is compared to any other individual. And when it is argued that in that first [instance] there is no quantity, and thus that [quantity] cannot cause that distinction, I say that in that first [instance] there is no quantity in the genus of material cause, because there is not yet [such distinction] inherently in the individual, but as such it is not the cause of matter's designation; indeed, on the contrary, designated matter is the material cause of quantity, because it is receptive to it. But I say that in that first [instance] quantity is in the genus of formal cause, and, as such, is the cause of the designation of matter, and is prior to the designation of matter, as is clear in the similar [case] of the substantial form susceptible of being received in matter, insofar as it is in potency for it, for the form in the genus of material cause is posterior to the potency of matter; in fact, at least with respect to the nature, matter has receptive potency for form before the form is received; however, in the genus of formal cause, form precedes matter's potency, because such potency is in matter in relation to form, so, as such, form is prior.[22]

It can be seen, then, that Javellus has tried to show the precedence of form with respect to quantity, because it is due to form that matter can receive accidents within a Thomistic framework. Thus, quantity can be in matter only as potentially prior form. But there is also another question or difficulty: An effect in act requires a cause in act, therefore, the designation of matter is in act in matter and is an effect caused by quantity; hence, there is quantity in matter, and it is in act, which is contrary to what was said at the beginning.[23]

Javellus answers to this that it is sufficient that the effect in act have a formal cause that exists in a radical manner, that is, not in itself, but *in its root;* for in that way, although such quantity does not exist in act in itself, it is in the *root* of matter, insofar as it has the capacity for that quantity and not for another; and it has this capacity through the action of the producing agent. And he adds that the quantity that exists as its root in the matter is not the form of designation, but the formal notion of it (i.e., that without which there would be no such designation); and, although the cause of an effect in act must be in act, it is not necessary that that from which its formal notion is taken be in act, as is clear in the case of active powers or faculties.[24]

A last difficulty or question attracts Javellus's attention. If by designated matter is understood matter with a receptive potency to a certain quantity, it follows that it is an aggregate of substance and accident, because matter functions there as substance and the potency for an accident—as quantity is—is also accidental and functions there as an accident. But something different had been said before, namely, that designated matter is something substantial and not accidental.

Javellus's answer is that the potency is in the same genus as the act it receives only in a primary way and not in a secondary way (otherwise, the soul would be in the category of quality, as its faculties, and not in that of substance). Accordingly, Javellus concludes: "Therefore, I say that the potency of matter whereby it is receptive to this quantity, is substance, and it is the same thing as the matter, because primarily and of itself expresses a relation to this or that substantial form; but, since it cannot receive such a form, unless [the said form] were receptive of such quantity, then it is related in a secondary manner to this or that quantity."[25] On this point Javellus refers to Cajetan, making sure that he agrees with him on this interpretation.

B. Logical Consideration of the Individual

According to this consideration, the principle of the individual is that whereby the individual, insofar as it is one in number, becomes categorical under the *species specialissima;* for below it is the level of individuality. And such level, in this logical consideration, cannot be designated matter. In fact, designated matter is *part* of the individual, while that level expresses the *whole* substance of the individuals. Moreover, from such level is taken the individual difference, which is predicated *in recto* of the individual, after the fashion in which the specific difference is predicated *in recto* of the species.[26]

To that could be objected that to posit individual differences is to fall into Scotus's position; but Javellus says that he does not agree with him with respect to the principles from which the individual differences are taken. For

Scotus takes them from the side of form, believing that just as the specific difference contracts the generic nature, so the individual difference contracts the specific nature, even when there is no designated matter. Such is the reason why he posits individual differences in immaterial beings, that is, beings separated from matter; and thus it turns out that in individual differences there can be many numerically distinct things under the same species. In contrast with Scotus, Javellus maintains the relation of matter in individual differences. That is, the presence of designated matter produces the individual difference, because without it it is not certain that the specific nature not be multipliable; thus the individual difference causes that the individual be constituted in a category under its species and be distinguished from any other individual.

In other words, the principle of the individual, considered logically, is the individual difference (*differentia individualis*).[27] Javellus proves this alluding to the fact that a being is substantial prior to any accident; hence, quantity cannot contract the nature into an individual, because it would do it after it is substance. Nor is it designated matter, because what contracts something in the direct categorical line cannot be a part of it, and matter is a part. For that reason designated matter is not predicated *in recto* of the thing; however, the individual difference is predicated *in recto* of the thing, because the difference has the nature of a whole, not of a part. Hence, in the logical order, it is necessary to posit the individual difference (and not designated matter) as the principle of the individual.

1. Scotus's Opinion. As far as Scotus's opinion is concerned, Javellus proposes to expound it and analyze its strongest arguments in order to dissolve them. Scotus's main thesis is that the cause or principle of the individuality of the individual, that is, that the specific nature be contracted into an individual, is a positive and simply incommunicable entity, which he calls '*haecceitas*'. Such an entity is neither the matter nor the form, nor a composite of them, but the mode or end term of them all, which completes and fulfills them, and it is their ultimate reality. However, it is not distinguished from them by a real distinction, but by a distinction of another sort.[28]

The individuating principle is something positive for Scotus, Javellus explains, because the individual difference is something positive, since it is a property of being. Moreover, negation qua negation cannot contain real being. Hence, what distinguishes the individual must be something positive. Just as the constitutive element of the specific difference is something positive, so also must be the constitutive element of the individual difference, particularly if numerical unity is regarded as greater than specific unity.

In addition, such an individuating principle is of itself *this* or *this thing* ("*haec*"), that is, indivisible and incommunicable; because, just as the in-

dividual is constituted as incommunicable, so also is that whereby it is constituted as such. For the same reason the individuating principle is of itself
indivisible, and it is *this*.[29]

The individual difference agrees in some aspects with the specific difference, and in others it differs from it. They agree in that they are compared
to their superiors as act is to potency and they contract it; and they differ in
that the specific difference does not take away all divisibility (for it leaves
numerical divisibility). Also they agree in that both of them are taken from
form; and they differ in that the specific difference is sometimes taken from
different forms than the genus (given the plurality of forms that Scotus accepts in the individual), while the individual difference is always taken from
the ultimate reality of form. Likewise they differ in that the specific difference is present by reason of form, of quidditative being, and of the concept
of the species; for that reason, the specific difference is called "form" with
respect to the individual difference. On the other hand, the individual difference is present by reason of matter; hence, the individual difference is called
"material" with respect to the specific difference because it is neither in
quidditative being nor in the concept of the species.

Javellus considers Scotus's position to be imaginative, rather than intellectual or rational, and rather narrative than demonstrative, because it presupposes that the individual differences are taken from the ultimate reality of
the form. Javellus bases his criticism on the fact that, according to him, Thomism has proven that individuality cannot come from form, but must come
from matter. This seems like a rather arbitrary argument from authority by
Javellus. For he adds only the analysis of certain arguments that Scotus opposes to St. Thomas's thesis, according to which he rejects matter plus quantity as principle of the individual. Two principal reasons are given by
Scotus.[30]

The first argument given by Scotus against the Thomist thesis states
that the individual difference has the numerical difference as its primary effect; therefore, it is the principle of the said unity and, hence, of the individual. That it has such an effect is demonstrated because the said numerical
unity does not follow from the quiddity, since the quiddity is not of itself this
(*haec*) or from the specific difference, since the latter is principle of the specific unity only, which is lesser than numerical unity. Nor is some accident
the principle of the said unity, not even determinate quantity, because, just as
the substantial entity of the individual precedes naturally any accident, substantial unity precedes numerical or quantitative unity. Consequently, what
causes numerical unity is the individual difference (*haecceitas*) and it is the
individual difference that is the principle of the individual.[31]

Javellus answers the main argument by denying the antecedent. To the
proof of the antecedent he answers that it is based on an insufficient division

(or disjunction) because, in addition to the specified causes, designated matter would have to be posited, and designated matter is the principle constitutive of the material individual and its distinctness, that is, what distinguishes it from any other individual.

The second argument given by Scotus, as presented by Javellus, states that, since two individuals differ from each other in a proper way, it follows that their difference must be based in primarily diverse things. For Scotus, such primarily diverse things can be only their respective haecceities; thus they are the principles whereby individuals are constituted and differ. For the rest, Scotus's proof that only haecceities can be such primarily diverse causes is based on an exhaustive division (or disjunction)—according to Javellus: It is not the specific nature because it is precisely in it that the said individuals agree; it is not prime matter, because it has the same nature in both; it is not quantity, because two quantities can be diverse only by themselves or by their places.[32] Moreover, they are not different in themselves, because then they would have to be specifically distinct. Nor could their places be the source of difference, since place is of two sorts and neither of them works: one is categorical and another is the difference of quantity. Categorical places cannot be the source of difference, because they follow quantity, as the relative follows the absolute. And neither can the places distinctive of quantity, because they are distinguished in themselves or by something else; and they are not distinguished by themselves, because by themselves they are but this; and, if by something else, one may ask how that something else is made other, and so on into infinity.[33]

Javellus answers that two individuals have numerical distinction thanks to their quantities, which are their distinctive principles. But quantities differ by their places, insofar as place consists in the order of the parts in the whole. Besides, places differ according to the order of the parts; and orders are distinguished by themselves, because distinction belongs to the notion of order.[34]

2. Scotistic Arguments Against the Thomistic Principles of Individuation. Toward the end of his exposition, Javellus says that he will answer some arguments proposed by Scotists. In the first place, he makes clear that he will pay no attention to those arguments that conclude that the principle of individuation is not designated matter or matter as related to a certain quantity, for they do not go against what he considers to be the Thomistic thesis. He adds that those who wish to look at the arguments by Scotus, Aureol, and Durand that do not affect the Thomistic thesis, may consult Capreolus in *In II Sent.*, d. 3, q. 1, *contra 2am conclusionem*. So, he takes into account only one difficulty, according to which St. Thomas seems to contradict himself in the thorny theme of whether the quantity that designates matter is determinate or indeterminate. The dilemma is formulated thus: The quantity cannot be determinate, because there can be no quantity in matter before form. Nor can it be indeterminate, because it would follow that the child Socrates would not be the adult Socrates, since the determinate quantity present in the first does not remain in the second.[35]

Javellus answers that *determinate quantity* can be considered in two ways: (1) as the quantity that is constrained to a certain term and cannot be made larger or smaller, such as the quantity of the sky; and (2) as the quantity that is constrained to a certain term or degree but can be made larger or smaller, for example the quantity of this water. On the other hand, *indeterminate quantity* can be considered indeterminate in three ways: (1) because it is infinite in act; (2) because it has no certain term, even though it may not be infinite in act, for example because it is not of two or three, nor can it be designated by another number; and (3) because, even when, according to the nature of things, it is related to some term, it is not considered in relation to this or that term, but rather with a certain breadth. According to all of this, Javellus answers to the argument that indeterminate quantity is the principle of the individual, not in the first sense or in the second, but in the third. And he explains this sense—certainly difficult to understand—saying that

> even when the quantity whereby the matter of Socrates becomes divided from any other matter, it is always related to a certain term, because at the beginning it is, for example, [the matter] of a finger, later of a hand, later of an elbow, etc.; however, all this quantity, considered in all the breadth there is between the maximum and the minimum in relation to which the nature of a particular species can be preserved in a particular individual, is the principle of the individual. I say, moreover, that determinate quantity, insofar as it is opposed to indeterminate [quantity] of the first and second types, is the principle of the individual, because the magnitude of all natural things is determinate.[36]

And, since this seems to contradict some of St. Thomas's sayings, Javellus tries to show their agreement with it. For example, he points out that it agrees with what Aquinas says in *In Boethii De trinitatem*, that determinate quantity is the principle of the individual, because there he understands 'determinate' as opposed to 'indeterminate' in its third sense, since that is the way the quantity with a certain end is determined, and thus it is not principle of the individual, because, since it changes and receives another term, the same individual would not remain. It also agrees with what St. Thomas says in *De principio individuationis*, that determinate quantity is the principle of the individual, since there he takes 'determinate' as opposed to 'indeterminate' in its first and second senses. In fact, St. Thomas does not refer to indeterminate quantity insofar as it precedes form, nor does he posit it as principle of the individual. In accordance with it, it can be seen how St. Thomas preserves a role in individuation for both determinate and indeterminate quantities. For there is a sense in which determinate quantity designates matter, and also there is a sense in which indeterminate matter designates it. So, they are not opposed in the same sense or under the same aspect, and therefore, there is no contradiction in Thomas. Such is the way in which Javellus tries to solve the difficult question concerning the type of quantity that designates matter in the formula '*materia signata quantitate*', which is the principle of individuation according to Thomists.[37]

III. Conclusions

The views of Javellus and Ferrara illustrate the differences there can be concerning an issue within the same school. There were also such differences concerning other issues, for example, between Capreolus and Cajetan. Even more, history repeats itself here very closely, for—at least in part—Javellus's view is the same as Cajetan's and Ferrara's position is the same as Capreolus's.[38] Each add sharp distinctions and ingenious arguments to defend their respective views. Above all, Javellus defends the view that *materia signata* has a transcendental relation to quantity, that is, having quantity only in potency or "radically"; and he elucidates the question of the type of quantity to which matter is related, that is to say, whether it has to do with indeterminate or determinate dimensions. Moreover, he adds that the dimensions are indeterminate in some sense and determinate in another sense. In turn, Ferrara maintains that quantity has to be in act, that is, as form-of-quantity, for there to be numerical distinction (in addition to incommunicability) in the individual.

In fact, both Cajetan's position, represented by Javellus, and Capreolus's position, represented by Ferrara—defended with new arguments—have some truth (in that they do not unilaterally exagerate) and respond to the two distinct but complementary requirements of the Thomistic theory of individuality. Javellus is correct in excluding actual quantity from *materia signata,* a view compatible with St. Thomas's requirement that accidents be received in virtue of form and not without it. And, on the other hand, Ferrara is correct in saying that matter cannot be determinate if it does not have actual dimensions. There has been even an author who has said that these two requirements are not mutually exclusive and that they can be made compatible if *materia signata* is regarded as being under actual quantity, although not intrinsically, but only as something that occurs "radically", since quantity comes from matter as from its root and is actualized by the form.[39] And it is that, as he says, for St. Thomas quantity must be individualized before the individual body itself, in such a way that it makes matter relate only to a particular quantity; and what individualizes quantity is the *situs* or position. Now, quantity alone with *situs* is indeterminate dimension; because of that it is not sufficient to provide complete individuation; determinate dimension has to intervene in some way later. For that reason it is there that Javellus intervenes, rejecting that it be indeterminate dimensions alone, because that would be an Averroist thesis that Aquinas could not have accepted. The dimensions have to be determinate in some way—that is Ferrara's point—but that does not involve that they be absolutely determinate; otherwise, a man, who had particular determinate dimensions in childhood and different ones in adult life, would not be the same man in childhood and adult life.

In conclusion, regardless of how fine and acute these controversies have been throughout history, it cannot be said that all the difficulties involved in the Thomistic doctrine of individuation have been solved. Even today they need to be discussed, since in each age new problems are found; but the Thomist school continues to defend the Thomistic thesis and tries to solve the diverse issues that it encounters.

Notes

1. On the life and work of Javellus and Ferrara, see J. Quétif and J. Echard, *Scriptores Ordinis Praedicatorum* (Paris, 1719–1723, facs. rep. New York: Burt Franklin, n.d.), and the appropriate entries in *Dictionnaire de Théologie Catholique* and *New Catholic Encyclopaedia*. Also, see C. Giacon, *La seconda scolastica,* vol. 1 (Milano: Fratelli Bocca, 1944), pp. 37 ff. and 85 ff.

2. For Javellus, see Chrysostom Iavellus, *In omnibus Metaphysicae libros quaesita textualia* (Lugduni: Apud Gasparem a Portonariis, 1559) (abbreviated henceforth as *Quaesita*). For Ferrara, see Francis Sylvester Ferrara, *Commentaria in libros quatuor Contra gentiles S. Thomae de Aquino,* ed. I. Sestili (Rome: Orphanotrophii a S. Hieronymo Aemiliani, 1898) (abbreviated henceforth as *Commentaria*).

3. Aristotle, *Metaphysica* V, 6, 1016b32–33.

4. Javellus, *Quaesita,* pp. 91r–v; Ferrara, *Commentaria,* pp. 135 and 138–139.

5. Javellus, *Quaesita,* p. 91v: "Non potest autem dici quod hoc distinctivum sit quantitas, quoniam cum sit accidens posterior est substantia Sortis. Haec potest dici quod sit substantia Sortis cum quantitate quoniam ex his duobus non fit unum nisi per accidens. Superponitur autem individuum esse unum per se, et haec consideratio erit realis."

6. *Ibid.:* "Quantum autem ad considerationem logicam, quaerendum est, propter quid contrahitur species ad individuum ut reponitur in praedicamento, ita

quod principium contractivum dicat totam naturam individui, et de eo praedicetur in recto.''

7. Cf. St. Thomas, *De ente et essentia,* ch. 2 and *De natura materiae et dimensionibus interminatis,* ch. 3.

8. Javellus, *Quaesita,* p. 91v: ''Invenimus autem in dictis eius aliquando quod materia, ut stat sub dimensionibus signatis, est principium individuationis: ut patet in expositione illius tex. 12 in V *Metaph.* unum vero numero sunt, etc. Aliquando quod materia in ordine ad hanc vel illam quantitatem, ut patet in tract. *De principio individuationis.* Aliquando quod materia ut sub certis dimensionibus consideratur.''

9. *Ibid.,* pp. 91v–92r.

10. *Ibid.,* p. 92r: ''. . . quoniam entis et unius per se, non est assignandum principium quod sit unum per accidens, sed aggregatum ex materia et quantitate est unum per accidens, cum sint res diversorum generum et praedicamentorum: ergo, etc.''

11. Ferrara, *Commentaria,* pp. 136–137: ''Materia quidem, in quantum individuum est incommunicabile per exclusionem communicationis illius, qua universale communicatur particulari. Nam, quia materia primum subjectum est, in nullo receptum inferiori, ideo natura in materia recepta, ut sic, nulli inferiori communicari potest. Quantitas autem concurrit, inquantum individuum distinctum est a quolibet alio individuo ejusdem speciei, distinctione quantitativa et materiali. Unde sicut duo conveniunt individuo, scilicet, incommunicabilitas et distinctio, ita materia signata, quae principium individuationis est, duo includit, ipsam scilicet materiam incommunicabilem, et quantitatem ad quam primo, materialis distinctio pertinet; ita quod nec materia sola individuat, nec solo quantitas; sed materia quantitate signata et limitata, est illa quae individuat: ratione materiae dans incommunicabilitatem, ratione vero determinationis suae per quantitatem, naturaliter distinguens.''

12. St. Thomas, *Summa theologiae,* III, q. 77, a. 2, c.: ''. . . dicendum est quod individuationis principium est quantitas dimensiva. Ex hoc enim aliquid est natum esse in uno solo, quod illud est in se indivisum et divisum ab omnibus aliis. Divisio autem accidit substantiae ratione quantitatis, ut dicitur in I *Physic.* Et ideo ipsa quantitas dimensiva est quoddam individuationis principium huiusmodi formis, inquantum scilicet diversae formae numero sunt in diversis partibus materiae. Unde ipsa quantitas dimensiva secundum se habet quandam individuationem: ita quod possumus imaginari plures lineas eiusdem speciei differentes opositione, quae cadit in ratione quantitatis huius; convenit enim dimensioni quod sit quantitas positionem habens. Et ideo potius quantitas dimensiva potest esse subiectum aliorum accidentium quam e converso''. *In IV Sent.,* d. 12, q. 1, a. 1, sol. 3, ad 3: ''De ratione individui duo sunt, scilicet quod sit ens actu vel in se vel in alio; et quod sit divisum ab aliis quae sunt vel possunt esse in eadem specie, in se individum existens; et ideo primum individuationis principium est materia quo acquiritur esse in actu cuilibet formae sive substantiali sive accidentali; et secundarium principium individuationis est dimensio, qua ex ipsa habet materia quod dividatur. . . .''

13. Ferrara, *Commentaria*, p. 137–138.

14. *Ibid.*, p. 140: ". . . nisi in materia, quantitas praeintelligatur per quam efficitur hoc et distincta ab alia materiae parte."

15. Javellus, *Quaesita*, p. 92r: ". . . ergo singulare materiale est singulare ante omnem quantitatem receptam et permanentem in materia, non est ergo necesse, quod materia signata includat actu quantitatem." Ferrara holds the contrary; cf. *Commentaria*, p. 138.

16. Cajetan, *In De ente et essentia*, ch. 2, q. 5. See Chapter 19 on Cajetan in this volume.

17. Javellus, *Quaesita*, pp. 92r–v.

18. *Ibid.*, p. 92v.

19. *Ibid.*, p. 93r.

20. *Ibid.*

21. This is Cajetan's view; cf. Ferrara, *Commentaria*, p. 138. Javellus and Ferrara agree on this point.

22. Javellus, *Quaesita*, pp. 93r–v: "Et propterea teneo, quod in illo priori est distinctio quantitativa, individuo materiali comparato ad quodcumque aliud individuum, et cum arguitur, quod in illo priori quantitas non est, ergo non potest causare illam distinctionem. Dico quod in illo priori quantitas non est in genere causae materialis, quoniam nondum est inhaesive in individuo, sed ut sic non est causa signationis materiae, immo econverso, materia signata est causa materialis quantitatis, eo quod est receptiva eius. Dico autem quod in illo priori quantitas est in genere causae formalis, et ut sic, est causa signationis materiae, et est prior materia signata, sicut patet in simili de forma substantiali receptibili in materia, ut est in potentia ad ipsam, forma enim in genere causae materialis est posterior quam potentia materiae prius enim saltem natura, materia habet potentiam receptivam formae, quam recipiatur forma in genere, tamen causae formalis forma est prior, quam potentia materiae, eo quod talis potentia est in materia in ordine ad formam: ergo ut sic, forma est prior."

23. This objection resembles that of Ferrara in *Commentaria*, p. 136.

24. Javellus, *Quaesita*, p. 93v: "Sufficit effectu in actu habere causam formalem existentem non in se, sed in radice sua, nam illa quantitas etsi non sit in actu in se, est tamen in materia, ut in radice, prout fit capax huius quantitatis et non alterius actione agentis. . . ."

25. *Ibid.:* "Dico igitur quod potentia materiae qua est receptiva huius quantitatis, est substantia, et est idem re cum materia, quoniam primo et per se respicit formam hanc vel illam substantialem, sed quia non potest recipere talem formam, nisi sit receptiva talis quantitatis, ideo secundario respicit hanc vel illam quantitatem."

26. *Ibid.:* "Qui gradus differt a materia signata, quoniam illa est pars individui, iste autem gradus, dicit totam substantiam individui, a quo gradu sumitur differentia individualis, quae praedicatur in recto de individuo, sicut differentia specifica praedicatur in recto de specie."

27. *Ibid.*, p. 94v.

28. *Ibid.*, p. 95r.

29. *Ibid.*

30. *Ibid.*, p. 95v.

31. *Ibid.*, p. 96r.

32. Since place (*situs,* or position) is what individuates quantities and other mathematical entities.

33. *Ibid.*

34. *Ibid.:* ". . . ordines autem distinguuntur seipsis, eo quod de ratione ordinis est distinctio, et hic est status."

35. *Ibid.*, p. 96v.

36. *Ibid.*, p. 97r: ". . . licet quantitas, qua redditur materia Sortis divisa a quacumque alia materia, sit semper sub certo termino, quia in principio est, puta unius digiti, deinde unius palmi, deinde unius cubiti, etc. tota tamen haec quantitas considerata secundum totam latitudinem, quae est inter maximum et minimum, sub quibus potest servari natura talis speciei in tali individuo, est principium individui. Dico insuper quod quantitas terminata ut opponitur interminatae, primo, et secundo modo est principium individui, eo quod omnium naturalium est terminata magnitudo. . . ."

37. On the difficulties with this formula, see A. G. Fuente, "Interpretaciones tomistas de la fórmula 'materia signata quantitate' ", *Estudios Filosóficos* 10 (1961): 461–470.

38. Cf. S. Assenmacher, *Die Geschichte des Individuationsprinzips in der Scholastik* (Leipzig: Verlag von Felix Meiner, 1926), pp. 53–58.

39. Cf. A. Gazzana, "La *materia signata* di S. Tommaso secondo le diverse interpretazione del Gaetano e del Ferrarese", *Gregorianum* 24 (1943): 80.

21

FRANCIS SUÁREZ
(B. 1548; D. 1617)

JORGE J. E. GRACIA

The importance of Suárez's views in the history of the problem of individuation can hardly be overstated.[1] Not only did he write one of the most extensive systematic treatises on individuation ever produced, but his discussion of the topic displays a sophistication rarely found in treatments of it. Among scholastic works on individuation, none can match its breadth of topics, incisiveness of thought, clarity of exposition, and systematic arrangement. There are, indeed, plenty of discussions of individuation in the later Middle Ages, as the present volume illustrates, but none among them surpasses or even equals Suárez's analysis. True, one may find that this or that author produces a better argument here and there, or that his thought is clearer on some points, or still that his position on a particular dimension of the problem of individuation is theoretically superior to that of Suárez. But, on the whole, Suárez's philosophical effort in the area of individuation can be seen only as far superior to anything accomplished before him. And it is not clear that we can find subsequent writers who have surpassed it. These statements may sound exaggerated, but even a summary survey of the literature on individuation will show the relative poverty of the existing materials and the richness of Suárez's contribution by comparison. Indeed, even in our century, where considerable attention has been focussed on individuation, most of the treatments are short, superficial, and often repeat obvious mistakes.

Apart from philosophical value, Suárez's analysis of individuation also has value for the historian of ideas, since he discusses most of the important historical views on individuation that preceded him. His text contains a wealth of historical information that helps to reconstruct the broad outlines of the history and development of the problem of individuation in later scholasticism.[2] This should not be interpreted, however, as meaning that

Suárez's treatise is a scholarly work on the history of the problem of individuation, for nothing could be further from the truth. Suárez's analysis of individuation is found in Disputation V of his *Disputationes metaphysicae.* This work is systematic in character and displays no sense of historical development, and in this it is no different from other philosophical works produced at the time. Suárez's age is not aware of the history of philosophy as a separate enterprise, and Suárez is no exception to this attitude. His interest is not in the history of ideas, but in ideas themselves and their value. That he finds them in historical figures who preceded him, and that he is able to present a systematic map of those ideas and their authors does not change the fact that he treats them and their authors as contemporaries. Still, the information that he gives concerning various historical positions and authors can be considered valuable for those who study the history of philosophy, since his analysis of those authors and their views is generally insightful and often leads to a greater understanding of them.

Our discussion in this chapter will be divided into five parts, following the order and topics raised by Suárez in Disputation V. The areas to be covered are as follows: (I) the intension and extension of 'individual'; (II) the ontological status of individuality; (III) the principle of individuation of substances; (IV) the principle of individuation of accidents; and (V) the presence in the same subject of accidents differing only in number. Sections IV and V will be dealt with only briefly both because they are less important in this context than the others and also because of the need to keep this chapter to a manageable size. Before we enter into the discussion of Suárez's views properly speaking, however, I shall make some propaedeutic and general remarks about Suárez's approach that should be helpful for the understanding of the procedure he follows. At the end of the chapter I shall add a few overall conclusions concerning the import of Suárez's views.

Disputatio metaphysica V, where Suárez presents his views on individuation, is entitled "Individual Unity and Its Principle". It is one of fifty-four disputations that make up the monumental *Disputationes metaphysicae,* first published in Salamanca in 1597.[3] From its place in the *Disputations* one can gather the importance Suárez attaches to its subject matter. Only four Disputations precede it. The first deals with the nature of metaphysics (also called 'first philosophy' by Suárez); the second discusses the essential nature or concept (*de ratio essentiali seu conceptu*) of being; the third deals with the general characteristics of being, its so-called trancendental attributes, that is, unity, truth, and goodness; the fourth concerns transcendental unity; and the fifth is devoted to the examination of our topic, namely, individual unity and the issues that are involved in it. Only after Suárez has discussed individual unity does he turn to formal and universal unity. From the place given to it, it is clear that unity is the first and most basic attribute of being; truth and goodness are discussed only later. And individual unity is more fundamental than universal and formal unity, since it is discussed before them. Thus we have an early indication of the superior importance Suárez attaches to the individual over the universal in his metaphysics. While some scholastics ignore individuality altogether and many deal with it only in the context of universality, Suárez not only gives individuality separate treatment, but regards it as more fundamental than universality. Not only does this go against the standard procedure followed in the early Middle Ages, it is also contrary to the way in which many other late scholastics, such as Duns Scotus, deal with these issues.[4] Some do not deal with individuality separately because they may have considered it a less fundamental notion, while others do not because they may have thought that its analysis was impossible.

The translation into English of Disputation V covers over 100 pages of text and is divided into nine sections:[5]

Sect. 1:   Whether all things that exist or can exist are singular and individual.
Sect. 2:   Whether in all natures the individual and singular thing as such adds something to the common or specific nature.
Sect. 3:   Whether designated matter is the principle of individuation in material substances.
Sect. 4:   Whether the substantial form is the principle of individuation of material substances.
Sect. 5:   Whether the existence of the singular thing is the principle of individuation.
Sect. 6:   Finally, what the principle of individuation is in all created substances.
Sect. 7:   Whether the principle of individuation of accidents is to be taken from the subject in material substances.
Sect. 8:   Whether it is incompatible for two accidents, diverse only in number, to be simultaneously present in the same subject owing to their individuality.
Sect. 9:   Whether it is incompatible with the individuation of accidents that many accidents differing only in number be successively present in the same subject.

From the titles of the sections it should be clear that the core of Disputation V, comprising Sections 3–7, has to do with the principle of individuation of substances and accidents. Sections 1 and 2 seem to be devoted, respectively, to what I referred to in the Introduction to this volume as extensional and ontological issues, although, as will become clear later, Section 1 also deals with the conception of individuality. Finally, Sections 8 and 9 raise issues that apply only to accidents and that surface in the context of certain views concerning their individuation.

Suárez does not devote a separate discussion to the problem involved in the discernibility of individuals, but what he says at various points of Disputation V makes clear that he is aware of it and thinks it has nothing to do with the metaphysical problem of individuation. Indeed, he clearly distinguishes between three issues, dealing respectively with (1) "the principle of individuation considered by itself and in itself", (2) "the principle whereby one individual is distinguished from another with respect to us", and (3) "the occasion of the distinction [of one individual from others]".[6] The first issue concerns "being and the proper constitution of a thing . . . and therefore is most a priori and proper to this science [of metaphysics]".[7] But answers to the last two issues provide "only either a posteriori signs or occasions of distinguishing . . . individuals", which are, therefore, "very deficient and exceedingly equivocal".[8] Epistemic issues, in Suárez's view, are not appropriate in what is a purely metaphysical context and, therefore, need not be addressed in a metaphysical treatise such as the *Disputationes metaphysicae.*

Also to be left out are theological matters. Suárez, like most of his scholastic contemporaries, regards theology highly and considers revelation a knowledge superior to natural knowledge. Indeed, he often and consciously brings theological considerations to bear even in his purely philosophical works. But he understands quite well that philosophy and theology have independent spheres of operation and that their methods and concerns are different. The *Disputationes* were written to set down the metaphysical foundations for a supernatural and divine theology, and he explicitly notes in them the need to develop a "Christian philosophy" that may serve divine theology.[9] Moreover, he acknowledges that he occasionally and marginally deals with purely theological problems in that work.[10] But he also makes clear that the *Disputationes* is a philosophical work and that his role in writing it was that of a philosopher, not of a theologian.[11] The ultimate purpose of a metaphysics for him is as a basis for theology, but that does not mean that it should be confused or mixed with theology or that the reasoning and arguments it uses should be theological, that is, taken from authority. Consequently, we find him in the *Disputationes* frequently setting issues aside because of their theological character and always trying to provide arguments that can stand on their own philosophically. This approach is quite different from the approach used by most of his scholastic predecessors and results in a work of metaphysics very different from the predominantly theological works produced by earlier scholastic figures. Suárez's explicit identification of his role as that of a philosopher sets him apart from Thomas Aquinas, Duns Scotus, and most other towering figures of scholasticism, who view themselves as theologians, and puts him in the camp of such future metaphysicians as Descartes, Spinoza, and Leibniz.

As already mentioned, the core of Disputation V has to do with the problem of individuation. But the treatment of that issue is preceded by two sections devoted to two other issues that Suárez regarded as propaedeutic. I characterized these issues above as extensional and ontological, adding that Section 1 also discusses the conception of individuality. All of this makes very good philosophical sense, for it would seem useful, if not necessary, to determine what individuality is—its definition and status in things—before asking what the principle of individuation is. In this, Suárez's procedure contrasts again with that followed by many of his predecessors, who do not always raise explicit questions concerning the intension of 'individual' and the ontological status of individuality in individuals. Duns Scotus, for example, in spite of the centrality that individuality occupies in his metaphysical thought, never presents a clear exposition of the notion of individuality, and neither does Thomas Aquinas nor William of Ockham. Indeed, most scholastic authors do not seem to have been aware of the importance that settling the intensional and ontological issues has for the solution to the problem of individuation; they are too concerned with the extensional issue, which they generally treat in the context of universals and as a result neglect other matters related to individuation.

I. The Intension and Extension of 'Individual'

In Section 1 of Disputation V Suárez accomplishes two things: First, he provides an analysis of the notion of individuality, and second, he commits himself to a certain view about which things are individual.

A. Transcendental Unity

As already stated, the term that Suárez uses to refer to individuality is 'individual unity' (*unitas individualis*). Therefore, to understand what individuality is we must begin by examining his conception of unity. Suárez discusses various types of unity in the *Disputations,* but the most fundamental of these in his view is transcendental unity. It is examined in some detail in Disputation IV. Following a well-established scholastic tradition, Suárez understands by 'transcendental unity' the unity that is "convertible with being."[12] What this "convertibility" means varies from author to author, but in general it is taken to mean at least that the terms 'being' (*ens*) and 'one' (*unum*) are coextensive: Everything that is a being is also one and everything that is one is also a being. Unity is regarded as a fundamental attribute of being (*passio entis*) that always accompanies it, even if it can be distinguished from it in some ways. In short, unity is a property of being if 'property' is taken in the technical Aristotelian sense codified by Porphyry in which what is proper to something (to a species, in his context) always accompanies it, as it happens for example with man and the capacity to laugh.[13] But to say that transcendental unity is a property of being does not clarify sufficiently its relation to being, and therefore, this issue was the subject of considerable speculation among scholastics.[14]

The controversy centered around three different views. One, attributed by Suárez to Avicenna, Duns Scotus, and Antoninus Andrea, holds that "unity adds to being a kind of positive accident distinct *ex natura rei* from being, although by itself following and concomitant with every being".[15] This position, then, maintains the coextension of 'being' and 'one', but also accepts that unity adds to being some kind of positive reality distinct from being.

A second position, attributed by Suárez to Bonaventure and Alexander of Hales, holds that "unity adds to being a kind of positive property not really, or *ex natura rei,* but distinct only conceptually from being".[16] Accordingly, 'being' and 'one' are coextensive, but their intensions are distinct because the notion of unity contains something positive that it adds to the notion of being.

Suárez disagrees with these two positions and adopts a third, which he attributes to a host of authors, including Thomas Aquinas, Cajetan, and Aristotle. According to this view, "unity does not add anything positive, whether conceptual or real, to being, nor anything *ex natura rei* nor only conceptually distinct from being".[17] But does this mean that unity and being are the same thing not only extensionally, but also intensionally? Is there no distinction at all between the notions of being and unity? For Suárez there is a distinction, but it is not a distinction in which the notion of unity includes something that the notion of being does not. Indeed, if that were the case, to be one would mean to be something more and, therefore, other than to be. And that would not make much sense for him.[18] "Unity and being are one and the same nature, because unity does not express any positive notion other than the notion of being."[19] Still, to be one is not the same as to be and the reason is that unity adds to being a kind of privative negation.[20] Indeed, Suárez goes on to explain that unity is distinguished from being "not only because it is one of its attributes, but because the names ['one' and 'being'] are not synonyms, and to them correspond diverse formal and objective concepts in the mind".[21] But what is the "formal and objective concept" of unity that differentiates it from being? In what consists the kind of privative negation about which Suárez speaks? The answer is "the negation of division in being itself".[22]

Unity means, then, indivisibility of being in itself. But this notion should not be confused with other negations. There are in particular two other conceptions of this negation that should not be confused with the correct one. According to one, unity means "undivided in itself and divided from everything else".[23] And, according to Suárez, some authors go so far as to interpret the division from others as prior conceptually to the division in itself. To be one is somehow to be separate or different from others, if we may translate Suárez's language into the language used in the Introduction to this volume. But Suárez rejects this view, since "to be divided from another is not a requisite of being one absolutely, but only of being one among many".[24] Indeed, God was one before creatures were created and yet he was not divided from anything, and even if nothing else existed but him, he would still be one.[25] True, if something is one it is also "fundamentally and in aptitude distinct from another", but that does not mean that unity consists in distinction from others. As Suárez puts it, distinction follows unity, just as equality and inequality follow from quantity.[26] Distinction, therefore, does not enter into the proper understanding of unity, but is rather a consequence of it.

One might wish to express Suárez's view on this by saying that to be one entails the capacity or potential to become distinct from others, but since it does not entail actual distinction from others, it cannot be said that to be one is to be distinct from others. Similarly, to be human entails the capacity for laughter but it does not entail laughter. Division from others, then, may perhaps be better understood in the Suarecian scheme as a property (in the technical Porphyrian sense) of things that are one, but not as being part of the definition of unity.

However, as we saw earlier, Suárez does not interpret the negation of division as a mere negation, but rather as "a kind of privative negation". For him and most other scholastics a negation is simply a lack. For example, for a man not to have wings is a negation. But a privation is the lack of what ought to be present in a thing, and what ought to be present in a thing is determined by its nature.[27] For example, blindness is a privation in human beings because it is in the nature of human beings to have vision. Now, according to Suárez, the negation of division is neither just a negation nor a privation, but "a kind of privative negation". It is not a privation strictly speaking because it does not consist in the lack of a form in a subject that has a natural aptitude for it. But it is not just a negation, because it attaches to being as to a real subject, something that does not happen with mere negations.[28] In short, transcendental unity is an attribute of being, coextensive with it, that adds to it a kind of privative negation of division.

B. Transcendental Unity vs. Individual Unity

Having examined the most general notion of unity, transcendental unity, now we must turn to the more specialized notion of individual unity.

And the first question that needs to be asked is whether individual unity and transcendental unity are the same. This is discussed by Suárez in Disputation IV, S. 9. The term he uses there to refer to individual unity is 'numerical unity'. There are two things to keep in mind about this difference of terminology. The first is that Suárez, following a well-established tradition, uses the adjectives 'numerical' and 'individual' interchangeably. The second is that he points out that the term 'numerical unity' can also refer to quantitative unity, that is, unity restricted to the accidental category of quantity. Understood in this sense individual unity and numerical unity are not the same thing by any means.[29] In the quantitative sense, numerical unity stands for "the principle of quantitative number", but when it is interchanged with individual unity, it is contrasted with generic and specific unity.[30] Apart from the special case when 'numerical unity' refers to quantity, however, it can be regarded as equivalent to 'individual unity', and that is how Suárez treats it in this context.

It might be appropriate to add here the parenthetical comment that Suárez does not establish any clear extensional or intensional distinctions between the notions of "singular unity" and "individual unity". Not all scholastics follow this procedure, however. As early as the twelfth century there are efforts to distinguish between singularity and individuality, and some texts of Boethius suggest a distinction between these notions and particularity.[31] But Suárez does not make any attempt to distinguish these notions and does not keep the terminology separate.

Now let us go back to the issue concerning the relation of numerical (i.e., individual) unity to transcendental unity. The questions that we must address are (1) whether 'individual unity' and 'transcendental unity' are coextensional terms, that is, whether they refer to the same thing in reality; and (2) whether they are cointensional, that is, whether they have the same meaning. Only three combinations among these possibilities need be taken seriously: (a) individual unity and transcendental unity are really (extensionally) the same but are conceptually (intensionally) different; (b) they are both really (extensionally) and conceptually (intensionally) the same; and (c) they are neither really (extensionally) nor conceptually (intensionally) the same. A fourth combination—conceptually (intensionally) the same but really (extensionally) different—is also possible, but it does not make much sense in this context and therefore need not take up our time.

Suárez raises the issue of the relation of individual unity to transcendental unity explicitly in Section 9 of Disputation IV, but he does not provide a definite answer to it and tells us that we must wait until he discusses the status of individuals and universals in Disputations V and VI, respectively, to find out his view on this matter.[32] Still, in Disputation IV he outlines a position that will turn out to resemble his own closely.

The position he outlines holds that numerical, individual, or singular unity is properly and in reality an attribute of being and therefore is the same as transcendental unity. The reason given in support of this view is that transcendental unity must be real, but in things there is only one real unity, namely, individual unity. Indeed, since in reality there are only individual beings, being becomes convertible with individual being and therefore individual unity is also convertible with transcendental unity.[33]

Clearly, then, this view holds that in reality transcendental unity and individual unity are one and the same; they are what we have been calling "coextensive". But the view does not make clear if there is to be an intensional distinction between these unities. Of course, if the view maintains, with Suárez, that transcendental unity is to be understood simply as the negation of division, and that individual unity is to be conceived as incommunicability, then we must infer that there is indeed an intensional distinction between the two.

This view has much in common with the views defended by Suárez in Disputation V, but, as already mentioned, he does not endorse it in Disputation IV. Rather, he states that, until other details are discussed, individual unity should be regarded as one type of unity that, along with universal, material, and formal unities, make up transcendental unity.[34]

As we shall see, however, he holds that every thing has individual unity, while also maintaining an understanding of individual unity as incommunicability. This indicates his position must be that 'transcendental unity' is coextensive with 'individual unity', although the two terms are intensionally distinct. With this in mind we can turn to Suárez's explicit analysis of individual unity and its extension.

C. Individual Unity

Suárez takes up the analysis of individuality, that is, of individual unity, in Sect. 1 of Disputation V. In a key passage, he states:

> That is called "common" or "universal" which is communicated to many entities or is found in many entities according to one single nature. On the other hand, that is called "one in number" or "singular" or "individual" which is one being in such a way that, according to that nature of being through which it is called "one", it is not communicable to many entities. For example, to those that are lower to or placed below it, or to those that are many under that nature . . . [35]

This text emphasizes the point already made that Suárez uses the terms 'one in number', 'singular', and 'individual' interchangeably. It also makes clear that 'individual' is opposed to 'universal'. But most important of all, it presents Suárez's understanding of individuality as incommunicability. To be individual is to be incommunicable, but not to be incommunicable in just any way. This is already tacitly suggested by the examples contained in the passage cited but is later made explicit, when he adds: "No other negation of division or divisibility that may complete the notion of an individual and singular entity can be thought, except that which has been explained by us, namely, that the entity be such that its whole nature may not be communicable to many similar entities or, what is the same, that it may not be divisible into many entities such as itself."[36] Thus, for example, "human being" is not individual, since it is divisible, that is, communicable to many entities in each of which the whole nature of human being is found. But "this human being" is individual, because it cannot be divided into, or communicated to, other entities that are also human beings.

The term 'incommunicable' has a long history. It was first used in the context of individuality by Boethius, who spoke of the "quality" of individuals such as Plato and Socrates as being "incommunicable".[37] But the term fell quickly into disuse until it was brought back into philosophical discourse in the thirteenth century.[38] Being a negative term, its meaning was never discussed to the extent that its complement, 'communicable', was discussed. Early on Boethius raised the question of the correct understanding of 'common',[39] and by Suárez's time there were many discussions concerned with various interpretations of the terms 'common' (*communis*), 'communicability' (*communicabilitas*), 'commonality' or 'community' (*communitas*), and 'communication' (*communicatio*).[40] Indeed, Suárez himself discussed some of these terms in Disp. XXXIV, S. 5, 54–57. For our purposes, however, it is sufficient to note that he understood incommunicability as a negation of the sort of community proper to universals: An individual cannot be divided into entities specifically the same as itself, while a universal can.

Now we see how individual unity differs from other sorts of unities even though all unity consists in the negation of division, as we saw earlier. For the indivision characteristic of individuals has to do with incommunicability, while not every type of unity implies incommunicability. For example, the universal "human being" is one formally and universally, according to Suárez, and therefore undivided as a form or universal, but it is not incommunicable, since it can be "communicated" to many things specifically the same.

It is important to understand that Suárez is aware that other scholastics who precede him hold different notions of individuality. In particular, the view that individuality has to do with distinction or difference and the view that it has to do with multiplicity within the species were both quite widespread, and Suárez explicitly rejects them. This does not mean, however, that he thinks that these notions are unrelated to individuality. In Section 1 of Disputation V, where Suárez presents his own view of individuality, he does not mention at all the notion of ''distinction from others'', but he refers to ''multiplicity within the species'' in the answer to an objection. There he states that ''whether a spiritual substance and nature can or cannot be numerically multiplied within the same species has nothing to do with [its individuality]''.[41] Elsewhere, moreover, he explains exactly how distinction is related to individuality:

> Although a thing's being one in itself [i.e. individual] is by nature prior to its being distinct from others, nevertheless the latter follows intrinsically from the former without any positive addition being made to the thing itself that is one, but only by negation, by which, having posited the other term, it is true to say that this is not that. Accordingly, the same positive thing that is the foundation of unity with respect to the first negation or indivision in itself, is subsequently the foundation of the later negation consisting of distinction from another. In this sense it is usually said with great truth that a thing is distinguished from others by that whereby it is constituted in itself, because it is distinguished by that whereby it is. . . . Therefore, likewise in the case of individual unity, what is a principle of the individual with respect to its constitution and its incommunicability or indivisibility in itself is also a principle of its distinction from others; and, conversely, what is a principle of distinction must also be a principle of constitution.[42]

Individual unity is *naturally prior* to distinction from others, but distinction follows *intrinsically* from individual unity by negation alone. For this reason whatever is the foundation of one is the foundation of the other. Individuality is not to be understood as a kind of distinction, although if something is individual it will be distinct from other individuals, provided that such individuals exist. This is why it is said that distinction follows intrinsically from individuality. At least two conditions are necessary, then, for something to be distinct from others: (1) It must be individual and (2) there must be other individuals. But for something to be individual, no condition other than incommunicability is necessary. This explains why the foundation of individuality and distinction in a thing is the same while they are not intensionally equivalent. Clearly, Suárez's views on the relation between individuality and distinction mirror his views on the relation between indivision and distinction discussed earlier in the context of transcendental unity. For that reason they need not be elaborated further here.

The common view that conceives individuality as somehow having to do with multiplicity within the species is also rejected by Suárez. Both in the text given earlier concerning this matter and while discussing Thomas Aquinas's view on individuation, he separates the notion of individual unity from the multiplication or production of individuals within the species.[43] To be a member of a species that has or can have several members is not a necessary condition of individuality by any means. Indeed, Suárez adheres to the view, maintained by Thomas Aquinas and others, that each angel constitutes a whole species, while holding also that angels are individual.[44] The same holds for God, who is unique and also individual.[45] Neither multiplicity within the species nor distinction from others, then, is to be considered part of the notion of individuality.

D. Extension of 'Individual'

Having clarified Suárez's conception of individuality, we can turn to the issue ostensibly treated in Section 1: the extension of the term 'individual'. This issue is introduced with the question: "Whether all things that exist or can exist are singular and individual?"[46] And the answer is quite clear:

All things that are actual beings or that exist or can exist immediately are singular and individual. I say 'immediately' in order to exclude the common natures of beings, which as such cannot immediately exist or have actual entity, except in singular and individual entities. If these [individual entities] are removed, it is impossible for anything real to remain.[47]

Suárez's text echoes the standard medieval formula inspired by Aristotle: Everything insofar as it exists is individual. But what does the formula mean? To what exactly does 'everything' refer for Suárez? It refers to every entity except natures such as human being, white, tall, and so forth. Everything else is individual: purely spiritual beings, composite beings, material beings, and all their features, principles, and components. This becomes even more clear as the disputation progresses and Suárez identifies the principles of individuation of matter, substantial form, substantial modes, substantial composites, spiritual substances, and accidents. Every entity, therefore, has individual unity for Suárez. Even God is "singular and individual, since he is one in himself in such a way that he cannot be multiplied or divided into several [beings] similar [to himself]".[48] Indeed, God's individual unity is the model for all others, since his indivisibility is essential.[49] If God could be divided into beings specifically the same as himself he would not be one but several gods, at least in potency, a doctrine abhorrent both to faith and reason, in Suárez's view. Similarly, Suárez holds that angels are indivisible in this sense because they are not communicable to many "supposits", that is, they are not universals that can be instantiated.[50] And he criticizes those authors (some interpreters of Aristotle and Thomas Aquinas) who hold views that imply the nonindividuality of purely spiritual beings.[51] Indeed, for Suárez the notions of "individual" and "universal" are exhaustive and mutually exclusive.[52] Everything is either one or the other but not both, and individuality belongs to all that exists "immediately". Suárez's understanding of the extension of 'individual', then, is maximal as far as existing things are concerned; he rejects all restrictions upon it.

There is, indeed, only one kind of *actual* unity in the universe, individual unity. And since unity is convertible, that is, coextensive, with being, everything that is an actual being must necessarily have individual unity. As Suárez puts it, "to be an entity [i.e., one being] and to be divisible into many entities [i.e., capable of becoming many beings of the same specific kind as the original being] implies a contradiction".[53] All actual beings, then, possess individual unity, but universals and forms do not.[54] The latter two have unity, but their unity is conceptual. Scotus's view that in an individual there are, as it were, two unities, the unity of the individual and the unity of the nature, is completely rejected by Suárez. For him the unity of the nature in the individual is the same in reality as the unity of the individual; their distinction is the result of mental consideration alone.[55] And the unity of the nature apart from the individual unity is only conceptual.[56]

In Suárez's universe, then, all beings have individual unity. This doctrine contrasts with that of Thomas Aquinas, since it seems that for the latter the unity proper to each level of being is different and concordant with it. God, whose essence is to exist, and who is therefore unique, has no individual unity, so to speak. His unity could only be one proportional to his being; it might be called, using a term coined by some twentieth century Thomists, 'existential'. Angels, who are composed only of form and their act of existence (*esse*)—each of them being a complete essence or species in itself—do not have the same kind of unity as material beings. Their unity is proportional to their essence, and thus, according to some of Thomas's critics, it can be called "essential". Finally, material beings, composed of form, matter, and their act of existence (*esse*), have, properly speaking, numerical unity, a result of their quantified matter (*materia signata*), and this makes possible the existence of many separate individuals within a species.[57]

It would be inaccurate, however, to say that Thomas and the other scholastics who seem to have restricted the extension of 'individual' in some sense would consequently hold that the substances which did not have individuality were divisible into units of their same specific kind, that is, they were universal. For it would be inconceivable that any scholastic should entertain the possibility of a divisible God or even of a divisible angel. What Thomas Aquinas seems to have rejected, along with many others, is that God and angels are numerically different, understanding by this that they are numerically discrete beings within a species. For they may have understood individuality primarily as a distinctive characteristic of material beings. And Suárez would agree to this extent: If individuality is primarily difference understood as distinction from other beings and multiplicity within the species, then it is clear that God is not individual and it is quite probable that angels are not individual either. But he would disagree with their conception of individuality; he would argue that their view is limited by their failure to distinguish between indivisibility on the one hand and distinction and multiplicity within the species on the other.

II. The Ontological Status of Individuality

The issue concerned with the ontological status of individuality is raised in Section 2 of Disputation V with a familiar issue: "Whether in all natures the individual and singular thing as such adds something to the common or specific nature."[58] The way in which Suárez responds to this issue indicates that in his mind the issue has three aspects. The first has to do with whether there is an addition whereby the individual adds something to the common nature. Or we might put it differently: Whether an individual is something more than the common nature as, for example, 12 is 5 more than 7. Thus, for Socrates, we ask whether Socrates adds something to, or is something more than, "human being", considering that "human being" is both his nature and the nature he has in common with other human beings. The second aspect of the question concerns the ontological character of what is added: Is it something real or something merely conceptual? In our example, is what Socrates adds to "human being" something in reality or merely a concept? Or, put differently, is Socrates something more in reality than "human being" or is he only conceptually something more than "human being"? And third, is what the individual adds to the common nature distinguished from the common nature really or only conceptually? That is, is an individual (such as Socrates) something more than the common nature (in this case "human being") in reality or only conceptually?

Before we proceed, let me clarify further the issue at stake in three ways. First, it is important to keep in mind that the term 'common nature' as used in this context should not be understood to refer to the concept that we may have in our minds when we think of a thing. It is true that the term was sometimes used to mean just that. For example, the common nature "human being" would refer to the concept that, say, Aristotle has when he thinks about a human being such as Socrates. But, if the common nature is understood in this way, as a concept in someone's mind, then the question at hand would pose no great difficulty, and I surmise that almost everyone in the later Middle Ages would agree to its answer. Apart from the substantial or accidental individual, such as Socrates or the color of his hair, there would also be an individual quality in, say, Aristotle's mind—his concept of human being. And almost everyone would agree that the substance "Socrates" and the accidental quality "color of Socrates's hair" are really distinct from a quality of Aristotle's mind, and that Socrates and the color of his hair are in reality something more than the quality in Aristotle's mind. Hence, there is no issue, or at least not one that would raise strong disagreement, when this matter is formulated in terms of an individual on the one hand and the common nature understood as a concept in someone's mind on the other.

Naturally, this is not what concerns Suárez. He is interested in the common nature as it is found in individual things—the humanity of Socrates and Plato, for example—and not in the concept of human being that Aristotle has in his mind when he thinks of them. It is the status of what the individual adds to, or is over and above, this nature that is involved. True, Suárez understands the common nature as "what is conceived abstractly and universally by us",[59] but this should not be taken to mean that it is the concept that, say, Aristotle or Plato have of a nature such as "human being". What Suárez has in mind is rather the intension of a term, to which he refers elsewhere as an "objective concept".[60] Naturally, this understanding of a common nature is different from the understanding that Thomas and Scotus have, for example, and it makes a difference with regard to their answers to the question Suárez poses in this section of Disputation V. But Suárez's interpretation of the term should not obscure the fact that the common nature is not to be understood as a quality of someone's mind.

The second point to bear in mind is that the terms 'individual' and 'singular' as used in Suárez's formulation of the issue refer not only to primary substances, such as Socrates or this chair, but also to their features, such as Socrates's color of beard and this chair's weight. As we have already seen, individuality for Suárez extends to every kind of reality including the features of primary substances. The discussion centers around primary substances for reasons of convenience more than anything else: It is easier to deal with substances alone in this context, rather than to discuss both substances and accidents. But this should not obscure the fact that at least some conclusions at which Suárez arrives concerning substances are also applicable to features and other components of substances.

Third, what is at stake here, according to Suárez, is the ontological status of what serves as the basis for the distinction between an individual and the common nature. According to him, everyone accepted the view that the notion of individual involves the negation of division of an entity into entities naturally similar to itself and, therefore, to be an individual and to be a common nature are two different things. The issue in question, as Suárez puts it, "concerns rather the foundation of that negation" and its status.[61]

Having clarified the issue at stake, we can now turn to its solutions. Suárez considers three different solutions to it in addition to his own. The first, which he attributes to Duns Scotus and Fonseca among others, holds that "the individual adds to the common nature a real mode, distinct *ex natura rei* from the nature, and, together with it, it makes up the individual".[62] We can now present this view in terms of the three aspects of the issue identified earlier: (1) There is an addition, that is, the individual adds something to the common nature; (2) what the individual adds is something real, which Suárez calls "a mode"; and (3) this mode is distinct *ex natura rei* from the common nature. This is the Suarecian way of presenting the Scotistic view that individual things have a formality, the "thisness" (*haecceitas*), which is formally distinct from the common nature and responsible for individuating it.[63] It is "formally" rather than "really" distinct from the common nature because neither the nature nor the thisness are realities "as thing and thing". The unity and the being of the common nature are not the kind of unity and being proper to individual things (i.e., substances or their accidents); the unity of the common nature is "less than numerical unity" and its being is proper to itself.[64] Thus, according to Scotus, the nature and the thisness cannot be distinguished as two things are, nor as two concepts. Their distinction follows from their ontological character as formalities with a being and unity of their own, and thus it is less than real but more than conceptual; it is formal.

The second position, attributed to Ockham, Henry of Ghent, and Gabriel Biel, holds that "the individual adds absolutely nothing positive and real to the common nature, whether really or conceptually distinct from it, since every thing or nature is by itself, primarily and immediately individual".[65] According to this position, (1) there is no addition of any kind that the individual makes to the common nature; (2) nothing real or conceptual is added by the individual; and (3) since nothing is added by the individual to the common nature, there is nothing conceptually or really distinct from it. For Ockham the individual is real but the nature is not. Unlike Scotus, Ockham does not accord to the nature a unity and being proper to itself. The only unity and being in reality are individual unity and being, and these are proper only to individuals, not to natures.[66] Moreover, what causes the individuality of the individual is not a formality added to it, as it is for Scotus. Indeed, nothing causes the individuality of the individual, for the individual is such by virtue of itself.[67] Suárez interprets this to mean that there is nothing real added and, more radically, that there is no conceptual distinction between an individual and its nature. The reason is that the individual is essentially individual, which means its very nature is to be individual and, therefore, there can be no distinctions of any kind between the two.

The third position is supported with texts of Aristotle and Thomas. It maintains that an immaterial thing is individual in itself and "adds nothing to the common nature, while it is not so with a material thing",[68] for in material things the individual adds designated matter, that is, matter under the accident of quantity.[69] Thus, this position is similar to the second one in regard to immaterial things, while it resembles the first with respect to material beings. As presented by Suárez, it can be described as maintaining that in material beings, (1) the individual adds something to the common nature; (2) what it adds is real; and (3) what it adds is really distinct from the common nature. Indeed, what an individual is over and above the common nature and what grounds its individuality is quantified matter, and both matter and quantity are categorical realities really distinct from the common nature with which they unite to constitute an individual thing. By contrast, immaterial individuals are identical to their essences, since they have no matter that can introduce distinctions among members of the same species. Therefore, it is not possible to maintain that an immaterial individual add any thing real or even conceptual to the common nature.

This third position, then, shares in the two previously described views. On the one hand, like Scotus, it holds that what the individual adds to the common nature is something real, that is, the feature that individuates the nature. For Scotus, however, it was *haecceitas,* while for the third position it is designated matter (i.e., matter under the accident of quantity). Consequently, what the individual adds to the common nature is not only real, but also something really distinct from the nature, since quantified matter is a reality distinct from the reality that is the nature. The nature "man" and the individual "Socrates", therefore, differ as the undetermined and the determined, that is, as (1) a nature undetermined by individual characteristics (designated matter), and (2) the nature considered together with those very characteristics.[70] For Thomas this should not be taken to mean that the nature is found separate from individuals, or that it is not part of the individual, or even that it has a unity and being other than the unity and being proper to the individual. However, it does mean, according to Suárez, that the distinction between nature and individuality (what the individual is over and above the common nature) is a real one, based on the way things are and not on the way the mind considers them. For in an individual the quantified matter that distinguishes it from other individuals is real and is as really distinct from the nature as matter is from form or as accidents are from substance.

On the other hand, like Ockham, this position maintains that at least in some things the individual is identical to the common nature. Thus an angel is nothing but its nature. Note, however, that there are two things Suárez does not take into account which greatly distinguish Thomas's view with respect to immaterial substances from Ockham's general position. The first is that, for Ockham, the individual is identified with the common nature, based on his view that everything is essentially individual; while for Thomas one can say that immaterial substances are the same as their essences, not because they are essentially individual, but because they lack matter. Second, it is not strictly true that for Thomas immaterial substances are equivalent to their essences, since they are composites of essence and existence.[71] And Ockham, of course, does not subscribe to that view.

Suárez's own position differs in important respects from the three views he criticizes. He sets it out in four parts:

> I say, first, that the individual adds something real to the common nature, by reason of which it is such individual and there comes to it the negation of divisibility into many [individuals] similar [to itself].[72]

The individual adds something real to the common nature by reason of which the individual is indivisible. This reality added by the individual to the common nature is, as the title of Disputation V reveals, a kind of unity, that Suárez calls "individual unity" in Section 1. Naturally, since unity and being are convertible, and to be real is to be, the unity the individual adds to the common nature must be considered something real.

> I say, second, that the individual as such does not add anything distinct *ex natura rei* from the specific nature.[73]

But what is added by the individual to the common nature, namely, the individual unity, is not distinct *ex natura rei* from the nature. Indeed, if that were the case, there would be a composition in the individual of at least thing and mode or even thing and thing. However, this cannot be the case, for the common nature, say "human being", is not a thing; that is, according to Suárez it is not something real apart from the individual. What is real (and here we see the Ockhamist influence) is the individual human being, not the nature "human being". The nature is an abstraction. Therefore, it is not possible for the nature to be either really or modally distinguished from the individuality of the individual, that is, from individual unity, even though the individual with its individual unity be real. For, to be so distinguished, the common nature and the individual unity would have to fall into a relation of thing to thing or thing to mode.

But if the distinction between the common nature and what the individual adds to it is not real, then it must be conceptual. And, indeed, this is what Suárez concludes:

> I say, third, that the individual adds to the common nature something conceptually distinct from it, belonging to the same category and metaphysically composing the individual as an individual difference which contracts the species and constitutes the individual.[74]

Still, what is added is not a concept, for individuality, or as he puts it, individual unity, is not something conceptual. On the contrary, it is real, the most real constituent of anything, since, as he notes in Section 1, individuality extends to all and only real things. Certainly there is no reason why a conceptual distinction should hold only between mental entities or concepts. In fact, Suárez holds that conceptual distinctions do not hold between mental entities. They are grounded in reality, although only in one thing that is considered by the mind in two ways. Suárez puts it as follows:

> This sort of distinction does not formally and actually hold between the things designated as distinct, as they exist in themselves, but only as they exist in our concepts, from which they receive their nature.[75]

This is the distinction that holds between two attributes in God, for example, or between the terms of the relation of identity when one says that Socrates is the same as himself. For God's attributes are not really distinct from each other since his nature is simple, nor is Socrates something distinct from himself, although to identify him with himself it is necessary for the mind, as it were, to duplicate him.

It should be emphasized, then, that the distinction is not between conceptual entities. Suárez is explicit in pointing out that the terms of the conceptual distinction are different aspects of the same thing, and that these different aspects arise either through mental repetition and comparison or through some inadequacy in conception. In either case they are grounded in a real thing and as such are not misleading as long as the distinction is understood to be conceptual and not real.

From all this it can be seen that a conceptual distinction between the common nature and what the individual adds to the common nature does not require that individual unity be a mental being or concept. Moreover, for individual unity to be real does not require that the distinction between it and the common nature also be real, for real things can be the basis of conceptual distinctions. The individual and what it adds to the nature are conceptually distinguished from the nature, but in reality the nature and the individual are one and the same, just as Socrates is still himself when we distinguish him from himself.

Using an example, we may illustrate Suárez's view in the following way. We have, on the one hand, an individual thing, say Socrates, and, on the other, the intension of 'human being', which is what Suárez understands Socrates's nature to be. (He calls it an abstraction.) Now, according to Suárez, Socrates adds something real to the intension of 'human being', since Socrates is something real over and above the intension of 'human being', which is not itself something real. But what Socrates adds to it, that is, what he is over and above "human being", is not something really distinct from "human being", since there are not two real things to be distinguished, but only one real thing, Socrates, and his nature, which is an abstraction.

Finally, this doctrine applies both to material and immaterial beings and, therefore, is to be distinguished from the position that Suárez attributes to Thomas:

> I say, fourth, that the individual adds something conceptually distinct to the species not only in material things and accidents, but also in created and finite immaterial substances.[76]

Suárez's view, then, is that the individual is really something more than the common nature; it adds something real to it. But the individual and what it adds are not really, but only conceptually, distinct from the common nature. Moreover, this applies to all created things equally, whether material or immaterial, substances or their accidents. This latter point separates Suárez's position from the view he attributes to Thomas. His rejection of an *ex natura rei* distinction between the individual's individuality and the common nature distinguishes his view from that of Scotus. Finally, his acceptance of a conceptual distinction between the individuality of the individual and its common nature separates him from the view he attributes to Ockham.

III. The Individuation of Substances

As mentioned earlier, the bulk of Disputation V is devoted to the discussion of the principle of individuation in both substances and accidents. Four of these sections, Sections 3–6, deal with the individuation of substances and one, Section 7, with the individuation of accidents. In addition to his own view, Suárez discusses three other views of the individuation of substances: a material view, a formal view, and an existential view. But he does not discuss the views of Scotus or Ockham in this context. He discusses the views of those two authors under a different heading, the issue concerned with what I have called the "ontological status of individuality". In the case of Ockham the reason is obvious: Anyone who holds that individuals are such *per se* and immediately does not have to identify a principle of individuation. And in the case of Scotus the reason is that, for Suárez, Scotus's so-called thisness is not a principle of individuation properly speaking but rather the very individuality of the individual. As such the Scotistic view does not really offer a theory of individuation.[77]

A. Individuation by Designated Matter

The first view of individuation discussed at length identifies designated matter as the principle of individuation. This was not only a popular view at the time among Thomists, it also was the source of much debate and misunderstanding. Suárez discusses three different interpretations of it. The first (I) is the position of what might be called "orthodox Thomists." [78]

> The first interpretation is that matter designated by quantity is nothing other than matter with quantity or matter affected by quantity. For they hold that the principle of individuation is, as it were, composed of these two, so that matter may give incommunicability and quantity distinction. [79]

But there are two versions of this position. According to the first, "quantity is not in prime matter but in the whole composite and is destroyed when the substance is corrupted and is newly acquired for the generation of substance". [80] According to the second, "quantity is in prime matter and remains the same in what is generated and corrupted". [81]

Suárez finds many faults with both versions of this view, but we cannot dwell on them here. Let it suffice to say that most of Suárez's objections spring from the fact that quantity is an accident and as such must be posterior to substance. It is inconsistent, then, to think that quantity is the cause of an intrinsic feature of substance, namely, individuality. [82] This objection also militates against all other views of accidental individuation—bundle views, relational views (space-time, place, position), and so on, for which reason Suárez dismisses them in passing. [83]

A second interpretation (II) purports to understand designated matter as "not intrinsically including quantity itself, but rather as the term of the relation of matter to it". [84] This interpretation comes out of the discussion of indeterminate quantity found in Thomas's *Commentary on Boethius' De trinitate*. There Thomas states:

> Dimensions can be understood in two ways. In one way inasmuch as they are determinate, and by this I mean that they have a definite measurement and shape. In this sense, as complete beings, they are located in the genus of quantity. Now, when dimensions are understood in this way they cannot be the principle of individuation. . . . In another way dimensions can be taken as indeterminate, simply as having the nature of dimensions, though they can never *exist* without some determination. . . . In this way dimensions are located in the genus of quantity as something incomplete. It is through these indeterminate dimensions that matter is made to be this designated matter, thus rendering the form individual. [85]

Thomists, concerned about the problems created by the accidental nature of quantity, find support in this and other similar passages for the view (II-A) that the sort of quantity which is to be considered part of the principle of individuation is not accidental quantity, such as "three feet wide". Rather, they identify the quantity which is to be considered part of the principle of individuation with the potency contained in matter for accidental quantity— the capacity of matter to be three feet wide. In a sense, this view seems more concordant with Aristotle's casual statements about the issue, since it tends to put the principle of individuation back into prime matter.[86] But it is difficult to see how such an interpretation can be reconciled with many other texts from Thomas in which he explicitly identifies the principle of individuation of this man, for example, with his flesh and bones.[87] Indeed, many followers of Thomas do not wish to have anything to do with this view, as Suárez himself points out, and they preferred a different way of speaking (II-B), although Suárez does not see it as very different:

> Matter is the principle of individuation not insofar as it is in potency to this quantity, but insofar as it virtually pre-contains this quantity or is the root and foundation of this quantity.[88]

Apart from (II-B) there is a third version (II-C) of this interpretation, which holds that:

> Designated matter is nothing other than matter immediately disposed to this form, because it is not disposed except by quantity affected by particular qualities.[89]

But even this last version may be interpreted in two different ways, depending on whether (1) the view presupposes "that quantity and other dispositions inhere and remain in matter and absolutely precede in the order of nature the introduction of form";[90] or (2) the view "presupposes that quantity and other dispositions are not in matter, but in the composite, and that, as they produce the last disposition, they follow form."[91]

Suárez's rejection of the three versions (A–C) of this interpretation (II) of Thomas's position is based primarily on the unintelligibility and uselessness of the distinction on which this view rests between the potency for quantity in matter and the actuality of quantity present in matter. The inadequacy of the distinction is a result of the fact that the potency and act of a kind (in this case, quantity) fall within the same category in the Aristotelian framework. As such, the distinction does not add anything to the first interpretation, as Suárez sees it.[92]

Finally, the interpretation of a third group of Thomists (III) is explained in four parts. First, "they hold that matter designated by quantity is not the principle constituting the individual in reality, and from which the individual difference contractive of the species and constitutive of the individual is truly taken".[93] Second, they maintain "that matter is the principle and root of the multiplication of individuals in material substances".[94] Third, they hold "that matter, designated by quantity, is the principle and root, or at least the occasion, of the production of this individual as distinct from the rest".[95] And, fourth, they state "that matter, designated by sensible quantity, is called the principle of individuation in relation to us, because by it we know the distinction of material individuals among themselves".[96]

The problem that Suárez sees with this position is that, even if designated matter were a good principle of individual distinction and discernibility from our point of view, such an answer would leave unresolved the original (ontological) problem concerning the principle of individuation. Moreover, this view would not account for the individuality of spiritual beings.[97]

B. Individuation by Form

The second view of individuation, discussed by Suárez in Section 4 and suggested by some texts of Averroes and Durand of St. Pourçain, is that the principle of individuation is the substantial form.[98] In a man, for example, it is his humanity that is responsible for his individuality. The support for this view is derived from the general Aristotelian doctrine that regarded form as the vehicle for all actuality and existence in the individual. It is only fitting, some concluded, that form should also be the principle of an individual's most basic unity, its individuality.

Suárez, however, finds it difficult to explain, among other things, how substantial form, so different a principle from matter and accidental forms, could individuate these other components of the individual.[99] This leads him to reject this view insofar as it holds form alone to be the full and adequate principle of the individuation of things. According to him, form is only the principal one.[100] Matter, as we shall see, also plays an important causal role in individuation.

C. Individuation by Existence

In Section 5 of Disputation V, Suárez discusses the last of the views he rejects. Here again, as with the formal view of individuation, he finds himself in partial agreement with it, provided the terms in which it is expressed are understood correctly. The view in question holds that the principle of individuation is existence, and Suárez finds support for it in texts of Scotus, Soncinas, and Henry of Ghent, although he does not attribute it to anyone in particular.[101]

This alternative becomes viable after the introduction of the Thomistic doctrine of the real distinction between essence and existence. In a phoenix, for example, what the phoenix is and the act whereby it exists are really distinct, for there is nothing in the definition of a phoenix that implies its existence. The latter answers the question 'Is it?' (*an est*) rather than the question 'What is it?' (*quid est*).[102] Although not all implications of this view are easy to see, and some ideas commonly thought to follow from it are clearly contrary to the import and intention of Thomas's original doctrine, at least one of which could be thought to follow easily. Could it not be argued that the real distinction of existence from essence introduces another element in the constitution of an individual, and since existence is "incommunicable", existence is the principle of individuation?

Suárez discusses three versions of this view, depending on three different interpretations of existence. One version, following the Thomistic view, asserts that "existence is distinct *ex natura rei* from the essence of the individual".[103] But Suárez finds this difficult to reconcile with the notion of an individual possible being.[104] Conceptually, according to him, there is no difference between an existing Paul and a nonexisting, possible Paul. How can one hold, then, that existence individuates? A possible Paul does not exist, but is every bit an individual as the actually existing Paul.

The second version interprets existence as subsistence, which in turn can refer to the supposit, the nature, or the individual insofar as they belong to a particular species.[105] But in none of these interpretations does Suárez find comfort for this view. Since his arguments are too long to be analyzed here, we shall have to omit consideration of them, turning instead to the third interpretation of existence he discusses: existence considered as entity. But, if existence is interpreted as entity, Suárez tells us, there is little difference between this position and his own, except for the unfortunate misuse of terminology.[106] To his view we now turn.

D. Individuation by Entity

The first two of the three theories discussed by Suárez address the question of individuation in the context of material substances. This is indicated by the titles of the sections in which they are discussed: "Whether designated matter is the principle of individuation in material substances" and "Whether the substantial form is the principle of individuation of material substances". Spiritual substances are excluded. The reason for this exclusion is the identification of individual unity with the numerical distinction of the individual from other individuals within the species characteristic of material entities. This identification, mentioned earlier, is made by many of Suárez's predecessors.

The third view, when interpreted correctly, according to Suárez, coincides with Suárez's own. It identifies existence as the principle of individuation and assumes that individuality extends to all beings, not only to material substances. This is no doubt a consequence of Suárez's careful distinction between the notion of individuality as indivisibility, on the one hand, and the notion of individuality as numerical distinction and plurality within the species, on the other. In Sections 5 and 6 of Disputation V, then, Suárez is able to discuss all created substances. He excludes God, the only uncreated substance, because, as he points out elsewhere, "the divine substance . . . is individual by itself and essentially; whence, there is no more reason to look for a principle of individuation in it than for a principle of its essence or existence."[107] In short, God is individual in the sense Ockham said all things were: *per se*. To ask what makes him individual is superfluous. The case of other spiritual substances is different, however. For, although they are not numerically multiplied within the species in the way material beings are, they do have an essence and common nature to which individuality is added: An individual angel is really more than its angelic nature, even if there can be only one angel of each.

But God, angels, and material composites are not the only substantial entities in Suárez's world. His world also contains matter, substantial forms, and substantial modes. In all of them the principle of individuation is the same: the entity. "It seems that every singular substance is singular in itself, that is, by its entity, and needs no other principle of individuation in addition to its entity, or in addition to the intrinsic principles that constitute its entity."[108] If the things in question are simple, as is the case with form, matter, or a mode, then their simple entities are the principle of individuation.[109] And if they are composites, as material substances are, then the principle of individuation is the individual matter and the individual form of which they are composed, united to each other. Of these components, as we said earlier, the form is primary, but not sufficient by itself.[110] Individuality in material beings requires both matter and form. The causes of the individuation of individuals are the intrinsic principles that constitute them. In simple beings, it is the beings themselves as they exist; in spiritual beings, it is the form as it exists; and in composite beings, it is the principles that compose them.[111]

This is what Suárez means by saying that the principle of individuation of a thing is a thing's entity. For a thing's entity is nothing but "the essence as it exists".[112] In simple beings it is simple, but in composite ones it is the composite as it exists. And since what exists is individual, we must conclude that it is the individual that is the principle of its own individuation. Indeed, Suárez points out clearly that it is not "form" and "matter" that individuate this composite of which they are parts, but "this form" and "this matter".[113] And what makes this form and this matter individual? Their entities, that is, the form and matter themselves as they exist in reality.

But then, one may ask, is Suárez's view of the principle of individuation any different from Ockham's? After all, Ockham says that individuals are individual by themselves. The differences between the two views are not easily discernible, but nonetheless they are there. In the first place, Ockham speaks of the individuality of individual composite substances apart from the individuality of their components. But Suárez analyzes the individuality of composite substances in terms of the individuality of their components. Second, Ockham considers the individual to be individual *per se,* and this not only means individual by itself, but also *essentially.* There are no essences aside from individual essences. Consequently, there is in fact no individuation. To speak of individuation presupposes that there is such a thing as a nonindividual that may become individual through something else, and this, for Ockham, is absurd. But Suárez does not have individuality attach to individuals essentially.[114] Individuality is *per se* in simple entities, *per aliud* (i.e., their components) in composite ones, but in neither case is it something essential. What is essential to an individual is what is common to it and all other members of its species and genus. Consequently, Suárez can speak of individuation since he still holds on to the notion of essence as what is common, even if this, considered as such, is only an abstraction, as we saw previously.

In spite of these differences, however, it is clear that Suárez's view of individuation is closer to that of Ockham than to the views of Thomas Aquinas and Duns Scotus.

IV. The Individuation of Accidents

The inquiry into the principle of individuation of accidents is briefly undertaken and settled by Suárez in Section 7 of Disputation V. Contrary to a widespread view (supported among others by Thomas Aquinas[115]) that accidents are individuated by their subject, Suárez, following the general principle stated in Section 6, holds that they are individuated by their own entities.[116] Socrates's black color of hair, for example, is the individual black color of hair that it is because of its own entity, not because it is Socrates's color of hair.

Suárez's rejection of the individuation of accidents by the subject is based on the nature of the subject-accident relation. As he puts it, "The subject cannot be said to be the intrinsic principle of the individuation of accidents, as intrinsically and essentially composing the accident . . . since the accident is certainly not intrinsically composed of the subject."[117] The relation between subject and accident is, within the context of Aristotelian metaphysics, an extrinsic one, that is, extrinsic to the subject (which may or may not have the accident in question) and extrinsic to the accident (which may or may not be attached to a particular subject). It would not do, then, to explain the individuality of an accident, which is something intrinsic to it and tied to its very nature and entity, by reference to something extrinsic. Peter's black color of hair is not this black color because it belongs to Peter; it is this black color of hair because it is "a this" by itself. That it belongs to Peter is an accidental matter, since it could have belonged to someone else.

V. The Presence of Accidents Differing Only Numerically in the Same Subject

In the last two sections of Disputation V, Sections 8 and 9, Suárez takes up a problem of widespread concern among scholastics, a problem related to the individuation of accidents. This issue concerns the manner, if any, in which accidents differing only in their individuality, and therefore belonging to the same species, can be present in the same subject. For example, how can two numerically different whites be present in Paul? The two logical possibilities of dealing with this question are explored in Sections 8 and 9 respectively. In the first, the case is put in terms of simultaneity; in the second, of succession.

With respect to the first, Suárez considers five different opinions that oppose in some measure the view that accidents differing only numerically can be present simultaneously in the same subject.[118] The views most opposed to the simultaneous presence of numerically different accidents derive their opposition from their doctrine concerning the principle of individuation. If, for example, accidental individuation is caused by the subject, then it would certainly be impossible for two accidents differing only in their individuality to be present at the same time in the same subject. In such a case, their difference would spring from the subject, and this being the same, the two accidents would have to be the same. If the black color of Paul's hair is the individual black color it is because it belongs to Paul, it could not happen that Paul would have two black colors of hair that were exactly alike in kind but still distinct.

Since Suárez points to a different principle of accidental individuation, however, identifying it with the accident's entity, it becomes possible, irrespective of other considerations, for two numerically different accidents to be present in the same subject at the same time even though they are not different in any other way. If that were an impossibility, Suárez points out, it would have to be derived from some factor other than individuation.[119] Accordingly, and with a great deal of caution, he proposes (1) that the proposition, "No plurality of accidents of the same species can be present in the same subject [at the same time]", is not to be accepted without exception, and (2) that the occurrence of a plurality of accidents of the same species in the same subject at the same time does not occur naturally.[120]

The answer to the second problem, posed in Section 9, whether accidents differing in number can be successively present in the same subject, follows easily from this one. For, if it is possible that they do so even simultaneously, it would be even more possible for them to do so successively. Indeed, Suárez holds not only that it is possible, but also that it does happen in the natural order.[121]

VI. Conclusions

In conclusion, Disputation V provides us with a masterful, systematic, and comprehensive discussion of the metaphysics of individuality. At the center of Suárez's view is the doctrine that the principle of individuation is the entity of a thing. Other important elements of the theory are the conception of individuality as incommunicability, the commitment to the universal extension of the category of individual, and the view that individuality adds something real to the common nature, although it is only conceptually distinct from it. In all this the purely metaphysical character of Suárez's view is clear, and part of what distinguishes his approach from more contemporary positions is precisely this metaphysical character and his relative disregard for the kind of epistemic and semantic issues that have concerned contemporary philosophers. By contrast, part of what separates Suárez's approach from his contemporaries and predecessors is its complete reliance on philosophical rather than theological argumentation for the establishment and evaluation of philosophical views. Thus, while Suárez's thought and commitments are rooted in the scholastic past, his approach already anticipates the future.

Notes

1. For general information on Suárez and his works, see J. H. Fichter, *Man of Spain: Francis Suárez* (New York: Macmillan, 1940); J. de Scorraille, *François Suárez de la Compagnie de Jésus,* 2 vols. (Paris: Lethiellieux, 1912–13); C. Sommervogel, *Bibliothèque de la Compagnie de Jésus,* 9 vols. (Paris: A. Picard, 1890–1900); C. Riedl, *Jesuit Thinkers of the Renaissance* (Milwaukee: Marquette University Press, 1939); Francis Suárez, *On Formal and Universal Unity,* trans. J. F. Ross (Milwaukee: Marquette University Press, 1964); Cyril Vollert, *Francis Suárez. On the Various Kinds of Distinctions* (Milwaukee: Marquette University Press, 1947, rep. 1976); and Francis Suárez, *On the Essence of Finite Being as Such: On the Existence of That Essence and Their Distinction* (Milwaukee: Marquette University Press, 1983). For specific discussions of individuation, see A. F. de Vos, "L'aristotélisme de Suárez et sa théorie de l'individuation", *Actas. Congreso Internacional de Filosofia, Barcelona, 1948,* vol. 3 (Madrid: Instituto Luis Vives de Filosofia, 1949), pp. 505–514; Jorge J. E. Gracia, "Suárez's Criticism of the Thomistic Principle of Individuation", *Atti. Congresso Internazionale di Filosofia nel suo VII Centenario, 1974*

(Rome, 1978); Jorge J. E. Gracia, "What the Individual Adds to the Common Nature According to Suárez", *New Scholasticism* 53 (1979): 221–233; Jorge J. E. Gracia, *Suárez on Individuation* (Milwaukee: Marquette University Press, 1982); Walter Hoeres, "Wesenheit und Individuum bei Suárez", *Scholastik* 37 (1962), 181–210; Juan Rosanas, "El principio de individuación, según Suárez", *Ciencia y Fe* 6 (1950): 69–86; Reiner Specht, *Francisco Suárez. Über die Individualität und das Individuationsprinzip*, 2 vols. (Hamburg: Meiner, 1976); and Engelbert Ssekasozi, "A Comparative and Critical Analysis of the Metaphysical Theories of William of Ockham and Francis Suárez as Regards the Principle of Individuation" (doctoral dissertation, University of Kansas, 1976).

2. Vollert has already noted the importance for the history of philosophy of Suárez's discussion of authors who preceded him. See *Francis Suárez,* p. 8.

3. The *Disputationes* underwent twenty editions within a few years of its publication, and there have been other editions since then. For our purposes we shall use the text found in volumes 25 and 26 of Suárez's *Opera omnia* (Paris: Vivès, 1856–1866).

4. In the early Middle Ages individuality was frequently discussed in the context of the problem of universals (see, for example, Peter Abailard's *Logica ingredientibus*), and Duns Scotus discussed individuality in the context of angelology (see *Ordinatio* III, 1).

5. My *Suárez on Individuation* contains a full translation of the text.

6. Disp. V, s. 3, 28: "principium per se et in se individuationis . . . id quod in ordine ad nos est principium distinguendi unum individuum ab alio . . . occasio talis distinctionis."

7. *Ibid.,* s. 7, 4: "in ordine ad esse et ad propriam rei constitutionem . . . quae maxime a priori est, et maxime propria huius scientiae."

8. *Ibid.,* s. 3, 34: "valde diminute, et cum magna acquivocatione . . . solum . . . vel signa a posteriori, vel occasiones distinguendi . . . individua."

9. In "Ratius et discursus totius operis ad lectorem".

10. *Ibid.*

11. *Ibid.:* "In hoc opere philosophum ago. . ."

12. Discussions of the convertibility of unity and being are frequent after the middle of the thirteenth century, although the doctrine of convertibility goes back to the Greeks. For a well-known example, see Thomas Aquinas, *Summa theologiae* I, 11, 1.

13. Porphyry, *Isagoge,* in Boethius, *In Isagogen Porphyrii Commentorum, editio secunda,* ch. 15, ed. S. Brandt, in *CSEL,* vol. 48 (Vienna: Tempsky, 1906; rep. New York: Johnson, 1966), p. 275.

14. See, for example, D. H. Pouillon, "Le premier traité des propriétés transcendentales. La 'Summa de bono' du Chancellier Philippe", *Revue Néoscolastique de Philosophie* 42 (1939): 40 ff.; G. Schulemann, *Die Lehre von den Transcendentalien in der scholastischen Philosophie* (Leipzig: F. Meiner, 1929); Jorge J. E. Gracia, "The Convertibility of *unum* and *ens* according to Guido Terrena", *Franciscan Studies* 33 (1973), 143–170; and the various articles in an issue of *Topoi* devoted to the transcendentals edited by me in 1992, v. 11. For Suárez, see my "Suárez and the Doctrine of the Transcendentals", *Topoi* 11, no. 2 (1992): 121–134.

15. Disp. IV, s. 1, 1: "unum addere supra ens accidens quoddam positivum, ex natura rei distinctum ab ente, per se tamen consequens et concomitans omne ens."

16. *Ibid.*, s. 1, 2: "unum addere supra ens proprietatem quamdam positivam non realiter, vel ex natura rei, sed sola ratione ab ente distinctam."

17. *Ibid.*, s. 1, 6: "unum nihil positivum addere supra ens, nec rationis, nec reale, neque ex natura rei, neque sola ratione ab ente distinctum."

18. *Ibid.*, s. 1, 7–11.

19. *Ibid.*, s. 1, 6: "unum et ens esse unam ac eamdem naturam, quia nimirum nullam rationem positivam dicit praeter rationem entis."

20. *Ibid.*, s. 1, 12: "unum addere supra ens negationem aliquam per modum privationis."

21. *Ibid.:* "unum aliquo modo distingui ab ente, quia et est passio eius et illa nomina non sunt synonyma, sed diversi conceptus formales et obiectivi illis in mente respondent."

22. *Ibid.*, s. 1, 13: "negationem divisionis in ipsomet ente."

23. *Ibid.*, s. 1, 14: "indivisum in se, et divisum a quolibet alio."

24. *Ibid:* "esse divisum ab alio non requiritur ut ens sit absolute unum, sed solum ut sit unum ex multis."

25. *Ibid.*, s. 1, 16.

26. *Ibid.:* "Et hoc modo esse distinctum ab alio aptitudine et fundamentaliter potest dici convenire omni enti, qua unum est; tamen hoc ipsum non intrat formaliter rationem unius, sed consequitur illam, sicut consequitur ad quantitatem ut sit fundamentum aequalitatis vel inaequalitatis."

27. Disp. LIV, s. 3.

28. Disp. IV, s. 1, 19.

29. *Ibid.*, s. 9, 11.

30. *Ibid.*, s. 9, 12.

31. See Gracia, "The Legacy", in this volume.

32. Disp. IV, s. 9, 14.

33. *Ibid.*, s. 9, 12.

34. *Ibid.*, s. 9, 14.

35. *Ibid.*, s. 1, 2: "Commune enim seu universale dicitur quod secundum unam aliquam rationem multis communicatur seu in multis reperitur; unum autem numero seu singulare ac individuum dicitur quod ita est unum ens, ut secundum eam entis rationem, qua unum dicitur, non sit communicabile multis, ut inferioribus et sibi subiectis, aut quae in illa ratione multa sint."

36. *Ibid.*, s. 1, 3: "Nulla autem alia negatio divisionis seu divisibilitatis excogitari potest, quae compleat rationem entitatis individuae et singularis, nisi ea quae a nobis explicata est, scilicet, quod entitas talis sit, ut tota ratio eius non sit communicabilis multis similibus entitatibus, seu (quod idem est) ut non sit divisibilis in plures entitates tales qualis ipsa est."

37. Boethius, *In librum Aristotelis De interpretatione,* in *PL* 64.462–464.

38. Thomas Aquinas, for example, speaks of the "communicability of names" in *Summa theologiae* I, 13, 9.

39. Boethius, *In Isagogen,* Bk. I, ch. 10, pp. 160–161.

40. See, for example, Cajetan's *Commentary on Thomas' 'On Being and Essence'*, q. 10, trans. L. H. Kendzierski and F. Wade (Milwaukee: Marquette University Press, 1964), p. 199.

41. Disp. IV, s. 1, 7: "ad hoc nihil refert quod spiritualis substantia et natura posit intra eamdem speciem secundum numerum multiplicari, necne."

42. *Ibid.*, s. 3, 12: "licet res prius natura sit in se una quam sit distincta ab aliis, tamen hoc posterius intrinsice sequitur ex primo absque additione ulla positiva quae fiat ipsi rei quae est una, sed solum per negationem, qua, posito alio extremo, verum est dicere hoc non est illud. Itaque illud idem positivum quod fundat unitatem quoad primam negationem seu indivisionem in se, fundat consequenter posteriorem negationem distinctionis ab alio, quo sensu dici solet, et verissimum est, per illud rem distingui ab aliis per quod in se constituitur, quia distinguitur per id quo est . . . ergo similiter in unitate individuali id, quod est principium individui quoad constitutionem eius, et incommunicabilitatem seu indivisibilitatem in se, est etiam principium distinctionis eius ab aliis; et e converso, quod est principium distinctionis, debet etiam esse principium constitutionis."

43. Disp. V, s. 3, 12 and 34.

44. *Ibid.*, s. 1, 7.

45. *Ibid.*, s. 1, 6.

46. "Utrum omnes res quae existunt vel existere possunt singulares sint et individuae."

47. Disp. V, s. 1, 4: "res omnes, quae sunt actualia entia seu quae existunt vel existere possunt immediate, esse singulares ac individuas. Dico 'immediate', ut excludam communes rationes entium, quae ut sic non possunt immediate existere, neque habere actualem entitatem, nisi in entitatibus singularibus et individuis, quibus sublatis impossibile est aliquid reale manere."

48. *Ibid.*, s. 1, 6: "divina natura est ita in se una ut multiplicari non possit aut in plures similes dividi."

49. *Ibid.*, s. 1, 7.

50. *Ibid.*

51. *Ibid.*

52. *Ibid.*, s. 1, 6.

53. *Ibid.*, s. 1, 5: "implicat contradictionem esse entitatem et esse divisibilem in plures entitates."

54. *Ibid.*, s. 1, 4.

55. *Ibid.*, s. 2, 10.

56. This will become clear in the next section.

57. See, for example, *De ente et essentia* 5, where Thomas discusses individuation only in the context of material substances. Immaterial substances, except for the human soul, which is naturally joined to matter but can exist without matter (i.e., without a body), are not multiplied within the species; they are only "limited" by their nature and their being (*esse*). This seems to imply that they are not individual or at least not individual in the same sense in which material beings are. However, Thomas states elsewhere (*Summa theologiae* III, 77, 2, in Marietti, vol. 5, p. 140a) that "separate immaterial substances are individuated by themselves", a statement that implies that they are indeed individual. Suárez himself believed that Thomas accepted the individuality of immaterial substances (Disp. V, s. 2, 6). The question at stake, then, is not whether he accepted it, but (1) how he interpreted it, (2) what importance he attached to it, and (3) how he was able to account for it.

58. "Utrum in omnibus naturis res individua et singularis, ut talis est, addat aliquid supra communem seu specificam naturam."

59. Disp. V, s. 1, 1: "communem naturam seu quae a nobis abstracte et universe concipitur."

60. Disp. II, s. 1, 1: "The thing or nature which is properly and immediately known or represented by a formal concept [the formal concept is the act itself whereby

the intellect conceives a thing] is called an objective concept. For example, when we conceive a man, the act which we produce in the mind to conceive him is called a "formal concept". However, the man known and represented in the act is called an "objective concept"; it is called a 'concept' by extrinsic denomination from the formal concept, through which its object is said to be conceived, and hence it is correctly called 'objective' because it is not a concept as a form intrinsically ending [i.e., determining] the conception, but as the object and matter about which the formal conception is, and to which the whole power of the mind tends . . . the formal concept is always a true and positive thing and, in creatures, a quality inhering in the mind, but the objective concept is not always a true positive thing. . . ."

61. Disp. V, s. 2, 7: "sed est de fundamento illius negationis."

62. Disp. V, s. 2, 2: "individuum addere communi naturae modum aliquem realem ex natura rei distinctum ab ipsa natura et componentem cum illa individuum ipsum."

63. Duns Scotus, *Ordinatio* II, dist. 3, qq. 5–6, reply to the first objection.

64. *Ibid.*, q. 1.

65. Disp. V, s. 2, 5: "individuum nihil omnino addere communi naturae quod positivum et reale sit, aut re aut ratione distinctum ab illa, sed unamquamque rem vel naturam per se esse individuam primo et immediate."

66. Ockham, *On the Sentences* I, Dist. 2, q. 4, answer to the question.

67. *Ibid.*, q. 6, answer to the question.

68. Disp. V, s. 2, 6: "in immaterialibus res singularis nihil addit supra naturam communem; in materialibus vero aliquid."

69. Thomas, *De ente*, ch. 2, and *Expositio super librum Boethii De trinitate*, q. 4, a. 2, ed. B. Decker (Leiden: Brill, 1959), p. 143.

70. Thomas, *De ente*, ch. 2.

71. *Ibid.*, ch. 4.

72. Disp. V, s. 2, 8: "Dico primo: individuum aliquid reale addit praeter naturam communem, ratione cuius tale individuum est et ei convenit illa negatio divisibilitatis in plura similia."

73. *Ibid.*, s. 2, 9: "Dico secundo: individuum, ut sic, non addit aliquid ex natura rei distinctum a natura specifica."

74. *Ibid.*, s. 2, 16: "Dico tertio: individuum addere supra naturam communem aliquid ratione distinctum ab illa, ad idem praedicamentum pertinens, et individuum componens metaphysicae, tamquam differentia individualis contrahens speciem et individuum constituens."

75. Disp. VII, s. 1, 4: "Et est illa distinctio rationis, quae formaliter et actualiter non est in rebus quae sic distinctae denominantur, prout in se existunt, sed solum prout substant conceptibus nostris, et ab eis denominationem aliquam accipiunt."

76. Disp. V, s. 2, 21: "Dico quarto: individuum non solum in rebus materialibus et accidentibus, sed etiam in substantiis immaterialibus creatis et finitis addit aliquid ratione distinctum supra speciem."

77. *Ibid.*, s. 2, 31 and s. 3, 2, and Woosuk Park, "Common Nature and *Haecceitas*", *Franziscanische Studien* (West Germany) 71 (1989): 105–123.

78. Suárez refers to texts of Capreolus, Ferrara, and Soncinas. See Disp. V, s. 2, 9.

79. Disp. V, s. 3, 9: "Prima expositio est materiam signatam quantitate nihil aliud esse quam materiam cum quantitate seu quantitate affectam; ex his enim duobus censet hoc principium individuationis quasi integrari, ut materia det incommunicabilitatem, quantitas distinctionem."

80. Disp. V, s. 3, 10: "quantitatem non esse in materia prima, sed in toto composito, et destrui corrupta substantia, et novam comparari ad generationem substantiae."

81. *Ibid.*, s. 3, 11: "quantitas inest materiae primae et manet eadem in genito et corrupto."

82. *Ibid.*, s. 3, 10–17.

83. *Ibid* and Disp. V, s. 6, 2.

84. *Ibid.*, s. 3, 18: "non includere quantitatem ipsam intrinsice, sed ut est terminum habitudinis materiae ad ipsam."

85. Q. 4, a. 2, answer to the question, p. 143. In Thomas Aquinas, *Faith, Reason and Theology*, trans. A. Maurer (Toronto: PIMS, 1987), pp. 97–98.

86. For a discussion of the problem of individuation in Aristotle, see W. Charlton, "Aristotle and the Principle of Individuation", *Phronesis* 17 (1972): 239–249.

87. *De ente*, ch. 2, and *Summa theologiae* I, 29, 3 and 30, 4.

88. Disp. V, s. 3, 18: "non materiam ut est in potentia ad hanc quantitatem, sed ut virtute praehabens hanc quantitatem, seu ut est radix et fundamentum huius quantitatis, esse principium individuationis."

89. *Ibid.*, s. 3, 19: "materiam signatam nihil aliud esse quam materiam ultimo dispositam ad hanc formam, quia non disponitur nisi quantitate talibus qualitatibus affecta."

90. *Ibid.*, s. 3, 19: "quantitatem et alias dispositiones inhaerere et manere in materia, et simpliciter praecedere ordine naturae introductionem formae."

91. *Ibid.:* "supponendo quantitatem et alias dispositiones non inesse materiae, sed composito, et ut conficiunt ultimam dispositionem consequi formam."

92. *Ibid.*, s. 3, 20–27.

93. *Ibid.*, s. 3, 28: "de principio constituente in re individuum, et a quo vere sumitur differentia individualis contractiva speciei et constitutiva individui, negat haec opinio materiam signatam quantitate esse principium individuationis."

94. *Ibid.*, s. 3, 29: "materiam esse principium et radicem multiplicationis individuorum in substantiis materialibus."

95. *Ibid.*, s. 3, 30: "materiam signatam quantitate, esse principium et radicem vel saltem occasionem productionis huius individui distincti a reliquis."

96. *Ibid.*, s. 3, 33: "materiam quantitate sensibili dici principium individuationis quoad nos, quia per illus nos cognoscimus distinctionem individuorum materialium inter se."

97. *Ibid.*, s. 3, 34.

98. *Ibid.*, s. 4, a. See chapters by Wippel in this volume.

99. *Ibid.*, s. 4, 2–6.

100. *Ibid.*, s. 4, 7.

101. *Ibid.*, s. 5, 1.

102. *De Ente*, ch. 4, pp. 12–13 and 18–19.

103. Disp. V, s. 5, 2: "existentia esse ex natura rei distinctam ab essentia individui."

104. *Ibid.*, s. 5, 3-5.

105. *Ibid.*, s. 5, 6.

106. *Ibid.*, s. 5, 2.

107. *Ibid.*, s. 3, 1: "divinam substantiam . . . illa per se et essentialiter individua est, unde non est quod in ea quaeratur individuationis principium, magis quam essentiae vel existentiae ipsius."

108. *Ibid.*, s. 6, 1: "omnem substantiam singularem [se ipsa, seu per entitatem suam, esse singularem] neque alio indigere individuationis principio praeter suam entitatem, vel praeter principia intrinseca quibus eius entitas constat."

109. *Ibid.*, s. 6, 2–14.

110. *Ibid.*, s. 6, 15.

111. *Ibid.*, s. 6, 18.

112. Disp. VII, s. 1, 12 and 19.

113. Disp. V, s. 6, 2–13.

114. *Ibid.*, s. 6, 1.

115. *Summa theologiae* III, 77, vol. 5, p. 140a.

116. Disp. V, s. 7, 4.

117. *Ibid.*, s. 7, 3: "subiectum non potest dici principium intrinsecum individuationis accidentis, tamquam intrinsece et per se componens accidens . . . quia [accidens] non componi intrinsece ex ipso subiecto."

118. *Ibid.*, s. 8, 2–14.

119. *Ibid.*, s. 8, 20.

120. *Ibid.*, s. 8, 15–16.

121. *Ibid.*, s. 9, 3–4.

22

JOHN OF SAINT THOMAS (B. 1589; D. 1644)

JORGE J. E. GRACIA AND JOHN KRONEN

John of St. Thomas must without a doubt be counted among the most faithful followers of Thomas Aquinas.[1] Whether his interpretations of Thomas's views accord in fact with the letter and spirit of the Angelic Doctor's doctrines is, of course, a matter of scholarly debate, but it is clear that he openly intended to explain and develop the teachings of the master whose name he had adopted. Indeed, he went so far as to explicitly identify the marks of a true disciple of Thomas in his *Cursus theologicus*.[2] They are the following: (1) the continuation of and adherence to a long tradition of disciples that included Hervaeus, Capreolus, Cajetan, Ferrara, Victoria, Soto, and Flandria; (2) the energetic defense and understanding of Thomas's doctrines; (3) the exposition and acceptance of his views; (4) the arrival at conclusions that coincide with those of Thomas, as well as the attempt to reconcile any apparent inconsistencies among them; and (5) the promotion of harmony and agreement among other followers of the master.

Considering this overall aim, John of St. Thomas's views on individuation must be taken as an interpretation of the Thomistic view on the same subject, although some Thomists would disagree and others have in fact done so on at least two counts: They question not only the accuracy of John's interpretations of Aquinas's views but also their viability.[3]

John of St. Thomas's most important discussion of individuation is contained in the *Cursus philosophicus Thomisticus*. In this work, published in Madrid and Rome in 1637 and later in Cologne (1638), Lyon (1663), and Paris (1883), are contained his most important philosophical ideas.[4] John's theology is primarily developed in several works, including a multivolume commentary to Thomas Aquinas's *Summa theologiae* entitled *Cursus theologicus*. Although there are also several apologetic and devotional works published in Spanish, these have nothing of importance to say about individuation.[5] The commentary on Thomas's *Summa* contains, as would be expected, occasional remarks pertinent to this subject. However, the usefulness of those remarks is somewhat limited insofar as their principal aim is theological, and they lack the systematic and philosophical character displayed by the discussion of this topic found in the *Cursus philosophicus*. The present analysis, therefore, will be based primarily on the key texts of the *Cursus philosophicus*, although it will make reference to at least one section of John's commentary on the *Summa* that deals explicitly with individual unity.

The *Cursus philosophicus* is a comprehensive and systematic work divided into two parts: "Ars logica" and "Naturalis philosophia". The latter is in turn subdivided into four parts: "De ente mobili in communi", "De ente mobili incorruptibili", "De ente mobili corruptibili", and "De ente mobili animato". Only the first, third, and fourth of these parts are found in the published editions of the *Cursus philosophicus*.[6] This is unfortunate, for the second part would probably have had something to tell us concerning the individuation of separate substances.[7] As things stand, however, the only extended discussion of individuation contained in the *Cursus philosophicus* that we can use to understand John's views is found in the third part of the "Naturalis philosophia", which is concerned with corruptible and movable being. The pertinent discussion is part of Question 9, whose explicit topics are the subject of accidents and the principle of individuation. It is the last three articles of the question (three, four, and five) that are of interest to us. Articles 3 and 4 deal with the principle of individuation of material substances and article 5 is concerned with the individuation of accidents. In addition, a section in the *Logic* is pertinent to our subject, for it deals with the proper definition of the individual. The section occurs in Part II of the *Logic*, entitled *De instrumentis logicalibus ex parte materiae*, under q. 9, "De individuo", aa. 1 and 2.[8]

Our discussion will be divided into four parts: the intension of 'individual', the individuation of material substances, the individuation of accidents, and conclusions.

I. The Intension of 'Individual'

A. Transcendental and Individual Unity

Like Suárez, whom he frequently cites, John understands individuality as a kind of unity and therefore discusses its relationship to transcendental and formal unities. He does so in his commentary to Thomas's *Summa theologiae*, where the question is raised as to the various types of unities that there are and how they differ from transcendental unity.[9]

There are, according to John, three types of unity: transcendental, formal and individual. Transcendental unity, he tells us, is "the unity and indivision of a being insofar as it is a being'',[10] adding later that "it is nothing other than a thing insofar as it is undivided in the notion of being".[11] Formal unity is the unity or indivision of something considered formally and quidditatively. Finally, numerical unity, that is, individual unity, has to do with "a determined and incommunicable, that is, material, indivision".[12] Individual unity differs from formal unity in that the individual is related materially and as a subject to all higher predicates; that is the reason why this unity is called "material". It is called "determined and incommunicable" because there is no further predication or communication beyond it in the predicamental tree.[13]

Clearly there are intensional distinctions among these three unities. The question that arises, however, is whether there are also extensional ones or whether, as Suárez did, John will understand transcendental and individual unities as the same in reality. And, indeed, his answer to this question seems quite unambiguous: "From all this it is clear that transcendental, formal and individual unity are found in the same subject and individual: nor are there three unities simply and absolutely, just as neither are there three entities, but rather the same entity is fully and completely undivided in every aspect."[14] Indeed, no unity whatsoever is possible without individual unity: "if individual unity is removed, neither formal nor transcendental unity remains".[15]

From these texts it seems clear that John adopted a view similar to that of Suárez with respect to the relation between transcendental and individual unities: They are intensionally different but extensionally the same. With an understanding of this relation, then, we may turn to John's conception of the individual.

B. Conception of the Individual

As would be expected, John's discussion of the concept of the individual is contained in his logic rather than in his natural philosophy, where the principle of individuation is discussed. The identification of the principles and causes of individuation is a problem in natural philosophy (physics) for John, who follows standard late scholastic practice in this matter; concepts, on the other hand, and thus the definition of individuality, are analyzed in a logical context.

Two problems mar many scholastic discussions of individuality, as already mentioned in this volume. The first is the confusing use of 'individuatio' ('individuation') to refer both to individuality and the process whereby individuality accrues to an individual. John does not differ from many of his predecessors in this respect, but we have tried for the sake of clarity to keep the two senses of 'individuatio' separate by translating the term by 'individuality' in contexts where it seems to be the clear sense of the text.

The second problem consists in the failure to distinguish clearly between individuality and the principle of individuation. Suárez, as can be seen
in the chapter devoted to him in this volume, distinguishes between the two,
and points out that Scotus identifies them and thus fails to provide a proper
explanation of individuation. John echoes Suárez's view on this, although he
does not refer to him at this juncture and provides an even clearer distinction
between the two.

> The principle of individuation is something different from the individ-
> uality that is caused by such a principle. Saint Thomas identifies the
> principle of individuation of composite things with matter designated
> by quantity and that of accidents with a relation to it. Moreover, in
> things that lack matter he teaches that the form . . . is the principle of
> individuation. . . . But the formal individuality caused by the principle
> of individuation is metaphysically the individual difference itself and
> physically it is the numerical and individual unity whereby a being is
> one so that it is not further divisible or communicable through other
> contracting differences.[16]

Individuality, that is, individual or numerical unity, is to be distinguished
from the principle of individuation as an effect is distinguished from a cause.
When one deals with the principle of individuation, then, one is dealing with
something different from individuality. Indeed, the definition of individuality,
that is, of what it is to be an individual, is not the definition of the principle
of individuation. This is quite clear in John's texts. However, the talk about
the "definition" of individuality does raise a difficulty, since individuality is
not a nature like horseness and dogness and, therefore, presumably cannot be
defined strictly speaking.

I suspect this difficulty is one of the reasons why many scholastics deal
with the concept of individuality neither explicitly nor separately. Of course,
there are exceptions. Ockham devotes a chapter to it in the *Summa logicae*,
and Suárez discusses it in the disputation devoted to individual unity. John is
also an exception and holds that it is possible to offer a definition of the individual qua individual. An individual may be understood in two ways: (1) as
designated and determined, in the way Peter and Paul are, and (2) as vague
and in general (*vagum seu in communi*), in the way a man is.[17] It is in the
second sense that a definition of the individual is possible,[18] for the individual considered vaguely and in general "signifies the common nature with
the determinate way of being characteristic of singulars".[19] Now, although
this vague concept of the individual considered in general expresses something real,[20] it is an analogical concept "since individual differences are im-

mediately diverse and there is nothing univocal in the notion of individual difference".[21] The general concept of an individual, therefore, can be defined based on the analogical concept gathered from actually diverse individuals. Individuality is not a nature, but it has sufficient conceptual content to have a definition.

Having presented John's distinction between individuality and the principle of individuation, and his response to those who object to any attempt at offering a definition of individuality, we may turn now to his view of individuality. He begins the discussion by introducing two distinctions that turn out to be quite useful, according to him, in sorting out the various definitions of the individual already given by various authorities. The first is the distinction between individuality "conceived *generally,* as found in all things, whether substances or accidents", and the second is individuality conceived "specially, as found in the genus of substance".[22] The second is the distinction between two ways of considering the individual: "first-intentionally or second-intentionally".

Neither the distinction between substance and accident nor the distinction between first and second intentions is new at the time of John's writing. The former is already present in the first Latin texts of the Middle Ages and goes back to Aristotle, and the latter has roots in the Islamic tradition and is standard in scholastic works from the thirteenth century onward. Nor is it new to speak of the individuality of substances and accidents separately. However, what is new, as far as we have been able to determine, is the idea of applying these distinctions to the definition of the individual and seeing how the various definitions given by previous authorities ought to be understood in those terms. The use of the distinction between a general definition of individuality applicable to all individuals and a more restricted one applicable only to substantial individuals allowed John to distinguish between, for example, Porphyry's view that to be an individual is to have "a collection of features not found in anything else",[23] and Thomas's view that an individual is what is "indistinct in itself and distinct from others".[24] The first definition is clearly applicable only to substances, since only substances can have features, while the second is broader.[25] Of course, John adopts Thomas's definition, for two reasons: First, it is more general and therefore applies both to substances and accidents; second, it is essential, while he regards Porphyry's definition as merely descriptive because it presupposes a "constituted individual essence", since features presuppose something of which they are features.[26]

Most scholastic authors before John do not quite know what to do with Porphyry's understanding of the individual. Their objections usually repeat the Abailardian point that this view is incompatible with a substance-accident ontology of the Aristotelian sort, an objection that John repeats in other places. Consequently, Porphyry's understanding of the individual is rejected in the end in spite of Porphyry's stature and authority. But John's clever use of the mentioned distinction does allow a place for Porphyry's view, for John points out that Porphyry's definition is applicable to substances and is a descriptive rather than an essential definition.

A similar procedure was adopted to deal with another nuisance that had been around for more than a thousand years by the time John was writing. The way John deals with it indicates how good he is at sorting out and keeping separate metaphysics and logic. The nuisance in question is that, in addition to the understanding of individuality already discussed, Porphyry also gives a definition of the individual as "what is predicable of only one" and adds, moreover, that "the individual is contained under the species and the species under the genus".[27] The difficulty that medieval and scholastic authors encountered involved these two definitions and how to take them.

In the early Middle Ages, as pointed out elsewhere, the two definitions tended to support the rise of two different ways of dealing with individuality, one metaphysical and the other logical (and linguistic). But most authors understood both ways to have metaphysical implications. Of course, this attitude, particularly with respect to the second definition, was challenged by some. Ockham explicitly said that if the individual is defined in the way Porphyry had done (as what is predicable of only one), it cannot be considered a thing, and must be understood as a word.[28] And John, of course, agreed. He applied the distinction between first and second intentions to the concept of individual.[29] "The individual considered as a first intention expresses the real singularity or individuality found in reality which is nothing other physically and really than the numerical unity whereby a thing is one, undivided in itself and divided from everything else."[30] The individual considered first-intentionally, therefore, is the real unity, the individuality that individual things have. As such, it is defined as a unity in virtue of which a thing is undivided in itself and divided from everything else.

On the other hand, the individual may also be considered second-intentionally, and then the definition that applies to it is the Porphyrian definition that involves predicability. For here we are dealing with concepts and logic, not with reality (being) and metaphysics. This, of course, does not mean that it concerns something fictitious or arbitrary; it means only that it has to do with logic rather than metaphysics. Thus with John we have an unambiguous acceptance of two different approaches to individuality. Modern philosophy was to remain indecisive, but the twentieth century, at least within the Anglo-American tradition, seems to have come down overwhelmingly on the side of the logical approach.

Having established John's understanding of individuality we may now turn to the problem of individuation properly speaking. For that, of course, we have to leave his logic and turn to his natural philosophy.

II. The Individuation of Material Substances

A. Formulation of the Problem

John begins the discussion of the individuation of material substances by presenting his own formulation of the problem. He clarifies the meaning of individuality and its principle. Recapitulating some of his thoughts from the *Logic,* he tells us that individuality can be considered metaphysically, logically, and physically. Metaphysically, it indicates the lowest categorical level in the series of predicates where the genus is the highest, and it is neither a concept nor a unity in things. Logically, it is a second intention, a concept that refers to "the relation of subordination to higher predicates and the relation of predicability to one [thing] only, that is, to itself".[31] Finally, "physically, it is the very numerical unity whereby something is one in such a way that it is indivisible in itself and divided from everything else",[32] and John refers to a text of Thomas Aquinas in the *Summa theologiae* to support this point.[33] In this last sense, as Suárez had already clearly pointed out, individuality entails two things: on the one hand, incommunicability and indivision and, on the other, distinction from other individuals within the species.[34] Because individuality involves distinction within the species John thinks he must also discuss the notion of multiplication, for distinction within the species entails the possibility of there being more than one individual belonging to it. But note that all this concerns the individuality of *material* substances. The case with immaterial substances is entirely different, as Thomas himself had made clear.[35]

The second term whose meaning John clarifies is '*principium individuationis*' (principle of individuation), allowing him to identify what he takes to be the problem of individuation. According to him, the principle of individuation is the foundation or root of individual unity, and he understands such unity physically as involving both indivisibility into many and division from other things that also possess individual unity. Thus the individuality that has to be accounted for is neither logically nor metaphysically conceived. The question of whether the principle of the physical unity characteristic of individuals is to be found "among the constitutive principles and properties of the nature" or "outside the concept of the nature" must be answered.[36] All of this, of course, is in keeping with the view of the individual presented in the *Logic* and of individual unity adopted in the *Cursus theologicus.*

Now, according to John, there are two conditions that the principle of individuation must fulfill: First, it must pertain to substance and produce a substantial unity and, second, it must "multiply substances substantially and not essentially or formally".[37] It is the substance that is individual, and the substance remains essentially and formally the same as other substances. That is, an individual man, for example, is not formally or essentially different from any other man in virtue of his individuality, since in fact he is essentially and formally the same as other men.

These two conditions are significant. The first indicates that John is impressed by the old Abailardian argument that in a substance-accident metaphysics the principle of individuation must be substantial.[38] Consequently, John's interpretation of Thomas attempts to eliminate any trace of accidentality in the principle of individuation. The significance of the second is that he is not impressed by formalist interpretations of Thomas's view, an indication that he maintains individuality is not concerned with form.[39] We shall see later how John's interpretation seeks to satisfy these conditions.

Finally, John makes clear that the end term of individuation is subsistence, which is essentially found only in substantial individuals. Accidents do not have subsistence and are not by themselves complete (*terminationem*), although they are completed by their relation to substance.

In sum, the problem of individuation of material substances involves identifying the principle of the physical unity proper to those substances, and John's task is to come up with a viable interpretation of Thomas's view on the subject. But such an interpretation has as conditions that the principle be substantial and not formal.

B. Contemporary Opinions

After formulating the problem and clarifying some of the terminology associated with it, John proceeds to discuss in standard scholastic fashion the main solutions available. He mentions five different positions, two of which are subject to various interpretations.

1. Entity. The first view dismissed by John, which he correctly attributes to Suárez, holds that "each thing is individuated by itself and from its own entity and just as the thing itself has formal unity and all unity is an attribute of being, so [this view] posits that very entity as the principle of individuation".[40]

2. Thisness. The second view rejected by John holds that "individuation is the result of something distinct and as it were extrinsic that comes to the nature and that [this view] calls 'thisness'.[41] The formal effect of such thisness is to render a nature indivisible into subject parts. The nature in itself is potential and indifferent to being this one or that one, but becomes individual through the addition of an external entity. As expected, John attributes this view to Scotus.

3. Form. The third view rejected by John holds that the principle of individuation is form. In one interpretation, the form in question is substantial, and John reports that this version is attributed to both Averroes and Avicenna.[42] But others hold, according to him, that two things are required for individuation: incommunicability to many and numerical distinction from others. The form of quantity is responsible for the latter. John reports that this view is attributed by Scotus to Godfrey. John also claims that several Thomists, such as Soncinas, Capreolus, and Ferrara, adopt this position because Thomas himself favors it in some places.[43]

4. Matter and Form. The fourth position, like the third, distinguishes between incommunicability and distinction. It holds prime matter to be the principle of incommunicability. However, since matter in itself is purely potential and indifferent to any individual and species, and since individuation presupposes a constituted specific nature, this view adds that a principle of distinction is also required. Some adherents to this point of view identify the principle of distinction with substantial form, so that the principle of individuation becomes matter together with substantial form.[44] Others reject this view and posit matter designated by quantity, that is, matter with a relation to quantity, as the principle of individuation. And this, John reports, is not only what Thomas says but also what Thomists hold, although there is great variety in the interpretation of what is meant by the "designation" of matter by quantity. Sometimes it is interpreted as quantity itself considered as actually informing matter, sometimes as quantity radically preexisting (*praehabita*) in matter, and sometimes as quantity only connoted in, and as a kind of implied condition of, matter.

5. Existence. Almost as an afterthought, John refers to the view that existence or subsistence is the principle of individuation, although he does not discuss this. He cites Scotus's report of this view as his source, although it is more likely that it is Suárez's discussion of this position that he was using, since it is Suárez who refers to subsistence when speaking about this view; Scotus speaks only of existence.[45]

C. Criticism of Non-Thomistic Opinions

1. Criticism of Entity as the Principle of Individuation. Before giving his own position, John criticizes each of the views he rejects. Of these he spends the most time on the first, that of Suárez. He attacks Suárez's view by undermining what he calls its "foundations". The first of these foundations is the following argument: Since unity is an attribute of being, real unity follows real entity. But real unity is necessarily singular because in reality there is no abstract unity. Therefore, the unity that is an attibute of being (i.e., transcendental unity) is, insofar as it is real, the same as numerical unity, and individuation must follow entity. The second foundation is also an argument: Individuation pertains to the metaphysical order. But metaphysical order follows entity, that is, form and whatever pertains to it. Thus individuation cannot be the result of anything other than a thing's entity. Finally, the third foundation consists of Suárez's arguments against views that identify the principle of individuation with accidents and matter and his arguments in favor of the role played by form in individuation.

John's objections against the foundations of Suárez's views are extensive and, therefore, cannot be discussed here in any satisfactory detail. For present purposes, however, it should be sufficient to note that John accepts unity as a transcendental attribute of being, although he does not accept the idea that this implies the identification of transcendental unity with numerical unity and of the principle of individuation with entity. He reasons, as we saw earlier, that being is subject to multiple considerations to which a multiplicity of unities also correspond. Although numerical and transcendental unities are one and the same in reality, they differ conceptually. Moreover, although individuation pertains to the metaphysical order and thus to entity, it does not follow that entity must be the principle of individuation. According to John, the aspect under which entity is considered in relation to individuation "connotes something accidental, upon which individuation depends". Finally, John agrees with Suárez that accidents are not the principle or radical cause of individuation, but contrary to Suárez adds that they are "required conditions" of it. Again he agrees with Suárez that "matter in itself, separate from all form" is not the principle of individuation, but contrary to Suárez maintains that matter is the principle of individuation when it is considered in relation to the accident of quantity. As far as form is concerned, John disagrees with the key role Suárez gives it in individuation. Although matter is actualized through form, it is matter that distinguishes the individual "materially and incommunicably" and not form.

2. Criticism of Thisness (Haecceitas) as the Principle of Individuation.
The second opinion which John considers and rejects is that of Scotus, according to which the species is contracted to the individual by means of a principle (the thisness lying ouside the species as such) in the same way as the species contracts the genus by means of the specific difference. But the notion of thisness according to John can be interpreted in two ways. In one way (I) it means simply the "individual difference" or "numerical unity" of an individual. In this sense, as noted by Suárez, to accept the doctrine of *haecceitas* is nothing more than to accept that individual things have an individual unity distinct from the individual unity of other things, a fact accepted by everyone.[46] On the other hand, *haecceitas* may also be interpreted

(II) as "a form coming from without", modifying and contracting the species, as whiteness modifies a substance in which it inheres. Understood in this way, John says, the doctrine is unacceptable, for then "thisness" is either an accident (A), a substance (B), or a substantial mode (C). If an accident (A), it is either proper (A') or common (A"). But it cannot be proper (A'), since proper accidents proceed from the form or essential nature and are hence convertible with it. Since John has already shown that the essence of a thing as such, being common to many, cannot be the principle of individuation, neither can any essential properties. Only common accidents (A") therefore remain; but these, everyone admits, are not essential to the subject in which they inhere and can come and go without the subject ceasing to be (e.g., the color of the skin of a human being changes in summer or winter, while the human being remains). "Thisness", however, cannot come and go without the substance ceasing to be, since thisness, by hypothesis, is what makes the substance an individual substance. On the other hand, if "thisness" is not any kind of accident, it must be the substance itself (B) or a substantial mode (C). Both of these fail, however. It cannot be the substance itself (B), because it would then be intrinsic and not extrinsic as Scotus claims. Nor could it be a substantial mode (C), for substantial modes originate in substance and are therefore also intrinsic to the substance. In short, *haecceitas* fails to meet the requirements of a proper principle of individuation.

3. Criticism of Form as the Principle of Individuation. The final position John considers before defending his own is the position that form, substantial or accidental, is the primary and radical principle of individuation. According to him, neither substantial nor accidental form can function as the principle of individuation. Substantial form fails because form considered as such is a specific principle and, therefore, communicable to many. Form cannot be incommunicable of itself unless it be immaterial and unrelated to matter, whereas form is often in matter and related to matter and, therefore, communicated to it. But to be individual is precisely "to be incommunicable to many" and the principle of individuation must also be incommunicable, facts that disqualify form from this role.

The view that accidents, including quantity, are the principle of individuation, is also easily dismissed by John. For the accidents of a substance, far from individuating it, depend upon it. The substance must exist as an individual before its accidents. It is necessary that the principle that individuates substance be substantial and not accidental. With respect to quantity in particular, John adds that, since it is a material form, it is communicable to many in exactly the same way as substantial form. This is another reason why quantity cannot be the primary and radical principle of individuation, although it may be a condition of it.

D. John's Position

From what was said earlier concerning John's attitude toward Thomas Aquinas's thought and the rules he prescribes for Thomas's disciples, we should expect his position to be presented as concordant with Thomas's statements and also with the interpretative tradition composed of the views of well known and respected Thomists. But not all Thomists who precede John agree on their interpretation of Thomas's doctrine of individuation, and some of them even hold different views at different times. John's task was by no means easy.[47] He needed to find a formulation that fits Thomas's texts while encompassing the views of his followers, leaving some room for his own interpretation and contribution to the issue. Finally, also in accordance with the rules he prescribes for Thomists, we should expect John to present an interpretation that answers some of the charges brought against Thomas's view. We need to be reminded that Thomas's doctrine of individuation is not only one of his most criticized theories, but also one that has been subjected to a considerable variety of interpretations. A brief look at the chapters contained in this volume that present the views of Thomas, Thomists, and critics of Thomas's position will substantiate this claim.

John's strategy is quite in line with his goals. He begins by presenting a brief, standard formulation of Thomas's position followed by references to pertinent texts. He also tries to show that Thomas's formulation is in line with the role Aristotle gives to matter in individuation, in spite of Scotus's arguments to the contrary. This is followed by a more detailed formulation that is supposed to encompass the variety of relevant opinions among Thomists. Finally, he denies two misconceptions when explaining what he takes to be the correct rendering of Thomas's position.

The first step in John's strategy, then, is to present Thomas's formulation: *matter designated by quantity is the principle of individuation.*[48] The adoption of this formula puts John squarely in the camp of those who regard designated matter as the principle of individuation in Thomistic metaphysics. It also pits him against those who emphasize the role of form or of matter by itself.

The second step is to present an analysis of this brief formula that is concordant, at least in general, with the variety of opinion among Thomists:

> The designation of matter is not carried out formally by quantity considered as a form inhering in matter that produces this designation, but rather *it is produced by an intrinsic relation of matter to quantity considered as a dividing and separating form.* Thus quantity is the end term of the designation of the matter to which it is related, rather than an intrinsically designating form. Hence, it is said to be related [to it]

as a condition and connotation of individuation. And considered as such, that is, as a condition, quantity is the first, although matter is [both] the first and radical individuating principle. So, matter designated by quantity is the same as matter related to quantity considered as dividing. This division, although not produced without the information of quantity, since quantity as a certain disposition comes from form, nevertheless under the aspect of division precedes the form itself in the genus of material cause.[49]

John considers this analysis consonant with traditional interpretations of Thomas's position. Of these interpretations he lists three that correspond to the three listed at the beginning of article 3. The first holds that the principle of individuation is matter plus quantity, matter being responsible for the ultimate incommunicability of the individual, and quantity for its division and separation from others. Designated matter, then, is to be interpreted, according to this view, as matter informed by quantity, and John identifies Ferrara and Soncinas as its proponents. This accords with Suárez, who describes the same position and attributes it to these two and also to Capreolus.[50]

The second view, on the other hand, interprets designated matter as matter considered "in relation to this quantity".[51] Accordingly, the principle of individuation is not matter informed by quantity, as the first view holds. Obviously, it is not clear what the formula "matter in relation to this quantity" means, and John tells us there are two subviews under this general position. The first interprets the formula to mean that matter is determined to this quantity by a superadded substantial mode that somehow determines and designates it. The second, however, understands the formula to mean that matter is determined by a relation to and disposition for such quantity. This latter interpretation is the one John finally favors. He does not mention any authors who either subscribe to or defend the view of designated matter as involving a superadded mode, but Suárez refers to Javellus and Giles as defenders of the general view under which these two subviews are subsumed.[52]

Having presented what he considers to be the three most important traditional interpretations of Thomas's position, John is free to present his own as well as his justification for rejecting any other antagonistic view. He begins by making a distinction between two senses of 'designated', which we might call "epistemic" and "ontological". The epistemic sense he explains as pertaining to the appearance of something with respect to us, while the ontological he explains as having to do with the incommunicability of a thing and its separation and division from others.[53] John grants that, insofar as the appearance of things is concerned, it is without a doubt quantity, as well as other accidental features, that designates things. We become aware of individuals as individuals through their dimensions and other accidents. This position, he points out later on, is in perfect accord not only with Thomas's view, but also with those of his commentators Bañez, Cajetan, and González.[54] However, the issue under consideration is not the epistemic distinction of the individual from other individuals, but rather what John calls its "substantial individuation", that is, the ontological character of the individual as such and as separate from others. For the latter, John argues, what we have called here the "epistemic" understanding of matter's designation is not sufficient. But, then, we may ask, how is this designation to be interpreted?

First, John answers by telling us how it is *not* to be interpreted and only afterward does he explain how it should be. Matter's designation should *not* be interpreted as (1) just matter, (2) matter informed by quantity, or (3) an absolute mode added to matter. We have already encountered interpretations (2) and (3). They are two of the three ways John lists as important traditional interpretations of Thomas's position. It is here that he mentions interpretation (1) for the first time. Its importance derives from the fact that it was associated with Aristotle by some of his commentators and interpreters, and also because some texts of Thomas lend credance to it.[55] After listing these views John proceeds to argue against them.

1. Criticism of Matter. The view that matter by itself is the principle of individuation is rejected by arguments based on matter's disposition to form and other matter.[56] Because matter is disposed to form, it is potentially many things and cannot be the basis of individuation. Matter in itself is a generic principle and, therefore, is of itself common and potential to many forms by which it is determined and actualized.

2. Criticism of Matter Informed by Quantity. The view that matter actually informed by quantity is the principle of individuation is rejected for several reasons. The first is that quantity cannot *immediately* inhere in matter as such, and so it cannot mark it off for the reception of the substantial form. On the contrary, quantity can inhere only in the individual composite *already* constituted by the union of matter with substantial form. Informing quantity, far from grounding the individual substance, presupposes it. The second reason is that, even if the supernatural power of God were to separate the quantity from the substance, the substance would remain individual. Moreover, even separated accidents would remain individual by means of their relation to the subject. The third reason is that quantity is in itself universal, like all forms, and therefore it needs to be rendered individual to be the particular quantity of *this* individual. Nothing that is in itself universal, however, can ground individuation. And the final reason is that quantity, being an accident, could give only accidental being, while the principle of substantial individuation must give substantial being; substantial individuals must be distinguished substantially, not accidentally. This final reason gives John the opportunity to dismiss all accidental theories of individuation, including bundle theories.

3. Criticism of an Absolute Mode Added to Matter. The view that the principle of individuation is matter determined by some absolute mode related to quantity is disposed of more briefly by John. According to him, it violates the principle of parsimony by postulating an unnecessary entity. Matter in and of itself is the ultimate subject for all substantial and accidental forms, including quantity, and hence it is related to them without need of a superaded absolute mode.

4. The Designation of Matter as a Relation of Matter to Quantity. The way the designation of matter to quantity should be interpreted, according to John, is as "a relation of matter to quantity", for quantity divides and separates matter into parts.[57] John is aware that, within the Aristotelian framework generally adopted by scholastics, quantity is an accident and accidents do not inform matter directly, but rather inform the already constituted composite of matter and substantial form. This naturally creates a problem for all accidental theories of individuation, for the accidents that are supposed to individuate turn out to be posterior to the substantial individual. Therefore, it is not clear how they can function as individuators.[58] But John does not see this difficulty as insurmountable. Matter, according to him, can have a relation to quantity like the relation it has to dispositions, without presupposing the actual information of matter by quantity. This is enough for quantity to determine matter in such a way that it may function as the principle of individuation. As he puts it, "the potentiality of matter [whereby it can be this as well as that] is determined to this form [of quantity] rather than to another".[59] Quantity can do this because it not only produces extension in those things that have it, but also divides one portion of matter from another. Thus matter by itself, without a relation to quantity, is not the principle of individuation. Nor do the incommunicability and division characteristic of individuals result from quantity considered by itself. Rather they result from matter insofar as it is related to the form of quantity that it does not actually have, but toward which it has a disposition to be determined and divided in a certain way. For this reason John modifies Thomas's original formula 'matter designated by quantity' to 'matter *radically* designated by quantity'.[60] The addition of 'radically' is meant to indicate that the designation is not an actual informing of matter by quantity that is present in the composite substance, but that in matter we find the root of its designation arising from the disposition it has toward certain forms of quantity.[61] Quantity, therefore, is not an absolute principle of individuation, but rather a concomitant condition. As a concomitant condition, it cannot function formally as a cause of individuality. But it is to quantity, and not to other accidents, that matter is radically related in order to function as the principle of individuation; for none of the other accidents produce division, and division is a requirement of individuality.

But, we may ask, what does quantity mean for John? The manner in which John speaks of a disposition to "this form" in the context of quantity seems to suggest that he understands quantity as determinate dimensions, as Thomas does in several places.[62] But actually John is impressed with the well-known objection against this view based on a consideration of the required conditions to account for individual identity through time. The objection is found in Scotus, Suárez, and other critics of Thomas, and even Thomas himself raises it to argue for the view that the dimensions that are added to matter to turn it into a principle of individuation must be indeterminate.[63] Briefly put, the objection argues that matter designated by determinate dimensions cannot be the principle of individuation, for the dimensions of substances change and this would seem to entail that the identity of the individual would also have to change. But, since individuals do not change their individual identity when they change dimensions, the dimensions that individuate them cannot be determinate.

As pointed out elsewhere, this objection is ineffective. It confuses individuality with identity, failing to understand that the principle of one need not be the principle of the other, and therefore that, even if dimensions change, a different principle could ensure the continuity of the individual. But John, like Cajetan, is impressed by the objection and concludes, as a result, that the dimensions to which matter is related in order to function as the principle of individuation are indeterminate. Indeed, he goes even further than this by pointing out that indeterminate dimensions are nothing other than quantity.[64] In conclusion, *the principle of individuation of material substances is matter considered as radically related to indeterminate dimensions.*

III. The Individuation of Accidents

In article 5 John raises two issues: Whether individual accidents are individuated by the subject and whether there can be two numerically distinct accidents in the same subject. These are the same issues with which Suárez is concerned at length at the end of the disputation he devotes to individual unity.[65] For us only the first question is pertinent, and we shall deal with it very briefly since it does not contain much novelty.

John's answer is unequivocal: "According to Thomas it is most certain that the individuation of accidents is taken from the subject in which they are; that is, [individuation is taken] in relation to it."[66] This is, indeed, Thomas's view, which John supports with appropriate references. However, he considers three other possibilities as well. The first holds that accidents are individuated by themselves, the second maintains that prime matter and not the substantial composite is the principle of individuation of accidents, and the third argues that at least quantity is individuated by itself.

Contemporaneous to John's writing, the two major theories of the individuation of accidents are the substantialist view, defended by Thomas's followers, and the view that accidents are individuated by themselves, defended by Suárez. John's allegiance is clear, although he does not really answer Suárez's objections to his position.[67]

IV. Conclusions

As mentioned earlier, John perceived his task as finding a solution to the problem of individuation that was in keeping with Thomas's view and with those of his traditional interpreters, while providing for its defense against any possible objections. His solution was to provide an interpretation of the designation of matter as the radical relation of matter to indeterminate dimensions. This position may be described as a middle ground between the views that make matter the principle of individuation and those that identify matter plus the addition of a form or mode as the principle of individuation. This intermediate position allowed John to keep the substantiality of the principle of individuation, to maintain its nonformal character, and at the same time to avoid the objection against the determinacy of dimensions based on their changing character.

From the point of view of the preservation of an orthodox Thomism, again this position may be considered at least partly successful within the Thomistic tradition for two reasons: first, it preserves the well-known formula "individuation by designated matter", and second, it adopts a view quite concordant with one of the two positions adopted by Thomas with respect to the interpretation of quantity. Moreover, there had been previous attempts at similar solutions by other Thomists, or pseudo-Thomists, such as Giles, Hervaeus, Cajetan, Javellus, and Ferrara, a fact that gave credibility to John's interpretation. It should be clear that John's position was an *interpretation* of the Thomistic view, going well beyond what Thomas actually said, and it is partly for this reason that it has been criticized by some Thomists.

If, however, one looks at John's position from an independent philosophical point of view, some troubling issues remain. The most important of these can be formulated in a question: How can the relation of matter to indeterminate dimensions be sufficient to account for something being "a this"? It is simply not clear how matter can be related to something indeterminate or, even if that were possible, how a relation to something indeterminate can be responsible for the determinacy characteristic of individuals. Indeed, if one looks at John's very text, the problem becomes quite evident, for he concluded that "quantity and other individual properties. . . . are required" for individuation.[68] And it is repeated elsewhere that the division of quantity is a required condition of individuation because it gives rise in matter to the determinate substantial incommunicability that substantially individuates.[69] But to say that the division brought about by quantity is a necessary condition is certainly not to say that it is a sufficient condition of individuation. This inadequacy is the weakness of John's position; even if we were to grant that he identified a necessary condition of individuation, we are still missing the most important parts of the puzzle.

There are also other problems. For example, even though John presented a rather sophisticated discussion of the notion of individuality in the *Logic,* he did not attempt to deal with the questions of extension, ontological status, and discernibility that had concerned so many other scholastics before him. Indeed, if one compares Suárez's discussion of individual unity in Disputation V with John's discussion, the latter is somewhat anticlimactic.

From an independent philosophical standpoint, therefore, John's view leaves something to be desired, although his distinction between the logical, metaphysical, and physical definitions of individuality constituted an important landmark in scholastic discussions of the individual. John's importance, it must be admitted, is primarily historical. He provided (1) perhaps the last important scholastic formulation of the problem of individuation unmixed with the epistemic elements that were going to characterize early modern discussions of that problem. He also presented (2) an interpretation of Thomas's view that was going to find its way into the thought of many subsequent Thomists.

Notes

1. For information on John of St. Thomas's life, works, and thought, see John N. Deely, *Tractatus de signis; The Semiotic of John Poinsot* (Berkeley: University of California Press, 1985).

2. *Cursus theologicus, Tractatus de approbatione et auctoritate doctrinae angelicae divi Thomae,* Disp. II, a.5 (Paris: Desclée, 1931), vol. 1, pp. 297–301.

3. See, for example, the criticisms of Umberto Degl'Innocenti in "Il principio d'individuazione dei corpi e Giovanni di S. Tommaso", *Aquinas* 12 (1969): 59–99, particularly pages 65, 77–80, 85, and 92. See also M. D. Chenu, *Introduction à l'Etude de Saint Thomas D'Aquin* (Montreal: Institut d'Etudes Médiévales, 1950), p. 280; W. R. O'Connor, "The Natural Desire for God in St. Thomas", *New Scholasticism* 14 (1940): 225; and H. de Lubac, *Supernaturel* (Paris: Aubier, 1945), p. 138.

4. *Cursus philosophicus Thomisticus secundum exactam, veram, genuinam Aristotelis et Doctoris Angelici mentem,* ed. B. Reiser, 3 vols. (Turin: Marietti, 1933).

5. Best known is *Explicación de la doctrina cristiana y la obligación de los fieles en creer y obrar.*

6. The edition we use has the following inscription in the place where the second part should have been included: "Secundam partem, quae tractat de ente mobili incorruptibili, quod est coelum, auctor non edidit." *Cursus philosophicus,* vol. 2, p. 531.

7. Also unfortunate is that the edition of the work we are using is missing the parts of Part I, q. 9, dealing with matter, form, and angels, where again John of St. Thomas may have said something pertinent to individuation. This is not a case of the neglect to write the text, but rather of some pages being dropped and others being put in their place during the production of the volume. However, in q. 8, a. 3, of Part II, he makes clear that he follows Thomas in holding that angelic substances are individual, although there is and can be only one individual per species. Angelic natures can be conceived as having a kind of indifference and potentiality to individuality, which is totally lacking in the divine nature. *Cursus philosophicus,* vol. 1, p. 413a.

8. *Cursus philosophicus,* vol. 1, pp. 424–435.

9. *Cursus theologicus,* Part I, q. 11, a. 2, vol. 2, pp. 112–117.

10. *Ibid.*, p. 112a: "unitas et indivisio entis ut ens est."

11. *Ibid.*, p. 113a: "non esse aliud quam rem ut indivisam in ratione entis."

12. *Ibid.*, p. 112a: "indivisio terminata et incommunicabilis, seu materialis."

13. *Ibid.*, p. 112b.

14. *Ibid.*, p. 114a: "Ex quibus patet unitatem transcendentalem, formalem et individualem in eodem subjecto et individuo reperiri: nec facere ibi tres unitates simpliciter et absolute, sicut nec tres entitates, sed eamdem entitatem plene et complete reddere indivisam ex omni parte."

15. *Ibid.*, p. 115b: "remota individuali unitate, dicimus quod non manet unitas formalis vel transcendentalis. . . ."

16. *Cursus philosophicus,* vol. 1, p. 427a–b: "aliud esse principium individuationis, aliud individuationem ipsam, quae a tali principio causatur. Principium individuationis sumit Divus Thomas in rebus compositis ex materia designata per quantitatem et accidentia vel per ordinem ad illam. In rebus autem a materia separatis ipsammet formam, ut incommunicabilis est materiae, docet esse principium individuationis. . . . At vero individuatio ipsa formalis, quae a principio individuationis causatur, metaphysice est ipsa differentia individualis; physice autem est ipsa unitas numeralis et individua, qua aliquod ens taliter est unum, quod non est amplius divisibile seu communicabile per alias differentias contrahentes. . . ."

17. *Ibid.*, p. 424b. The term '*vagum*' is documented as early as Albert the Great in connection with individuation in the Latin tradition, but the notion of a

"vague individual" is found even earlier in the Islamic tradition. See the pertinent chapters in this volume.

18. *Ibid.*, p. 428b.

19. *Ibid.*, p. 430a: "significat naturam communem cum determinato modo essendi; qui competit singularibus. . . ."

20. *Ibid.*, p. 430b.

21. *Ibid.*, p. 431b: "cum ipsae differentiae individuales sint primo diversae, nihil illis univocum dari possit in ratione differentiae individualis."

22. *Ibid.*, p. 425a: "*generaliter* accepta, prout in omnibus generibus invenitur, tam substantiae quam accidentis . . . specialiter, prout in genere substantiae invenitur. . . ."

23. *Ibid.*, p. 425b: "collectio numquam in alio eadem erit."

24. *Ibid.*, p. 426a: "indistinctum in se et distinctum ab aliis."

25. *Ibid.*

26. *Ibid.*, p. 426b.

27. *Ibid.*, p. 428a: "quod de uno solo praedicatur . . . individuum continetur sub specie, species autem sub genere."

28. William of Ockham, *Summa logicae* I, ch. 19: "Porphyry says that a particular is what is predicated of only one thing, but this definition does not make any sense if it is interpreted to apply to something existing outside the mind."

29. For John "a term of *first intention* is one that signifies something according to what it is in reality or in its own proper status, i.e., independently of the status it has in the intellect and as having been conceived—such as *white, man* as they are in reality. A term of *second intention* is one that signifies something according to what it has from being a concept of the mind and in its intellectualized status, e.g., *species, genus* and other like things that the logician deals with." *Cursus philosophicus*, vol. 1, p. 13a. In John of St. Thomas, *Outlines of Formal Logic*, trans. Wade, p. 36.

30. *Cursus philosophicus*, vol. 1, p. 425a–b: "Individuum quantum ad *primam* intentionem dicit ipsam singularitatem, prout a parte rei invenitur, quae singularitas seu individuatio realis non est aliud physice et in re quam ipsa unitas numerica, qua aliquid ita est unum, quod est indivisum in se et divisum a quolibet alio."

31. *Cursus philosophicus*, vol. 2, q. 9, a. 3, p. 769: "Logice dicit relationem subicibilitatis ad praedicata superiora et praedicabilitatis de uno tantum, id est de seipso."

32. *Ibid.*: "Physice est ipsa unitas numerica, qua aliquid ita est unum, quod est indivisivum in se et divisivum a quolibet alio."

33. *Summa theologiae* I, q. 29, a. 4. Actually what Thomas says is as follows: "Individuum autem est quod est in se indistinctum, ab aliis vero distinctum." (In Marietti ed., vol. 1, p. 209). This is quite different from the formula used by John, since the notions of *indivisivum* and *indistinctum* are different. The first involves indivisibility strictly speaking, while the second concerns sameness, but John uses the notions of division and distinction (and their opposites) interchangeably.

34. For Suárez's distinction between these notions, see the previous chapter in this volume.

35. For Thomas's view see *De ente et essentia*, ch. 5; *De substantiis separatis* 8. For John's views, see note 7.

36. *Cursus philosophicus*, vol. 2, p. 769: "ex principiis constitutivis et propriis ipsius naturae, an vero ex aliquo, quod sit extra conceptum naturae. . . ."

37. *Ibid.:* "multiplicet substantiam substantialiter, quod non essentialiter nec formaliter." Note the use of 'multiply' where one would have expected 'individuate', indicating further John's understanding of individuality as involving multiplication within the species in addition to indivisibility and distinction.

38. See note 58.

39. For formalist views see the chapters on Godfrey, Peter of Auvergne, John Baconthorpe, and James of Viterbo in this volume.

40. *Cursus philosophicus*, vol. 2, p. 771: "unumquodque individuari seipso et ex propria entitate, et sicut seipsa habet unitatem formalem, et omnis unitas est passio entis, ideo ipsam entitatem ponit pro principio individuationis."

41. *Ibid.:* "individuationem fieri per aliquid distinctum et tam quam extrinsecum adveniens naturae, quod vocavit haecceitatem." We are taking some liberties with the translations of these texts.

42. Indeed, Suárez did so in *Disputatio metaphysica* V, s. 4, 1.

43. See the chapter in this volume on Godfrey, Peter of Auvergne, John Baconthorpe, and James of Viterbo.

44. There are many authors whose positions could be interpreted in this way. Indeed, such authors as Burley and Suárez might qualify. See the chapters on them in this volume.

45. For Scotus, see *Opus oxoniense* II, d. 3, p. 1, q. 3. For Suárez, see *Disputatio metaphsica* V, s. 5.

46. Suárez, *Disputatio metaphysica* V, s. 2, 7.

47. A case in point is Cajetan. See the chapter on him in this volume.

48. *Cursus philosophicus*, a. 4, vol. 2, p. 781.

49. *Ibid.*, p. 782: "Signatio materiae non fit formaliter per ipsam quantitatem tamquam per formam inhaerentem materiae et afficientem ipsam, sed fit per intrinsecum ordinem materiae ad quantitatem ut ad formam dividentem et separantem, et ita quantitas potius est terminus signationis materiae, ad quam dicit ordinem, quam forma intrinsice signans, et hoc modo dicitur se habere ut conditio et connotatio individuationis. Et in isto genere, scilicet ut conditio, quantitas est primum, licet materia sit primum et radicale individuandi principium. Itaque materia signata quantitate idem est, quod materia ordinata ad quantitatem ut dividentem, Quae divisio licet non fiat sine informatione quantitatis, et quantitas, ut dispositio quaedam est, dimanat a forma, tamen sub ratione dividentis praecedit in genere causae materialis ipsam formam. . . ." Our emphasis in the translated text.

50. Suárez *Disputatio metaphysica* V, s. 3, 9. See also pertinent chapters in this volume.

51. *Cursus philosophicus,* vol. 2, p. 782: "materiam ut ordinatam ad hanc quantitatem."

52. Suárez, *Disputatio metaphysica* V, s. 3, 18. See pertinent chapters in this volume.

53. *Cursus philosophicus,* vol. 2, pp. 782–3. This distinction between a principle of individuation and a principle of distinction is clearly stated by Suárez in *Disp. metaphysica* V, s. 3, 28 and 33.

54. *Cursus philosophicus,* vol. 2, p. 785.

55. See Suárez, *Disp. metaphysica,* V, s. 3, 34. John may have Cajetan in mind for the first position since Cajetan's final view on this subject seems to have been that matter by its very nature is the principle of individuation. See the chapter on Cajetan and Degl'Innocenti, "Il principio d'individuazione," as well as the latter's "Animadversiones in Caietani doctrinam de corporum individuatione" and "Del Gaetano e del principio d'individuazione", *Divus Thomas* (Piacenza) (1948): 19–45, and (1949): 202–208.

56. *Cursus philosophicus,* vol. 2, p. 783.

57. *Ibid.*, p. 784: "signatio materiae explicanda est per ordinem ad quantitatem ut dividentem et separantem ipsas partes materiae."

58. This sort of reasoning was frequently used by scholastics who opposed accidental theories of individuation. As already noted, it goes back to Abailard's *Logica ingredientibus,* ed. B. Geyer, in *Beiträge zur Geschichte der Philosophie des Mittelalters,* vol. 21, parts 1–3 (1919–1927), pp. 13 and 64. See also the chapters on Scotus, Cajetan, Ockham, and Suárez in this volume.

59. *Cursus philosophicus,* vol. 2, p. 784: "ipsa potentialitas materiae determinatur respectu istius formae potius quam alterius."

60. *Ibid.*, p. 785: "Et sit intelligo materiam signari radicaliter quantitate."

61. Cajetan had used the term '*radix*' in connection with the principle of individuation, but he had actually held that matter was the *radix* of quantity, rather than that matter is *radicaliter* designated by quantity. The views are quite different in spite of Degl'Innocenti's claims to the contrary in "Il principio d'individuazioni dei corpi e Giovanni di S. Tommaso", p. 64.

62. For example, in *De ente et essentia,* ch. 2.

63. Thomas Aquinas, *Expositio super librum Boethii De Trinitate,* q. 4, a. 2, ed. B. Decker (Leiden: E. J. Brill, 1959), pp. 142–143. St. Thomas Aquinas, *Faith, Reason and Theology: Questions I–IV of His "Commentary on the 'De trinitate' of Boethius,* trans. A. Mauer (Toronto: Pontifical Institute of Mediaeval Studies, 1987), pp. 97–98.

64. *Cursus philosophicus,* vol. 2, p. 787.

65. *Disputatio metaphysica* V, s. 5.

66. *Cursus philosophicus,* vol. 2, p. 789: "In sententia S. Thomae certissimum est individuationem accidentium sumi a subiecto, in quo sunt, seu in ordine ad illud."

67. Suárez, *Disputatio metaphysica* V, s. 7.

68. *Cursus philosophicus,* vol. 2, p. 785: "quantitatem et proprietates individuales . . . sunt . . . conditiones requisitae. . . ."

69. *Ibid.:* "nascitur ex ipsa materia incommunicabilitas determinata substantialis et substantialiter individuans, posita tamen illa divisione quantitatis ut conditione requisita."

23

THE SCHOLASTIC BACKGROUND OF MODERN PHILOSOPHY: *Entitas* AND INDIVIDUATION IN LEIBNIZ

IGNACIO ANGELELLI

Dies war die philosophische Umwelt, in der Leibniz heranwuchs

—(*Wundt*, p. 143)

Leibniz's *Disputatio metaphysica de principio individui* has been already recognized as part of the second scholastic[1] intensive work on the principle of individuation.[2] A special monograph has been devoted to the relationship between the *Disputatio* and its sources.[3] The interest of such an essay, written when the author was a teenager, lies mainly, of course, in that it reveals the background and starting point of an outstanding thinker.

The central problem of the *Disputatio*, as well as of many other texts on individuation, in my view is, the understanding of the term '*entitas*'. The thesis defended by the young Leibniz is that individuals are individual by their *entitas*. The term '*entitas*' occurs in the *Disputatio* about sixteen times. The two following remarks can be made on the basis of an examination of the various occurrences of the term.

First, '*entitas*' occurs in the grammatical construction '*entitas* of'; it appears that for any individual I*x*, there is a *y* such that *y* is an *entitas* of *x*, and everything indicates that there is at most one *y* for each *x;* that is, we may talk of "*the entitas*" of an individual. A second interesting feature of *entitas* is that somehow it has parts; it is possible to consider the whole (*tota*) *entitas* or just part of it.

I will not consider here other, less prominent features of *entitas* in the *Disputatio*. Just one of the two mentioned characteristics, namely, that *enti-*

tas is *of* something (whether of something *else*) or not is apparently not said in our text) is sufficient to reveal a contrast with our contemporary use of 'entity', as described in the following passage from Russell:

> Whatever may be an object of thought, or may occur in any true or false proposition, or can counted as one, I call a term. This, then, is the widest work in the philosophical vocabulary. I shall use as synonymous with it the words unit, individual and entity. The first two emphasize the fact that every term is one, while the third is derived from the fact that every term has being, i.e. *is* in some sense. A man, a moment, a number, a class, a relation, a chimaera, or anything else that can be mentioned, is sure to be a term; and to deny that such and such a thing is a term must always be false.[4]

From Russell we learn that each individual is an entity. Combining the old and the new senses we obtain the rather surprising phrase 'entity of an entity'. Leibniz's thesis becomes "the principle of individuation of each entity is its entity". The *Oxford English Dictionary* points out that 'entity' began with an abstract sense, "but, in accordance with the tendency of such words, it early acquired a concrete sense (= *ens*), which predominates in modern use".

A well-known translation of Descartes manages to render the old *entitas* by means of the new entity. The Latin text of Descartes is, "Per realitatem objectivam ideae intelligo entitatem rei representatae per ideam. . .";[5] the French version is, "Par realité obiective d'une idée, i'entens l'entité ou l'estre de la chose representée par l'idée . . ."[6] Haldane and Ross translate this as follows: "By the objective reality of an idea I mean that in respect of which the thing represented in the idea is an entity. . ."[7] This translational acrobacy may well be, in the final analysis, correct (in that the *entitas* of an entity is that in respect of which the thing is an entity, i.e., an *ens*), but it is not fair to offer to the modern reader of Descartes the result of the acrobacy without an account of how it was accomplished.

We are interested in determining the meaning of the old term '*entitas*', especially in connection with Leibniz. Is it satisfactory to say, with the just quoted acrobatic translators of Descartes, that '*entitas*' means that in respect of which a thing, an individual, is an *ens*, is a being? Correct as this is, it is not sufficient, because of the notorious ambiguity of 'being', '*ens*', and 'is'. The first guess of an educated reader, such as Russell, who in the preeceding quoted text suggests *existence* as what makes an entity entity, turns out to be wrong, at least with respect to the background of Leibniz, as well as with respect to Leibniz himself. Leibniz regards *existentia* as only a *part* of the *entitas tota*.[8] Suárez says: *entitas rei nihil aliud est quam realis essentia extra causas posita*.[9] (7, 1, 12). This text is quoted by Gracia, who however prefers to leave his general definition of '*entitas*' in scholastic thought as "the character or property of being", that is, rather uncommitted.[10]

An examination of other sources close to Leibniz confirms the "essential" emphasis on *entitas*. Eustachius a Sto. Paulo, author of the *Philosophia quadripartita*, the second-scholastic manual mentioned by Descartes[11] and known to Leibniz through the *Breviarium* of his teacher Scherzerus (sections 13, 19 of the *disputatio*) includes '*entitas*' in his index of terms for the fourth section, on metaphysics. *Entitas quid:* What is *entitas?* If then we turn to page 30 of the metaphysics, we see a very short *Quaestio de entitate*, with the following opening words: *entitas quasi entis quantitas, non se tenet ex parte existentiae . . . sed ex parte essentiae.*

Eustachius, in his *quaestio* on *entitas*, goes on to say that the entity of a thing is identical *realiter*, although not *formaliter*, to the essence of the thing. But even if the meaning of "the essence of a thing" were perfectly clear, this identity would be of little help, insofar as the "formal" difference between the entity of a thing and the essence of the thing remains greater than might be expected.

Eustachius devotes most of his *quaestio* to explaining what is *entitas formaliter sumpta;* that is, in what sense does entity differ from essence, in spite of being "really" the same. The *entitas* of a thing has a *quantitative* aspect that is not shared by the essence. This is anticipated by the previously quoted first words of the *quaestio: entitas [est] quasi entis quantitas.* Later on Eustachius gives a striking example, according to which a dense piece of matter has more *entitas* than a rarefied piece of the same size. The *entitas* of a thing is viewed as a whole, which has parts, *partes entitativae.*

Perhaps Eustachius exaggerated this quantification of the *entitas*. Scherzerus criticizes him in this respect: *Quid sit entitas? respondeo verbo: est entis essentia, seu formalis ratio entis ut sic. Stolida est autoris* [Eustachius] *etymologia: entitas est quasi entis quantitas.*[12] At any rate, Leibniz's *entitas* reflects the quantitative conception in that, as said, the *entitas* is a *whole* with *parts*. Leibniz's thesis is that *omne individuum sua tota entitate individuatur* and the various views on the principle of individuation are generated by him according to whether the *tota entitas* or just a part of it is regarded as the *principium*.

Moreover, Leibniz's strongest indirect defense of his thesis, as well as his best attack on the views that identify the principle of individuation of x with a "positive" part of the *entitas* of x (existence, haecceity), consists in pointing out the difficulties created by the "other" part of the entity, the *pars altera*, that is not the principle of individuation. These difficulties are mentioned in sections 6 and 23 of the *disputatio:*[13]

Posset quoque aliquis pro omnibus sententiis adversis ex eo fundamento quo a nobis differunt, respondere, fieri unum numero per suam Entitatem, sed non totam. Verum obstat, quod altera quoque pars intrinsece est una numero, et sequeretur, si principia interna unius et Entis differunt ut totum et pars, unum et Ens quoque ut totum et partem differre, imo Ens aliquid addere supra unum (section 6).

Si non sunt universalia ante mentis operationem, non datur compositio ante mentis operationem ex universali et individuante. Non est enim realis compositio, cujus non omnia membra sunt realia. Sed verum prius. E. Minor probo. Omne quod ante mentis operationem realiter ab altero ita differt, ut neutrum sit pars alterius vel ex toto vel ex parte, potest ab altero separari. Nam in adaequate differentibus neutrum altero ad suum esse indiget. E. potest separari per potentiam Dei absolutam, et solum pars a toto ita ut id permaneat, est simpliciter inseparabilis. Min. prosyll. probatur, daretur enim linea realiter neque recta neque curva, quod absurdissimum. v. Ruv. Logic. de universal. q.4. (section 23).

In the first passage, from section 6, Leibniz assumes that "the other part"—the part of the entity that is *not* the principle of individuation—is an individual; in the passage from section 23 he assumes that "the other part" is a universal. Under the tacit assumption that everything is either individual or universal, these two cases are exhaustive, and Leibniz shows that in either case something absurd follows.

I am not clear on how to reconstruct the deduction that leads to the *absurdum* in the text from section 6, and I find some difficulties in fully analyzing the analogous deduction in the passage from 23 (particularly the phrase "*ut neutrum sit pars alterius vel ex toto vel ex parte*"). The absurdities themselves, however, are clear: In the first case the predicate '*x is an ens*' would turn out to be definable as the conjunction of the predicate '*x is one*' *and* some other predicate, that is, *being* would be a particular species of a more general concept. In the second case universals would exist in reality.

From the two quoted passages we learn that anything falling short of the *whole* entity of *x*, any *proper part* of the entity of *x,* will not do as a principle of individuation of *x*. As a matter of fact, this is precisely the thesis defended by the young Leibniz: The principle of individuation of *x* is the whole *entitas* of *x*.

Our search for the (Leibnizian) meaning of '*entitas*' however has led us nowhere. We appear to be lost in a maze of unconvincing answers to that question: *Entitas* is existence, *entitas* is essence, *entitas* is a "quantified" essence, *entitas* is all of this together.

The question about the *entitas* of a thing is, in its form, identical to the typical mathematical question about the definition of a function: Given *x* as input, what is $f(x)$? Given Socrates, what is the *entitas* of Socrates?

I would like to conjecture that "the *entitas* of *x*" is, to continue with the mathematical terminology, just the identity function, namely, the *entitas* of *x* = *x*. For example, the *entitas* of Peter, and especially the emphatic "*tota entitas* of Peter*" is the same as Peter.

Needless to say, such a conjecture provides an unexciting finale to our quest for the meaning (in Leibniz) of '*entitas*'. It also forces us to rewrite Leibniz's thesis on the principle of individuation as a rather dull statement:

1.   The (whole) *entitas* of *x* = *x* [conjecture]
2.   The (whole) *entitas* of *x* = the principle of individuation of *x* [Leibniz' thesis]
3.   The principle of individuation of *x* = *x* [from 1 and 2].

Thesis 3 is not surprising relative to the Leibnizian text. We find the "self-individuation" terminology in, for example, section 12 of the *Disputatio:* the supporters of the view that makes negation the principle of individuation fail to see, according to Leibniz, that *natura possit individuare seipsam*. Indeed, I view this self-individuation language as a confirmation of the conjecture.

Perhaps another confirmation of the conjecture is found in the modern English concrete use of 'entity'—the use by *les logiciens anglais,* as Lalande's *Vocabulaire* puts it.[14] The fact that at a certain point 'the entity of Peter' designates the same object as 'Peter' may account for the modern usage, according to which Peter is an entity.

Once we accept thesis 3 as a representation of Leibniz's view, the issue arises whether such a view deserves being regarded as an answer to "What is the principle of individuation?" or rather should be considered as (a) leaving the issue unresolved or perhaps even as (b) amounting to the denial of the existence of a principle of individuation. The latter interpretation (in form (a) or (b)) becomes obligatory for anyone who wants the principle of individuation of *x* to be different from *x*. Historically, there is much plausibility to it.

DeWulf, in his history of medieval philosophy, repeatedly refers to this elimination of the problem of individuation implied by the type of thesis defended by the young Leibniz. Commenting on Ockham, he writes: "Every being is individual by all it is . . . the problem of individuation becomes void of meaning";[15] commenting on Durand: "the problem of individuation vanished".[16] Both DeWulf[17] and DeRaeymaeker[18] quote, in connection with Peter Aureolus, the impressive statement "*nihil est quaerere*": To ask for the principle of individuation is to ask for nothing. In the second scholastic period, referring to the kind of thesis that we find in Leibniz, Fonseca writes: "Itaque, etsi haec sententia primo aspectu quibusdam videtur facilima, est tamen omniun implicatissima, et quae, si tandem ad verum sensum reducatur, quaestionem insolutam relinquet."[19] In the third scholastic period, DeRaeymaeker observes: "Auctores plures individuum tota sua entitate individuari autumant; et proinde quaestio principii individuationis nulla esset."[20] Thus, when we read in Thomasius's Preface to Leibniz's *Disputatio:* "Se maxime placet hic Nominalium Entitas, quae simplicissima, sed eadem simul, uti judico, verissima decisione totum hunc nodum, et in eo spinosissimas tricas dissecat"[21] we may agree that the thesis defended by Leibniz is *simplicissima* (*verissima* is another matter), but in the very peculiar sense of proclaiming that the principle of individuation of any individual is the individual itself.

As a final remark, I would like to point out that Leibniz counts Suárez as a supporter of his thesis (even though this is not presented by Leibniz as an obvious fact but rather as something needing some argument, see section 4). This classification of Suárez has been endorsed by DeRaeymaeker[22] and is certainly encouraged by Suárez's own self-individuation language: *unamquanque entitatem per seipsam esse suae individuationis principium.*[23] Thus, the interpretation proposed in this chapter would transform Suárez's answer to his solemn question, *Quod tandem sit principium individuationis in omnibus substantiis creatis,*[24] into the dull assertion, *principium individuationis* of $x = x$. As said, this amounts to a nonanswer or even to a covert denial of the existence of a principle of individuation, under the reasonable assumption that the principle of individuation must be different from the individual. But such an interpretation of Suárez would be immediately objected to by, for example, Gracia (who argues that for Suárez there is a principle of individuation[25]) and by Suárez himself (who strongly replies to the previously quoted Fonseca's criticism[26]). The further discussion of this topic, involving not only Leibniz but also Suárez, will not be attempted here.

Notes

1. I wish to emphasize the convenience of this terminology: "first", "second", and "third" scholasticism, introduced by Carlo Giacon in the Preface to *Filosofia. Il pensiero cristiano* (Milan: Universitá Cattolica del Sacro Cuore, 1943). The first coincides with the medieval period and the third corresponds to the so-called neoscholastic phase. The term 'second' is especially useful rather than the misleading or poor 'late', 'later', 'postmedieval', etc. (for example, 'late' = 'spät' has been already assigned for the last *medieval* segment). The second scholasticism includes not only the relatively better known flowering in Catholic European areas, but also the protestant schools (cf. Max Wundt, *Die deutsche Schulmetaphyski des 17. Jahrhunderts,* Tübingen: J. C. B. Mohr, 1939) in Europe as well as the surprising production in the Iberian colonies of America.

2. L. DeRaeymaeker, *Metaphysica generalis ed. al.* (Louvain: E. Warney, 1935), p. 399; M. DeWulf, *Storia della Filosofia medievale* (Florence: Libreria Editrice Fiorentina, 1944), p. 143.

3. L. McCullough, "The Early Philosophy of Liebniz on Individuation: A Study of the "Disputatio metaphysica de principio individui" of 1663" (doctoral dissertation, University of Texas at Austin, 1976).

4. B. Russell, *The Principles of Mathematics*, 2nd ed. (London: Allen and Unwin, 1937), p. 47.

5. Descartes, *Oeuvres*, ed. C. Adam and P. Tannery (Paris: L. Cerf, 1897–1910), vol. 7, p. 161, in the short "geometrical" piece at the end of the *secundae responsiones*. Also *The Philosophical Works of Descartes*, trans. E. Haldane and G. Ross (London: Cambridge University Press, 1970).

6. *Ibid.*, vol. 9, p. 124.

7. *Ibid.*, vol. 2, p. 52.

8. W. G. Leibniz, *Disputatio metaphysica de principio individui*, section 3, in Sämmthiche Schriften und Briefe, VI, no. 1 (Darmstadt: Otto Reichl Verlag, 1930).

9. F. Suárez, *Disputationes metaphysicae* VII, 1, 12 (Salamanca, 1597).

10. Jorge J. E. Gracia, "Entity", in Glossary of *Suárez on Individuation* (Milwaukee: Marquette University Press, 1982).

11. Descartes, *Oeuvres, Correspondence*, iii, pp. 185, 196. For Eustachius a Sto. Paulo, see *Summa philosophiae quadripartita* (Coloniae, 1616).

12. *Breviarium Eustachianum, Metaphysica, quaestio* xxxv (Frankfurt-am-Main, 1665).

13. The passage I quote as belonging to section 6 belongs in the Gerhardt edition to a "double" section 7.

14. A. Lalande, *Vocabulaire . . . de la philosophie*, 5th ed. (Paris: Presses Universitaires de France, 1947).

15. DeWulf, *Storia*, p. 379.

16. *Ibid.*, p. 374.

17. *Ibid.*, p. 375.

18. DeRaeymaeker, *Metaphysica*, p. 398.

19. P. Fonseca, *Commentariorum . . . in libros Metaphysicorum Aristotelis tomi quatuor*, v, vi, iii, 2 (Coloniae, 1616).

20. DeRaeymaeker, *Metaphysica*, p. 397.

21. Preface to Leibniz's *Disputatio*.

22. DeRaeymaeker, *Metaphysica*, p. 399.

23. Suárez, *Disputatio* V, 6, 1.

24. *Ibid.*

25. Gracia, *Suárez on Individuation*, p. 137, n. 3.

26. Suárez, *Disputation* V, 6, 1: "Eam vero referens Fonseca . . . dicit . . . esse omnium implicatissimam, et quae si ad verum sensum reducatur, quaestionem insolutam relinquit. Mihi autem videtur omnium clarissima. . . ."

Epilogue:
Individuation in Scholasticism

Jorge J. E. Gracia

The complete and detailed history of the development of the problem of individuation in the scholasticism of the later Middle Ages and the Counter-Reformation still remains to be written. But the chapters contained in this volume should provide a provisional chart of the most important landmarks in that development, indicating the main directions it took and the basic positions adopted during the period.

The discussions of the problem of individuation in the period that concerns this volume looked back on three important sources that preceded them: the Latin texts of the early Middle Ages, and the Islamic and Jewish works produced before 1150. The works of Islamic and Jewish writers became available to the Latin West through the translations made primarily in Spain beginning around the middle of the twelfth century. As we saw in the introductory article dealing with the legacy of the early Middle Ages, by 1150 medieval authors in the Latin West had already covered considerable ground with respect to individuation. The original casual remarks about individuation that one finds in the very early centuries of the early Middle Ages became transformed in later centuries, and particularly in the twelfth, into rather sophisticated views, analyses, and criticisms. The criticisms were directed against mostly accidental views of individuation and against other aspects of what I have called "The Standard Theory of Individuality", and the views formulated leaned toward positions that considered individuality to be "primitive". The strong realistic tendencies common in the earlier centuries suffered a decline toward the end of the period, although no consensus on the proper understanding of individuality was ever achieved. Nevertheless, it is quite clear that authors were becoming more conscious of the distinction between the epistemic issue of discernibility and the ontological issue of individuation. Thus, the importance of the legacy of the early Middle Ages and its influence on the thought of the later Middle Ages should not be underestimated. True, the philosophical vocabulary of the early Middle Ages

lacked the richness of the scholastic vocabulary developed later, and the sophistication of later discussions was missing prior to 1150. But the impact of
the early period was nonetheless important, although it was generally more
negative than positive. By this I do not mean to say that it was regressive. On
the contrary, the influence of the early Middle Ages in the development of the
problem of individuation was quite salutary in many ways. What I mean to
say is that what the later Middle Ages inherited from the earlier period were
mostly negative conclusions concerning various approaches and solutions to
the problem of individuation: Accidents cannot individuate, universals do not
exist, the problem of individuation is not the problem of individual discernibility. These conclusions must have played an influential role in later discussions of individuation, because the overwhelming opinion of later
centuries is in accord with them.

A more positive source for the development of the problem of individuation in the later Middle Ages is found in texts produced by Islamic authors,
and to a lesser extent in the work of Jewish authors, whose writings became
available to the Latin West during the period of translations. In the work of
Avicenna (Ibn Sina) and Averroes (Ibn Rushd) in particular, and to some degree in that of Maimonides and Avicebron (Ibn Gabirol), twelfth century
scholastics found important conceptual tools related to the problem of individuation. In all four they found detailed discussions of the roles of matter
and form in the constitution of material substances and interpretations of
Aristotle's thought on the issues. But in the texts of Avicenna and Averroes
they found not only such conceptual tools, but also explicit discussions of
the problem of individuation, presentations of alternative solutions to it, and
defenses of the views that the authors themselves favored. With these tools
in hand, scholastics were ready to address the problem of individuation
by themselves.

Even a cursory look at the work of Avicenna and Averroes will reveal
how heavily Latin discussions of individuation relied on Islamic sources. The
view that substantial form is the principle of individuation can be easily
traced to the commentaries of Averroes on Aristotle, and the prominent position given to existence in individuation is clearly evident in texts of Avicenna. Indeed, until the very end of the period that concerns us, Averroes
was identified as the source of the first and Avicenna as the source of the
second. As we have seen in an earlier chapter in this volume, Suárez follows
in this tradition. But it was not just doctrines of individuation based on substantial form and existence that Latin authors found in Islamic sources. They
also found views concerning the role of matter, considered as prime matter or
as matter under certain determinations. Early medieval authors had not really
explored these possibilities. No one in the early Middle Ages seems to have
thought of substantial form, existence, or even matter as principles of indi-

viduation. As already stated, the views of authors from the period tended to fall into two camps—versions of the bundle view, often understood in accidental terms, and the view that understood individuals to be individual *per se*. Echoes of similar positions are found in texts of Islamic writers, but these texts do not seem to have had as much influence as others that spoke of form, existence, and matter.

In addition to Islamic authors, scholastics from the thirteenth century and later also found useful materials related to individuation in Jewish authors such as Maimonides and Avicebron. Of these, the work of Maimonides seems most directly related to individuation. In it scholastics found important comments about the bearing of individuation on such views as creation, the immortality of the soul, the problem of the various intellects involved in the process of cognition, and the resurrection of the body. Some of these issues had also been discussed by Islamic writers, but in the Latin West they had not been explored. Western discussions of individuation generally had occurred in the context of the problems of the Trinity, original sin, and universals.

The history of the development of scholastic views on individuation during the period that concerns us here may be roughly divided into five stages: a stage of absorption (1150–1225), a stage of consolidation (1225–1275), a stage of maturity (1275–1350), a stage of decline (1350–1450), and a stage of rebirth (1450–1650). Of these five stages in two there seems to have been relatively little development with respect to the problem of individuation. One of these is the stage of absorption. Several major figures during this time paid no attention to the problem of individuation, and those who did mentioned it only in passing. None of the important figures of the times, such as Domingo González (active ca. 1150–1200), Amaury of Béne (d. ca. 1207), William of Auvergne (ca. 1180–1249), or Robert Grosseteste (ca. 1168/75–1253), for example, seems to have dwelled on the details of the problem of individuation. Their concerns appear to be elsewhere, particularly with the explanation of the *fluxus entis* and the relation of the created world to the uncreated divine entity. The seeds of the thought of Avicebron, some Islamic thinkers, and such early medieval writers as John Eriugena may have played a role in their conceptual struggles and steered them away from individuation. Of course, most of them did make comments pertinent to the issue of individuation, and some, like William of Auvergne, for example, seem to have had something explicit to say about it, but in general their efforts were directed toward other, more pressing matters.

The other stage at which there seems to be limited interest in individuation is the hundred years that began with the middle of the fourteenth century. The reasons for the relative lack of interest in the problem of individuation at the time may be related to three factors. First was the black death, an epidemic of bubonic plague of enormous proportions that decimated the population of Western Europe. The ranks of the faculties at the various universities were devastated, and thus we find a general decrease in scholastic work during this period that naturally also affected discussions of individuation. Second, a renewed interest in science, political theory, and ethics detracted from metaphysics. Since the problem of individuation is fundamentally metaphysical, interest in it decreased and fewer occasions arose for its consideration. Third, the humanist movement promoted Platonism, a philosophy that pays very little attention to the individual and, therefore, contributed to the neglect of the problem of individuation.

The historical stages when discussions of individuation occur more frequently include the period that extends from the second quarter of the thirteenth to the middle of the fourteenth centuries (which I have divided into the periods of consolidation and maturity), and the period that comprises the Renaissance and the Counter-Reformation. These periods had a strong interest in metaphysics, although such an interest should not necessarily be interpreted to mean that it went unchallenged. The fourteenth century in fact contained strong antimetaphysical currents, but even the antimetaphysicians dealt with metaphysical issues. Thus, in spite of the adverse climate, there was an extraordinary surge of interest in the problem of individuation between 1275 and 1350.

The period from 1225 to 1275 witnessed the transformation of the problem of individuation from a marginal issue into an important issue: The issue in fact became "consolidated". Individuation attracted the attention of most major scholastic writers, such as Albert the Great, Roger Bacon, Bonaventure, and Thomas Aquinas. Indeed, Roger Bacon complained about the excessive attention given to this problem, which, according to him, had a rather simple solution.

In spite of all this attention, however, there are indications that individuation was still considered only a secondary philosophical problem at the time. In the first place, very few textually independent discussions of individuation were undertaken. For the most part no treatises or even separate questions and disputations devoted to the issue of individuation were written. Individuation was generally discussed in the context of other problems and was usually textually integrated with them. Its importance was always dependent on the importance of something else. During this period scholastics did not seem to have realized the philosophical weight that individuation has in and of itself. Indeed, most of the solutions given to the problem tried to explain away individuality or to analyze it in terms of other more fundamental notions. Thus, for example, Bonaventure explained individuality in terms of form and matter, and Thomas analyzed the individuality of corporeal substances in terms of matter and quantity. Finally, and in spite of Roger Bacon's complaint, it was not at all the case that everyone during the period discussed individuation. Yes, there were many discussions of it and even more references to it, but still many authors seem not to have dealt with it at all.

This situation changed drastically in the period that extended from 1275 to 1350. During those seventy-five years individuation established itself not only as an important philosophical problem, but also as a central one. There are three differences between an important problem and a central problem. The first is that the solution to a central problem is fundamental for the solution to other problems. The second is that a central problem functions as a seminal source for the development and creation of other hitherto unknown problems. And the third is that the central problem functions either as an umbrella under which other problems are discussed or is a problem whose solution and discussion come first in the logical organization of a philosophical system.[1]

There are clear indications that the problem of individuation became a central problem after 1275. In the first place, its treatment became textually independent of the treatment of other problems. Suddenly, self-contained treatises appeared that dealt with individuation, such as *De principio individuationis,* attributed to Thomas Aquinas, and Bedersi's *Treatise on Personal or Individual Forms.* Of course, individuation was not always discussed in separate treatises. In most cases it was treated, like most other issues of the Middle Ages, within large comprehensive works, such as commentaries and *summae.* But it is significant that, even within such works, individuation, contrary to previous practice, became a separate subject of discussion, so that textually separate parts (treatises, questions,) were devoted entirely to it within larger works. And this is not all, for individuation slowly established its logical precedence over other philosophical issues, even over issues to which it had been previously subservient. One of the most dramatic examples of this development occured in the *Opus oxoniense,* where Duns Scotus devoted an entire part of a distinction, constituting a rather complete and self-contained treatise, to individuation. In this same text he also offered his most important discussion of universality. If one remembers that it is precisely universality that originally provided some of the impetus for the discussion of individuation and furnished the locus for its discussion, one can see how far things had changed by the end of the thirteenth century and the beginning of the fourteenth. For Boethius, Gilbert of Poitiers, Abailard, and even some thirteenth century figures, individuation was something to be discussed in the context of, and after, universals. But for Scotus this pattern is turned around.

It is also important to note that every major and many minor figures of the later Middle Ages discussed individuation, a clear sign that individuation was regarded as one of the major philosophical topics. Even more significant, the three most important philosophical traditions of the later Middle Ages, Thomism, Scotism, and Ockhamism, developed explicit views on individuation that became the subject of continued controversy and discussion. Indeed, individuation became in many cases the measuring stick used by some authors to determine the degree of orthodoxy of the members of these traditions.

Finally, the most important of all of these developments is that individuality tended to be looked at as a primitive notion and not, as it had been regarded before, as a notion subject to further analysis. Thus, individuation became not only a fundamental problem, but individuality was to be regarded as a fundamental and primitive component of reality. The two major philosophical figures of this period seem to have agreed on this very point in spite of their fundamental disagreements on other matters. For Scotus, individuality, that is *haecceitas,* was not subject to further analysis; indeed it was not even subject to definition. And Ockham was not far from this position when he maintained that individual things are individual essentially, for, if individuality is a matter of essence, it cannot be subject to analysis. Thus Scotus explained individuation in terms of a primitive and unanalyzable principle, and Ockham indicated that individuality needs no explanation because everything is individual by itself. All of this led Suárez to point out that neither Scotus nor Ockham had addressed the problem of individuation, since in fact what they had done was to agree that things are individual and nothing more.[2] Regardless of whether Suárez was right or wrong in his assessment, it is clear that both Scotus and Ockham, and per force their orthodox followers, adopted a view of individuality that turns it into a fundamental notion in the explanation of reality and one that is not subject to further analysis.

In spite of the interruption to which scholastic discussions of individuation were subjected after the middle of the fourteenth century, they resumed with renewed vigor in the latter part of the fifteenth. There was a general resurgence of scholasticism during the period, first in Italy and later, during the Counter-Reformation, in Spain. This was a period of great commentaries on classical medieval texts, such as Thomas's *Summa theologiae,* and of great syntheses. The most important of the syntheses was the *Disputationes metaphysicae* by Francis Suárez. In this work the gains that had been made with respect to individuation in the fourteenth century were incorporated. Suárez devoted one of his disputations to individuality, which he interpreted as a fundamental kind of unity; indeed, he placed the disputation in question before the one devoted to formal unity, revealing the thrust of his thinking in favor of the individual. Scotus's displacement of the problem of universals by the problem of individuation was therefore complete.

An overview of the development of the problem of individuation in the Middle Ages shows a progressive understanding of the fundamental character of individuality and its centrality in metaphysics. The few lines devoted to individuation by Boethius at the beginning of the Middle Ages turned into treatises that, like Suárez's, expanded to more than 150 pages and dealt with the subject matter independent of other issues. This surprising development surely calls for an explanation. Unfortunately, I have none to give that would meet rigorous scholarly criteria, but I suspect that this development is a direct result of the introduction of Christianity in the West. The reason is simple: Christianity exalts the importance of the individual. Individual human beings have immortal souls and a supernatural end; God loves them and even subjected himself to excruciating pain and suffering in human form because he loves them. Moreover, God's love and attention is not restricted to human beings; it extends also to animals and inanimate nature. He created all things out of infinite love, endowing them with dignity and worth. And such a unique relationship between God and the world also gives rise to speculation concerning creation, personal immortality, the resurrection of the body, the nature of angels, original sin, and the Trinity—all doctrines that in one way or another raised questions concerning the individual and individuation. Indeed, the deep importance that Christianity bestows on the individual, whether human or not, explains the Franciscan phenomenon. The appearance of St. Francis would be unintelligible dislodged from its Christian background.

Nor can I find any bases for the emphasis on the individual in the Greek background of the philosophical thought of the Middle Ages that would undermine my suspicion. As already stated elsewhere in this book, the Greeks had very little concern for the individual in their philosophy. Their concern was reserved for the universal, for the principles that would ground morality and knowledge. The history of philosophy in the Middle Ages reveals that every time there was an infusion of Greek thought, there was a corresponding decrease in the discussion of individuality. Only after Greek thought had been digested and adapted to Christian needs in each instance do we find a resurgence of a concern for individuality. This occurred at the end of the twelfth century, during the period of translations, and also after the middle of the fourteenth, when the influence of Platonism was especially strong. In the particular case of individuation, Greek philosophy had just the reverse effect on medieval thought that Gilson credits it with having concerning philosophical developments.[3]

In short, it is primarily in Christian thought that one finds the extraordinary emphasis on the individual that makes intelligible the appearance of and the level of development reached by the problem of individuation in the Middle Ages. Therefore, it makes sense to say that, at least philosophically speaking, the individual was discovered by the Middle Ages and that such a discovery was largely due to the extraordinary influence of Christian doctrine on the thought of the period.

Notes

1. I have discussed these differences at greater length in "The Centrality of the Individual in the Philosophy of the Fourteenth Century", *History of Philosophy Quarterly* 8, no. 3 (1991): 235–251. For a discussion of the theory of the development of philosophical ideas that supports this historical analysis, see my *Philosophy and Its History: Issues in Philosophical Historiography* (Albany: State University of New York Press, 1992), ch. 6.

2. See Suárez, Disp. IV, s. 2, 7; and Woosuk Park, "Common Nature and *Haecceitas*", *Franziskanische Studien* 71 (1989): 188–192.

3. E. Gilson, *History of Christian Philosophy in the Middle Ages* (New York: Random House, 1955), p. 540.

BIBLIOGRAPHY

This bibliography includes only works to which reference has been made in chapters of this volume.

Abailard, Peter. *Incipient Glossae secundum magistrum Abaelardum super Porphyrium* and *Logica nostrorum petitioni sociorum*, in *Beiträge zur Geschichte der Philosophie und Theologie des Mittelalters*, vol. 21, Parts 1–3 and 4 (1919–1927 and 1933).

———. *De generibus et speciebus*, ed. V. Cousin. Paris, 1836.

Adams, Marilyn McCord. "Ockham on Identity and Distinction." *Franciscan Studies* 36 (1976): 5–74.

———. "Universals in the Early Fourteenth Century." In *The Cambridge History of Later Medieval Philosophy,* ed. Norman Kretzmann, Anthony Kenny, and Jan Pinborg, eds. pp. 411–439 Cambridge: Cambridge University Press, 1982.

———. *William Ockham,* 2 vols. Notre Dame, IN: University of Notre Dame Press, 1987.

Aegidius Romanus. *See* Giles of Rome.

Albert the Great. *Opera,* ed. Petrus Jammay. Lyon: Claudius Prost, 1651.

———. *Opera omnia,* ed. A. Borgnet. Paris: Vivès, 1890.

———. *Opera omnia,* ed. Institutum Alberti Magni Coloniense. Münster im Westphalia: Aschendorff, 1951 ff.

Alexander of Aphrodisias (pseudo). *In Aristotelis Metaphysica commentaria,* ed. M. Hayduck. Berlin: G. Reimer, 1891.

Alfarabi. *Kitāb Al-Ḥurūf [Book of Letters],* ed. Muhsin Mahdī. Beirut: Université Saint-Joseph, 1969.

Allaire, Edwin B. "Bare Particulars". *Philosophical Studies* 14 (1963): 1–7.

Allen, Elliott B. "Hervaeus Natalis: An Early 'Thomist' on the Notion of Being". *Mediaeval Studies* 22 (1960): 1–14.

Altmann, A. "Ibn-Bajja on Man's Ultimate Felicity". In *H. A. Wolfson Jubilee Volume,* ed. S. Lieberman, pp. 47–87. Jerusalem: American Academy for Jewish Research, 1963.

Anawati, M. M. "St. Thomas et la Métaphysique d'Avicenne". In *St. Thomas Aquinas*, vol. 1, ed. E. Gilson, pp. 449–465. Toronto: Pontifical Institute of Mediaeval Studies, 1974.

Anonymous. *Trois commentaires anonymes sur le Traité de l'âme d'Aristote*, ed. M. Giele, F. Van Steenberghen, and B. C. Bazán. Louvain and Paris: Publications Universitaires, 1971.

Anscombe, G. E. M. "The Principle of Individuation". *Berkeley and Modern Problems, Proceedings of the Aristotelian Society*, suppl. vol. 27 (1953): 83–96.

Antoninus Andreas. *Expositio textuali librorum Metaphysicorum*. In *Joannis Duns Scoti Opera omnia*. Paris: Vivès, 1891–1895.

Aristotle. *Aristotelis opera cum Averrois commentariis*. Venice, 1562–1574.

———. *Aristoteles graece, ex recensione Immanuelis Bekkeri*. Berlin: Academia Regia Borussica, 1831.

———. *The Complete Works*, ed. Jonathan Barnes. Princeton, NJ: Princeton University Press, 1984.

Armstrong, D. M. *Universals and Scientific Realism*, 2 vols. Cambridge: Cambridge University Press, 1978.

Arway, R. "A Half Century of Research on Godfrey of Fontaines". *The New Scholasticism* 36 (1962): 192–218.

Assenmacher, S. *Die Geschichte des Individuationsprinzips in der Scholastik*. Leipzig: Verlag von Felix Meiner, 1926.

Averroes. *Aristotelis opera cum Averrois commentariis*. Venice, 1562–1574.

———. *Epitome in librum Metaphysicae Aristotelis, Aristotelis opera cum Averrois commentariis*, vol. 8. Venice, 1562–1574; rep. Frankfurt-am-Main: Minerva, 1962. Arabic text, ed. C. Rodriguez. Madrid, 1919.

———. *In Aristotelis libros Metaphysicorum commentarius, Aristotelis opera cum Averrois commentariis*, vol. 8. Venice, 1562–1574; rep. Frankfurt-am-Main: Minerva, 1962. Arabic text, ed. M. Bouyges. Beirut: Inprimerie Catholique, 1938 ff. (*In Met.*)

———. *Commentarium magnum in Aristotelis De anima libros*, ed. F. Stuart Crawford. Cambridge, MA: Mediaeval Academy of America, 1953.

———. *De substantia orbis*, trans. A. Hyman. In *Philosophy in the Middle Ages*, ed. A. Hyman and J. Walsh, 2nd ed. Indianapolis: Hackett, 1983.

Avicenna. *Logica*. In *Opera philosophica*. Venice, 1508; rep. Frankfurt-am-Main: Minerva, 1961.

————. *Metaphysica*. In *Opera philosophica*. Venice, 1508; rep. Frankfurt-am-Main: Minerva, 1961.

————. *Sufficientia*. In *Opera philosophica*. Venice, 1508; rep. Frankfurt-am-Main: Minerva, 1961.

————. *Al-Najāt*, ed. M. Kurdī. Cairo: Government Press, 1938.

————. *Al-Ishārāl wa'l Tanbīhāt*, ed. S. Dunya. Cairo: Government Press, 1947.

————. *Al-Madkhal*, ed. I. Madkhour, *et al*. Cairo: Government Press, 1952.

————. *Al-Maqūlāt*. Cairo: Government Press, 1959.

————. *Ilāhīyyāt*, ed. Anawati, *et al*. Cairo: Government Press, 1960.

————. *The "Metaphysica" of Avicenna*, trans. P. Morewedge. New York: Columbia University Press, 1973.

————. *Liber de philosophia prima sive scientia, divina*, ed. S. Van Riet. Louvain: E. Peeters, 1980.

Ayer, A. J. "The Identity of Indiscernibles". In *Philosophical Essays*, pp. 26–35. London: Macmillan and Company, 1954.

————. "Individuals". In *Philosophical Essays*, pp. 1–25. London: Macmillan and Company, 1954.

Bäck, Allan. "Avicenna on Existence". *Journal of the History of Philosophy* 25 (1987): 351–367.

————. *On Reduplication*. Munich: Philosophia Verlag, forthcoming.

Bacon, Roger. *Fr. Rogei Bacon opera inedita (Rerum Britannicarum Medii Aevi Scriptores*. London, 1859.

————. *Opera hactenus inedita Rogeri Baconi*, fasc. 2 *Liber primus Communium naturalium Fratris Rogeri*, ed. Robert Steele. Oxford: Clarendon Press, 1905[?].

————. *Opera hactenus inedita Rogeri Baconi*, fasc. 10, ed. Robert Steele. Oxford: Clarendon Press, 1930.

————. *Opera hactenus inedita Rogeri Baconi*, fasc. 11, ed. Robert Steele. Oxford: Clarendon Press, 1932.

Baeumker, Clemens. "Roger Bacons Naturphilosophie, in besondere seine lehre von Materie und Form". *Franziskanische Studien* 3 (1916): 1–20.

Balić, C. "Henricus de Harcley et Ioannes Duns Scotus". In *Mélanges offerts à Étienne Gilson*, pp. 93–121, 701–702. Etudes de Philosophie Médiévale, new series. Toronto and Paris: The Pontifical Institute of Mediaeval Studies and J. Vrin, 1959.

Bärthlein, Karl. *Die Transzendentalienlehre der alten Ontologie.* Berlin: De Gruyter, 1972.

Baudry, Leon. "Les Rapports de Guillaume d'Occam et de Walter Burleigh". *Archives d'Histoire Doctrinale et Litteraire du Moyen Âge* 9 (1934): 157–175.

Bazán, Bernardo. *Trois commentaires anonymes sur le Traité de l'âme d'Aristote.* Louvain and Paris, 1971.

Beckmann, Jan P., ed. *Ockham-Biblographie, 1900–1990.* Hamburg: Felix Meiner, 1992.

Bedersi, J. *A Treatise upon Personal or Individual Forms,* fol. 66a–93b. Paris: Bibliothèque Nationale Man. 984 Heb.

————. *Sefer Behinat Olam.* First printed in Mantua, before 1480.

————. *The Letter of Apology.* In *She'elot uTchuvot . . . Rabbenu Shelomo ben Adret* (Hanover, 1610), 65d–67a (416–418).

Bergmann, Gustav. *Logic and Reality.* Madison: University of Wisconsin Press, 1964.

————. *Realism: A Critique of Brentano and Meinong.* Madison: University of Wisconsin Press, 1967.

Bigi, C. "La struttura dell'essere secondo s. Bonaventura". *Collectanea Franciscana* 32 (1962): 209–229.

Bittremieux, J. "Distinctio inter essentiam et esse apud s. Bonaventuram". *Ephemerides Theologicae Lovanienses* 14 (1937): 302–307.

Black, Max. "The Identity of Indiscernibles" *Mind* 61 (1952): 153–164.

Bobik, J. "La doctrine de saint Thomas sur l'individuation des substances corporelles". *Revue Philosophique de Louvain* 51 (1953): 5–41.

————. "Dimensions in the Individuation of Bodily Substance". *Philosophical Studies* (Maynooth) 4 (1954): 66–79.

————. "The 'Materia Signata' of Cajetan". *The New Scholasticism* 30 (1956): 127–153.

Boehner, Philotheus. "The Realistic Conceptualism of William Ockham". *Traditio* 4 (1946): 307–335; rep. in his *Collected Articles on Ockham,* ed. Eligius M. Buytaert, pp. 156–174. St. Bonaventure, NY: Franciscan Institute, 1958.

Boethius. *In Categorias Aristotelis libri quatuor.* In *Patrologiae cursus completus. Series latina,* vol. 64. ed. J. P. Migne. Paris: J. P. Migne, 1891.

————. *In librum Aristotelis De interpretatione.* In *Patrologiae cursus completus. Series latina,* vol. 64, Ed. J. P. Migne. Paris: J. P. Migne, 1891.

————. *In Isagogen Porphyrii commenta.* In *Corpus scriptorum ecclesiasticorum latinorum,* vol. 48, ed. Samuel Brandt. Vienna: Tempsky, 1906; rep. New York, Johnson, 1966.

————. *The Theological Tractates and the Consolation of Philosophy,* ed. and trans. H. F. Stewart and E. K. Rand, rev. S. J. Tester. Loeb Classical Library Series, 2nd printing. Cambridge, MA, and London: Harvard University Press and Heinemann, 1978.

Boetius of Dacia. *Quaestiones super librum Topicorum,* ed. N. G. Green-Pedersen and J. Pinborg. Copenhagen: Librarium G. E. C. Gad, 1976.

Bonaventure. *Opera omnia,* 10 vols. Edita studio et cura pp. Collegii S. Bonaventurae. Florence, Ad Claras Aquas (Quaracchi): Ex Typographia Collegii S. Bonaventurae, 1882–1902.

————. *Collationes in Hexaëmeron et Bonaventuriana quaedam selecta,* ad fidem codicum manuscriptorum ed. F. M. Delorme. Bibliotheca Franciscana Scholastica Medii Aevii, vol. 7. Florence, Ad Claras Aquas (Quaracchi): Ex Typographia Colegii S. Bonaventurae, 1934.

Booth, Edward. *Aristotelian Aporetic Ontology in Islamic and Christian Thinkers.* Cambridge: Cambridge University Press, 1983.

Bridges, John Henry. *The Opus maius of Roger Bacon,* 2 vols. Oxford and London: Clarendon Press, 1897. London and Edinbourgh: Williams & Northgate, 1900; rep. Frankfurt-am-Main: Minerva, 1964.

Brown, Stephen F. "Walter Burleigh's Treatise *De suppositionibus* and Its Influence on William of Ockham". *Franciscan Studies* 32 (1972): 15–64.

————. "A Modern Prologue to Ockham's Natural Philosophy". *Miscellanea Mediaevalia,* 13, no. 1 (1981): 107–129.

Buridan, Jean. *Quaestiones subtilissimae super octo Physicorum libros Aristotelis.* Paris, 1509; rep. as *Johannes Buridanus: Kommentar zür Aristotelischen Physik.* Frankfurt-am-Main: Minerva, 1964.

————. *Quaestiones in Metaphysicam Aristotelis.* Paris, 1518; rep. as *Johannes Buridanus: Kommentar zür Aristotelischen Metaphysik.* Frankfurt-am-Main: Minerva, 1964.

————. *Quaestiones in De caelo et mundo libros Aristotelis,* ed. Ernest A. Moody. Cambridge, MA: Mediaeval Academy of America, 1942.

————. *Tractatus de suppositionibus* (the fourth treatise of the unedited *Summulae de dialectica*), ed. Maria Elena Reina, in "Giovanni Buridano: 'Tractatus de suppositionibus' ". *Revista critica di storia della filosofia* 14 (1959): 175–208 and 323–352. Trans. inp. King, *John Buridan's Logic* (Dordrecht: D. Reidel, 1985).

————. *Tractatus de consequentiis,* ed. Hubert Hubien in "Philosophes médiévaux", vol. 16. Louvain: Université de Louvain, 1976. Trans. in King, *John Buridan's Logic* (Dordrecht: D. Reidel, 1985).

————. *Sophismata* (sometimes considered the ninth treatise of the unedited *Summulae de dialectica*), ed. T. K. Scott, in *Grammatica speculativa,* vol. 1. Stuttgart and Bad Cannstatt: Fromann-Holzboog, 1977. Complete trans. in T. K. Scott, John Buridan: Sophisms on Meaning and Truth (New York: Appleton-Century-Crofts, 1966); partial trans. in G. E. Hughes, *John Buridan on Self-Reference* (Cambridge: Cambridge University Press, 1982).

————. *Quaestiones in Praedicamenta,* ed. Johannes Schneider. Munich: Verlag der Bayerischen Akademie der Wissenschaften, 1983.

————. "Quaestiones in De anima secundum tertiam lecturam." Unpublished partial ed. and trans. by J. A. Zupko (Book III, q. 8 and q. 10).

Cajetan. *In De esse et essentia D. Thomae Aquinatis commentaria,* ed. P. M. H. Laurent. Turin: Marietti, 1934.

————. *Commentaria in Summa theologiae.* In *S. Thomae Aquinatis Opera omnia,* iussu Leonis XIII edita, vols. 4 and 5. Rome: Ex Typographia Polyglotta, 1882–1948.

————. *Commentary on Thomas' 'On Being and Essence',* trans. L. H. Kendzierski and F. Wade. Milwaukee, WI: Marquette University Press, 1964.

Callus, D. "The Origins of the Problem of the Unity of Form". *Thomist* 24 (1961): 257–285.

Carré, M. H. *Realists and Nominalists.* London: Oxford University Press, 1946.

Castañeda, Héctor-Neri. "Individuation and Non-Identity". *American Philosophical Quarterly* 12 (1975): 131–140.

Catto, J. I., ed. *The Early Oxford Schools,* in *The History of the University of Oxford,* vol. 1, general ed. T. H. Aston. Oxford: Clarendon Press, 1984.

Chappell, V. C. "Particulars Re-clothed". *Philosophical Studies* 15 (1964): 60–64.

Charlton, W. "Aristotle and the Principle of Individuation". *Phronesis* 17 (1972): 239–249.

Chenu, M. D. *Introduction à l'etude de saint Thomas D'Aquin.* Montreal: Institut d'Etudes Medievales, 1950.

Chisaka, Yasuo. "St. Thomas Aquinas et Avicenne" In *Thomas D'Aquino nella Storia del Pensiero,* vol. 1. Naples: Edizioni Domenicane Italiane, 1974.

Chrysogone du Saint-Sacrement. "Maître Jean Baconthorp. Les sources, la doctrine, les disciples". *Revue Néoscolastique de Philosophie* 34 (1932): 341–365.

Cicero. *De natura deorum*. In A. J. Kleywegt, *Ciceros Arbeitsweise im zweiten und dritten Buch der Schrift "De natura deorum"*. Groningen: Wolters, 1961.

Copleston, Frederick. "Ockham to Suárez". In *A History of Philosophy*, vol. 3. Westminster, MD: The Newman Press, 1963.

———. *A History of Medieval Philosophy*. New York: Harper and Row, 1972.

Crowley, Theodore. *Roger Bacon: The Problem of the Soul in His Philosophical Commentaries*. Louvain and Dublin: Editions de l'Institut Supérieur de Philosophie and James Duffy & Co., 1950.

———. "Roger Bacon: The Problem of Universals in His Philosophical Commentaries", *Bulletin of the John Ryland's Library* 34 (1951–52): 264–275.

Cunningham, F. A. "Richard of Middleton, O.F.M., on *esse* and Essence". *Franciscan Studies* 30 (1970): 49–76.

Da Altari, C. "Individuo e principio di individuazione in S. Bonaventura". *Studi Francescani* 58 (1961): 264–286.

Dales, Richard C. "Henricus de Harclay. Quaestio 'Utrum mundus potuit fuisse ab eterno' ". *Archives d'Histoire Doctrinale et Littéraire du Moyen Âge* 50 (1983): 223–255.

———. "Henry of Harclay and the Infinite". *Journal of the History of Ideas* 45 (1984): 295–301.

De Corte, M. *La doctrine de l'intelligence chez Aristote*. Paris: J. Vrin, 1934.

Deely, John N. *Tractatus de signis; The Semiotic of John Poinsot*. Berkeley: University of California Press, 1985.

Degl'Innocenti, Umberto. "Il pensiero di San Tommaso sul principio d'individuazione". *Divus Thomas* (Piacenza) 45 (1942): 35–81.

———. "Animadversiones in Caietani doctrinam de corporum individuatione". *Divus Thomas* (Piacenza) (1948): 19–45.

———. "Del Gaetano e del principio d'individuazione". *Divus Thomas* (Piacenza) (1949): 202–208.

———. "Il principio d'individuazione dei corpi e Giovanni di S. Tommaso". *Aquinas* 12 (1969): 59–99.

De Guimarēs, A. "Hervé Noël (d. 1323), Étude Biographique". *Archivum Fratrum Praedicatorum* 8 (1938): 5–81.

De Lubac, H. *Supernaturel*. Paris: Aubier, 1945.

De Mercin, L. "Notes sur le problème de l'être selon saint Bonaventure". *Études Franciscaines* new series, 11 (1961): 2–16.

Denifle, H., ed. *Chartularium Universitatis Parisiensis,* vol. 1. Paris: Delalain, 1889.

De Raeymaeker, L. *Metaphysica generalis,* rev. ed. Louvain: E. Warney, 1935.

De Rijk, L. M. "On Buridan's Doctrine of Connotation". In *The Logic of John Buridan,* ed. Jan Pinborg, pp. 91–100. Copenhagen: Museum Tusculanum, 1976.

Descartes, R. *Oeuvres,* ed. Charles Adam and Paul Tannery. Paris: L. Cerf, 1897–1910.

————. *The Philosophical Works of Descartes,* trans. E. Haldane and G. Ross. London: Cambridge University Press, 1970.

De Vos, A. F. "L'aristotélisme de Suárez et sa théorie de l'individuation", in *Actas. Congreso Internacional de Filosofía, Barcelona, 1948,* vol. 3. pp. 505–514. Madrid: Instituto Luis Vives de Filosofía, 1949.

De Wulf, M. *Un théologien-philosophe du XIIIe siècle. Étude sur la vie, les oeuvres et l'influence de Godefroid de Fontaines.* Brussels: Hayez, 1904.

————. *A History of Medieval Philosophy,* trans. E. Messinger. New York: Longmans, Green, 1926.

————. *Histoire de la philosophie médiévale,* 6th ed. Louvain: Institut Supérieur de Philosophie, 1934–47.

————. *Storia della filosofia medievale,* Italian trans. Florence: Libreria Editrice Fiorentina, 1944.

Di S. Brocardo, N. "Il profilo storico di Giovanni Baconthorp". *Ephemerides carmeliticae* 2 (1948): 431–543.

Dod, Bernard. "Aristoteles Latinus". in *The Cambridge History of Later Medieval Philosophy,* ed. N. Kretzmann et al, pp. 45–79. Cambridge: Cambridge University Press, 1982.

Duhem, P. *Études sur Léonard de Vinci. Ceux qu'il a lus et ceux qui l'ont lu,* 3 vols. Paris: Hermann, 1906–1913.

Durand of Saint Pourçain. *Durandi a Sancto Porciano . . . Petri Lombardi Sententias theologicas commentariorum libri IV.* Venice, 1571.

Durandellus. *Evidentiae contra Durandum.* Vatican Library, MS Ross, 161.

Emden, A. B. *A Biographical Register of the University of Oxford to A.D. 1500,* 3 vols. Oxford: Clarendon Press, 1957–1959.

Etzwiler, J. P. "Baconthorpe and Latin Averroism". *Carmelus* 18 (1971): 235–292.

————. "John Baconthorpe, 'Prince of the Averroists'? ". *Franciscan Studies* 36 (1976): 148–176.

Eustachius a Sto. Paulo. *Summa philosophiae quadripartita*. Coloniae, 1616.

Fakhry, Majid. *A History of Islamic Philosophy*. New York: Columbia University Press, 1970, 1983.

Faral, E. "Jean Buridan: Maître dès arts de l'Université de Paris". In *Histoire Littéraire de France*, vol. 28 part II, pp. 462–605. Paris: Imprimerie Nationale, 1949.

Feldman, Seymour. "Gersonides' Proofs for the Creation of the Universe". *Proceedings of the American Academy for Jewish Research* (1967): 113–137.

———. "Platonic Themes in Gersonides' Cosmology". In *Salo Whitmayer Baron Jubilee Volume*, pp. 383–405. Jerusalem: American Academy for Jewish Research, 1975.

Ferrara, Francis Sylvester. *Commentaria in libros quatuor Contra gentiles s. Thomae de Aquino*, ed. I. Sestili. Rome: Orphanotrophii a. S. Hieronymo Aemiliani, 1898.

Fichter, J. H. *Man of Spain: Francis Suárez*. New York: Macmillan, 1940.

Fonseca, P. *Commentariorum . . . in libros Metaphysicorum Aristotelis tomi quatuor*. Coloniae, 1616.

Freudenthal, G. "Cosmogonie et Physique chez Gersonide". *Revue des Études Juives* 65 (1986): 295–314.

Gäl, Gedeon. "Gualteri de Chatton et Guillelmi de Ockham controversia de natura conceptus universalis". *Franciscan Studies,* new series, 27 (1967): 191–212.

Gauthier, Léon. *Ibn Rochd*. Paris: Presses Universitaires de France, 1948.

Gazzana, A. "La *materia signata* di s. Tommaso secondo le diversa interpretazione del Gaetano o del Ferrarese". *Gregorianum* 24 (1943): 78–85.

Ghisalberti, A. *Giovanni Buridano: dalla metafisica alla fisica*. Milan: Vita e Pensiero,1975.

Giacon, Carlo. *Il pensiero cristiano con particolare riguardo alla scolastica medievale,* Guide Bibliografiche. Milan: Universitá Cattolica del Sacro Cuore. Milan: Societá Editrice "Vita e Pensiero", 1943.

Gilbert of Poitiers. *The Commentaries on Boethius*, ed. N. Häring. Toronto: Pontifical Institute of Mediaeval Studies, 1966.

Giles of Rome (Egidio Colonna). *Quodlibeta*. Venice, 1503.

———. *De gradibus formarum*. Venice, 1502. Ed. J. S. MaKaay. "Der Traktat des Aegidius Romanus über die Einzigkeit der substantiellen Form." Ph.D. dissertation. Würzburg: St. Rita-Druckere, 1924.

———. *Sententias*. Venice, 1521.

————. *Aegidii Romani Theoremata de esse et essentia,* ed. Edgar Hocedez, S. J., in Section Philosophique 12. Louvain: Museum Lessianum, 1930.

————. *Theorems on Existence and Essence,* trans. Michael V. Murray. Milwaukee, WI: Marquette University Press, 1952.

————. *Quodlibeta.* Louvain, 1646; rep. Frankfurt-am-Main: Minerva, 1966.

Gilson, Étienne. "The Road to Scepticism". In *The Unity of Philosophical Experience,* pp. 61–91. New York: Scribner's, 1937.

————. *Jean Duns Scot.* Paris: J. Vrin, 1952.

————. *History of Christian Philosophy in the Middle Ages.* New York: Random House, 1955.

————. *Le thomisme,* 6th ed. Paris: J. Vrin, 1965.

————. and T. Langan. *Modern Philosophy: Descartes to Kant.* New York: Random House, 1963.

Glorieux, P. *Répertoire des maîtres en théologie de Paris au XIII siècle,* 2 vols. Paris: J. Vrin, 1933.

————. *La littérature quodlibétique de 1260 à 1320,* 2 vols. Kain and Paris: Le Saulchoir and J. Vrin, 1925–1935.

————. *La faculté des arts et ses maîtres au XIIIe siècle.* Paris: J. Vrin, 1971.

Godfrey of Fontaines. *Les Quodlibet Cinq, Six, et Sept,* ed. by M. de Wulf and J. Hoffmans. Les Philosophes Belges, vol. 3. And *Quodlibet neuf,* vol. 4. Louvain: Institut Supérieur de Philosophie de l'Université, 1914.

Goichon, A. M. *La distinction de l'essence et de l'existence d'apres Ibn Sina.* Paris: Descleé de Bouwer, 1937.

————. *La philosophie d'Avicenne et son influence en Europe médiévale.* Delhi: Wotilal Banarsidass, 1969.

Goldfeld, Lea Naomi. *Moses Maimonides' Treatise on Resurrection: An Inquiry into Its Authenticity.* New York: Ktav Publishing Co., 1986.

Gómez Caffarena, José. *Ser participado y ser subsistente en la metafísica de Enrique de Gante.* Analecta Gregoriana, vol. 93. Series Facultates Philosophicae, sectio B, n. 8. Rome: Apud Aedes Universitatis Gregorianae, 1958.

Goodman, N. "A World of Individuals". In *The Problem of Universals,* ed. Charles Landesman, pp. 293–306. Notre Dame, IN: Notre Dame University Press, 1956.

Gracia, Jorge J. E. "The Convertibility of *unum* and *ens* according to Guido Terrena". *Franciscan Studies* 33 (1973): 143–170.

————. "Suárez's Criticism of the Thomistic Principle of Individuation". In *Atti. Congresso di S. Tommaso d'Aquino nel suo VII Centenario,* pp. 563–568. Rome, 1977.

————. "What the Individual Adds to the Common Nature According to Suárez". *New Scholasticism* 53 (1979): 221–233.

————. *Suárez on Individuation*. Milwaukee: Marquette University Press, 1982.

————. "Individuals as Instances". *Review of Metaphysics* 37 (1983): 39–59.

————. *Introduction to the Problem of Individuation in the Early Middle Ages*, 2nd rev. ed. Munich and Vienna: Philosophia Verlag 1988. First ed., 1984.

————. *Individuality: An Essay on the Foundations of Metaphysics*. Albany: State University of New York Press, 1988.

————. "The Centrality of the Individual in the Philosophy of the Fourteenth Century". *History of Philosophy Quarterly* 8, no. 3 (1991): 235–251.

————. *Philosophy and Its History: Issues in Philosophical Historiography*. Albany: State University of New York Press, 1992.

————. "The Transcendentals in the Middle Ages". *Topoi* 11, no. 2 (1992): 113–121.

————. "Suárez and the Doctrine of the Transcendentals". *Topoi* 11, 2 (1992): 121–134.

————. and Woosuk Park. "Llull y el principio de individuación", in *Studia Lullistica: Miscellanea in honorem Sebastiani Garcias Palou*, ed. Sebastià Trias Mercant, pp. 35–46. Palma de Mallorca: Maioricensis Schola Lullistica, 1989.

Gredt, Josef. *Elementa philosophiae aristotelico-thomisticae*, 7th ed. Freiburg: Herder, 1937.

Guillelmus Alvernus. *De universo*, in *Opera omnia*. Aureliae, 1674.

Gutiérrez, D. "De vita et scriptis Beati Jacobi de Viterbio", *Analecta Augustiniana* 16 (1937–1938), 216–224; 282–305; 258–381. Published with slight modification as *De B. Iacobi Viterbiensis O.E.S.A. vita, operibus et doctrina theologica*. Rome: Analecta Augustiniana, 1939.

Hackett, Jeremiah. "Practical Wisdom and Happiness in the Moral Philosophy of Roger Bacon". *Medioevo* 12 (1986): 55–109.

Halkin, A. S. "Yedaiah Bedersi's Apology". In *Jewish Medieval and Renaissance Studies*, ed. Alexander Altmann, pp. 165–184. Cambridge, MA: Harvard University Press, 1967.

Hamelin, O. *La théorie de l'intellect d'apres Aristote et ses commentateurs*. Paris: J. Vrin, 1953.

Henninger, Mark. "Peter Aureoli and William of Ockham on Relations". *Franciscan Studies* 45 (1985): 231–243.

————. "Aquinas on the Ontological Status of Relations". *Journal of the History of Philosophy* 25 (1987): 419–515.

————. *Relations: Medieval Theories 1250–1325.* Oxford: Clarendon Press, 1989.

Henry of Ghent. *Summa quaestionum ordinariarum,* 2 vols. Paris, 1520; rep. St. Bonaventure, NY: Franciscan Institute Press, 1953.

————. *Quodlibeta magistri Henrici Goethals a Gandavo doctoris solenis,* 2 vols. Paris, 1518; rep. Louvain: Bibliothèque S.J., 1961.

————. *Quodlibet II,* ed. R. Wielockx. Louvain: Leuven University Press, 1983.

Henry of Harclay. *In I Sententiarum.* Vatican Library lat. 13687, fols. 13v–97v; Casale Monferrato, Biblioteca del Seminario Vescovile b 2, fols. 1r–84r.

————. *Quaestiones ordinariae.* Vatican Library Borghese 171, fols. 1r–32v; Worcester, Cathedral Library F. 3, fols. 181v–215v; Assisi, Biblioteca Comunale 172, fols. 125r–131v, 133r–136r, 149r–153v.

————. "Question on the Univocity of Being", ed. Armand Maurer. *Mediaeval Studies* 16 (1954): 1–18.

————. "Questions on Immortality", ed. Armand Maurer. *Mediaeval Studies* 19 (1957): 79–107.

————. "Questions on the Divine Ideas", ed. Armand Maurer. *Mediaeval Studies* 23 (1961): 163–193.

————. "Quaestio de significato conceptus universalis", ed. Gedeon Gál. *Franciscan Studies* 31 (1971): 178–234.

————. "Disputed Question on the Plurality of Forms", ed. Armand Maurer, in *Essays in Honor of Anton Charles Pegis.* ed. J. Reginald O'Donnell. pp. 125–159. Toronto: Pontifical Institute of Mediaeval Studies, 1974.

————. "Questions on Divine Prescience and Predestination", ed. Mark G. Henninger. *Franciscan Studies* 40 (1980): 167–243.

————. "On the Formal Distinction in the Trinity", ed. Mark G. Henninger. *Franciscan Studies* 41 (1981): 250–335.

————. "Question on Relations", ed. Mark G. Henninger. *Mediaeval Studies* 49 (1987): 76–123.

Hervaeus Natalis. *Subtilissima Hervei Natalis britonis theologi acutissimi quodlibeta undecim.* Venice, 1513.

Hissette, R. *Enquête sur les 219 articles condamnés a Paris le 7 mars 1277.* Louvain: Publications Universitaires, 1977.

Hocedez, E. "Les 'Quaestiones disputatae' de Richard de Middleton". *Recherches de Sciences Religieuse* 6 (1916): 493–513.

————. *Richard de Middleton, sa vie, ses oeuvres, sa doctrine.* Louvain: Specilegium Sacrum Lovaniense, 1925.

——. "La théologie de Pierre d'Auvergne". *Gregorianum* 11 (1930): 526–52.

——. "La vie et les oeuvres de Pierre d'Auvergne". *Gregorianum* 14 (1933): 3–36.

——. "Une Question inédite de Pierre d'Auvergne sur l'individuation". *Revue Néoscolastique de Philosophie* 36 (1934): 355–386.

Hödl, L. "Die Quodlibeta minora des Herveus Natalis O.P. (d. 1323)". *Münchener Theologische Zeitschrift* 6 (1955): 215–229.

Hoeres, Walter. "Wesenheit und *Individuum* bei Suárez". *Scholastik* 37 (1962): 181–210.

Hughes, G. E. *John Buridan on Self-Reference* (ed. and trans. of *Sophismata* VIII). Cambridge: Cambridge University Press, 1982.

Ibn Gabirol, Solomon. *Mekor Hayyim [Fountain of Life]*. In S. Munk, "La Source de Vie", in *Mélanges de philosophie juive et arabe*. Paris: Librarie Universitaire, 1857; rep. 1955.

Ivry, Alfred. "Averroes on Intellection and Conjunction". *Journal of the American Oriental Society* 86 (1966): 76–85.

——. "Maimonides on Possibility". In *Mystics, Philosophers and Politicians*, ed. Jehuda Reinhartz *et al.*, pp. 77ff. Durham, NC: Duke University Press, 1982.

——. "Maimonides on Creation". In *Creation and the End of Days*, ed. Norbert Samuelson and David Novak, pp. 185–214. New York: University Press of America, 1986.

James of Viterbo. *Disputatio prima de quolibet*, ed. E. Ypma. Würzburg, 1968.

Jammer, Max. *Concepts of Space*, 2nd ed. Cambridge, MA: Harvard University Press, 1969.

Javellus, Chrysostom. *In omnibus Metaphysicae libros quaesita textualia*. Lugduni: Apud Gasparem a Portonariis, 1559.

John Baconthorpe, *Quaestiones in quatuor librum sententiarum et quodlibetales*, 2 vols. Cremona, 1618; rep. Farnborough: Gregg, 1969.

John Damascene. *De duabus in Christo voluntatibus*. In *Patrologiae cursus completus. Series graeca*, vol. 95, ed. M. Lequien. Paris: Migne, 1864.

——. *De fide orthodoxa*, ed. E. M. Buytaert. St. Bonaventure, NY: Franciscan Institute, 1955.

John Duns Scotus. *Opera omnia*, 26 vols. Paris: Ludovicum Vivès, 1891–1893.

——. *Opera omnia, studio et cura Commissionis Scotisticae (ad tidem codicum edita)* praeside P. Carolo Balić. Vatican City: Typis Polyglottis Vaticanis, 1950–1982.

————. *God and Creatures: The Quodlibetal Questions,* trans. with an Introduction, notes, and glossary by Felix Alluntis and Allan B. Wolter. Princeton, NJ: Princeton University Press, 1975.

John of Salisbury. *Metalogicon,* ed. Clemens C. Webb. Oxford: Clarendon Press, 1929.

John of St. Thomas. *Cursus theologicus.* Paris: Desclée, 1931–1946.

————. *Cursus philosophicus Thomisticus secundum exactam, veram, genuinam Aristotelis et Doctoris Angelici mentem,* ed. B. Reiser. Turin: Marietti, 1933.

————. *Outlines of Formal Logic,* trans. with an Introduction by Francis C. Wade. Milwaukee, WI: Marquette University Press, 1955.

Jung-Palczewska, E. "Le problème d'Averroîsme de Walter Burley dans son Commentaire sur la 'Physique' ". *Studia Mediewistyczne* 24 (1986): 101–109.

Kellner, Menachem. "R. Levi ben Gerson: A Bibliographical Essay", *Studies in Bibliography and Booklore* 12 (1979), 13–23.

King, P. *Jean Buridan's Logic* (trans. of the "Treatise on Supposition" and the *Tractatus de consequentiis*). Synthese Historical Library. Dordrecht: D. Reidel, 1985.

Klinger, I. *Das Prinzip der Individuation bei Thomas von Aquin.* Muñsterschwarzacher Studien, No. 2. Münsterschwarzach: Vier-Türme-Verlag, 1964.

Klubertanz, G. "*Esse* and *exsistere* in St. Bonaventure". *Mediaeval Studies* 8 (1946): 169–188.

Koch, Josef. *Durandus de S. Porciano O.P.: Forschungen zum Streit um Thomas von Aquin zu Beginn des 14. Jahrhunderts.* Beiträge zur Geschichte der Philosophie des Mittelalters 26 (1927).

————. *Kleine Schriften,* 2 vols. Storia e Letteratura, vols. 127–128. Rome: Edizioni di Storia e Letteratura, 1973.

Köhler, T. W. *Der Begriff der Einheit und ihr ontologisches Prinzip nach dem Sentenzenkommentar des Jakob von Metz O. P.* Rome: Herder, 1971.

Kraus, J. "Die Universalienlehre des Oxforder Kanzlers Heinrich von Harclay und ihre Mittelstellung zwischen skotistischem Realismus und ockhamistischem Nominalismus". *Divus Thomas* (Freiburg) 10 (1932): 36–58, 475–508; 11 (1933): 76–96, 288–314.

Krempel, A. *La doctrine de la relation chez saint Thomas.* Paris: J. Vrin, 1952.

Kretzmann, Norman. "Aristotle on Spoken Sound Significant by Convention". In *Ancient Logic and Its Modern Interpretations,* ed. John Corcoran, pp. 3–21. Synthese Historical Library, vol. 9. Dordrecht: D. Reidel, 1979.

————. *et al.*, eds. *The Cambridge History of Later Medieval Philosophy.* Cambridge: Cambridge University Press, 1982.

Kuksewicz, Zdzislaw. "The Problem of Walter Burley's Averroism". In *Studi sul XIV Secolo. In Memoriam di Anneliese Maier,* pp. 341–378. Storia e Letteratura, vol. 151. Rome: Edizioni di Storia e Letteratura, 1981.

————. "The Potential and the Agent Intellect". In *The Cambridge History of Later Medieval Philosophy,* ed. N. Kretzmann *et al.* Cambridge: Cambridge University Press, 1982.

Lalande, A. *Vocabulaire technique et critique de la philosophie,* 5th ed. Paris: Presses Universitaires de France, 1947.

Leff, Gordon. *William of Ockham: The Metamorphosis of Scholastic Discourse.* Manchester: Manchester University Press, 1975.

Leibniz, W. G. *Dissertatio de stilo philosophico Nizolii.* In *Opera philosophica,* ed. J. E. Erdmann. Berlin, 1840.

————. *Disputatio metaphysica de principio individui.* Samtliche Schriften und Briefe, vol. 4, part I, ed. Willy Kabitz. Darmstadt: Otto Reichl Verlag, 1930.

————. *Selections,* ed. P. P. Wiener. New York: Charles Scribner's Sons, 1951.

Levi ben Gershon (Gersonides). *Milhamot ha-Shem [Wars of the Lord].* Leipzig, 1866.

Levi ben Gershon. *The Wars of the Lord, Book I,* trans. by Seymour Feldman. Philadelphia: Jewish Publication Society of America, 1984.

Lewry, Osmund. "Boethian Logic in the Medieval West". In *Boethius: His Life, Thought and Influence,* ed. Margaret Gibson. Oxford: Basil Blackwell, 1981.

Lindberg, David C. *Roger Bacon's Philosophy of Nature: A Critical Edition, with English Translation, Introduction, and Notes, of De multiplicatione specierum and De speculis comburentibus.* Oxford: Clarendon Press, 1983.

Lloyd, A. C. "Aristotle's Principle of Individuation". *Mind* 79 (1970): 519–529.

Long, D. C. "Particulars and Their Qualities". *Philosophical Quarterly* 18 (1968): 193–206.

Lottin, O. *Psychologie et morale aux XIIe et XIIIe siècles.* Louvain: Abbaye de Mont Cesar, 1942–1960.

Loux, M. J., ed. *Universals and Particulars: Readings in Ontology,* 2nd ed. Notre Dame, IN: Notre Dame University Press, 1976.

————. *Substance and Attribute: A Study in Ontology.* Dordrecht and Boston: D. Reidel, 1978.

Lukasiewicz, J. "The Principle of Individuation". *Proceedings of the Aristotelian Society,* suppl. vol. 27 (1953): 69–82.

Macierowski, E. M. and R. F. Hassing. "John Philoponus on Aristotle's Definition of Nature: A Translation from the Greek with Notes", *Ancient Philosophy* 8 (Spring, 1988): 73–100.

Madkour, I. *L'Organon d'Aristote dans le monde Arabe.* Paris: J. Vrin, 1934.

Maier, Anneliese. "Ein Unbeachteter Averroist des 14. Jahrhuderts: Walter Burley". In *Medioevo e Rinascimiento,* Festschrift B. Nardi, pp. 477–499. Florence: Instituto de Filosofia della universitá di Roma, 1955.

Maierú, A, ed. *English Logic in Italy in the Fourteenth and Fifteenth Centuries.* Naples: Bibliopolis–Edizioni di Filosofía e Scienze, 1982.

Maimonides. *Ma'amar tehiyyat ha-meytim (Treatise on Resurrection,* ed. J. Finkel. New York, 1939.

———. *Makálah fitehiyyat ha-metim* [*Treatise on Resurrection*], ed. Joshua Finkel. New York: American Academy for Jewish Research, 1939. Trans. F. Rosner. New York: Ktav Publishing House, 1982.

———. *Moreh Nebukhim,* Modern Hebrew Edition, ed. E. Shemuel. Jerusalem, 1959.

———. *The Guide for the Perplexed,* trans. and ed. Shlomo Pines. Chicago: University of Chicago, 1963.

———. "Maimonides' Arabic Treatise on Logic", ed. Israel Efros. *Proceedings of the American Academy for Jewish Research* 34 (1966), supplementing a previous publication in *PAAJR* 8 (1938).

———. *Treatise on Resurrection,* trans. A. Halkin. New York: JPS, 1984.

Maloney, Thomas S. "The Extreme Realism of Roger Bacon". *The Review of Metaphysics* 38 (1985): 807–837.

———. *Three Treatments of Universals by Roger Bacon—A Translation with Introduction and Notes.* Binghamton, NY: Medieval and Renaissance Texts and Studies, 1989.

Mandonnet, P. *Des écrits de S. Thomas d'Aquin.* Fribourg, Switzerland, 1910.

Manekin, Charles. *The Logic of Gersonides.* Dordrect: Kluwer Academic Publ., 1992.

Marenbon, John. *From the Circle of Alcuin to the School of Auxerre.* Cambridge: Cambridge University Press, 1981.

Markowski, Mieczyslaw. "Die Anschauungen des Walter Burleigh über die Universalien". In *English Logic in Italy in the 14th and 15th Centuries,* ed. Alfonso Maierú, pp. 219–229. Naples: Bibliopolis-Edizioni di Filosofia e Scienze, 1982.

———. "Johannes Buridans Polemik gegen die Universalienlehre des Walter Burleigh", *Mediaevalia Philosophica Polonorum* 26 (1982), 7–17.

Martin, Conor. "Walter Burley". In *Oxford Studies Presented to Daniel Callus*, pp. 194–230. Oxford Historical Society, new series, 16. Oxford: Clarendon Press, 1964.

Martine, B. J. *Individuation and Individuality*. Albany: State University of New York Press, 1984.

Maurer, Armand. "St. Thomas and Henry of Harclay on Created Nature". In *La filosofia della natura nel medioevo: Atti del Terzo Congresso Internazionale di Filosofia Medievale*, pp. 542–549. Milan: Società Editrice "Vita e Pensiero", 1966.

———. "John Baconthorp". *New Catholic Encyclopedia*, vol. 7, pp. 1020–1030. New York: McGraw-Hill Book Company, 1967.

———. "Method in Ockham's Nominalism". *Monist* 61 (1978): 426–443.

———. "William of Ockham on Language and Reality", in *Miscellanea Mediaevalia: Sprache und Erkenntnis im Mittelalter*, 13.2, ed. A. Zimmermann, pp. 795–802. Berlin: Walter de Gruyter, 1981.

———. "Ockham's Razor and Chatton's Anti-Razor". *Mediaeval Studies* 46 (1984): 463–475.

———, trans. *St. Thomas Aquinas: Faith, Reason and Theology*. Toronto: Pontifical Institute of Mediaeval Studies, 1987.

McCullough, L. "The Early Philosophy of Leibniz on Individuation: A Study of the 'Disputatio metaphysica de principio individui' of 1663". Doctoral dissertation, The University of Texas at Austin, 1976.

McInerny, Ralph. "Albert on Universals". In *Albert the Great Commemorative Essays*, ed. F. Kovach and R. Shahan, pp. 3–18. Norman: University of Oklahoma Press, 1980.

Meiland, J. W. "Do Relations Individuate?" *Philosophical Studies* 17 (1966): 65–69.

Merlan, Philip. *Monopsychism, Mysticism, Metaconsciousness*. The Hague: Martinus Nijhoff, 1963.

Miller, Barry. " 'Exists' and Other Predicates". *The New Scholasticism* 53 (1979): 475–479.

———. "Existence and Natures". *The New Scholasticism* 56 (1982): 371–375.

Minges, Parthenius. *Ioannis Duns Scoti doctrina philosophica et theologica*. Ad Claras Aquas: Ex Typographia Collegii S. Bonaventurae, 1930.

Monahan, A. "Quaestiones in Metaphysicam Petri de Alvernia". In *Nine Mediaeval Thinkers: A Collection of Hitherto Unedited Texts*, ed. J. Reginald O'Donnell, pp. 145–181. Toronto: Pontifical Institute of Mediaeval Studies, 1955.

————. "Peter of Auvergne". *New Catholic Encyclopedia*, vol. 11, pp. 211–212. New York: McGraw-Hill Book Company, 1967.

Moody, Ernest A. *The Logic of William Ockham.* New York: Sheed & Ward, 1935.

Müller, J. -P. "Un cas d'éclectisme métaphysique: Jean de Paris (Quidort) O. P.". *Miscellanea Mediaevalia* (Berlin) 2 (1963): 651–660.

————. "Eine quästion über das Individuationsprinzip des Johannes von Paris O. P. (Quidort)". In *Virtus politica. Festgabe zum 75. Geburtstag von A. Hufnagel*, ed. J. Möller and H. Hohlenberger, pp. 335–356. Stuttgart and Bad Cannstadt: F. Frommann, 1974.

————, ed. *Le Correctorium corruptorii 'Circa' de Jean Quidort de Paris.* Rome: Herder, 1941.

Munk, A. "La Source de Vie", in *Mélanges de philosophie juive et arabe.* Paris, 1857; repr. 1955.

Murdoch, John E. "Henry of Harclay and the Infinite". In *Studi sul XIV secolo in memoria di Anneliese Maier*, ed. A. Maierù and A. Paravicini Bagliani. Storia e Letteratura, vol. 151. Rome: Edizioni di Storia e Letteratura, 1981.

Normore, C. "Buridan's Ontology". In *How Things Are: Studies in Predication and the History and Philosophy of Science*, ed. James Bogen and James E. McGuire, pp. 187–200. Dordrecht: D. Reidel, 1984.

O'Connor, W. R. "The Natural Desire for God in St. Thomas". *The New Scholasticism* 14 (1940): 213–267.

Ockham, William. *See* William of Ockham.

Owens, Joseph. "Common Nature: A Point of Comparison Between Thomistic and Scotistic Metaphysics", *Mediaeval Studies* 19 (1957): 7–13.

————. "Judgment and Truth in Aquinas". *Mediaeval Studies* 32 (1970): 138–158.

————. "Existence as Predicated". *The New Scholasticism* 53 (1979): 480–485.

————. "Natures and Conceptualization". *The New Scholasticism* 56 (1982): 376–380.

————. "Thomas Aquinas: Dimensive Quantity as Individuating Principle", *Mediaeval Studies* 50 (1988): 279–310.

Park, Woosuk. "The Problem of Individuation for Scotus: A Principle of Indivisibility or a Principle of Distinction?" *Franciscan Studies* 48 (1988): 105–123.

————. "Common Nature and *Haecceitas*". *Franziskanische Studien* (West Germany) 71 (1989): 188–192.

————. "*Haecceitas* and the Bare Particular". *Review of Metaphysics* 46 (1990): 375–398.

Paulus, Jean. *Henri de Gand. Essai sur les tendances de sa métaphysique.* Paris: J. Vrin, 1938.

Pegis, Anton C. "Concerning William of Ockham". *Traditio* 2 (1944): 465–480.

———. Pelster, Franz. "Heinrich von Harclay, Kanzler von Oxford und seine Quästionen". In *Miscellanea Francesco Ehrle* I, pp. 307–356. Studi e Testi, 37. Rome: Biblioteca Apostolica Vaticana, 1924.

———. *Declarationes magistri Guilelmi de la Mare O.F.M.* Melle:Aschendorf, 1956.

Perreiah, A. "Buridan and the Definite Description". *Journal of the History of Philosophy* 10 (1972): 153–160.

Peter Aureoli. *Scriptum super primum Sententiarum.* Vatican Library MS Borghese 329, fols. 317v–345v.

———. *Commentariorium in Primum Librum Sententiarum pars prima auctore Petero Aureolo Verberio ordinis minorum archiepiscopo Aquensi.* Rome, 1595.

———. *Scriptum super I Sententiarum,* ed. E. M. Buytaert. St. Bonaventure, NY: Franciscan Institute, 1952.

Peter Olivi. *Quaestiones in Secundum librum sententiarum,* 3 vols., ed. B. Jansen. Ad Claras Aquas (Quaracchi): Ex Typographia Collegii S. Bonaventurae, 1922–1926.

Peter Palude. *In II Sententiarum.* Vatican Library, MS lat. 1073.

Pinborg, Jan. "Walter Burleigh on the Meaning of Proposition". *Classica et Mediaevalia* 28 (1967): 394–404.

———. *Logik und Semantik im Mittelalter; ein Überblick.* Stuttgart and Bad Cannstatt: Frommann-Holzboog, 1972.

Pines, Shlomo. "Individual Forms in the Thought of Yedaya Bedarsi". In *Harry A. Wolfson Jubilee Volume,* ed. S. Liebermann, pp. 187–201. Jerusalem: American Academy for Jewish Research, 1965.

———. "Scholasticism After Thomas Aquinas and the Teachings of Hasdai Crescas and His Predecessors". *Proceedings of the Israel Academy of Sciences and Humanities* 1, no. 10. (Jerusalem, 1967), pp. 1–101.

Plotinus. *Enneads,* ed. P. Henry *et al.* Paris: Descleé de Bouwer, 1951ff.

Popper, K. R. "The Principle of Individuation". *Proceedings of the Aristotelian Society* 27 (1953): 107–112.

Porphyry. *In Categorias scholia in Aristotelem,* ed. C. Brandis. Berlin, 1836.

———. *Porphyrii Isagoge et in Aristotelis Categorias commentarium,* ed. A. Busse. Berlin: G. Reimer, 1887.

————. *Isagoge,* trans. Boethius, ed. Lorenzo Minio-Paluello in the series Aristoteles latinus I, 6–7. Paris: Desclée de Bouwer, 1966.

Pouillon, D. H. "Le premier traité des propriétés transcendentales. La 'Summa de bono' du Chancelier Philippe". *Revue Néoscolastique de Philosophie* 42 (1939): 40–77.

Praepositinus. *Summa,* cod. Vat. lat. 1174.

Pseudo-Scotus. *Super librum I Posteriorum.* In *Joannis Duns Scoti Opera omnia.* Editio nova juxta editionem Wadding. Paris: Vivès, 1891–1895.

Quétif, J. and Echard, J. *Scriptores Ordinis Praedicatorum.* Paris, 1719–1723; rep. facsimile, New York: Burt Franklin, h. d.

Quine, W. V. O. *From a Logical Point of View.* Cambridge, MA: Harvard University Press, 1953.

Quinn, J. F. *The Historical Constitution of St. Bonaventure's Philosophy.* Toronto: The Pontifical Institute of Mediaeval Studies, 1973.

Quinton, A. *The Nature of Things.* London: Routledge and Kegan Paul, 1973.

Renan, Ernest. *Averroés et l'averroîsme,* 4th ed. Paris: Calmann Levy, 1882.

————. *Les écrivains juifs francais du XIVe siècle.* Paris: Histoire Litteraire de la France, 1877.

Richard of Mediavilla. *Clarissimi theologi magistri Ricardi de Mediavilla super quatuor libros Sententiarum Petri Lombardi Quaestiones subtilissimae,* 4 vols. Brescia, 1591.

————. *Quodlibeta doctoris Eximii Ricardi de Mediavilla Ordinis Minorum.* Brescia, 1591 (end of vol. 4 of his *Sentences* commentary).

————. *Quaestiones disputatae.* Vatican Library MS. lat. 868.

Riedl, C. *Jesuit Thinkers of the Renaissance.* Milwaukee: Marquette University Press, 1939.

Robert, P. *Hylémorphisme et devenir chez saint Bonaventure.* Montreal: Librarie St. Françoise, 1936.

Roensch, Frederick J. *Early Thomistic School.* Dubuque: Priory Press, 1964.

Roger Bacon. *Opera quedam hactenus inedita.* Rolls Series, ed. J. S. Brewer. Rerum Britannicarum Medii Aevi Scriptores. London: Green, Longman and Roberts, 1859.

————. *Opera hactenus inedita,* fasc. 2, ed. Robert Steele. Oxford: Clarendon Press, 1905.

————. *Opera hactenus inedita,* fasc. 10, ed. Robert Steele. Oxford: Clarendon Press, 1930.

————. *Opera hactenus inedita,* fasc. 11, ed. Robert Steele. Oxford: Clarendon Press, 1932.

Roger Marston. *Quodlibet,* ed. G. F. Etzkorn and I. C. Brady. Ad Claras Aquas (Quaracchi): Ex Typographia Collegi S. Bonaventurae, 1968.

Roland–Gosselin, M.–D. *Le "De ente et essentia" de S. Thomas d'Aquin.* Kain: Le Saulchoir, 1926; Paris: J. Vrin, 1948.

Rosanas, Juan. "El principio de individuación, según Suárez". *Ciencia y Fe* 6 (1950): 69–86.

Rosenberg, Jean R. *The Principle of Individuation: A Comparative Study of St. Thomas, Scotus, and Suárez.* Washington, DC: Catholic University of America Press, 1950.

Rosenberg, Shalon. "Logic and Ontology in Jewish Philosophy in the Fourteenth Century". Unpublished Ph.D. dissertation. Hebrew University, Jerusalem, 1974.

Rucker, P. Palmaz. *Der Ursprung unserer Begriffe nach Richard von Mediavilla. Ein Beitrag zur Erkenntnislehre des Doctor Solidus.* In Beiträge zur Geschichte der Philosophie und Theologie des Mittelalters, vol. 31, Part I. Münster: Aschendorff, 1934.

Rudavsky, T. M. "Individuals and the Doctrine of Individuation in Gersonides". *The New Scholasticism* 51 (1982): 30–50.

————. "Divine Omniscience and Future Contingents in Gersonides" *The Journal of the History of Philosophy* 21 (1983): 513–536.

Russell, Bertrand. *The Problems of Philosophy.* Oxford: Clarendon Press, 1912.

————. *The Principles of Mathematics.* London: Allan and Unwin, 1937, 2nd ed.

————. *An Inquiry into Meaning and Truth.* London: Allen and Unwin, 1940.

————. *Human Knowledge: Its Scope and Limits.* New York: Simon and Schuster, 1948.

Samuelson, Norbert. "Gersonides' Account of God's Knowledge of Particulars". *The Journal of the History of Philosophy* 10 (1972): 399–416.

————. *Gersonides: The Wars of the Lord: Treatise Three: On God's Knowledge.* Toronto: Pontifical Institute of Mediaeval Studies, 1977.

Scherzerus, J. A. *Breviarium Eustachianum.* Francofurti ad Moenum, 1665.

Scorraille, J. de. *François Suárez de la Compagnie de Jésus,* 2 vols. Paris: Lethiellieux, 1912–1913.

Schlanger, Jacques. *La philosophie de Salomon Ibn-Gabirol.* Leiden: E. J. Brill, 1968.

Schulemann, G. *Die Lehre von den Transcendentalien in der scholastischen Philosophie.* Leipzig: F. Meiner, 1929.

Scott, T. K. *John Buridan: Sophisms on Meaning and Truth* (translation of the *Sophismata*). New York: Appleton-Century-Crofts, 1966.

Sellars, Wilfred. *Science and Metaphysics.* London: Routledge and Kegan Paul, 1967.

Shapiro, Herman. "A Note on Walter Burley's Exaggerated Realism". *Franciscan Studies,* new series, 20 (1960): 205–214.

———. "More On the 'Exaggeration' of Burley's Realism". *Manuscripta* 6 (1962): 94–98.

Sharp, Dorothy E. *Franciscan Philosophy at Oxford in the Thirteenth Century.* Oxford and London: Oxford University Press and Humphry Milford, 1930.

Siger of Brabant. *Quaestions sur la Métaphysique.* Louvain: Éditions de l'Institut Supérieur de Philosophie, 1948.

———. *Quaestiones super librum Metaphysicae,* ed. C. Graiff. Louvain: Publications Universitaires, 1948.

———. *Les Quaestiones super librum De causis de Siger de Brabant,* ed. A. Marlasca. Philosophes Medievvaux 12. Louvain: Publications Universitaires de Louvain, 1972.

———. *Quaestiones in tertium De anima, De anima intellectiva, De aeternitate mundi,* ed. B. C. Bazán. Philosophes Médievaux 13. Louvain: Publications Universitaires de Louvain, 1972.

Sirat, Colette. *A History of Jewish Philosophy in the Middle Ages.* Paris: Edition de la Maison des Sciences de l'Homme, 1985.

Sommervogel, C. *Bibliothéque de la Compagnie de Jésus,* 9 vols. Paris: A. Picard, 1890–1900.

Spade, Paul V. "Some Epistemological Implications of the Burley-Ockham Dispute". *Franciscan Studies* 35 (1975): 212–222.

Specht, Reiner. *Francisco Suárez. "Über die Individualität und das Individuationsprinzip,* 2 vols. Hamburg: Meiner, 1976.

Ssekasozi, Engelbert. "A Comparative and Critical Analysis of the Metaphysical Theories of William of Ockham and Francis Suárez as Regards the Principle of Individuation". Unpublished Ph.D dissertation, University of Kansas, 1976.

Staub, Jacob J. *The Creation of the World According to Gersonides.* Chico, CA: Scholars Press, 1982.

Stella, P. T. "Illi qui student in Scoto: Guglielmo di Alnwick et la 'haecceitas' scotista'', *Salesianum* 30 (1968): 614–637.

Stout, G. F. "The Nature of Universals and Propositions". *Proceedings of the British Academy* 10 (1921): 157–172.

Strawson, P. F. "Particular and General". *Proceedings of the Aristotelian Society* 54 (1953–1954): 233–260.

———. *Individuals*. London: Methuen and Company, 1959.

Suárez, Francis. *Disputationes metaphysicae*. Salamanca, 1597.

———. *Disputationes metaphysicae*, ed. C. Berton. In *Opera omnia,* vols. 25 and 26. Paris: Vivès, 1861.

———. *On Formal and Universal Unity,* trans. J. F. Ross. Milwaukee: Marquette University Press, 1964.

———. *On Individual Unity and Its Principle,* trans. Jorge J. E. Gracia. In *Suárez on Individuation,* pp. 29–173. Milwaukee: Marquette University Press, 1982.

———. *On the Essence of Finite Being as Such: On the Existence of That Essence and Their Distinction,* trans. Norman Wells. Milwaukee, WI: Marquette University Press, 1983.

Tachau, K. H. "The Problem of the *Species in Medio* at Oxford in the Generation after Ockham'', *Mediaeval Studies* 44 (1982): 394–443.

Thomas Aquinas. *Opera ommia,* Leonine ed. Rome: Ex Typographia Polyglotta Vaticana, 1882–.

———. *Scriptum super libros sententiarum magistri Petri Lombardi,* ed. P. Mandonnet. Paris: Lethielleux, 1929.

———. *Scriptum super libros sententiarum magistri Petri Lombardi,* ed. M. Fabianus Moos. Paris: Lethellex, 1947.

———. *De principiis naturae,* ed. John J. Pauson. Louvain: E. Nauwelaerts, 1950.

———. *In duodecim libros metaphysicorum Aristotelis expositio*. Rome: Marietti, 1950.

———. *Aristotle's De anima in the Version of William of Moerbeke and the Commentary of St. Thomas Aquinas,* trans. K. Foster and S. Humphries. New Haven, CN: Yale University Press, 1951.

———. *Truth,* trans. Robert W. Mulligan. Chicago: Henry Regnery, 1952.

———. *Quaestiones disputatae,* ed. M. Cacaterra *et al.* Rome: Marietti, 1953.

———. *Opuscula philosophica,* ed. Raymund M. Spiazzi. Rome: Marietti, 1954.

————. *De ente et essentia,* ed. Raymundi M. Spiazzi. Turin: Marietti, 1954.

————. *De unitate intellectus contra averroistas,* ed. Raymundi M. Spiazzi. Turin: Marietti, 1954.

————. *Opuscula theologica,* ed. Raymund A. Verardo. Rome: Marietti, 1954.

————. *Quodlibeta,* ed. Raymund Spiazzi. Turin: Marietti, 1956.

————. *Expositio super librum Boethii De trinitate,* ed. B. Decker. Leiden: Brill, 1959.

————. *Summa contra gentiles. (Liber de veritate catholicae fidei contra errores infedelium),* ed. Ceslai Pera *et al.* Turin: Marietti, 1961.

————. *Treatise on Separate Substances,* ed. and trans. Francis J. Lescoe. West Hartford, CN: Saint Joseph College, 1963.

————. *De spiritualibus creaturis.* In *Quaestiones disputatae,* vol. 2. Rome: Marietti, 1965.

————. *In octo libros physicorum Aristotelis expositio,* ed. P. M. Maggiolo. Turin: Marietti, 1965.

————. *Summa theologiae,* ed. Blackfriars. London: Eyre and Spottinwoode, 1965.

————. *On the Unity of the Intellect Against the Averroists,* trans. B. Zedler. Milwaukee: Marquette University Press, 1968.

————. *On Being and Essence,* trans. A. Maurer, 2nd ed. Toronto: Pontifical Institute of Mediaeval Studies, 1968.

————. *Quaestiones de anima,* ed. James H. Robb. Toronto: Pontifical Institute of Mediaeval Studies, 1968.

————. *Commentary on the Posterior Analytics of Aristotle,* trans. F. R. Larcher. New York: Hamilton Printing Co., 1970.

————. *Questions on the Soul,* trans. James H. Robb. Milwaukee, Marquette University Press, 1984.

————. *Faith, Reason and Theology: Questions I–IV of "Commentary on 'De Trintiate' of Boethius,* trans. with Introduction and notes by Armand Maurer. Toronto: Pontifical Institute of Mediaeval Studies, 1987.

Touati, Charles. *La pensée philosophique et théologique de Gersonide.* Paris: Les Editions de Minuit, 1973.

Tweedale, M. M. *Abailard on Universals.* Amsterdam: North Holland, 1976.

Uña Juárez, Agustín. *La filosofía del siglo XIV: Contexto cultural de Walter Burley.* Madrid: Real Monasterio de El Escorial, 1978.

Van Steenberghen, F. *Aristote en Occident: les origines de l'aristotélisme parisien.* Louvain: Édicions de l'Institut Supérieur de Philosophie, 1946. Trans. L. Jonston, *Aristotle in the West: the Origins of Latin Aristotelianism.* Louvain: Nauwelaerts Pub. House, 1970.

———. *La philosophie au XIIIe siècle.* Louvain: Publications Universitaires de Louvain, 1966.

———. *Maître Siger de Brabant.* Louvain: Publications Universitaires de Louvain, 1977.

Veatch, Henry. "Essentialism and the Problem of Individuation". *Proceedings of the American Catholic Philosophical Association* 47 (1974): 64–73.

Vignaux, Paul. "Nominalisme". In *Dictionnaire de théologie catholique* 11, 1, pp. 718–783. Paris: Letouzey et Ané, 1931.

———. "Occam". In *Dictionnaire de théologie catholique* 11, 1, pp. 863–889. Paris: Letuzey et Ané, 1931.

Vollert, Cyril. *Francis Suárez. On the Various Kinds of Distinctions.* Milwaukee: Marquette University Press, 1947; rep. 1976.

Walter Burley. *De puritate artis logicae tractatus longior,* ed. P. Boehner. Franciscan Institute Publications, Text Series No. 9. St. Bonaventure, NY: The Franciscan Institute, 1955.

———. *De diffinitione,* ed. H. Shapiro and F. Scott. *Mediaeval Studies* 27 (1965): 337–340.

———. *Expositio super artem veterem Porphyrii et Aristotelis.* Venice, 1497; rep. Frankfurt-am-Main: Minerva, 1967.

———. *De formis,* ed. Frederick J. Down Scott. Munich: Bayerische Akademie der Wissenschaften, 1970.

———. *In Physicam Aristotelis expositio et questiones.* Venice, 1501; rep. New York: George Olms, 1972.

Walter of Chatton. *Reportatio et Lectura super Sententias,* ed. J. C. Wey. Toronto: PIMS, 1989.

Washell, Richard F. "Logic, Language and Albert the Great". *Journal of the History of Ideas* 34 (1973): 445–450.

Weisheipl, James A. "Albertus Magnus and the Oxford Platonists". *Proceedings of the American Catholic Philosophical Association* 32 (1958): 124–139.

———. "Ockham and Some Mertonians". *Mediaeval Studies* 30 (1968): 163–213.

———. "Albertus Magnus and Universal Hylomorphism". In *Albert the Great: Commemorative Essays,* ed. Francis J. Kovach and Robert W. Shahan, pp. 239–260. Norman: University of Oklahoma Press, 1980.

Wiggins, David. *Sameness and Substance.* Oxford: Basil Blackwell, 1980.

William of Ockham. *Opera philosophica,* 6 vols., ed. G. Gál *et al.* St. Bonaventure, NY: Franciscan Institute, 1974–1984.

———. *Opera theologica,* 10 vols., ed. S. Brown and G. Gál, *et al.* St. Bonaventure, NY: Franciscan Institute, 1967–1986.

Williams, D. C. "The Elements of Being". *Review of Metaphysics* 7 (1953): 3–18 and 171–192.

Winiewicz, David. "A Note on *alteritas* and Numerical Diversity in St. Thomas Aquinas". *Dialogue* 16 (1977): 693–707.

Wippel, J. F. "Godfrey of Fontaines: Disputed Questions 9, 10, and 12". *Franciscan Studies* 33 (1973): 351–372.

———. "The Dating of James of Viterbo's Quodlibet I and Godfrey of Fontaines' Quodlibet VIII". *Augustiniana* 24 (1974): 348–386.

———. *The Metaphysical Thought of Godfrey of Fontaines.* Washington, DC: The Catholic University of America Press, 1981.

———. "The Relationship Between Essence and Existence in Late Thirteenth-Century Thought: Giles of Rome, Henry of Ghent, Godfrey of Fonataines, and James of Viterbo". In *Philosophies of Existence: Ancient and Medieval,* ed. P. Morewedge, pp. 131–164. New York: Fordham University Press, 1982.

Wolfson, Harry A. *Crescas' Critique of Aristotle.* Cambridge, MA: Harvard University Press, 1929.

———. *The Philosophy of Spinoza,* 2 vols. New York: Schocken Books, 1969.

———. *The Philosophy of the Kalam.* Cambridge, MA: Harvard University Press, 1976.

Wolter, A. B. "Duns Scotus on the Natural Desire for the Supernatural". *New Scholasticism* 23 (1940): 281–317.

———. "Duns Scotus on Intuition, Memory and Our Knowledge of Individuals". In *History of Philosophy in the Making,* ed. L. J. Thro, 81–104. Washington, DC: University Press of America, 1982.

———. *Duns Scotus' Early Oxford Lecture on Individuation.* Santa Barbara, CA: Old Mission Santa Barbara, 1992.

———. and M. M. Adams. "Duns Scotus' Parisian Proof for the Existence of God". *Franciscan Studies* 42 (1982): 248–321.

Wolterstorff, Nicholas. *On Universals.* Chicago: University of Chicago Press, 1970.

Wundt, M. *Die deutsche Schulmetaphysik des 17. Jahrhunderts.* Tübingen: J. C. B. Mohr (P. Siebeck), 1939.

Wyss, Joseph M. *"De natura materiae" Attributed to St. Thomas Aquinas.* Louvain: Nauwelaerts, 1953.

Xiberta y Roqueta, B. M. *De scriptoribus scholasticis saeculi XIV ex ordine Carmelitarum.* Louvain: Bureaux de la Revue, 1931.

Ypma, E. *La formation des professeurs chez les Ermites de Saint-Augustin de 1256 à 1354; un nouvel ordre à ses dèbuts théologiques.* Paris: Centre d'Études des Augustins, 1956.

Zavalloni, Roberto. *Richard de Mediavilla et la controverse sur la pluralité des formes.* Philosophes médévaux, vol. 2. Louvain: Editions de l'Institut Supérieur de Philosophie, 1951.

SIGLA

BGPM: *Beiträge zur Geschichte der Philosophie des Mittelalters*
CCSL: *Corpus christianorum, series latina*
CSEL: *Corpus scriptorum ecclesiasticorum latinorum*
PG: *Patrologiae cursus completus. Series graeca*
PIMS: Pontifical Institute of Mediaeval Studies
PL: *Patrologiae cursus completus. Series latina*
SUNY: State University of New York

CONTRIBUTORS

Ignacio Angelelli. Professor, Universidad Nacional de Buenos Aires; Ph.D., University of Fribourg (Switzerland). Professor, University of Texas at Austin. Publications: *Studies on Gottlob Frege and Traditional Philosophy* (Dordrecht: Reidel, 1967); "The Techniques of Disputation in the History of Logic", *Journal of Philosophy* 67 (1970); "On Saccheri's Use of the *consequentia mirabilis*", *Akten des II Internationalen Leibniz-Kongresses, 1972*, vol. 4 (Steiner Verlag, 1975); "The Substitutivity of Identicals in the History of Logic", *Studien zu Frege*, ed. M. Schirn, vol. 2 (Frommann Verlag, 1976); "The Aristotelian Modal Syllogistic in Modern Modal Logic", *Konstruktionen versus Positionen*, ed. K. Lorenz, vol. 1 (Berlin, 1979).

Ivan Boh. M.A., Fordham University, 1956; Ph.D., University of Ottawa, 1958. Professor, The Ohio State University. Publications: "Problems of Alethic and Epistemic Iteration in Later Medieval Logic", *Philosophia Naturalis* 21 (1984): 492–506; "Belief, Justification, and Knowledge: Some Late-Medieval Epistemic Concerns", *Journal of the Rocky Mountain Medieval and Renaisance Association*, 6 (1985): 87–103; "Propositional Attitudes in the Logic of Walter Burley and William Ockham", *Franciscan Studies* 44 (1984): 31–59; "Metalanguage and the Concept of *ens secundae intentionis*", *Thomas von Aquin, Miscellanea Mediaevalia* 19 (1988): 53–70; "John of Glogovia's Rejection of Paradoxical Entailment Rules", *Die Philosophie im 14. und 15. Jahrhundert. In Memoriam Konstanty Michalski (1879–1947)* (Amsterdam: Verlag Grüner 1988): pp. 373–383; On Medieval Rules of Obligation and Rules of Consequence", *Anuario Filosofico* 21 (1990): 39–102; "Bradwardine's (?) Critique of Ockham's Modal Logic", in *Historia Philosophiae Medii Aevi*, (Amsterdam and Philadelphia: Verlag Grüner, 1991), pp. 55–70; *Epistemic Logic in the Later Middle Ages* (New York: Routledge, 1993).

Allan Bäck. Ph.D., The University of Texas at Austin, 1979. Associate Professor, Kutztown University. Publications: *On Reduplication* (Munich and Vienna: Philosophia Verlag, forthcoming); "Anselm on Perfect Islands", *Franciscan Studies* 43 (1983); "Aquinas on the Incarnation", *New Scholasticism* 56 (1982); "Avicenna on Being and Existence", *Journal of the History of Philosophy* 25 (1987); "Existential Import in Anselm's Ontological Argument", *Franciscan Studies* 41 (1981); "Philoponus on the Fallacy of Accident", *Ancient Philosophy* (1988); "Ibn Sina on the Individuation of Perceptible Substance", *Proceedings of the PMR Conference*, vol. 14 (1989); "Sailing Through the Sea Battle", *Ancient Philosophy* 12 (1992); "Avicenna's Conception of the Modalities", *Vivarium*, 30 (1992): 217–255.

Mauricio H. Beuchot. Licentiate, M.A., and Ph.D., Universidad Iberoamericana de México. Professor, Universidad Iberoamericana de México and Universidad Nacional Antónoma de México. Publications: *Elementos de semiótica* (Mexico City, 1979); *Ensayos marginales sobre Aristóteles* (Mexico City, 1985); *La filosofía del lenguaje en la edad media* (Mexico City, 1981); *El problema de los universales* (Mexico, 1981); *Filosofía analítica, filosofía tomista y metafísica* (Mexico City, 1983); *Lógica y ontologiá (en la filosofía medieval y analítica* (Guadalajara, 1986); *Aspectos históricos de la semiótica y la filosofía del lenguaje* (Mexico City, 1987).

Stephen F. Brown. Ph.D., Université de Louvain (Belgium). Professor, Boston College. Publications: Editor of the *Opera omnia* of William of Ockham; articles on Ockham's sources and critics—Henry of Ghent, John Duns Scotus, John of Reading, Walter Burleigh, Richard of Conington, Robert Cowton, and Walter Chatton.

Jorge J. E. Gracia. M.A., University of Chicago, 1966; M.S.L., Pontifical Institute of Mediaeval Studies, 1970; Ph.D., University of Toronto, 1971. Professor, State University of New York at Buffalo. Publications: (ed.) *Com usar be de beure e menjar: Normes morals contingudes en el "Terç del Crestià"* (Barcelona: Curial, 1977); *Suárez on Individuation* (Milwaukee: Marquette University Press, 1982); *Introduction to the Problem of Individuation in the Early Middle Ages* (Munich, Vienna, and Washington, DC: Philosophia Verlag and The Catholic University of America Press, 1986, 2nd ed. 1988); *The Metaphysics of Good and Evil According to Suárez: Disputations X and XI*, with Douglas Davis (Munich and Vienna: Philosophia Verlag, 1990); *Individuality: An Essay on the Foundations of Metaphysics* (Albany: State University of New York Press, 1988); *Philosophy and Its History: Issues in Philosophical Historiography* (Albany: State University of New York Press, 1992); (ed.) *"The Transcendentals in the Middle Ages,"* issue of *Topoi* 11, no. 2 (1992).

Jeremiah M. G. Hackett. M. Phil., University College, Dublin, 1975; M.S.L., Pontifical Institute of Mediaeval Studies, 1980; Ph.D., University of Toronto, 1983. Associate professor, University of South Carolina at Columbia. Publications: (ed.) *Dictionary of Literary Biography: Medieval Philosophers*, vol. 115 (Detroit and London: Gale Research Inc., 1992; (coed.) *A Straight Path: Studies in Medieval Philosophy and Culture, Essays in Honor of Arthur Hyman* (Washington, DC: The Catholic University of America

Press, 1988); "The Attitude of Roger Bacon to the *scientia* of Albertus Magnus", in *Albertus Magnus and the Sciences: Commemorative Essays 1980,* ed. James A. Weisheipl, O.P. (Toronto: Pontifical Institute of Mediaeval Studies, 1980), pp. 53–72; "Roger Bacon", *The Dictionary of the Middle Ages,* vol. 2, ed. Joseph Strayer (New York: Scribners, 1983), pp. 35–42; "Moral Philosophy and Rhetoric in Roger Bacon", *Philosophy and Rhetoric,* 20, no. 1 (1987): 18–40; "The Practical Philosophy of Roger Bacon", *Irish Philosophical Journal* 3 (1986); "Practical Wisdom and Happiness in the Moral Philosophy of Roger Bacon", *Medioevo* 12 (1986): 55–109; "Philosophy and Theology in Roger Bacon's *Opus Maius*", in R. James Long, ed. *Philosophy and the God of Abraham: Essays in Honor of James A. Weisheipl, O.P.* (Toronto: Pontifical Institute of Mediaeval Studies, 1991), pp. 55–70.

Mark G. Henninger. M.A. Fordham University; Ph.D., University of California at Los Angeles, 1984. Associate professor, Loyola University of Chicago. Publications: *Relations: Medieval Theories 1250–1325* (Oxford, 1989); numerous articles in medieval philosophy. Currently working on a critical edition of the *Quaestiones ordinariae* of Henry of Harclay.

Linda L. Peterson. Ph.D., University of California at Irvine, 1985. Associate Professor, University of San Diego. Papers presented: "Necessary Accidents and the Individuation of Intellectual Souls", colloquium session on the History of Medieval Philosophy at the Eastern Division Meeting of the American Philosophical Association, Boston, MA, 1986; "St. Thomas and the Intellectual Soul: Historical and Contemporary Reflections", invited paper presented at the April 1988 meeting of the International St. Thomas Society of the American Catholic Philosophical Association.

Peter Overton King. Ph.D., Princeton University, 1982. Associate professor of philosophy and adjunct professor of classics, The Ohio State University. Publications: *Jean Buridan's Logic* (Dordrecht: D. Reidel, 1985); *Peter Abailard and the Problem of Universals in the Twelfth Century* (Ithaca, NY: Cornell University Press, forthcoming); also several articles on medieval philosophy.

John Kronen. Ph.D., State University of New York at Buffalo, 1990. Assistant Professor, University of St. Thomas, St. Paul, MN. Publications: "Essentialism Old and New", *The Modern Schoolman* 68, no. 2 (1991); "Substantial Unity and Hylomorphism", *The American Catholic Philosophical Quarterly* 65, no. 3 (1991); "Can Leclerc's Composite Actualities be Substances?" *Process Studies* 1 (1992).

Armand A. Maurer. M.A., 1943; M.S.L., 1945; Ph.D., 1947. Professor emeritus, Pontifical Institute of Mediaeval Studies and University of Toronto.

Member of the Royal Society of Canada. Publications: *Medieval Philosophy*, revised ed. (Toronto: Pontifical Institute of Mediaeval Studies, 1982); *Recent Philosophy: Hegel to the Present*, in collaboration with E. Gilson and T. Langan (New York: Random House, 1966); *St. Thomas and Historicity* (Milwaukee: Marquette University Press, 1979); *About Beauty. A Thomistic Interpretation* (Houston: Center for Thomistic Studies, University of St. Thomas, 1983); (ed.) *Siger of Brabant. Quaestiones in Metaphysicam* (Louvain: Editions de l'institut Supérieur de Philosophie, 1983).

Joseph Owens. M.S.D., Pontifical Institute of Mediaeval Studies, 1951. Professor emeritus, Pontifical Institute of Mediaeval Studies. Publications: *A History of Ancient Western Philosophy* (New York: Appleton-Century-Crofts, 1959); *The Doctrine of Being in the Aristotelian Metaphysics*, 2nd ed. (Toronto: Pontifical Institute of Mediaeval Studies, 1963); *An Elementary Christian Metaphysics* (Milwaukee: Bruce, 1963); *An Interpretation of Existence* (Milwaukee: Bruce, 1968); coauthor, *The Wisdom and Ideas of St. Thomas Aquinas* (Greenwich, CT: Fawcett, 1968).

Tamar M. Rudavsky. M.A. (1974) and Ph.D. (1976), Brandeis University. Associate Professor, The Ohio State University. Publications: (ed.) *Divine Omniscience and Omnipotence in Medieval Philosophy*, Synthese Historical Library (Dordrecht: D. Reidel, 1985); "The Doctrine of Individuation in Duns Scotus, Part I", *Franzikanische Studien* 58 (1978): 320–377; Part II, 62 (1980): 62–83; "Divine Omniscience and Future Contingents in Gersonides", *The Journal of the History of Philosophy* 21 (1983): 513–536, rep. in *The Philosophers Annual* 6 (1983); "Divine Omniscience, Contingency and Prophecy in Gersonides", in *Divine Omniscience and Omnipotence in Medieval Philosophy*, pp. 161–181; "Creation, Time and Infinity in Gersonides", *Journal of History of Philosophy* 26 (1988).

John F. Wippel. M.A. (1960) and S.T.L. (1966), The Catholic University of America, 1966; Ph.D., University of Louvain, 1963; *Maître-Agrég'e de l'Ecole Saint Thomas d'Aquin*, Louvain, 1981. Professor, The Catholic University of America. Publications: (coed. and coauth. with Allan B. Wolter) *Medieval Philosophy: From St. Augustine to Nicholas of Cusa* (New York: The Free Press, 1969); *The Metaphysical Thought of Godfrey of Fontaines: A Study in Late Thirteenth-Century Philosophy* (Washington, DC: The Catholic University of America Press, 1981); *Metaphysical Themes in Thomas Aquinas* (Washington, DC: The Catholic University of America Press, 1984); (trans. and intro.) *Boethius of Dacia: 'On the Supreme Good,' 'On the Eternity of the World.' 'On Dreams'* (Toronto: Pontifical Institute of Mediaeval Studies, 1987); (ed. and author of ch. 6) *Studies in Medieval Philosophy* (Washington, DC: The Catholic University of America Press, 1987).

Allan B. Wolter, O.F.M. M.A., 1942, and Ph.D., 1947, The Catholic University of America; Lector Generalis, The Franciscan fInstitute, 1954. Professor emeritus, The Catholic University of America, and research associate, University of California at Los Angeles Center for Medieval and Renaissance Studies and the Franciscan Institute of St. Bonaventure University. Publications: *The Transcendentals and their Function in the Metaphysics of Duns Scotus* (St. Bonaventure, NY: The Franciscan Institute, 1946); *John Duns Scotus: Philosophical Writings* (Indianapolis: Hackett, 1987); *John Duns Scotus: A Treatise on God as First Principle,* 2nd ed. with commentary (Chicago: Franciscan Herald Press, 1983); *Duns Scotus on the Will and Morality* (Washington, DC: Catholic University Press, 1986); *John Duns Scotus: God and Creatures: The Quodlibetal Questions,* with F. Alluntis (Princeton, NJ: Princeton University Press, 1975); *The Philosophical Theology of John Duns Scotus* (Ithaca, NY: Cornell University Press, 1990).

INDEX OF AUTHORS

This index includes translators and editors in addition to authors. It was prepared by James McCarthy.

INDEX OF SUBJECTS

This index records only some of the most important places where particular subjects or terms are discussed or mentioned. No attempt has been made to record all the places, not even all the important places, where those subjects and terms are discussed or mentioned. It is also intended to record the diversity of terminology used by medieval authors and scholars of medieval thought in their discussions of individuation. Occurrences of Latin terms in Latin quotations given in footnotes have not been recorded. No occurrences of terms appearing in titles of books or articles have been recorded.